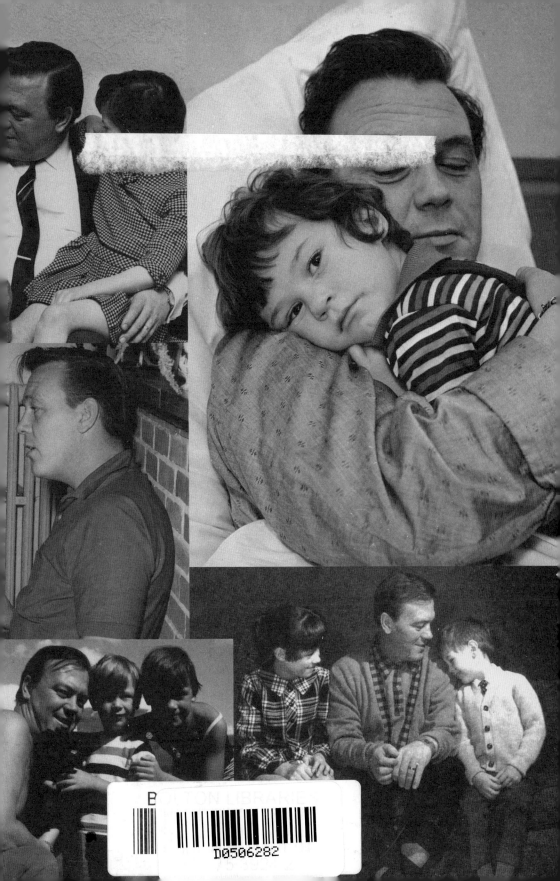

THE SINGER'S SINGER

THE LIFE AND MUSIC OF

MATT MONRO

THE SINGER'S SINGER:
THE LIFE AND MUSIC OF
MATT MONRO

ISBN 9781848566187

Published by
Titan Books
A division of
Titan Publishing Group Ltd
144 Southwark Street
London
SE1 0UP

First edition January 2010
1 3 5 7 9 10 8 6 4 2

Visit our website:
www.titanbooks.com

To receive advance information, news, competitions, and exclusive Titan offers online, please register as a member by clicking the "sign up" button on our website: **www.titanbooks.com**
Did you enjoy this book? We love to hear from our readers. Please e-mail us at: **readerfeedback@titanemail.com** or write to Reader Feedback at the above address.

A CIP catalogue record for this title is available from the British Library.

Printed in the UK by CPI William Clowes Beccles NR34 7TL.

THE SINGER'S SINGER

THE LIFE AND MUSIC OF

MATT MONRO

MICHELE MONRO

TITAN BOOKS

OVERTURE

Michele & Max

This book is dedicated to my father
I wanted to honour his life and tell his story
It is not about my life with my father
It is not written from my point of view
But that of many family members, friends and fans around the world.

This book is also for my son Max, who never knew Matt Monro.
It is an integral part of life to know your origins and family roots.
I hope this book brings insight into the man, the singer, the husband,
the father and makes Max proud to know this then was
his grandfather.

To my beautiful mother: who always enables me to live out my
dreams even though hers are temporarily adrift.
You were joined in life and will meet again – all is not lost.

To daddy: No goodbyes. Just passages of time. Until later.

xxx

SOFTLY... AS I LEAVE YOU

C romwell Hospital:
  Tossing and turning, then stillness, a vision begins to form, a room, stark, white, clean, clinical, almost virginal in its sterility. The odour of disinfectant is overpoweringly noxious with its undiluted presence. A clock, its only function to make the minutes pass too quickly, draining the body of life each time the second hand moves, an eternity. A stricken face lying on top of the sheets, like a dressmaker's dummy, unstirring and as white as the linen itself. The inevitable drip attached to the mannequin's arm, in perfect synchrony with the motion of the timepiece. Time itself has become the enemy, the judge and the ultimate hangman.

Genderless people move in and out between the life support systems as if on a crudely man-made obstacle course, each one careful not to intrude on the other's duties, carefully playing with a myriad of dials and instruments on bleeping and blinking electronic meters. A game: if played in the right sequence, the ultimate prize – life itself – one false move, a splinter of error, then the booby prize.

Malignant cells spreading their vicious poison, a failed hepatic transplant because an extensive spread was not found until after the incisions were made – a bit bloody late to realise that, don't you think. Thirty-two nameless people in a remedial tag-team who just lost the relay race against the devil. Someone's vital organs now lying discarded and useless, thrown into a sterile tray marked for incineration.

A hand reaches out and touches, contact, warmth, feeling, sympathy, pulling me down an endless corridor of clinical detachment. Hundreds of people, faces merging together in an infinite maze. Everyone looking, peering, staring, their eyes boring into mine, searching for answers to unanswerable questions, heads tilting in mock sympathy.

Claustrophobia, a pressing heat, parched throat, cold clammy droplets of sweat dribbling from the creases of my brow, utter panic, legs moving, running faster than they can possibly go. Eyes blink, a mirage, doors, no, two doors, quite normal looking in their appearance but disguising the escape route I desperately crave, a trick of the light or a cruel optical illusion? Pressing, pushing, opening, falling and then the wonderful night air enveloping me with its coolness, the breeze embracing me with its fingers. The stars ablaze with compassion and understanding, their inner peace, calmness and serenity engulfing me with their tranquillity. A deep laboured breath, then another, each one urging my soul for the courage to face the clock. His scars will heal, but will mine?

Minutes, hours or days, no difference, still that same hospital room to be faced each time. I sit looking at the clock, wondering if yesterday has gone or is it already tomorrow. My eyes are heavy, weary with the hypnotism of the stillness. Holding the mannequin's hand, sharing our sorrow with each other's touch, without having to say the painful words. Sleep, an end to the nightmare of consciousness. My eyes open, just a fraction, just in case the set has changed. If things have altered I will close them again, maybe forever. Everything is exact, as before. I can wake to face reality. I glance down at the motionless figure, our fingers as entwined as a spider's web. Our hearts no longer beating as one, mine: pulsating with youth, vitality and eternal love, his: slower with age, riddled with disease and lost vigour, but with no less love.

Movement, just out of the corner of my eye, rubber soles connecting with stone floors. It is lunchtime at the zoo. Hands reach to reconnect the new drip, tubes like spaghetti junction, sending the sterile saline solution, infused over thirty minutes, on its weary travels. Not too fast, not too slow, just at the precise speed. Do not pass go, do not collect £200, go directly to jail.

Tick tock, tick tock. I think they have turned the sound up on the clock; the monophonic pitch drowns out my thoughts. I must turn the volume down or think louder. I love you, I need you and love conquers all, doesn't it? Even the evil spirits of the timepiece? Where there is life there is hope, what else do they say? Nothing, words are but empty letters formed together in vague meaningless sentences.

No single person can speak and cure the emptiness inside, the numbness that engulfs my limbs is all consuming. There is but a void, full of hot air, rage and bitterness. Is life that unfair that just when I am old and wise enough to understand the power of love and to have learnt what it is to be able to return it with complete unselfishness, it is taken away? The final gift vanishes before it has been given.

The pupil is unable to show the teacher what she has been taught. Empty lessons... No, that is not what is required. The lessons must continue but from a different tutor. The lesson must be acknowledged from life itself. Hard or easy, the road must be travelled, wheels in motion towards the unknown. Not too fast, not too slow, just the precise speed, do not pass go... STOP, I've played that game before, rewind, the synapses are working in reverse, like a video in backward motion, the incessant celluloid holding vital caches of information. Memories of happier times, smiles, laughter, tears but this time with joy, running, talking, holding hands, unity, togetherness and love. I feel pain, heart pumping faster, breaths coming more quickly, tears welling up, panic. STOP. Buttons pushed, fast forward. The video stops at the required position, the present. I will concentrate on the present, on the future; I must not give up hope. We have been through worse, I think. Was there anything worse? Can't think straight at the moment, the cameras have stopped, the video has broken... NO – only the pause button was pushed for a split second – relief.

There it is, the inevitable sound of the timepiece. Life is as it was, no more yesterdays, just tomorrows full of loneliness.

Play the game, please continue. My move, or is it yours? We will play later. I must sleep as you have done for a million years. When I wake up it will be your move, don't forget.

Daybreak filters through my lashes, a glimpse of sunlight awakens my senses and I know it is a beautiful day. Another sound: music, harmony, a chorus line of skylarks on the windowsill running through their orchestration perfectly. Happiness has settled on the day. Fingers still entwined. Eyelids flutter, no, not mine, his, or just another illusion from the vestige of sleep. No, it's there. His eyes focus on mine, my fingers squeeze his, his smile promotes mine. My tears, for my eyes only. No time for words, so much to say, but mustn't tire him, they say he must rest. Rest, what else has he been doing for three days? Dying is their only reply, their excuse for not knowing the answers to my questions. The coma has passed, life has restored itself and the cocoon has burst, emitting a brilliance of colour, pouring out in never-ending rays of hope and achievement. The ultimate test has been passed. Full marks. The game nearly played out, just home base to reach and winner takes all. Well done, a brilliant manoeuvre. Letting your opponent think you were down and out, and just as defences were low, and reflexes off-guard, you pounced. The unexpected comeback, false tabs, a standing ovation to a full house, the orchestra plays on. Encore. Bravo.

The house is full of old friends, your chair beckoning its master, aged and frail pictures smiling at me with calmness and tranquility. Phone calls full of "I told you it would be alright", full of cheer and warmth and then stilted, not knowing quite what else to say, so we'll speak later. A promise of a good night's sleep, pleasant dreams, home sweet home, a welcome call away from the nightmares of yesteryear. I will return tomorrow, after my dreams have ended and I awake.

Sunshine streaming into frosted panes of glass, shards of light fighting their way through the closed curtains, which have been drawn to shut out the paparazzi and their pugnacious obscene lenses. The kettle whistling for attention, no bills in the morning mail, only hundreds of get well cards. Today so different from the rest, all the get-well wishers in the world who banded together have finally got their wish. The dream has come true. Getting better is the order of the day. Time to talk and listen to advice on how to travel the road to recovery. Clock ticking, faster and faster, but the fear is gone. It now races to heal the body of its ordeal. Chemotherapy now replaces the saline solution, its Mitozanthrone drip giving the body the power to fight the disease and break down the filthy cancer cells that threatened to destroy our lives. It is another day suffering one more treatment, a further experimental test and so on, etcetera, etcetera, etcetera.

Vomiting racks the frail body but this is expected, swelling in the right leg countered with an intravenous drip and stitches removed from the 'Mercedes Benz' incision wound. Hopes are high that no further side effects take hold and the patient can return home until the next dose of Mitozanthrone in a fortnight.

The warrior returns the victor, but in a blink of an eye the poison starts building again, the liver goes into failure, he can't eat and a drip needs to be attached to pump the body with nutrients, the pain is too much, morphine is administered and an ambulance called.

I wake up, something is wrong, masks come into focus and blue gowns break down the harshness of the endless white. I am led and draped in the same costume as the other players, to protect him, they say. Protect him from what? Us is the answer, our germs, our nefarious contamination. The chemotherapy has broken down the life destroying cells but they did not read the instructions on the packet. It could not differentiate the good from the bad and so has invaded them all. His white cells have faded and been destroyed by their own helper. The enemy has got the edge once again. Sleep again, pain, his, more drips. Chemo discarded like the joker in a pack of cards. Morphine to ease the burden of death. Can I have some please? I am dying inside, cell-by-cell.

That damn clock again, seeking its revenge, this time the victor, its hands drawing the final curtain across the stage of despair. The theatre emptying of its non-paying audience, the scene has been repeated once too often for them to sit there and watch the predetermined ending. At the first showing they reached for their hankies waiting for the tears that would fall, crying for the actors in the roles that they have been cast. Intermission. Time to stretch the legs, relieve themselves of the tensions of sitting on the edge of their seats for too long. A quick drink to quench the thirst of apprehension whilst the clock reaches the point where the second half beckons. The play resumes. The dialogue is being replayed like the video that re-runs the sketch. The cause of the deterioration is now bronchopneumonia and an intramuscular diamorphine cocktail is administered. This time no tissues, the crying was done in the first half. The audience ponder for just a fraction of a moment, as if to verify whether the author might have made a miscalculation. No, the scene is being played just as it has been written.

Fingers entwined, tears falling over the eyes that had hoped.

The clock finally comes to a standstill, its mechanism has at last worn out. The executioner has come to collect his prize. The waiting is over... or has it just begun?

Dreams or nightmares? Neither, just stark reality.
Goodnight daddy, I will miss you until the end of time itself.

Time of death 15.20pm: 7 February 1985.

A lone figure in a crowded arena, the face hung with misery and the burden of pain, a hundred tears falling silently onto the whiteness of the ground which has frozen into a crisp icy crust, just like my heart which even the warmest of sunlight rays couldn't thaw. It is so cold, the air freezing even as it leaves the mouth that utters empty words and promises of better days to come. I cannot remember a time of such steely weather that even the trees oscillate in disgust and the bleakness of the day conveys the thoughts of others. Tiny snowflakes drift down from the sky and I can only imagine that heaven must be crying too. I am alone in my grief even though there are a thousand faces looking on.

A blackness surrounds my being, am I asleep or dead? I feel in limbo where everything is blurry and disfigured and the world is running in slow motion. Bloody endless lines of people, pitying handshakes, mumbled condolences, silent tears and controlled hysteria. I want to go home and lock myself away from this wretched scene but… I don't want to leave him alone here in a place full of strangers and nowhere to rest undisturbed.

The service is over. I don't remember it beginning. Cameras flashing into the privacy of my soul and the long eternal walk down an aisle of no return. We are led to the best seats in the house, which is only fitting since we paid the highest price. All eyes watching… staring… at us, the mourners.

"The Lord is my shepherd", is he? The lull of a monotonous tone waffling on about his life, what do they know about it? Turn to page thirty-two in the hymnbook – or was it thirty-four? Who cares? All stand, all sit, bloody puppets on a string who are mechanically worked by a man uttering God's commands.

All eyes focus on THAT box, lying solitarily on its pedestal, the expensive one because that is what he deserved – the best – it's amazing that one inconsequential item can hold an entire audience captive. It just lies there and we wait until the final curtain closes and he has taken his final bow. Do we applaud his life or weep in his death?

I look around our home and all I see is him, his glasses by a crossword book, cigarettes in a green onyx box, a dressing gown hung so carefully by the shower waiting for its master to lay claim, his watch laying on his bedside table waiting for his return. This home that he built up for us to live in, is full of his being, his presence, but he is not really here at all. I feel so empty; no one will ever be able to explain any of this to me.

They say time heals, I say it is a burden. I'd give my life to turn the clocks back and start again but there are no fairy tale endings. Dreams are but lost causes and death is just an extension of life in another sphere, ashes to ashes, dust to dust.

A Portrait...

Matt Monro was one of the most distinctive singers to surface from the British pop scene in the early 1960s. In a career that spanned some of the most dramatic changes in popular music, Matt Monro stayed true to his musical style amid the growing popularity of heavy rock bands and guitar-smashing extroverts. That fact alone, coupled with his uniquely eloquent voice, earned him the admiration of his peers across the music business.

Along with The Beatles and the Bond phenomena, Monro was to become one of Britain's biggest exports, with his characteristic laid-back style, cool sophistication and trademark middle of the road songs. Yet he had not been born into the glamorous world of show business nor with the name that would make him famous.

Terence Edward Parsons, the youngest of five children, made his first appearance in the world on 1 December 1930 to parents Alice Mary (née Reed) and Frederick William Parsons. Arthur was the eldest sibling, followed by Alice, Reg, Harry and then Terry, who was nicknamed Bo by his father.

Terry was born in an East End area of London known as Shoreditch, a geographical circumstance that made him a true Cockney. During the inter-war period, Shoreditch ranked alongside Hoxton and King's Cross as one of the toughest areas in London. Thieving and violent crime were commonplace, shootings not infrequent, bloodstained clothing a boastful fashion and police always patrolled the area in pairs. Weekends saw vicious gang fights erupt in the streets. The most feared during that era was a bunch of Italians known as the Sabini Gang and during the 1950s and 60s there was another threat just three quarters of a mile east of the area – the infamous Kray brothers.

Terry's father, Frederick, was a chemical worker and packer for a drug company near the Angel Islington. He'd had the same job since coming out of the army,

Terry Parsons aged 6

where he fought in the trenches during the First World War. His wife, Alice, was petite, attractive and shyly self-assured; she was admired, consulted for advice and respected for her calm good sense by almost everyone who knew her.

Bringing up a large brood was expensive and Frederick worked long, arduous days. Alice, who cleaned during the day, set the tone at home. She was full of joy, loved having visitors and would go to great lengths to make them feel welcome. After dinner she would tackle the chores and stay up until everything was exactly as she wanted. She would then creep to bed in the early hours and grab a little sleep before going to work in the morning.

When Frederick became ill, his company offered to send him to Switzerland for treatment, but it was too late. He had suffered ill health after being gassed in the First World War and was incorrectly treated for malaria when he first became sick; it wasn't until much later that a specialist hospital diagnosed tuberculosis. Doctors gave him a year to live; he lasted two, but his quality of life was exceptionally poor.

Alice spent long periods in the hospital tending to her husband while Terry grew up fending for himself. Gang culture existed in the streets, with most youths carrying knives in a bid to maintain their reputation. Gang members felt invincible

In Ever Loving Memory

OF

FREDERICK WILLIAM PARSONS

Who passed away 12th May, 1934,

AGED 40 YEARS.

———

Interred at Chingford Mount Cemetery.   Grave No. CR 27816.

and as they grew older they crossed the line from petty theft to the horrors of drug abuse. They knew no other way of life, had no guidance from their elders and craved respect and protection from those around them. The Parsons lived in fear of the children either being attacked or tempted into the culture themselves, but the streets were their natural playground and there were no alternatives. They could only pray for their offspring's safety and their powers of resistance.

On 12 May 1934, after spending a year in hospital, Frederick died and although Terry hardly knew his father, he was devastated. He had vague images of visiting him in hospital and, on another occasion, of his father sitting on steps by a beach, but he was never sure whether these images were real or figments of his imagination.

Conditions in the underground mortuary where the body of Terry's father was kept before burial were still antiquated. The gas-lit flag-stoned corpse chamber was connected to the hospital by a disintegrating brick passage. The smell was stomach-churning, but family members had to suffer the nasal assault if they wanted to pay their last respects. A local undertaker in Southwark Bridge Road took care of the burial arrangements, and Frederick William Parsons was finally laid to rest at Chingford Mount Cemetery in a pauper's grave. He was only forty years old.

The Parsons family had already been living below the poverty line when Frederick was alive. As a widow with young children, Alice's circumstances forced her to accept menial low-paid work, and as a result she had to find rent-free accommodation.

Alice brought up the children single-handedly, managing on her pension of ten shillings a week, which she supplemented with cleaning jobs. The family moved around the area, living without electricity in gas-fuelled accommodation, though they did once have the luxury of one bath in a house occupied by several families. Those rooms were desperate places, with bugs breeding under loose wallpaper and rodents a regular sight. After several months, the family moved to Welby House at Hornsey Rise. The barrack-like property was built as four low-rise blocks, providing low-rent basic living, gas lighting and outside 'middens' (toilets), which were cleaned out once a week by the council. The flat was sparsely furnished and washing facilities were little more than a bath with a hinged wooden top in the scullery, impossible to use with any privacy in the crowded flat. The best thing about the place from Alice's perspective was that her children could play safely in the large open space between each block.

The kitchen was the hub of the home because it had a fire grate, which was black-leaded weekly with Zebo. The fire was the source for Alice's stew cooking and the routine boiling of the kettle. Terry's brother Reg was given the nightly ritual of banking the fire down, then raking over the embers in the morning to get it going again.

Reg and I used to huddle round the fire, which warmed us from the front but left a draught against our backs. I so wanted to warm my cold feet but resisted the temptation because of the painful itching that came from catching chilblains once before. — Matt Monro

Like all their friends, the Parsons had an outside lavatory. It would get hot in the summer, so Alice would hang herbs on the door together with squares of cut newspaper, and bitterly cold in winter, the seat so icy they had to work up the courage to sit down. At night it was a frightening place to visit. Reg remembers, "My brothers and I would hold out until we were desperate and then begged the others to come with us. We would wait for each other outside the door in the dark, scared stiff, urging the other to 'get on with it', with each strange noise bringing unbridled fear. Then we would run back to the safety of indoors, scuffing our skin in our panic not to be last in. I don't remember what my sister used to do, as she never asked for our help."

The children wore layers of clothing to keep warm, which were invariably ill-fitting as they were passed down from sibling to sibling. The bedroom was never heated and always felt cold and damp in the winter. It was a tortuous affair getting into bed until the chill had worn off. In fact, everywhere in the house was cold as

Terry Parsons aged 11 with his mother Alice

a result of the high ceilings and stone floors.

Daily shopping was necessary as there was nowhere to store groceries. The small boys carried the weight of sugar, flour and potatoes home each day. Terry loved going to the grocer and, if he was lucky, it might be a day for broken biscuits, when his mother would buy half-a-pound, a luxury for the brothers. The boys drooled over the smells of freshly baked breads and in later years, when coming home from secondary school, Terry would walk the mile to purchase stale buns sold at half price from a local baker.

Losing a father at the tender age of three turned Terry into a rebellious child, and having no brothers or sisters of a playable age intensified his solitude. Though Alice was not an outwardly loving woman and had difficulty showing the boy the affection he craved, she was desperately trying to make ends meet and Terry's attitude made it very difficult for her to cope. In later years Terry's need for an audience was always there and he discovered that his talent provided the ticket to a form of social acceptance that he needed.

Terry's early life was desperately unhappy and two years after losing his father, his mother, who was struggling to clothe, feed and house five children while also holding down a job, was taken seriously ill. There were no benefits or financial help from the State and suffering from exhaustion and a mental breakdown, Alice was removed to a sanatorium. Her two youngest children, Harry and Terry, were placed in a foster home in Ashes Wood, Sussex, under the care of Mrs Driver, who took in children of parents who were unable to cope.

Terry hated it; he felt abandoned and didn't understand that the placement was only temporary. He started biting his nails and became even more withdrawn.

After six months, Alice was released and, fearing that the Drivers were becoming too fond of her children, she immediately applied for their return. With their mother back at work, Alice and Reg were left in charge of Terry, who took to being very naughty, often escaping their watchful eyes and strolling in hours later without any attempt at an excuse or apology. His sister's room was off-limits but it didn't stop him from 'borrowing' her lipstick and using it as a writing implement or from hiding Reg's glasses. On one occasion, Terry's 'sitters' took him to the police station, where Reg was friendly with one of the sergeants, and Terry was locked in a cell for a couple of hours to teach him the consequences of bad behaviour. However, the exercise proved ineffective.

Harry was no angel either, and was in the habit of standing on local balconies and taking aim at pedestrian's heads with an arsenal of rotten eggs. Arthur, who was already out at work, also had his own idiosyncrasies. On Friday nights, after he had been paid, he would send Harry out to buy a new pair of socks, which he wore all week and then threw away.

Terry's education was as unsettled as his home life, and he was shuffled between no less than four schools in a three-year period. He started at Bath Street School, but three weeks later was moved to Duncombe School. Then, less than seven weeks after starting his scholarly existence, he was admitted to hospital with infective hepatitis with a brace of birthdays celebrated in not the most congenial of surroundings, taking two years to recover.

It toughened me up. It made me count my blessings — when I had any to count. — Matt Monro

Terry then went to Parliament Hill Open School to convalesce. The Open Air School Movement marked a new period in preventative medicine. The schools took under-nourished slum students and children with serious illness and provided them with food and wholesome surroundings.

> **Terry wasn't very interested in school and didn't take to discipline very well. He was as sharp as a tack but lazy. Fantastic sense of humour and we laughed a lot; there wasn't much that happened in life that wasn't funny to us. The school doctor gave him his annual examination for symptoms of the prevalent TB and declared him fit to return to school. — Harry Parsons**

Terry finally returned to Duncombe School but his distaste for the institution was blatant, as the school attendance register would indicate. His proudest boast during his schooldays was that by crafty manipulation and intense scrutiny of the attendance officer's habits, he succeeded in attending class for only one solitary week in a whole year, and even that was only so he could grab second place in the school diving championships.

He also had to attend choir practice, but wasn't allowed to sing as he was so out of tune he put the other children off.

Perhaps Terry could be forgiven for his lack of enthusiasm, as not every member of his family set the best of examples. Harry had won a scholarship to one of the better grammar schools but was expelled soon after for scrumping apples.

In 1938, Terry was moved to Hugh Middleton in Clerkenwell. The school had separate entrances for boys and girls and although it catered for both sexes there were no mixed classes, much to Terry's chagrin. Though the dungeons under the school were out of bounds, Terry spent many a day with his friend Ben exploring the cellars that led to other corridors and passages, many of which had been blocked for years.

Eight months later, Terry was re-admitted to Bath Street. Existing records reveal no reason for this constant upheaval but with this sort of commitment to learning there was no danger of Terry becoming a serious student. It wasn't his mother's fault but circumstances that forced the situation. Despite Alice's best efforts to provide a stable environment for the children, her situation forced yet another change when the family moved to Wenlock Street.

In those pre-pubescent days Terry had an inclination towards football. At seven he was scuffing his shoes in the streets running after the ball. His mother was always worried about the cost of new shoes, but lengthy lectures did nothing to curtail Terry's enthusiasm for the game. By age eight he was a solid little player. His street friends recognised his potential, and his speed and ability with the ball earned him a place on the local team.

A big match was arranged on a neighbourhood field and as word of the event grew, so did the number of spectators. Not long into the game Terry missed an important goal, much to the disapproval of the partisan crowd, who started booing from the sidelines. With the score still nil-nil after half-time, the crowd grew boisterous again when the opposing team gave a penalty. But Terry refused to take it, fearing scorn from his newfound friends if he repeated his mistake of earlier. His team elected another player who lined up for the shot and promptly missed as well. The crowd became abusive with a divide forming between the supporters of the two teams, resulting in the police being called. The match resumed and moments before the final whistle, Terry had a clear run opportunity of sprinting the ball up the field and without a moment's hesitation kicked the ball into the back of the net. The whistle blew, the crowd went mad, he was hoisted onto the shoulders of his team and for the first time in his life Terry felt a confidence in himself that had never been there before. He felt like a giant.

Though it was to be Terry's last football match, those memories stayed with him for the rest of his life.

The only thing that featured in Terry's life more than football was music. Turning on the kitchen's battery-powered Bakelite wireless produced an orange glow behind its large display, and as the valves warmed, a low drone would follow and slowly a muffled sound emerged from the gold, meshed material covering the jaws of the speaker. Permanently tuned to Radio Luxembourg, it proudly showcased popular and big band music like Benny Goodman, Artie Shaw, Tommy Dorsey and Ella Fitzgerald. This was Terry's first introduction to the musicianship of Bing Crosby, Fred Astaire, Perry Como and Frank Sinatra, but it wasn't just the Americans that were impressing. In the United Kingdom, bandleaders Joe Loss, Harry Roy, Ambrose, Roy Fox and Ray Noble all had orchestras which featured the most famous band singer of the time, Al Bowlly.

These were good times, but the small machine that housed the magic of music would also bring devastating news a year later.

A Childhood Interrupted

By the summer of 1939 war was imminent. School halls issued gas masks and the stench of rubber, when the masks were forced over children's faces, resulted in coughing, choking and in some cases vomiting. A square cardboard box, housing the offending item, was given out with a compulsory order to carry it at all times. The school then announced that the children would be evacuated as a unit, and drills were practised so that assembly points were known. Children were required to hang a card around their neck listing their seat number on the bus. Practice was relentless, but they had no idea when they would be forced to leave their families.

Along with their identity label and gas mask hanging from their neck, each child also had a small bag for clothing and food for the day. They left in the early hours of the morning under the umbrella of darkness. As parents and guardians were not allowed to go with the children, the police were brought in to enforce the policy.

The first school children were evacuated on 1 September 1939 – the day that Germany invaded Poland – in a manoeuvre named Operation Pied Piper. In the first three days of September nearly three million people, mostly children from inner cities, thought to be the most vulnerable to Nazi bombing raids, were transported to the countryside. The railway platforms were crammed with the uproar of shouting officials and sobbing children who had no idea of their destination. As they departed, the children thought they would be home for Christmas.

More disorientation followed, as after their arrival, the children were lined up against a wall and local residents, acting as foster parents, were invited to take their pick. This was just one of the moments of humiliation for the evacuees. The government campaigned with posters and advertisements, to convince parents to send their children to a better place, on the mistaken assumption that there was enough accommodation to house everyone. For many it was an experience which gave them a better life, but others were not as fortunate, suffering beatings, mistreatment and abuse at the hands of 'carers' who were only looking for cheap labour. Under the conditions of indiscriminate evacuation, Terry was one of thousands of artificial orphans created by the war, and his memories of the trauma of separation were so painful that he rarely talked about it later in life.

Terry was evacuated to Cornwall but immediately made the decision that he wasn't staying. After enduring quite enough of his enforced exile he made his own way home, arriving on the doorstep and declaring he wasn't going back.

A child's perspective of life in wartime London was very different from their parents; for them, it was an incredible adventure. Shrapnel from the bombing raids was collected as keepsakes on the way to school. One evening an incendiary bomb fell and hit the cover of the manhole outside Terry's home. Although it damaged the cover, it didn't detonate and the appearance of men in special overalls who came to remove it caused great excitement among the neighbourhood boys.

During the Blitz, huge areas of London's East End were reduced to rubble, the brunt of the attack being focussed on the East End Docks. The area was in chaos as smoke and flames engulfed the Parsons' neighbourhood. Terry's family were bombed out on more than one occasion and they routinely had to pack up and move. They were also forced to spend several nights in the communal shelter. It was noisy and the air was hot and stank, so when the 'all clear' siren sounded they were thankful to climb back into their own beds.

At a new school – and there were many during the early years of the war – bullying was commonplace, although Terry could hold his own. Swimming and boxing had strengthened him and, after defending his corner on a couple of occasions, he was left alone while they targeted a weaker child. Schools were overcrowded, as many of them had been requisitioned as makeshift morgues, and working class life was hard and brutally competitive – individualism was what kept your head above water.

The constant bombing, petrol and food shortages and the blackout meant that most people spent a lot of time in their homes. Terry's mother still went to work, making just enough money to feed the gas meter and buy some coal. She had already sold the few possessions they had to make ends meet. To combat the terror of the raids and claustrophobia of the home, people also took refuge at the cinema, where for one or two pennies they could escape reality for a few hours. More often than not the kids couldn't afford the ticket price and would 'bunk in', picking the lock on the fire safety doors with a bent piece of wire.

I remember during the war going to Crouch End Broadway. We used to bunk in every Sunday. I remember sitting through two or

three performances just to see a film and walking home during the air raids with all the shrapnel falling around. — Matt Monro

Harry had also returned home briefly, but he and Terry were soon evacuated again, this time together, to South Luffenham. Arriving in the countryside after living in a big city was alarming. Although there were woods, fields and open spaces, the village itself felt small and unfamiliar to the two boys. Instead of the characteristic red beacons of London, the countryside buses were grey and only ran once a day. It was another huge upheaval for young Terry. However, the brothers only stayed a few weeks since the village didn't have the facilities to educate Harry.

After South Luffenham, Harry was next shipped to Linslade, Leighton Buzzard, this time to the Pantlings' residence at 90 Soulbury Road. Terry was put on a train from London and turned up at the three-bedroom council house asking for Harry, and the family put him up for two nights. Alice asked Hilda Pantling if she could help find lodgings for Terry so that he could be near his brother and she turned to her close friends Bob and Liz Watson, who lived with their children Grace and Joan on the same road at number 76. On Terry's arrival there was a freshly-made cake and lemonade waiting in the kitchen and a small, neatly made up bedroom at the top of the house. Terry had never had a room of his own before, or a cupboard or even a drawer. This was a luxury not even afforded to adults in his family.

Terry went to The Boys School in Leopold Road under the watchful eye of headmaster Mr Samuel, while Grace Watson attended The Girls School. They did the regulatory arithmetic, spelling, writing and reading. Both schools were very strict – naughty children were kept in at the end of the day and in extreme cases the cane would come out of hiding. Although Terry was not a lover of church he sang in the boys' choir with three other evacuees at St Barnabas' Church. When Christmas came Terry joined others to tour the village singing carols.

Sunday was considered a day of rest, so the children were not allowed to play, but as a rare treat they would go for walks along the canal. The river was the best place to fish and the boys often competed against each other for the most impressive catch. When the weather dictated, although lacking in trunks, they would swim in the icy waters to cool down. If they heard anyone coming they would hold their breath under the water until the strollers had passed so as not to get in trouble.

At the back of the house was an expanse of fields, including Bluebell Woods, and Grace and Terry used to go there to climb trees, go apple scrumping and fool around under the hayricks. Terry started smoking at eleven and persuaded Grace, who was older than him by a few years, to try it out, then bribed her to buy him packets of Woodbines – threatening to spill the beans to her parents if she refused.

At fourteen years of age, Grace started work for Aquascutum as a machinist making uniforms for the troops and receiving fifteen shillings a week. Terry found work in the cellars of the local pub, The Clarendon, by lying about his age. The two children spent nearly all their time together. Terry was the younger brother Grace never had and Terry shared her affection.

The village was fairly quiet and there was very little to remind the children that a war was going on apart from occasional army manoeuvres through the small street. If they wanted information on the outside world they would visit the cinema to watch the *Pathé News*.

Terry stayed at Linslade Junior School and he and Harry would occasionally go to the cinema together in Leighton Buzzard. Their mother had a friend who worked on the railways and sometimes got privilege tickets, which was how she managed to visit the boys every few months. On one visit she took Harry home with her. He was four years older than Terry and it was time for him join the workforce as a plumber's mate.

Terry didn't pass the eleven plus exam. Those that failed were moved into another building and remained there another two years, until they were released from school at the age of fourteen to become shop assistants, errand boys, apprentice tradesmen or Watney's Brewery girls. Terry left Linslade before he was fourteen after a stay of two years.

Terry arrived home to find streets of abandoned houses. Many of their neighbours had not fared well and had left their homes for safety elsewhere. Terry had seen a lot of collapsing buildings since the war started, but it was nothing like seeing this, right by his own home. He took to the streets with his old friends and little gangs formed, who set up base and played imaginary war. The boys climbed through shattered windows and found a disused wonderland of enormous houses and empty flats. Other small gangs had the same idea, and it was often a race to see who could claim the spoils of war first. The friends scrambled through the rubble, collecting items left behind by previous owners, amassing what they could in the hope of a quick sale to earn a few pennies. They were very inventive when it came to ways of making money.

We used to go 'coking' at the weekend, down to the gasworks.
We'd collect sacks of coke and earn a farthing for every sack.
People needed it to eke out their coal, which was in short supply.

South Luffenham School

If you had an old pram or a pushchair you could fetch more than one sack at a time. — Matt Monro

Alice was not happy about Terry being home. She felt it was only a matter of time before he would get into trouble in London, so in 1943 she made arrangements for him to be billeted out of the city with a middle-aged couple, Charles and Rosetta Hudson, who already had a young lad living with them in South Luffenham. Alan Fox had been in an orphanage before being fostered by the Hudsons and with Terry's arrival he had company for the best part of a year.

South Luffenham was a small village in the county of Rutland, with only two shops, a combined Post Office and general store, and a provisions store and greengrocer. Rose and Charlie lived at number three in the middle of a row of five cottages called Flower Terrace. They were an elderly couple who had never had children of their own and felt that by taking in evacuees they were helping the war effort. They were strict but caring and gentle people and Terry grew very fond of them. The cottage had a long, large garden complete with outhouses and a pigsty. There was no electricity or telephone, only paraffin oil lamps and candles. Cooking was done on a hob on one side of the fire grate with a water tank on the other, both heated by an open fire burning wood or coal. There was no fridge but they had a sizeable larder that kept the food cool. The cottage had three bedrooms, the main one for the Hudsons and two double beds in the other two. Alan shared with another evacuee, Ray Harper, and Terry shared with Ray's brother, Malcolm.

The Post Office shop took me on to deliver papers and I collected two shillings and sixpence in tips, which I used towards buying myself my first long pair of trousers. — Matt Monro

The rector of the parish church was Reverend Brown, but the boys called him Biff. He was extremely fond of his 'vacs', as he called the children, and used his car to take them on regular swimming outings to Peterborough and visits to Wickstead Park in Kettering. He also allowed the boys the use of his bicycle, teaching most of them how to ride. All the children were obliged to attend church every Sunday and Aunt Rose encouraged her charges to join the choir. She had a lovely singing voice herself and had been a member of the Uppingham Choral Society in her younger years. One of her choirmasters was Malcolm Sergeant, who went on to become a renowned conductor. Alan and Terry were both members of the church choir, and the Reverend took full advantage of their abilities, repeatedly selecting them for solo parts, which they secretly enjoyed.

The village school housed two large classrooms, one for infants, the other for the over sevens. Mrs Tebbutt, the headmistress, would arrive from nearby Stamford, where she lived, and the girls would go over the fields to meet her. The boys would accompany them, mainly to enjoy the freedom of the open air and run alongside the riverbanks that cut through the fields. The school cook was Mrs Russingham and all the evacuees stopped at school for dinner. On a child's birthday she would make their favourite pudding, which was guaranteed to earn her a smile.

When they weren't in school or singing in the choir, the boys had plenty of chores to keep them busy. They trekked up to the woods to collect logs and small branches to make kindling to light the fires. They fetched the milk from farmer Bellamy and helped plant vegetables in Uncle Charlie's two allotments. Charlie was head herdsman on Pridmore Farm and the children would help out by taking the cattle to Stamford market, a walk of nearly eight miles. There were no stand pipes in the area, so all the water had to be fetched from the spring that flowed into a well in the middle of the village. Terry filled six buckets with drinking water each day and kept a large outside tank topped up for washing and cleaning.

Breeding rabbits was one of Uncle Charlie's sources of income and every day Terry and I had to fill four sacks of rabbit-grub containing dandelions, cow parsley, sour thistles and cloves from the fields and hedgerows. — Alan Fox

Aunt Rose was an excellent cook, making up meals of vegetables, homemade bread, butter, jam and cakes. She even made her own wine in flavours ranging from rhubarb, elderberry, ginger, parsnip and carrot. They would have meat twice a year when Uncle Charlie selected one of the pigs for slaughter. Local butcher Bitty Lake would come and kill the animal in the garden, cutting it into hams and flitches and providing bacon, sausages and pork pie, though the lion's share always went to the grown-ups. The cuts would be put on flat trays, preserved in salt and put in the long pantry. When the pigs were being fattened all the people in the village who didn't keep animals would bring their scraps around to help with the feed. They knew that Pig's Fry – a mixture of kidney, liver, and pork belly with bacon on the top – would be doled out to them later, taken home on a plate covered with a napkin. It was a good time for the whole neighbourhood and everyone got a decent meal.

The children under Rose and Charlie's care formed a close-knit group and often used nicknames for each other. Alan's was Tester, as he was always chosen to go and try things first. Terry earned his moniker, Bramble, on one of his many trips to Spano Aerodrome. The runways were close to the perimeter fence and were in disrepair, with huge cracks spreading across the tarmac. Within the cracks, blackberry brambles grew in circles very low to the ground. There were loads of blackberries and very large ones too, so the boys often stripped off their shirts and set about collecting the fruit. A good haul might make them some pocket money. Terry was a good deal shorter than the other boys and instead of leaning over the brambles to pick them he noticed a small gap in the bush and crawled through to grab some extra juicy ones. When the boys had enough and were getting ready to go home, Terry found he couldn't find the gap he had crawled though and became trapped in the middle of the bramble bushes. The boys all wore short trousers so couldn't get in to help their mate without getting ripped to shreds by the thorns. They called on the help of some beet workers in the surrounding fields who came and cut him out, laying coats over the brambles to prevent being caught in the thorns. Laughing at Terry's predicament, they assured him they would soon have him out, calling out, "come on Bramble, let's be having you". The nickname stayed with Terry throughout his teenage years and ended up gaining Alan access to Terry twenty years later.

Once again, it was time for Terry to return home to London. The city had been left badly damaged and the buildings that remained standing looked shabby and in desperate need of repair. In that spring of 1945, Terry had a strong sense that his childhood was over.

**I remember Mum's face, full of tears, full of joy at having me home
again. This woman who had lived through two world wars, still
stood upright with open arms. — Matt Monro**

Terry came back to a very different family scene. Harry had entered the Royal Air
Force as soon as he had turned eighteen, ending up as Acting Sergeant Instructor
at Lyme Regis, as had Reg. Harry and Terry would often visit Reg at Mill Hill
Barracks where he was based and they were always guaranteed a few free drinks.
Arthur, the oldest, was married and both he and Alice were working.

Terry's war heroes were the RAF boys Alice brought home. It used to cost her
a packet of chewing gum or a chocolate bar to get rid of him so she could steal a
kiss and a cuddle.

Fourteen was the earliest age you could leave school and Terry was forced to so
he could go to work. He found himself undertaking a succession of mundane jobs;
his first was with the Imperial Tobacco Co, where he started in the factory as an
offal boy collecting waste tobacco and sweeping up the debris from the cutting
machines. Terry recalled that the post-war tobacco shortage was greatly increased
by his own personal consumption at source. Terry kept five shillings of each week's
salary before handing the rest over to his mother but she wasn't left with much as
she insisted on paying her son's fares and dinner money.

Terry was always enthusiastic about starting a job but boredom quickly set in. He
drove a lorry delivering Guinness for the Bulldog Brewers, but that only lasted a
week. A series of jobs followed, including office worker, apprentice to a master builder,
fireman on the old London North Eastern Railway Line from King's Cross, as well
as a plumber's mate, decorator's mate and a plasterer's mate. Terry kept searching for
the one elusive job that could hold his interest. Next came attempts as an electrician,
coalman, bricklayer, truck driver, kerbstone fitter, factory floor sweeper, stonemason,
milkman, baker and even a general factotum in a custard factory. Terry even claimed
to have put the heating system into Vauxhall's at Luton. Jobs came and went. In one
year he held a total of fifty-three jobs. He detested all of them.

The music scene saw many changes nearing the late 1940s. Discs were played on
78rpm records, pressed on shellac (a brittle material that was easily scratched) and
played on wind-up gramophones that pushed the sound through steel needles.
Recording methods had their limitations and lack of space on the disc meant that
no piece of music could exceed three minutes. The elite could afford all-electric
gramophones with loudspeaker amplification. In America, the jukebox became all

the rage, launching a clutch of young stars by repeated playing of a song along with continual requests on wartime radio shows, which helped sell the idea of the hit record. American radio show *Hit Parade* began playing the top selling music of the week and *Billboard* magazine also published its first Music Popularity Chart. 'I'll Never Smile Again' by Tommy Dorsey, with vocalist Frank Sinatra, was the first ever 'Number One' record, an achievement honoured by the presentation of a gold disc. Thereafter it became every artist's aim.

Terry's love of music hadn't waned and his childhood years were spent listening to the magic that emanated from the radio. At first he was unimpressed by Sinatra, but in later years firmly believed him to be the best interpreter of a song. He also loved Perry Como and remained a great admirer of the man throughout his life.

> I used to listen to Peter Potter on *Voice of America* through the American Forces Network. Perry Como was the singer and hearing 'Prisoner of Love' set my sights on a musical career. I've never seriously learnt to play a musical instrument but I wish I had.
> — Matt Monro, *Hong Kong Sunday Post-Herald*

From the age of fourteen Terry spent as much time as he could either practising his singing or performing for other people. The first time he sang with a group was in his teens at the Tufnell Park Palais in North London with The Bill Evans Band. He was trying to impress a girl he was dancing with, hoping to escort her home, and began singing in her ear. She told him that if he really had to sing he should get up on the stage. Being dared by friends and with his confidence boosted by a few beers, the young boy took his youthful courage into his hands and did just that. He asked Evans, who played saxophone, if it was all right to sing a number. Like all good fairy tales, Evans was so impressed with the impromptu performance that he gave Terry a regular Saturday night spot with the band, singing two songs for ten bob a night. One of the numbers, 'I Wonder Who's Kissing Her Now', was Terry's star turn.

> I always used to hang around the ballrooms like the other guys when I was about fifteen years old. As with other local kids, I used to go into the pub to have a few pints, then the lads used to say, "Why don't you get up and sing a song?" and I did and people seemed to like it. That was more or less the start of it. Every kid seeks admiration and that was my ego trip. — Matt Monro

Another one of Terry's favourite singing haunts was The Brecknock Arms, conveniently located near to where he lived at Kingsley House on the Brecknock Road Estate. Harry recalled also going with Terry to a pub in York Way. People often referred to him as Perry Como, because Terry had modelled himself on him. "It was only later that he developed his own style. Bowie, as he was known to family and friends ever since our father nicknamed him, never owned any records because he was always broke but listened to the radio all the time. It was only when I heard him sing at The Boston that I realised how good he was, then at Hornsey Town Hall. He was very popular with the girls. One rang the house and after the required small talk she asked Terry to sing to her down the phone, but Terry kept saying no. He told her if she sang to him first, then he would sing to her. My brother-in-law, a telephone engineer, hooked up the telephone to the valve speaker on the radiogram and this girl sung and made the most frightful noise you've ever heard in your life – we all had a laugh. After that he was obliged to sing her a few notes."

Nobody else in the family could sing. In my case God saw that I couldn't do anything and had nothing else going for me. So he decided: "I've got to do something to help this poor bastard".
— Matt Monro

When Terry was sixteen, Harry came home on leave from the Air Force and, having a few bob in his pocket, Terry latched onto his brother for an evening out. They went to The Belmont and Harry bought them a pint each. Terry didn't waste any time in grabbing the microphone at the piano for a song, and it wasn't long before he had people flocking around him and buying drinks. Although Harry didn't buy another drink for the rest of the night, he went home alone while Terry went home with the girl.

The weather was brutal in the early part of 1947, as Britain was gripped by an Arctic freeze that lasted two months and nearly brought the country to a standstill. According to records there wasn't a single day when it didn't snow somewhere in the United Kingdom, but it didn't stop Terry trudging to various public houses in pursuit of his dream.

Terry was singing most nights at The Boston in Tufnell Park with their resident trio. The atmospheric venue boasted a huge lounge at the back, capable of holding two hundred people. One of Terry's regular songs was 'There's a Tree in the Meadow', because it was a big Dorothy Squires hit at the time. The Tufnell Park

Terry at 16

Palais was above The Boston and Terry and friends would often practice there. Terry's pay was a much-needed seventeen shillings and sixpence. He was always broke and never held a day job for very long. As a consequence he was always borrowing money from both his sister Alice and brother Reg.

> **Bowie, Bob Weedon, Johnny Bromberg, Leo Kennedy and myself were called the 'Tufnell Park Indians' and we tried to emulate the Four Freshmen. I wasn't allowed to sing as they said I sounded like a rusty saw, so I stuck to my bass. — Chris Day**

In the post-war years conscription to the armed forces began at eighteen, but it was possible to volunteer to serve in the forces as soon as you turned seventeen, which Terry did. Prior to his departure, his mother bought him a St Christopher's medallion, the patron saint of travellers, to keep him safe. He wore it throughout his life. Although he had often dreamt of travel, his incentive for joining the

Reg and Jean's wedding.

Regular Army in 1948 on a five-year engagement wasn't just the promise of adventure in far-away lands.

> **I had somebody's husband after me for a start. He was a villain. I was also out of work and I didn't know what to do with myself. It all seemed a good idea at the time, but I've no regrets. — Matt Monro**

The night before he enlisted in the army, and encouraged by friends and a few pints, the young Terry Parsons took to the stage at The Boston, to his sister Alice's initial horror and subsequent amazement. As he was going to stay the night in Tottenham Court Road, a place where they put the troops up, Terry had invited Alice and his brother Reg and wife Jean for a farewell drink. As soon as they were settled some of the older ladies started shouting out, "Bowie, give us a song," and Terry went up on stage. Alice and Jean went to the toilets totally embarrassed; they had no idea he could sing. Then they heard the lyrics of 'The Ring Your Mother Wore', and it was so good that they came out to hear the song properly. They realised that people had stopped dancing and were listening, which was unheard of in the North London pub. It was the first time Alice had heard her brother sing.

PRIVATES ON PARADE

Terry joined the REME (Royal Electrical & Mechanical Engineers) as 2233273 Craftsman Parsons after filling in application forms at a London Recruiting Office in Montague Street. He was initially stationed in Britain, first passing his driving test, then a mechanic's course and an advanced driver's exam, resulting in an upgrade to instructor. After an interminable wait for his medical, he was finally approved fit to serve. Terry was marched down to the NAAFI and ordered to spend eight shillings six pence on essentials like boot polish, Blanco, Brasso and toothpaste, leaving just one shilling six pence to be misspent.

Terry trained at Bovington, an army camp in Dorset, and also spent time doing Light Aid Detachment (LAD) work at various places like Perham Downs and Blackdown in Mill Hill. A lot of the camps were scattered around the Stonehenge area, as the ground was good for tank training. His basic soldier instruction included marching, billet cleaning, drilling, use of hand grenades and shooting with all manner of guns. After six weeks of basic training he began his trade instruction as a tank driver at Perham Downs.

As the camp was only eighty-five miles away from home, Terry tried sneaking off on a Friday and hitchhiking back to London. On his first attempt, a few of them got a lift on an open topped lorry where they froze for about an hour. The only alternative was to take the official coach, which left from the guardhouse every Saturday lunchtime. The cost was eighteen shillings return. Getting back had its own set of problems and many a time a cold and tired group of soldiers could be seen trudging down a pitch black road towards their second home at 3.30am on a Monday morning.

One of the lads tried arranging a coach for the return trip to London at a discounted cost of twelve shillings. Not surprisingly, there were many takers. Come the Saturday a rather tired rickety coach turned up at the camp gate and those sitting at the front found they were treated to diesel fumes coming off the engine. On the Sunday night they assembled at King's Cross Station for their return trip back to camp. There were always extra takers for that leg of the journey, as there was otherwise no sure way of getting back in time, which would have them marked down as AWOL. The seats were highly uncomfortable, but at a reduced fee of six shillings it was worth it.

All trainees were 'potential' officer material, but any potential Terry had disappeared the minute he broke curfew. He was promoted to Lance Corporal but lost his stripe a week later. He often got himself in trouble while serving, as he frequently went AWOL. His mother and sister routinely had the military police knocking on their door demanding to search the house for him – until Alice (who was fiercely protective of her youngest son) learnt from a soldier friend that they had no right of entry. She could now refuse access.

Terry was frequently on 'jankers', or prison time, being punished for his various indiscretions. Once, he returned late for duty whilst he was at Mill Hill and living at nearby Tufnell Park in London. Terry was awarded twenty-nine days' detention and forfeited thirty-six days pay for being AWOL on 14 February 1949. It must have been a memorable Valentine's date!

At the end of trade training they were given postings to operational units. The most coveted postings were overseas to such exotic places as Singapore and Hong Kong, where they were led to believe there was a generous amount of spare time that could be spent lazing on the beaches. The reality was quite different. There was a surplus of mechanical engineers and most postings were in England. Terry was required to rough it in exotic locations like Blandford and Blackdown, each of which seemed to have a rain cloud permanently tethered over the town. The day was a catalogue of boring routines, such as the NATO exercise, guard duty, fire picket, and periods spent on fatigues, which often involved emptying dustbins around the officer's marital quarters.

While serving at Wyke Bridging Camp, Craftsman Parsons entered a talent competition on Weymouth Pier, called the Carroll Levis Discoveries. He came second to a blind pianist performing the Warsaw Concerto. Terry won a table thermometer, which he took home to his mum, who continually heated it up over the gas stove to see if it was working properly.

Terry had already requested an overseas posting on entry to the army and after two years he was sent to Hong Kong for three years as a mechanic and tank instructor. He flew to Singapore on 18 October 1950, but not on quite the same routing as a modern day airline. The first stop, taking just over seven hours, was

Terry and his unit visit San Miguel Brewery, Hong Kong 1952

Malta, and from there they took the scenic route landing at Cyprus, Bahrain, Karachi, Bombay and Ceylon, before finally disembarking at Singapore. Because they travelled over neutral territories they were the first troops to fly out as civilians. Having been issued with 'civvies' that were rather larger than Terry, he turned up for parade looking like a pea on a drum. The trousers were turned up to the knee, his sleeves were turned up to the elbow and his coat came to his ankles. Even Terry's commanding officer couldn't stop a small smile escaping his lips.

They were housed in Changi (an ex-prisoner of war camp) for the first three weeks before their transfer to Sham Shui Poi Army Camp in Kowloon Tong. The freighter took fifteen days to complete a four-day journey, courtesy of the tail end of a hurricane. Terry was stationed under the watchful eye of his Adjutant Aubrey Whent and Provo Sergeant Don Butt who were responsible for the troops of 6FOD (Forward Ordinance Depot). It was now five years after the war had ended and the country was going through a rebuilding period, which was all very exciting for someone who had never been further than Sussex.

Terry was a vehicle mechanic; he worked in the first aid department for vehicles. The Light Aid Detachment REME personnel were placed there to carry out first line repairs. Tom Mulcahy also worked in the unit and he and Terry spent the next year together travelling all over the country, picking up parts for machines and tanks. Contrary to what Terry told everyone, he worked hard and was often given the added responsibility of Duty Driver, taking the orderly officer to Sham Chi Po. This was a unit on the docks, which had to be manned twenty-four hours a day.

Upon arrival Terry hooked up with George Clegg, Steve Hiscott, 'Rocky' Morrison, John Danbury, Peter McEvoy, Maurice Renshaw and Harry Killey. They shared a billet together along with five other men. Another friend Terry made was Full Corporal Edgar Francis James who came over to Hong Kong in 1952. He was a tank driver with ordinance and part of LAD. Terry and Ed used to go for long walks up to Lion's Rock, which overlooked the camp.

The men would be up at 6.00am, have breakfast on the half hour and first parade at 7.30am. If you were not present at parade you were declared AWOL. Duty would finish at 5.00pm and dinner would shortly follow. After that your hours were your own, and with no entertainment provided for the soldiers in camp, the boys would catch the number ten bus to Kowloon, often visiting the YMCA, popular because it served cheap beer.

Stationed in Hong Kong with the Royal Engineers, Terry discovered a profitable sideline, singing in battalion and local talent shows. Every Saturday night all the lads travelled on the Star Ferry to the Cheero Club, a serviceman's hangout at Murray Barracks that stood where the Hilton now looms. The *Beginners Please* contest was sponsored by the Philip Morris tobacco company, and the winner received two hundred of the company's cigarettes and a paltry ten Hong Kong dollars. But the big draw was the grand prize of a half hour show on Rediffusion, which was the local commercial radio station.

Terry took part in the club's weekly talent night and won. After an unprecedented seven wins, the organisers banned him from entering the competition as the sponsors were worried the contest would look crooked. The promoters solution was to offer Terry his own residency on one of their programmes on Radio Hong Kong and eventually Rediffusion gave him his own programme, *Terry Parsons Sings*.

> **One of the first places we went was the Cheero Club and Terry entered a talent contest. I was totally out of my depth but Terry was completely at home. He was born to do it, nothing fazed him. It was the best three years of my life. — Peter 'Yorky' McEvoy**

Terry Parsons Sings was broadcast to all those sensible enough to have acquired a Rediffusion radio set. The programme was a regular feature and Craftsman

Bing Rodriguez and band members

Parsons became reasonably well-known as a result. Terry's success led to several job offers, from troop entertaining to cabaret spots. At one such gig, while singing in one of the servicemen's clubs, he was spotted by Bing Rodriguez and asked to front his dance band at a local club in The Star Hotel. The band consisted of a local pianist and bass player, with Terry on vocals, Bing playing tenor sax and Tony Carpio on guitar. When their contract came to an end, they were offered a similar gig at the Ritz, a nightclub in the North Point district of Hong Kong. Bing went on to become one of Terry's dearest friends; it was a friendship that lasted a lifetime.

Craftsman Parsons finished the last eighteen months of his career in Hong Kong singing with the dance bands. His weekly army wage was sixty Hong Kong dollars, his dance band salary five times the amount; he always said he was the highest paid squaddie in the British army.

There was a strict 1.00am curfew in place and Terry was frequently busted as most of his gigs didn't finish until 01.15am. The rules dictated that he sign in and out of the guardroom, but more often Terry was able to sneak out of the front gate as he knew most of the guards on duty – unfortunately he couldn't get back in as easily. The front gate was too risky, so he used to come in over the wire at the back of the compound. The night before his first Rediffusion broadcast, Private Parsons returned to his unit rather later than his pass allowed. Coming in over his usual spot on the perimeter fence, he jumped straight into the arms of the RSM (Regimental Sergeant Major) and was promptly placed under house arrest and sent to the cells. Luckily for Terry he was on fairly good terms with his CO and persuaded him to allow his appearance on the pre-booked programme. The condition: two armed guards escorted Private Parsons to the radio station and stood either side of him throughout the broadcast. The story goes that the CO listened to the radio show. He must have enjoyed it for the charges were dismissed. He laughingly joked, "The army interfered with my career." Terry loved his time abroad. He thought that Hong Kong had to be the best posting in the British Army.

> You always remember the good things but I cannot for the life of me remember any really bad things about my army career. Of course, I did 'jankers' but that was the extent of my punishments. I never ever got sent away. The army taught me self-discipline and a great deal about comradeship. I was always conscious of being well turned out and I became very adroit at dodging people, especially when it came to getting back into camp after curfew. — Matt Monro

Capitalising on his newfound fame, Terry formed a small theatrical group in Hong Kong called The Doh-re-mis with Dorothy Hart-Baker and Mena Silas. They performed regular troop shows every Saturday night at the YMCA in Salisbury Road, Kowloon. In fact, Terry cut his first ever disc singing *Pagliacci* with Mena at piano at one of these shows.

> I also divided my time entering talent contests and singing in the YMCA on Saturdays. As soon as I got paid for warbling, I began to take it seriously, until then it had all been a bit of a joke. — Matt Monro

Terry was offered a nightly gig at the Imperial Ballroom in Nathan Road singing with Filipino Mistra Ray and his band. He was accepted socially and invited to all the big functions, moving in circles he hadn't known existed before. Singing for local radio one evening and then a cabaret the next, he was regularly arrested by army police for 'being adrift', often ending up with a seven-day stint in the cells for breaking curfew. Terry was escorted to the cookhouse to collect his meals but had to eat in his cell. Although the area was small with only a metal bed, a mattress and a sheet, it was the only part of camp that was equipped with fans, so it at least stayed cool in the stifling heat. The 'prisoners' had to work during the day – on

Parsons & Duval

more than one occasion Sergeant Don Butt made Terry cut the camp grass using a pair of hand scissors.

Sergeant Derek Billingham was nine months older than Terry and constantly in trouble for turning a blind eye during guard duty while Terry climbed over the wall to sing at one of the clubs in Kowloon. Derek and Terry had a third musketeer called 'Scouse' Woosey, an amazing saxophonist who could play every instrument under the sun. Derek and Scouse used to wait for Terry to get up and then set up drums and piano in the NAAFI and the three of them would play for two hours at a time.

Kessick Withey worked for the Admiralty and moved to Hong Kong in 1949 with his wife Irene and daughter Jean. He was an amateur comedian and formed a concert party to entertain the troops at The Seaman's Mission and the China Fleet Club. They also put on a talent night, which Kessick emceed. Terry, being a familiar face at these contests, had occasion to meet Kessick and later joined the Concert Party on a tour of the New Territories.

Most of the entertainment around Hong Kong was for the benefit of the troops, with regular dances held in the Forces Clubs. The bands across the colony took

Concert Party, New Territories (Kessick Withey is in the back row, third from right).

turns in playing at these gigs and The Kings Shropshire Light Infantry Dance Band was a familiar sight. Having joined the group in 1949 playing alto sax and clarinet, Corporal Bill Griffiths persuaded Lance Corporal Parsons (Terry having been promoted again) to join the band and act as Master of Ceremonies. One of their regular bookings was the weekly dance held in the Chatham Road NAAFI Club in Kowloon, which paid the men the princely sum of eight dollars a performance. Terry enjoyed that period of his life and stayed with the band until Bill's unit was moved to Korea in 1951.

> **We can distinctly remember Terry singing with us as a guest singer on quite a few occasions. One thing I remember is the fantastic applause he used to receive whenever he performed. He was a good-looking soldier, with a voice that was quite distinctive and appreciated by all the young girls, who always gave him a rousing ovation each time he sang. I feel very proud to have been on the same stage as him. — Bill Griffiths**

Bill had married a Chinese girl after meeting her on a blind date in 1950. She attended all of the band's gigs and often brought along a friend to keep her company while her husband was on stage. She was responsible for introducing

Terry to Doris Barton, who immediately became his long-term girlfriend.

Richard Crook was in the Royal Navy at the beginning of the 1950s. It was around this time that he bumped into young Terry Parsons at the Cheero Club opposite the enormous Hong Kong and Shanghai Banking Corporation building – now known as the HSBC. They instantly hit it off and regularly spent evenings together over the course of a couple of months, until Richard's ship returned to England.

> From time to time I would see Terry, and on one of these occasions he had just won fifteen Hong Kong dollars at a talent contest and I helped him spend most of it. We used to meet in the Wanchai district, have a few drinks in the Universal Club, followed by a meal, or we might go to the Jockey Club. Everywhere we went people knew Terry, including the local Chinese. He was doing some programmes for the Silver Network of Radio Hong Kong, which he later invited me to. — Richard Crook

Most evenings Terry was still actively moonlighting, with the army's knowledge he said – but he didn't always sneak away to sing. Neville Clark worked for the Whampoa Docks in Kowloon as a clerk, but was also responsible for booking the entertainment at one of the more celebrated clubs in the area. Neville was credited with giving Terry his first break, singing at the HK Kowloon Lawn Bowls Club. The ex-patriot community was fairly small after the war and the club was the social centre of the neighbourhood. They had a swimming pool, several lawn bowls greens, a cricket pitch and inside the clubhouse a restaurant, bar and several meeting rooms. Neville and his wife Margaret became great friends with the young soldier, treating him as one of the family. Margaret was forever making sure Terry had something to eat. In return for Neville's support, Terry often helped him out with babysitting duties.

Another person he grew very close to was Ray Cordeiro, who music lovers across the country knew as Uncle Ray. Their friendship grew while Terry was working at Radio Hong Kong. Ray started out as a bank clerk, which bored him to tears, but the evenings gave him the chance to pursue his real passion: music, especially jazz. He formed Ray and his Band, with himself as the trio's drummer, and continued to do the two jobs for a few years. But burning the candle at both ends began to take its toll and on the advice of his brother, who worked at the newly formed Rediffusion, the first cable radio station in Hong Kong, he took a job as a scriptwriter, a job he knew nothing about it. Under the guidance of his American boss Frank Harris, Ray made a name for himself, rising through the ranks and eventually becoming one of the company's DJs.

Ray often tagged along in the evenings with Terry and his army pals, taking in a show or sharing several drinks. It was not unusual for the lads to drink four or five pints a night and Ray desperately tried to keep up with them. In November, enjoying a rare night off, Terry and Ray were invited by John Wallace to see a show at The Lee Theatre featuring Caesar Velasco and his Skyroom Band in *Band Show*. Most locals were familiar with the Parsons face and reputation and it wasn't long before Caesar invited Terry up on stage for a guest spot. In fact, Terry was so familiar to the local population that most private function requests came from Chinese and Portuguese couples wanting the singer to entertain their wedding guests.

Army pal Ken Brown in the Royal Artillery (45th Field) first met Terry in Hong Kong and they joined forces as *Parsons & Duval*, a vocal comedy act performing at the local YMCA. Ken's surname had been changed to Duval as Brown didn't sound theatrical enough. Both men had enlisted at the same time, but Ken had been sent to fight in Korea while Terry was posted to Hong Kong.

Returning to Hong Kong and now officially attached to a combined services entertainment unit, Ken immediately looked to make contact with people interested in show business. At the first opportunity, he went to see one of the Saturday night shows at the YMCA, which featured about half a dozen acts. He wandered backstage after the performance, and the first person he met was Terry. The two soldiers immediately became friends; there was an instant chemistry between them as if they had known each other for years.

By the time Ken met Terry, the singer had already won several talent competitions and been featured on local radio programmes. Ken watched his newfound friend perform at the YMCA one evening and both thought it would be a great idea to team up as a double act. They set about rehearsing a suitable routine, *Comedy and Songs,* and took on John Wallace as their manager. As well as his job on the radio station, Wallace also worked for the *South China Post* as a correspondent and had a variety of contacts. He set about the task of securing bookings for the duo.

Dozens upon dozens of people went to see *Parsons & Duval*, often performing on the American aircraft carriers that went in and out of Hong Kong. Each performance strengthened their friendship. On one occasion, Ken was confined to barracks for seven days for being late back to camp. Terry was asked to perform on the second day of his friend's incarceration but would only do so with his partner. Ken was released early.

If the duo were offered bookings, they took them, however awkward it was geographically. On one such occasion Terry and Ken were booked at a club in one of the far-reaching towns and flown in to the local airbase, with the airstrip smack-dab in the middle of open country and the gig several miles away. It was already dark and their escort was nowhere to be found. Terry took the liberty of 'borrowing' a car that had the keys conveniently left in the ignition. He drove it to the barracks and abandoned it next to the venue. As it turned out, Terry had inadvertently stolen the Chief of Police's car. Luckily the duo were never questioned about how they had travelled to the venue.

Laughter seemed to follow the boys everywhere. One of their shows was in a make-shift camp. A wooden stage had been hastily built and an army truck was parked against the stage to be used as their dressing room. Duval opened the act and, having warmed up the crowd, introduced Terry, who strolled on singing a romantic ballad. He intended to take the centre spot while Ken changed, but before the singer reached the mark, the stage collapsed taking most of his lower body with it. There was Terry, his outstretched arm extending out of the hole, still with microphone in hand, trying to finish the song. The crowd erupted, taking Ken with them on the wave of belly-laughter. It took six soldiers to cut Terry out of the wreckage and, although a dance troop performed in front of the collapsed stage, the audience were more focused on the rescue attempt.

On another occasion, Terry and Ken wrote a new script and asked the stagehand to place it somewhere easily visible, so he pinned it to the curtains. Of course, when the show started the curtains were drawn back and the script promptly flew out into the arena.

One weekend, the duo were joined by a girl singer, Patty Swift. Girl was rather a kind description, as she was most likely in her fifties. The opening gambit of Patty's act was to swing to the stage on a rope to the sounds of 'Hang on the Bell Nellie'. Waiting in the wings, Patty asked Ken and Terry to give her a push on line three of the chorus, vigorous enough to swing her right across the stage – but she came off mid-flight!

Despite all the laughs, the friendship had a serious side. Ken and Terry were parked outside the base one night talking about spiritualism. Confessing to previously being a complete sceptic, Terry admitted he was now a strong believer and as he talked his face suddenly transfigured to that of someone else. Though it

gave Ken quite a fright, the incident was evidence enough to make a believer of
him as well. Terry admitted that spiritualism had altered his outlook on many of
life's problems, but he mostly preferred to keep his spiritual beliefs private. In later
life he had several one-on-one sittings with mediums; he was advised that he would
marry twice and that his second wife would have a great influence on his career.

Ken used to stay in Terry's camp after the Hong Kong shows as he was stationed
out in the New Territories and it was too far to travel back late at night. They spent
two fun-packed years together, developing a fabulous friendship. The duo went
from success to success, building up to an appearance at Government House
before Sir Alexander Grantham and his wife – then the Governor of Hong Kong.
When the time came for them to be demobbed, the *South China Morning Post*
acknowledged their popularity.

> **Today Terry Parsons and Ken Duval are leaving for the United
> Kingdom. They have been without a doubt the most popular
> entertainers in Hong Kong for the last twelve months, and have
> always been asked to go back again wherever they have performed
> and described as Terry Parsons, England's answer to Frank Sinatra
> and Ken Duval, half Danny Kaye, half Jerry Lewis. At least we can
> say we saw them first. — *South China Morning Post***

Their time was over in Hong Kong. Ken went to Australia and Terry to England.
Terry had played nearly every venue in the country, worked black tie events, white
dinner jacket parties, concerts, broadcasts and sung at the Governor's party.

Terry actually volunteered to stay on in the army. He had done five years, but
had seven left on the reserve. His commanding officer explained that three years
was the maximum he could serve in the Far East. He would therefore have to go
back to England for a minimum of six months and then they would try and
reclaim him. Terry realised it was likely he would end up in Germany through the
winter and changed his mind, taking his discharge. The testimonial from his army
discharge papers stated that he was a willing worker with a good knowledge of
wheeled vehicles and capable of carrying through a job without supervision. He
had a high standard of ability as a vehicle inspector and was clean and well turned-
out.

Terry had been based in Hong Kong for three years, a location which was to
become the springboard for his aspirations as an international singer. He

acknowledged that his later success was moulded by his continual moonlighting engagements whilst in the army. Years later, at a concert in Manila and dressed in a beautiful barong, the traditional dress of the Philippines, he stated that his success in music was due to the Filipino musicians he'd met in Hong Kong in the 1950s.

> I can never forget Caesar Velasco, Bing Chambing, Bing Rodriguez and Chris Villa, who taught me how to sing well. We drank, dined, slept, laughed and stayed together in Hong Kong during my past wild days. Filipinos are always special people to me. — Matt Monro

AN ANAGRAM OF MORON

In June 1953, Terry's old life in Hong Kong ebbed away as every nautical mile of the six-week voyage took him closer to a Britain in the grip of Coronation fever. His buoyant optimism reflected the new mood of the country but his success abroad counted for little back home. An agent advised him to get a job in a nightclub and promised he'd come and see him work, but they proved to be empty words.

Terry had trouble staying in a regular job. His sister's husband Len Carron worked at the GPO on the telephone side and got Terry some work there. In the afternoon of Terry's first day Len received a telephone call to ask after Terry's whereabouts, as he had apparently not returned from his lunch break. Terry later told Len that it had been too boring. The young man was clearly single-minded about what he really wanted to do.

He joined a semi-pro band, The Jimmy Cavanaugh Trio, at the weekends working at Hornsey Town Hall under the pseudonym Terry Fitzgerald. Terry had worked out that if he sang a few songs at the dance hall he wouldn't have to pay the two shillings and sixpence to get in. Similarly, his friend, Len Farnell, struck a deal with the singer – Terry would adopt Len as his manager so he could get in for free as well, but Len would have to buy the drinks.

During this period, on 27 June 1953, Terry recorded 'How Deep is the Ocean' and 'All of Me' but it isn't clear how or who the acetate was cut with. It remains in the archives bearing nothing but the date etched into the disc.

Not content to give up his dream, Terry auditioned for Eric Delaney and Eric Winstone and worked for a short while with Stan Davis's Band, but the gigs weren't regular enough to provide an adequate income. Driving was the only skill he left the army with and when things looked bleak, which they did with sickening regularity, Terry drove to make ends meet. This time, instead of tanks, he drove a builder's lorry delivering cement to the many building sites that were trying to reconstruct war-torn Britain.

Terry was also back entering talent competitions in the local area. A record crowd of seven hundred people saw him win the contest at the Islington Town Hall, an achievement that was recorded in the local paper on 5 March 1954.

Saturday night would usually find Terry and his friends at the Tufnell Park Palais, but another hang-out was the St John's Distillery in Archway Road. It was a big pub with a dance hall at the back where on the weekend Ernie Oliver would play with his band The Oliver Trio. Ernie played piano, his wife Ella played double bass and Ted played the drums. Although the band was called a trio, Ernie often had friends that would join in, including Terry on vocals and trumpet-player Arthur Ewbank. Terry and Ernie became great mates, often going on auditions together.

It was during one of those weekends that he met Iris Jordan. This was Terry's first serious romance since returning home and after the loneliness of the last few years he confused companionship with love. The romance progressed to marriage after Iris informed her boyfriend she was pregnant and on 15 January 1955, Iris' father gave away his daughter's hand in marriage at the local registrar's office. Terry's mother wasn't too pleased about the situation and, knowing money was short, allowed the couple to live with her until they found their feet. Terry initially took a job long-distance driving on the London to Glasgow haul to provide for his new family, but soon gave the job up, as it meant he wasn't around for any evening singing gigs.

1954 had seen a new craze sweep over from America with the Crew Cuts giving the world 'Sh-Boom' and Bill Haley and the Comets releasing 'Rock Around the Clock'. If that wasn't enough to feed teenage hysteria, a good-looking lad called Elvis hit the charts with 'That's Alright Mama'.

In fact, music was to see a dramatic change over the next few years. In the 1940s, music was all about the big bands and the following decade saw artists like Frank Sinatra, Ella Fitzgerald and Perry Como commanding the adult market, but popular music was quickly turning into pop and new talents such as Pat Boone and Elvis Presley appealed in a booming teenage market demanding rock 'n' roll. And it wasn't just rock 'n' roll that carved out a niche for itself. 1955 saw Lonnie Donegan enjoy a number one hit with 'Rock Island Line', an upbeat version of a traditional song by the American Blues singer Leadbelly. The music industry woke up to the fact that there was a place for traditional music and, if marketed correctly,

Harry Leader Orchestra & Al Jordan.

folk music would be a big money earner.

Unaware of the changing market, Terry was still singing his brand of music at Hornsey Town Hall. Harry Leader – whose band had become popular because it deliberately set about to sound American – spotted the young man and convinced him to turn professional, signing him to sing with his band and drive the tour bus. Leader had originally taken a residency spot in the West End of London in 1942. Signed for a three-month try-out at the Astoria Ballroom in Charing Cross Road, his contract had seen him there for nearly thirteen years. It was a big step for Terry, working in the profession full-time, but he excitedly took on the challenge, taking the stage name of Al Jordan. His wife's maiden name was Jordan, which is probably where he came up with this pseudonym.

Harry auditioned the singer six times with the full band going out to a live audience. It took Terry a while to realise that while he was being auditioned, he wasn't getting paid. But that was Harry, always trying it on.

On 16 July 1955, Terry's son was born at the City of London Maternity Hospital and the newlyweds named him Mitchell Terence Parsons. When the time came for

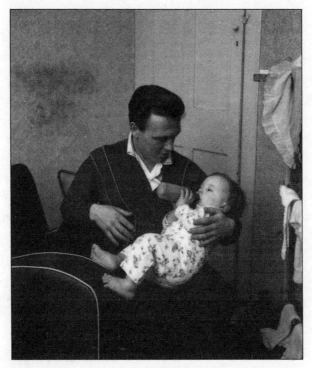

Terry & Mitchell

the birth certificate to be registered, Terry's profession was listed as 'milk roundsman'. With a baby to support, he took on additional driving jobs to earn extra money but continued to work with Leader in the evenings.

Although the couple had initially moved in with Terry's mother, the arrival of the baby prompted them to move to Windsor Road in Islington. Terry found it hard living with his mother's continuing disapproval.

Alice's disapproval didn't just apply to Terry and his wife. Harry was living with a woman, Pat, three years his senior who was estranged from her spouse. Alice Parsons was ashamed of her son and didn't approve of Pat one little bit and her view of the situation didn't improve much when the couple later married. She was slightly happier with Jean, her son Reg's choice of wife, feeling that she was more of her class, but ignoring the fact that her daughter-in-law didn't believe in lifting a hand when visiting.

Alice didn't actually disapprove of her daughter's marriage to Len Carron but was concerned that she was slightly detached from the real world. She was continually angry with her brother for joining the army, as she felt that he had deserted the family in his ambition to make good. In later years, Alice's jealousy would rear its ugly head in accusing her brother of stealing their mother's wedding ring on her deathbed. Her marriage gave her the opportunity of moving to Welwyn Garden City, which she did in the hope of distancing herself from the memories and poverty of her childhood. She didn't like to discuss her upbringing, while Terry was proud of his roots and remained so throughout his life.

Terry's mother was most content with Arthur's choice of spouse, Amelia, but didn't see the couple socially all that often. For his part, Terry kept his distance from all the family arguments and pettiness, preferring to immerse himself in the 'reality' of show business.

It was as Al Jordan that he gained his first commercial release when, on 10 August 1955, he recorded a cover of Frankie Laine's 'Strange Lady in Town' with The Harry Leader Band at IBC Studios in London for the American owned label Solitaire. Although Harry Leader arranged the recording, he couldn't take the credit for it being his protégé's first record, as Terry had already cut a version of 'On with the Motley' from *Pagliacci* in Hong Kong with Mena Silas on the piano – which was dreadful.

I came across Terry Parsons in 1955. I had been tipped off that there was a promising vocalist at Hornsey Town Hall. I went along there during my break off the stand at the Astoria. I knew at once that the singer was special and arranged for him to sing with my band on the American label Solitaire, renaming him Al Jordan.
— Harry Leader

Late September 1955 saw Harry announce he was taking the band on the road for a series of dates and a summer season in Bridlington Spa for July of the following year. For nearly six months Terry sang in a succession of one-night stands around the country and thought any job would be better. It meant month after month of travelling from one town to another and although he gained a wealth of experience, he wasn't earning enough money to justify being away from his young family.

On 4 April 1956, whilst playing at Green's Playhouse, Glasgow, Terry and a couple of the boys from the rhythm section, Spike Heatly on bass, Pete Smith at piano and Derek Fairblass on drums, decided to cut a private record to counteract the boredom of the day. They used Biggers Studios in the city centre and made *Polka Dots and Moonbeams*. The experience cost Terry thirty shillings and although he had been hugely excited about the prospect, his voice did not remotely sound as he had imagined it would and he was deeply disappointed. So there, for the time

being, his aspirations rested. Spike borrowed the track and in the interim Terry forgot about it.

> I wish I'd had a tape recorder in the early days. The fact is the voice one hears while actually singing and what comes out of a loud speaker bears little resemblance, that's what makes any playback so instructive. As far as singers are concerned it can offer harsh testimony, exposing bad intonation, errors of phrasing and breathing, as well as giving the first reliable evidence of the actual quality of a voice. — Matt Monro, *Melody Maker*

Being married with a child was a big responsibility and the long days away from home took their toll on Terry's relationship, forcing him to abandon his life on the road. He couldn't afford to stay with the dance band anymore, because although he was working five nights a week, driving the tour bus in the day and singing in the evenings, he was only earning twelve pounds a week. He was also expected to pay for his own digs and regularly shared with three other musicians, to reduce the bill and, on several occasions, he even slept in the bus.

Terry's next job would be associated with him for the rest of his life. An old schoolmate, Gordon Holland, suggested Terry try for a job at the London Transport Depot at Manor House, where he signed up as a driver for Holloway Garage.

Being only five foot six inches tall, he had quite a unique way of passing his test at Chiswick. The driving test was taken in a single-decker bus with a crash gearbox and he found that, once seated, he couldn't reach the clutch pedal, so each time he had to change gear he would stand up, rather like a jockey urging on his mount. Only after they had passed him did his supervisors tell him he could screw the seat down to accommodate his smaller frame. As a result of the incident, all his workmates soon nicknamed him Titch.

London Transport hired the aspiring singer and put him on a weekly wage of nine pounds. Allocated his bus badge (N46052), he regularly drove the number 27 Highgate to Teddington route and occasionally the number 14 route from Putney Bridge to Hornsey Rise. Both Terry and his regular conductor Nellie Mitchell had to be up at 4.00am to take the bus out at 5.00am.

Though his new work schedule was demanding, Terry still sought to establish himself as a band singer in the evenings, singing at a pub called The Favourite in Hornsey Rise. He also filled in with a Saturday night gig with Harry Pitch's band at the Hornsey Town Hall, where they would pass the hat around for him and there might be a couple of quid in it at the end of the night. Eventually the trio asked him to perform with them regularly for a fee of just over thirty-two shillings a night.

My brother Chris and I used to frequent the Favourite pub in Hornsey Rise, which was the terminus for the number 14 bus. They only had piano and drums but we both used to get up and give a song. We thought we were good. We realised Terry was well known in the pub because whenever he entered, whoever was next to be called to give a song had to wait until Terry had sung. On the first occasion we grumbled about the unfairness of this, but it was explained that Terry only had a limited amount of time because he had to get back in his bus. When we heard him sing, all our objections evaporated. He was so good that we used to make a point of going to the pub just to listen to him. He was a very nice, modest man, a great artiste – no gimmicks, no show, just a wonderful voice and personality. – George Skelly

Whilst Terry was working on the buses, Spike sent the Glaswegian disc to Winifred Atwell without telling his friend. Winnie was one of the biggest musical acts of the 1950s, Decca Records' most successful artist and an accomplished rag pianist with a series of boogie-woogie and ragtime hits. Out of the blue, Alice received a note from the Decca Recording Company addressed to her son, politely telling him that the record submitted had been unsuccessful. A couple of weeks later another letter arrived, telling her son that on Winifred Atwell's recommendation they had re-visited the disc and that they wanted to meet with him. It seemed if Winnie had faith in this young man's relaxed style then the label was prepared to have a little faith too.

Winnie had also sent a cable to the flat asking Terry to come and see her at the London Palladium where she was performing and he arrived in time to catch most of the Trinidadian's act. Her stage persona was of a gentle, rather aristocratic woman who came alive at the piano, with a dazzling smile that literally lit up the stage. Winnie's husband, former stage comedian Lew Levisohn, who was vital in shaping her career, was also watching from the wings. The couple had met in 1946 and became inseparable, marrying soon after. Lew took over the management of her career and had made an early decision that Winnie would open the show with a concert grand followed by honky tonk numbers played on her 'other piano', a beaten up old upright bought from a Battersea junk shop for fifty shillings. It was this piano that would later feature all over the world, from Las Vegas to the Sydney Opera House, travelling over half a million miles by air throughout Winnie's concert career. Winnie and Lew also made a business out of nurturing new stage and music talent and Terry was apparently next in line.

After the show, Terry chatted with the couple and it was decided that the young singer would audition at Decca with Dick Rowe, Winnie's recording manager. The label was every bit as enthusiastic about Terry as Winnie was, and they took the practically unheard of step of launching a new singer with an LP and a recording contract. The usual practice would have been a single disc release to test the waters. Terry left the audition with not just a recording contract with Decca, but also a management agreement with Lew Levisohn.

On 17 September 1956, Terry Parsons signed a contract with Decca for one year with two one-year options. He was so broke that the record company bought him a navy blue tonic suit, a plaid shirt, an overcoat and shoes with 'lifts', which were to be taken out of future royalties. He still used his two shirts and four starched collars, the only decent clothes he owned.

Less than six weeks after signing the new recording contract, Terry was booked in at the studios to cut his debut album *Blue and Sentimental* with The Malcolm Lockyer Orchestra. Terry, who was still driving the number 27 bus turned up at the studios on a chilly, miserable Sunday with a grade-A attack of nerves. Partly to keep himself warm and partly to have the comfort of familiar things around him, he kept on his heavy blue serge bus driver's jacket. It all looked a trifle bizarre: an aggregation of the country's finest musicians looking very professional, all the mechanical clutter of a recording studio looking very intimidating, and in the middle of it all, a bus driver wearing his pasteboard roundel indicating that he was licensed to drive a public service vehicle. No wonder the orchestra wore a 'now we've seen everything' look.

Certainly, Terry was a little uneasy upon recognising several top musicians in the room. The Malcolm Lockyer Orchestra warmed up in the recording studio ready to do a long stint in backing an unknown on his first long player. They ran through the first number. "Okay let's take this one" boomed a voice from the control box. They took it. They played it back. The musicians listened, looked at the not-so-tall singer and after a short pause, burst into applause.

Terry Parsons had satisfied the toughest, most cynical and certainly the most musicianly audience he ever had to face. He sang with a gimmickless freshness, as if the lyrics were his own personal thoughts, phrasing the song with a maturity that belied his inexperience. From that moment on, he was one of them. He loosened his tie, opened his collar, took off his bus driver's jacket and started a new career.

Decca soon decided Terence Edward Parsons needed a different name for his recording career and it took a matter of minutes to choose. 'Matt', taken from Matt White, an Australian Fleet Street journalist who worked for the *Daily Sketch* at the time and had written a centre-page spread of adulation about the singing bus driver, and 'Monro', from Winnie's father, Monro Atwell. Matt Monro was born.

In later years, Matt's name was legally changed along with his family, all except for his eldest son Mitchell, who retained his original birth moniker. But the constant misspelling came to irk him; it was either spelt Munro, Monroe or even Munrowe, sometimes as much as three different ways within the same article.

It's easy to remember, it's an anagram of moron! — Matt Monro

Laying down the album in one day, Matt recorded *Blue and Sentimental*, containing ten standards, his first commercial recording for a long-playing record. Most experienced artists took that amount of time over four or five titles. Decca released the long-playing record before he had even made a 78rpm.

First recording session with Decca

Producer John Browell heard a test pressing of 'Ev'rybody Falls in Love with Someone' at Matt's audition for Decca and was so excited about it that he agreed to attend an audition that Winnie had set up for Matt at the BBC's Variety Department. Only a few hours later, Matt had signed a contract to appear on *The Showband Show* with Cyril Stapleton and his orchestra, the most popular showband in Britain.

> Auditions were conducted in a studio, the panel that were listening to you were blocked off from the studio by a curtain so the artist couldn't see who they were performing to and the panel would allocate marks. Winnie arranged the audition and on hearing Matt, I was very impressed with him and subsequently I was able to offer him work with the BBC Show Band, conducted by Cyril Stapleton.
> — John Browell

Cyril Stapleton was a recognised orchestra leader, mainly due to his regular BBC broadcasts and recordings. His fame was assured when, in 1952, The BBC Dance Orchestra was changed to The BBC Show Band and Stapleton was appointed as its conductor. Despite initial criticism, under Stapleton's shrewd leadership it had become the BBC's prestige outfit for the playing of popular music, employing the finest musicians and arrangers and attracting not only top British singers, but American entertainers such as Frank Sinatra and Nat King Cole as well. Their importance to the music industry was demonstrated by the fact that at least one London publisher offered Stapleton the exclusive pick of all new songs several weeks before they were released to other performers.

On 10 November 1956, Matt recorded 'Ev'rybody Falls in Love with Someone' as his first single release. Decca hadn't given their new artist a great choice of material with which to launch his career. Although Matt's single had won the BBC's *Festival of Music*, Dickie Henderson and Don Rennie had both already recorded the track. At only one minute forty seconds it was rather short too.

Decca also dictated how Matt should sing, restraining him from letting go on all the high notes, and instead asking him to sing very quietly in the style of Perry Como. Although he adored Como, Matt didn't feel that was his style at all and that it was the worst thing he'd ever done.

> It would be unusual now for a hit record in the States to be taken up by another artist on this side of the Atlantic. In the 50s however all recorded versions of the same song came about on the same date. The practice was a reflection of the power of music publishers. In the mid-50s, the song rather than the artist or the record company was king. No singer could record a song without the publisher's agreement and their interest was primarily in the promotion of sheet music sales. Record charts had been introduced in the UK in 1952 but still played second fiddle to the sheet music listing. The consequence was that several different artists often recorded the top songs of the day. All the competing versions would be released on the same date. Sheet music copies regularly featured several different artists on the same cover. Sheet music sales of the big songs reached up to ten thousand copies per day, easily rivalling the number of records sold. — Ken Crossland, *The Man Who Would Be Bing*

Despite all the publicity, the single failed to sell, but Matt remained confident that his singing career had taken off. The BBC had officially announced that he would replace Dawn Lake as the featured singer in the Show Band from 3 December in their Light Programme. Preparing for a showband series in television was a major operation, like putting on a stage show. With forty-two musicians, thirty-five players and a choir of twelve, Cyril Stapleton had his work cut out for him and he needed his new singer to be available for run-throughs as soon as possible. So, without hesitation, Matt handed in his two-weeks notice at the bus garage.

Matt was still not earning much and relied on the five pounds a week Iris brought in as a dressmaker in the West End to pay the twenty-two shillings a week rent on their two-roomed flat at Windsor Road. The accommodation had green lino floors, naked electric light bulbs and the couple had to get their water by jug from upstairs as there was no bathroom or kitchen. Iris wasted no time in celebrating the BBC's announcement and arranged for a friend to look after fifteen-month-old Mitchell so she and her husband could enjoy a rare night out at the cinema on their own.

On the night of 30 November 1956, off-duty busmen and clippies (drivers and conductors) attached to Holloway Bus Garage gathered in strength at their dance in Athenaeum, Muswell Hill. The star entertainment of the evening was provided by their popular colleague Terry and towards the close of the evening the former Mr Parsons exchanged farewell handshakes with his friends and said an official goodbye to his old name and career.

The next day – on his twenty-sixth birthday – Matt met up with his new publicist, Les Perrin, who had been appointed by Decca to promote their new star. Perrin had recently left the Southern Music Group in Denmark Street and opened his own premises with Lew Levisohn on Bond Street. Matt was a marketing dream to Les, for as well as the 'overnight success' story of Matt and Decca, the fact that the singer was just about to start with Stapleton's Show Band gave him plenty of material to write about.

Things were certainly looking up for Matt Monro. On 2 December, Les had arranged for them both to go to Winifred Atwell's office to pick up the acetate for the new album and Matt was looking forward to hearing the master for the first time. Les had also extended an invitation to respected music plugger Mickie Schuller, who worked out of Mills Music on Denmark Street and was a great friend of the publicist. Les wanted her opinion on the new singer on the block.

It's Not How You Start...

Mickie Schuller's origins were very different from Matt Monro's. Originally from Germany, she began life named Renate Annette Daisy and was born on 19 July 1933, during the early days of Hitler's dictatorship. The child's grandparents, Anna and Max Halle, had flown over to Berlin just for the event. They had moved to England some forty years previously and didn't make the journey often, but this was a worthy occasion.

Evelyn Mira Halle had married Adolf Schuller, known affectionately as Dolly, on 18 October 1932 and Renate was almost certainly conceived on their honeymoon. Their joy was complete when two years later a boy, Ernest Harold, was born on 23 December 1935.

However, living under Hitler's hateful reign meant their happiness was short-lived. The German authorities took to pouncing in the dead of night, dragging families out of their homes, bundling them like cattle into unmarked vans heading towards the railway stations. Most were never seen again.

The implementation of the planned extermination did not officially begin until 1942, but the Jews had been living under the shadow of death from Hitler long before that, and fearing for the lives of their children, those that could, arranged for them to be sent out of the country.

Because Evelyn's parents had been living in England for the past forty years, their residency made it possible for the Schullers to obtain an exit visa for Renate and Ernie. It was a heartbreaking time for the family but an easy decision for the parents. They'd rather risk never seeing their children again, given the threat of almost certain death if they stayed in Germany.

On 30 December 1938 the Southampton boat train brought forty-one refugee children from Germany to London. Ernie, aged two years and six months, was the youngest in the party and was tired by the journey from Hamburg on the United

Refugee press cutting

States liner *Washington*. Ernie and Renate were just two of the twenty-seven boys and fourteen girls in the first batch to disembark at Southampton. They had fled from Germany, leaving their home and their parents.

Arriving at Waterloo Station, Ernie was crying. There was pandemonium in the waiting room where the children were assembled, and Ernie's tears set Renate off, until their aged Jewish grandparents found them and carried them off to Acton to start their new lives. The one-penny *Star Newspaper* and *The Daily Herald* marked the occasion with photographs for their readers showing the full extent of the horror, with bereft and bewildered children left like parcels, with tags round their necks, to be claimed by distant relatives or family friends.

Renate was devastated by the suffering her family had endured; the image of her father riding one tram after another to avoid being home when the Nazis came was etched permanently in her mind. Several members of the family were gassed or shot, and one of her last haunting memories before leaving Germany was of people running for their lives. What stuck in her mind most was the image of Freddie, her father's brother, being dragged away from the house to be murdered.

Anna and Max were kind souls who, in those first months of separation, had offered Renate and Ernie a lifeline of love during a very unsettled period. They put on a brave front for the sake of their grandchildren, but were frantically worried about the safety of their own children and prayed each night that they too would escape the ravages of their homeland.

Their prayers were answered when three months later Evelyn and Dolly also managed to flee Germany, but not before losing several loved ones in the gas chambers. They were incredibly lucky, being amongst the last Jews to escape. They stayed temporarily in Acton with their parents and children, before purchasing a house on Madeley Road on a mortgage. It contained two small flats upstairs from the main property, so they moved their family into the main house and rented out the flats.

The Schullers had not long settled into their new home before Renate's father, Adolf, was picked up for interrogation in England by Immigration and interned in a camp on the Isle of Man, where he was held until they determined he was a legitimate refugee and not a Nazi in disguise. Renate cried herself to sleep for nights on end and it would be more than a year before she saw him again.

On 19 September 1939 Renate started school at St Augustine's Priory at age six. Evelyn had approached the school and begged them to accept her daughter. The school administrators were compassionate and took pity on the small girl, which was extraordinarily generous given that it was a convent school for Catholic children.

Renate spoke no English when she started at St Augustine's but picked it up almost immediately. Ernie was also accepted by the school for a short time, but at the age of six he was taken by Hamilton House, a school for boys, and learnt quite quickly that his sister wasn't there to protect him anymore. Although both were private schools there was no possible way for Evelyn to pay the fees, so a bursary was established for both children.

Adolf had been a dental surgeon in his homeland but, being a refugee, was unable to practice in England. He therefore obtained funds from his close friend Charlie Jarvis and set up business as a dental technician making dentures. Taking on optician Laurie Lauder as a partner, he opened a little shop with upstairs premises in Praed Street, opposite St Mary's Hospital in Paddington.

The end of the war in 1945 was naturally a huge relief, but Renate's world was due another upheaval when her beloved father suffered a severe heart attack while at work and was rushed across the road to St Mary's Hospital. The medical team

Mickie and her father Dolly

did everything they could, but it was too late. There had been no indication that he was unwell and the news hit the family extremely hard. Evelyn's friends all rallied round but nobody could help fifteen year-old Renate. That date, 17 January 1949, remained forever etched in her mind. Her devastation was beyond the comfort of her mother; no one could talk to her and she mourned his loss for a long, long time.

In 1950, Renate left school and took temporary jobs with Shloer and Save the Children. Both offered her permanent positions, but her sights were set solely on the music industry. Arcadia was an English music publishing company affiliated with Mills Music of America and John Hendricks, a friend of her parents, knew the head of the company – Harry Ralton – personally. Renate had an interview at the firm and at age seventeen began her career in the music industry.

She joined Arcadia Music as a stamp-licker, tea-maker and switchboard operator, but soon found promotion to ledger accounts. Her boss was Harry Ralton, who gave her the nickname 'Mickie' after the cartoon character Mickey Mouse, as he could never remember her real name. From that moment on, she became Mickie to everyone. After Harry died, Fred Jackson was brought in as his replacement and Mickie became his secretary on the Mills Music side.

Fred Jackson had made quite an impression on Denmark Street in recent years and not without good reason. He had served with the Commandos during the war and took a military approach to putting Mills Music on top of the music world. In December 1953, Mickie became the assistant to the Light Music Manager Henry Croudson and, when he left the company, Fred put her in charge of the Light Orchestra and Music Department for Mills Music. From switchboard operator to Head of the Light Music Department in less than four years was an incredible achievement by anyone's standards, but Mickie Schuller had also succeeded in becoming Britain's first and only female plugger in the business.

A plugger's job was to sell the music. Once Mills accepted a piece of work from either a songwriter or composer, the primary aim was to get it recorded. Mickie would go around the country visiting radio stations attempting to gain airplay. Commercial radio stations rarely gave anything consideration unless approached by a plugger. Normally the music was sold to bands, orchestras and singers, so that they would play or sing the music on their radio programme. If selected, the sale of the music would generate royalties for composers, lyric writers and publishers and hopefully become a hit.

When posed the question: "What was the biggest break a new record could get?" Mickie replied, "To get it played on *Two-Way Family Favourites* or *Housewives Choice* for radio, and the television disc spots would be *Off the Record* and *The Jack Jackson Show.*"

Mickie considered the conductor her most important target, as it was ultimately his decision whether he liked a piece of music enough for his band or orchestra to play it. She often went out for lunch with Alan Ainsworth, who fronted the Northern Dance Orchestra, and Colonel Dunn, who was the conductor of The Royal Marines Band. Her job took her all over the British Isles doing a round tour of the principal cities at least once a year and her trips were certainly not without adventure. One incident, in February 1954, almost saw her plane forced down into the Irish Sea. On another outing, while returning from BBC Bristol, Fred and Mickie led a convoy of cars through a severe blizzard right into the thick of a snowdrift. They had to abandon the car and return by foot to the hospitality of The White Horse at Calne in Wiltshire.

Arcadia Music (front centre) Harry Ralton, Owner of Arcadia, (extreme left front) Henry Croudson Light Music Manager, (centre middle row) Mickie Schuller before promotion

Known as Tin Pan Alley, Denmark Street is a very small side street off the Charing Cross Road in the West End of London. It will be forever associated with music. In the 1950s every shop in the street was teeming with songwriters and music publishing companies. Mills Music, Dave Toff Music and Southern Music were just a few of the players. It was the hub of the British music industry, and the two cafés on the street – Julie's and the Suffolk Dairy – were regularly crammed with musicians, songwriters, agents and publishers complaining, gossiping, hustling and making connections in industry sales.

As well as Julie's Café, the White Lion and the Tin Pan Alley Club became the places to relax, drink and mingle with like-minded artists and workers in the industry. You could spot a dozen entertainment personalities at any given time and these watering holes functioned almost as a recruitment centre for jobbing musicians.

Earning Denmark Street the nickname of London's Tin Pan Alley in the 1920s, musicians had been flocking to this renowned corner of Soho since its origins as a sheet music supplier in Victorian times. Most of the buildings dated from the 1800s, when it was considered a fairly low-class area with its proximity to the theatres and pubs of Soho. Rent was cheap, which attracted struggling artists, composers and musicians. Music publishers set up their businesses here around the 1890s, supplying orchestral musicians at nearby theatres and music halls. There was no doubt that music publishers were still the principal players in the British music industry in the 1950s.

Music publishers placed songwriters under contract, securing the exclusive rights to publish their work. The market was analysed to determine which style of song was selling, and composers were then asked to focus their talents on writing in that style. The completed song would be tested with both performing artists and the buying public to help determine which should be published. Once published, song pluggers were employed to persuade artists to feature it in their act, thereby exposing the music to the public.

One young man named Hal Shaper had come to London from his native South Africa to pursue his dream of becoming a renowned songwriter. He was successful in persuading David Toff to take him on as a song plugger and was put under the watchful eye of Len Taylor. He stayed with Toff from the summer of 1955 until August 1958.

Mickie would often pop in to the White Lion pub with her friends Jo Wright, Pat Goddard and Zoë Rowland. In fact it was Zoë who later introduced Mickie to Bill Giles, a printer at Lowe and Brydon, whom she married at Chiswick Town Hall on 3 April 1954. Evelyn was not impressed with her daughter's choice of husband. In later years Mickie admitted: "I wasn't even sure why I married him, because he was really very boring and not much fun to be with." She was more in love with the idea of marriage than the actuality. Evelyn agreed to let the young couple move into one of the flats upstairs at Madeley Road, mainly to keep an eye on her daughter but also to help the couple with their finances.

Mills Music decided to part ways with Arcadia and open their own British division. On 12 February 1955, they announced the acquisition of their premises at 20 Denmark Street, London WC2. Fred Jackson awaited the arrival of his chief, Jack Mills, who had flown in from New York to open the new offices, furnished with the latest modern equipment. The entire organisation – which in the past was spread over four buildings – made the move just in time to really exploit 'Majorca', their first big hit that year, which had been picked up by Fred Jackson on one of his continental trips. Plugger Max Diamond, the manager of B F Wood Co Ltd, was geared up for the exploitation of a second continental hit, 'Blue Tango', scheduled for release in March. It was waxed in Britain by Frank Chacksfield and recorded by Leroy Anderson, who already boasted nine American top-line records. Mickie was put in charge of the Leroy Anderson catalogue and now had to ensure

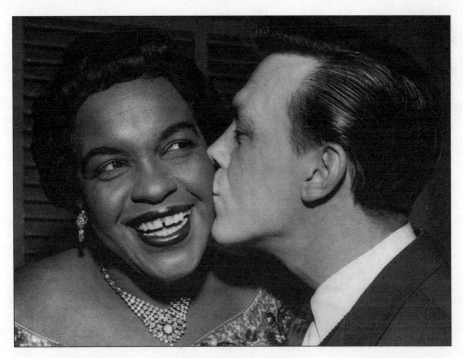

Matt & Winifred Atwell

that every tune got fair representation on the air.

Considered the Max Clifford of his day, Les Perrin was a hugely respected publicist, who worked out of his own premises in Bond Street. Les and Mickie had become great friends, and over drinks in The White Lion in November he told her about his new client, a singer Winifred Atwell had just discovered. Winnie's offices were in New Bond Street, which housed both her music business and an innovative product she had just marketed – hair and make-up for black skin – an entirely new concept in those days. Winnie was throwing a launch party for her new prodigy's LP the next evening and Les thought Mickie might enjoy the occasion, that and the fact that given her respect in the music business, Les was eager to gain her opinion on his new client. It was an event that would change Mickie's world, and definitely make her question her choice of husband.

Mickie waited for her day at Mills Music to finish. Although she had agreed to go to the record launch in the evening with Les Perrin she wasn't feeling her usual enthusiastic self and was having trouble concentrating. She'd had problems with her marriage almost from the beginning. The reality was that soon after her wedding she realised she didn't really love her husband and it was increasingly evident that they had different interests and ambitions. That morning, they'd had

Matt visiting Mickie at Mills Music

another argument about the hours she worked. He wanted a wife who would have dinner ready on the table when he came home and she was making excuses not to go home in the evenings. Mickie's work meant travelling and Bill was resentful of coming back to an empty flat. She couldn't blame him but the job was exactly what it had been prior to their union. Bill had made the assumption that once married he would change things but the presumption was misplaced. Mickie's mother had told her the marriage was a mistake before the paperwork was even signed, but she had ignored the advice and was now loathe to admit the error of her judgement.

Not wanting to let Les down, Mickie made the short journey to New Bond Street to meet him at the appointed time. She had only met Ms Atwell once before and found her to be great company. Winnie was terribly excited about her new discovery and with a simulated drum roll she played a few tracks from the new album that had just been delivered by Decca. Each track received enthusiastic approval from the guests and everyone agreed that Winnie had picked a winner.

It wasn't long before her new prodigy arrived and as Matt Monro walked through the throng, applause rippled the air and people vied for a chance to congratulate him.

Mickie had a different opinion. Having listened to the songs and the strong

Showband *rehearsals with June Marlow, a member of The Stargazers*

romantic voice, she imagined Matt to be tall and broad shouldered, with chiselled good looks – a real Adonis. Although she couldn't fault the voice, she was hugely disillusioned with the man. He was much shorter than the mental picture she had conjured up and he bit his nails. The girls in Winnie's office were swooning all over him, but Mickie thought he seemed cocky. Nevertheless, she loved the album.

Having spotted Mickie across the room, Les came over to say hello with the singer in tow. The publicist made the introductions and as Mickie examined Matt's features more carefully she noticed his clear hazel eyes, his mink coloured hair and broad shoulders. He was easy to talk to, but halfway through their conversation he was pulled away by Lew Levisohn to be introduced to some potentially important contacts. Mickie was niggled that everyone was fawning over him, but it didn't dawn on her that the instant dislike she felt probably sprang from the fact that deep down she was attracted to him.

A couple of days later Les and Matt popped into her office. Les practically lived in Tin Pan Alley, but Mickie hadn't expected to see his companion and was slightly put out. She was unaware that Fred Jackson had asked Les to bring the singer in for an introduction. If she was honest, her irritation largely stemmed from her not looking her best.

Mickie saw Matt several times over the next week. He was due to start with The Show Band shortly and would pop in to discuss his work and ask her advice. Each time he came to the office he asked Mickie if she wanted to go for a coffee, but she always turned him down, even with a crowd in tow. She soon realised that every time she heard his cheery voice greeting the doorman, she would reach for her powder compact and check her hair. She was even more agitated when she learned that, like her, he was married.

Despite Mickie's best efforts, events kept the two together. Mills Music was eager to add Matt's name to their list of contacts in an attempt to get the singer to feature their songs. They were throwing their annual Christmas party later that month and Mickie was asked by her boss to invite the singer.

Matt's BBC radio debut, and first taste of broadcasting, was to be pre-recorded on 9 December 1956 at Aeolian Hall in New Bond Street and he was incredibly excited about his first official day with The Show Band. Cyril Stapleton's *Showband Show* was on air three times a week; two were one-hour broadcasts mixed with comedy while the third was a two-hour airing on Friday nights. John Browell, the producer, introduced Matt to an array of artists who worked on the show: Bob Monkhouse and his comic partner Dennis Goodwin, Alfred Marks, Paddie O'Neil, Harold Smart, Bert Weedon, Dennis Wilson, The Showband Singers and The Stargazers (Cliff Adams, Fred Dachtler, Dave Carey, Bob Brown and June Marlow). These would be his work colleagues for the foreseeable future.

> **I always knew Matt would become a star from the first time I heard him. It was a combination of presence, particularly how to use the voice and how to present a song. He had a very good rapport with an audience. Coupled with the easy style of singing, he managed to make a song sound quite effortless and he would put all his feeling into the interpretation — he had this wonderful ability to step inside a song. — John Browell**

Bob Monkhouse and Matt quickly became firm friends. Apart from a mutual respect for each other's art, they both had the most wonderful sense of humour and would often be found creased up in laughter. Matt had never been to Aeolian Hall before and was unaware of the doorman/commissioner 'Peg the Pig', the nickname given to him by Bob. Nobody could understand this guy, he insulted everyone, was usually unshaven, unwashed, with a stained uniform and halitosis.

In the four years he'd held the job everyone had experienced the rough side of the doorman's tongue. On Matt's first day he arrived at the venue with Ivor Morantz, a gifted guitar player. Matt waved hello to the doorman and politely asked, "Excuse me, could you direct me to the toilets?" Peg the Pig gruffly replied, "Can't you find them yourself?" Matt, without missing a beat, said, "Actually, I was going on my sense of smell and it led me to you."

Rehearsals at Aeolian Hall usually kicked off at 2.30pm, with recording between 6.30pm and 7.30pm, and the final broadcast at 9.00pm. It was a long day, but Matt loved every minute of his new world. He was also delighted that *Melody Maker* had written a few lines about his appearance on Sunday evenings.

Matt adored Cyril and after a show the company would often go across the road for a well-earned libation. This didn't go down too well at home. Although Iris had initially been pleased with her husband's new job, she was constantly dissatisfied with the long hours he worked. He was never home and this was not the life she had envisioned for herself as a pop star's wife. Matt, on the other hand, had done his best. He'd married Iris out of a sense of duty, even though he hadn't planned on starting a family until he'd established himself. Iris had always known his aspirations but now she wanted him to give the business up just when it was coming good. He just couldn't bring himself to offer up the ultimate sacrifice – his dream.

Christmas 1956 loomed and the festive season brought with it numerous invitations to various social and industry events. The one Matt was most looking forward to was the Mills Music annual party. This was an important date in the music-publishing world's calendar and Matt was set to make the acquaintance of several people there that would later play an important role in his life. One was Pat Brand, editor of *Melody Maker*; another was Maurice Kinn, editor of *New Musical Express*. Maurice ran a column called 'Alley Cat' which was well known for causing great embarrassment to artists who were caught in compromising situations. There was also the small matter of spending a bit more time with one Mickie Schuller.

The party was littered with important contacts including Hal Shaper, David Toff and Bob Kingston from Southern Music, Ernie Ponticelli and Jimmy Phillips for Keith Prowse Music and Decca's representative, Dick Rowe, who made a late entrance with Winnie and Lew. The room was buzzing with talk of the new singer, with everyone wanting an introduction to the newest star. Matt's time was totally monopolised but Winnie managed to pull him aside to say she had something she wanted to discuss, and offered an invitation to her New Year's Eve party the following week.

The evening was hugely successful from Matt's point of view but not just because of the contacts he'd made. He had gone to the party alone, but left with Mickie. They'd shared their first kiss in the alley behind the Mills Music building, while a passer-by shouted for them to "get a room". Although they were both married, their attraction to each other was too powerful to resist. Sense and decency prevailed, however, and they resolved to carry on their friendship with phone calls through Mickie's office.

On New Year's Eve, Matt worked on the final *Showband Show* of the year. Finishing at 10.00pm, he didn't stop for the obligatory drink with the crew since he was expected at Winnie and Lew's party and wanted to arrive before midnight. He also had to pick up Iris en-route. The party was in full swing but soon after his arrival Winnie and Lew invited Matt into another room for a quiet word. They wanted him to appear with Winnie on her new Radio Luxembourg show, starting the following week. It was recorded on different days from Cyril's show, so there would be no problem scheduling the broadcasts. The year was starting on a high for Matt.

1957 started well. Although Matt was still living in Windsor Road, he had splashed out on a telephone, making it infinitely easier to deal with any business coming his way. Cyril signed him for a further thirteen weeks, to work from the Riverside Studios, with Winnie as the first guest, guaranteeing a great atmosphere in the studios. Matt was also excited by the arrival of his own copies of *Blue and Sentimental* and immediately forwarded one to Matt White, thanking him for the loan of the name. His biggest thrill came only two days into the year when he made his television debut with Cyril Stapleton on *Show Band Parade*. The contract was signed promising four monthly programmes in the series.

My very first television appearance: nervous as a kitten in the morning, bloody fed up by the evening. Duet with Janie Marden. Rucked by Iris, came home late. — Matt Monro, diary entry, 2 January 1957

Matt was indeed fed up by the evening. He had been genuinely excited about the prospect of appearing on television and, having worked with both Cyril Stapleton and Janie Marden on radio, didn't feel the media transition would be traumatic. He was told to sing a duet with Marden, which wasn't a problem – the crisis arose when he was made to sing 'Seven Brides for Seven Brothers' dressed up as a cowboy. Janie was a tall lady and wore ballet pumps, but to compensate for his short stature Matt was made to wear heeled cowboy boots. Unfortunately his duet partner was still taller than him! He felt ridiculous, but thankfully the press chose to focus on his natural talent: "Relaxed, poised and possessed of a great deal of easy charm, here was a home grown singer who could match vocal chords with any top line American."

The next day was very busy, with Matt getting ready for his first Radio Luxembourg broadcast on *The Winifred Atwell Show*. Winnie's usual guests were Teddy Johnson and Pearl Carr, but their pantomime season at Wolverhampton prevented them from making the recordings. Winnie introduced Matt to Geoff Love (who was backing him on the broadcast) and representatives from Curry's, the sponsors of the show. They had been funding the programme for the last five years, bringing Winnie and her two pianos to an audience every Sunday, and it remained one of the top shows on air. Now Curry's had decided to tour the new all-star show to their customers and friends, broadcasting from different locations around the country. Currently topping the bill in *Wonderful Winnie*, she had made a triumphant return to England after a sensational Australian tour. With top billing on television, two records ('Poor People of Paris' and 'Let's Have a Ding Dong') both selling over a million copies each, a wonderfully successful Palladium season and her new prime time radio show, Winnie's popularity was at its peak.

Luxembourg's first programme was broadcast from Stoke Newington Town Hall and Matt felt the day was quite successful. He had sung two songs, 'True Love' and 'Night Lights', which had both gone down well. The cast went to Archie May's in the evening to celebrate, where Matt got slightly boozed. Alcohol was a great way to unwind after a show and he'd graduated from the beer of his army days to Scotch on the rocks, which remained his favourite tipple throughout his life. Unfortunately, Matt had arranged to take Iris to the cinema to see *Oklahoma!* that night but, because it was the first show in the Luxembourg series, the day had overrun. His wife was kept waiting for nearly two hours and wasn't best pleased.

Although Matt stayed in constant contact with his mother and arranged a visit for the evening after the broadcast, the family unit was disintegrating. He rarely saw his siblings anymore, even though he made every effort to attend the get-togethers his mum arranged.

Am making this entry late, can't remember much about today.
Spent most of the day at Hornsey Rise just loafing. Alice's in the

evening, Reg and Jean didn't show up, they went to a party, Harry and Pat didn't show up, Chris had mumps, sat and watched television, Len took us home. — Matt Monro, diary entry, 5 January 1957

His own home life wasn't much better. Even the natural high of his success and the additional buzz of alcohol wasn't taking away the pain of an unhappy marriage. Iris was always dissatisfied and her misery was dragging him down. She was not supportive of the business and wanted him to get a 'real job' so he could come home every night. Trouble between the young couple escalated and Matt left before the end of January, moving back in with his mother. In the meantime, Mickie had also separated from her husband. Similarly, Bill wanted someone to come home to every night, but accepted defeat and moved back to his family. Matt and Mickie were now effectively single, and with a guilt-free consicence they arranged their first official date.

**Matt kept asking me out, I kept saying no. Then one day in January, when it was clear that both marriages were at an end – I said yes. How many times I have thanked the gods that I did.
— Mickie Schuller**

The second Radio Luxembourg show was at the Kursaal in Southend, where Winnie was also doing a week in Variety. Matt met Dickie Henderson and they arranged to catch up the following week for a drink in Tin Pan Alley. Matt didn't have his own transport and, coming back on the train together later that evening, Mickie persuaded him to come back to Madeley Road with her. Matt slept on the settee and Evelyn saw him off in the morning with a cup of coffee. Oddly enough, she wasn't cross with her daughter, just hugely relieved that Bill was out of her life. It also didn't hurt that by then Matt's face and name were plastered on billboards all over town, was appearing regularly on the radio and attracting headlines such as "Bus Driver makes good". Evelyn was quite impressed.

Matt's second single was to be 'Gone with the Wind', but although it was recorded and allocated a catalogue number with 'My Old Flame' as the B-side, it was shelved in favour of 'Garden of Eden'. Winifred Atwell had originally recorded the song in December 1956, but when four different versions suddenly appeared in the Top 30 in January of that year, Decca realised the song's potential and rushed their new star into the studio to record his version.

Had lunch with Ernie Ponticelli and fixed recording of 'Garden of Eden' with Dick Rowe for Saturday. I think we're a little late with this one. Already in the bestsellers. Here's hoping. — Matt Monro, diary entry, 10 January 1957

By the time Matt's version came out, the public had already placed Frankie Vaughan at number one in the charts with the same track and there didn't appear to be any room for a fifth rendering. However, Matt's adaptation reached the second spot in the sheet music charts alongside eight others, including Winnie's and one from The Billy Cotton Band (yet another Decca version). The papers wrote that Matt's choice of material was generally too predictable, not realising that he had no say in the matter. It certainly wouldn't have been his choice to compete against such established artists as Frankie Vaughan, Gary Miller, Dick James and Joe Valino. But the press still considered him a potential star in the making, especially with Les Perrin's publicity promotion and the recording guidance of Dick Rowe.

His next two Decca recordings came less than a week later when he laid down 'I Never Had a Dream Like This Before' and 'Mare Picola', both of which were never released. Although the tracks are listed on the main log at Decca, the tapes have never been located.

Matt had built up a steady work routine: recording with Stapleton and Atwell each week, regular meetings with John Browell to decide the next week's songs and habitual meetings with Dick Rowe at Decca. Several more dates with Mickie also followed, including a private showing of the Eddie Fisher-Debbie Reynolds film *Bundle of Joy*. Mostly they met in pubs for a drink and every Friday went to the Lyons Corner House for dinner. Mickie paid for most dates as Matt never had any money. Although he was constantly working, he was paying Iris maintenance each week and giving whatever he could to his mum.

Matt was prone to mishaps. His mother used to say he was an accident waiting to happen. Coming out of the Lyons Corner House late January he missed his footing on the steps. Matt and Mickie went down together in a heap and although they laughed the incident off, Matt still had pain in his right side days later. A trip to the hospital confirmed he had broken three ribs.

Matt tried his best to ignore his injury and went into the studio to cut an album for the American market. Although *Blue and Sentimental* had already been released in England, Decca decided to issue the disc in the States with two new tracks, 'The

One I Love' and 'My Old Flame'. Every note was sheer agony, but the pain didn't stop Matt singing at the three-hour session, nor at the two concerts and three broadcasts that followed. Amazingly, no one suspected a thing.

> **Tough morning at Decca making records for the States. Didn't turn out too bad but didn't like the songs very much. I don't think they will mean anything, I hope I'm wrong. Stapleton's birthday.**
> **— Matt Monro, diary entry, 31 January 1957**

The month finished with several press interviews and Matt even had his palm prints taken for *Valentine* magazine's horoscope page.

He received a call from Iris at the beginning of February informing him that Mitchell was ill with bronchitis and tonsillitis, so he promptly arranged for the doctor to visit. The failure of his marriage had no impact on the love he felt for his son and he stayed at the flat until the boy was fully recovered.

Mickie was also unwell. She had got up feeling sick, but went to work anyway and felt somewhat better. A week later she got out of bed and collapsed. The family physician Dr Nusbaum said he could smell an unusual odour in the flat and, after closer examination, it appeared that Mickie had suffered from carbon monoxide poisoning through fumes seeping out of an anthracite coal burner. Mickie had to remain off work for six weeks, causing her colleagues great concern. In the seven years she had been with the company she had never missed so much as a day's work. Matt was beside himself as his girlfriend (not feeling that she looked her best) had forbidden him from visiting her. But after a week's banishment she changed her mind, realising that she missed him more than she thought possible.

Although work was coming in, Matt's money wasn't. The producer John Kingdon offered him four shows on his radio series *Music About Town* starting on 28 February. This was the start of a long and happy working relationship between the two, but although the broadcasts offered great exposure they didn't pay very well.

Decca's next Monro offering was 'My House is Your House', but David Hughes at Philips and Mike Holliday at Columbia also recorded it, Holliday giving it its correct Spanish title 'Mi Casa, Su Casa'. The song was an Al Hoffman/Dick Manning composition written for Perry Como. They were an established partnership and had been responsible for many of the crooner's big hits, but on this occasion not even Como had much success.

Matt was constantly in demand and his next important invitation was for the

Ivor Novello Awards in April 1957 at the Camden Theatre. The musical accompaniment was supplied by the BBC Show Band and conducted by Stapleton, so naturally Matt was included in the show. Presented annually since 1955, these awards were the premier honours available to British composers and competition was fierce in Tin Pan Alley. Mantovani took the prize for the personality who had done most for popular music in 1956. The show also featured The Johnny Dankworth Orchestra, Vanessa Lee and Eamonn Andrews acting as compère. John Browell organised a celebratory drink after the show and several personalities went home with a heavy head.

Soon after the awards, favourable notices came in for the American version of *Blue and Sentimental* so a further two albums were requested. But Decca had other ideas. The label was beginning to have second thoughts about their new signing and pushed the project onto the back burner.

In June, Mills Music sent Mickie and Jack Jackson on a two-week business trip to The Venice Music Festival. Prizes were awarded to composers and publishers and Mickie was there in her capacity as music manager for her company, even though they were not up for an award.

I had known Matt for six months when my firm sent me to The European Light Music Festival, a wonderful trip to Venice and the French Riviera. My thoughts kept returning to Matt. One morning I strolled along the shore and watched a honeymoon couple walking hand in hand towards the beach and suddenly thought it would be nice if Matt were there with me. On impulse I went back to the hotel room and began a letter to him. It was just a chatty letter but at the end I put, I arrive at 7.30pm at London Airport on Friday. If you're free perhaps you could meet me there for that coffee you're always promising. I posted the letter and tried to put Matt out of my mind. He'll never get it in time, I told myself. But all the same I could no longer hide from myself that my feelings for Matt were changing. He was no longer just a business friend or a casual date. I wanted to know him better, much better, and my heart told me he felt as I did. When I stepped on the tarmac at London Airport I saw at once he was there waiting. He held out his hand. Silently I took it. From then on I never refused Matt's coffee invitations. — Mickie Schuller

It took that trip for Mickie and Matt to realise that their casual relationship was no longer casual anymore and that their feelings had deepened over the months. It wasn't long before Matt moved in to Madeley Road, much to the concern and dissension of his future mother-in-law.

The Showband Show was broadcasting three times a week, but this ended on 28 June 1957. In the face of widespread criticism, the BBC refused to reverse its decision to 'kill' the band. Although they'd terminated the contract, the BBC did decide to present a special tribute programme in celebration of the five years The Show Band had been broadcasting. The one-hour special was called *Show Band Cavalcade* and in addition to the resident singers, John Browell's plan was to book as many of the artists as possible associated with the series for the gala show. Browell also secured recorded messages from Rosemary Clooney and Frank Sinatra. The estimated cost of the show was six-hundred pounds and following the broadcast, Cyril arranged a private party at the Café Royal in London.

When Matt had started with the BBC Show Band in 1956, rockers like Cliff Richard and Elvis Presley were on the way up. It was the blue suede shoes era, and the ballad was in danger of being buried. It seemed like Matt's brand of music was on the brink of slipping into unjustified anonymity.

In the four months since Matt had signed a contract with Decca he'd issued three singles on 78rpm and 45rpm together with the 10" LP *Blue and Sentimental,* which has since become one of his most collectable releases. The Decca recordings would be repackaged on an *Ace of Club* LP in 1961 and again in *Decca's World Of* series ten years later. However, with three singles failing tó chart, Matt and Decca parted company. They liked his voice but told him ballad singers didn't stand a chance in the rock 'n' roll age.

After enjoying an initial rush of success, everything seemed to be going very flat for Matt Monro. Now with The Show Band defunct, Matt survived doing the odd broadcast with people like Dave Shand and Sid Philips. Money was scarce and he became desperate. He suddenly had doubts about his ability and decided to take a regular job. The dejected singer had renewed his Public Service vehicle license a few months back, simply because it looked as if he might have to use it again. Matt still believed in himself, but not as much as Mickie did. She was adamant that if he went semi-pro, he might easily miss a big job opportunity.

Decree Absolute

The press reported that three British record stars, Jimmy Young, Lita Roza and Matt Monro, had all split from Decca. The trio accused the record company of neglecting home talent in favour of the teenage craze for American rock 'n' roll. One of Decca's recent policies was to buy up ready-made hits from many of the two-thousand small independent American companies and market them in Britain. Jimmy Young moved to Columbia because they offered him a free choice of material and a better financial deal, while Lita Roza switched to Pye-Nixa.

In many ways Decca was just a pressing factory. I left them because I was neglected. They only offered me two songs in a year and neither of them were suitable. Decca never paid for any press or advertising, they left us to plug our own records. All we ever did was cover jobs for American music. — Lita Roza

Matt became one of the dream chasers, hanging around Tin Pan Alley desperately trying to get recording work, which is where he first met up with Don Black.

I used to make so many demonstration discs for fifty bob a time they used to call me the 'Demo King of Denmark Street'. — Matt Monro

I was a song plugger and Matt would sit around the office every day hoping to pick up the odd five quid for a demo. They did not come very often, so most of the day was spent playing cards in a haven called The Tin Pan Alley Club. To say that Matt was on the breadline would be an enormous overstatement. In those days a sausage roll

was a banquet. However, as is often said in this business, "it's nothing that a hit won't put right." — Don Black, *BASCA News*

The two became great friends. Don was still doing the odd gig for his brother Michael and Matt would watch him work. Michael had done extremely well for himself after a friend told him he was putting on a show at an American Air Force Base in South Ruislip and needed a compère. He readily accepted the position and was a smash, mixing comedy with impressions and earning himself a standing ovation. The commanding officer was suitably impressed and asked him back the following week. So Michael began the vast circuit of army and air force bases, putting on shows and booking acts. He was forever wheeling and dealing. Demand became so great that he would be juggling twenty-odd shows every weekend in bases across Europe, and where possible he would offer up work to his brother Don. That was how Michael Black became one of the most important agents in Britain.

Matt continually made the rounds. He went into any office where he thought there might be a chance of work. During those dire times he recorded for a few budget labels and, although he may have featured on one under his own name, Matt certainly used his Al Jordan pseudonym for a series of ten inch LPs on the Top Pop Club International label. He also sung on the odd demo for Bob Kingston at Southern Music, one being a track called 'Dreamdust'. It was rumoured that he sung for Embassy using an alias, though Hal Munro was not one of them.

We all recorded for Embassy, but under an alias, as we didn't want to be associated with a cheap label. I recorded under the name Jane Lowe. — June Marlow

Matt arranged an interview with Harris' paintbrushes, but Mickie wouldn't hear of it. She stood firm in her support of Matt's music career, even though the failed singer felt awful about not bringing any money to the relationship. Matt, always the self reliant, down-to-earth Cockney, had a simple solution – he would get a regular job. But Mickie, devoted and endlessly optimistic, resolved to be the breadwinner until Matt hit it big-time and of that she was adamant. She reasoned that if Matt was semi-pro, he might be unavailable to accept work and she knew beyond question that he would hit the jackpot soon. As far as she was concerned Matt had to put up a front, making it appear that he had all the work he wanted as a singer. That meant dressing well, being seen in the right places and keeping up with contacts.

Mickie bought a second-hand Hillman Minx with her own money, but gave it to Matt so he could get about more easily. Her gesture allowed Matt to take gigs further afield without relying on public transport timetables.

Fate intervened and Fontana signed him to a one-year contract with two one-year options, confident that Decca's loss was their gain. Fontana was a subsidiary of Philips and proclaimed great things for the disillusioned singer. Matt had nothing to lose – except his career.

Work flowed in now that Matt was associated with a major record label again. He received television offers solely on the strength of his own name rather than through association with The Showband. ITV's *Late Night Show* was aired in February and Matt's appearance went very well, boosting his flagging confidence. He was then offered a new thirteen-week radio series called *Music About Town* through his friend John Kingdon.

Matt's first venture with Fontana was 'The Golden Age' coupled with 'I'll Never Have a Sweetheart'. Perhaps Fontana had an attack of nerves about their new signing, as Matt's debut single was only issued on 78rpm. In this instance, the nerves were perhaps justified as the track didn't do much and Fontana's A&R Manager Jack Baverstock was left wondering what to throw at Matt next. Unfortunately for Matt the press assumed these 'new' songs were his suggestion, but as before he'd had no say in the matter.

> **Matt Monro, who joined the Fontana label after leaving Decca in a huff – saying he wasn't getting enough exploitation, went straight into direct competition with Decca's Terry Dene. Dene and Monro's version of 'The Golden Age' were released on the same day and Dene's version featured in his film 'The Golden Disc'. I say it's a false re-start for Monro. For his Fontana debut he should have found something original – not chosen a song that's bound to be associated with another star's name. He made the same mistake with Decca: his 'Garden of Eden' came out seven weeks after other artists had got it on to the hit parade. — *Picturegoer***

A Story of Ireland was his next disc, played over the credits of a series of films made by The Dublin Abbey Players. The films were shown both in England and Stateside, with the unrealised hope that they would also be aired on television. The song itself displayed a pleasing romantic mood – the middle break allowed John Gregory's string section a few bars to carry the melody until Matt returned with a chorus to close the song. But it wasn't enough to satisfy the public.

Times were changing at Broadcasting House. In 1950, the non-commercial BBC was only transmitting four hours of television a day, confined to areas where their two lone transmitters were placed: Alexandra Palace in North London and Sutton Coldfield near Birmingham. The 1953 Coronation of Queen Elizabeth saw television sales escalate when it was estimated that more than twenty million people tuned in to watch. However, the biggest transformation came with the arrival of the Independent Television Network (ITV). Not only did they offer innovative programming and a fresh approach, but unlike its state-funded rival, ITV existed as a commercial channel dependent on advertising revenue. The BBC was under fire and their immediate strategy was to transfer several of their radio shows over to television.

A two-year research programme commenced in 1956, which incorporated the installation of a second experimental colour camera at the BBC's North London site and saw the birth of a broader and more exciting schedule. Matt took part in the experimentation, which was filmed at Alexandra Palace over a thirteen-day period. The colour broadcasts were targeted at limited areas in the capital. If you were one of the lucky ones, you would have seen Matt on test colour television transmissions singing 'How Long Has This Been Going On'. Whatever the verdict, colour television wouldn't reach British shores until the late sixties. However, Matt's involvement did produce the following response from the programming controller of the network.

> **2 April 1958**
> **Sent to: Mr Russell Turner & Mr Denis Main Wilson - producers Six-Five Special**
> **I was impressed on Colour Television on Monday night by the performance of Matt Monro, who I understand is a bus driver or was. He seemed to me to have a pleasing, sympathetic personality and while his range may well be limited it did seem to me that he might be worth a bit of a build up in Six-Five Special. — Memo from Kenneth Adam, Controller of Programmes, Television**

Matt was several weeks into his *Music About Town* radio series when another television offer came his way. The show, *Top Numbers*, was filmed at the ABC TV Theatre at Chelsea Place. This time he was given his own dressing room, but the producer made him look like a pirate and stand in what was supposed to be the crow's nest of a ship, singing 'Catch a Falling Star'. He was on the verge of walking

out when they threatened to sue him for breach of contract. As Matt started singing, the microphone became caught up and no proper sound came out. He could only wait for the red transmission light to go out before help came to disentangle him. He was mortified. His next outing didn't fare much better. He was booked at the Commodore Theatre on the Isle of Wight, travelling alone since he was unable to afford a musical director. Matt arrived for rehearsal and asked the pianist to begin. There was nothing forthcoming. The musician's explanation: "I'm sorry I don't think I can read this music, I haven't got my chord glasses on." Another disaster.

The work offers were slow coming in. However, Matt was particularly looking forward to a charity concert at the London Coliseum because he was able to take Mickie along. They had little chance to get out, so it was a refreshing change for them to be seen in public together. During rehearsals, Matt went up to Harold Miller, one of Britain's top singing teachers, and asked if he could become one of the esteemed teacher's pupils. The wise Mr Miller smiled and said: "I can't teach you to sing because you do it naturally. You have a delightful, natural style. I can't teach you to breathe because you breathe in the correct way, through your diaphragm. You produce notes in exactly the right way for your type of singing. I think lessons might interfere with your style and probably change your voice completely and I advise against them." Matt respected the teacher's honest opinion and didn't presume to argue.

Fontana weren't rushing forward with any new material and phone calls to Jack Baverstock came to nothing. Matt spent months waiting to record another song. Fontana and Decca couldn't be more different: where Decca were churning tracks out every few weeks, Fontana preferred to let their artists sit twiddling their thumbs. Matt was frustrated. Away from Fontana, the BBC hired him to do four experimental stereophonic radio recordings and he picked up several song demos for music publishers that were then submitted to other artists for consideration. There was just enough activity to keep Matt optimistic, but barely enough work to sustain him.

His next offer through Lew Levisohn's Agency was a four-date tour for Granada. He was thankful for the Hillman Minx and the luxury of the car meant he didn't have to spend most of the day travelling to the venue. He especially enjoyed working with comedian Jimmy 'ay ay, that's your lot' Wheeler, impressed by the total ease with which he delivered his lines. This was also the first time he had worked with Johnnie Gray and his Band of the Day, although it wouldn't be his last.

Matt's year was full of disappointments. He was hired by Elstree Studios in May and duly rehearsed and recorded the song 'Merci Beaucoup' for inclusion in the 1958 motion picture *Girls at Sea*. But his version never appeared in the film, being sung instead by Teddy Johnson. While no explanation was offered, at least his fee of twenty-five guineas allowed him to send money to both Iris and his mum, and take Mickie out for a drink.

Sitting in the pub with his girlfriend, Matt lamented over his marriage and the maintenance he was paying at a time when he couldn't even afford to feed himself. In a frustrated outburst, he revealed that he would never marry again. Mickie became quiet for the rest of the evening. Although the thought of marrying Matt hadn't crossed her mind, she felt it was a very cold, unromantic remark to make. To Mickie, it seemed that she was good enough to go out, sleep and cohabitate with, but not good enough to marry. Matt was merely venting and hadn't aimed the comment at her, but the atmosphere was bleak for a day or two. An invitation to dinner by Pat Brand and his wife broke the ice.

The Brands always created a varied guest list to keep things interesting and this evening was no exception. There were ten guests who were all expected to chip in with the cooking. They all happily made fish balls of tinned salmon coated in batter and fried in oil. The allocated head chef was an unknown out-of-work actor. He arrived in an oversized woollen sweater unravelling at the seams and shoes that desperately needed resoling. Pat pulled him away from the kitchen to introduce him to Matt and Mickie. His name was Sean Connery.

Maurice Kinn was also at the dinner and over the months had become a great friend of Matt and Mickie. Pat and Maurice knew they were both still married to other people. That was taboo in those days and with Pat the editor of *Melody Maker* and Maurice running a gossip column called "Alley Cat" in *NME*, either one could have finished off Matt's career by writing about the extramarital affair. It was a great testament to their friendship that both journalists failed to mention this in print.

There was still nothing forthcoming from Fontana, but at least Matt was getting a few jobs and there was an offer to work three Butlins holiday camps. The brainchild of former travelling showman Billy Butlin, the camps accommodated holidaymakers in purpose built chalets built in long single-storey terraces, which looked more like an army barrack than a holiday resort. For an all-inclusive price, holidaymakers were offered three sit-down meals, refreshments and a huge range of programmed activities broadcast through the tannoy 'house' system each day. Most of the shows were staged in the Viennese Ballroom and Gaiety Theatre. However, the audience was there to drink and be entertained. If you were placed near the bottom of the bill, then the task of entertaining a hostile boozed-up crowd could be fairly thankless.

By contrast, there were a number of the worthwhile charity events up and down the country. However broke Matt was, he accepted every invitation. Cyril Stapleton, who was compèring the Daily Express Starlight Dance in association with the SOS at Harringay Arena with Vera Lynn, rang and asked Matt if he would sing a couple of songs. Matt was thrilled to be included in a bill that didn't really need his talents, as Stapleton had already secured Lonnie Donegan, Denis Lotus, George Melly, Petula Clark, Malcolm Vaughan, Lorraine Desmond and a dozen others. The line-up was wonderful, but then so was the cause as the proceeds were going towards a holiday home for spastic children. It was the biggest venue Matt had performed in, with a capacity crowd of ten-thousand excited fans in attendance. It was billed as one of the biggest pop music shows ever staged and among the bands that played for dancing were the amazing talents of Johnny Dankworth, Eric Delaney, Cyril Stapleton, Humphrey Lyttleton, Al Fairweather and Eddie

Thompson. But that wasn't the end of the celebrity line-up: Sam Wanamaker, Bob Monkhouse, Alfred Marks and Peter Sellers all sold programmes and signed autographs. Vera Lynn, chairman of the society and head of the event, even got the television company ATV to show a sixty-minute excerpt in place of *Saturday Spectacular*.

It seemed as if the earlier memo to Russell Turner and Denis Main Wilson, the producers of *Six-Five Special*, had produced the right results. Matt was invited to appear on a shortened edition of the show, representing Fontana. Larry Page was sent over from Columbia, Maurice Allen from Nixa and HMV showcased the newest addition to their stable, Barry Barnett.

However, all offers of work were disjointed; in fact Matt's life felt disjointed. The only constants were Mickie's unwavering faith in the man she loved and the lifeline John Kingdon's work offered. His new ten-programme radio show, *Once in a While*, recorded at Aeolian Hall, brought in a much-needed ten guineas a time. Working with John was a delight and Matt felt right at home as June Marlow – whom he hadn't seen since his days with The Show Band – was also on the show. Matt, June and Bill McGuffie were the resident artists throughout the series and the long days gave light relief to Matt's growing concern about his record label.

I was seventeen and working for Mellin Music, a small music publishing company. It was so small there were only three staff members: my boss Len Edwards, his secretary Pat Williams and myself. I made the tea, did the filing, ran errands and occasionally played piano for singers who would visit the office in search of songs. As well as getting new records played, music publishers wanted to have their new songs performed by the many singers working regularly for the BBC. Matt Monro was one of the best and one of the most popular BBC Radio stars. Len asked me to take a package of songs to him at the Aeolian Hall where he was recording a radio programme for the BBC. Matt was rehearsing as I entered the studio. There were a few chairs along one of the walls, so I sat down quietly and waited for an opportunity to introduce myself. The producer, John Kingdon, approached me and asked who I was and why I was there. I politely explained I was delivering music to Mr Monro. "Well", he said, "song pluggers aren't welcome in my studio so you'll have to leave immediately". Matt heard all this and promptly called out, "It's alright, John, he's my guest. I invited him".

**He then walked over, shook my hand and said, "You must be Tony.
Len said you were coming over." He didn't need to do this, but it was
a warm and caring gesture to a young lad and I've never forgotten
it. I spent the rest of the morning watching Matt and the musicians
working and loving every moment of it. — Tony Hatch**

Budding songwriter, Hal Shaper, had moved from David Toff to the more
prestigious Robbins Music, where he began his writing career under the guidance
of Alan Holmes and his assistant Joy Cannock. He spent the next seven years
gaining the best apprenticeship possible in the music industry. Credited as John
Harris on those early songs, Hal had no desire to be rich or famous – his only
aspiration was to write for a living.

Don Black, on the other hand, was still with Dave Toff. Matt continued to make
the rounds each week and always paid his friend a visit. During this time, the
struggling singer was particularly depressed. He had been offered work at Chester
Variety, but money was so tight he didn't have the funds to go. Don offered Matt
seven pounds, enough to get by until his next pay cheque, even though he didn't
have much himself. Though Matt paid his friend back as soon as his BBC cheque
was cashed, he never forgot the favour. Don admitted it was the best investment
he ever made. As soon as the opportunity came for Matt to have a manager he told
Don: "It's your gig, son."

Meanwhile Mickie had been in talks with Jack Mills, negotiating a substantial
salary increase that would take effect within the next few months. With her boss
Fred Jackson in hospital and the American counterparts in England discussing
imminent changes at Mills, the conversation made Mickie feel better about her
future with the company.

With money to buy petrol, Matt went to Chester for the week, staying at cheap
digs in Halkyn Road. He sent his mother a card and kept in touch with Mickie by
phone. Her calls and letters remained cheerful in an effort to keep her man's spirits
buoyant, but Matt, usually so upbeat, wasn't enjoying his time on the road.
Business wasn't good and the crowds were tough. He was glad to get back to
Ealing, where some good news awaited him. He received a letter from the BBC,
informing him that the company had decided to transmit the four experimental
sound programmes he had made and he would therefore be paid ten guineas each.
Nestlé's had also offered him a jingle for a thirty-second Christmas commercial and
Fontana had been in touch to tell Matt they had some work for him.

Mickie had some news of her own. Having previously suffered a miscarriage in the early days of her marriage, specialists had informed her that she was unable to have children so she was therefore understandably shocked to find she was pregnant. The last thing Mickie wanted was for Matt to feel he had to marry her and repeat the mistake he had made with Iris. But Matt didn't feel that way at all. He did however become even more desperate for a break and put everything into his newest session with Fontana, 'Have Guitar Will Travel'. This time the press were generous in their appraisal.

> **A mighty active guitar opens up the topside before the Ken Jones Orchestra establish the skiffle tempo for Matt Monro to sing, 'Have Guitar Will Travel'. Modulations help to lift the song to quite an exciting finale, with Matt delivering the lines powerfully and well.**
> **— Record Mirror**

Matt and Mickie went to the 1958 Tin Pan Alley Ball at the Dorchester Hotel full of hope for the future. Only that morning Matt had learnt that he'd been offered two *Saturday Clubs* before the year's end. The couple also attended the Philips/Fontana Christmas party, mingling with Anne Shelton, Robert Earl and Johnnie Gray, little realising it would be Matt's last attendance at a Fontana function.

None of the singles released by Fontana in 1958 charted, even though these records brought many kind words from reviewers and people in the business. No other material was recorded for the label, although the six songs re-surfaced on the bizarre coupling of *Tony Blackburn Meets Matt Monro* in 1969, released to capitalise on the singer's later success. Although Fontana had proclaimed great things for Matt, he only made three plug-starved discs for the label and was quietly dropped when the time came to renew contracts.

The music business was changing and not for the better. Matt was left with a shrinking audience and his own dogged belief in the music he loved. He was an artist in transition – and the change didn't look good. Matt was once again without a label and bearing the full weight of a long depression.

If Matt had thought the last two years were rough, then he was in for a shock. His flash of fame had burnt out and he returned to relative obscurity. The beginning of the year brought nothing. Word spread that he had been dropped by a second record label and no one wanted to touch him. He went back to auditioning and found some work at The Blue Angel, a hostess club in Little Portland Street. John Kingdon offered a lifeline with the offer of a few broadcasts.

In January 1959, both Matt and Mickie applied for a divorce, seeking a cross petition which involved only one set of papers and meant the cases would be heard on the same day. There were no objections, as both injured parties agreed to let their former spouses go. The usual wait was three months, but as the baby wasn't due until June it was thought there was plenty of time for the marriages to be dissolved and the couple to tie the knot before the birth.

Mickie was a petite five-foot tall and couldn't have weighed more than seven stone but no one even guessed she was four months into her pregnancy and the couple carried on as normal attending the Music Trades Ball on behalf of Mills Music.

In February Matt recorded 'Bound For Texas'. Charles Chaplin had asked him to sing the song on the soundtrack for his new feature-length film, which combined three of his old silent shorts, for Brunswick. It would be the first of many soundtrack themes recorded by the singer.

Matt was due to pick up a cheque from his *Swingalong* broadcasts and popped into the studio to see John Kingdon. Although Decca had given him a suit and a couple of items of clothing, he only had one pair of shoes and daylight was poking through from underneath. He needed to get them resoled, because when it rained his feet got wet. The last thing he could afford to do was get sick. John wanted him to meet his new secretary and talk about a few shows he had lined up in June. It was still months away, but Matt had no choice. He had to take anything that came his way. One thing that never came across was Matt's desperation and his temperament remained outwardly the same – calm, relaxed and a hell of a nice guy.

I first met Matt in 1959 when I started working for BBC Variety producer Johnnie Kingdon. The programme he was producing included pianist Bill McGuffie and singers Patti Lewis and Matt Monro. They weren't well known, but were terrific artists and the programme was delightful. Their fees used to come to the studio and we regularly went for a drink after the recording as the pub owner would cash pay cheques if he knew the artists. — Pam Cox

Mickie hadn't taken any time off work during her pregnancy, fully intending to carry on right through to her eight-month check-up, but it inadvertently turned out that she worked until the day before the baby was born. Having gone home she decided to clear out a cupboard, which hadn't been touched since moving in, when without warning Mickie felt too weak to carry on. That night she suffered nasty pains in her stomach, so went and had a long hot bath. An hour later, with Matt firmly ensconced

Matt & baby daughter Michele

in front of the television watching Russ Conway playing *Side Saddle,* Mickie stuck her head round the door to say she thought they needed to go to the hospital. Matt, not quite taking it in, asked her to wait until the end of the programme. Matt rushed Mickie to Perivale Hospital and at 10.25 am on 2 April their daughter Michele was born, albeit two months prematurely and weighing just over five pounds.

The couple were delirious with happiness. Both Alice and Evelyn competed for their granddaughter's attention and fussed over the new mother in their midst. Matt felt rather like a spare part and so he left the hospital early, going to the pub to tell all his mates the marvellous news. Of course, the couple hadn't thought the baby might come early and as such were still not married, but the following morning, five years to the day, Mickie's marriage to Bill was dissolved and Matt's followed soon after. The final paperwork arrived on 14 April and they arranged their wedding for the following day.

After four years in Australia, Ken Brown's first task upon landing on British soil had been to look up his former army pal. Tin Pan Alley was the logical place to go, and being such a close community it didn't take him long to re-connect with his mate. Ken's timing couldn't have been better and he soon agreed to be Best Man at Matt's wedding. Ken promptly organised a stag outing, but while the boys were out Mickie had second thoughts and made up her mind to call the wedding off. She felt that Matt had been forced into a similar situation in his first marriage and, as much as she loved him, didn't want him to feel bitter over events later on. They'd had a lot of rows lately, because Matt hated being supported by his girlfriend. Matt came back to be confronted with her decision but he wouldn't hear of it, adamant that he wanted her to be his wife. On 15 April, as arranged, they were married at Ealing Registry Office. Their daughter was thirteen days old. Mickie always glossed over the date of her marriage, as she didn't want anyone – especially the press – to know she'd had the baby out of wedlock. From that day on, the birth of their daughter was always assumed to be much later or their marriage much earlier.

The registrar's office had peeling paint on the walls and light bulbs missing in the fittings. When the registrar asked him, "Do you take Renegate Schuller to be your wedded wife?", Matt was momentarily unsure of who he was marrying. There was a short silence, broken only by giggling from the couple as they tried to laughingly explain that her name was actually Renate.

On the way home the couple stopped at a local photographer to have pictures taken of their special day. The studio was cheap and tacky, but Mickie wanted a photo to mark the occasion. Mickie bought her own ring, which they'd picked together at a jeweller's in Ealing, while Matt's mother gifted him her own wedding ring, which she had enlarged. He wore it every day of his life.

Matt was so broke that I lent him the money for the wedding license and bought my own wedding ring. When we came out of the registry office in Ealing, we tramped up and down in the pouring rain looking for a photographer's studio. We walked out of one because it was too expensive and eventually found a funny little place, which we could afford. It's a terrible picture, there's the leg of the tripod in one corner, and an expanse of bare lino stretching out behind us. — Mickie Monro

When the couple arrived back at Madeley Road, Michele was clutching a little bunch of posies and Evelyn was in her element playing the role of doting grandmother. Mickie's brother Ernie popped in and the boys celebrated with a few beers at the flat. Ken talked to Matt about putting the double act back together, but the idea didn't get off the ground, although the two old friends picked up the conversation as if they'd never been apart.

Maybe the marriage was an omen. Having just returned from his wedding

Mickie, Evelyn & Matt - wedding photo

ceremony, Billy Hill Bowen rang and asked if Matt wanted to do a commercial. Matt enthusiastically agreed. Billy asked for Matt's fee, but the singer had no idea of what to quote. After an awkward pause, Billy asked if seventy-five pounds would be agreeable. Matt quickly accepted, flabbergasted at the amount. It was a huge sum of money for the young couple, and couldn't have come at a better time. On the designated day, Matt went along to the studio and sang over a thirty-second piece of music. He was asked to sign a contract and was paid his fee.

With a new baby and wages needed for a live-in nanny, to enable Mickie to go back to work, Matt's fee for the commercial didn't last long. Funds were so low that most days the couple would toss a coin to see whether they ate lunch or bought a packet of cigarettes. Matt continued with broadcasts for John Kingdon, recording 'Swingalong', 'Once in a While' and 'Sing it Again'. He spent time in Don's office and Mickie settled back into her routine at work. Her brother Ernie popped round regularly and they often ended up playing poker. After marrying a woman named Diane, he was a father-to-be himself, and found the waiting agonisingly slow. In

September the wait was finally over and Michele had a little cousin called Gary.

Matt's contract had come to an end with Lew Levisohn and he didn't feel there was anything to gain in re-signing. Instead, agent/manager Don Read took over the personal management of Matt Monro. At the same time, the memos circulating in the BBC's offices at Wood Lane were none too generous about the singer's talents. In any event, the try-out mentioned in this disparaging memo never happened.

> **Memo to All Heads of Light Music Programmes**
> I have just noticed that Minute 59/486 of the Light Music Artists Committee Meeting of 12 November refers to Matt Monro. I had occasion to meet this artist when recording a Magazine Programme and can offer the information that he is a sincere, though exclusive 'pop' singer very much of the Sinatra style. His voice is naturally pleasing, though his sense of musicianship is not high and I feel that his use to this department would be limited. At best I would recommend a single date try-out with, say, the Lou Whiteson Orchestra. — Edward Nash, Senior Producer, 20 November 1959

Ironically, at the precise moment Matt was struggling to make ends meet, his voice could be heard several times a night on national television. His was the voice behind a high-profile advertising campaign for Camay, a popular brand of soap, which he joked about on talk shows in later years. Billy Hill Bowen rang him soon after, asking if he would be interested in a follow-up to the Camay campaign. Billy realised that Matt's fee must have gone up because of the ad's success and offered him double the amount received a few weeks before.

The couple didn't realise that, due to repeats, Matt's modest bit of singing about the soap, designed to make ladies "feel a little lovelier each day with fabulous pink Camay", would earn him ten thousand pounds over a three-year period. In fact, television jingles would feature heavily in Matt's life. Companies such as Pepsi Cola, Cadbury's, Bisto, Oxo, Shell, Nescafé and Woolworths would all be eager to sign him in the future. During a twelve-year span, he recorded over forty commercials for notable companies and became known as one of the most prolific off-camera television ad voices. But it wasn't just the phone call from Billy Hill Bowen that was fortuitous; the call that came next was to change Matt's whole life.

An Outing With Sellers

Peter Sellers made his recording debut in 1958 with a disc released by Parlophone Records. The session was produced by George Martin, later to find fame as The Beatles' record producer, who was at that time making a name for himself in the comedy-recording field, and it marked the beginning of a partnership that continued throughout most of Sellers' career.

George had started his career working as an assistant for Oscar Preuss, the head of EMI's Parlophone Records. EMI also had several other labels under their umbrella including Columbia, Zonophone and HMV, but they were all run as separate entities. Oscar was a heavy taskmaster and very possessive of Parlophone, but the strict rules he imposed had caused the label to lose a lot of artists, who had been moved from one label to another. One such rule meant that Parlophone couldn't record a musical show, these had to be made by HMV.

A change happened after the British and American Columbia labels split from each other, causing EMI to lose their American imported artists. RCA, who had issued their records on HMV in England, also moved away and started their own company. EMI were forced to find new artists and the Artists and Repertoire (A&R) men were given the task of rebuilding the label's roster.

George Martin's role was to find a commodity and new sound for the label, but that wasn't always an easy task, as Oscar preferred things done in a certain way – his way. He was fastidious in his approach and had certain reservations about tampering with proven techniques. But George found an ally in Stuart Eltham, a tape operator at Abbey Road. They'd immediately become friends and found a common goal in obtaining a new sound and improving the quality of 78 records.

Oscar always liked the voice to be well forward as is on most 78s records and I remember once we'd recorded a musical show called

Matt & George Martin

Wedding in Paris. George and I were very pleased and I thought we'd
done a marvellous job but when Oscar heard it he was horrified. The
voices weren't loud enough for his taste and he gave me a bit of a
ticking off when he next saw me. I told George that Oscar didn't like
the sound and he said yes I know, he's threatened me with the sack
– we were convinced we had a good sound. — Stuart Eltham

Despite such disagreements, when Oscar retired in 1955 he promoted George to
Head A&R Manager. George's first years were spent recording classical and baroque
music, but his sights eventually turned to comedy and producing novelty records,
working with Rolf Harris, Flanders and Swann, Spike Milligan, Harry Secombe,
Michael Bentine and Peter Sellers.

In autumn 1959, George rang Mickie at Mills and told her about a small job he had
for Matt, which would require him to record a take-off of Sinatra. A song had been
written for the opening track on the second Peter Sellers album he was working on
and the intention was that Sellers should sing it with a voice as near as possible to

Sinatra's. British songwriter Ken Hare provided a new song in the swinging Sinatra manner, Graham Fisher (George's pseudonym) wrote the music and Ron Goodwin wrote and recorded an appropriate accompaniment.

Although Peter couldn't sing terribly well, it was thought he could use his great powers of mimicry so that it would actually sound like someone doing an impression of Sinatra, adding comic significance to the title of the LP, *Songs for Swingin' Sellers*. However, Sellers was doubtful that he could pull off the task, admitting that he could manage ordinary impressions but not vocal ones. Although he wanted to phrase it like Sinatra would, he didn't know how to achieve the effect and, being a new song, Sellers had no Sinatra version to compare it to. George's solution was to look for someone who had a voice like Sinatra – he didn't want an impression but to hear it sung the way that Sinatra *might* sing it. He came up with two possibilities, Denis Lotus and Matt Monro. He'd heard of Matt through his Decca recordings and decided he had the better voice and sounded more like the American singer, so he offered the session to him.

At first Matt was thrilled to get another offer from a record company, but the feeling soon turned to one of disappointment and then to anger. He didn't want to imitate anyone. He wondered why, if he apparently wasn't good enough for regular work, was he good enough to impersonate just about the greatest singer in the music industry at the time. The actual recording was never intended for the album but was only to be used as a guide for Seller's own impression. Matt was seething with frustration and he wanted so much to record in his own right that he nearly turned the job down, but Mickie managed to cool him off. She persuaded him to take the job by insisting that they could never tell where it might lead or where the breaks might come from.

It was a privilege to work with Matt because he was such a good singer. We worked a system out for recording it. It was difficult because we had woodwind and a full brass section to do a dance band sound. We had strings to fill in which meant you got a lot of spill over on the string microphones and from the brass because it was all done live, it wasn't overdubbed. — Stuart Eltham

He came in and did the job like the professional he was and he was so good at the job and so easy to work with. I paid him a measly twenty-five pounds and he did the job very quickly and very efficiently as he always did. I had to give him a pseudonym and

Fred Flange came to mind. 'Flange' was one of my favourite nonsense words and (indoctrinated by Spike Milligan) when John Lennon asked me how does artificial double tracking work? I said to him, "It's very simple John, all you have to do is put the voice into a double bifurcated sploshing flange". From then on he would say to me, "Let's flange the voice shall we?" and so a new verb was formed. — George Martin

Matt did the job and he did it well and upon hearing the recording, Sellers – a master of impersonation – admitted he could never approach Sinatra's style so accurately or do such justice to the song. He thought the test number was great and suggested they use Matt's version as the opening track on the album. George rang Matt again and explained the situation. George only wanted him for the one job, to sing a single song and then disappear, with no credit. Matt got the dead needle as nobody was going to know who the artist was; it seemed a complete waste of time. Nevertheless, Matt agreed to the use of his voice under the guise of a pseudonym and made a return trip to the studio to record the final cut.

Matt didn't realise what he'd taken on until he did that second session. Unlike the first take, this recording was intended for release and all he could do was imagine how Sinatra might approach a new song. Sinatra had influenced practically every singer worth his salt but Matt had never consciously copied him and felt the elements that make Sinatra so unique were elusive. The balance room technicians tinkered with the track to get it closer to the 'Capitol' sound.

> **When I heard the playback it sounded exactly like me and nobody else, but apparently that's just the way I heard it. — Matt Monro**

Though the experience was demoralising for Matt at the time, the only lasting regret he had about the experience was that, having admired Sellers greatly, he never got the chance to meet the comic genius.

For the benefit of the record and to keep the true identity of the artist under wraps the album sleeve read: "In 'You Keep Me Swingin' you will hear some very familiar, and expensive, tones. No it's not Peter Sellers this time. For mainly political reasons, however, the real identity of this performer must be kept secret. No prizes are offered for the correct solution."

Released at the end of 1959 with the memorable album cover featuring a body hanging from a tree, it caused something of a furore in professional circles. Billed as a 'Capitol' singer, the publicity pictures taken of Matt from behind with a hat on created a huge buzz in the industry.

After the initial comedic value had been appreciated, the press association, DJs, agents and producers all wanted to know how Parlophone had managed to get clearance to use the vocal talents of Mr Sinatra. Second thoughts told them the voice couldn't be Sinatra's as the copyright laws would have prevented the use of his voice, but the alternative was just as unbelievable. Had Sellers, the man of many parts, excelled himself to carry off such a convincing pastiche? Parlophone were besieged with phone calls and letters, with record buyers and press wanting to know who the mystery singer was.

Once the true identity of the impersonator got out, the industry tabloids were awash with admiration and offers to give Monro work flooded in.

> **Monro's voice is behind the cleverest and most irreverent impersonation of a singing idol ever recorded – a diabolically ingenious spook of Frank Sinatra and The Nelson Riddle Orchestra for Peter Sellers' new LP *Songs for Swingin' Sellers*. So exact is Monro's copy of a typical punchy, cockahoop Sinatra lyric that I would expect Ava Gardner to be taken in by it. The phrasing, accent, slurs, the suspicion of a rasp here and there is backed with all the impatient brassiness so true to life. — *Reuters News Agency***

Fred Flange marked a peculiar beginning to a twenty-five-year relationship with EMI for Matt Monro. George Martin was impressed with the way Matt had approached his work on that session. "He was extremely professional, had no tricks and no temperament and only had to be asked to do something once. When he sang he just expanded and the notes would come out and go on forever."

It didn't take too long for George to ask Matt if he would like to record under his own name. He presented the singer with a generous contract and became his recording manager. It couldn't have come at a more opportune time. The end of 1959 was rock bottom for Matt, he was a thousand pounds in debt and he and Mickie had toasted the New Year in with cooking sherry. But the couple weren't about to get their hopes up just yet as Matt had already been handed the chance of stardom twice before. What worried him slightly about the deal was that Parlophone was known as the comedians' label and had no singers signed to it.

Having signed Matt under their Parlophone label, finding a song was as important as having the right tools of the trade to record it. George's office on the fourth floor of Great Castle Street was equipped with an upright piano, and seeing music pluggers was one of his top priorities. They would visit the main A&R players, and showcase their latest songs in the hope that one of them would be the right choice for one of the record label's artists.

> In the old days, there was an unwritten law, you had an A&R man and you went to see them with the best of your songs. The A&R men then were real music people with a real love for songs – people like Wally Ridley, Norman Newell, and George Martin at EMI, and Johnny Franz at Philips. There was no greater pleasure than to take good songs into good music people – they loved them, it transcended their job. To find a great song for whoever the artist was, was an art in itself, and they never used to toy with it. — Hal Shaper

Sheet music was still the stronghold of the music business, with the market counting for a significant share of the overall industry revenue, and as a result, the music publishers still had immense influence and power. Songwriters were still considered to be at least as important as the pop stars, if not more so. The pop stars might bring in the teenagers but without the songs, they were nothing, and in the pre-Beatles era, singers were singers and songwriters were songwriters and the two rarely crossed over.

George's role as A&R manager was to ensure the record sounded as close as

George Martin (extreme left), unknown, unknown, Cyril Shane (Mills), Johnny Franz (Philips), Matt

possible to the live sound. The process of 'producing' was still in its infancy but George's role would grow very quickly.

> **The job encompassed lots of administration too. It was like being a label manager and an artist manager in one. I was responsible for negotiating and managing the artists' contracts and even for paying their mean royalties. We generally gave artists a penny per double-sided record. — George Martin,** *Playback*

George had trained as a musician and was extremely knowledgeable about both the musical and technical side. He knew how to use a microphone to achieve the best possible resonance, how to place it to achieve a certain sound and what differences came from using different sized bands.

> **Apart from the pleasure of hearing how woodwind should really be played, I also gained from these sessions an early lesson in recording. By careful placing of the instruments, it was possible to record using only one microphone. The natural acoustics of the studio gave the**

recordings their fine sound, and I learned that to obtain a natural sound one should use as few microphones as possible, a principle which I believe still holds good today. — George Martin, *All You Need is Ears*

Ron Goodwin was the chosen arranger for Matt's first session and a familiar face to the singer as they had both worked together on the Sellers album. Another recognisable talent was EMI's senior recording engineer Stuart Eltham, who would come to work on all of Matt's Parlophone albums over the ensuing years.

George had selected three of four songs as possibilities for a first release but his initial priority was to introduce Matt to the unique elements of his studio. The original structure started life as a Georgian townhouse and was converted into studios when the Gramophone Company acquired the building. When the company later amalgamated with Columbia Graphophone to form EMI, the studios became known as EMI Studios (the name change to Abbey Road didn't officially happen until 1970). Studio 1 took pride of place. It had been built with classical music in mind and could easily accommodate a full symphony orchestra. The second studio was smaller and much less grand than its counterpart, but it established a reputation in the industry for providing top-class acoustics.

Studio 2 was Matt's first introduction to the recording world of George Martin. The men routined several numbers and the choice was made to lay down two songs, 'These Things Happen' and 'I'll Know Her'. Matt commanded the studio and settled down comfortably when he realised that George was going to allow him to sing in his natural voice, something that he hadn't been permitted to do with either Decca or Fontana. His technique was effortless, sustaining long notes for an eternity and it was soon evident that George and Matt would make a fearsome team.

He had the most wonderful microphone technique. A lot of singers get too close to the mike, so that the final consonant on a lyric comes across too strong. Mike Holliday along with Matt Monro were the two most naturally gifted microphone singers that I ever recorded. It was a total gift; their diction was perfect. — Stuart Eltham

Although George had free reign in the studios and access to whatever orchestrations and backing he required, there was an unspoken rule regarding finance. There were no actual budgets in place but expensive procedures would need the permission of his superior. John Burgess, one of Columbia's producers, recalls that the only thing that was an issue was the amount of tape used when the records were cut. In the backrooms of EMI's studios, there was a silent army of technicians in white coats who would start complaining about the waste of valuable supplies if you used up too much tape, as it was an expensive medium. This was 1960 and recording technology was still stuck in the Dark Ages. Recordings were made using one track directly onto tape, so if you didn't get it absolutely right on the first take, that was it, you just had to record again and risk the wrath of the men in white coats. The necessity to record everything in one take meant they all worked under immense pressure.

Taking direction from his producer, Matt laid down the first track, 'These Things Happen'. Although Matt thought it went well, he hated singing with headphones on because both the orchestra and his own voice were piped straight back into his ears. He didn't feel it was a natural way to record, and it was the first and only time he used the method during his career.

Without the encumbrance of the earphones, he recorded the second of the two songs, 'I'll Know Her', and felt much happier. George was delighted with the session and the musicians shared the sentiment.

It was great to go into a studio with someone who knew totally what they were doing. Put the music up and 'Bang!' the thing was done, instead of take twenty-five like so many others. Matt was always perfect, absolutely right. — Tony Fisher, session musician

On reflection, George didn't think the two songs were strong enough for a single release and so a second session was booked. He also changed arrangers, booking another familiar face for the second gathering, Tommy Watt. Matt and Tommy had worked together many times over the previous two years on programmes such as *Band Waggon* and *Time For Watt*.

George chose a further two songs for the new session, hoping that these might be stronger. 'Love Walked In' was the last song that George Gershwin had composed before his death at the age of thirty-eight. Martin thought it a perfect choice; it had an understated piano and string arrangement, which allowed Matt's voice to be the driving element. The second song was Johnny Worth's 'Fare Thee Well My Pretty Maid'. Although recorded, the song was shelved and at the time of writing remains unreleased.

After a long deliberation, George decided that out of the four tracks recorded during the two sessions he would couple 'Love Walked In' with 'I'll Know Her'. He had found out that Adam Faith was due to release the Johnny Worth composition on

EMI Recording Session

a new EP as well as his debut album and didn't want Matt's former problems, of another version of the same song acting in direct competition to Matt's release, to resurface. 'These Things Happen' wouldn't in fact be released until 2006, when the Matt Monro Estate included it on *The Rare Monro,* an album of previously unissued material.

Matt's new record was finally pressed and ready to be dispatched to the shops. Then, at the last minute, someone noticed that the name had been spelt MUNRO, so all the labels had to be changed. As it transpired, the misspelling of his name would follow him throughout his life.

The record wouldn't set the world alight, but the most important thing to come out of those initial sessions was the friendship between George and Matt. It would sustain them, both professionally and personally, and become an unbreakable bond until death.

PRELUDE TO A STORM

The success of *Songs For Swingin' Sellers* saw an avalanche of work pour in for Matt. He was booked for nightclub cabaret in London, Manchester, Birmingham, Glasgow, Dublin and Belfast. He made his debut at Le Condor Club in Wardour Street and his first night performance was so successful that his season there was extended. In early January, Matt signed as the featured singer with Johnnie Gray and his Band of the Day for its American tour in March.

Johnnie Gray had started his Band of the Day – an excellent eight-piece – some years back. Musicians working with him were cut down to size if their musical or social behaviour wasn't up to par. One trombonist made the mistake of being drunk on the stand, and Johnnie literally threw him out of the hall. If his musicians were late they were fined one pound and at the end of the month it was shared out amongst the boys who'd been punctual, Johnnie not taking anything for himself. His proud boast was that, in nearly forty years, he'd never been late, broken a contract, knocked a fellow musician or broken his word. He was always dressed immaculately in Savile Row suits and his behaviour was impeccable. His motto was: "If you want to be a professional, act professionally."

Johnnie had met and worked with Matt back in 1958 on the Granada Theatre circuit. The singer went to see Johnnie in his offices in Tin Pan Alley when the Peter Sellers disc broke.

A small man came into my agency in Denmark Street. I heard him sing and immediately took him on a tour of the States with my band. I had to change many of his keys as he'd only been used to singing with piano and drums. On our return I recommended him to my record label. The singer was Matt Monro. My greatest mistake was that I failed to sign him. — Johnnie Gray

Johnnie Gray and his Band of the Day

Rehearsals with the bandleader started in February. Apart from a couple of meetings with George Martin and his debut recording sessions booked with Parlophone, Matt's time was free during the day.

Johnnie had to pull a few strings in England to get Matt on the tour. This involved Matt becoming a member of the Musicians Union, a pre-requisite for all professionals in the business. The rules were strict on both sides of the Atlantic and the Union would only allow Johnnie and his Band to play for cabaret. They were not allowed to play as a dance group, so Ray McKinley, leading the Glenn Miller Band, was booked to kick off proceedings. They would play for forty minutes and then, after a short break, be followed by the main act, billed as 'Johnnie Gray and his Band of the Day with Matt Monro and Kerri London.'

Matt's 1960 visit to the States was on a special exchange agreement. The Musician's Union stated that any artist working Stateside had to have an equivalent agreement, allowing one of their artists to work in the reciprocating country. Matt was exchanged for Ella Fitzgerald and Johnnie Gray for Louis Armstrong.

The press pictured Johnnie leaving Heathrow for his fourth American tour with his vocal team. Terry Bracknell was sent out as road manager, Johnnie was on saxophone, Johnnie Edwards on brass, Bob Kevin on drums, Ken Hogston on bass and Laurie Holloway on piano. It was Laurie's first professional job and he stayed with Johnnie for seven years, learning the trade.

They flew out of Heathrow North – which Johnnie described as "a bit of a shed" – with all their family and friends providing a big send off. They went via Iceland, where the plane was due to stop for a refuel. It was a seventeen-hour flight, but the weather was so bad that snowstorms prevented them from landing, so they had to turn round and fly back. Matt hadn't been too pleased from the start, as the airline was El Al. Not being Jewish, he hated cold meats and orange juice for breakfast and, worst of all, no milk for his tea. They landed in Prestwich, Scotland. They then all had to go through customs, even though they hadn't been anywhere or gotten off the aircraft! Johnnie immediately phoned Harold Davison, the agent that was representing him on the trip.

I am not sure what strings they pulled, but the next day a KLM flight was diverted from Heathrow to Prestwich to pick us up. One of the passengers was Queen Filipina and she was not amused. We were relieved as otherwise we would have been in breach of contract, something that was taken very seriously throughout the bases. — Johnnie Gray

They were diverted from New York to Washington. It was bitterly cold with sub-zero temperatures and it soon became evident that no one was expecting them. No one knew the aircraft had been diverted and after several frustrating hours they finally caught a connection back to New York. On arrival, the agency didn't even know who they were, never having heard of Johnnie Gray or Matt Monro. They were told to stay in the airport and, after much waiting, were told that their first engagement was in… Washington, in two days time!

Cold, wet and tired, the band was taken to the President Hotel on 42nd Street in the heart of New York. Matt had never been to America and loved being in a hive of activity. The most exciting part of the trip, though, was seeing Eartha Kitt at the Latin Quarter. Matt's contract allocated a ten pound salary per day, plus full board and lodging. Most of his spending money went that first night, but the experience was well worth it. After years of listening to the greats on radio, to see such a star live was a huge thrill.

The travelling had been exhausting and on arrival at Bolling Air Force Base, Johnnie discreetly approached Matt, explaining that he didn't want to share with one of the boys in the band. They were staying in bachelor officers' quarters and he justified his decision by saying that as Matt was the vocalist it was more appropriate if he shared with him. The singer suffered badly from sinus problems, causing him to snore rather loudly, which Johnnie soon found out. He lay awake in the next bed all night, occasionally mumbling "Jesus Matt, shut up." Johnnie checked out the very next morning and Matt had the room to himself.

Let me bring you up to date on the great American tour. Texas has been cancelled. We stayed in New York overnight and then went to Mitchell Field, which is about thirty miles out. We stayed overnight there and then flew in an Air Force plane out here to Washington and now this is where we are going to stay. Today is Wednesday and we still haven't worked yet.

I haven't been too well and had to visit the base hospital for a very sore throat, also that funny mild blister rash that I sometimes get on my hands is no longer mild and has now covered my whole hands. The doctor said it was nothing serious and wasn't infected. We are all living in the officers' rooms, they're great, private bathrooms and showers. Then we eat in the officers' club, which is just like a first class restaurant and nightclub. You would hate this country, everything seems so false and unreal and everything is so expensive. To cut expenses when we were in New York I shared a room with two of the boys and even then it cost 25 cents. — Matt Monro, letter from Bolling Air Force Base, Washington

Matt and Johnnie were particularly tickled by their road manager's antics. Terry Bracknell had travelled without a suitcase, just taking a small holdall with him. Every time his shirt became dirty, he would buy another one. When questioned about this quirkiness, he simply explained that clothes were very cheap in America.

The weather played havoc with the band's travel plans, causing shows to be cancelled. They once again found themselves back in Washington, but Matt was just grateful that he was being paid. The base had no facilities at all and boredom set in amongst the boys. There was only so many hours of pool, cards and spoof you could play.

We were supposed to be working tonight but due to bad weather all transport has been cancelled. I showered, got all dressed up in my dinner jacket and went to the club only to find it called off. I was well pleased as you can imagine. I would welcome work now

just to break the routine. I've still got the rash on my hands but it's now all over my body as well though it's a different type, more like prickly heat. A couple of the boys have also got it so I don't think it can be anything serious. — Matt Monro, letter from Bolling Air Force Base, Washington

Within a couple of days the weather started to improve, the snow thawed enough to make ground transport possible and the runways were deemed safe enough for landing. Matt's lethargy ebbed away as he was allowed to do what he did best — perform. He enjoyed working the bases and, although they were not known to the audience, the shows went down very well. The smaller clubs enabled a performer to develop an intimacy with the crowd and after two years of British radio, Matt found it refreshing to perform in front of a live audience.

Washington became their base and from there they travelled to Texas, Baltimore, Pennsylvania and, for a second time, New York. They were eating in the officers' mess of the airbase one evening when Matt spotted a James Stewart look-a-like. He was amazed at the similarity between the star and one of the officers, who was one of Matt's idols. The matter was clarified when the film star came up after the show to speak to the artists.

At last the weather has started to improve. It's still freezing but the sun is shining like mad. We did our first job last night (Friday) at a service club about sixty miles from here and it went like a bomb. Johnnie got them all going in about two minutes and from then on it was easy. I can't stand being away from you any longer than I have to. I wish you could have been with me. I think then that I would have liked the USA a lot better. — Matt Monro, letter from Bolling Air Force Base, Washington

Matt had been worried about entertaining the American troops and was genuinely thrilled to find the shows going down a storm. But the days were long and hard for him. He hadn't really been apart from Mickie since they'd met and he was feeling the pain of separation. He looked forward to her letters. The latest one revealed that his first disc for Parlophone would be released on 25 March and everyone shared in his excitement. Mickie had finally left Mills Music due to internal politics. Les Perrin, who had opened up his own company Les Perrin Associates in Denmark Street, asked her to work for him, which was too tempting to turn down. Mickie stayed busy at work

Les Perrin

and in the evenings Les came over to help put together a press manual on Matt. They would post it to over a hundred journalists, newspapers, disc jockeys and television producers.

There was talk of the singer staying on in New York to make a few business contacts and meet some of the American agents, but he thought it a bit premature and wanted to get home. Mickie had told him that she had just paid the electricity bill and begged him to go easy because the cash register read nil.

The tour's second week saw the most exciting news arrive. Members of President Eisenhower's personal aircrew had heard Matt sing when visiting the Washington base and invited him and the band to perform for them at The Pentagon. He was the first pop vocalist to receive such an invitation and no one else has performed there since. What amazed both Johnnie and Matt was the apparent lack of security. Band members went in and out with all their instrument cases and crated music stands, and not one of the security detail checked any of the contents.

We made history. We gave the first ever concert inside the Pentagon. Everything, FBI, security, the lot and in the audience

were the personal aircrew of the President. The only music they have in there is chapel music. I've just looked out of the door and we have a snowstorm on our hands. The forecast is eight inches. I just hope it doesn't ground us on Friday morning. Sitting at the next table through dinner was James Stewart. He looks much the same as he does on the screen but a lot older.

We had a party last night in the officers' club. Your husband got himself drunk and staggered off to bed about 1.30am. There's one thing about getting drunk on this beer: you don't get a hangover. — Matt Monro, letter from Bolling Air Force Base, Washington

We fly out of here tomorrow for New York, stay there the night and then come home. We have two shows to do tonight, one in the service club and one in the officers' club. This should be a stormer as it's St Patrick's Day which is a big thing over here though I don't know why, probably because everyone claims Irish, Welsh, Scottish or English descent. The showroom has been transformed into a green odyssey; everything is green including the beer.

In the act I've been using a very posh accent, which has been going down like a bomb, the people seem to like what I do. We haven't come across any anti-British feeling, which surprised me, but I can't tell you how strong the colour feeling is. It really amounts to open hate. About seventy percent of the population of Washington are coloured and the slums are indescribable, just piles of sticks and stones. — Matt Monro, letter from Bolling Air Force Base, Washington

The tour ended in New York. Matt and Johnnie had enjoyed their time together and built up a great professional relationship. In subsequent years Matt would often leave a drink waiting behind the bar for his friend, if Johnnie was following him into a theatre.

Matt returned to England to find that his new record hadn't fared that well. The disappointment of yet another flop, this time with his third record company, didn't sit too well on Matt's conscience. He'd seemed to have had all the breaks, but was beginning to think that perhaps he just wasn't meant to be a singer. Yet again Mickie became his rock, giving him the encouragement to remain positive.

At least work had poured in following the success of *Swingin' Sellers* and it looked as if Matt would enjoy some steady income. Billy Hill Bowen rang, asking if he was interested in doing another set of ads for the Camay campaign, and the offer of more jingles came in for a Bisto campaign. Les Perrin had done a good job at getting press coverage. He sent out over a hundred press packs while Matt was in America, which secured the occasional television appearance, including *Easy Beat,* Granada's *People and Places* and *Cool For Cats.* Matt accepted every offer that came in, including a couple of clubs on the Manchester circuit. His main port of call after every trip was Tin Pan Alley, and he was still managing to pick up the odd demo.

Towards the end of April Matt had dinner with American agent Norm Riley. Les Perrin was convinced that, when the elusive hit record came, they had to be ready to spread their wings overseas and Matt was persuaded to sign a one-year contract.

Ken Brown had taken on the management of Terry Dene, a singer cum comedian, and invited Matt, Michael and his brother Don to see his new show at the Condor Club in Wardour Street. Mickie felt it was important and equally prudent for Matt to be seen out on the town and she was happy for her husband to go out with the boys.

Matt loved good comedy and Terry was adept at storytelling. He soon had the place jumping with an Elvis Presley number before singing his latest release, 'Geraldine'. Kenny Baker's gags and harmonica maintained the party spirit and Matt was persuaded to step up from the audience to sing 'Old Black Magic' and 'Way Down Yonder in New Orleans'. This was just the right setting to lift Matt's spirits and help him unwind, whereas Michael found it difficult not to talk shop – even on a night out. There was always a sense of excitement with Michael and it was often hard for anyone else to get a word in when he was in full throttle. Don, on the other hand, was the complete opposite. He was slimmer-framed and certainly the introvert of the family.

These evenings out were important and enabled Matt to make new business contacts. He constantly met new artists and, although they might only see each other on the circuit occasionally, they were important associations. Being constantly away from home meant those friendships were vital when on the road, as they kept you sane and dulled the heartache of being away from loved ones.

One such contact arranged a night out at the Pigalle in London. Matt had never been there and was looking forward to the evening, but his excitement reached untold levels when he learned they were going to see Sammy Davis Jr. Arriving in Piccadilly and seeing his idol's brightly lit name outside the venue gave Matt such an adrenalin rush that he found himself in need of a drink to steady his nerves.

Sammy was in London to appear on the Royal Variety Show and his agent had added a series of television spots and a week of cabaret at the Pigalle. The club was packed and the few empty seats at Matt's table were soon taken when Bruce Forsyth and his party arrived. The established comic had hotfooted it across town once the curtain came down on the royal show he had been compèring. It didn't take the two men long to get acquainted and it was obvious that Sammy was also one of Bruce's favourite performers.

The lights dimmed and a sense of expectation filled the room. The build up was such that when Sammy's opening music started and he walked out on stage, you expected to see a giant of a man. The reality was a small, underweight, extrovert showman dressed in a beautiful black silk shirt laden with gold jewellery. The performance was magical.

Matt's evening became even more magical when he was invited, with a few others on the table, to go back to Sammy's hotel after the show. He spent an hour with 'Mr Wonderful' and that meeting marked the start of a long and meaningful friendship. Sammy invited Matt to see the show again that week so he could also meet Mickie.

The days following those special evenings were something of a come down. However, one piece of good news was the announcement that Matt would be one of the five singers competing in the six-nation contest for the European Cup, a singing competition being staged at the Casino Knokke-le-Zoute in Belgium at the end of July. Apart from himself, the other four representing Britain would be Steve Martin, Valerie Masters, Jimmy Lloyd and Wally Whyton. In addition to holding the Cup, the winning team would also share a thousand pounds of prize money.

On the rare occasion when he wasn't working, Matt would relax in the White Lion playing darts. He was a founding member of the Tin Pan Alley darts team, otherwise known as 'The Honourable Company of Dart Throwers and Arrow Bungers'. This was an aggregation of show folk who played darts weekly in the local pubs around London in aid of charity. The team included Alma Cogan, Pearl Carr, Ivy Benson, Lorie Mann, Michael Ingrams, Teddy Johnson, Bryan Johnson, Johnny Duncan, Wee Willie Harris, Carl Barriteau, Al Saxon, Johnny Dankworth and Jimmy Young.

Matt's appearance in June on BBC's *Tempo 60* was followed the week after by a four-day booking on ATV's *Lunch Box*, which was filmed in Birmingham. Jerry Allen was originally booked as musical director and co-host with Noele Gordon for its run of six weeks, but it proved so popular that it ended up running for eight years. Matt became a regular on the programme and loved working with Jerry and his trio. Jerry played the organ, Ken Ingarfield was on bass, Lionel Rubin was the drummer and Alan Graham was on vibes. June Marlow often worked with Matt on the show and

Lunch Box *rehearsals with Matt, June Marlow & Roy Edwards*
(Alan Graham of Jerry Allen and his Trio on Vibes (at back))

it was a happy association.

June and Matt arrived at the studio at six-thirty every morning to rehearse, and the usual format was they'd perform a couple of songs each and a duet. The production team usually made the song selection in advance, although they obviously asked both artists for their thoughts. Matt nicknamed June and himself 'Tweedle Dum and Tweedle Dee' and over the ensuing months their duets included 'Fancy Meeting You Here', 'Let's Get Away From it All', 'Anything You Can Do I Can Do Better', 'Together Wherever We Go' and 'Can't Take That Away From Me'.

Matt travelled up to Birmingham on a Sunday night, taking the train so that Mickie could use the car. The show usually finished by mid-afternoon and June, Matt, Jerry and his boys would pop to the pub for an early dinner and a few well-earned drinks.

In my opinion Jerry Allen is the finest organ player in the country, while his group is the best quartet we have. There isn't a quartet that plays together like they do. They know instinctively just what

> **you're going to do when they're providing the backing. I worked with them on *Lunch Box* in Birmingham; one week in every month for the six months I spent on the show. I had a great time. — Matt Monro**

Matt enjoyed his time on the programme immensely, not just because of the professionalism of the cast and crew, but also for the fantastic camaraderie. And he certainly made an impact on one of the viewers.

> **I first saw Matt on *Lunch Box* when I was about thirteen years old. He hadn't had any big hits of his own to begin with, but he just came over as a lovely man with a fabulous voice. I bought all his records on the day they were released; I even had a standing order with the man in our local record shop. I had to save my pocket money to buy the records and it was even harder when EPs and LPs came along, but if I hadn't saved enough the owner would still call me into the shop on my way home from school and let me have the record and the sheet music. I even struggled home with a promotional board he let me have. — Sue Parker née Maull**

From that moment Sue became a life-long fan, travelling the length and breadth of the country to see Matt perform. But in 1960 she was still at school. Even though it took her fifteen minutes to get home, she would make the extra trip at lunchtimes just to see Matt on *Lunch Box*.

Sue was originally a big Doris Day fan, with copious photographs covering her bedroom wall, but gradually that collection made way for the new man in her life. Her father was never allowed to decorate her room and there wasn't an inch of wallpaper to be seen. She poured over the pages of *NME* and *Melody Maker* and collected every press cutting she could lay her hands on. With those first articles she started a scrapbook and over the years it grew into a huge collection of books she proudly stored in the safety of her home.

Matt couldn't have asked for a more loyal fan. However, despite the number of times she watched him on the television and waited for him outside the ATV studios in Aston during the school holidays, she couldn't bring herself to speak to him or ask for his autograph. It would take several more years before she had the nerve to approach the singer and even then, it was only because she was forced into the situation.

British Entry, Six-Nation Cup Knokke-le-Zoute – Steve Martin, Jimmy Lloyd, Wally Whyton & Matt

Matt next travelled over to Belgium for the Knokke Festival, which was Mickie's first trip abroad with her husband. They had been together for more than three years, so Matt was thrilled to be taking his wife with him on the eight-day trip. It wasn't to be the honeymoon they'd never had, because Matt insisted it would be a great idea to take Evelyn, his mother-in-law. She'd endured a hard life and had been very lonely since losing her husband, and the gesture was Matt's way of thanking her for all the help she had given him and Mickie. Even though the British team were eliminated in the first round, Matt still enjoyed the rest of the week with Mickie and Evelyn. They treated the time as a partial holiday, exploring the coastal city in the mornings while taking advantage of the casino games in the evenings.

The first week of August was hot and sticky, but things were set to get stickier for Matt in the ensuing months. It began with his first season at the Astor Club for Michael Black.

A Sting in the Tale

Michael Black was now working for Bertie Green who owned the world-renowned Astor Club in Berkeley Square, London. The venue was littered with prostitutes, which the club politely called hostesses, who'd wait for a table to be filled and then order champagne for the guests at £2.00 a bottle. They'd get a pound for each bottle purchased, earning up to a tenner on good nights. Michael was responsible for booking the entertainment at the club and had free reign, but with the condition that he mustn't book any male singers; Bertie felt the club was for girls, saucy comics or speciality acts.

Michael had many of his acts already booked at the hundreds of American bases throughout Britain and felt it wouldn't hurt to have an extra entertainer at the ready, so he arranged an audition for Matt at the Astor. Knocked out by the singer, Michael immediately got on the phone to the Sergeant at South Ruislip NCO Club where he booked acts every Friday, Saturday and Sunday. Michael wasted no time in selling *The Matt Monro Show* into the base. The clubs were hard work, in part because the audience was segregated and because men who were stationed there were far from home and the club opened in the mornings. If the men were off duty they would open a bottle of Budweiser early on and sit there drinking all day.

The night of the booking, Michael picked Matt up at the Astor and drove him to the base, where there was a mixed crowd. The sound equipment amounted to a microphone with an 'on and off' switch, with no control for reverb, sound, bass or treble. The crowd were noisy and the room was filled with cigarette smoke. Secretly, Michael was worried that the crowd would eat the singer alive. But Matt was fearless; he just walked out and sang. And he absolutely tore them apart.

Being a little fellow, I remember how dismayed the Colonel was when

Entertaining a Saturday night crowd.

he saw me. After the concert had been a riotous success the Colonel came up to me and said "You know something, son. When I first saw you I got a terrible feeling in my stomach. I thought man, what will these boys do to this poor little guy up there." — Matt Monro

A lot of audiences had the same first impression as that US Air Force Colonel. They saw Matt walk on stage, a short, stocky fellow who didn't look anything special until he sang. Over the months Matt settled into a comfortable routine working a circuit of NCO and Airmen's Clubs. Part of his regular cabaret act was to ask a lady to come up on stage and sing 'Nice 'n' Easy' with him and Mickie had often laughingly threatened to come up herself one night. No one was more shocked than she, when at South Ruislip NCO Club one evening, Mickie volunteered herself, just to shock Matt. But once she was on stage she soon realised her error. She was shaking with nerves and crying with laughter and could hardly sing a coherent note. Matt took full advantage of the situation, laughing at her with the audience, and although the envy of every woman in the audience, Mickie was mortified.

Arthur Lowe's agency was based at the Astor, but he ultimately worked for Bertie Green. Michael would send a contract out on behalf of the Arthur Lowe Agency offering Matt a ten-pound fee and free transport. It meant Matt had to travel to the Astor Club for the pick-up but was ferried back and forth from the bases along with the other artists on the bill. Michael decided to take a chance and put Matt on at the Astor without Bertie's permission. His boss was prone to wandering in and out of the club without warning, but he hadn't been around for a few days.

The hubbub surrounding Parlophone's new signing had quietened down. Matt's single had come out and hadn't fared well, so he was prepared to take whatever work came in. He opened at the Astor and did remarkably well considering the circumstances. Several nights into his contract, Bertie walked in, saw the singer and thought he was fantastic. Luckily for Michael, Bertie decided to overlook his booker's disregard for his 'no male singer' rule and announced that he wanted to sign Matt to his agency.

Matt had now been working for Michael through the Arthur Lowe Agency for some months and the American base work came in thick and fast. There seemed no reason for Matt not to sign a more permanent contract with the Agency. Matt's manager Don Reed had hit the road, having failed to deliver much of the work he had promised, and Matt was now convinced that he had nothing to lose by signing with the Agency. He was most definitely wrong. Bertie's legal man went through every contract with a magnifying glass, ensuring they were watertight. Bertie couldn't lose; every artist who signed was on a six-month probationary period enabling him to get rid of anyone he wished, but they were prevented from leaving until he was ready to let them go. He had also taken the precaution of putting the club in his wife's name to prevent any lawsuits. It wasn't the best decision that Matt could have made.

Bertie wasn't one of nature's gentlemen. He had a very bad reputation as a villain and he used to sign artists up with the sole intention of doing nothing and then suing them. He did it to four or five people. It took a long time to get disassociated from Bertie. When I finally went on my own he put so many blocks up, but in the twelve years I'd been booking the clubs, all anyone saw was me – nobody else. What do I think of Bertie Green? – A greedy bastard, a greedy no-good bastard. You'd get a bad name just through being associated with him, your credibility stood for nothing. – Michael Black

Bertie had Matt signed for five years, but didn't give the singer any work, other than what he'd already been getting him as an agent. The only difference was that

now Matt was paying a management's commission instead of the lower agency fee. Word spread, but too late, that this was the usual practice of the man. Regrettably the contract Matt signed was watertight and he was forced to buy himself out of the agreement for a whopping three-thousand pounds, but he did it just in time. Unfortunately this wasn't the end of Matt's legal problems that year. He would soon come up against Ember Records.

Between Matt's work at the airmen's bases and the Astor Club he was still peddling his talents on Denmark Street. Sitting in the White Lion he got talking to Merrick Farren. Merrick was looking for a singer who could lay down six demonstration discs to sell to the BBC as a broadcast. On 9 August 1960, Matt went into Maida Vale Studios with Merrick and sang the tracks, which included 'Ghost of Your Past' and 'Quite Suddenly'. The session finished and Matt left with his fee, thinking nothing more of it. He accepted another two weeks' work for the television show *Lunch Box* in August, but before leaving for filming in Birmingham he met with George Martin to discuss the next session. The producer was convinced he had come up with a winner and a date was set for 2 November 1960.

Matt was working four-day weeks for ATV's *Lunch Box* and on the days when the set went dark he filmed two consecutive shows for Southern TV. Although the lunchtime shows' rehearsals took place at Max Rivers Rehearsal Rooms in London's Great Newport Street, Michael Black was unaware that the actual filming was taking place in Southampton, some eighty miles away, and booked Matt into Croughton NCO Club the same night.

Matt got very little sleep over the next two weeks, as these lunchtime shows required early morning starts and the evening club work meant very late finishes. *Lunch Box* ended, but there was no breathing space as immediately after, Matt recorded a radio and a television programme with Malcolm Mitchell and His Trio.

Matt was running on autopilot and found the only way to unwind while away from his family was to have a few drinks. Alcohol provided solace, making the loneliness more tolerable. This was the occupational therapy that he needed and it wasn't a solitary affair. Show business was a social activity and fellow artists and company crews expected Matt to have a drink with them once a show was wrapped. He was only too happy to oblige and avoid the alternative – an empty room in a strange town.

A lot of Matt's bread-and-butter work came from television and radio adverts. Although the weekly music papers reported the latest trends in record buying, they were not necessarily an indication of the top songs being sung or whistled in offices and homes throughout the country. There was a special type of song that was being hummed more frequently than any other composition to emerge from Tin Pan Alley, and that was the advertising jingle.

The principal object of a jingle is to fix a product firmly in the mind of the public. It is a specialised art from both the writers' and recording artists' perspectives, for their singing must be confident, reassuring and persuasive. Such importance was attached to the making of commercials that enormous sums of money were spent securing the top session men in the business.

In an average year over two-thousand-five-hundred different commercials were screened and the majority included music or jingles of some kind. Some of pop's best-known names were used. Many of them appeared on camera, such as Gary Marshal and Humphrey Lyttleton for Crunchie Bar, Dave King for Corona Squashes, Jim Dale for Nux Bar and Benny Hill for Schweppes Table Waters.

Cliff Adams was another top jingle man but in his case most of the singing went to the artists connected with him such as The Stargazers and The Adams Singers, but occasionally he would go outside his own camp, as with Rosemary Squires, who was heard for Fry's Turkish Delight and Bon Coffee, as well as Matt Monro for Player's Cigarettes, Wills Tipped Woodbines, 7 O' Clock Blades and Strand Cigarettes.

It was Johnny Johnston who developed the jingle into a fine art. He wrote so many that it is impossible to list them all, but firm favourites were Bird's Eye, Bulmer's Cider, Cadbury's Milk Tray and Campbell's Soups. Some of these were the most memorable jingles featured on television and, for the most part, featured Johnny's own artists The Keynotes and The Johnston Singers, with the distinctive voice of Jean Campbell clearly evident.

Another team who strongly featured on the scene were John and Joan Shakespeare, who constantly commanded attention with their easy-on-the-ear jingles for products like Drene Shampoo, Lyons Maid Ice Cream, Spangles, Bird's Custard, Orangillo and Player's Cigarettes. Matt became a favourite with the husband and wife song writing team and featured on an untold number of jingles over the years including Milk Extra-Pinta, Babycham, Hartley Peas, Butlins, Coates and Zal.

Matt stipulated, as he always did for demonstration sessions, that the disc should not be released commercially. But news had filtered through that Merrick Farren had sold the six numbers that he had asked Matt to record for a BBC broadcast to Ember Records, and the company was intent on releasing two of the tracks. The reason for Matt's stipulation over demos and his subsequent argument with Jeff Kruger, head of Ember Records, was that the recordings were not of a good enough quality to be released. They had been produced for a totally different purpose.

When questioned, Kruger insisted that someone with the tapes had approached him, and as they were free of any contractual obligations, he had bought them. He further added that as they had been made before Matt was officially signed with

EMI, they were his property.

A solicitor issued a writ to stop the release of the six songs, which the recording star had taped for a fee of twenty pounds. 'Ghost of Your Past' and 'Quite Suddenly' had already gone to press, which created a real sense of urgency. Matt was furious with the record label, but his anger was slightly misdirected, since Jeff Kruger had bought the tapes in good faith. The case rested with the solicitors and a court date was set for January 1961. There was nothing Matt could do except wait for the outcome.

> **I first met Matt in one of the numerous offices in Denmark Street where so many of the then music publishers were located – this was a few hundred yards north of my then offices at Cambridge Circus. Mine was the only real independent label and we were up against the might of the monopoly comprising EMI, Decca and Philips who did all they could to put us out of business. We were successful and had a hit with The Harry Simeone Chorale singing 'Onward Christian Soldiers', 'Little Drummer Boy' and a recording of 'The Madison' we cut with Ray Ellington. Subsequently we bought other recordings to consider releasing and one of these was a demo Matt did. — Jeff Kruger, Ember Records**

The Monros took a well-earned holiday in Cornwall during the last week of September. Matt was exhausted and plagued by regrets. Although he had worked flat out, he had no money to show for it. All he wanted to do was sing; he didn't want to deal with the day-to-day realities of the business. The taxman wasn't interested in Matt's earnings after expenses, just what he had made over the year. Mickie felt that her husband had more than enough on his shoulders without worrying about administrative matters, so each week she put aside a small amount to cover the Government's tax bill. Over time Mickie took on anything she considered an excess burden on Matt. He would hand over any income less his daily expense money and for that sacrifice he would never have to think about a bill again – Mickie took care of everything.

Even though he had been stung, Matt still went ahead with several demos, one for Tin Pan Alley Music called 'Blue Eyed Boy' and others for Don Angus, Michael Carr and Don Black. He went back to the studios, but this time for the National Benzole advertisement campaign. They used Cine Tele Sound Studios (CTS) in

Caravan Holiday Cornwall

Bayswater in what had previously been an old Wesleyan chapel. The building had unusual acoustics but it was still considered to be one of the best recording studios in London and rapidly achieved a near monopoly of the TV jingle market. Matt still had to earn a living and couldn't afford to be picky. He couldn't know that as the year was drawing to a close he was weeks away from a life-changing event.

Brother Can You Spare a Dime?

On 2 November 1960, history would be made, and this time there would be no going back for Matt Monro.

On previous recording sessions for Matt, George Martin had selected Ron Goodwin and Tommy Watt as the arrangers, but for the upcoming session he decided to use Johnnie Spence, a new kid on the block who had just been signed to Parlophone as a musical director. A meeting was arranged between Matt and Johnnie and the two hit it off straight away.

> **Johnnie Spence was one of the best musicians I've ever known. He was a marvellous arranger, a great band man, and his scores for brass, saxes, rhythm and strings were the best I've ever had, much better than I could do. His work with Matt Monro was one of the highlights, one of the joys of my life. He always turned up with a very tasteful score; he was also a lovely man, a great character. He did tend to burn the candle at both ends though, and in the middle! It was a great tragedy when he died, it was such a shock, he was so young. — George Martin**

George selected three or four songs as potential new releases, and arranging a routine session was the first item of business.

> **Routining meant that I would collect a number of songs I thought would be suitable for the artist, and then they would come to the office and we would run through them on the piano. Having agreed on the numbers they would sing, we would work out which keys they would be sung in, what the shape of the recording would be, how**

many choruses they would have, what kind of orchestral backing, what kind of beginning and ending and so on. — George Martin

The original Abbey Road paperwork records that the producer booked for the session was actually Ron Richards, George's assistant. However, George evidently had a change of heart, as he attended the session personally and changed the paperwork to reflect this.

George was convinced he had *the* song for Matt. He told the singer to do the number with a Nat King Cole sensibility, but Matt was adamant that he didn't want to do any more impressions. George agreed and explained that Matt could perform the song however he wished, but that was the sort of treatment he wanted to achieve. Matt remained unconvinced that the song would do very well and thought it one of the most uncommercial songs he'd ever heard. But even the greatest of singers have been wrong: Frank Sinatra turned down 'Mona Lisa' and Nat King Cole 'Love is a Many-Splendored Thing'. The chosen song had started out as an instrumental, penned by Columbia recording manager Norman Newell and written by orchestra leader Cyril Ornadel. The title – 'Portrait of My Love'.

Charlie Katz was the fixer for the orchestra. He played violin himself and his brief was to book all the musicians for the session at Abbey Road. They had to be booked as far in advance as possible because any musician of good standing would get retained very quickly, some of them doing up to three sessions in a single day. Charlie selected Kenny Clare on drums, Kenny Powell on piano and Roy Willox on lead alto sax, all of whom became favourites for many future sessions.

Vic Fraser was also involved in that momentous session. He'd first met Johnnie Spence whilst working for the music publisher Campbell Connelly in Denmark Street in the late 1950s. Johnnie had been the accompanist to the singer Anne Shelton and would bring the arrangements he'd done for her to Vic for copying. Vic had subsequently left the publishers and turned freelance but he and Johnnie had become friends and kept in touch. George had asked the arranger to do a treatment on 'Portrait' and, once written, Johnnie dropped the score off with Vic for copying. From that original score it was Vic's job to copy all the parts for the individual instruments. As Vic had been studying music arranging he was keen to hear the new score performed, so Johnnie got permission for Vic to attend the recording.

Stuart Eltham knew there was no set rule for uncovering talent – you just had to keep your ear to the ground. He knew George had taken Matt under his wing after an unsuccessful record debut and stood ready in the studio. After routining the song and getting the arrangements written for each member of the orchestra, they were finally ready to record. There was a nervous anticipation in the air and although Eltham tried to look cool and blasé he admitted he always got a tingle of excitement waiting for the band to swing into the music for the first time.

George threw everything he had at 'Portrait'. He made the unique decision to record in stereo rather than the mono used for Matt's first session. The other trick up his sleeve was to use a twenty-three-piece orchestra to give the song a big sound. To justify the costs he split the session to divide the expenditure and appease the finance department – Keith Kelly took the morning and Matt the afternoon.

Everyone was excited by the way the session had gone. John Burgess had been quietly sitting in the control booth and was mesmerised by the unknown's voice. He could not possibly know that several years later he would take over the job as Matt's A&R manager.

Matt had laid down a great track but he remained unconvinced.

> 'Portrait' was given a Nat King Cole treatment, musically. Orchestrally we changed it a little bit, but only the middle eight. We didn't change the melody; we just changed the note values. I loved the song but didn't think there was a chance for it in today's market. There was Cliff, Adam Faith, Presley, Tommy Steele and Rock with the Cavemen, that was the sort of music that was selling so I didn't think it stood a snowball in hell's chance. George rang three weeks later and said, "Keep your fingers crossed, we might be in the charts next week", and we were. — Matt Monro

'Portrait' had been chosen as the A-side from the very beginning, but that left a dilemma over the flip side. After consideration, George and Matt agreed to use 'You're the Top of My Hit Parade', which they felt complemented the ballad perfectly. The second track was laid down with comparable ease.

Matt had a knack for making each session appear easy, but it didn't hurt that the best tools in the trade – a marvellous song, a great producer, great orchestrations and great musicians – supported him. He would never presume to think that the process could be successful without the whole team effort. Recording was hard work and the demands of having to deliver a track in as few takes as possible were immense. There was a great deal of pressure on Matt to deliver first time round.

It wasn't just the phrasing, or his timbre, or his flawless musicality, to

Matt & Johnnie

a man who had to channel his most intimate emotions into his recordings, if only as a release, the performance was everything.
— George Martin

George, Matt and Johnnie found the ultimate weapon for sustaining them through the subsequent long days and nights spent in the studios and alleviating session tension and anxiety – laughter. They all shared a similar sense of humour and each session would see one or all three of them rolling about the floor in stitches.

The session was over at last; the tape in the can, and musicians, producer, engineers, arranger, copyist and assistants all joined Matt for a well-earned celebratory drink. An hour later, the cast thinned and George invited a select few to dinner. He also arranged for Mickie and Johnnie's girlfriend Marion to meet up with them in the restaurant.

From that moment on, Johnnie Spence became Matt's Musical Director, his name as closely associated with Matt Monro as Nelson Riddle's was with Sinatra. Johnnie went on to become one of the most respected arrangers, conductors and composers in the business, rivalling the best work of Richard Wess and Billy May in the States. He was able to arrange for all kinds of moods, but he was to be most remembered for his hard-swinging orchestrations. On record he accompanied such artists as

Richard Allen, Sheila Buxton, Craig Douglas, Perry Ford, Paul Hanford and Janet Richmond. But he found his greatest success in teaming with Matt, whom he backed on all the singer's Parlophone recordings. An unbreakable bond developed between the arranger and the singer, who shared something very special and understood one another completely.

The official date of release for Matt's record was 25 November, which seemed a long way off, but all they could do was wait. Matt carried on working, making two demos for Marilyn Music Company, unaware that another demo was about to upset the applecart a few weeks later.

Matt was working the American bases the week prior to the release of the record and Michael Black was delighted to announce that Matt's fee had been pushed up to fifteen pounds. There was no denying that Matt would have a tough fight on his hands, competing in a music chart that also included entries from Adam Faith, Tommy Steele, Cliff Richard and The Shadows, and Johnny and The Hurricanes. The swinging sixties had truly arrived, complete with pop groups, amplifiers and electric guitars.

One of the few people in the media who recognised rock 'n' roll as a major new phenomenon was Jack Good. He was steadfast in his conviction that the musical style was there to stay, observing that the kids were hanging out in coffee bars kitted out with jukeboxes which were churning out rock 'n' roll and nothing else. Even Tin Pan Alley, which had remained stuck in the era of big bands for so long, had changed by the early sixties and the crooners were being swept away in a tidal wave of younger artists, managers and hustlers.

Captivated by the phenomenon, Jack Good was anxious to expand on his vision of bringing the music to a wider-reaching media: television. He had met with the BBC who had been impressed by his enthusiasm and energy and agreed to give his ideas a shot. There was an hour of dead screen time, with children's programmes ending at six in the evening and adult programming beginning at seven, and he was given that hour on a Saturday night to produce a programme aimed at the teenage market. Good came up with a winning concept that became *6.5 Special*, bringing an unpredictable, chaotic live studio show featuring bands and interviews to the masses. It was the only one of its kind on television, and as the sole pop show it had unrivalled power to introduce new acts.

Jack Good also wrote a highly influential column in *Disc* magazine. His word was considered sacred at the time, and everyone waited to hear what he would make of Matt's new release. When 'Portrait' hit the streets he gave the disc a glowing review and, with *Disc*'s influence, that was enough to help sales extensively. Matt's good friends Pat Brand and Maurice Kinn also wrote appreciative reports in their respective papers, *Melody Maker* and *NME*, and Max Diamond at Kassner Music did a fantastic job of plugging the record. In fact there wasn't a bad review from any of the press. Another key champion of the record was disc jockey Brian Matthew, who touted it on the turntables of his Saturday morning show, *Saturday Club*. Prior to both *Top of the Pops* and Radio One, *Saturday Club* and *6.5 Special* were the only programmes on air to play pop music and, with that widespread exposure, it had the power to create hits.

The press reviews were fabulous and the unforgettable 'Portrait of My Love' entered the list of British best-selling records in December 1960, selling two-hundred copies and reaching number three in the charts. It stayed there for sixteen weeks. It was Matt's eighth single and was a smash, establishing him as one of the best singers in the country.

> Matt's version of 'Portrait' was a wonderful record, he sang it beautifully and it is one of my happiest memories. Matt's sense of phrasing, his understanding and reading of a lyric was the best you could get from England. I think his musicianship was marvellous. No, I think the only thing you can say against Matt is that he isn't very tall.
> — George Martin

The only slight disappointment was that Matt Monro was unable to repeat the feat on the other side of the Atlantic.

> 'Portrait' was taken into the best sellers by an alternative version by Steve Lawrence. Naturally I'm disappointed that I didn't click there with 'Portrait'. The trouble was that the company who were originally going to issue the record in the States simply sat on it and did nothing at all. By the time Warwick came along and took over the record, Steve's disc had a four-week start. — Matt Monro

In later years, Matt met up with Steve Lawrence when he was appearing at London's Pigalle nightspot with his wife Eydie Gorme. Steve sang 'Portrait' and prefaced it with a few words about Matt, introducing him to the nightspot's audience. Later, over drinks, Steve admitted that having already whipped in to grab 'Portrait' for the American market he was then tempted to do the same again with 'My Kind of Girl', but he didn't have the nerve to do it to Matt twice.

Matt was getting calls of congratulation from everyone he knew, those in Tin Pan Alley were genuinely pleased for a man they thought was too good to record demonstration discs for other artists and drinks were lined up everywhere he went. Don and Michael Black were ecstatic, Michael more so as some weeks before he had pre-booked Matt into the Astor Club for a week's cabaret in the period immediately following the record's release. Matt's name was everywhere and Michael came across as the golden boy. Lyricist Norman Newell was delighted, as secretly he had thought the words of his song were too sophisticated for a hit, but the Monro magic proved them all wrong. Having heard the record, Tony Christie thought England had finally produced a top-class artist.

The accolades poured in and the phone rang off the hook as Matt was besieged with songs from all over the country. He had become a star overnight! But nothing had immediately changed for him on the money front. When Matt and Mickie were invited to attend a prestige charity event in Battersea Gardens they both certainly looked the part, but what the public didn't see was Mickie's brother Ernie pulling up in his battered second-hand white transit van around the corner from the event. Ernie sprang out of the driver's seat to let Matt and Mickie out of the back and, having dusted themselves down, they proudly made their grand entrance.

Soon enough, though, the record's success brought about a complete transformation to the Monros' lives. At last the indefatigable Mickie felt she might safely leave her job. She was ecstatic that Matt was finally getting the exposure and appreciation he so richly deserved.

There was one change, however, that the couple were not prepared for – they had been together nearly twenty-four hours of every day since they'd met and suddenly this was all going to change radically. Even with the luxury of not having the time restrictions of a job, Mickie was a mother with a small child and couldn't just get up and leave to tour with Matt. They were destined to endure long forced separations, which they didn't like at all.

Matt was getting heavy attention for his chart hit and within days of the record climbing high in the charts, Ember Records released 'Ghost of Your Past' and 'Quite Suddenly'. Matt hated the tracks, they were never meant for commercial release and he resented their intrusion on his newfound success, worrying that they might damage his credibility. However, there wasn't a thing he could do about it until the court hearing date.

EMI spent thousands promoting a hit recording and I took – as they saw it – advantage of their efforts. I recall Matt was not happy about

the release but it was perfectly legitimate even if I was riding on other people's efforts. It could not hurt Matt [as I saw it] since every mention of his name over the BBC and Radio Luxembourg was a plus. No one belittled the recording and disc jockeys always then mentioned or played his new EMI record. — Jeff Kruger

The reviews of the record were mixed and it failed to register in the charts.

Matt Monro now makes a bold bid to consolidate his newfound success with the first coupling for the new Ember International label, 'The Ghost of your Past' and 'Quite Suddenly'. Bold because these are not what you call commercial titles. The backing is unusual enough to attract considerable attention to the disc — violinist composer Merrick Farran, who is responsible, brings an almost 'serious' approach to it in the form of violin and cello accompaniment.
— *Reuters News Agency*

Matt couldn't dwell on the situation though, as offers were pouring in and he had already made several commitments prior to the record's release. The day after his thirtieth birthday he attended rehearsals for *Rendezvous With Rosemary*, an Associated Rediffusion variety programme. He had first met the host, Rosemary Squires, when they recorded several 'open end' radio station announcements for American Radio stations. This was the second series Rosemary had worked with for Rediffusion and she was allowed to choose a different male guest each week. Once Rosemary heard Matt's voice she wasted no time in getting him on the show, with the wholehearted agreement of the producer Daphne Shadwell.

He was very busy but I got him eventually and coincidentally he had just cut his first record. He came to my house for rehearsals carrying the record under his arm. We asked him what he was going to do and he produced the record 'Portrait' almost apologetically — he thought that with all the rock 'n' roll around it didn't stand a chance. He played it to my manager, the producer Daphne Shadwell and we were all knocked out. We said, "You've got to do it — it's bound to be a hit". We later recorded it in the studio and the rest is legend. It is one of my proudest moments that this great hit was first aired on my show on 9 December 1960. I can honestly say that working with Matt on TV

Acetate Rendezvous with Rosemary

was one of the joys of my career – he was so easy and loved by everyone, artistes, producers and crew alike. — Rosemary Squires

His appearance was such a success that Rosemary invited Matt to do two more guest appearances in later shows. During one spot the two sang a duet called 'Mama Will Bark'. The aired programme showed a close-up of just their heads with ears stuck on and paw mittens on their hands. Matt would do anything for a laugh and to ensure they made good television, which sometimes needed variation to keep things visually interesting.

Sinatra himself recorded the same novel little rumba about romancing dogs and, although he hams it up for all he's worth, he drew the line at performing the canine howls, that privilege went to Donald Baine.

Matt's other appearance on the show featured a pastiche of a classic silent movie sequence with Matt as the hero, rushing in to rescue the damsel in distress, backed of course by dramatic piano music. The sketch opened with Matt sitting in a director's chair with the name 'Matt Monro' splashed across the back. He then swung round to camera and sang a chorus of 'You Ought to Be in Pictures'. The camera then faded into the caption like an old-time film, with a violin and piano playing 'Hearts and Flowers'. The camera pans in to show Rosemary in a broken-down cottage with a shawl around her head and a baby in her arms, her father threatening to throw her out into the snow. Rosemary pleads with him as the villain – played by Rosemary's manager David Mostyn – enters and demands the rent. Suddenly, the door opens with a big fanfare of music and in swoops the hero, Matt, saying, "I'll pay the rent". A fight ensues and Rosemary is next seen being tied to the railway lines by the villain. In the background dramatic music plays as the train approaches.

> **Enter Matt to free me just in time and the screen caption is "My hero", and Matt and I embracing as they play 'Chattanooga Choo Choo'. Then it flashes back to the director's chair and together we join in the singing of the song 'You Ought to Be Pictures'. It all sounds corny – as it was – but actually it worked out very well and was a good piece.**
>
> **Matt's impact on the business was enormous; he was arguably the greatest UK male vocalist of his time. He was underrated then but, like others, we were victims of the time, when popular music as we had known it changed almost overnight. — Rosemary Squires**

Matt was doing rather well; he had his own *Just For You* series on BBC's Transcription Service, appeared regularly on *Lunch Box* and was in constant demand for cabaret dates. Promotion for the record was fiercely demanding, but it certainly paid off with his disc first going silver and then gold.

> **I first met Matt in the 60s when his first record came out and he was doing a programme at ATV in Birmingham called *Lunch Box*. We did lots of one-nighters together, all in big theatres. I used to go on before Matt and introduce him. It was excellent fun and we had a lot of good times together, loads of laughs and, of course, stopped a load of alcohol from going bad. He was a great singer and a super bloke, one of the best. — Kenny Cantor**

The week of Christmas 1960, Matt was booked for a Light Programme series, taking the place of Frank Ifield as resident singer for *Stringalong*, which was to be aired in the New Year. Pianist Bill McGuffie was another resident attraction for the show's thirteen-week run. Matt was also invited to do Light Programme's new Wednesday series, *Parade of the Pops* by his friend, and producer of the show, John Kingdon. He'd first appeared on the show back in October and it would become a regular occurrence right through to 1968. Launched in August 1960, it quickly gained the second-highest rating figure for a pop music show, with an average listening audience in excess of four million each week.

Matt was overwhelmed by the success of the song, but his delight was tinged with a feeling of apprehension. He realised he was riding on the crest of a wave and was genuinely thankful, but he also knew full well that times could become sticky in as little as a year. His biggest thrill was in knowing that his hit had been with a quality song – he felt it was one of the best that had been written in his lifetime. Because the song itself was of such a durable nature, he hoped the public would react to the singer in the same way. In his estimation it was a remarkably healthy trend from the point of pop music. Although there was a percentage of beat numbers in the Top 30, ballads and good tunes were taking a firmer hold than they had succeeded in doing for years. This dovetailing of idioms and styles was a refreshing change from the long period of rock dominance.

Matt had nothing against rock, he thought it had many factors to its advantage and although he had never considered himself the type to indulge in the strictly beat-type music, he had every admiration for the youngsters who had made the grade in that field. He did confess though, that the tidal wave of rock had caused him many disappointments in the past. After all, he'd been knocking around in show business for some time and although he'd been fortunate, in that he'd always managed to make a living, it was only now that he'd managed to boost his career to the heights he had always aspired to. In fact, before 'Portrait' came along he had practically abandoned any hope of becoming a star. His thoughts were that to be accepted as a really big name, you had to click when you were young and fresh and he'd seriously believed that his initial impact had failed and that he would have to be content to remain a sort of 'good trouper' who had never quite made the grade.

He knew that the work rolling in for him now was solely attributed to the record being a hit, but as to the reason why it should happen now, in this way, after such a long time of knocking at the door, he credited to George Martin and the song writing team of Ornadel and Newell. Matt couldn't believe that out of all the artists associated with the EMI Group he was the one to land 'Portrait' and was grateful to George for sticking by him even though he had recorded several times for him without any noticeable effect. There was a film doing the rounds titled *The Singer Not The Song* and Matt couldn't help thinking that in his case, it was the song and not the singer. But George had always stuck to his belief that one day Matt would succeed in getting away on disc and that belief was now paying off handsomely. George, like others in the industry, was delighted for the singer. Matt had been around for so long in a role of also-ran that people were genuinely thrilled something big had finally happened for him.

The big question now was – could Matt build upon this initial record success? His

Recording Session Johnnie, Matt & George

future aspirations weren't simply to have a follow-up hit, or indeed a string of disc hits, his deepest wish was to be recognised as an international entertainer and there were many facets of the business to be conquered before that could happen. Cabaret and stage performances had to be undertaken and he was hoping for more rewarding exposure on television. Although he had worked in both fields extensively already, he hadn't been featured as a major attraction. There was also the film world to consider – he was hoping to undertake a role in musical comedy, though he strongly suspected that his height would work against him. But lack of inches wouldn't prevent him from becoming an entertainer, as opposed to solely a singer, and his ambitions were firmly set.

One-nighters, cabaret appearances and television dates were already being lined up for him. Whether or not it would prove to be lasting, only time would tell. If the current flush of success proved to be only fleeting, he would naturally be disappointed, but not broken-hearted, for he had never harboured any false illusions.

There are three things that have always struck me about Matt. One is that he was never bitter about rock 'n' roll – though it came at exactly the wrong time for him. Second he has always been able to joke about his shortness. Thirdly, he is a very modest man. He once told me he

Don Black, Don Rennie & Barry Barnett (seated) in Don's office in Denmark Street

would be embarrassed in the company of opera singers, because of the vast technical skills and dedication they have. In other words, he would be inferior to them. — Mickie Monro

Three days before Christmas, Matt invited Don Black to lunch. They had become great friends and the singer had a proposition for the young songwriter. He brought up the subject of management and asked Don if he would consider leaving Denmark Street to take the job. Don was understandably nervous; he had a family to support and was earning a regular salary with a relatively new position at music publishers Film Music. Matt explained that he would be earning good money and that as his manager he would receive a percentage of all work that he took on. Don didn't debate the issue for very long, reasoning that the job would also be a good outlet for his song writing. It was a job that Don never relinquished, even when he was too busy and really had no time to look after Matt, he could never bring himself to break away.

Just a few years previously, Don's brother Michael had got him a job at the *New Musical Express* (*NME*), which was run through impresario Maurice Kinn, a quietly spoken man with a strong aura that screamed power and money. Don rose through the ranks, but the work was tedious and the money awful. Then Michael unexpectedly came to his brother's aid – when he needed a compère for one of his shows, he offered Don the job. Billed as "Britain's slowest-rising comedian", he loved the spotlight but wasn't a great success. It was also not the profession for a young man wanting to settle down and, aged just twenty, Don proposed to his girlfriend Shirley. On 7 December 1958, they were married at Brenthouse Road Synagogue.

Kinn's offices were a who's-who of the world of show business, with Dickie Valentine, Frankie Laine and Billy Eckstine passing through regularly, so Don used the opportunity to get to know the Alley's music publishers and hang around their offices. He quickly became fascinated with the art of song writing and the people who made it happen. These were dream-chasers who doggedly pursued publishers with their latest effort, toughened from constant rejection but resolute in their goal to produce a hit.

Don had become friendly with lyricist Mike Hawker, who had written the Helen Shapiro hit 'Walking Back to Happiness'. He confided in Don that his latest royalty cheque had topped a thousand pounds and encouraged him to pursue his song-writing dream. After a few failed attempts, 'April Fool' was selected as the B-side on Al Saxon's new release and Ivy League picked up 'Crazy Over You'. While Don didn't earn a fortune, the ten-pound cheques that filtered through from the PRS were equivalent to a week's wages.

Don went back to the streets of Tin Pan Alley. But this time the street was to be the start of a genuinely new direction. He left *NME* and went to work for music publisher David Toff as a song plugger. It was ruthless and adrenaline-fuelled and he loved it, and in professional terms, the move was the start of everything, for it was there that Don first met Terry Parsons.

As the years progressed and Matt's good fortune climbed ever higher, Don was able to come to terms with living in the shadows while someone else took the spotlight, though self-effacement would never come easily to him. However, despite that fact there was not a moment when this agent, with shrewd eyes behind tinted glasses, was not prepared to fight Matt's corner, but the relationship between the two was never without its difficulties.

Don may have given him encouragement and guidance but he initially lacked the qualifications to go the whole way. Having been a comic and in the spotlight himself it took him a while to adjust to the spotlight favouring someone else. In the early years of their

partnership he could never entirely ignore an opportunity for his own self-promotion. Don's shortcoming was his inability to spot the occasional window of opportunity that could have enhanced Matt's career at any given time. — Mickie Monro

The contract that existed between Don Black and Matt Monro was little more than an offer of employment and a handshake, but this agreement proved harder to break than any that had gone before, bolstered by the weight of a seven pounds loan Matt had extracted from Don in 1958. Matt was a totally moral man, brought up to believe one must stand by one's principles. At times he was racked by guilt and found it too hard to leave Don behind on his ever-growing journey to stardom. They had started out together, and Matt was loyal, even though he increasingly felt that Don was not the right person to further his career.

In the early days, ten or fifteen percent was a fair enhancement on an agent's typical return if management duties were involved as well, but Don would later hedge his bets and go into business with Vic Lewis, which saw the percentage rise to twenty percent. Initially the dates were sporadic, and though the names might have sounded glamorous, like the Embassy, the Astor and Quaglino's, they represented for the most part superficial sophistication and B-movie glamour. More often than not, the reality was putrid digs with cold, soiled dressing rooms in strange, washed-out clubs where the atmosphere was heavy with smoke and the smell of alcohol and violence clung to the walls. Mostly heavy-drinking environments, clubs like the Astor unashamedly encouraged their customers' alcohol ingestion with a bevy of girls expert in persuading clients to part with their money. The artist had to compete with the chink of glassware and incessant prattle of the waitresses and call girls selling their wares.

In each artist's career you can point to one strong individual working behind the scenes. In Matt's case it was his wife Mickie who truly gave that selfless dedication to promoting his career.

Mickie has been the real driving force in my career. On occasions I've lost hope of making it and decided to quit the business and she would say "Look you've struggled so far, so struggle on a bit further, you'll make it one day." I don't know what I would have done without her encouragement. She is the woman behind me, the girl with the financial brain, who is my wife, my manager, my cashier, my booking agent and my budgeteer. I'm a nit with money. — Matt Monro

LA DI DA

With a new manager in tow, the Monros felt confident that they could leave the business side to Don, but as it transpired, Mickie was never able to hand over the reins completely. She still kept copies of all the contracts, ensured the accounts were up-to-date, replied to the fan mail and answered hundreds of calls. One such call was an enquiry from the business magnate Len Matcham. He needed a cabaret artist between 24 and 27 December at his hotel in Jersey. The booking was accepted. It meant that Matt and Mickie would be together for Christmas.

Len Matcham was a self-made millionaire. Matcham had become increasingly concerned about the punitive impact of the British Death Duty on persons of standing, and had just relocated to Jersey, where he acquired the Water's Edge, Woodville and Washington hotels. He ran his empire from the penthouse suite of the Water's Edge, interrupted only by the ninety days he was allowed by statute to return to British soil.

Matcham had only recently bought the hotels and realised that the Woodville didn't have a big name booked for the Christmas season. Having contracted Matt at the last minute, he wasn't able to attend the show himself but was overwhelmed by the feedback he later received from staff and clientèle about the singer and his performance. He rang the couple and apologised for not being there personally. Before leaving, Matt agreed to perform again at Easter, but this time he would do the gig for nothing, in exchange for a small holiday. They had thoroughly enjoyed their time in Jersey and would have liked to extend the trip by a few days, but Matt was contracted to appear on *The Russ Conway Show* the following day and rehearsals started at 2.00pm.

He arrived at Wood Green Studios and met up with Colin Clews, the producer. They ran through the show's outline, which was to be taped between 8.30 and 9.00pm. Russ introduced himself by his real name, Trevor Stanford, and Matt noticed that he was missing half of one of his fingers. The pianist later revealed that two of Matt's other friends Bill McGuffie and Dave Allen also shared this unusual attribute and he had subsequently set up a club called 'The Niners'.

The year ended with a feature spread for the *Record Mirror*. Although Matt saw the New Year in alone at the American base at Brize Norton, he reasoned that with more money coming in, the new year could only be better. Matt's aspirations were becoming a reality. Mickie had shared his dream and become deeply immersed in them. In a time of widespread discouragement and insurmountable obstacles, the young couple were both steadfast in their optimism. This was the reason Matt would hold his wife so close for the rest of his life, because she'd been there from the beginning, without a negative word and without making the burden heavier. Mickie was a very proud woman who recognised her own importance. She knew that her husband couldn't have held himself together without her motivation, conviction, trust and support. By supporting him financially, she had allowed him the freedom to pursue every opportunity the business threw at him and enabled him to follow his destiny. Matt was young and attractive, but even with his fame he was never seduced by his own celebrity and needed an anchor. He ached for someone to come home to after weeks on the road – and that someone was Mickie.

1961 saw Matt named Top International Act by *Billboard* magazine, an American publication dedicated to the music industry. It maintained a number of internationally accepted music charts that tracked the most popular songs and albums in a range of categories. Its most famous chart was the Billboard Hot 100, grading the top 100 songs by combining single disc sales and radio airplay regardless of genre.

The *New Musical Express*' chart survey described Matt as the artist who had restored class to commerciality. 1961 also saw Matt in the charts with no fewer than four singles.

Matt met with George Martin and a date was set for the beginning of January to record for a compilation album that Parlophone was putting together. Matt was added to the cast of the all-star disc, which was based on the *Parade of the Pops* radio series. The LP was waxed under the supervision of recording manager Norman Newell, and made in EMI's Hampstead studio before an invited audience. Other contributors included The King Brothers, Russ Conway, Janet Richmond, Garry Mills and Bob Miller and The Millermen, who were one of the mainstays of the radio series. Matt recorded two tracks, 'I Should Care' and 'I'm a Fool to Want You', in the one day. Although the album *Parade of the Pops* was recorded exclusively for Parlophone, people mistakenly assumed, because of the title, it had been made by the BBC.

George wanted Matt back in the studio to record the next single but had to wait until Matt's weekly appearance at the Piccadilly Club in Glasgow was honoured. Matt was, however, able to arrange an evening session in between his *Lunch Box* commitments. The choice of recording studio is a matter for the artist and producer to decide on, but EMI were very protective over who used Studio 1. Their use was determined by status and when 'Portrait' hit the charts Matt was finally allowed to record in the prestigious setting. George and Matt met for lunch to discuss the next choices; it was a difficult decision as it was important not to let the success of 'Portrait' pale against another flop.

The making of a record would start with myself and say Matt having lunch together and talking for a couple of hours about what should be on the next record. The suggestions might come from him or I might give him something from all the material that the publishers used to bring us. Then we would discuss who would be orchestrating the pieces, when the recording would take place and what size of orchestra he wanted. It would be my job to organise all those things... But when the appointed day came, it was really the engineer who was in charge. They had great experience in the placing of the microphones and the acoustics of the studio... Settling the way the pieces were to be performed was the prerogative of the performer. The recording was the engineer's baby and the ultimate aim of the engineer in those days was simply to recreate the sound as faithfully as possible. — George Martin

George, Johnnie and Matt spent the day in Abbey Road laying down 'Come Sta' and 'Love is the Same Anywhere'. They were both pretty songs but were nothing exceptional, and once they were in the can it was decided to wait for the Ember Records court hearing before releasing anything. The last thing they needed was an Ember release competing against their hope of a second hit single.

Although Matt was only part way through his thirteen-week commitment to the radio series *Stringalong* and *Just For You*, he found the time to fly to Dublin. Through careful scheduling, he managed a night at the Crystal Ballroom, five at the Roof Top Club and a television appearance on Ulster TV's *Roundabout*.

Matt's absence this time around wasn't too long, but Mickie was beginning to feel the pain of not seeing her husband. When they were unable to be together Matt would stay in constant touch by writing postcards and phoning. He was methodical about ringing, adding substantial amounts to his hotel bill, but he needed to hear his wife's voice at the end of the day. She kept him informed about Michele's progress, doctor's appointments and the more mundane aspects of their everyday life. Mickie would only tell him a problem if she couldn't handle it on her own, and even then she'd wait until the right time. She never resented his fame but did see it as an intrusion on their time together. These separations became increasingly long and Matt was always eager to get home.

> **I tried to spare him the burdens of fatherhood. He was diligent about the phone. I can't remember him missing a day, regardless of the number of time zones between us. — Mickie Monro**

In the last week of January the BBC named Teresa Duffy, Bryan Johnson, Valerie Masters, Mark Wynter, Anne Shelton, Steve Arlen, Ricky Valance, The Allisons and Matt Monro as the nine artists who would compete for Britain's entry in the 1961 Eurovision Song Contest. The British entry for the Eurovision final at Cannes would be decided on 15 February, when 120 voters in different parts of the country would judge the merits of the nine songs. Their votes would be telephoned to BBC-TV studios in London where the show would be transmitted. The three record companies involved with the event were EMI, Decca and Philips. All the songs in the contest were being specially written for the event and would be in the record shops the day after their television debut.

Matt was thrilled at being chosen for the event as it would undoubtedly mean enormous exposure and the chance to represent his country. A huge disappointment was to follow when, through a lot of mismanagement, he was unable to perform the number and Craig Douglas took his place. Matt's only consolation was that 'The Girl Next Door' finished joint last in *Song For Europe*. He was understandably furious with the cock-up, and half-heartedly agreed to sing in the British Song Contest in February.

Things were not to get much better. Although injunctions restraining Jeff Kruger and his Ember International label were enforced and prevented the company from publishing or advertising a record made by Matt, two of the titles were already out in the market place.

On 15 February, arrangements were made for settling the action. There was nothing to be done about the two songs already released, but Mr Justice Lawton, who was sitting in Chambers in the High Court, ordered that the other four songs were not to be published. The tapes were to be returned and then destroyed, but they were never found. However, a letter did arrive from Ember promising that the tracks would not be issued, although it didn't stop the company later placing 'Quite Suddenly' and 'Ghost of Your Past' on their new album *Don Rennie and Matt Monroe* [sic].

In an industry coup, John Barry joined Ember as head of A&R in 1963. He never had ownership over the label, but he was personally responsible for several high profile projects and was a driving force in gaining Ember recognition within the business. The relationship wasn't to last as Kruger and Barry's personalities clashed from the outset. The coupling of Don Rennie and Matt Monro was something that Barry wanted, and since Kruger published some of the songs he wanted to use, he didn't oppose the release.

The album was a transparent attempt to cash in on Matt's success, but the issue was slapdash, with Matt's name spelled two different ways on the cover. The disagreement continued when on 4 November 1965 an injunction was sought to stop Kruger publishing the records in the United States, as Matt and his management felt it could do untold damage. The solicitor argued that once issued in America, Matt could spend a fortune with American lawyers in trying to suppress it. The injunction was upheld.

Jeff Kruger bears no grudge over the events that happened in the 1960s and when asked, his comments were extremely complimentary.

> **He should have made it to the very top. He was without doubt a hell of a talent and so much better than his contemporaries of the time. He made his way successfully against the stream and he certainly had a chance, perhaps his advisors at the time were not influential enough to take him to his potential zenith. He had a feeling for a lyric the others couldn't get close to. He certainly was a man to be very proud of and a super artist who made it against tremendous odds. — Jeff Kruger**

'Portrait' continued to be in demand, with radio and television companies vying for the artist's appearance. Matt remained loyal, choosing *Saturday Club* over a competitor because they had used his services before his success. He debated 'Angel on My Shoulder' as his follow up single instead of 'Come Sta', but remained unconvinced about the song and decided to wait for the outcome of the upcoming British Song Contest. Associated Rediffusion aired the first of four heats to find the best British song, with each heat winner going through to the final that coming Friday.

In that first heat, Matt was pitted against The Dallas Boys, Jill Day, The Three Barry Sisters and Craig Douglas. Matt won the first round, the song given top placing

ITV Song Contest

by all nine regional panels. He was due to record the number for Parlophone as one side of his next release. The song was 'My Kind of Girl'.

There were three days of further heats. Lorrie Mann won on the Tuesday evening with 'Keep it That Way' and Mike Preston came first the night after with the song 'Marry Me', gaining a clear twenty point lead over his closest rival, Ronnie Carroll. Mike Desmond suffered considerably on the evening with extensive pain from a fractured jaw he sustained in a car accident two days before, but he'd made the decision not to have it set until after the contest. Frank Ifield won the last heat with the song 'I Can't Get Enough of Your Kisses'.

The final took place at the Royal Festival Hall, organised in co-operation with The Music Publishers Association. They'd lined up a whole host of names to promote their first British Song Contest, competing with the BBC's famous Eurovision Contest for screen audiences. They had gone to great lengths to ensure that all the songs submitted fairly represented most genres, from the wildest rock to the quietest romantic ballad. More than five hundred songs were received, from which the best twenty were selected, performed and judged.

On the final day, there remained four songs from which to choose the overal winner and runners up. The jury were members of the public and several panels, each made up of sixteen people, sat in various ITV centres outside London, with their decision relayed to a central scoreboard. Mike Preston won the competion with the song 'Mary Me' and matt came in a respectable second.

Matt, George and Johnnie rushed into the studios to record 'My Kind of Girl', the song penned by composer/librettist Leslie Bricusse. The slot for the session had been last minute, which was unfortunate for Vic Fraser as Johnnie had a habit of being late with the scores. He had dropped the music off with Vic at the eleventh hour and the copyist was frantically trying to finish the parts for the orchestra. They took the B-side first, a song called 'This Time', which Johnnie had written himself.

> **Johnnie was always late getting the scores finished, which often meant working late into the night. On this occasion I was copying the last of the three scores on a table in the corner of the studio. The first title had been recorded and they were working on the second. After a take George said, "That's fine Matt, let's move on". Matt looked at me and mouthed the words "Are you finished?" I shook my head and Matt said, "Let's do another take George," just to give me more time. — Vic Fraser**

On 3 March 'Portrait' departed the charts but was replaced the very next week by 'My Kind of Girl'. Earlier in the year Warwick Records president Morty Craft had paid a visit to George Martin at Parlophone. The fate of Mr Monro was once again set to be altered. These two top record producers from different continents banded together for one common cause, to make the voice of Matt Monro number one throughout the world and, after months of hard work, success was soon to be their reward. The single reached No 5 in England and gave Matt his first American hit where it peaked at No 18, an achievement that was noticed by Capitol Records.

It was a testament to the tune's popularity that both Sinatra and Sammy Davis Jr later recorded the track. The unique quality of Matt's voice made him a star amongst the stars and earned him the title 'The Singer's Singer'. After hovering on the fringe for several weeks, Matt's hit recording of the Leslie Bricusse composition finally made the grade, giving him the honour of being the first British singer to reach the American Top 20 in over three years (the last being Laurie London with 'He's Got the Whole World in his Hands' during April 1958). For all its success, Matt never did receive any royalties from America.

With two top ten hits in quick succession, there was no shortage of offers for appearances. It wouldn't be long before Matt had his own television and radio series. Every country wanted a piece of him, but because of the huge impact he'd made in America it was decided that Matt's priority had to be the offer of respected agent and booker, Mark Leddy, to appear on *The Ed Sullivan Show* later in the year. The booking

Matt & Bert Weedon at Record Shop Promotion

would be coupled with a four-week engagement at the Fremont Hotel in Las Vegas.

Even with two hits under his belt, Matt wasn't commanding the big money. Of course his fees went up considerably, but he had been contracted for quite a lot of work after the success of his first hit and they were all on a lower salary than he could have charged now. On the other hand, he was getting a lot of experience in live cabaret, which helped to round out his future prospects. Johnnie Spence was involved with a few projects of his own, and as such it was impossible to commit fully to life on the road with Matt. But he had introduced Russ Shepherd to the singer, and it was agreed they would use him when Johnnie wasn't available.

Having his own musical director was a huge step forward for the singer. After months of being backed by inadequate musicians, Matt reasoned that at least one person would now be able to read his dots even if that person was in his employment. It provided a sense of security that he had at least one ally on the stage with him. He was able to put this to the test when he worked at the De La Warr Pavilion. Matt's support was ace guitarist of 'Ginchy' fame Bert Weedon, and Ricky Valance who'd struck it big with 'Tell Laura I Love Her'.

I only met Matt once, when he was doing a one-nighter at the De La Warr Pavilion, Bexhill. He was superb and being in the front row,

my friends and I had a great view of the stage. The pianist was quite short and during the evening the girls got the giggles as his feet hardly touched the pedals of the grand piano. After the show we went to the stage door and met Matt. He asked the girls why they were laughing and we explained it was just a silly moment watching the pianist. "That's good" he said, "I thought my zipper was undone." — Keith Cowper

Mickie rang Matt during the week to tell him Decca had released an LP called *Portrait* on their low-price Ace of Clubs label, which looked to all like a cynical attempt to take advantage of Matt's recent successes. The title itself was certainly not a coincidence, being a re-release of the LP he had recorded for Decca four years before. Luckily the press was generous considering it had been his first time in a recording studio and he wasn't allowed to sing comfortably.

Decca have done the steadily growing army of Monro fans an enormous service in making available several excellent tracks. Most of them were originally issued on Matt's first professional recording, a 10 inch LP, four years ago, and Decca should be given the credit for being quick to find an outlet for Monro's talents. A pity they didn't persevere with them. Occasionally he nervously rushes a coda yet there is sensitivity and charm in everything else he does. This is surely the best quid's worth on offer this month. — *Melody Maker*

There were two labels Matt couldn't shake off when it came to the press: one was the singing bus driver tag, the other was Britain's Frank Sinatra. In his early career he felt the comparison with the great singer was a compliment, but the routine connections were slowly starting to grate on him. Pete Murray reversed the situation when broadcasting his show with the introduction, "Now here's a record by Frank Sinatra, the Matt Monro of America." Matt thought it was marvellous of Pete and it really tickled him to hear it put the other way round.

There is no denying that Sinatra has influenced me, but so have Perry Como, Tony Bennett and Dick Haymes. A singer simply has to listen to the masters, you learn so much in this way. I don't try to copy these people, that would be pointless. I have simply learnt things from them and have tried to incorporate these things into

my singing. — Matt Monro

David Jacobs introduced the star-studded cast at the sixth annual *Daily Express Record Star Show* at Wembley's Empire Pool. There were two performances in aid of SOS Holiday Home for Spastic Children and every seat was sold out. David Jacobs had made his first public appearance broadcasting in the BBC's *Navy Mixture* series in 1944. He did impressions but Charles Maxwell, the producer of the show, suggested that he focus on announcing, as his parodies were truly awful. Matt also thought the broadcaster's impressions were awful and they used to crack up over them. Whenever they met they would always end up in fits of laughter; in fact it was exactly because of this that David was fired from the BBC in 1948 as a newscaster – for laughing too often. They had a great working relationship and a mutual admiration for each other. David staunchly maintained that Matt flew the flag for Britain.

David received an invitation to have dinner at Sinatra's house in Palm Springs. Having watched a film in the home cinema they retired to the den for drinks. Jacobs asked his host, "You know we all love your voice, but who do you like?" Sinatra responded, "That's not difficult to answer: Ella Fitzgerald, Tony Bennett, Vic Damone, and your Matt Monro has the best set of pipes in Britain." One thing David did think the two singers had in common was that they both cared about the words they sang. He wasn't alone in that assumption.

> **Matt had the rare gift of getting to the heart of a lyric and delivering it in such a way that it became a personal message to his audience. Matt's sense of phrasing, his understanding and reading the lyric, was the best you could get in England. It was a real privilege to work with him and to know him so well, marvellous man. — George Martin**

At long last a holiday awaited Matt and his family as guests of the Woodville, the hotel where he had played cabaret at Christmas. Just before leaving for Jersey, Matt and Mickie received the news that 'Portrait of My Love' had won an Ivor Novello Award for 'the most outstanding song of 1960'. A panel of eight show business personalities, including David Jacobs, Anne Shelton and Joe Loss, representing the Songwriter's Guild of Great Britain conferred the honour, and Matt received the award in a special programme televised on Whit Monday. Matt was thrilled.

The couple's plane landed in Jersey, and Len Matcham was there to greet them personally, together with his assistant Sue Groves. Len had employed Sue the

Ivor Novello Award BBC TV Studios – Front row l to r Ron Grainer, Anthony Newley, Matt & Tony Osborne.
Back row l to r Cliff Richard, Paddy Roberts, Catherine Boyle, Helen Shapiro, Billy Butlin & Johnny Dankworth

previous year and there was an instant rapport and chemistry between the two. She became his companion until the end of his life.

One of the reasons Matt's friendship with the millionaire grew was that Len was a down to earth self-made man who hated the tag 'millionaire' but readily admitted he was "pretty well off". There was nothing showy about Len; he loved Irish stew and Lancashire hot pot, smoked incessantly and popped a pill each day for his blood pressure.

Len and Sue spent the next few days in Matt and Mickie's company, arranging a multitude of different outings to keep the couple entertained. Len owned a stable of horses on Jersey and everyone was invited for a day out at the races. His host also arranged for Matt and his friend Bruce Forsyth to spend the day fishing.

In the original agreement it was arranged that Matt would perform one show in the hotel's main ballroom. Len and Sue made up a table of ten, inviting their friends to witness the vocal marvel. They were certainly not disappointed; Matt stormed the room and was besieged by fans after the show asking for his autograph.

Matt and Mickie had a fabulous time and as the moment approached for them to

Len Matcham introducing Matt to hotel manager at Water's Edge Hotel

return to London, Len took them out for a farewell dinner. The meal was a real treat and after the plates were cleared away Len presented Mickie with a mink stole. The couple were stunned by the businessman's generosity but it was just his way of showing the deep feeling and respect he had for them. Prior to moving to Jersey, Len had lived in Bournemouth and reared minks in a dedicated farm he owned. He was brimming with pride when he explained that the stole was from his own farm and that he had commissioned the garment especially for Mickie. If she wasn't quite convinced by the story she changed her mind when she saw her name embroidered into the lining in the most exquisite gold stitching. Len also arranged to sell his grey Bentley to Matt for a nominal fee. It was the car Len drove when he was in London, but it was hardly used anymore and the magnate thought Matt should have something more fitting to drive now he was a chart success.

Returning to London, word had been leaked to the press about Matt's forthcoming trip to the United States and his imminent guest appearance on one of America's foremost television programmes, the celebrated, coast-to-coast *Ed Sullivan Show*. Don was trying to string together several television and radio interview spots to coincide with the trip, and he was also negotiating for the British star to take part in the TV presentation of the Ivor Novello Awards the following month. Warwick Records were also lining up dates for a lightning promotional tour in conjunction with the release of

'My Kind of Girl'.

But first there was the business of thirteen one-nighters for agent Arthur Howes. Jess Conrad and Matt were to top an all-star package, which opened at the Regal in Colchester. Jess had been an instant hit, earning the title of 'teen idol' after appearing on television's *Oh Boy*. Armed with a Decca recording contract, he had just had hits with 'Cherry Pie' and 'Mystery Girl' and was voted England's most popular singer in 1961's *NME* poll. He had played the London Palladium, Wembley Pool and toured throughout the world with friends and fellow rock stars Eddie Cochran, Gene Vincent, Brenda Lee, Marty Wilde, Johnny Kidd and Eden Kane. Interestingly, Matt was participating in a rock 'n' roll show and so the smooth sounds the audience had come to expect from the singer initially seemed out of place. The tour started without a hitch and the two singers got on famously. Instead of becoming a stereotype 'rocker', Jess had formed the *La Di Da Star Club* throughout his travels. Members were encouraged to take on a Noel Coward persona and stroll backstage in their dressing gowns while garishly waving their cigarette holders in the air. Having recruited Shane Fenton and Eden Kane in the past, he endeavoured to enrol Matt as a *La Di Da Star*, making for a lot of fun and amusement amongst the crew.

> **There was I in my red shirt and white jacket, white moccasins and pink socks standing against Matt in his suave dinner suit. We were the Elvis Clones and Matt had the Bing Crosby look. But he had just had a huge hit with 'Portrait' and someone obviously thought the show was a good idea and to be fair it worked. — Jess Conrad**

Matt opened the show and did the first half with Jess topping the bill and closing, but the young rocker never adopted an 'I'm a star attitude' with Matt. Contrary to the image his publicist conjured up, he was not like that in person. They considered themselves two London lads who enjoyed a laugh and were great mates.

The tour was hugely successful and they were just past the half way mark when they arrived in Lincoln. Friends of Jess' came backstage after the show and caught up for an hour before moving on to continue their chat over drinks in a small club until the early hours. Jess and Matt arrived at their digs to find they had been locked out. This was not that surprising as most digs had strict curfews in place and no amount of knocking would gain them entry. The boys were at a loss until Jess came up with the bright idea of sleeping in the car. He had a beautiful bright red Jaguar with black leather interior and it certainly looked more appealing than walking the streets all night. Jess was a bit of a 'Dapper Dan' and was known on the circuit for 'looking

ABC Savoy Theatre, Lincoln: Matt, Jess Conrad, theatre manager and fans

good'. Not wanting to crease his clothes, he changed into silk pyjamas and a matching dressing gown.

Matt donned these funny old striped pyjamas but he didn't have a dressing gown. We made ourselves comfortable and settled down for the night. — Jess Conrad

A loud rap on the glass frightened the living daylights out of the boys, especially as they couldn't see outside the steamed up windows. Jess rolled the pane down a touch to see a not-so-friendly policeman looking suspiciously at him. At three in the morning he wanted to know what was going on inside the car, and Jess explained the bizarre situation as best he could. At first the policeman didn't believe it was Jess Conrad, but with a bribe of an autograph for the Mrs, he was slightly mollified. At that point he noticed a movement in the back of the car and asked Jess for clarification. Jess explained that it was his co-star in the show, Matt Monro. The local cop quite simply didn't believe this story and felt there was more going on than he had been led to believe. He made Matt get out of the car, resplendent in his Marks and Spencer striped bed wear. To prove his identity the half-asleep singer was made to sing several bars of 'Portrait'.

A broad smile spread across the copper's face as he realised he had just had a private audience with two of the biggest names in town. After the boys had explained the situation, the officer took them back to the police station, gave them a cell each kitted out with sheets and warm blankets while serving them both a steaming mug of coffee before calling out goodnight. A rap on each cell in the morning saw them both delivered a full English breakfast. Washed and fed, they thanked the local constabulary and went on their way to the next gig. It was a story they both dined out on for weeks, and even a small passing comment about policemen would see the boys rolling about the floor in laughter.

Even though he enjoyed himself immensely on the tour, Matt missed Mickie every lonely hour and as soon as he got home, he arranged for them to have a night out at London's Pigalle. Tony Bennett was performing a four-week season at the restaurant and the British singer was eager to make the American's acquaintance. Al Burnett, Pigalle's chief, was booking huge names into the room in a bid to make the Piccadilly showplace London's top night out. Bennett invited them backstage, having been told Matt was in the audience, and the men swapped telephone numbers before the evening was over.

The Jess Conrad tour was not the only rock 'n' roll show Matt was involved with. The BBC announced a galaxy of British jazz and pop talent for two events at the Royal Albert Hall. The shows, widely known as the *BBC Festival of Dance Music*, had been renamed the *BBC Beat Shows*. The first typified radio's *Saturday Club, Go Man Go* and *Sing It Again* whilst the second represented *Parade of the Pops, Jazz Club* and *Easy Beat*.

The first show aired on 8 April and the second two weeks later, with Matt performing in the latter among such familiar faces as Adam Faith, Acker Bilk's Paramount Jazz Band, Bob Miller and The Millermen, The Raindrops, The King Brothers and Bert Weedon. Matt said in a later interview that with the fifty other acts being nearly all groups, he felt like the old man of the sea. Brian Matthew, who was compèring the show, had worked with Matt on numerous occasions, including *Saturday Club*. They were also due to do a series of Sunday concerts at the North Pier Blackpool in July, with Matt topping the bill and Bert Weedon closing the first half.

I used to compère mammoth pop concerts at the Royal Albert Hall and at one of these Matt had just scored a hit with 'My Kind of Girl'. It was decided that he would make his entrance at the back of the ground floor of the Albert Hall and start singing as he walked through the audience. Matt was petrified and I had to stand

**with him and try to keep his spirits up before he made his
entrance. — Brian Matthew**

Matt was working every day, this time in a series of one-nighters on the Granada
circuit. The production was called *Showtime*, with Matt pitted against top comedy star
Frankie Howerd and top vocal group The Mudlarks. There was absolutely no
breathing room. Sandwiched in between those appearances, Matt had to fit in a
recording session for George. The best that could be arranged was a session between
2.30-5.30pm as he was taping a commercial for 7 O'Clock Blades in the morning.
Matt recorded 'Can This Be Love' and 'Why Not Now' for his next single release.
The earlier recorded 'Come Sta' and 'Love is the Same Anywhere' had been shelved
as future singles with the decision to include them on Matt's first LP. With two tracks
in the can he added 'Such is My Love' for his forthcoming album before jumping in
his new Bentley and belting up the motorway to Granada Aylesbury for the two
shows that night. George wanted to get Matt's first Parlophone album ready for print,
and sessions were placed anytime the singer had a few hours to himself. His schedule
was gruelling.

Matt had the unusual experience of guesting in two major BBC TV series on
successive Sundays during June. Although the booking for Joan Regan's *Be My Guest*
was telerecorded on 14 May for transmission four days later, it wasn't actually
transmitted until 18 June, one week after he appeared with Anne Shelton in *Ask Anne*.
He was also booked for *Thank Your Lucky Stars,* a new twenty-five minute ABC
television show. Hosted by Pete Murray, it was being heralded as an important spot
for British pop music.

   These were Matt's bread and butter jobs, but he still had to attend non-paying
prestigious events. The invitation to be guest of honour at the fifth annual Golden Disc
Variety Club Luncheon at the Dorchester Hotel was one such affair. Star speaker
Sophie Tucker had the room in stitches, while Joan Regan, Cliff Richard, Tony Bennett
and Matt treated everyone to a song. Humphrey Lyttleton gave an excellent muted
trumpet solo, and The Beverley Sisters, who sang unaccompanied, harmonised
smoothly through a couple of numbers, while Pete Murray and David Jacobs indulged
in some funny backchat. Matt was certainly feeling no pain by the time he left early
evening; he had enjoyed the day thoroughly and made his way to Great Castle Street
to meet George and Johnnie, stopping by John Burgess's office for a quick hello.

   Most of George's ideas paid off solidly. But not the one that had the producer
suggesting a late night session at the studio to highlight Matt's relaxed way with a

song. They decided they should first have a drink and a meal, but the trouble was that by the time they were ready to record, everyone was a little too relaxed. The session was done with rhythm accompaniment only, directed by Johnnie in Studio 3 and, although only booked until midnight, it was nearly an hour later before they left. Of the six titles recorded, none made it to the *Love is the Same Anywhere* album. Engineers Stuart Eltham and Richard Langham could only look on in amusement as most of the tape used contained hoarse laughter. George returned to the normal approach after that failed experiment.

> **'No One Will Ever Know', which Matt recorded in 1961, was a song I had written with Jerry Lordan and it needed a very sensitive artist to perform it. Matt did a test recording of it with Johnnie on piano. Later the song was issued with full orchestral accompaniment scored by Johnnie on Matt's Parlophone LP, *Love is the Same Anywhere*, but it was that early piano demo that remains my favourite. A case of less is more, I think. — George Martin**

Several of the tracks were re-recorded at a later date, while others emerged on *The Rare Monro* in 2006. One of those, 'The Wrong Time', was a great swinger, with Matt and Johnnie letting rip. Recorded in one take, it shows Matt in a rare jazz moment and it's a shame it didn't surface much earlier.

'Why Not Now' was picked as the new Parlophone single and was vastly different from his previous hits, based on a traditional Spanish melody, which many people knew as 'Ay Ay Ay'. David Greer adapted the music while Peter Ling penned the new English lyrics. Just before release, Matt and his recording manager began wondering whether the reverse coupling, a beautiful new Graham Fisher/Herbert Kretzmer ballad titled 'Can This Be Love', was the stronger of the two sides. Even on release a tremendous amount of interest was being shown in 'Can This Be Love' and it was hoped it would make the chart grade too. Matt had every reason to be happy as the growing popularity of the disc meant that he had completed a hat-trick of consecutive hits. It was quite an achievement considering that only five months before Matt was struggling among pop music's also-rans.

> **Another of my favourite performances from Matt is a song I wrote under the pseudonym of Graham Fisher along with Herbert Kretzmer, who later wrote all the lyrics for *Les Misérables*. 'Can This Be Love' was issued as a single in 1961 and shortly afterwards**

was included on Matt's EP 'Matt's Kind of Music'. — George Martin,
Playback

Cliff Richard and Matt Monro were neck-and-neck in the two most important sections of the *Melody Maker's 1961 Pop Poll.* And it was Matt with 'Portrait of My Love' who just pipped Cliff with 'Please Don't Tease' to the Top of the Vocal Discs. Cliff did, however, beat Matt into second place as Top Male Singer.

With three top chart hits and appearances all around the country, there was no question Matt was a giant in the performance stakes. But television was quite another thing altogether.

**Matt was the guest on my television series *Be My Guest* and the producer, John Street, asked Matt to stand on a box during the recording, as I towered above him. We sang 'Swinging on a Star'.
— Joan Regan**

Matt's nickname for Joan was 'Regan' and they had become good friends over the years, consistently working together or seeing each other at show business events and charity evenings. Matt was known for his good sense of humour and he would be the first to make comic reference to his own height. If he didn't, others surely would. A few years later he was singing in Australia and Joan went along to see him. He opened the show with 'Once in a Lifetime' and when he got to the line "I feel like a giant", he glanced over at Joan and said "and you can shut up for a start".

Straight after Joan's show had been taped Matt was on his way to the North Pier Pavilion, Blackpool for a series of Sunday concerts presented by Bernard Delfont that would take him right through to the beginning of September. The seaside had retained its appeal to holiday makers through its piers, traditional slot machines, Punch and Judy shows and donkey rides on the sand. Blackpool had wanted to break away from the traditional seaside town stereotype and added their own version of the Eiffel Tower, an electric tramway, three piers, and a multitude of shops to extract money out of the tourists. With the addition of its famous illuminations, the town's relentless promotional drive paid off. They attracted millions of visitors each year, targeting July, August and September as their main trading months. Competition was fierce amongst the venues, with each trying to better the other when booking the big draw names.

Bruce Forsyth says that on his first *Sunday Show* concert the running order and timing of the show was very important, because the Lord Chamberlain's laws governing

Backstage at Blackpool North Pier

Sunday entertainment meant that all shows had to finish – no matter what was happening on stage – before 10.00pm. Even if you were in the middle of the last song, that was it. Ten o'clock you were off.

There was a series of top-line acts joining Matt at the Pavilion, including the brilliant guitarist Bert Weedon, The Gaunt Brothers who played the piano, and Lyn Cornell, Decca's personality songstress. Brian Matthew strung the twice-nightly shows together, with Matt filling twenty-five minute spots. They were a great success from the start, and Matt was amazed that after each performance there would be a throng of people waiting for his autograph at the stage door. A few months previously he could walk down any street in complete anonymity, but now it was impossible to take the same steps without being stopped or people pointing, laughing and shouting greetings. By June 1961, the name Matt Monro had become a guarantee of full houses at concert halls and the entertainment clubs that were springing up all over Britain, and there was no shortage of enquiries. Matt's profile had grown enormously in a short time and with the security of nearly a years' work in the diary, Matt and Mickie felt it safe to take the first step towards home ownership.

Estate agents Stephen Hiscott & Co helped in the search for the property. Having served with him in Hong Kong, Hiscott assisted his old army pal by making the purchase as easy as possible. From a limited space to four bedrooms was pure luxury, and the semi-detached house in Ewell, with its Tudor leaded windows and spacious garden for Michele, was a definite step up the housing ladder. It had been difficult living in one room in Evelyn's house and, although grateful for her generosity, it was now time to make the move. Michele had just seen her second birthday and space had definitely been a challenge. With keys in hand, the young family opened the door of 14 Ruxley Lane and called it home.

MEET MATT MONRO

Matt was working on his first Parlophone album, a collection of new British compositions of ballads and swingers that George wanted to release later that year. The album *Portrait*, recently brought out by Decca, had been well received by critics and was steadily amassing sales, but Matt wasn't thrilled with it. He could, of course, understand why the record company had wanted to put the album out. However, he took exception to Decca titling the release "Portrait" in a blatant attempt to cash in on his first Parlophone hit – a song also called 'Portrait'. Matt was adamant that his singing on that album lacked poise and assurance, demonstrating a limited range. It was, after all, his first-ever professional record and he felt that it sounded amateurish in comparison to his more recent recordings. It might have been a shrewd business decision from Decca's point of view, but Matt thought the release was a mistake.

In recent months, Matt had been chalking up big successes touring Britain in a variety of rock-based package shows, but his ambitions began to move elsewhere. He had nothing against rock music, it just irked him that rock groups seldom provided the right sort of backing for his material. In particular they didn't tend to carry a string section, which Matt used on several of his songs. The intimacy and scope of nightclub work appealed to him, as did the freedom of experimenting with different material. He wanted the chance to tackle little-known standards and new works by contemporary writers. The big challenge of cabaret work was to stop an audience from talking, drinking or dancing and *make* them listen to you.

Matt was thrilled when an offer came through from Radio Luxembourg asking him to record thirteen fifteen-minute programmes in their 1961 Autumn schedule, but by far the most exciting prospect was another offer to host his own thirteen-week

Mel Torme & Matt

television series called *Meet Matt Monro* between 12 June and 28 August 1961. It would replace Michael Holliday's series and air at peak viewing times, with Johnnie Spence arranging and conducting the proceedings.

Matt wasted no time in developing his new show, setting up a meeting with Johnnie and Mel Torme. Although Mel was immensely busy at the time – in rehearsals for his appearance on *Sunday Night at the Prince of Wales* – Matt got him to agree to a tele-recorded appearance on one of the show's episodes. Since Associated Rediffusion didn't want another male vocalist competing against the talents of their host, they arranged for Matt to conduct an interview with the American singer, after which Matt sang some of his best-known songs.

Director Daphne Shadwell arranged for some of the best musicians in the business to back Matt, with favourites Kenny Clare, Kenny Powell, Judd Procter and Roy Willicks appearing on a regular basis. The twelve-piece orchestral backing gave Matt the perfect vehicle to sing his kind of music and each episode saw him open with a verse of his signature tune 'Portrait', sing four songs and end with a few lines of 'It's a Pity to Say Goodnight'.

If you put a bunch of musicians into the same room on a regular basis you are bound to be in the firing line of pranks from time to time, and sure enough high energy lit up the set of *Meet Matt Monro* each week.

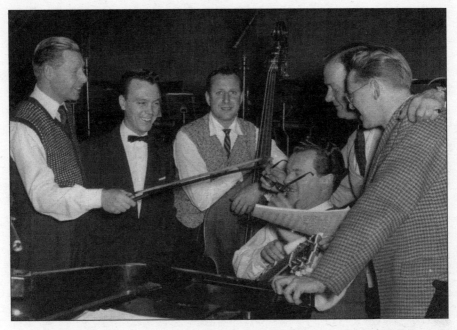

Showband members Cyril Stapleton, Matt, Joe Mudele, Bert Weedon, Jack Cummings & Dennis Wilson

A particular line-up was wanted to produce a particular sound – right angles to each other, four or five instruments parallel to the other four or five. One guy was on a sousaphone, which was shaped like a bell and faced forward. During rehearsals one musician aimed a sweet wrapper at the instrument and threw it into the hole. There were sniggers all round but the sousaphone player remained unaware of the prank. Others soon joined in with all manner of rubbish they could lay their hands on, including cigarette packets. Unfortunately someone threw in a live cigarette and the paper caught fire and there was smoke everywhere! — Vic Fraser

Following this incident everyone in the studio was in stitches, and it took quite a while to clear the studio of both the smoke and the smell! Daphne wasn't amused and called a lunch-break, hoping that the musicians would return with a more professional attitude. Unfortunately for her, the sousaphone player had a debt to settle. While at the pub, he bought several sausages and upon his return to the studio, rammed them into the trumpet piece!

Cyril Stapleton & Matt rehearsing for Showband Show

BBC's Light Programme's fourteen-week radio series, *Matt's Kind of Music* was a different concept altogether. Matt had the dual role of singer and compère, introducing a different guest instrumental group each Tuesday night. Producer John Browell, who was a friend of Matt's, organised Don Lang & His Frantic Five as the first week's guests; while the final show saw the Show Band reunited, with Bert Weedon, Bill McGuffie, Harold Smart and Cyril Stapleton all taking the stage. Johnnie Spence led a specially assembled ten-piece band, which was showcased each week in front of a studio audience.

The BBC were always pushed for time, the programme had to be live; there was a three-hour rehearsal and a half-hour break between the end of rehearsal and transmission. Matt was very professional in the application of his act. The producer was always interested in whether they knew their job and were able to perform and come to the studio knowing their material. So therefore all you had to do is get arrangements, voice and balance married up together with the presentation of the programme to make sure the whole thing was going to work out to an exact twenty-nine minutes and thirty seconds, which was required for a

thirty-minute broadcast. — John Browell

The show wasn't recorded until early evening so in the short break between the rehearsal and transmission Matt, Johnnie and Browell would nip around to the pub and have a quick drink while the audience were being seated in the studio. Five minutes before going live they would do the audience warm up and introduce the artists and musicians.

> **On one occasion we were coming back from the pub and the entrance to the studio was down a long flight of stairs. Unfortunately Matt fell down the flight of stairs and broke his ankle. He was in a lot of pain. I asked if he could still sing, he said yes, and as we were live with minutes to go it was absolutely necessary for him to go on. He looked very grey and was perspiring very heavily, but he performed and not a soul in the audience knew a thing was wrong – incredible. — John Browell**

Matt's accident wasn't an isolated incident and over the years he suffered some terrible misfortunes. On this occasion, he had no choice but to perform, and wait until the show was over before going to the hospital.

When word got out that Matt was to star in his own television show, he was inundated with material, everyone wanting him to sing their original composition. He'd play them all, sorting the wheat from the chaff, picking out the two or three that interested him. However, by that time, the majority of groups were writing their own material. Music publishers were finding the need to print material obsolete, and this eventually meant an artist like Matt only heard new music after it had been recorded. Johnnie wrote a lot of music himself, and, in fact, 'In the Still of the Night' sung against the bands' intriguing counterpoint 'My Guys Come Back' was one such composition, written especially for the show.

Despite having the luxury of his own series, Matt took on any work he could, fearing his success could all end tomorrow. Matt accepted a personal appearance at The Ideal Home Exhibition in Olympia. Staged annually by *The Daily Mail*, its aim was to bring together everything associated with having an 'ideal' home. Mike Foster had been the set designer for the Gas Council's stand for several years and suggested that the presence of a pop star would entice visitors. Matt was booked and happily signed autographs and posed for photographs with the crowd. Mike Foster's nine

Caroline Foster and Matt at The Ideal Home Exhibition

year-old daughter Caroline presented the singer with a small gift as a mark of the Gas Council's appreciation.

> My father arranged for me to have the day off school and I was allowed to wear my best party dress. I wasn't really aware of who Matt Monro was. My father had given me a gold cigarette lighter to give to Mr Monro and at the given time I made the presentation. He had a voice that melted your heart. He was stunningly good looking and he had these gorgeous eyes, almost as if he was looking right into me. It was a magical moment that I will always cherish. — Caroline Foster

Matt next worked on Associated Rediffusion's *Summersong,* a carefree outdoor piece of entertainment, during which he sang a medley with Cleo Laine, Dennis Lotis and Craig Douglas. Matt was a great fan of the comedian Dudley Moore, who also appeared on the programme, and was anxious to catch his show – *Beyond the Fringe* – at the Fortune Theatre. Unfortunately, the only evening he had off was booked with a prior invitation to the opening night of the West End production *Stop the World – I Want to Get Off,* starring Anthony Newley.

Stop the World was a huge success and the press were out in force. Matt had a quick drink with Newley after the show, but not wanting to outstay his welcome he made his excuses. Over the years Matt recorded several Newley compositions, including 'Who Can I Turn To', which Newley himself thought was one of the best versions he'd heard.

During the last week of August 1961, Matt laid down the finishing tracks for his debut album, *Love is the Same Anywhere*, which was due to be released in October. The track 'I'll Dream of You' is one of only two songs Matt wrote with Mark Dan. The other was 'I'm a Limey', which, although never recorded, was used in his cabaret bookings.

August that year also saw the American disc scene get a shot in the arm as both Matt Monro and Lonnie Donegan had records high in the American Top 20 – Matt with 'My Kind of Girl' and Lonnie with 'Does Your Chewing Gum Lose Its Flavour'. America was now firmly in Matt's sight and, although he had accepted a booking for *The Ed Sullivan Show* in October, another booking in the States had unexpectedly come in for the end of August. Matt had been asked to film a series of television and radio advertising jingles for the powerful Pepsi Cola Company and, with trepidation, he boarded a flight for New York. The promotion was for Teem, a lemon and lime flavoured soft drink introduced to the market as Pepsi's answer to 7 Up and Coca Cola's Sprite. The singer flew a six-thousand mile round-trip for just a couple of minutes work, each Teem jingle being only sixty seconds long, but for Matt it was well worth the effort, as it gave him the opportunity to record with a fifty-piece orchestra led by renowned American conductor Hugo Winterhalter.

On arriving at the studios and after pleasantries, Hugo asked Matt if he knew the song. Matt responded, "Give me a minute, I'll run through it with the pianist." Mr Winterhalter replied in a heavily sarcastic tone, "Yeah, right". These sentiments were also mirrored under their breath by the other musicians. But to their amazement, that's exactly what Matt did.

"It's here, it's here, it's crystal clear" sang Matt, giving the soft sell to the soda drink on the commercials. That session earned him the nickname 'One Take Monro'.

It was a good opportunity for me to gain a quick all-expenses-paid visit to New York. I was able to have a look at the Round Table where I start a month's season on October 2 and arrange for the Ed Sullivan TV shows. It would have cost me a lot to do all this but the

commercial paid for it. — Matt Monro, *Disc Magazine*

The Round Table was quite a place. Although not the biggest nightspot in New York, it was certainly large enough for Matt's US debut cabaret performance. London had nothing like it and it would certainly be a challenge. He would also have to deal with the Sinatra comparison all over again.

> **They seem to know me over there but they tend to accept me as an answer to Sinatra. A New York columnist headed her article — "Is Matt Monro a New Sinatra?" And then went on to say that I didn't always sing like Sinatra, but if I didn't continue to do so I would disappoint my fans. It reminded me of the time when an American agent came over to England with an offer for me to go to the States as a Sinatra impersonator. He wanted me to wear the hat, carry the drink, the raincoat, the lot. I told him where to put his offer! I'm getting sick of the Sinatra comparison but I suppose I'll just have to let it ride for a while in the States. — Matt Monro,** *Disc Magazine*

Entertainment journalist Earl Wilson had written in his *New York Post* column that while Matt was over in America he had confessed to being influenced by Sinatra. However, he had conditioned this statement by pointing out that you would be hard-pressed to find a singer who hadn't been influenced by Sinatra, other than opera singers and the worst of the rock 'n' rollers. Of course Matt was influenced by Sinatra, as it was the music he grew up with but at no time did he ever try and copy the American singer, although he regularly hailed him as the best at what he did. Matt took umbrage to the comparisons, as did many others in the business.

> **I don't think he sounds like Sinatra at all. Because Britain lacks standard singers, you tend to make comparisons all the time. We have so many standard singers in the States we don't make comparisons. It's a load of crap to say he sounds like Sinatra. — Scott Walker**

> **While Monro's nickname as the "British Sinatra" lingers on, there is quite a marked difference in the two singers. Much of that talk was because Monro popped on the music scene at the same time as the other Sinatra disciples, and it was easy to use his Britishness**

> as a lazy differentiator. Vocally, there was a wide gulf: Sinatra
> famously approached songs with an evenly aggressive attitude,
> while there was a disarming humility in the Englishman's delivery
> that allowed his big notes to explode with breathtaking drama. For
> that reason, a music critic recently used the unlikely term "edgy"
> to describe the singer's style. Monro's 1968 recording of
> 'September Song' is a perfect example of this actual differentiating
> quality in Monro's style. — Steve Ellis, Performing Rights Society

The fact is that Matt recorded very few songs associated with the American star. There were popular tunes that they both covered, but Monro never went after Sinatra's songs, choosing instead to seek alternative sources for his material. But regardless, the comparisons followed Matt throughout his life. To be second best wasn't good enough for a singer of Monro's stature, but he found it difficult to shake the Sinatra tag off and eventually learned to live with the routine comparison.

> Ever since I begun to hit it big, the Sinatra 'tag' has hung on me like
> an albatross and frankly I'm getting a little tired of it. I don't mind
> when people say I sound like Sinatra, after all it is a compliment,
> but the insinuation that I consciously try to imitate him is not only
> unfair it's ridiculous. I sing like Matt Monro. If by singing like Matt
> Monro I happen to sing a little like Sinatra, that's great, as I've said
> it is quite a compliment. — Matt Monro

Having vetted the Round Table, where he was to play a three-week season that October, and on his way to the airport for his return flight to England, Matt stopped off at Mercury Artists Corporation and signed a contract with Frank Musciello and Joe Little, making them his personal representatives and agents covering America, Canada and Mexico.

Matt's flight back to England was uneventful until they were only an hour out from landing at Heathrow Airport in London. Matt was due in at 7.00am and a car was ready to take him for a personal appearance, opening a store at Worcester. But fog delayed the plane, forcing an unscheduled landing at Shannon Airport in Ireland. Ron Randall of EMI's promotional department, arranged for Matt to get a seat on the first plane back to London.

The singer finally landed at Heathrow but the fog persisted, and it was soon realised that Matt would not be able to make the opening in time if he went by car.

Ron rang Gatwick Airport's heliport booking centre and within the hour a helicopter was en-route to pick up its patient guest but unfortunately it suffered radio trouble and had to return to base. Eventually Matt was picked up at the special VIP landing strip – used by the Queen and Prime Minister – and set off for Worcester. The route was still foggy however and when the pilot landed at what he thought was a Worcester sports ground, Matt found himself in the middle of a cricket match at Redditch, several miles off target!

Shortly after his return from Worcester, Matt met up again with Anthony Newley and discussed the possibility of recording one of the songs from his show. When 'Gonna Build a Mountain' had first been shown to Matt, he rejected it completely, but after visiting the opening night of *Stop the World* in July, he began to have second thoughts. He looked at it again and decided to try it out as a swinger instead of its original form as a spiritual number – it took four arrangements before Matt was satisfied with the song. In September the song came out as Matt's follow-up single. The A-side builds from a steady casual opening to a big swinging climax, while the flip side, 'I'll Dream of You', is slow, melodious and romantic.

Nearing the end of his radio and television series, Matt was about to leave for New York when, out of the blue, Sinatra's Reprise label asked him to sign with them.

> **The offer also includes a Hollywood film and a cabaret season at the Cal-Neva nighterie on the north shore of Lake Tahoe. It sounds like a good offer. It's a lump sum deal, rather like a transfer for a football player... It's really up to EMI whether they accept the offer or not. I shall have to leave it to them. But I don't see much hope of it happening as EMI seem to be happy with Morty Craft at Warwick. He does a lot to push my records in the States. — Matt Monro**

When Sinatra first launched his label in 1960, he signed a number of world-ranked artists to his stable. Reprise quickly acquired famous names who would guarantee quality performances and lucrative sales. Stars like Sammy Davis Jr, Dean Martin, Rosemary Clooney and Bing Crosby. However, as far as is known, only one British star was invited to sign, and that was Matt Monro.

Matt turned down the offer, which had come at a time when he was clicking healthily in the charts on both sides of the Atlantic. There was no clear explanation given to the press for Matt's decision to stay with a British company. Don Black gave an interview saying that by teaming Matt with Sinatra's company, Reprise would have two singers of the same ilk on the same label. Don also pointed out that Ella Fitzgerald, Andy Williams, Perry Como, Vic Damone, Sammy Davis Jr and Frank Sinatra were among those who had paid Matt the ultimate compliment of recording songs that he had originally introduced. And he added, "that not one of them has yet been able to better the original version."

> **Matt would have loved to have signed with Reprise, it might have even given him the chance to work with Sinatra, but too many people were genuinely worried that this might not be the innocent offer it seemed. We could have been tied to a recording contract that didn't want to record Matt, and that would have been both costly to his career and our pocket. We felt we had no option but to decline, but it was one of things that stayed with you, niggled away, and posed the question "what if?" — Mickie Monro**

Matt's last commitment before flying back to the States was his debut performance on ATV's *Sunday Night at the Palladium*. The show's format never changed throughout its run: the curtain opened with the glamorous, high-kicking Tiller Girls, followed by a warm welcome from the host, a sprinkling of variety acts before 'Beat the Clock' brought the first half to a close. The second part brought another liberal offering of acts followed by the 'top of the bill', before the full cast waved goodbye from the famous revolving stage in the finale. In its heyday, the show commanded twenty-eight-million viewers, nearly half the population of the UK at the time.

A live show of this kind couldn't escape one or two problems from its notable guests. Judy Garland refused to go on the revolving stage because she was said to be too 'emotional'. The Rolling Stones also refused, saying that it would upset their anti-establishment image. Mario Lanza accidentally punched his own bodyguard and Harry Secombe fell through a trap door.

On the 28 September 1961, Pan American flew Matt to New York for his American cabaret debut. Mickie accompanied him along with musical director Ralph Dollimore. Both Johnnie Spence and Russ Shepherd were unable to make the trip. Don had extricated a ticket out of CBS in the capacity of Matt's manager and his brother Michael had paid for his own flight so he could tag along. Matt first met David Berglas, a member of the Magic Circle, on that flight and the illusionist ended up joining them. Don and Michael persuaded David to show them a trick whilst they were in mid-flight over the Atlantic. Berglas asked one of his fellow passengers to pick a card and sign it. He then somehow made it appear on the outside of one of the plane's windows!

The week before Matt's arrival, American agent Bill Downs was interviewed for *Disc Magazine* and offered the opinion that the singer was going out to the States too late. He said that he should have been there at the height of 'My Kind of Girl''s popularity. Matt, however, disagreed.

> I read the article and I didn't agree. If Presley came over here would it be too late? Personal appearances and television can make or kill you. It's happened to American artists in Britain. Take Robert Horton. He couldn't have been more popular when he came over here but when he went on tour he died a death. — Matt Monro

Upon arrival at John F Kennedy Airport, Matt was faced by a press reception of four-hundred journalists, all eager to get the first story on the British singer in America. However, one article published on 6 October 1961 was maliciously cruel and totally unfounded.

> English singer Matt Monro is beginning to sound like a bit of a bore, even before we Yankees get a chance to see him perform in the flesh. He's been imported here for one reason; he had a hit record 'My Kind of Girl' which was a hit solely because he managed to make himself sound exactly like Frank Sinatra singing a Nelson Riddle arrangement. Now this one-record star is reported (by his own management) to have turned down a tour of outdoor concerts with the comment "The only people who should work arenas are tennis players and prize fighters." Mr Monro, the only people who should work arenas are people who can fill them – people like Judy Garland and Harry Belafonte. — Dorothy Kilgallen, *New Castle News*

Interestingly, this journalist didn't mention Frank Sinatra playing an arena – maybe she thought he couldn't fill it either! With comments like that it is not surprising that Matt was more than a little nervous over the reception he would get.

Matt's schedule was certainly hectic. He was contracted for three shows a night:

two thirty-five minute performances and one twenty-minute set, with a musical running order that Matt thought fitting for an American audience who preferred middle of the road fare.

The singer was delighted with the last minute inclusion of 'Gonna Build a Mountain' in his repertoire. All numbers from the Anthony Newley show, including Matt's new single, had recently had a ban imposed on them in the States. The consolation was that all American versions had been banned, so nobody could beat Matt to the release. It's unknown why the boycott was introduced. Two likely reasons are Jerry Lewis recorded songs from the show without permission, and the Broadway version of the show was not due to open until 3 October 1962.

Opening night saw a packed house turn out for the former bus driver. Having gone through a pre-set routine in his dressing room, he stood in the wings smoking a cigarette with a calm demeanour concealing the fact that he was petrified. Matt's musical intro struck up, with Ralph conducting the orchestra. Every light was angled on the lone artist; each set of spellbound eyes was trained on him in anticipation. The silence was only ended when Matt broke it with a song. A man of mercurial moods – self-critical, emotional and sentimental – Matt had no gimmick to fall back on other than his voice. His singing was a tapestry of warm colours with orchestrations that animated each note of his faultless performance.

Matt's voice was genuinely untrained – singing lessons refused. He smoked forty cigarettes a day, could stay up all night but could still sing like a bird. Phrasing incredible. There was a class to his voice – he was a very ordinary East End guy, but when he sang it was a cultured and cultivated voice. — Don Black

Opening night was a resounding success, but throughout his life there was never a performance which Matt didn't analyse to see how it could be improved or bettered. He was a perfectionist in his art, feeling every audience deserved his best performance.

If his opening night success at The Round Table nightery is anything to go by, Matt Monro will be welcome in New York any time he cares to call. His debut was a great personal success and should ensure packed tables for the remainder of his three-week season at the venue. The audience on Monday were warm and responsive. Towards the end of Matt Monro's performance patrons were roaring for encores... Matt's style was slick, polished and professional and he came across as a warm, high-spirited and constantly tasteful performer. Instead of a copy of Sinatra, he displayed an unpretentious individuality in his singing... Matt opened with a clever, novelty-flavoured original titled 'I'm a Limey' during which he introduces himself as a newcomer to the American show business scene, wearing a bowler hat. His opening was certainly a striking success and in the opinion of veteran show business observers, Matt should have a durable career here, since his professionalism can carry him through, even during periods when he doesn't have a hit record. — Nat Hentoff from New York for the *Musical Express*.

When he opened to a celebrity-packed Round Table, Matt became the third Briton in three weeks, alongside Shirley Bassey and Tubby Hayes, to take New York by storm. Top DJs and show business personalities jammed the cabaret spot to watch a bowler-hatted Monro go through his paces. The audience were with him all the way and he received a marvellous reception. When Matt broke into 'My Kind of Girl' the audience reacted as though it was as familiar as Crosby's 'White Christmas'. Bassey caught Matt's opening night and Matt and Mickie returned the compliment by visiting her at the Hotel Plaza. The Round Table was known for taking pride in presenting top quality musical artists, such as Sarah Vaughan, Louis Armstrong, Dave Brubeck and Carmen McRae. Matt Monro was no exception.

Matt was stunned by his success. Rather than taking the credit for himself, he put it down to Johnnie Spence's superb arranging, demonstrating a modesty not often seen in show business circles. He read the reviews with relish, but one in particular made him extremely happy.

> **One could be forgiven for going to Matt's act expecting to see someone impersonating Sinatra, but after seeing his act most of them have stopped making comparisons and accepted his style as individual and not copied from anyone. — Reuters News Agency**

After his first performance Morris Levy, one of The Round Table's owners, threw a party at the club in Matt's honour. Mickie was absolutely stunned by the reception they received. It was overwhelming and slightly surreal. Everyone had laid out the red carpet for Matt Monro.

It was early morning before Matt and Mickie fell into bed but Mickie couldn't sleep, she was floating on cloud nine. "We'd struggled for years while Matt tried to break through. New York was like a million accolades being thrown at once. I couldn't stop crying. Matt had followed his dream and it had just come true."

A dramatic incident marred Matt's otherwise hugely successful stint in New York. Halfway through his season, Ben Selwyn of RCA Records and his promotional team invited the singer and his wife for a meal in a nearby restaurant to discuss a potential business deal. The entrées had just been cleared when suddenly three guys burst into the eatery and started shooting. Matt and Mickie were thrown to the floor by the waiter and remained under the table for the duration of the gunfight, which lasted little more than a minute. Emotions were swept aside in their haste to leave the restaurant before the morgue employees came to collect the body of a well-known Mafia hood. Less than an hour later, Matt was back in the hotel excitedly recounting the incident, while Mickie had gone to bed with a sedative. They never did complete a deal with RCA.

It's All Talk

The day after Matt's stint at The Round Table had finished he was preparing for the first of three appearances on *The Ed Sullivan Show*. Each Sunday night millions of Americans tuned into CBS at 8.00pm Eastern Standard Time for an hour-long edition of the show. It was completely unpredictable, but it was television at its tumultuous best.

Given the nickname 'Mr Sunday Night', Ed Sullivan presided over each show. There was always a run-through in the afternoon in front of a studio audience, during which Mr Sullivan would offer encouragement to the anxious guests but he was equally anxious himself before each performance. Each show had to be perfect and if Sullivan didn't feel that the artists met his high standards, they were paid off at rehearsals. Fortunately, Matt made the grade. Billed as 'Britain's singing sensation', his American television debut saw him wow the audience with a flawless presentation of 'My Kind of Girl'.

With the first show under his belt, Matt met up with Shirley Bassey and Lonnie Donegan at the Hotel Plaza for tea. It was great seeing a few British faces and they happily compared notes about their month abroad. Matt also had cause to celebrate, as Mickie had just told him his new album *Love is the Same Anywhere* had just made 'Record of the Week' and hadn't received one bad review. His favourite write-up was from *Tit-Bits* magazine which, apart from citing the album as the best British prestige disc for a long time, stated that Matt's style and musicianship were better than anything Sinatra himself had done of late. It boosted his belief that his type of music would have a permanent market.

Record of the Week: 'Love is the Same Anywhere' could find its way to the top of Nelson's Column and even that wouldn't list it high enough in my estimation. In the first place I have never enjoyed

Lonnie Dunegan, Shirley Bassey and Matt at the Hotel Plaza, New York

Matt's singing more, not even with 'Portrait'. And secondly he has had the courage to do something no artist has done; he has chosen NEW songs, new British songs for this album. His only concession to American writers is the inclusion of a couple of numbers from the pen of Irving Berlin... A special word of praise for the work of musical director Johnnie Spence who was responsible for all the arrangements. Magnificent is the only word to describe his musical genius, which together with Matt's impeccable singing makes this the finest vocal LP I have received in a long time. — Gerry Kilgallon, *Evening News*

Unlike today's market, where albums are full of singles, in 1961 tracks on an album were rarely released that way. Instead, singles were often coupled together to form EPs (Extended Plays). Both sides of Matt's first album for Parlophone contained the cancelled singles 'Love is the Same Anywhere' and 'Come Sta', but none of his hits. Several of the tracks were written by people who would later present Matt with possible entries for *A Song For Europe* in 1964. Al Saxon wrote 'April Fool' together with Don Black under the pseudonym Berg, and although they had known each other since the end of Matt's years with Decca, this was the first time that Don had written for him. Matt's self-titled EP and the single 'Gonna Build a Mountain' were

Matt & Don in Times Square for Matt's first New York engagement at the Hotel

released at the same time as the album. Despite Matt's commercial success during the previous twelve months, neither the album nor the EP charted and the single failed to climb any higher than forty-four in the hit parade.

Following on from his success in New York, Matt flew to Ontario, Philadelphia and Detroit while Mickie flew back to England to be with Michele. Although Matt's records had been successful, monies were paid three months in arrears so that record sales could be established. Their income was therefore reliant on Matt's club work, which wasn't enough to justify Mickie travelling with him all over the world.

However, Matt found the distance between them agonising. He was considered a good-looking man, and with his stunning voice and pop star status he garnered plenty of attention from female fans desperate to spend time with him. But Matt was genuinely not interested. He was a loyal husband and one who was madly in love with his wife. At these times of utter despair Matt found solace in a bottle.

After riding on the crest of a wave for months Matt was quite unprepared for his next shows.

> **Business is terrible, no advertising, especially in Detroit where all his business comes from. He's blaming us but the staff say it has been like this for weeks. 'Tambouritzans' - 12 people open the show, which comprises a gypsy and three singers, dancers and all that jazz for forty minutes. Then a comic does forty minutes – so it's eighty minutes before I get on stage. Before I start they've had enough – only another ten days. — Matt Monro, letter from the Metropole Hotel, Ontario, Canada**

Mickie's daily letters and phone calls perked Matt up and kept him in touch with what was going on back home. George wanted him to do another album and a single, but was still looking for the right song. 'Why Not Now' was number 78 in the *Cashbox* chart, the album was selling extremely well and everyone was pleased. Indeed, Parlophone had sent a letter giving notice to extend their contract for another year.

Matt grabbed the opportunity to see Connie Francis at the Latin Casino in Philadelphia. After Connie's singing, the thing that impressed him most was the venue itself, which was big enough to hold a twenty-five piece orchestra and three-thousand people sitting. Connie and Matt ended the evening drinking at the Rickshaw Inn lobby bar, a well-known after-hours hangout.

Matt was delighted to fly back to England. His second *Ed Sullivan Show* wasn't until the end of December and he had numerous commitments in the diary before then, including another *Parade of the Pops,* two programmes for Radio Luxembourg, *Pop Pourri* and the track for the film *Tahiti* at CTS. In November, Matt opened at Harrison Gibson's Room at the Top Restaurant for a two-week appearance, attracting one of the largest opening night audiences for some time. It was a far cry from the memory of Canada.

Working for John Browell was proving to be unlucky. While recording a BBC Christmas show in London, Matt tripped on some wires that lay across the studio floor; the duct tape had come loose and Matt's foot had caught the protruding flex. He'd broken the same foot only a few months previously, and this time suffered two chipped bones. There wasn't time to go to hospital, as he was due on stage at Ilford. That night he was carried on to the cabaret floor and performed either sitting down or leaning against a stool. He was later taken to hospital, where they applied a plaster cast up to his knee with a rocker. The next morning he realised he couldn't get any trousers on over the rocker and Mickie had to take him back to the hospital to have

Marion & Johnnie Spence with Mickie

it taken off so he could appear on stage in his characteristic formal wear.

After a quick interview with the *Daily Sketch* and an appearance on *The Benny Hill Show*, Christmas was nearly on top of them. Matt and Mickie were invited to the EMI Christmas party, where they spent their time mingling with Marion and Johnnie and George and his girlfriend Judy. George introduced Matt to Rolf Harris, with whom he had done some early recordings. In fact, Rolf would work with Johnnie two years later when he was arranging the release of 'Tie Me Kangaroo Down, Sport'.

Still in his early twenties, Johnnie was rapidly building a reputation as one of the country's most brilliant and imaginative musical directors. Parlophone was so impressed that they recorded him conducting his orchestra under his own name.

Matt, Mickie, Johnnie and Marion spent Boxing Day together at Ruxley Lane; in fact this became a yearly ritual. Vic Fraser popped in for a drink, as did George and Judy. The producer was in fact still married so had to be careful where he was seen out, but he could be himself with the gang and they spent many happy times together. The boys played poker and settled down for a long leisurely afternoon while the girls cooked. Matt got ash in his scotch and instead of trying to spoon it out he threw it on the fire. Although it caused an almighty flare up of flames, which took a liking to the curtains his wife had just hemmed, it was several days before a very unhappy Mickie found the hole in her new curtains. It was years before Matt owned up that it had been his fault.

On the 27 December, the day before Matt was due to fly back to New York, George, Johnnie and Matt were back in the studios. The first track they ran through was 'Is There Anything I Can Do?' The other track on the schedule was 'Softly As I Leave You', an English title and lyric to an Italian melody. It hit big when Matt took it up, and Shirley Bassey and the American stars followed almost immediately. It made the writers a lot of money – not least Hal Shaper who became sufficiently financially secure to form his own publishing company.

The song's original title was 'Piano' and an Italian success when it was first performed by Mina, the country's top singer, at the San Remo Song Festival. Robbins Music boss Alan Holmes subsequently heard the song after Mina released it as a single in 1960 and sent it to George Martin who thought the song might do quite well in England. George wrote to enquire whether the girl could sing in English, and there the matter rested for a couple of months. Then, out of the blue, George rang Alan Holmes and told him that if he could get an English lyric by the following morning Matt would record it.

Lyricist John Harris went to work altering the original Italian lyrics to suit a male vocalist. Within hours, Hal Shaper was flying to Milan to get the publishers to approve the project so he could write English lyrics to the melody. Hal Shaper remembers the story slightly differently.

I was in Italy in 1961 and Tony de Vita was playing me a symphony in three movements that he had written. I loved the tune in the second movement and brought it back to England. I made a piano demo of it and gave it to Matt Monro; and about three months later he rang me and said "I've been playing the tune endlessly. We are going to record it, so can you have the lyrics over at George Martin's office by 10.30 in the morning?" Luckily I came up with a lyric for the following morning, and Matt recorded it. I didn't think the lyric on paper was all that wonderful, but Johnnie Spence's arrangement rolled down, Matt did one take, and we all looked at each other and said, "Well, that's it, I guess." The song started slowly in America, although it was a Top 40 success... Then in 1964, Frank Sinatra recorded it and it was that version which kicked the song off into glory, although I have never heard anyone sing it better than Matt. I've

always loved his version. — Hal Shaper

One story that surrounded the song was that Elvis Presley had been in Las Vegas and heard Jerry Vale singing it. Jerry told Presley that the songwriter had scribbled down the tune on his deathbed. Elvis believed this to be true and the song became a great favourite of his in his act. Shaper never corrected him in case he stopped singing it.

The year ended on a high with Matt returning to New York to record the second *Ed Sullivan Show* for New Year's Eve. Sullivan seemed genuinely pleased to see the British singer again and Matt was far more relaxed the second time around, though he admitted later to Mickie that he didn't know any of the other guests appearing with him on the show. While in the States, Matt grabbed the opportunity to catch up with his friend Sammy Davis Jr, and also found time to meet Louis Armstrong, Perry Como and Adam Wade.

What a personality and what a performer. Meeting Satchmo is something you never forget, he's dynamic! He strikes you at once as being even more flamboyant than his reputation. He is loaded with personal magnetism. I went down to Basin Street with a friend to see him. After the show we went backstage and met him. He'd heard some of my work and liked it. We chatted for some time about this and that. It was a very pleasant and memorable evening. — Matt Monro

The demand for Matt's music continued unabated throughout 1962. The turnaround in the singer's fortune in a little over twelve months was enormous. Matt knew he was earning big money but setting aside enough to meet any future tax demands was a problem, as he had no experience of managing earnings on this scale. Mickie had taken the reins for a while but now the bookwork was proving quite complicated, with different sets of revenue earned from television, radio, advertising, personal appearances and record royalties. The couple took advice from an accountancy firm and set up two companies: Matt Monro Enterprises for the UK-based work and Melody Management for overseas earnings.

Matt was voted Most Promising Male Singer of 1961 as well as Most Popular Foreign Artist by the American trade paper *Billboard*. 'My Kind of Girl' was rated sixth in the Favourite Records category and fifth in the Favourite International Song Poll. Matt was also voted *Melody Maker*'s Number One Singer, *Weekend Magazine*'s Singer of the

Year and Top International Star as well as Top Newcomer in *Billboard*'s disc jockey poll.

'My Kind of Girl' won an Ivor Novello award as the most performed work of the previous twelve months and incredibly 'Portrait' was runner-up; an amazing achievement considering it had been voted the most outstanding song the previous year.

Matt flew to Cologne to entertain the British troops in Germany, recorded a couple of jingles and crammed in another *Parade of the Pops*, all while anxiously waiting to see how his new release, 'Softly As I Leave You', would be received. The surprising result came in the last days of January as reporterd by John Wells.

> Look through the Top 20s for the past three weeks and one thing should strike you – there is an intruder in them... That disc is Matt's 'Softly' and it doesn't fit because, although when it was issued everyone seemed to agree that it was a great number, they also thought it was album material and would have needed far too many plugs to be a commercial bet as a single. 'Softly' lacks the immediate appeal of Matt's two big hits, 'Portrait' and 'My Kind of Girl' and so it was perhaps not so surprising that the Juke Box Jury panel of 27 January voted it a miss. So what happened?... According to Pete Murray the answer to that is simple – the personality of the singer. It's an excellent record, I'd say one of the three best he's ever made but I think it's selling on his own personal popularity and tremendous artistry. Matt is a wonderful singer and puts a great deal of feeling into a song. Anyone else singing 'Softly' and it would have been a miss, I'm sure of this. — John Wells

With the verdict in, and another hit under his belt, Matt could breathe a sigh of relief. It all helped cement his ever-growing popularity and he was now being hailed in the press as 'Britain's number one male singer'.

Matt was helping Mickie prepare lunch one day when he heard Carole Carr announce a request for his latest disc on *Two-Way Family Favourites*. It was such a thrill hearing his records on air and it was something he never tired of. He was equally excited when Roy Parker, the editor of *Record Retailer*, threw a party in his honour. EMI followed suit with their own celebratory reception, taking the opportunity to award Matt with two gold discs representing the success of 'Portrait' and 'My Kind of Girl'.

Matt had been gracing the Luxembourg 208 airwaves every Tuesday night for several months with his distinctive, lush style of singing. Now there was news that he was to have two extra fifteen-minute slots on a Sunday. Radio was the perfect medium to advance record sales; that was at the forefront of every artist's mind. Overseas sales were equally important and although 'My Kind of Girl' had been a big hit the year before on the Warwick label, the label's executives had agreed in February that Liberty would look after any future releases.

Matt was delighted with the work that was pouring in. 1962 saw him take on his first summer season in Weymouth, a trip back to Hong Kong and his third *Ed Sullivan Show*. Don's phone was ringing off the hook. He ran through all the offers with Matt and, once a decision was made, executed the contracts and entered dates in the diary. It was a far cry from his nine-to-five job in Denmark Street.

The most important tool for any songster is the song itself and Matt had been lucky with his choices so far, although he would be the first to admit that he didn't have an immediate eye for a hit. He hadn't thought 'Portrait' a possible commercial success and then made a monumental mistake in turning down an exclusive on 'The Shadow of Your Smile' long before Tony Bennett cut the 1965 Academy Award winner. The song's author had sent the composition to Matt but the singer didn't think it would appeal to the mass market. When it appeared in the film *The Sandpiper*, Tony Bennett sent Matt a thank you note.

Although Don had been dabbling in song writing himself, it was not something he had taken too seriously. Matt openly encouraged his friend as he could see potential in the youngster and had already recorded 'April Fool' as a favour to the budding lyricist. "If Lionel Bart can do it son, why can't you?" Matt enthused. It was the money motivation, his love of music and Matt that kept him at it.

There were many prestigious venues throughout England, but for Matt none quite as alluring as London's Talk of the Town in Leicester Square. He was one of only two artists (the other being Frankie Vaughan) who performed there a record-breaking ten times. Lofty accolades came consistently from both the paying public and the critics. Matt always swore he would be the one to break the record but unfortunately the venue closed down, declaring the 'contest' a draw.

Talk of the Town was the brainchild of theatrical producer Robert Nesbitt. After staging the first ever revue show at the Dunes Hotel in Las Vegas, he wanted to bring that same sensibility home to Britain. On his return to London, he told leading impresario Bernard Delfont, "I've been to this place called Vegas and that's the future of entertainment, not people sitting in rows of seats, but dining while they watch entertainment. It will be a sensation and this is what we need to do." They joined forces with leading restaurateur Charles Forte, cast their eye around the West End, and came across the Hippodrome. The venue wasn't faring too well and had become something of a white elephant, but it seemed perfect for their vision. It re-opened to modest success, showcasing a steady succession of speciality acts presented in two parts during the course of the evening. Later it was decided to drop one of the floorshows and present headliners for the second half of the evening. The dance floor was raised during the show to provide a dramatic apron to the formidable stage. It was a resounding success. The only serious competition came from the Savoy Hotel, another London spot that regularly showcased big names.

Billy Marsh was the booker for the room. As probably the best agent during this period, he certainly had the pick of a huge arsenal of stars who loved to perform there. With his guidance the venue became synonymous with the best in nightlife entertainment and earned international renown as one of the truly great nightspots in the world.

Matt's first appearance at the venue was on 13 February 1962, deputising for singer Joan Regan, who had been taken ill in the middle of her run. Matt replaced her at a few hours' notice. Having worked the room he was eager to be booked under his own merit, but it would be another three years before that ambition became a reality.

That week Matt's new single entered the *NME* Top 20 and *Melody Maker* crowned him Top British Singer in their nationwide poll. The good news didn't end there. While attending *Weekend Magazine*'s 'Date with the Stars' ball, editor Howard French presented him with the Singer of the Year award. During the evening Matt was introduced to Sid James, who he was particularly interested in talking to, since he had recently agreed to do several shows with Tony Hancock later that year.

Sid James had met Hancock on the set of British comedy remake *Orders are Orders*. It was Hancock's film debut unlike James who was by then, an old hat at it, notching up over forty film credits. They became firm friends and Sid joined the cast of Hancock's new radio show *Hancock's Half Hour*. Sid quickly learned that Hancock was not an easy man to work with. The comic was a nervous character who worried about everything and over the years he seemed to feel threatened by Sid's growing popularity. Without warning Hancock dropped his co-star from the series. Although Sid explained to Matt that he bore no ill will towards Tony, the incident had left him feeling betrayed. Matt liked the cards-on-the-table, chain-smoking South African and

Matt with his new green Jaguar outside Weymouth Pavilion

before departing for the evening promised to stay in touch.

Matt was booked for a season in Weymouth and reasoned to Mickie that he needed a more reliable car than the Humber Super Snipe. Matt had a passion for cars and as his earnings escalated so did the status of his car. Matt took a hire purchase agreement out on a brand new Jaguar. Being superstitious he'd never wanted a green car, but the only way he was going to get the Jaguar D-Type Sports reasonably quickly was to accept one in that colour. Not long after, he was out looking for a small car for Mickie and spotted a little red Mini. The fact that it carried the license plate 8929 MM sealed the deal. A few weeks later Mickie had the number plate transferred to Matt's Jaguar. From then, however many cars he owned, Matt kept the number plate and it remains in the family today.

After all the trouble with Bertie Green, Matt parted company with his agent Michael Black but retained Don as his personal manager. There was little time to lament the change as Matt was about to open at La Reserve in Sutton Coldfield for a week. Staying at the Metropole Hotel in Birmingham, he was only a short distance from the club. He drew up outside the entrance and, leaving the car in neutral, ran in to ask where he should park. Having been directed to the venue's private facility, Matt went outside to move his Jaguar only to find that it had been broken into and his wallet and gold and silver cufflinks stolen.

Throughout Matt's travels, Mickie wrote to him every night before going to sleep as it made her feel closer to him, but Matt couldn't bear writing long letters so he would send endless postcards. After months of receiving these postcards, Mickie told him she longed to have an envelope to open. While he was away in Birmingham an envelope arrived for Mickie – inside was a postcard!

> I was so excited when I knew he was going to appear at the La Reserve, Sutton Coldfield. The show was wonderful and I waited to speak to him afterwards. He was wonderful and from that moment on I was smitten. — Joan Jowett

Sue Parker also travelled to La Reserve to see her idol and although she loved the show she still couldn't pluck up the courage to ask for his autograph. Being so young she wasn't allowed to travel to the venues on her own and would often rope her mother into coming with her. If that failed, then her father would have the task of escorting her.

Mickie rang Matt after the show one night to confirm that the contract had arrived for his tour with The Four Freshmen. She also thought to tell him that the new Steve Lawrence album was called – *Portrait of My Love*!

After the show closed, Matt grabbed a few well-earned days at home. With a long season coming up he took the opportunity to get fitter and decided to give up smoking. It took a lot of will power to kick his forty-a-day habit, but having made the decision Matt banned his wife from keeping any cigarettes in the house and threw a party to celebrate. The next post brought a letter saying that the sponsor of his forthcoming Radio Luxembourg programme would be a cigarette firm. He started smoking again.

BIG NIGHT OUT

Impresario Vic Lewis organised the eagerly awaited tour by America's ace vocal team, The Four Freshmen, and American pianist/vocalist Jeri Southern. Lewis teamed Danny Williams and a specially-formed Kenny Baker Orchestra with Matt as special guest for a series of ten one-nighters. The Four Freshmen included Ross Barbour and his cousin Bob Flanigan, Ken Albers and Bill Comstock. Matt was knocked out by their personalities both on and off the stage. The show was well received at every venue and the accolades poured in from the press. Then disaster struck as Jeri Southern was forced to pull out of the tour. She was struck down by a severe case of jaundice and was lying seriously ill in a New York hospital after being flown home from London, but thankfully the tour was strong enough to carry on in her absence.

I first heard Matt at our manager's house. He had a record of 'My Kind of Girl'. I was astonished because I had not heard a voice of that quality in popular music for some time. I realised I was hearing, in my estimation, the next great vocal star. We first met when Vic Lewis put together a tour with Matt, singer Jeri Southern, a young singer named Danny Williams and a band put together by the marvellous trumpet player Kenny Baker. We toured England for about three weeks. During that time we became fast friends with Matt and gained a great appreciation and respect for his exceptional talent and persona. There were quite a few 'pub adventures' along the way, all in the name of sightseeing of course.
— Bill Comstock, The Four Freshmen

After the tour ended, Matt desperately needed a day off but returned to Windsor Road to see his ex-wife and play with his son. Things were better between Matt and

The Four Freshmen

Iris, as the long separation seemed to have defused the tension. He took Mitchell for a walk to Hornsey Rise and then on to see his grandmother. Even with Matt's success, Alice remained totally independent and kept working until very late in life, despite all of her son's efforts to dissuade her. Matt would give her money and she would put it in a cupboard. Two weeks later, the money would still be in the closet, untouched.

Matt and Mickie's very first holiday abroad – which didn't involve work – was to the top hotel Pez Espada a little way up the coast in Torremolinos, Spain. It was the first luxury hotel on the Costa del Sol to open its doors in the 1950s and occupied a prime location next to the beach promenade. Matt and Mickie knew they'd made the right choice when they walked in and saw that actor Anthony Quinn was also staying there. Although expensive, Matt and Mickie felt the trip was worth every penny. They both needed to get away from the business and were desperate to spend some quality time together. They strolled through the Spanish quarter, with its many tapas bars and fish restaurants, and spent a glorious afternoon at Benalmadena's upmarket marina.

returning bronzed and rested, it was only a few hours before Matt was back in the studios recording his next single, 'My Love and Devotion', along with a couple of tracks for a future album. George told him that 'Softly' had been released on Liberty in America that week, the first British record to be issued on the label.

Matt continued in holiday mode by watching a couple of jazz bands and playing golf while on a six-night Scottish tour. On his return, he gave Mickie an ultimatum. He had bought his wife a new Mini six weeks earlier but she still hadn't learned to drive. This was mandatory, as the couple were going to Weymouth in a few months and couldn't all fit in one car. Matt threatened to sell the car and said Mickie would have to stay in London. A few weeks later, she took the driving test and passed on her first attempt. She was twenty-nine years old.

The 16 March saw Matt back working with The Four Freshmen, Danny Williams and Kenny Baker at The Charlie Chester Music Hall. The only new face was Rosemary Squires. The Freshmen all trooped back to Ruxley Lane after the show, poured drinks, sat on the floor and sang songs most of the night. Nursing a hangover, Matt flew to the Netherlands the next morning for his first big continental television spot, flying back a few hours later to headline a week in Torquay.

It was turnaround weekend at the Palladium. Shirley Bassey and The Temperance Seven were in the process of packing their belongings and tidying their dressing rooms to make way for the artists taking over on Monday 14 May for the second and last variety bill of the short season. The new occupants were not exactly in strange surroundings, for both Helen Shapiro and Matt Monro had previously broadcast from the location, though it was their first appearance in a seasonal show there.

Helen had, in an amazingly short time, developed into England's top female singer, rivalling even Cliff Richard, Adam Faith and Billy Fury for teenage appeal and record sales. Her final dress rehearsal at the theatre was scheduled for Monday morning under the leadership of conductor Eric Tann. Tann was filling in for resident musical director Reg Cole, who was rehearsing with Bruce Forsyth for the Palladium's summer show at the time. Backed for the most part by a rhythm section taken from the main pit, the most intriguing feature of Helen's act was her medley, during which she accompanied herself on a specially-made tenor banjo.

After four years with The Malcolm Mitchell Trio, pianist Russ Shepherd was leaving to join Matt as his permanent accompaniment. Although Russ had worked with Matt before, filling in when Johnnie couldn't appear, Matt now needed a more permanent

Matt & Helen Shapiro

replacement for Johnnie. Ironically, The Mitchell Trio and Matt were both on the current variety bill at The London Palladium.

Bernard Delfont presented the show, with Matt closing the first half and Helen topping the bill, and a mixed bag of artists making up the variety side. During Matt's fortnight residence at the Palladium he was kept fully occupied during the daytime at Abbey Road, completing his second album for the Parlophone label.

> **London Palladium this month is that splendidly original phenomenon in 1962, a singer with a fabulous voice. He has no gimmicks, he doesn't need a mike to reach the second row of the stalls, he doesn't need an echo to boost his vocal range, he doesn't need to wear his hair on his shoulders. He doesn't paw the ground, tear his hair or dislocate his pelvic girdle while delivering a number. — *Reuters News Agency***

It wasn't just the press who were impressed with Matt's singing. Helen Shapiro was also a great fan. Being still very new to the business, her parents travelled with her on most of the tour dates. Matt recognised this might be an overwhelming experience for such a young girl and made a point of calling at her dressing room to see if she needed anything. He regaled her and her parents with funny stories in between shows and after the performance they hung out at the Lotus House.

On the first night, I was surprised when Matt walked in, between shows, wearing a silk dressing gown. I wasn't aware that this was a theatre tradition. He looked so funny with his black socks and shiny black patent leather shoes! He would sit and tell us funny stories. Matt was so much fun to be with backstage; always good-humoured, with jokes and anecdotes. I would stand and watch him from the wings at every performance, and when he sang 'Softly as I Leave You', it never failed to move me to tears. What a voice! And such feeling! I believe he was one of the best singers this country has ever produced. He had immense talent and charm but remained totally unspoilt. — Helen Shapiro

Both artists thoroughly enjoyed the experience. One person, however, wasn't entirely happy. *The Record Mirror* published a reader's letter asking someone to explain why Matt Monro, a singer of international stature, was billed below Helen Shapiro, whose success was confined to the British market. The letter argued that at the very least they should have shared joint billing!

Another song was already in the can for release as Matt's follow-up single, but on the spur of the moment George changed his mind and asked Matt to come into the studio the next day to record 'When Love Comes Along'. Matt had to go into the studio session completely 'cold', without knowing either the words or the melody. He coped admirably and it was perfectly recorded in half a session. The song was quite a change from some of his earlier sentimental ballads. Behind Matt's smooth, slightly nasal vocal, Johnnie rang the changes by setting up a rather novel instrumental backdrop. He used a tinkling, staccato piano between his string section figures and the whole song took on a delicate country shade. The keyboard effects, plus a hard percussive beat, fall away later as the strings gather strength and Matt's voice climbs to an impressive climax.

The flip side, 'Tahiti', was included because Matt had sung it over the credits of a soon-to-be-released travelogue film. With the session over, Matt was delighted when Don presented him with tickets for a very special Sinatra concert. As part of a world tour to raise money for children's charities, this was to be the performer's first public appearance in England since 1953. Matt went to Sinatra's opening night at the Festival Hall and was so thrilled with the performance that he made plans to attend the second show at the Gaumont at Hammersmith. Steve Whiting later interviewed Matt for an article that appeared in both *The Echo Pop Special* and *The Sinatra Music Society Magazine*.

> **Now this week British singer Matt Monro – the man Sinatra asked after when he arrived in London and the man who coined that phrase 'The Guv'nor' – took time off between rehearsals at The Pavilion Theatre, Weymouth, to give *Pop Special* the low-down on Frank Sinatra. Of Frank's performance, Monro said: "This was the first time I had seen Sinatra in the flesh, and after seeing him, I have even more respect for him than ever." Believe me, he more than lived up to his reputation. No other man in the world could have given a performance like he did. — Steve Whiting**

When Sinatra granted one of his rare interviews during his visit, he asked the reporter, "How's that guy Matt Monro who made that great disc a couple of years back?"

Billed as "The Show of Stars", the cast at the Pavilion Theatre, Weymouth, was conventional summer fare with the usual variety bill, including Mike and Bernie Winters, The Springfields, Derek Dene, Sandra Peters, Kenet & Jani and Les Franky Babusio. Matt was top of the bill with a twenty-minute spot of his own, singing six songs twice nightly for just over three months. Sundays were filled with concerts, personal appearances, charity work and recording sessions. Matt looked forward to returning to Weymouth, the town that probably gave him his greatest fillip on the way to stardom. He had been placed second in a talent competition there and was the first to admit that the splendid reception he first received gave him the encouragement to pursue a stage career.

> **When he was doing Summer Season in Weymouth time was so tight he was doing two shows a day, then driving to London and into the studios to cut a few sides of his *Hoagy Carmichael* album. Incredible – he used to drive himself everywhere, he liked driving. I don't know anybody else that could do that schedule, amazing stuff. — Jeff Hooper**

Relocating your life for a fourteen-week period is not easy for any performer, but add

PAVILION WEYMOUTH
ENTERTAINMENT MANAGER S.A.PERRY F.I.M.E.M. TEL 3225
Bernard Delfont and Richard Armitage present
Twice nightly at 6·0 & 8·30
Box office open daily 10·0 a.m. to 8·0 p.m.
FOR THE SUMMER SEASON
THE SHOW of STARS
The International Singing Star
MATT MONRO
T.V. Comedy Stars
MIKE & BERNIE WINTERS
The popular T.V. & Recording Trio
THE SPRING-FIELDS
The Summer Show
Wonderful Time!
for the whole family
the show maidens
the pavilion orchestra
DEREK DENE
Kenet & Jani
LES FRANKY BABUSIO
AND HIS COMEDY WONDER TAXI
STALLS 8/6 · 7/6 6/0
CIRCLE 8/6 · 7/6 6/0 · 4/0
PLUS full supporting cast
A brilliant night out!
GRAND OPENING !! FRIDAY JUNE 8 at 8·0 p.m.
PRODUCED BY JOHN LYNDON • DEVISED BY ALAN CROOKS • CHOREOGRAPHY BY ESME BROWNE
BOX OFFICE: WEYMOUTH PAVILION
Postal Booking form
Date............................
Please forward...........STALLS 8/6 7/6 6/-...........CIRCLE 8/6 7/6 6/- 4/-
for the EVENING performance 6-0/8-30 on..
I enclose stamped addressed envelope and P.O./Cheque value £ s : d
NAME..
ADDRESS..
Printed by Electric (Modern) Printing Co. Ltd., Manchester 8.

Matt & musical director Russ Shepherd

a wife, a daughter and an au-pair and it becomes an even more difficult proposition. The trip necessitated the family taking two cars and renting a lovely house for the summer at Rodwell, overlooking the bay. They soon settled in and Matt went to explore the theatre and attend rehearsals. He now had a new pianist in Russ Shepherd, who he thought was a great acquisition.

Russ and Matt established a good rapport. It seemed that anyone who spent time with the singer was infected with his sense of humour and Russ was no exception. Sometimes the humour extended to the stage and on one occasion Matt jokingly asked Russ to shave his ginger beard off in case they were mistaken for Nina & Frederik.

The Winter boys were two opposites who complemented each other perfectly and the camaraderie between Matt, Mike and Bernie became very strong indeed. Away from the theatre the trio tended to spend all their time together. Mike was the most grown-up of the threesome, and was repeatedly telling Matt and Bernie off for giggling too much, although he found it impossible to stay cross with them for any length of time.

Mike, Bernie and Derek Dene provided the bulk of the comedy throughout the

Freddie Garrity, Matt & Dusty Springfield

season but The Springfields also joined in the fun of the show. The Springfields were a pop-folk vocal trio made up of Dusty Springfield, her brother Tom and Mike Hurst. The artists worked tremendously hard for very little and when the final curtain came down each night there were sighs of relief from the cast.

> **In those days we were on farming contracts. Farming is what agents and producers do to artists: they sign them for a 3/5 year contract for little money, then build them up (like farm animals) until, with luck, the artist is worth a lot more than they are getting. The true salary goes to the agent/producer. I don't think the joint weekly wages of Mike and Bernie, Jimmy Tarbuck and Matt came to a thousand pounds. We all needed to remain successful for at least three years to see out our contracts so that we would make the big money. — Mike Winters**

The shows put everyone under a great deal of pressure and each person had their own way of coping with the stress. One night Mike and Bernie were in their dressing room after the show when a terrible noise came through the ceiling. The following night, they heard the same racket again. It transpired that the Springfields' dressing room was directly above theirs and when Dusty and her brother came off stage they routinely smashed a set of crockery to pieces. Mickie saw them coming back from Woolworths in the daytime with bags full of teapots, cups, saucers and plates. No one quite knew why they went through this ritual, as they were all too embarrassed to ask them about it.

Mickie spent a great deal of time with Siggi Winters, Bernie's wife, while their husbands went off to play snooker. The boys used to play for half a crown a game. On one occasion, they played all through the night and Bernie ended up owing Matt twenty-six-thousands pounds. The bill was never settled!

During the last week of June, Matt went down to London to record with George. As well as a new single, Matt was laying down tracks for his next album *Matt Sings Hoagy Carmichael*. Noël Coward was in the building while Matt was recording 'I Get Along Without You Very Well', and hearing the rendition insisted on finding out who was singing so beautifully. He followed the sound to a studio and found Matt – they became friends.

To beat an imminent advertiser's strike ban, Matt was rushed to London to record a commercial backing track between performances of his summer show in Weymouth. Together, Matt, Peter Marsh and Rod Allen of Osborne-Peacock and composer John Shakespeare captured the Mackintosh's Weekend jingle, averting disaster. Most Sundays Matt was either working on the album or engaged in Sunday concerts and taped radio broadcasts. And there was also the important matter of Matt, Mike and Bernie judging the Miss Weymouth annual bathing beauty contest.

One rest day necessitated Matt and the Winters brothers flying to Jersey for a charity show. On the return trip the following morning, Matt and Bernie played a cruel trick on Mike. Disembarking the plane ahead of his brother, Bernie pulled Matt along and claimed their place in the customs line. They glanced round to see Mike several places back in the queue. On approaching the desk Bernie told the officials that the guy behind them had been acting suspiciously and Matt piped in that "he looked the guilty type". The two men were grinning from ear to ear as Mike was led away to an official search, having no idea why he was under suspicion.

Matt enjoyed his fame but it never went to his head. He was a part

**of a small group of us who felt privileged and lucky to be accepted
by the public. Matt and I worked together many times. Each time
was fun and full of laughter. Not once did a spiteful or nasty
comment pass our lips. Weymouth, Yarmouth, Blackpool, that's
about fifty weeks we spent together over a four or five-year period.
— Mike Winters**

Holiday Town Parade was a brand new television show, which toured northern
resorts and featured artists from summer shows, with Mike and Bernie as regular
guests. Technical faults held up filming for one show, and the boys ad-libbed for
nearly half an hour while technicians fixed the problem. Phil Jones, the producer,
was delighted and offered them their own series.

Big Night Out was an instant hit with its mixture of comedy and headline guests,
and featured Matt in no fewer than three episodes. The boys themselves did most
of the stunts, but that carried certain risks. On one show, Bernie had to break
through a wall in a deluge of plaster, saying the lines "Good evening everybody,
welcome to *Big Night Out*". Unfortunately the wall was too robust, and with Bernie
wedged halfway through, three stage hands had to hoist him out while a nurse
tended to his bleeding wounds. Only minutes later Bernie, who had somehow
made his costume change, was introducing the next sketch.

While Matt was waiting to film one of his spots on *Big Night Out,* he stood in the
wings watching Mike and Bernie's new sketch. Bernie was playing 'Big John' in a
staged cowboy fight and the scene called for Mike to strike his brother across the
head with a 'scored' bottle. The bottle turned out not to be scored, and it took
some time until Bernie regained consciousness. Matt fell about laughing.

Just before the season ended, Don announced he had another pop star in his
charge, one Barry Barnett. The press were citing similarities between Matt and
Don's new protégé in relation to their struggle up the ladder of fame. The likeable
nephew of famed old-time vocalist Sam Browne had made his first disc three years
earlier – when balladeers were a tough sell – and now was looking to make a fresh
start.

Don was expanding and instead of handling just Matt's work he was branching
out by combining forces with the Vic Lewis Organisation. But where artists such
as Bruce Forsyth had managed to negotiate their fees down, Matt's went up. The
comic had bought his way out of his contract with agent Miff Ferrie after a year of
torment and signed with Billy Marsh instead. In place of the inflated fifteen percent
agent's fee he'd been paying, Billy took only ten percent. On the flip side, Matt had

Airport Arrivals

been paying Don either thirty pounds or ten percent a week, whichever was the greater. Now Matt was also required to pay the Vic Lewis Organisation ten percent, inflating his fees to a significant twenty percent.

HANCOCK

In 1962 George Martin signed a promising new Liverpool pop band, little realising that his decision would soon turn Parlophone into one of the world's most famous and sought-after record labels. From the minute Brian Epstein brought George an unknown group called The Beatles, he was so excited that he developed insomnia. Once he took over, Martin arranged all The Beatles' music, coaxing, shaping and polishing, taking a three-bar snatch of guitar strumming by Paul to a full-length score for the symphony orchestras they used as backing. 11 September 1962 is a date that George Martin is unlikely to forget; it was on that day that he produced The Beatles' first record, releasing it less than four weeks later. Their success won the producer complete artistic freedom.

The Beatles may have arrived at Epstein's office in the benchmark rebel uniform of the day – jeans, t-shirts and black leather jackets – but after Epstein moulded their look they became known as much for their appearance as for their music. They presented themselves identically, clean-shaven with neat mop-head haircuts, white shirts and dark ties, with sharp creases down the front of their trousers. The only slightly unconventional part of the dress code was their collarless jackets, but that was hardly novel, as Sammy Davis Jr had already pioneered the Nehru look.

In this instance, Matt didn't have to catch up with the trend – his style had always favoured the shirt and tie approach. On stage, he was always elegantly presented in a beautiful tuxedo with shirt cuffs extending half an inch from the jacket sleeve, and perfectly crisp trousers breaking just above the shoe. His dress suit trousers would never be sat down in, and after he had taken his final bow, everything was hung beautifully, ready for the next performance.

He was equally meticulous in adhering to the superstition that anyone whistling in his dressing room would bring bad luck. If the ultimate crime was committed, the perpetrator had to leave the room, turn around three times in the corridor and then knock three times before coming back in. It was always done to protect the performance.

With George busy with his new signing, Matt readied himself for his upcoming tour with Tony Hancock. The comic had an enormous following, built on the strength of the now-legendary *Hancock's Half Hour* programmes, broadcast first on radio and then television.

Matt had looked forward to this engagement as he was knocked out by Hancock's genius. Three separate weeks of theatre followed, opening first at the King's Theatre in Southsea on 8 October, followed by the Liverpool Empire and the Brighton Hippodrome. The autumn tour, billed as *The Hancock Show* and presented by Bernard Delfont, was designed as a two-man vehicle, with Matt opening the first half and Tony performing in the second. As well as accompanying Matt, Johnnie Spence also had a small spot in the show, having just climbed the charts with his composition of the *Dr Kildare* theme.

> **I first met Matt and Mickie at the King's Theatre, Southsea. I'd been pushing Tony for months to scrub the old variety act and get a more modern one. I got Terry Nation in to write a new act for him. I started managing Tony from about the end of 1960 to approximately 1965. — Roger Hancock**

Hancock recruited Terry Nation, who had been successful writing for Frankie Howerd. Tony wanted new material for this tour and over a ten-day period they fashioned numerous sketches. But as opening night neared, Tony got a bad case of nerves.

He arrived in Southsea in a very large American chauffeur-driven car with Terry Nation and Glyn Jones, the Delfont agency's road manager. As usual, Tony insisted on going straight to the venue. Most entertainers have a stringent ritual in place prior to a performance. If the venue is an unknown quantity, they will endeavour to feel it out beforehand so it isn't an unwelcome stranger on the night. And Tony was no exception. He stood on stage and smelled the room, taking in how far away his audience would be and memorising any pillars or quirky foibles. Matt followed a similar ritual, pacing the stage and counting out the time it would take to walk to the wings or to his pianist. He searched the lighting and took in his surroundings as best he could, for when he was on stage he would have zero visibility. Behind the footlights could be a very lonely place as there is no opportunity to create intimacy, you can't

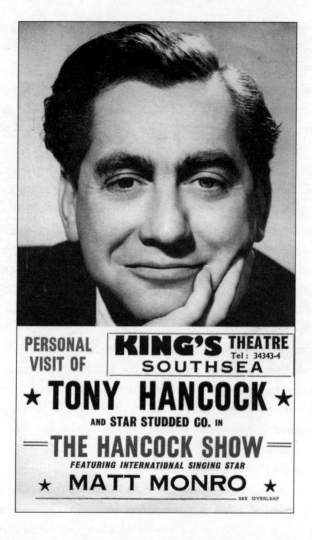

read the audience's expressions or see if boredom is setting in, you can only be led by the applause you hear.

> **The first magic moment is when people applaud what you do. Applause and the feeling you get on stage is something you cannot describe to anybody; it's not a feeling or experience you can share, it's a purely selfish moment of your life when people applaud what you do. Nothing compares, you can't buy it and you can't share it. — Matt Monro**

The next morning, Matt and Tony woke up in the same hotel unaware that the other was already there. Matt woke up mid-morning, read the morning papers, did the

Tony Hancock

crossword, phoned Mickie and got ready to head to the theatre for rehearsals. By contrast Hancock had risen at dawn and woken Terry Nation up. He was shaking and covered in sweat and obviously in torment about the performance. Arriving at the King's Theatre, Tony sat through the day's rehearsals, mumbling his lines and hurling pages of his script across the stage. By the end of the day, most of the new routines had been put to one side in favour of his older, more trusted material.

Hancock had always been a perfectionist, with performances preceded by hours of mental agony. Painful memories from his youth included an engagement in Sidmouth. His feeling of optimism had turned to fear when he couldn't find his name advertised anywhere, and it didn't abate even when he realised that he'd arrived a week early. Tony found no humour in the incident and, with money extremely tight, the three pence fare to get home was begrudgingly paid. His humour didn't fare any better when, while performing in a pantomime, he was given a piggyback by the other 'ugly sister' and during the ride the pair fell into the orchestra pit. The audience thought it hysterical, but Tony was completely mortified.

Hold anything green up in front of Hancock before a performance and he would anticipate doom. He even made his wife throw away her new green dress on the eve of his Royal Variety Performance. In view of Hancock's feelings about the colour, it was understandable that Matt would share his recent stories about his green Jaguar. He'd bought the car ready for his season in Weymouth and after less than three months it had already been broken into, scratched down the side and reversed into, courtesy of the Pavilion Theatre's girl dancers. That was the end of the car. Matt intended to get the vehicle repaired and sell it – vowing never to buy a green car again!

During the show's run at the King's Theatre, Hancock ad-libbed for more than forty wonderful minutes, virtually without props. Impersonations of Noël Coward at tea, Long John Silver and Charles Laughton's Captain Bligh had the audience virtually in convulsions. The highlight of the impeccably-timed performance was a parody of a Fred Astaire and Ginger Roger's dance routine, at the end of which Hancock of East Cheam and the girls of Scooter Teague Dance Assembly were completely lost in thick mist.

Some of the press were rather unkind, but the audience's reaction demanded that the show go on, that and the fact that Tony and Matt had pulled in over twenty thousand paying patrons in that first week. With twelve performances, it averaged out at over eighty percent capacity for each show.

On one memorable occasion, Tony wanted to try out a new sketch with Matt for the show, which required the singer to stamp on the comic's foot. But each time Matt did it Tony demanded that he do it harder. Matt was scared that he would hurt his co-star, but Hancock insisted that he try it with even more aggression. Matt slammed his foot down so hard that he gave himself a painful injury and the sketch was abandoned.

Virgins to Hancock's modus operandi were often surprised to find him slightly miserable and uncommunicative when he was working, but the comic was a complex character. His nerves overwhelmed him on a regular basis, and his resulting need to concentrate often gave outsiders the impression of detachment. Unlike Matt, it was never a good idea to see Tony before a show. He liked to take an hour before any performance and nurse his own company – the presence of anything other than a stiff drink was unwelcome.

Despite Tony's shortcomings, Matt loved the comic and didn't try to understand him; he just enjoyed his company. While Matt could be shy about accepting compliments on his performance, no amount of accolades could convince the comic that his gift was priceless. Yet Hancock's talent for making laughter – with an inflection in his voice, a change of expression on his pliable face – was innate. But his perfectionism was at the root of his neurosis and he became dependent on alcohol to relieve the tension and dull the loneliness. His marriage had deteriorated as alcohol became a habitual crutch and the situation was exacerbated when Tony took Freddie Ross as his mistress. It would be 1965 before he divorced his first wife and married Freddie.

Hancock didn't need to look very far for a drinking partner, with both Matt and Johnnie prone to a tipple themselves, and after each show the three would drink a place dry while dissecting their own performances. A ritual was established after the curtain came down, with each star giving time to their fans before joining the band members at the bar for a quick drink. Hancock, Matt and Johnnie would then leave for the hotel, arranging to meet within the hour, giving them ample time to shower and change. And there was one other thing the trio regularly did – each felt the need to phone their partner to say goodnight before a drinking session broke out, so as not to provoke a lecture.

The three-week show run cemented Matt and Tony's friendship, and over the years there were numerous invites volleyed back and forth between them. When Matt and Mickie visited Hancock's home, they found it odd that it looked to be furnished from a flea market or yard sale, with an old leather chair with the stuffing spilling out, an oddment of seating and, in one residence, underfelt on the floor. On one occasion, despite having no children himself, Tony threw a lavish children's party for Christmas with no expense spared.

An incident purported to have occurred between Matt and Tony was reported in Kenneth Williams's diary. He admitted he had heard the story third-hand when he was sitting with Sidney James and a few other cast members during the filming of *Carry on Abroad*. It seemed that Sid had talked at length about Hancock's antics, including claiming that Matt had told the story of an incident when he'd woken up one night to find Hancock attempting to give him fellatio, and that the singer had "given him a right hander".

Hancock and Matt were certainly in high spirits by the end of the second week of the tour. Feeling the need to carry on celebrating the success of the shows, they decided to catch the overnight sleeper rather than drive from Liverpool to London, where they would enjoy a brief stopover before going onto Brighton for the third leg of the tour. Joining them was Tony's entourage: Glyn Jones, the show's road manager, and Terry Nation, the show's scriptwriter. Terry's job was in fact defunct as the scripts had been dealt with, but he was retained at a fee of a hundred pounds per week just to keep the comic company.

Even before the train pulled away from the platform at Liverpool, the party was in evidence. It wasn't really that drinking had started early, more likely that it was carrying on from earlier in the evening. The men were clearly enjoying themselves,

Matt & Sid James

and as they readied themselves for the whistle's blow they toasted their good fortune and hoped for similar success in Brighton.

Cliff Goodwin's book *When the Wind Changed* also mentions the episode. It seems that in the early hours of the morning Nation was awoken by the sounds of raised voices coming from the next compartment, and on investigation found Hancock cowering in the corner naked. Nation stated that it was obvious from Matt's distaste that the comic had tried to sexually molest his friend while he was asleep. Hancock was taken back to his berth, while Nation attempted to pacify the enraged star, who was threatening to abandon the tour without further notice and initiate legal proceedings. The scriptwriter spent an age trying to change Matt's mind and eventually they both agreed it was better all around if the incident was never mentioned again.

Did the incident happen? Well, Matt and Tony certainly did a three-week tour together, they did drink together and they did come back to London on the same train. But did Tony approach Matt in an improper way? If he had, and if the incident had left Matt with so much distaste, it is doubtful he would have ever worked with the star again. If the allegations were in fact true, would Matt and Mickie have socialised with Tony in a family setting? Matt certainly never told his wife about such an incident and he tended to tell her everything. It is also questionable as to whether Sidney James would have relayed anything of such a delicate nature to Kenneth Williams, considering he loathed his co-star. This dated back to the very first shows Sid and Kenneth worked together on, which coincidently were the Hancock shows. There was open hostility between the two *Carry On* stars and, although it remained hidden from the public for the next twenty-odd years, it was evident to anyone who knew the men personally. More importantly, Sid had a problem with Kenneth's habit of flaunting his homosexuality and hated his effeminacy.

Matt had no such qualms about homosexuality. He knew and worked with many gay performers. If Tony had drunkenly made a pass, Matt would have laughed it off, knowing that the comic would have no recall the next morning, and he would most certainly have milked the story by sharing those antics with his friends. By the same token, Terry Nation was a good close friend of Tony's brother Roger, his wife Annie, Matt and Mickie. These friendships carried on until Nation's death but he never discussed such a story with any of them.

> I can tell you what the tours were like; they were hilarious from morning to night. We never went to bed and it was just one long laugh and I have very fond memories of Mr Tony Hancock.
> — Matt Monro

OPERATION SANTA CLAUS

*M*att *sings Hoagy Carmichael* was released on 15 November 1962 to universal success, and the composer even wrote to Matt complimenting him on the greatest rendition of his songs ever recorded. Bing Crosby lavished praise on the modest Londoner, saying that 'I Get Along Without You Very Well' was the most beautiful recording he had ever heard. With fine arrangements from Johnnie Spence, it remains to date not only one of Matt's finest album offerings, but was also one of his own personal favourites.

> I think Matt Monro sings a song just about as good as anybody I know. He doesn't put too many furbishes or furbuloes or too much lacy handling but he sings a song straight and he sings it in tune and with great clarity and good diction. I always liked this song ('I Get Along Without You Very Well') very much. I think he gives the best possible demonstration of how this song should sound. This is not the easiest song in the world either and you notice the range. He gets right down there to a note towards the end, which is not in my territory ... I couldn't get up there; I'd get a nosebleed. — Bing Crosby

Having flown back from New York after his third appearance on *The Ed Sullivan Show*, Matt and Mickie managed a social evening with Siggi and Bernie Winters. In a world that is full of fly-by-night gatherings, they were determined to nurture their relationship into something more than a brief 'hello' in-between tours.

A week later Matt's new single, 'My Love and Devotion', had climbed into the hit parade but while he should have been celebrating he was confined to bed on medical advice. Matt had pulled a muscle in his chest on the way back from the States, which was extremely painful, and on top of that, he now had a touch of jaundice.

Memories of Matt's army days came flooding back when his radio pal Ray Cordeiro rang garbling an excitable message about him having to come back to Hong Kong and to expect a follow-up call from Ted Thomas. The call came, arrangements were made and Matt left for the Orient on 17 December to take part in *Operation Santa Claus* – a three-day charity concert involving a journey of nearly twenty thousand miles. It was something of a sentimental journey for Matt, remembering the great times of his youth.

Donald Brooks, Controller of Broadcasting for Radio Hong Kong and one of the organisers of the event, saw him off the plane. Speaking at a press conference at Maxim's, Matt said, "Returning to Hong Kong was one of the biggest thrills of my career. I've always had an ambition to come back here." Matt was there at the invitation of the radio station as the star attraction of the station's annual three-day Drive-for-Dollars to aid the Colony's poor children. The climax of the event took place on the Thursday with Matt appearing at the city's Concert Hall in a live broadcast.

Bing Rodriguez and Ray Cordeiro went over to Matt's hotel room to greet the star. He was unpacking and Bing admitted to liking Matt's new shirts. Matt told him to help himself even though they were dress shirts and Bing didn't own a dress suit. Ray said "that's the way Matt was, always so generous".

Returning to Hong Kong as Matt Monro, he headed straight for Jimmy's Kitchen in Kowloon to treat his mates. It was a really expensive restaurant, and one he couldn't afford on his army wages all those years ago.

The weather here is fabulous. Went to my old army camp this morning, also did radio interview with John Wallace. Was out with my old friend Bing Rodriguez last night, great. — Postcard from Matt

The crowds built over the course of the day and Matt had hoards of children and families following him around the streets of Hong Kong. By the time it came to the show, the venue was jammed tight and full of expectancy. Spotlights lit the lone man on the platform and the room was still. The eyes of the singer were closed as musical words of romance spilled from his lips across an audience of silent worshippers. He didn't look like any other idol of his world of jukebox Gods, being short and stocky with a haircut that made him look square in the eyes of the teenagers whose whims created and toppled the Top 10. The singer had no tricks, no clanging guitars stimulated the voice, and no withering hips or flaying arms to supplement the spot-lit spectacle. Here was a singer whose only gimmick was his outstanding vocal talent. Matt Monro simply closed his eyes and sang songs of love, and suddenly defied the rules of jukebox stardom. By the time he left Hong Kong for a second time, Matt had become one of the best known and most in-demand entertainers in the Crown colony.

The theatre is the end; it's like a miniature Festival Hall with better acoustics. The Filipino boys have really gone mad at the fact that I remember them all and took the trouble to look them all up. Most of the old places that I used to work in are now gone, it's very modern here and a lot more expensive now than it was. I talked to Harry Odell, the Columbia Pictures boss over here who also books a lot of Far Eastern tours and he is very interested in me coming back next year to do Singapore, Japan and then Hong Kong. I'm having dinner with him tomorrow night to talk about it. — Letter from Matt Monro, The Ambassador Hotel, Nathan Road, Kowloon.

The beginning of the British Beat Boom in 1963 marked the end of the BBC Light Programme and its easy listening format. Though many changes were underway, Matt's world was only changing for the better. He never stopped working; his days were full with guest appearances on both television and radio, bookings at theatres and clubs up and down the country and another summer season in the diary. He was inundated with interview and photo shoot requests, as well as invitations to open garden fetes, record shops and Girl Guide headquarters. His schedule was manic but he didn't want to waste one minute of it, he was a man on a mission and he wanted that elusive number one spot.

January saw Matt at Abbey Road to record a new single 'One Day'. Major changes in technology meant that George was now recording to four-track tape and this allowed Matt to still sing live with the orchestra, but George could delay the decision of mixing mono and stereo until a later mix-down session. In the past when recordings were made the voice was 'locked' into the mix. If vocals were too low or high in level, no matter how good the take was, a new recording would be required to rectify the problem. Another benefit was that on rare occasions when Matt could not attend orchestral sessions, vocals could be added later.

'One Day' didn't make Emrys Bryson the millionaire he dreamed of being, but more than forty years on he is still earning royalties from the song. That previous summer, the Nottingham Playhouse put on a revue called *Yer What* in a small and poky theatre on Goldsmith Street. The show was a humorous look at Nottingham pioneering the Common Market and was written by Emrys and Australian musician Lance Mulcahey. Before opening night the director, Frank Dunlop, impulsively decided that he needed another song for the show.

Emrys got to work during his lunch hour and knocked out a verse and chorus about a lover who promises his lady that he will sail around the world discovering new lands for her – one day. With the Bryson lyrics in hand, Mulcahey worked equally quickly on the score and finished by teatime, with the cast rehearsing the number late afternoon. The revue only ran for three weeks and passed into obscurity with everyone going his or her separate ways. Months later, a friend of Emrys heard the song, sung by Matt on Radio Luxembourg, and excitedly rang him. For weeks Emrys tuned into the 208 frequency and inhaled the sweet smell of success. DJ Sam Costa plugged the record everyday and the writer was thrilled to hear his own lyrics emanating from the radio.

> **You can't get better than sheer perfection, which is what fabulous Matt is on this single. 'One Day' is a beautiful ballad, beautifully sung, beautifully arranged, and beautifully backed. The flip side is 'I've Got Love'. — *Reuters News Agency***

The thrills kept coming and the record was featured on *Juke Box Jury* and voted a hit. Matt was interviewed and gave the opinion that the song could be as big a hit as 'Softly'. Emrys was swept away by his own euphoria, buying up dozens of the single and continually playing it to anyone who would listen. He even began cutting the small reviews out of the music periodicals and started his own scrapbook. Emrys remembers the song with fondness and enjoyed his taste of show business success. His only regret was that he never met Matt personally. The single wasn't a hit regardless of the magnificent reviews, and even though his last six releases had charted, Matt was still disappointed with the result. While taping the *Ted Heath Show* during the usual round of television and radio broadcasts to showcase the single, Matt was delighted to meet up with Sarah Vaughan. There were several artists Matt admired greatly, and Vaughan was one of them and he regretted never working with her. Another of Matt's early ambitions was to sing with the Ted Heath Band, nothing could be better. He couldn't know then that years later the band would be his backing on broadcast.

Gambling and entertainment venues had sprung up all over the Midlands and the North of England in the last year and there was no shortage of venues to play. In early February, Matt was booked at Dolce Vita in Newcastle for a week. Also in town, working a different venue was a man who was to become one of Matt's closest friends – Dave Allen.

I did a week with Matt in Newcastle – he was one of those people you just laugh with, not because something funny has been said – if someone asked us what we were doing clutching our sides with laughter, you couldn't explain it to them or it would mean absolutely nothing to them … He was very funny, very dry; he was the ultimate pro, just a great character. We were in the same town and sometimes we got involved with each other's show. He had come back from a tour and he came on stage, sang the opening number, then talked explaining he had been away and had got Montezuma's Revenge saying he might have to nip off for five minutes. After twenty-five minutes, while singing a love song, he said "excuse me" and ran off: It is perhaps the biggest most sustained laugh I have ever heard in the theatre and when he came back on again the audience loved it and any mention or innuendo they fell about. — Dave Allen

There was an instant rapport between the two entertainers, they would work together many times over the years and would always endeavour to stay in the same hotel if they knew they were working near each other. They popped in to each other's shows, wound down together, played poker through the night, drank and smoked incessantly, laughed until it hurt and then started the process all over again.

We used to play poker together and that's about as intimate as you can get with anybody – when you're playing poker for money with your friends then that's close, that's a marriage in a sense. I love the man deeply. — Dave Allen

March brought a nineteen-date concert tour presented by William-Victor Productions, starring Shirley Bassey with Matt booked as special guest. William-Victor Productions was a branch of Vic Lewis's organisation that had just merged with Alan Blackburn and was lining up the Continental side of the deal. Together they would represent GAC, one of America's biggest booking offices, handling Chubby Checker, The Everleys, Paul Anka, Pat Boone and Nat King Cole.

The tour kicked off on 8 March at Colston Hall in Bristol with Russ Shepherd backing Matt in the first half, and Shirley opening the second half with her musical director Raymond Long. Battling a sore throat, with frequent excursions off-stage to gargle away the rough edges, Bassey was able to give full value to a wildly enthusiastic capacity second house. She attacked each note of every number with the same dynamic vigour and zest, and her powerful voice reached every corner of the venue. Having met Shirley on several occasions, Matt had given her the nickname Bert. With his characteristic sense of humour, he used to make fun of her and she allowed him to get away with things that others couldn't.

This performance marked a memorable event for Matt's most ardent fan Sue Maull. Sue had travelled all over the country seeing numerous performances, but still hadn't met the singer face-to-face. However, on this occasion a friend arranged for her to go backstage during the interval. She was sick with nerves, but having spent ten minutes with the star she left on cloud nine. Sue had finally met her idol! It was just a shame that she'd forgotten to ask for his autograph.

With very little space in the diary, Matt and Mickie didn't know when they would be able to have a proper holiday, but they managed a long weekend in Paris for their anniversary. Most couples would have been more than happy to share a romantic getaway alone but Matt and Mickie went off with Penny and Bruce Forsyth. Being a celebrity, it was hard to keep your movement's covert but the press weren't in evidence when the foursome were taken to a sex show and while two girls were writhing on stage Bruce was asked if he would like to participate!

More than twenty million viewers were puzzled when Bruce blushed and laughed in obvious embarrassment when John Lennon handed him a note during The Beatles' historic *Sunday Night at the London Palladium* appearance in October of that year. Lennon had evidently heard the story, and the note he handed Bruce simply said: "Would you like to participate?"

Bruce and Matt took another trip to the French capitol in 1964 to see Sammy Davis's show at Paris Olympia.

> Sammy was so showbiz, I loved him and everything he did. I remember being in Paris on one occasion with Matt Monro and a coupe of other guys, and we went to see Sammy's one-man show at the Olympia. Because he was worried that the French audience would not understand him singing in English, he cut the show to the bone – didn't include any parts where he would be speaking for too long – which, sometimes, he did! I had also seen Sammy in some wonderful cabaret appearances in Los Angeles, Las Vegas and Atlantic City, but his performance that night in Paris was superb, the best performance I ever saw him do. — Bruce Forsyth

Michael Holliday & Matt

Booked on the same bill as The Beatles, Shane Fenton and the Fentones and Del Shannon for the Royal Albert Hall's *Swinging Sounds 63,* and hours before he was due to walk on stage, Matt was told not to perform. He'd severed a blood vessel in his throat and the specialist who made the diagnosis of a ruptured vein caused by too much smoking and overstrains told the singer to cut down on his cigarettes. So for the meantime Matt cut down to four or five a day and took to smoking a pipe. Lance Percival took his place in the show.

To console himself during these trying times, Matt invested in a new Ford Galaxie convertible finished in white. It didn't matter to Matt that it was American or that it was an 'in your face' statement, a totally arrogant machine, or that it was twice the width and length of the average saloon, or even that it ate petrol twice as fast as the Jaguar, it was a symbol of his well-earned success and he loved it.

Of course he didn't stay resting very long as commitments were profuse and he didn't want to let anyone down. The Bassey tour wasn't on consecutive nights but spread across the month and he insisted on honouring the contract closing in Cardiff at the end of April. But after that, Mickie put her foot down, got Don to re-arrange the diary and booked them on a trip to Majorca for two weeks.

They stayed in Arenal and soon bumped into Michael Holliday and Adam Faith, who was with Mandy Rice Davis. Matt and Mike got on very well – they were both recording for EMI and although they had waved in the corridors of the studio, they had never had the chance to actually sit down and talk. They spent a lot of time relaxing by the pool talking about the business. Mickie left them to it, exploring the shops and looking for presents for the family. Coming back late in the day she would find the boys in exactly the same position as when she'd left them. Matt found Mike to be a troubled soul, but as the week went by he visibly relaxed and became more animated.

Matt returned to England fully recovered and rushed straight back into meetings with George and Johnnie, as well as his usual run of radio and television appearances. Matt and Mickie had managed to send Bassey a telegram from Spain the week before for her opening at Talk of the Town and were due there themselves on 9 May for Sammy Davis Jr's farewell charity show. Bassey also attended the event, mingling with the celebrities that littered the room from Elizabeth Taylor, Richard Burton and Lionel Bart to Alma Cogan, Dickie Valentine and Leslie Bricusse. Sammy encouraged Matt on stage to sing a number, after which he announced to the audience: "Matt Monro is the best singer there is – I mean the best." Matt was stunned – it was quite an accolade coming from one of show business' greats.

Matt never forgot his performing roots and the revitalisation of the British club scene led to many great nights in the North and seasons on the seaside circuit with British greats like Morecambe & Wise, Bruce Forsyth, Tony Hancock, Jimmy Tarbuck, Tommy Cooper and Dave Allen. His summer season outing this year was Blackpool. Billed as *The Show of Stars 1963*, it featured Morecambe and Wise, Lena Martell, juggling acrobats the Strong Brothers and ventriloquist Daisy May and Saveen.

Matt and Mickie rented a house in Ullswater Road and it didn't take Mickie long to arrange things just so. These seasons involved long periods away from home so she felt it important that they be as comfortable as possible.

> **Nothing against Blackpool, it's just that walk up and down the pier in the gales. It seems to stretch halfway to the Isle of Man. There's no train there, nothing. I used to live in the town but I'd leave at three to park my car and walk down the pier to get to a show at six. As you walk down the pier, the audience is sitting each side of you in chairs. It's like a fashion parade for a quarter of a mile. The longest catwalk in the business. You get to the theatre windswept and soaked. — Matt Monro**

Eric Morecambe, Matt & Ernie Wise judging Miss Blackpool

By the time Matt was packed up for the night, most of the audience were long gone. It was a long walk to the small back street where he was allowed to park his car and the area was not very well lit. Just as he was getting into his vehicle two guys viciously attacked him. Matt managed to close the door on one of the guy's heads and said to the other "Do you want some of this?" The other guy ran off. For all Matt's bravado he didn't stop shaking all night.

Matt quickly established a routine for the summer starting with a brisk swim in the public baths, adding on an extra length each day. His strong point was diving, and as a schoolboy he had won several medals. After breakfast, Matt was off to the golf course with some of the other stars that were appearing in Blackpool for the summer. His greatest golf rival was Eric Morecambe.

> It's marvellous. Every time I tee up Eric sticks his hand under my chin and says "Get out of that". I'm usually laughing so much by the time I make my stroke I miss the ball completely. But I was strongly tempted to give up golf as a bad job the other day. The club where I play is very friendly; some of the members take the game more seriously than I. I was driving and putting like Arnold

Matt, Eric Morecambe & Ernie Wise Blackpool Summer Season

Palmer, well almost, right round the first 16 holes. On the 17th, I bunkered myself under the clubhouse window and it took me six shots to get out. Everybody was watching. When I went in to the clubhouse a couple of the members asked for an introduction, so I told them I was Ernie Wise and sneaked out. — Matt Monro

He arranged to take Mickie out to dinner for her thirtieth birthday together with a few other people from the show. A champagne bottle appeared with an emerald cut diamond hanging around its neck with ribbon. This was the first ring Matt gave his wife other than her wedding ring, which she had paid for anyway.

On a rare Sunday off, Matt and Mickie went to see Nat King Cole's show at the Liverpool Empire. They were invited backstage and the two singers chatted amicably together. Unfortunately, this was the only time the two would meet. There were so many social invitations that it was impossible to attend them all, but there were exceptions made for friends. The couple attended Roy Castle's wedding and nearly missed the show trying to get back in time. It wasn't the driving that was ill timed but the long walk up the pier.

Sue Maull introducing Matt to her father in Blackpool

Sue Maull had come down to Blackpool determined to get the singer's autograph. Meeting the star for the first time, her father quipped, "She has dragged me over one -hundred and eight bloody miles to see you, you had better be good." Sue was so embarrassed she wanted the pier to swallow her up. One of the highlights of the evening was watching a skit involving Matt and Morecambe & Wise who were on stage donning tutus and doing the dance of the Sugar Plum Fairies.

Summer seasons seemed to be a jinx to Matt. He was leaving by the stage door after his show in Blackpool. The weather conditions were atrocious and high winds whipped across the North Pier. Gales swept many Northern seaside resorts, and in several areas ships sheltered in bays away from the rough seas. One of Matt's favourite hats flew off and in trying to retrieve it, he was physically lifted up by the wind and deposited rather harshly in a lateral position – resulting in one broken arm. Unfortunately, he was to injure the other one when several days later in Coventry, whilst forcibly trying to open a window in his dressing room, he pushed rather too hard. The result – the window frame was still jammed but his arm had gone straight through the glass.

Matt Monro fractured his left wrist, hurt his other arm, strained his back and lost a valuable gold watch last night, all for the sake of a hat. As he left the North Pier Theatre after the second performance, his

hat blew off. He tried to catch it but the strong gusts of wind knocked him over twice. It was that second time he really hurt himself. He had a sleepless night and this morning he was taken to Victoria Hospital to get his fractured wrist put in plaster. — *Reuters News Agency*

For all the work Matt was getting, he still wasn't offered the more prestigious television spots. The *Palladium,* the *Royal Variety* or his own television series, all eluded him. His roots were firmly embedded in England and he was deeply hurt every time he lost out to an American entertainer. It started eating at him. It wasn't just paranoia, even the press had noticed.

Of course we know the trouble with Matt Monro. He's just too darned good as a singer. Matt was promised a *Palladium* TV spot during the run of his brilliant 'One Day' single. The date was kept clear. But an American was hustled in at the last moment. On another occasion, he drove through the snow and slush from Newcastle-upon-Tyne to London, merely to stand by in case Frankie Vaughan was unable to make a *Palladium* showing. Everybody seems grateful to Matt, but not grateful enough to slot him in the show immediately afterwards. He hasn't been on for TWO YEARS and this for the man most folks in the business laud as our best male vocalist... Matt has become an international star, but the stark truth is that he's rated higher in other countries than here when it comes to getting the big shows. He could easily make a prosperous living in the States but he feels himself an Englishman and this makes him tolerant, to an extent, of some of the thinly-disguised insults he's been handed by top telly bookers here.
— Peter Jones, *Record Pictorial*

A BONDING SESSION

In the 1960s James Bond was a phenomenon and the impact was felt at box offices all over the world. The sound of Bond is unquestionably the sound of John Barry, the composer responsible for eleven James Bond film soundtracks. However, for the first film, *Dr No*, released in 1962, the producers hired songwriter Monty Norman to compose the incidental music and a title theme that would work for the whole series. Norman flew to the Jamaica location and drew on traditional Jamaican folk music for the recurring 'Underneath the Mango Tree' song. It wasn't what anyone was expecting and editor Peter Hunt suggested John Barry as a replacement. He delivered the perfect sound to fit the film, a sound that would form part of the identity of the Bond franchise, a unique combination of dominant guitar twang with the brass-heavy jazz style of the American pianist Stan Kenton. Barry had originally only been hired to arrange Monty Norman's title theme and expected to see that reflected in the movie, but it seemed that Peter Hunt had loved the score so much that he used it throughout the film. Although Barry challenged the original contract, the producers wouldn't budge on giving him any more money – or indeed that elusive writing credit. They did, however, offer Barry the promise that if the film was successful, and there was a follow-up, they would then contact him with the offer of further work.

With *Dr No*'s success, the producers started work on a follow-up, *From Russia with Love*. They had already commissioned Lionel Bart to write the title song, but hired Barry to score the rest of the film. Barry retained Peter Hunt's idea of weaving the theme throughout the film and brought two other key elements to bear on the piece: the technique of writing orchestral variations on the title theme and the addition of Barry's own 007 theme, an alternative to the main soundtrack. This was a delicate endeavour, as he had to ensure it was distinctly dissimilar from the original, while maintaining some of the uniform traits. Barry's answer was to use a grouping of hard, military-style percussion and brass for the main driving force, while transferring the

Recording Session with George, Matt & John Barry

melody to sweeping high-register strings in the middle. He then used the same energy in the arrangement of Lionel Bart's title song.

When the producers decided they wanted a theme song for every Bond film, they called on Matt to start the tradition. His voice was to feature on the soundtrack of *From Russia With Love*, the first Bond movie to have its own dedicated song.

Johnnie Spence was asked to arrange and produce Matt's version. He recorded the orchestral backing, which required twelve takes, while Matt's vocal – along with an overdub of Johnnie's tack piano – was done a couple of days later in just two takes. The flip side was 'Here and Now', written by John Junkin and Dennis King.

Interestingly, the producers didn't feel Matt's vocals fitted well over the opening titles, so Barry was asked to arrange an instrumental version with his 'Bond' sound. Matt's recording could be heard within the film and also over the closing credits.

We actually saw the movie for the first time in Paris. When Matt's vocal didn't come on at the beginning of the film, I thought they must have taken it out without telling us. Then during the film I heard Matt sing the title track but instead of over the film, it was coming out of a transistor radio very faintly while Bond is lying by the river. It lasted about six seconds. I couldn't believe that was all there was, I was terribly upset. Matt loved the Bond films and was avidly watching the action. He seemed immersed in the movie so I didn't voice my upset,

but knew he must have felt disappointed himself. Then right at the very end at the closing credits his voice filled the cinema and in the space of seconds I went from feeling decidedly dejected to euphoric.
— Mickie Monro

John Barry released the instrumental version as a single backed with the Seven and his orchestra, putting the '007 Theme' on the flip side. The track fared well in the British charts, reaching thirty-nine, whilst Matt's version made it to number twenty, giving him another major hit. It was inevitable that because of the explosive success of the film in the United States, and Matt's association with it, work would come flooding in from that side of the world.

The film was playing to capacity houses throughout Britain, rivalling Cliff Richard's *Summer Holiday* as the top box office attraction of 1963. Although Matt may have made better records, Bond's adventures boosted his latest release in a huge way and earned him another gold disc.

The success of *From Russia with Love* in autumn 1963 established the Bond films as a worldwide hit. Barry would go on to score eleven of the next fourteen Bond films and film music became a common bond between Barry and Monro.

The day after the Bond premiere, Matt travelled to Coventry Theatre to appear in their *Birthday Show* with Bruce Forsyth for the next eight weeks. Also on the bill were international opera singing star Adele Leigh, Yorkshire comedian Freddie Frinton, The Rastellis, a continental team of trampoline artists who scored a big hit with their amazing clown act, and Johnny Hart with his magic show.

Joan Davis managed to blend the mixture into a composite programme lasting nearly three hours with a surprising degree of continuity. Bruce's versatility was endless, laughing and clowning one minute, and then dancing, singing and playing the piano the next. He was barely off the stage and it was a punishing schedule, especially as he was also compering *Sunday Night at the Palladium*. Another member of the cast was Bob West, a vocalist with the Derek Taverner Singers. The team of twelve girl dancers and eight boy singers were probably the busiest of the artists as they had umpteen routines to learn that were scattered throughout the production. It was here that Bob met Matt Monro.

Matt had broken his wrist a few weeks previously in Blackpool and his arm was in a plaster cast, which prevented him from driving. He asked Bob whether he would drive him to London one night after the show as he had to record a broadcast the next morning. Mickie was meeting Matt at the Lotus House Chinese restaurant in Marble

Bob West, Kenny Clayton, Compere & Matt at Quaffers in Stockport

Arch and after dropping off his charge, Bob took the car back to his home in Pimlico.

Over the season the friendship grew. Matt, Mickie and Don discussed the possibility of asking Bob to work for Matt full-time as his road manager. Speaking to his partner Peter about the proposition and having to clear his diary of obligations, Bob finally took the position at the end of the year. Matt recalls this season as some of the happiest days of his show business life, with golf every day (once his cast had come off), great dressing rooms and hot food delivered from the theatre restaurant. Another reason he had for being over the moon was that Mickie had conceived in Blackpool and the baby was due in April 1964.

On 22 November, Matt was watching television in his dressing room when news came in of John F Kennedy's assassination. Although Matt was shocked by the President's death, a decision was made not to tell the audience until after the curtain had come down. Another incident that had upset Matt greatly was the death of Michael Holliday in October that year. The public knew Mike as a relaxed, easygoing entertainer – an impression created by his records and television shows – but this façade concealed an inveterate worrier with a nervous disposition reminiscent of Tony Hancock. He died from a suspected drugs overdose.

Two weeks before Christmas, Matt was booked in Manchester for a week at Mr
Smith's Club. It was here the press announced that Matt would sing all six songs
written for the British heat of the ninth *Eurovision Song Contest*. In the past, different
artists had sung different entries but now the press were speculating that with this
sensational change in format for the national heat, Britain was going all-out to win the
next competition. Matt was proud to be representing his country, and hoped fervently
that nothing would screw it up this time. He celebrated Christmas at home with
Johnnie and Marion. Mickie had held back one of Matt's presents and in front of their
best friends he opened the gift: Craig Douglas' version of 'From Russia with Love'!

Three days after Christmas Matt went into the BBC Studio to appear on *Juke Box
Jury*, which was presented as a live show. The panel consisted of Matt, Polly Elwes and
Jimmy Saville, with David Jacobs in the chair. The audience were seated at 5.45pm
when the producer introduced the host and David did a 'warm up' to relax both the
audience and himself. Once David was behind his desk the show started and his main
task was in asking the panel to cast their vote on whether a disc was a 'hit' or a 'miss'.

As soon as Matt came out of the studios he had to hotfoot it to the NCO Club in
South Ruislip for a late show. He'd only been there ten minutes when he received a
phone call from his sister Alice. He knew something was wrong as she would never
have rung him when he was working without due cause. The news was devastating
– his mother, who had been the picture of health the last time he'd seen her, had died
suddenly of a brain lesion. There had been no warning, no chance to say goodbye
and now he had to perform within minutes of hearing the tragic news. He knew his
mother would have wanted it that way – she had been very proud of her little boy.
Matt was shocked at the speed with which his mother was taken; there was no way
of knowing that morning that a few hours later his life would feel so much emptier.
He was bereft. The funeral was during the first week of the New Year, the same day
that Matt opened at the Odeon Leicester Square with Shirley Bassey and John Barry
and his Orchestra. It was the hardest show of his life, especially as one of the songs in
his repertoire was 'For Mama'.

Since 'From Russia with Love', John Barry had left EMI. Even though the record
company did acknowledge his arranging talents on the song and promote him to A&R
Director, he wasn't getting what he really wanted, the recognition and prestige that
came with having a named credit for his role. With his contract up for renewal he was
ready to re-negotiate, but EMI let it expire. John continued working with the Seven
until an offer came in – from Matt's old sparring partner at Ember Records, Jeff
Kruger. Ember Records offered John a proposal he couldn't refuse – complete

freedom to produce the records he wanted, an increase in salary plus expenses, a producer's royalty and that elusive producer credit. Barry had already produced two projects for the label and for the third release he called on Johnnie Spence to arrange and conduct an album of bebop jazz by singer Annie Ross. Now firmly entrenched in the job, John decided to broaden his options and set about establishing Topline Artists, his own management agency, with the help of two partners. Running the agency on a day-to-day basis was Tony Lewis, an obsessive music fan who knew everything and everyone in the business. While running the record company and writing Bond scores, Barry also carried on touring and working as musical director for other artists. Capitalising on the success of the Bond records, he agreed to go on the road with Monro and Bassey. He played the opening half of the bill with his own orchestra, finishing with the 'James Bond Theme', and then accompanied Bassey and Monro for the headlining second half.

John lived a sort of Bond-esque lifestyle himself. A handsome guy, he surrounded himself with a bevy of beautiful girls, cruised the clubs of London and ensconced himself in an enviable apartment. Favourites on the social circuit were Alvaro's, Terrazza or the Ad Lib Club. These havens for the in-crowd were popular because they were the only places open after the curtain came down in London's theatre district. Another main hang out was the Pickwick Club in Great Newport Street. It was opened by Wolf Mankowitz, Leslie Bricusse and Sammy Davis Jr, and was available to members only. Press photographers were strictly forbidden, so it became an immediate retreat for stars eager to escape the tabloid headlines. Barry's office was across the road, so he became a permanent fixture.

If something other than a club atmosphere was required then you could always pop into Stafford Court, Alma Cogan's flat in Kensington High Street. She knew and worked with everyone, being a notable star herself, and every Saturday she adopted an 'open house' policy. Stars from all the shows headed there after the theatres came out. Although Matt was not a habitual visitor, he did frequent most of the establishments from time to time, favouring the Lotus House, a huge, dimly lit Chinese restaurant in Edgware Road owned by Johnnie Koon.

While we were at the Talk of the Town and after the show we often went to the Lotus House, which was one of our favourites. Johnnie Koon, who was a lovely mate, ran it, and one evening I was there with Norma, Mickie and Matt. Matt was talking about how many years he had spent in Hong Kong and explained that if you want to tell the waiter you've had a good meal and good food, just say "Foykay Mai

Marion & Johnnie's Wedding

Dun'ah", so I'm rehearsing this through the rest of the meal and once they start clearing away the plates I go "Foykay Mai Dun'ah". The waiter came back with the bill and I had to pay for the whole thing. The English translation of course was "Waiter, my bill please" in Chinese, but that's Matt, I loved him for that. He just sat there and said "Thank you Kenny my son, thank you". — Kenny Clayton

On 5 January 1964, the day after the Bassey and Barry show, Matt and Mickie arrived at St Mary's Church in South Kensington to witness the marriage of their dear friends, Marion Horton and Johnnie Spence. Matt was best man and his daughter, four-year-old Michele, was chosen as bridesmaid. It was a beautiful ceremony and several days later the newlyweds took up residence in Ewell, Epsom, just minutes from Matt and Mickie. It would be the perfect arrangement for the girls; having each other's company would ease their loneliness when the boys were away on tour.

Matt left for Australia on 10 January, whilst Johnnie stayed behind to work on the *Tommy Steele Show*. Matt was following singer Frank Ifield in to the Chevron Hilton Hotel in Sydney for a three-week run, where he was booked for two shows a day, six days a week. Although that didn't faze him, having no clothes did – the airline seemed to have misplaced his luggage and was having a hard time locating it.

Don rang Quantas about your luggage and had a big row, telling them how annoyed you were. They said it had gone on the plane after yours. This went via God knows but should be in Sydney now. You're still number 36 in the charts and this is the eleventh week in the hit parade. — Letter from Mickie to Chevron Hotel, Sydney, Australia

Matt thought Sydney one of the most beautiful places he'd ever visited. The bays were spectacular, the natives friendly, and the food was good. Some of their clubs were fantastic – like small villages, with bowling alleys, restaurants, cinemas and squash and badminton courts.

I went out to the SS Oronsay today before she sailed with Kathy and Alan, Tony Cooper and Gerry Gibson. We had a few jugs while we were there and sort of carried on when we got back to the hotel. So I am now a little drunk and it's now 2.30 in the morning. Went out last night with Dave Allen and a few other people and really had a ball. We went to a great restaurant called the Bistro – it was the 'in' place for show business people, models and such like. On Sunday been invited to a Maori Party by the Maoriti Five where they cook food in the ground. Looking forward to that like mad! — Matt Monro, Letter from Chevron Hotel, Sydney, Australia

Dave Allen had a flat at Potts Point, one of the classier suburbs of inner Sydney, since he spent long periods of time in Australia. Having flown back in January, he was due to be there for eleven months filming a television series for Channel Nine, *Tonight With Dave Allen*, before returning to England in December. Matt went out with Dave most days. The comic's routine was strict; he'd have lunch every day with just one beer, and the rest of the afternoon was spent reading every newspaper and local gazette in preparation for his show. Once filming was finished, he would always meet up with Matt or pop over to the Chevron. Sport was one of the comic's great passions and he always laid a wager on the big events. He loved to gamble, but was hopeless at picking winners and usually lost whatever money he staked. Matt and Dave often had silly wagers between them – they couldn't help themselves. They bet on how long it would take an ice cube to melt or what colour socks the next person who walked in the club would be wearing, or how many times they could use the word 'fish' when ordering a round of drinks. It might have been completely ridiculous, but they thought it was hilarious.

Matt & Dave Allen

Dave had just interviewed a young actress, Judith Stott, on his show. The young comic, miles away from home, was smitten. She was a divorcee who had a son from her previous marriage and Dave pursued her. Following a whirlwind romance they were married on 9 March, just three months after their first meeting.

The night before his opening, Matt went to see Frank Ifield's closing show. In Frank's dressing room after the performance Matt was introduced to John Ashby, a man who eleven years later would find himself responsible for the singer's diary.

Just before Matt's return to England, Mickie rang to tell him that he had retained his title as Best Male Singer in the *Melody Maker* Jazz Poll, with a ten per cent lead over George Melly. It surprised a lot of people when Matt won the title first time around, but they were even more surprised when he held onto it.

> **Matt's jazz influences are clear; take 'Lulu's Back in Town' on The Rare Monro, which sticks very closely to Mel Torme's arrangement. Whilst he still interprets the song in his own way, he never strays too far from the composer's intentions. 'Birth of the Blues' – now that's a jazz performance. I think calling Matt a ballad singer is putting him in a specific box, which he really didn't deserve to be in. He was far more flexible than that. He could swing as well or better than many of his contemporaries. — Richard Moore, sound engineer**

Song Contests

Following the 1962 *Eurovision Song Contest*, the BBC had been stung by criticism for being too heavily influenced by record company interests. Aware of the difficulties involved in attracting the best songwriters and singers to the competition, they decided to change tactics. In the past, the BBC had worked in conjunction with the Music Publishers' Association and the record industry, and the year before it had invited seven leading songwriters to write seven songs, which were then performed by different artists. On that occasion they had placed the onus on the songwriters, allowing them to choose their own singers, but this approach was fraught with problems.

In 1964 the BBC had decided to implement a different system. Instead of an open final, they would first select the singer to represent the United Kingdom and then invite songwriters to submit songs. They felt that by offering a singer a guaranteed place in the Eurovision Song Contest, it would be easier to secure a top name to take part. Their choice was Matt Monro. He'd been working for the BBC for seven years, ever since his first television appearance with the Show Band back in 1957 and wasn't a stranger to the song contest process. Even though he'd lost out to Mike Preston in ITV's *British Song Contest*, it was 'My Kind of Girl' that had climbed the charts, giving him his second top five hit, leaving the winning entry 'Marry Me' trailing behind in the number 14 spot.

Matt was eager to perform in the contest, having lost out a few years before due to mismanagement. In January 1964, Matt signed the paperwork guaranteeing him a total of four-hundred and fifty guineas plus expenses for both *ASFE* (*A Song for Europe*) and the *ESC* (*Eurovision Song Contest*). He was allowed to select his preferred writers from a list supplied by the Songwriter's Guild of Great Britain and invited each to submit a new number for him to sing.

THE SONGS AND SONGWRITERS

'Choose' 02'33"- Lyricist: Lionel Bart - Composer: Lionel Bart - Arranger: Johnny Pearson - Publisher: Apollo Music

Lionel Bart had already scored several successful musicals including *Blitz* and *Oliver* and written hits for Shirley Bassey, Cliff Richard and Adam Faith. Matt was familiar with Bart's work, having recorded 'As Long as I'm Singing' and the recently penned Bond theme 'From Russia With Love'. In previous years, Bart had turned down the offer of submission from the BBC, but Matt's involvement made it tempting, and so he decided to throw caution to the wind.

'It's Funny How You Know' 02'22" – Lyricist: Norman Newell – Composer: Philip Green – Arranger: Geoff Love – Publisher: Mutual Music (Record Retailer lists the publisher as Ardmore and Beechwood)

Norman Newell began his career selling sheet music, before eventually joining EMI and becoming A&R manager for Nina & Frederik, Danny Williams and Russ Conway. Newell was also head of the Columbia label for years working with Russ Conway, Petula Clark, Marlene Dietrich, Gracie Fields, Geoff Love, Noël Coward, Shirley Bassey and the Beverley Sisters, before leaving EMI in the mid-1960s to become a freelance producer and focus on his writing career. He wrote the lyrics to Matt's hit 'Portrait of My Love', which in 1999 received its two millionth airplay and won both an Ivor Novello Award and the American BMI Award. He'd also co-written Matt's first recording for Decca, 'Ev'rybody Falls in Love With Someone'. His career honours included a Grammy, an Emmy, three Ivor Novello Awards, and six British Music Industry Awards.

The song's composer Philip Green won a scholarship at the tender age of thirteen to London's Trinity College of Music. Upon graduating, he became London's youngest West End conductor at the Prince of Wales Theatre. Working for EMI, he directed and played piano and harpsichord on 78s with many leading bands. During the Second World War, he made several recordings for Decca and went on to write the scores for over 200 films. Such was his prestige in the British film industry that Green was eventually appointed resident musical director of the Rank Organisation.

'I Love the Little Things' 02'23" - Lyricist: Tony Hatch - Composer: Tony Hatch - Arranger: Johnny Scott - Publisher: Welbeck Music

Tony Hatch was educated at the London Choir School and was Head Chorister at All Souls, Langham Place for four years. After starting work in a music publisher's office, he joined Top Rank Records as assistant recording manager and since 1960 had been recording for Pye. His first international hit was 'Look For a Star' sung by Gary Mills, which reached the Top 10 in the charts. One of his most recent successes had come with The Searchers' recording of 'Sugar And Spice'. He would shortly go on to produce a string of hits with Petula Clark, including 'Downtown' and 'Don't Sleep In The Subway'.

Seven years after first meeting Matt at the Aeolian Studios, Tony had the opportunity to write a song for him to sing in the contest. He says, "I knew that I was writing for Matt's voice but I had to follow the guidelines and they wanted something bright with an instantly catchy hook. So, I thought, put the hook right up front."

'I've Got the Moon on My Side' 2'47" – Lyricist: Mitch Murray – Composer: Mitch Murray – Arranger: Les Reed – Publisher: Robbins Music

Mitch Murray had only started writing popular songs a couple of years previously. However, during the year leading up to the contest, his songs 'How Do You Do It' and 'I Like It' had both been number one hits for Gerry and The Pacemakers. Murray also penned the Freddie and The Dreamers' hits 'I'm Telling You Now' and 'You Were Made For Me', which reached numbers two and three respectively. 'I'm Telling You Now' also reached the number one spot in America in 1965.

'Ten Out of Ten' 02'54" – Lyricist: Leslie Bricusse – Composer: Leslie Bricusse – Arranger: Johnny Scott – Publisher: Essex Music

Former Cambridge Footlights president Leslie Bricusse had contributed to the musicals *Stop The World I Want To Get Off* and *Pickwick*. He'd also had hits with 'What Kind Of Fool Am I?' and the previously mentioned 'My Kind Of Girl'. He later contributed to the scores of a number of well-known films including *Doctor Dolittle*, *Scrooge*, *Willy Wonka and the Chocolate Factory*, *Victor/Victoria*, *Home Alone* and *Hook*, all of which received Oscar nominations, with *Doctor Dolittle* winning the award for Best Song and *Victor/Victoria* winning for Best Music Score. Bricusse's best-known song is probably 'Goldfinger' from the Bond film of the same name. The song he submitted for this contest was originally recorded by Eden Kane in 1962, although it was not released until 1964.

'Beautiful Beautiful' 03'14" – Lyricist: Hal Shaper – Composer: Hal Shaper – Arranger: Les Reed – Publisher: Robbins Music

Hal Shaper wrote songs that were recorded by artists such as Joan Regan, Petula Clark, The Brook Brothers, Malcolm Vaughan, Cilla Black and Diana Dors. By the 1960s, he had already won an Ivor Novello Award. He wrote Monro's hit 'Softly As I Leave You', the financial success of which had enabled him to set up his own publishing company, Sparta Music. Headliners such as Elvis Presley, Shirley Bassey, Bing Crosby, Barbra Streisand, Morrissey and Frank Sinatra have all recorded Shaper's songs.

The Broadcast: A Song For Europe
Friday 7 February 1964 – 9.25-10.00pm – BBC1

Up until 1960, the British elimination heats were known as the *Festival of British Popular Song*. In 1961, it was renamed *A Song For Europe*, and for the next three years various famous names competed, sponsored by their respective record companies, with regional juries deciding the winner. From 1964 until 1975, the Head of BBC Light Entertainment selected one artist or group to perform all of the songs, with the viewing public deciding the winner by a postal vote. These performances were showcased on the major television variety shows of the day. In 1976, the BBC decided to return to the previous format of different artists for each song judged by the regional jury system. In 1988, the UK entry was decided by a viewer's telephone vote, a practice that continues to this day.

David Jacobs was the BBC's choice to compère the show in 1964, and to commentate the ESC in Copenhagen. Mike Samms was also contracted to provide eight backing singers for SFE and although not featured in shot they provided the chorus on five of the songs with the exception of *Ten out of Ten*.

Rehearsals took place on Tuesday and Wednesday and then on Thursday in the Television Theatre, Shepherd's Bush, from where the show was broadcast live the following night. Matt was required to attend rehearsals on all three days, as well as a photo shoot on Thursday afternoon, appearing on the cover of *The Radio Times* that same week. Each song was allocated a forty-minute slot, after which the cast and crew broke for dinner, returning at 8.00pm for a two-hour camera rehearsal of all six songs. Although Matt was needed at this time, the orchestra and choir were absent and the tracks were played from a record instead.

Matt wasn't required at the camera rehearsal scheduled for the Friday morning, although David Jacobs was needed in the afternoon for the last of the camera dry-runs. The all-important scoreboard was tested twice during the day and with everything finally set to go the audience were seated by 9.15pm, when the producer Harry Carlisle took them through a warm-up routine before the actual transmission.

The show started with a fifteen second fanfare, consisting of a five second rising sequence followed by a ten second tremolo, written by Dennis Wilson. With the fanfare playing, a caption with *A SONG FOR EUROPE* appeared on the screen, and producer Harry Carlisle introduced the show and the master of ceremonies. David Jacobs made his entrance during the *Song For Europe* theme written by Alan Bristow and introduced Matt, saying there was nobody who could do the job of singing all six songs better than him.

The sixteen regional juries were each made up of twelve members of the public. So as not to rush the judges, the producers Harry Carlisle and Yvonne Littlewood arranged for them to hear each song three times before transmission. David Jacobs then asked each jury in turn for their scores and number of votes each song had received.

Unfortunately there were delays due to problems with the scoreboard, which often showed the wrong marks but with the voting finally over and the scores verified, 'I

Love the Little Things' by Tony Hatch was declared the overall winner. Matt reprised the winning song at the end of the show and once the transmission was over, he attended a photo call and press conference with one very bemused composer. Hatch still couldn't believe that he had won when interviewed ten minutes after the results were announced.

> Matt's performance was spot-on and it was a wonderful moment for me when the National Judging Panels chose the song as our Eurovision entry. — Tony Hatch

The show received twenty-one percent of the viewing figures, which accounted for approximately 10.4 million viewers. The concept of one singer performing all the chosen songs was created so the judges couldn't be influenced by the personality of the singer and would concentrate on the song itself. The BBC's viewing panel approved of the format change and agreed it was the fairest way of presenting the songs. However, they did find that it lacked entertainment value visually. Matt Monro was well-liked as a singer, and many felt that he coped well with a succession of unfamiliar songs, although the fact that they were so similar was a definite drawback for some viewers. While some had thought 'I Love the Little Things' was the obvious winner, others were of the opinion that despite the calibre of the songwriters it was just the best of a mediocre bunch.

Choose	16 points	4th
It's Funny How You Know	11 points	6th
I Love the Little Things	87 points	1st
I've Got the Moon on My Side	43 points	2nd
Ten out of Ten	15 points	5th
Beautiful Beautiful	20 points	3rd

> Sometimes I wish I'd never entered the contest. People in the singing profession criticised the choice of the six composers... I think the contest is something you should only do once in your career. It was very hard work. I recorded all the songs for the British heat before I went on a tour of Australia. By the time I came back I had forgotten the songs. — Matt Monro

THE RECORD

An EP of all six songs, simply entitled *A Song For Europe*, was released shortly after ASFE aired. The EMI factory was put on standby to rush release the winning single, which hit the shops during the last week of February 1964. *Record Retailer* described it as "beautifully put together... a lighter, catchier song than most of Matt's releases".

Unsurprisingly, the single failed to chart, largely due to it being released after the *Song For Europe* EP. The six track extended play had sold well, reaching No. 16 in the EP charts, so few people were inclined to buy the seven-inch version as well.

A row broke out over Matt's six shillings and six pennies record released by EMI over the coupling of the tracks. Critic Bernard Braden maintained that the rightful B-side should have been the Mitch Murray runner-up song 'I've Got The Moon on My Side', as had previously been announced by the press. Instead the track chosen was 'It's Funny How You Know', written by EMI recording manager Norman Newell and Phil Green. This meant that the composer's royalties for the B-side went to the men whose song came bottom in the competition. It was one of the most heated debates in the music business for many years, with much of the criticism aimed at Norman Newell. The implication was that the real reason his song was chosen over the runner-up was because of his connection with EMI.

In reaction to this Tom Sloan, head of BBC TV Light Entertainment, told the *NME*: "After striving for years to help try and increase the standard of British song writing by means of this competition, I very much regret EMI's action and have told them so. This type of behaviour in my view can only lead to a situation where no leading composer will take part in such a competition in the future." Leslie Bricusse also hit out at the record company saying: "What EMI has done is costing Mitch money and giving Norman Newell a free ride on the back of a song that's a pre-sold hit." Even Matt was disgusted, believing it to be an insult to both Mitch Murray and the song writing profession.

Norman was asked by *NME* about the implication that he frequently put his own compositions on the B-sides of records to the exclusion of other writers. Newell hit back, denying he excluded others and saying that he was all in favour of giving British composers every opportunity. So why wasn't Mitch Murray's song on the B-side of Matt's latest release? Newell stated: "It's not up to me to answer that. It wasn't my decision. I had absolutely nothing to do with it. I can only say that I know of no guarantees whereby the runner-up was automatically assured of the B-side."

In fact Newell had nothing to do with the decision, which was taken by EMI Chairman Sir Joseph Lockwood. He told the *NME*: "...the BBC is not necessarily the best judge of the tunes we should release on our records. I heard 'It's Funny How

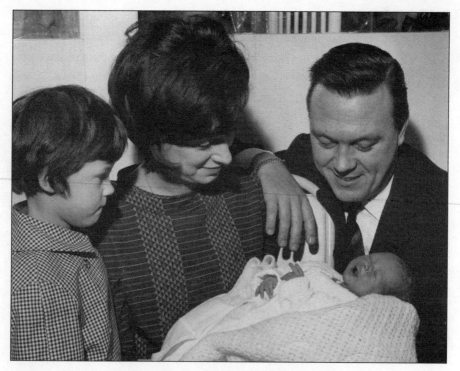

Michele, Mickie & Matt with new addition to the family

You Know' before the contest and chose it, with the song that won, as the best two saleable songs. The fact that it was voted last has no bearing on our decision to issue it. If we chose discs according to voting panels like *Juke Box Jury*, we would be bankrupt in no time."

THE INTERIM

Matt was delighted with the success of the contest and thought the song would do well. All he could do now was wait for Copenhagen. In the interim, he had a barrage of radio, television and publicity appearances, as well as a tour of one-nighters for agent Billy Forest.

While Mickie was in the final trimester of her pregnancy, Matt arranged to have a whole month free, two weeks before and two weeks after the birth, so that he would be sure of being with his wife and helping out with the new arrival. The baby decided differently and on the 21 February Matt's third child was born – a month prematurely. The first Matt heard of it was when he walked into a Bristol theatre for an evening performance to be met with the words: "You've got a son," which sent him rushing to the phone.

Weighing five pounds twelve ounce, the baby seemed healthy, but within a week he wasn't taking his food properly and his weight plummeted. Matt called the doctor and within hours his wife and son were rushed by ambulance to the hospital. The baby was immediately incubated and a specialist called. A constriction was found and the concern was that it might have prevented enough oxygen from getting to the brain. Test results confirmed there was no lasting damage, but it was three long weeks before the medical staff felt the infant could safely be discharged. Understandably, Matt and Mickie were nervous about leaving the safety of the hospital, but within days their fears eased and with things finally settled they decided on the boy's name – Matthew. A few weeks later the newborn developed eczema and had to go back into hospital, and it wasn't until the middle of April that he eventually came home for good.

Congratulations, heard you had a little man in your bed last night.
— Telegram from Eric Morecambe

Feeling confident that all was well with his family, Matt left on 24 February for his week's engagement at Mr Smith's Club in Manchester with Bob West now officially ensconced in his employment as road manager. Bob was so good for Matt. Whatever was asked of him he did without question, pre-empting Matt's every need. The luggage was taken to each dressing room, dress suits hung and shoes polished. He arranged backstage passes, took phone calls, collected the fan mail, arranged the hospitality in the dressing room and fended off unwanted press attention. He diarised live radio interviews whilst on the road, got the car valeted, drove when Matt was tired and, above all, was great company. When he finally left Matt four years later to pursue other ambitions, Matt never re-advertised the position. He said no one would ever be able to live up to Bob's legacy.

Another appearance on *Big Night Out* with Mike and Bernie Winters, the recording of the *Billy Cotton Show* and a promotional tour of the Netherlands, Germany and Belgium were all completed in the following weeks. However, Matt had to decline an offer to co-star with comedian Mort Sahl at New York's famous Copacabana nightclub due to his Eurovision commitments.

On 15 March, Matt headed to Abbey Road to record a new single and several tracks for the *From Hollywood with Love* album. With ten titles to record, the studio was booked for two consecutive days. George hired Buddy Bregman to write a few arrangements, even though technically, he was under contract to the BBC as a producer and director and wasn't allowed to work anywhere else. It was only because

Bruce Forsyth and matt Monro, Heathrow Airport en route to Eurovision

of George's association with The Beatles that David Attenborough, head of BBC2 at the time, approved the project. Buddy arranged and conducted four of the songs on the session, including 'Charade', ' The Second Time Around', 'The Green Leaves of Summer' and 'Around the World'.

> We met for ten minutes, ran over the songs and a few days later I came back to conduct my charts and it was GREAT. 'Second Time Around' is one of my favourite arrangements ever and 'Charade' has some of my best string work. I had forgotten how great they were and that my arranging and the music still hold up after all these years. Kenny Claire was spectacular on drums. — Buddy Bregman

Instead of flying out to Copenhagen as planned, Matt was recovering from a road accident after his white Ford Galaxie was involved in a collision. Although not badly hurt, he suffered from shock, and so was unable to use the flight tickets issued for 17 March. Fortunately Matt flew out only one day later than planned, and was confident that he would still have enough time to prepare.

The Eurovision Song Contest
21 March 1964 — 9.00-10.35pm — BBC1

The Eurovision Song Contest has been broadcast every year since its inauguration in Lugano, Switzerland. It was the brainchild of Frenchman Marcel Bezencon who, while working for the European Broadcasting Union (EBU), thought that a song festival could unite the nations of Europe, by transmitting one television programme simultaneously to all the countries in the union. In 1964, the Contest was held in Copenhagen, the city of the previous year's winners Grethe and Jørgen Ingmann. The beautiful concert hall in the Tivoli Gardens was the perfect venue for the most spectacular event in the pop music world calendar.

A large British contingent accompanied Matt to Denmark, including BBC TV Head of Light Entertainment, Tom Sloan, conductor Harry Rabinowitz, BBC Light Head of Music Kenneth Haines, BBC's Gramophone Department Chief Anna Instone, music publisher Don Agnes, producers Yvonne Littlewood and Harry Carlisle, the editor of *NME* Andy Gray, as well as David Jacobs, George Martin and Don Black. The mood was buoyant and optimistic.

For the live broadcast to run smoothly, the Contest required each performer to have perfected their act before the start of the show. In addition to rehearsals in his or her homeland, every participant was given the opportunity to rehearse on the stage in the Eurovision auditorium.

Rules specified that live singing and accompaniment were mandatory, and the host country was obligated to provide a full orchestra for each participant's use. This rule stayed in place until 1973, when pre-recorded backing tracks were allowed for the first time, though whatever instruments were present on a backing track had to be visible on stage to give a feeling of authenticity. This rule changed in 1997, and two years later the host country was released from having to provide an orchestra.

> **No idiot cards or other memory-aids are allowed so should I forget the words I'll have to fit in others. I have no special method of learning, just constant repetition. — Matt Monro**

Each song could be no longer than three minutes, although the rule wasn't put in place until after the first contest, which also allowed any number of performers on stage singing in any language. In later years, the rules enforced a maximum of two singers per entry who were required to sing in one of the recognised official languages of the competing nations. That restriction was lifted in 1973 when performers had the freedom to sing in any language of their choosing. Another important rule is that prior to submission to the national heat, each song must not have been published, recorded or performed.

Each participating broadcaster would elect a Head of Delegation, whose job it was to synchronise the movements of the participants, and who acted as that country's spokesperson to the EBU in Copenhagen. Members of the delegations included performers, lyricists, composers, official press officers and if required, a conductor. A commentator was also present if needed: each broadcaster could supply their own commentary for their television and or radio feed, to be broadcast in each country. The rules dictated that each participating broadcaster had to air the show in its entirety, including each country's performance, voting and reprise.

Three dress rehearsals were held over the days before the live transmission, after which the delegates met with the show's artistic director in the video viewing room to watch back their rehearsal performance, discuss camera angles, lighting and any choreography issues.

Lastly, there was the matter of the media. All questions and answers transcribed from each country's press conference were handed out to all journalists so they could go to print before their deadline. Business concluded, each delegation was invited to a party that was traditionally given on the Monday before the event by the Mayor, officially acknowledging that Eurovision has come to the city. A Eurovision-themed nightclub called Euroclub was also held each night of the week, to which all delegations were invited.

The UK wasn't the only country sending a top recording star. Annette Gronloh from Holland, Arne Bendiksen from Norway, and Anita Traversi from Switzerland were all chart toppers in their native lands.

Sixteen nations came to Copenhagen to compete on Saturday 21 March 1964, although there was one change to the final line-up. Industrial action by the Musician's Union meant that Sweden was unable to compete. Portugal, a newcomer to the competition, took their place.

Once all the performances were over, and the points calculated, the presenter called upon each voting country in turn and invited them to announce the results of their vote. The announcements were made over telephone lines, with the audio piped into the concert hall and broadcast across European radio and television airwaves. The points were then displayed on a scoreboard on the side of the stage.

Presentation Award for Eurovision Song Contest

In 1988, as technology progressed, the outmoded system was superseded by an electronic display which could be viewed on the television screen.

Mickie took baby Matthew's carrycot into the office with her to watch the programme, thinking it would bring Matt luck. Michele, who was one of her father's most faithful fans, sat for several minutes staring suspiciously at the screen. She approached it, peered closely into Matt's face, heaved a sigh of disgust and stamped off to find something that made more sense to her.

Matt's uniform quality, range and selfless performance gave the song an equal chance of winning but despite his excellent presentation he finished a distant second place. The winner of the 1964 Eurovision Contest was the youngest contestant, sixteen year-old Gigliola Cinquetti representing Italy with the song 'Non Ho L'Eta'.

Matt did a terrific job in Copenhagen and I think we were all a bit disappointed to be beaten into second place. — Tony Hatch

The after-show parties were crammed with delegations either celebrating their success or commiserating the fact they would be going home without the trophy. The show had been watched by 24% of the UK's population. Overall, it was thought the songs were poor in quality and that Cinquetti's performance – rather than the song itself – had influenced the juries.

Matt didn't agree. On the morning of the competition, the artists had heard one another's songs for the first time, and they all felt that the Italian girl would win.

THE AFTERMATH

The Evening News correspondent James Green was of the opinion that Matt had done as much as he could with the British song, and Andy Gray representing *NME* wrote that the contest had produced "no great tune" but was nevertheless exciting to watch. He felt the contest was important as a way of bringing together singers, conductors, composers and television executives from all over Europe, leading to an exchange of ideas.

Regretfully, no archival film exists of the recording, the only one missing apart from the inaugural contest. As well as the historic loss of the 1964 performance this was the first and only broadcast to be interrupted by a protestor, who had been hiding backstage as a stagehand. The camera only captured a few moments of the demonstration before the director cut to a shot of the scoreboard.

Matt stormed into the airport in London on the 23 March. He had an aircraft-sized bone to pick with British European Airways. Not only should he have flown home the day before with a four-strong BBC party, but he had also missed an engagement the previous night. They had all travelled to Kastrup Airport to check-in for the BEA flight to London the day before, arriving forty-five minutes before departure time. With their tickets accepted they went through customs, but at the aircraft gate both Matt and Tom Sloan were stopped by a BEA staff member and told that they couldn't travel on the flight as it had been overbooked. The airline's official statement was that they understood there was a breakdown in the electronic flight check-in system at Copenhagen and were investigating the matter. In the interim, they put the stranded passengers up at a local hotel for the night, but not their luggage – that had left without them.

> **What really crowned it was that Harry Rabinowitz, their musical director, offered to stand down and let me have his seat. In the space of time it took me to turn around and get my ticket from a bag the seat had been given to someone else. — Matt Monro**

When the party finally flew home in a Scandinavian Caravelle, they found that BEA had laid on VIP facilities. They were escorted to an empty customs channel where their baggage was waiting and cars were laid on to take them all home.

Song Contest photo session

A MATTER OF ASSOCIATION

The song that Matt really fancied from the 1964 *Eurovision Song Contest* was the Austrian entry 'Warum nur Warum' by Udo Jürgens. That it didn't score well didn't deter Matt; he felt the tune was a winner and all it needed was some decent English lyrics. Udo was a hugely popular composer in Austria. He'd sit at the piano and sing wonderful, melodic, Jewish-gypsy tunes that appealed to Matt.

He had first met the composer in July of 1960 when he was competing in the six-nation contest at Knokke-le-Zoute. Back then Udo was officially writing for Germany, but he had now just written the Austrian entry for the latest Eurovision contest. Matt asked Udo if he could take the song back with him and have an English lyric written for the score. He asked several people to attempt the project, including Hal Shaper – who had previously translated 'Softly' from the Italian song 'Piano'. He submitted a lyric but Matt didn't like it at all. "It had a literal translation; it didn't have the impact that I thought the melody should have so I got Don to attempt it." Don had already dabbled in song writing and the two sat down to discuss the project together.

In the interim, Matt had a regular roster of commitments, this time preparing for the opening on 27 March at the London Palladium of a Vic Lewis production called *A Song for Europe* with Kathy Kirby, Bob Monkhouse and Bob Miller and his Millermen. Before signing the contracts for this show, Leslie Grade had told Bob Monkhouse that he would be top of the bill. Grade brought out the proof of the boarding and Matt was on the left and Bob on the right. Bob said to Matt, "that makes you top of the bill". Matt replied, "not to Arabs".

As a singer, he was the ultimate professional, commanding respect amongst his peers, and offstage – always a gentleman.
— Kathy Kirby

Bob Monkhouse & Matt

Matt loved Bob; their sense of humour was very similar, although Monkhouse wasn't averse to borrowing other comic's gags and punch lines, having little conscience when it came to appropriating other performers' material. The lifting of comedy material was an accepted and recognised facet of the vaudeville and variety circuit. That didn't mean Bob wasn't funny in his own right, he certainly was. The way he worked an audience, editing the act on the balls of his feet, cutting a piece of material, adding a line or throwing in an ad-lib that might never be used again was masterful. He sat ensconced in his own private world scribbling away in a little writing book he carried everywhere, conducting his own research whether in hotels, clubs, showrooms or simply watching television in his room. This was blatantly in evidence one night in Miami when Matt and the family took Bob and Jackie to see the stand-up Woody Woodbury, who was working at a local club. Bob copied down most of Woody's act.

Matt and Bob became great friends, they just clicked and they were always delighted to find themselves booked on the same bill. Bob thought Matt to be a great talent and was forever complimenting him on his performance because he knew all too well that however good other people perceive you to be, there were always moments of self-doubt and Matt was no exception.

We were appearing at the Palladium and Matt was top of the bill. I was first half closing and compère. Matt had a knack for asking you things out of a clear blue sky that were always unanswerable. I knocked on the No 1 dressing room door, Matt beckoned me in and said, "Only what do you think, should I make records because I'm listening to one I just made and it sounds tinny, my voice sounds tinny, is it tinny?" The singer really wanted me to answer him and if I had agreed with him I swear Matt would have taken me seriously. Matt was quite distraught but I pointed out to him that he had balanced a whole load of things on top of the record player including two tin ashtrays so they were rattling and the disc had a sibilant tone. I removed the various items to which Matt said, "Oh yes that's better, it's rather good isn't it." — Bob Monkhouse

On 28 March, the night after their appearance at the London Palladium, Matt and Bob were booked for a week in the Wimbledon Theatre's show *Easter Parade* with Russ Shepherd accompanying the singer. It seemed that Matt's accident-prone nature rubbed off on anyone keeping his company. On the way to the venue, Russ insisted on driving across a roundabout instead of around it, and as the underbelly of the car struck the central island he had to slam down on his brakes to control the vehicle. He carried on to the gig not realising he had just broken his ankle. It was unfortunate, as he'd only recently recovered from a head injury, which had happened when Matt and Johnnie were rehearsing for the *Song For Europe* production – Russ had popped in for drinks. Later that evening, Marion arrived to pick up her husband, who then took over the driver's seat. Russ stuck his head through the open car window to say a further goodnight when Johnnie inadvertently leant on the button that controlled the electric windows, accidentally trapping Russ' head in the window frame.

Monkhouse was brilliant in a live show and completely different from his clean-cut television persona. In Wimbledon, he acted as a compère of sorts and had three long spots to himself. He was fast-talking and a bright and breezy teller of sophisticated stories, his dimples and excessive smiling vanishing only momentarily as he awaited a double entendre or sly innuendo to sink in. Equipped with a smattering of saucy stories, he told all with the slickness and polish of an expert.

Mickie was waiting in Matt's dressing room while he was on stage. Bob came in for a chat, as he often did, when suddenly Mickie took ill and, fearing she might pass out, Bob put his arm around her to support her tiny frame. Matt walked in and totally misread the situation. His body stiffened and just for a second looked as if he might strike the comic. Matt soon understood the reality of the situation when Mickie collapsed, prompting producer Arthur Lane to call an ambulance. She was taken straight to hospital, diagnosed with internal bleeding, swept straight into surgery and remained a patient for the next fortnight. She was discharged the day before Matt joined Shirley Bassey for an eight-date nationwide tour. Marion came over to stay with her and keep her company so Matt went off relatively untroubled knowing his wife was in safe hands. It would be three months before she was pronounced fully fit.

The Vic Lewis presentation was a refined, classy, package show. The tour was also meant to feature John Barry and his Orchestra, but Barry didn't turn up, so Vic Lewis stepped in and conducted the musicians on Barry's behalf. Bassey was a powerhouse, striding onto the stage in a tight, backless tangerine dress closing her forty-five minute act with her powerful 'I Who Have Nothing' to rousing applause. Matt interwove some comedic patter between well-known numbers, and for contrast threw in a snappy 'Bill Bailey' and the topical and witty 'A Matter of Association', whose lyrics were changed weekly to reflect the news in the gossip columns. Everyone was hand clapping or foot tapping so it didn't matter that the orchestra supplied far too full a backing for the finale number 'If I Had a Hammer'.

> **During the song Matt would reach in to the piano and take out a newspaper and pretend to read it. One evening the musicians pasted pictures of various nude ladies on the page. Matt opened the paper and there they were, staring at him. Since the show was live, he had to carry on singing whilst trying to stifle a laugh. It was quite a feat. — Vic Lewis**

One of the tour's stops was the Astoria at Finsbury Park. There used to be a theatre called the Finsbury Park Empire near to where Matt lived, and it was one of his earliest ambitions to play there if he ever made it big, but the venue closed before he had the chance. Playing the Astoria with Bassey was, however, the next best thing and Matt thought the evening was wonderful.

> **Real friendship is a rare commodity in today's world and I remember Matt as a true friend. We worked together many times and shared a great working relationship. Apart from being a wonderful singer and marvellous entrepreneur of lyrics, he was also the ultimate professional – with his records he will always be with us. — Shirley Bassey**

Just before the end of the tour, Matt got the news that the paperwork legally changing his name had now been stamped – he was no longer Terry Parsons. Other news was the confirmation of the tribute show for Michael Holliday at the Prince of Wales Theatre. Pianist Russ Conway, who organised the whole affair from start to finish with the aid of a committee, was brilliant in the self-effacing role of Master of Ceremonies, accompanied by Norrie Paramor's superb orchestra. Jessie Matthews was in excellent voice, while comedians Bruce Forsyth, Frankie Howard, Benny Hill, Max Bygraves and Peggy Mount were all on top form. With the poise and polish of Alma Cogan, dynamic energy of Dorothy Squires, vibrant force of Shane Fenton and the vocal delights of Matt bringing the show to an impressive conclusion, all heralded the success of the *Night of 100 Stars*. But undoubtedly the night belonged to two unseen stars, the late well-loved singer himself and Bing Crosby, whose recorded message was deeply moving and entirely without concessions to sentimentality.

While Matt was on the road, Don worked on the English lyrics of the song the singer had brought back from Copenhagen. Matt liked the treatment Don had come back with but there were some musical fill-ins that he thought were still needed to strengthen the score. In translation the beautiful, agonised lyric became 'Walk Away', and Matt was convinced they had a hit on their hands. He spoke to George Martin about recording the song, but the producer advised against it, unconvinced of the tune's potential. Nevertheless, Matt felt very strongly about the track and insisted that it was a winner. George eventually gave in to his request.

> **The A&R man's job is to mould the record with the artists. Take a Matt Monro session. Once decided on the titles, we plan every song with the arranger and decide what kind of treatment we want. We pool ideas. The format is worked out with Matt present so he knows what he is going to do. Sometimes the arranger will arrive at the session with something quite different but it generally works quite well. — George Martin, *Melody Maker***

The studios were booked for 28 April and without much further ado, the future hit was laid down coupled with a swinging rendition of 'Around the World'. With the tracks in the can, Matt and the family went to Benidorm for a much-needed rest, joined by their friends Johnnie and Marion. It didn't take long for the families to head to the swimming pool. Michele was emphatically told not to go towards the deep end, a command she promptly ignored. Noticing his daughter was out of her depth, Matt panicked and jumped into the water fully clothed with his cigar

l to r Derek Dene, Three Monarchs, Matt, Sheila Buxton and the Dallas Boys

still firmly in his mouth.

Although not a working holiday, the singer did agree to appear on a Spanish televised variety show called *Amigos del Lunes*, which was filming in Barcelona. Having got to the studios, Johnnie was furious to find there was only a five-piece orchestra. The producer promised the musicians were all capable of doubling up, and they might have been, but not on the same performance! It was absolute chaos. At rehearsals, the boys stood in the wings waiting for a bird act to finish. When it was time for them to take their turn, Matt was dismayed to find bird shit all over the floor, some of which then rubbed against the back of his good jacket. After the run through, Matt went to complain to the director and to find out when they were due on set for the actual performance. The answer was not what he wanted to hear. What the duo thought was a dress rehearsal was actually a full take and they left the studios fuming.

Returning to England, Matt and Mickie were soon re-packing for their June move to Branksome Park in Poole, which afforded easy access to Bournemouth's Winter Gardens. The rental property had a large garden for the children and was only five minutes from the seafront.

George and Alfred Black presented the twice-nightly ten-week *Five Star Show* and guesting with Matt were The Dallas Boys, Sheila Buxton, Derek Dene and The Three

Monarchs. Matt thought Bournemouth was so civilised; there were no one-armed bandits on the pier, no cockle sellers on the front and not one kiss-me-quick hat in sight. The town was slightly more sophisticated than any of his previous summer seasons and teeming with theatres, bistros, restaurants and two art deco cinemas. Bruce Forsyth was opening down the road at the Pavilion with *The Big Show of 1964,* Thora Hird and Freddie Frinton were starring in *Their Favourite Comedies* at the Pier Theatre, while Sundays featured artists such as Larry Adler, Winifred Atwell, The Bachelors, Russ Conway, Diana Dors, Adam Faith, Joe 'Mr Piano' Henderson, Susan Maughan and Ruby Murray.

Bruce Forsyth, who was renting an apartment only a few roads away from Matt, attended the singer's opening night, as his own show didn't open till the Thursday, and the two boys were soon making social arrangements for the summer. Playing golf each week at Parkstone Golf Club was mandatory and most nights after their respective shows they would go and grab something to eat. They always met outside the theatre or in the town itself as Bruce didn't much like people coming to his dressing room either before or after a show. Like Matt, he preferred that time to focus his energy. How they both felt after a show depended largely on how well they thought they'd performed. If the show had been well received the adrenalin rush would last several hours. If not, then they would analyse each part of the performance trying to determine how it could be improved. It didn't matter how many things had gone well, they would only remember and brood over the things that had not. Once they had left the sanctuary of the dressing room, it was business as usual, signing autographs, seeing friends or grabbing something to eat.

A gang of them would often go ten-pin bowling, competing against each other. They even assembled a Showbiz team for a special match, with the proceeds going to charity. The midnight game saw the team led by Bruce, Matt, Derek Dene, Johnny Shack and Les Voules playing against the Christchurch Licensed Victuallers' Association. The men met regularly at Bruce's flat for a game of cards and one night after the show Matt was running slightly late. The boys were sitting waiting patiently, watching the fish and chips Bruce had picked up get cold, when finally the buzzer rang. Bruce went to the door to find Matt standing there with open wounds all over his face and his suit torn to shreds. In his haste, Matt had rushed into the front of the building and straight through a plate glass window. The boys all went down to the lobby to help clear up the debris, and there amongst the shards of glass was Matt's splattered cigar; Bruce couldn't stop laughing. Matt finally sat down to a game of poker with bits of toilet tissue dotted about his face!

Bournemouth Showbiz Bowling Team

Amid the whirl of social activities, the show was doing exceedingly well. Opening night had seen seven hundred and fifty-six members of the South Coast Dairies Sports and Social Club make up the largest ever block booking at the Winter Gardens, when they saw the second performance of the *Five Star Show*. Travelling in seventeen coaches, the convoy arrived in Bournemouth at ten-minute intervals, being marshalled by the Bournemouth police.

Now considered by some to be Britain's first boy band, The Dallas Boys opened the show. Derek Dene came through clowning, joking, juggling and dancing and had the audience roaring for more. Matt went through his regular mix including a few new numbers, 'Exodus', 'Me and My Girl' and 'The Trolley Song', finishing with a tambourine in his hand for his finale of 'If I Had a Hammer'. One night piano star Russ Conway made a flying visit to Bournemouth and played a joke on Matt. It happened in the finale when the singer was introducing the cast of the Winter Gardens show. He called for the Dallas Boys to take their final bow and on the five of them bounced. Matt did a double take – there were only four Dallas boys, and one Russ Conway. The audience roared in approval.

Matt did his usual round of Sunday work, including concerts at the Opera House

Blackpool and both the Margate and Morecambe Winter Gardens, in addition to several television, radio and charity spots. On the first Sunday in August, Matt travelled to Ryde on the Isle of Wight to headline a show at the Commodore Theatre. The show was an unusual combination of acts – Matt, the island's local band The Cherokees, The Chimes, Kenny Lynch and The Pretty Things. The combination of one of Britain's post-war singers and a hard-edged rock group certainly caused a stir, especially when The Pretty Things purposely played a song that wouldn't end, prompting the stage manager to pull the curtain and stop their performance. Later, during Matt's closing spot, their drummer Viv Prince and his cohorts kept poking their heads around the curtains distracting both the artist and the audience. In the end, Matt changed the lyrics of his Eurovision song to 'I Love the Pretty Things', which had the audience creased up with laughter.

Returning home from a successful season with a day to spare, Matt was around to see Michele start at St Augustine's Priory, the same school her mother had attended when she first arrived in England. Michele hated the daily catechism business. Going to confession and May devotions with the compulsory straw boater pushed firmly down on her head was not one of her happiest memories. The school was snobbish and exclusive and you had to be the right kind of girl to be accepted. Boys were only allowed for the first five years, then it became an all-girl secondary school. Her brother Matthew was also enrolled at the age of five, but he escaped early by gently being asked to leave. In a state school the more recognised term was expulsion!

Within a few days of the school term starting, Matt's new single was available in the shops. 'Walk Away' was released on 4 September and was an enormous hit, selling eleven thousand copies on the first day alone. The disc rested comfortably in the charts alongside Manfred Mann, Sandie Shaw, The Searchers, Roy Orbison and The Hollies. Once again, the panel on *Juke Box Jury* had got it wrong, declaring it didn't stand a chance of seeing the Top 20. It had been three years since Don Black had written 'April Fool', but this new offering would become a milestone in both artists' careers. 'Around the World', the Victor Young composition featured on the flip side, had been given a new arrangement. With an upbeat orchestral treatment from Buddy Bregman, and Matt giving a rousing interpretation of the track, it wasn't surprising that the song was so well received.

Gorgeous, delicious, superb and any other superlatives you care to mention. They all apply to Matt Monro's 'Walk Away'. A warmly appealing ballad, exquisitely tailored by Matt, who extracts every

shred of meaning from the lyrics, aided by a throbbing rhythm and cascading strings. A quality record by any standard, though whether it will succeed is anyone's guess. If it doesn't happen it will be an injustice. 'Around the World' is a revival with a difference. There's a brash, brassy backing to this bouncy, bubbling, swinging interpretation. — Derek Johnson, *Musical Express*

By the last week of October, 'Walk Away' was sitting in the number four position in the British charts and number three in the Irish charts as well as jumping swiftly up the US Hot 100. In the Philippines, 'I Dream of You' was in the number one position, as was 'From Russia with Love' in Japan. The 007 number was also edging up the Top 10 in Hong Kong, finally reaching the highly coveted number one spot in February of 1965, beating both The Beatles with 'I Feel Fine' and Elvis Presley's 'Roustabout', which sat in second and third position respectively. Not bad for a few weeks' work!

Laryngitis and similar throat complaints are the bane of a pop singer's existence. They can strike at a moment's notice, and leave an artist croaking uselessly at the most inconvenient time. Matt fell prey to laryngitis like several other top pop stars. But despite the unpleasantness and inconvenience, laryngitis had a strange good-luck quality for Matt.

I had an attack of laryngitis at the time I was recording 'Softly'. I just about got it done before my voice went completely. And the same thing happened with 'Walk Away'. I got the track in the can with three takes. If there had been a fourth, my voice would have gone altogether. — Matt Monro

'Walk Away' spent four months in the British charts and earned Matt another gold record. It was much harder in the 1960s than it is today to accomplish the quarter of a million sales for a silver record, and half a million sales for gold. Allegedly Frank Sinatra also recorded 'Walk Away' but declined to release it when he heard Matt's version. Matt would later record the song in Spanish and – never one to ignore a winning formula – would turn to the Udo Jürgens songbook several more times during his career.

One of the few recordings where Matt Monro's vocals start from the very beginning and last until the final note. What a treat! All

Top of the Pops

**possible levels of emotional depth are included in his perfect
vocal. It would not be an overstatement to qualify 'Walk Away' as
the singular most outstanding vocal of all time. — Jeffrey Paul
Hayes, pianist**

At 6.35pm on the first day of January 1964, the BBC Television service broadcast the
first ever episode of *Top of the Pops* live from a disused church in Manchester known as
Dickinson Road Studio. Scheduled to make only a few appearances, the show
surpassed all expectations to become the longest running music programme in the
world. The format was simple; chart artists would perform their latest release, and the
finale would showcase the number one record. If an artist or group were unavailable,
dance troupes would perform a routine to the number, though this practice became
obsolete over the years with the advance of technology allowing artists to pre-record
their appearances or insert a promotional video.

The featured artists would gather at the studio each week, many of them flying up
from London to appear and returning on a late evening flight. It was on such a flight

at the beginning of October that Matt first met Val Doonican, and the two became great friends. Val was very much in the early stages of his 'solo' career and was on the show to plug his first record 'Walk Tall'. It wasn't long before the popular Irishman had his own Saturday evening television show, and Matt became a regular guest. Like most artists, Val began his career touring clubs around the country. He always took his own stool along since many of the venues didn't have anything appropriate.

> **A very talented friend of mine suggested that a 'folding type', similar to a photographer's tripod would be a good idea. He then proceeded to produce the perfect answer and after some forty odd years I still use it everywhere I perform. Matt saw me use this when he next joined me on TV and said he's always wanted something similar. The outcome was a Matt Monro stool from the same craftsman. While working up north a while later I noted that Matt was working a week at 'The Fiesta Club' in Stockton-on-Tees, so I went along to enjoy his show featuring his new stool.**
> **— Val Doonican**

Matt used the stool in every one of his live performances, and it travelled with him around the world many times over. It became a standard feature of his act, and he was never without it. Val and Matt worked together many times and they often performed in the same town but at different venues. On one such occasion, returning late to a near-deserted hotel while working in Porthcawl in Wales, Val heard a voice from nowhere shout goodnight. It had come from the night porter's small den by the door. Popping his head in to bid his own goodnight, Val found Matt having a drink and playing poker with the concierge!

On 9 October, Matt was back in the studio, this time with a song that had originally been recorded in French as 'Adios a la Mama' by its co-composer Charles Aznavour, and for a second time Don provided an English lyric. 'For Mama' wasn't due out until December, and in the meantime the diary was full with dates in Liverpool, Wolverhampton and Nottingham. Unfortunately, on 21 October, Matt collapsed at the city centre hotel he was staying at just as he was preparing to leave for rehearsals at the Stork Club in Nottingham. A doctor diagnosed acute laryngitis and yellow jaundice and several dates had to be cancelled.

For anyone self-employed, failure to work, whatever the reason, meant no salary. Even if the performer was living hand-to-mouth, their main concern was that they would be letting their audience down – the paying public who can be relentlessly unforgiving. There was not one occasion when Matt took his audience for granted, and thankfully he wasn't out of work for long. Five days later was able to fulfil a charitable engagement for the Stars Organisation for Spastics (S.O.S.). Outside, in Lewisham High Road, crowds were thronging the pavements. The theatre's frontage glittered like Piccadilly as it screamed the star-studded bill in lights. It was indeed a big occasion for S.O.S. chairman Harry Secombe and vice-chairman David Jacobs. The sense of excitement in the heaving auditorium escalated as the Cyril Stapleton Orchestra took their place on the podium to start the overture. By the time Matt left the stage, after finishing off his set with his current chart entry, the applause that followed was completely justified.

George wanted Matt in the studio on 3 November so he could lay down some tracks for the next album. The time on the studio clock said 2.40pm when the singer walked into the control-room and apologised for being late because he couldn't find a car parking space. He rubbed his hands together ready to start the three-hour-long session. Johnnie Spence was already in the studio, smoking one cigarette after another, coaxing the musicians into doing what he wanted. The brass blew in with a swing from the jacket-less musicians, who charged EMI seven pounds seven shillings each for the afternoon. George, sitting in the tightly shuttered control room with his recording engineer, was hoping to record four songs that afternoon. The sounds in the studio were relayed back to the control room where knobs, gadgets and microphones controlled, deadened, cut out and swelled the sound that George was looking for. Matt went into a cut-off 'dookit' separating him from the thirty-strong orchestra, and after a few false starts, 'It's a Breeze' was in the can and Johnnie and Matt joined George in the control room to hear the playback. If they didn't think the sound was fat enough or there was too much violin in places and not enough viola, they would go back for another take. Several hours later the last song, 'All My Loving', sung the Matt Monro way, was completed to the satisfaction of everyone. Slipping on his camel hair coat and with a few last words to Johnnie and George, Matt took his leave. Watching these three masters in a recording session was amazing; they were intensely dedicated, completely professional and totally opposed to leaving any aspect of the recording to chance.

Matt understood how to sing a lyric, but he knew it wasn't enough to just be a good singer; you also needed a great musical director, great orchestrations and great musicians to make a good record. He always felt an immense sense of achievement after an Abbey Road session; it was exactly what he'd always wanted to do. He also got a kick when Sinatra released his version of 'Softly As I Leave You' on the Reprise label and it didn't get that good a review. A reporter asked if he would comment on the disc but he was loathe to as he didn't want to be unflattering, but when pushed, responded by saying, "It seems to me that either he doesn't have the voice anymore, or alternatively he recorded it on a very bad day."

Matt's *Eurovision* appearance prompted a three-day November booking for a television spectacular in Rome, which spearheaded a hectic worldwide tour. On 13 November, Matt flew direct from Italy to Los Angeles to appear on the *Hollywood Palace* and *Lloyd Thaxton* television shows. Former wrestler and club owner Billy Kerfoot flew from Manchester to join the British singer on tour. Billy adored the business and, being a close friend, had inveigled an invitation to join Matt.

During this hectic visit to the States, Matt was the subject of countless press interviews and media requests. He was also invited to a number of receptions laid on by industry executives. Liberty Records chief Al Bennett threw a champagne press party for the star, welcoming him to the West Coast and Robert Skaff hosted a Cantonese supper in Matt's honour at Arthur Wong's Far East Terrace in North Hollywood.

Matt's diary was crammed full, but somehow he was able to squeeze in an ABC Network show called *Shindig*. It was an all-star kiddie bash headed by Matt and featuring the popular Chad and Jeremy duo, Neil Sedaka, Donna Loren, Tina Turner and The Righteous Brothers. Filmed on a Hollywood film set it had an unexpected guest in the audience – Bobby Darin.

> **The week in LA was very successful and everyone is convinced that the record is going to be top 10. Al Bennet of Liberty threw a big cocktail party for me last night and all the DJ's were there. Afterwards I was invited out to Universal Studios where Bobby Darin and Donald O'Connor had a party to celebrate the finish of a picture. There was a cabaret by a comedian called Larry Storch and a great new singer who got an ovation named Matt Monro! It was great and went so well. — Matt Monro, letter written on plane en-route to Japan**

Matt flew into Japan on 19 November for an eight-day sequence of concert, radio and television appearances in the country where his waxing of 'From Russia With Love' was still sitting in the number one slot. Matt was contracted to work seven days out of the eight, give fourteen personal appearances in Tokyo and work two shows a day in either nightclubs or military installations.

Donald O'Connor, Matt & Bobby Darrin

Bruce (Forsyth) phoned and sent his love and thanks for the telegram. His show had rave notices everywhere. He invited me to the opening but I didn't want to go on my own. Ron Goodwin phoned and invited us to go to the SOS Ball. He asked if you wanted to be a member and said there seems to have been an oversight in you not having been asked before in view of all the work you have done for them – just what we said after the last concert. — Letter from Mickie to Hotel New Japan, Tokyo

On his way back from Japan, Matt stopped off in Hong Kong to celebrate his birthday, visiting several of his favourite restaurants and nightclubs. He ended up at the Savoy and sang an unrehearsed version of one of his recent hits with the band. This was greeted with enthusiastic applause, and the audience refused to let him leave until he had sung three more songs.

The flight from Tokyo wasn't too bad except that it was delayed for over an hour and a half and we didn't reach Hong Kong until about

11.30pm. The strange thing I found in Japan is that on the back of 'From Russia with Love' was the James Bond Theme by John Barry. Oh well it takes all sorts but I must say I was surprised. I'm sorry I didn't come home with Russ but it seems a shame to come all this way and not stay for a few days. I'm going to make the rounds tonight and see all the faces again. 'Russia' is showing here at the moment and has been for about three months and you just can't get a seat. Needless to say you can't get the record either. Great EMI, and it isn't because they have sold out; you work it out.
— Matt Monro, letter from the President Hotel, Hong Kong

Matt returned from Hong Kong laden with a new wardrobe and a mink coat for his wife. Mickie used to say when they were broke that even if they ever had the money, she wouldn't want one, but she soon changed her mind. She had also arranged a birthday present for her husband; she had commissioned the artist John Baker to paint a portrait of Matt, which still hangs in the house today.

Before the year's end, Matt filmed a sequence for the film *Pop Gear* (aka *Go Go Mania*). Joan Shakespeare wrote it while Harry Field, the General Manager of British Pathé, directed the project. The line-up included The Animals, The Beatles, The Rockin' Berries, The Four Pennies and Herman's Hermits, among others.

Pop Gear made its debut at the Sky-Vue Drive-In Theatre in America with a general release throughout Britain forecast for February. It was expected to prove one of the biggest box-office attractions of 1965. The film has no plot, being an unashamed attempt at satisfying the popular demand for that particular type of rhythm and harmony. Matt, indisputably the dramatic principle and elder statesman among the younger acts, whose baritone glides effortlessly over the bouncy rock beat of the title song, treats us to 'Walk Away' and 'For Mama' in this sixty-eight minute special. The year ended with 'For Mama' in the Top 30 and although it is regarded as a classic now, the song was seen as something of a commercial failure. The flip side was the snapping swinger 'Going Places', which Black and Spence wrote together.

THE BIG DOME

At the beginning of 1965, Johnnie Spence started working on the *Tommy Steele Show*, but he still made the time to attend BBC's *Saturday Club*, and go back in the studios to lay down the tracks for Matt's forthcoming album *I Have Dreamed*. Matt recorded another song by Udo Jürgens, who had returned to *Eurovision* in 1965 with 'Sag Ihr, Ich Lass Sie Gruessen'. This time the song finished fourth and once again Don Black wrote an English lyric. The result was 'Without You', which failed to live up to expectations. Despite critical acclaim, it didn't climb any higher than No 37.

> Haunting melody blended with a thoughtful Don Black lyric, beat-ballad 'Without You' is impeccably handled by the stylish Matt Monro. If there's one fault, it is that the lavish scorings, shimmering strings, horns and harp – is just a shade overdone. But this is a quality disc, which deserves recognition. Contrasting brash swinger 'Start Living' has a twist beat, and is rendered just as competently. — *Reuters News Agency*

Although not seeing much chart movement in England, Matt's record *All My Loving* was number one in the Philippine Islands. While his career spawned numerous number ones around the world, one of Matt's biggest disappointments was never having the same recognition in his own country.

Who were the top personalities in show business in 1964? The *Melody Maker* presented the first annual Pop Writers' Poll, in which journalists voted, not necessarily for the most successful artist or record of the year, but for their favourites. The Beatles emerged winners of album of the year with *A Hard Day's*

Night and were also voted the top vocal and instrumental group. Matt Monro and Dusty Springfield took home the titles of top British male and female singers.

Things were changing in England, certainly in the world of show business. The centres of live entertainment were switching to local working men's clubs that until recently had been the strongholds of such male activity as snooker, darts and dominos. Greasbrough Social Club, on the outskirts of smoky Rotherham, was Yorkshire's proudest example of the new clubland. It was estimated they would spend thirty thousand pounds that year on providing entertainment for the members and their wives, paid for by a five-shilling entrance fee and the profit from the bar. Four years prior the club was little more than a wooden hut. With compensation it had received when its original building was pulled down for road widening, the club had built new premises with a concert room seating eight hundred, a dance hall and an enormous lounge. Matt's first booking at Greasbrough Social Club was interesting. Halfway through his act, the club was plunged into total darkness and the village was left without electricity for over an hour. Playing to a full house, Matt slipped quickly off the stage and returned with a lit candle, finishing his number without a microphone. He was given a standing ovation.

After a three-year wait, Matt was finally set to make his debut on 1 February in London's West End Talk of the Town. He opened a fortnight run accompanied by his regular pianist Russ Shepherd on keyboards, and Johnnie Spence piloting the Sydney Simone Orchestra through a raft of superb arrangements. Even though he had worked the room before, deputising for Joan Regan, it was still a nerve-racking occasion, with a plethora of showbiz personalities in the audience. Russ Conway, Alan Freeman, David Jacobs, Pete Murray, Georgia Brown, Joan Turner, Billy Walker, Freddie Davies and Bruce Forsyth (who had just made his debut in the room a few months back) had all turned out for Matt's big night. Matt also had his own personal supporters in Mickie, Don and Michael Black and George Martin. In earlier days, when second or third on the bill, it wasn't Matt's responsibility to fill the room, but now it was his name out there, and the onus was on him to make the night a success. Clubs were more difficult to work than theatres, as the artist had to compete with the bar for the audience's attention. Later that year Matt had a clause built into his contract specifying that when he was playing a club, waiter service would be suspended for the duration of his act.

Matt opened with 'Somewhere' and ran through 'Walk Away', 'Bill Bailey', 'Portrait', 'My Kind of Girl' and 'All My Loving'. After a dignified introduction to 'Softly', he broke into his Horniman's Dividend Tea and Pink Camay jingles. He came off stage to tumultuous applause. When Bruce Forsyth took to the stage to present Matt with his *Melody Maker* Press Award, which he'd won as Britain's best singer, the applause thundered round the room for a second time. Michael Black thought Matt's opening to be the biggest sensation of all time and certainly his success those first weeks led him to play the room a further eight times.

> I enjoy cabaret very much indeed. I'm much nearer the audience and find it more intimate. A cabaret audience is the hardest to conquer. So I look forward to it because it's a challenge to get them with you. You never experience it in a theatre. — Matt Monro

Rosalyn Wilder remembers that night. "Matt was extremely professional and understood that, with Robert Nesbitt, he was in the hands of someone who cared hugely enough about making everyone who appeared at the Talk of the Town into the best star they could be. He was quite relaxed, but not 'laid back' – that, I think would imply 'not worried', and he did care that it all came over well. The whole ambience of the 'Talk' was fun, we all worked incredibly hard but it was highly professional, we all respected each other and it was a marvellous atmosphere. We spent ages in the Star Suite after the show, loads of friends would pop in for a drink (or three) and chat, it was great fun. There were so many wonderful artists that performed in the room over the years. Sammy [Davis Jr] was tremendously exciting. He was completely off the wall; he spent more time worrying about how many girls he could get into his dressing room and how much stuff he could shove up his nose and into various other parts of his body, but he was a tremendous talent, you had to put up with all the nonsense that went on around it. He was quite incredible, but there is a little fault line that runs through a lot of these people that makes them vulnerable and difficult."

With the success of his West End appearance still smoking, Matt started rehearsals in London for *Go Go with Monro,* the brainchild of John and Joan Shakespeare. The rest of the shoot was to take place in Rome the following week and while packing for the trip, Matt received the news that Nat King Cole had died. Matt was choked by the reports, realising that the man who had fought racism all his life and refused to perform in segregated venues was no more. The iconic pop star cemented his popularity with such hits as 'Nature Boy', 'Mona Lisa' and his signature tune 'Unforgettable'. The revenues from 'Unforgettable' fuelled much of Capitol's success, and were believed to have played a significant role in financing the distinctive Capitol Records building on Vine Street in Los Angeles.

Completed in 1956, it was the world's first circular office building, and became known as 'the house that Nat built'. Matt had no idea that Cole's passing would play such an important role in his career.

Matt and Mickie left for Rome on 22 February for the first pilot of what was hoped to be a new television series. The shoot went well, the weather was kind and with a few hours to spare the Monros went walking down the Via Veneto. Matt spied Perry Como walking into a shoe shop with his wife. Mickie was so excited that she persuaded her husband to follow them in, and began to try on a number of shoes. She actually ended up buying a beautiful pair of suede ankle boots, which were exorbitantly expensive – though when the couple flew home the following morning, Mickie discovered the shop had mistakenly given her one black and one navy boot.

The next time Mickie remembered meeting Como was when they went to see him at The London Palladium and went backstage to introduce themselves properly. After knocking on the door, they were ushered in to find Como standing there wearing nothing but his dress shirt, long socks and suspenders. It seemed that all the bigger artists had the habit of taking their 'standing up' trousers off straight away.

When *Go Go With Monro* was released as a film short in cinemas across the country later that year, Matt and Mickie crept into the back row of The ABC Forum in Ealing, watched the film and snuck out again.

A barrage of television spots followed, culminating in ABC's *Big Night Out*. It was baffling what purpose the fancy scenery in so many shows served. Matt had to walk through such a forest of pillars, it's a wonder he didn't get lost! He had grown to hate the medium. There was no intimacy and no rapport with the audience. In the theatres and clubs you could sneak a look at the crowd, get a feel for the room and bask in the applause. Television was like being under a microscope, where all your mistakes were amplified and caught on celluloid to play back time and time again. The camera angles were never sympathetic to his height and occasionally the close-ups would aim right up his nose, or pick out the foundation line that the make-up department had overlooked. Blue lighting could make Matt look like he'd slowly asphyxiated some weeks prior, and red made him look like he'd suffered a bad sun-bed session, it was all so unforgiving. There was always a sense of dissatisfaction with television, everything was so clinical and detached; there was no spontaneity. You were well and truly 'produced'. You had to stand on the taped cross, and you couldn't wear certain colours or stripes as that would interfere with the transmission. Even if there was a live studio audience present, they were

Filming in Rome – Trevi Fountain

directed when to clap; nothing was left to chance. There were so many past instances of embarrassing sketches Matt was asked to partake in, or the obligatory duet with the host who, more often than not, couldn't sing a note. If the show was a bomb then you were the fighter carrier who dropped it. You weren't hired as a guest, but as a scapegoat for poor ratings or bad reviews. Yes, Matt hated television but he was forced to do it, lest someone should think his absence from the small box in the living room meant that he had died. At least radio was more refined, you could wear mis-matched socks and the audience wouldn't know, they wouldn't snigger because you'd tripped on your entrance or gasp because of a forgotten lyric. It was definitely the lesser of the two evils.

The British music scene was hugely different from America. In England, you are measured by the success of your last record. If it didn't hit the charts then your appearance wasn't required – anywhere. In the States, crooners could work the strips of Las Vegas and Atlantic City for years with only one hit under their belt.

Thankfully, Matt had scored more than one lone hit, and with that success he splashed out and bought a four-bedroom house in Hanger Lane, Ealing, through estate agents Roberts and Cleave. The Georgian property was built before the war and perched on the crest of a hill, with beautiful panoramic views across London. It was Matt's dream house and he knew he wanted it the minute he set eyes on it. He didn't want a stuffy show house where everyone had to walk on eggshells, he was looking for a comfortable home where the family could all relax and be themselves. A lot of the proposed renovations to the house were drawn up to Matt's own specification, particularly the lounge, which was to be extended to twice its size out into the back garden. It was a convenient base within easy reach of most mainline stations, several motorways, Heathrow Airport and London's West End, and it wasn't far from the golf course either. There were only three houses in the road, but they all looked like any other building in the area. The house wasn't ornate or ostentatious, nor did it look like the home of a pop singer, lacking the stereotypical private gated enclosure. Matt had no delusions of social grandeur and didn't adorn the home with fancy works of art. There were no lavish parties, or music blaring, or people leaving stoned in the middle of the night. Matt was not a great fan of parties, his idea of a perfect evening was the company of a few friends for dinner. In the absence of guests, he liked nothing better than a good movie. His favourite film was *The Magnificent Seven*, and he was a compulsive round the clock small screen viewer. He once said the worst fate that could befall him was to be stranded in a town without a television set.

> **To me, the most amazing thing about Matt is that he hasn't changed one iota from those Denmark Street days to becoming an international singing star. Matt was just as happy having a game of cards or watching TV as he was singing at the Palladium. I spent some of the best times of my life with Matt. He was a funny man. If you ever said anything funny yourself he was the audience you would dream of. He could literally fall down laughing.**
> **— Don Black, *BASCA News*, 1985**

The one thing Matt did treat himself to was a new car, this time a Rolls Royce Silver Cloud, which sat comfortably in the driveway of Dallas Road. Unfortunately, new car or not, Matt had to leave home almost immediately and in

March – armed with a special visa – he was granted entry to Singapore. He flew over earlier than needed in order to acclimatise. This proved prudent, as although he arrived safely, his luggage didn't. He was booked for a two-week engagement at Singapore's Goodwood Hotel, followed by a week in Manila and three weeks in Hong Kong. Mickie was left to cope with two children, a new house, and a set of builders whose job it was to build an extension, re-wire the entire building, upgrade the central heating system and redecorate every room. Once that was done, all Mickie had to do was await the furniture delivery.

> **John Crouch made me a visiting member of the Jockey Club so on Saturday afternoon I went to the races. At one time I was winning about eighty dollars (Singapore that is) and then over the last two races I blew all but nine dollars of it (Singapore that is). Then went out and had a Chinese meal (Singapore that is) in the heart of town. The unfortunate thing is that half-way through the meal the Indonesians let off a bomb, the third one this week, and damaged the water supply. As John is an officer in the riot squad, we had to finish our meal and get out of there in a hurry. There wasn't much to see as it was pitch black anyway and no one was hurt, but it did make for a little excitement. We met up with a few musicians (Singapore that is) and all finished up at the airport, which is the only place that has a bar open until 4.00am. — Matt Monro, letter from Goodwood Hotel, Singapore**

Mickie relied on Matt's letters to keep her up-to-date with the Singapore news. She was eagerly counting the days until she flew out to meet her absentee husband in what was to be her first trip to Hong Kong. Matt had bought the ticket as a wedding anniversary present. The house was taking up all of her time, that and the fact that her best friend Marion was heavily pregnant with her first child. As Johnnie was working at Wembley Studios doing the first of the *Ready Steady Go* live shows, it didn't seem like such a good idea to leave Marion on her own in Epsom, so Johnnie dropped her off at Dallas Road on his way to work. The two girls talked long into the night, finally going to bed at four in the morning. Three hours later Marion woke up with a terrible backache, but she thought it was because her dog Mandy had been in the bed with her. When Michele came down for school and saw the way Marion looked, she ran to get her mother. The birth wasn't easy, as the baby was facing the wrong way and the nursing team had to use forceps to

assist the delivery. In their haste they cut an artery and Marion ended up having a blood transfusion and stitches inside and out. Sarah Jane Spence was finally born on 2 April, the same day as her best friend's daughter Michele.

Mickie rang to tell Matt that Marion and Johnnie were now proud parents and that his EP *Somewhere* was sitting in the charts at No 19 but it was to be Matt's final EP appearance there. Two months later, *I Have Dreamed* made its debut in the album chart. It wasn't surprising that an EP of the same name featuring four of the album's tracks failed to make the hit parade.

The shows were packed out and, as well as being available for radio and press interviews, Matt managed a day at the REME Training Centre in Singapore. He also paid a visit to the EMI Studios in Singapore and met up with the chart-hitting beat group, The Quests. As they were the first local group to play with an international star, the event caused quite a stir in the press.

I've been seeing quite a lot of the army guys; in fact I'm going out with them this afternoon waterskiing. They have a big boat from the army so it should be a great day. Got your letter about the record, it's great isn't it? The shows are going like a bomb and it's a great room to work. Shirley Bassey arrives here on Sunday and

I've arranged to do a concert with her at the National Theatre. I think it will be a sell out. Anyway, everyone is waiting for me and we have to catch the right tide. — Matt Monro, letter from Goodwood Hotel, Singapore

Shirley Bassey was flying from London to Sydney via Singapore. Seizing on the opportunity, impresario Freddie Yew booked the National Arena, contracting Matt to do the first half and Bassey the second. The show sold out. Kenny Clayton had been working as musical director for the irrepressible diva for nearly a year. Having seen Kenny work that night, Matt thought of Mr Clayton when the time came to change musical directors.

Matt was reeling from the reception he'd received at the National Arena. The crowd had spent most of their time on their feet, and the singer was genuinely overcome with emotion. Sadly, his time in Singapore was at an end and the next day would see him fly to Manila for the next leg of his world tour, but he was ill-prepared for what awaited him.

To his astonishment, his adulation in the Philippines had reached Beatles proportions. On the eve of his trip he'd worked late into the night, sharing several beers with his musical director after the show. As a result they had nearly missed their flight from Singapore. They crawled onto the plane unshaven, hungover and feeling like death. When the PAL Sampaguita jetliner landed at 2.45pm, Matt, who was about to disembark the plane, turned to Russ and asked, "Who on earth is on this plane, look at those people out there, can you believe that?" He had no idea that the thousands of people that had gathered on the airfield were there for *him* – and if that wasn't enough to digest, they had strewn the most magnificent flowers all over the tarmac and had laid out a 'Welcome Matt'. He couldn't believe it and scolded himself for not having had a shave. He never forgot the incident.

A tour in the Philippines was quite unlike one anywhere else in the world. Once under contract the promoters tended to feel that they owned you for the duration. The organisers met Matt airside, and as he was led out of the luggage hall and through the airport doors he was besieged by thousands of screaming fans. An itinerary was thrust into his hand indicating that on arrival at the hotel he was to do the first of dozens of live radio interviews. He had bypassed customs and was taken to a ten-car motorcade. Each car was loaded, although Matt had no idea who sat in the other cars. As the motorcade started off, a swarm of media-hungry press followed in hot pursuit. The airport arrivals lounge, which only moments earlier

had been teeming with over-zealous screaming teenyboppers, had cleared in seconds as the majority of pubescent teenagers had stampeded an exit route to waiting cars and second-hand motorbikes in their eagerness to take chase.

The first time I played in the Philippines was during the elections, and one-hundred-and-twenty-five people were killed. It's a bit frightening because people were waving guns about everywhere I went; I had to have a two-man bodyguard unit. 'Walk Away' became a theme song of sorts for the incoming administration of President Ferdinand Marcos. The Filipino lyrics of the song made 'Walk Away' read 'Go Away', which was Marcos' message to the previous leader. — Matt Monro

1965 was an election year and the country was filled with political campaigning and pledges, but the people were excited by what Ferdinand Marcos was bringing to the table, with promises of new roads, bridges and public works, a generator with electric power and water services to eight regions. Even more exciting was his promise to fight crime, smuggling and corruption in the Government. But there was one obstacle in his path. President Diosdado Macapagal, who had promised not to run for re-election in 1965 and support Marcos' candidacy for the presidency, went back on this assurance, causing Marcos to resign from the Liberal Party. With the support of his wife Imelda Romualdez Marcos, he joined the Nacionalista Party and became its standard-bearer, with Senator Fernando Lopez as his running mate. 'Walk Away' had been playing on the radio for months, and the Filipinos adopted the song as a message to Diosdado to get out.

Every minute of Matt's day was taken up with something. There were interviews at the gig with radio stations, magazines and newspapers, which ran articles in ten languages across the continent. Local television channels were also begging for his time. Some of the television appearances were scheduled from six in the morning when he was expected to sing live on air. DJ's were referring to Matt as 'Double M'. Everyone wanted a little piece of him. Every interview brought with it the same questions and the same comparisons. Even the small amount of time off he was afforded was allocated to some major request, which couldn't be turned down. Hours were wasted travelling to a different town where the promoters insisted he meet certain dignitaries or important sponsors. As a result of this trip to Manila, Matt insisted in future contracts that, when arriving in a country outside of Europe, he would have the first day to himself to recover from the flight.

Matt was booked to play one night at the Araneta Stadium (The Big Dome). Mickie had thought him quite mad to accept the engagement, as it was a huge venue to fill. The next thing she recalls is receiving a telegram from her husband to say, "Held over for another four nights, twenty-six-thousand people a night, sold out. Love you."

Leaving the hotel to go to the Araneta was a major operation and much more chaotic than any other tour Matt had been on. There were thousands of girls waiting for him outside the hotel and his security had to fight their way through the crowds to get Matt to his car. As they pulled away, the crowds ran alongside the vehicle, banging on the doors and windscreen. They screamed, they cried; it was pandemonium and Matt worried that someone would get hurt. When he arrived at the venue it was the same routine but in reverse. After Matt had taken the last bow and left the stage for the night, the crowds were even more highly strung, having worked themselves into a frenzy. Once the security detail's ordeal of actually getting him into the car was over, a police escort was needed to get him

The Big Dome

out of the area. It was both exhilarating and exhausting.

The special Easter presentation at the Araneta ran six shows over four days. The Big Dome authorities, the main sponsors of the event, hadn't wanted to take a chance on the British balladeer and struck a deal with Ching Imperial and Ramon Ramos Jr of Cavalcade promotion, leaving themselves with only twenty-five per cent of the gross. It was a bad decision as after the sell-out shows, Matt ranked alongside Neil Sedaka and Ricky Nelson when it came to gross profits at the Big Dome. When the promoters of the show approached Pepsi Cola to sponsor the presentation, the proposition was warmly received. Matt Monro was just about the biggest recording star in the Philippines and the most consistent hit producer during the past few months, with his discs at the top of all the local charts. Matt's songs were being played in every conceivable place throughout the country, and sung by every known band and vocalist in the area. Since 'From Russia with Love' hit the top of their charts and stayed there for several weeks, Matt had not been out of the Top 10, placing as many as four of the most-played ten at the same time. In recent weeks, 'Walk Away' and 'For Mama' had kept Matt among the Top 5, coming on the heels of 'Somewhere, I'll Dream of You' and 'Exodus'.

The two-hour musical extravaganza also featured Pilita Corrales (the country's leading female singer) and Nino Robles, the fabulous nine-year-old Filipino performer, who combined his prowess on the bongos with both singing and tap dancing. Starting out in show business at the age of eighteen months, he had appeared on all of the top American television shows including *Jack Paar*, *Ed Sullivan* and *Ozzie & Harriet Nelson*. Twenty of the best bands in the country were also performing, vying for cash prizes and the title of *Combo of the Year*. The opening overture of the *Matt Monro Show* was followed by selections on the vibes by the Panlaqui Brothers, wizards of the xylophone. The combo contest followed, with four combos playing two selections each. The first half ended with Pilita singing her latest hits, 'A Million Thanks to You', 'Cucuru-Cucu', 'Amor' and 'La Ultima Noche'. She was one of the most effective torch singers Matt had ever performed with, crooning the pain out of her slim body and driving the mournful lyrics like nails into her audience. However tortured her performance sometimes appeared, she underwent a total transformation whenever she sang a zippy tune, becoming vibrant and effervescent. The second hour of the show featured a special medley by the Danny Holmsen Orchestra, and just when the audience couldn't bear the wait any longer, the star of the show was finally introduced.

Matt's opening number 'Around the World' was followed by 'Portrait', but when the first chords of 'From Russia with Love' rang out, the roof almost lifted off with the crowd's applause. He thanked the crowd in Tagalog (maraming salamat po) and delighted his audience by singing a duet with Pilita in their local language. The audience stood up in the middle of the ballads and every time Matt did a key change or held a long note, they stood again, cheering, stamping and screaming. At the closing of one song he left the stage. The crowd erupted, refusing to accept the show was over, but it was nothing compared to the noise that was made when he returned, wearing a barong, the national dress. Matt sang a total of fifteen numbers, breaking another record at The Dome and that didn't include the two additional renditions of 'Walk Away' he had to sing in order for the crowd to let him go. To be embraced by the people of a different culture is always an honour, and Matt was overwhelmed by the public displays of affection. Although entertainment had been booked at The Dome for six days, Matt had only been contracted for one of those shows. Having outsold The Beatles, Joe Quirino (the Coliseum's spokesman) issued an immediate statement "Due to persistent public demand, *the Matt Monro Show* has been extended to 21 April." The phones rang off the hook.

Our arrival in the Philippines was phenomenal; we broke every box office record held by everybody that has been here, including Nat King Cole. Reception fantastic. Last night in two shows played to

sixteen-thousand people. Today expect to play to thirty-thousand. See you in Hong Kong. — Matt Monro, postcard from the Hotel Filipinas

Matt was invited to meet Ferdinand Marcos, who had just been elected President. Matt serenaded the First Couple at their residence. After the meeting, Imelda Marcos sent a leather-bound album containing pictures of Matt with her and the children over to his hotel. It was something he always treasured.

The promoters begged Matt to stay a bit longer and he agreed to the addition of two more shows at Chandelier Hall. On the last night, Matt came out from his dressing room still in his dress suit and sat on a stool talking to some of the promoters. A guy behind him kept trying to interrupt, and Matt told him to wait as he was talking. The man proved somewhat impatient and, losing his temper, poured red wine over the singer's dress suit. With that, Matt swivelled round on the stool and knocked the guy out. Matt was flying out very early the next morning but was strongly advised to have extra security laid on, as the guy seemed to have rather unpleasant connections!

Have the acetate of your new LP and will bring it with me. George says 'knock out'. He wants to start a new album straight away – you record on the 27th, move to Yarmouth on the 28th and start in summer season on 1st June! You've won a National Record Award for the Best Light Vocal Record of 64' with 'Walk Away' and a AGRRA Award presented by Record Retailer. — Letter from Mickie to Hong Kong Hilton

Matt flew to Hong Kong for his engagement at the Hilton's Eagle Nest supper club, which he nicknamed 'the Vulture's Room', with the backing of Bading Tuason and his Orchestra. Two of Matt's many friends, radio broadcaster John Wallace and disc jockey Ray Cordeiro, were waiting for him at the airport and it was just like old times – the friendship that is, not the island. Matt was shocked by how much the area had changed since his army days. It didn't seem that many years ago that he'd regularly come back from the island late at night, scampering for the last ferry because if he missed it, he'd have to catch a 'walla' boat across, which cost one HK dollar.

First time I came to Hong Kong was by troop ship. This time I sat

Matt & Russ Shepherd

in the cockpit and watched the landing. It was amazing. Used to
stand at The Peninsula and look across the harbour, which you
can't do now as they have turned it into a planetarium. Hong Kong
being so small has no option but to build upwards but while you've
got to have progress it does spoil the naturalness of places. I went
up to Lion Rock today and what used to be unspoilt natural beauty
beyond Kowloon Tong is now high-rise buildings and apartments.
There's now access through Lion Rock to the New Territories, and
Cross Harbour Tunnel now has a subway, which goes across to the
island as well as Chung Wan Kuntong. It's an improvement for
commuters but spoils the romanticism. — Matt Monro, letter from
Hong Kong Hilton

The shows opened to packed houses and widespread acclaim. Don Butt, Matt's
old Provo Sergeant, came to see the show with his wife and was knocked out by
Private Parson's success. Mickie had arrived the night before and was amazed by
the awe with which people regarded her singing husband. The support wasn't just
confined to Hong Kong either: just before leaving England she'd had supper with
Tony Bennett and all he'd talked about was Matt.

> **Matt is so good that his Eagle's Nest clientele refuse to let him off so easily; they keep clamouring for more, then emcee Kit Masters steps back into the picture and tells them if they wish to hear more of Matt, they can come back tomorrow night – everybody laughs and the scene closes. Needless to say Matt is a big hit.**
> **— Reuters News Agency**

On her first morning in Hong Kong, Mickie answered the door to room service to see six cans of beer included in their breakfast order. The following day the same thing happened. The day after she changed the order to 'coffee' only!

Matt didn't use alcohol as a crutch to see him through a performance. He drank because he enjoyed drinking. In the early years, he'd been unable to afford the expense, but success had given him the freedom to indulge whenever he wanted. He felt it was a well-earned luxury. Unlike the average person who finished work at six o'clock, Matt habitually didn't finish until midnight and it was an unwritten rule that he would buy the members of the band a drink. There were also a hundred fans, promoters, stage crew, press and co-stars who wanted to raise a glass with the star. The social aspect was always appealing, but then there were also those impossibly lonely moments in a strange hotel room, thousands of miles from home, when a drink would help bring comfort. The erratic demands of his working schedule never allowed him the time to properly eat or sleep, and Matt loved nothing more than staying up into the early hours unwinding. If he did have 'one' too many, the only outward sign was that his eyes would glaze and he would invariably fall asleep.

> **I travelled the world with the man but never saw many sights – only the bars. He was a great drinker. When he stopped drinking I thought the firm of Johnnie Walker would go under. I used to tell the odd gag about Matt going for a medical – he had a urine test and they found an olive in it. Matt's drinking never really bothered me. I never once saw it affect any performance. It was an astonishing transformation. Drinking merrily in his dressing room, chain-smoking, suffering from sinus problems and colds, yet he would walk out and sing like an angel. — Don Black, *BASCA News* 1985**

With Mickie's arrival in Hong Kong, Matt had all the natural highs he needed.

There was someone to share his hotel room with, and no lonely periods to medicate with drink. Mickie wasn't against drinking; she indulged herself, and most of their time was spent in social situations. Michael Black had flown out on this trip and stayed at the Hilton. He had one of his acts, Dave Clinton, working there and after a show they would all meet up and go to Nathan Road together. Len Matcham and Sue Groves also flew out especially to see Matt perform, with the group regularly going out for a meal and a few drinks in town.

Matt loved the Far East, but all too soon it was time to head home. There was no room in the schedule to extend his stay, as he was due to open in summer season in five days' time, which meant that the whole family had to temporarily relocate to Yarmouth before the first show opened.

SHOWTIME

Matt opened at the Wellington Pier, Yarmouth on 4 June 1965, the same day that his new album, *I Have Dreamed*, was released.

> **The perfectionist strikes again. Matt in ballad mood touches new heights of artistry on this positively delicious set. His slowed down 'All my Loving' is a gem, so is the title track. 'Exodus' arranged by Johnny Scott... the rest by Johnnie Spence. There isn't any criticism one can make. This is superlative balladeering, crystal clear, phrased to perfection. Dig not the ballad eh? You still can't knock Matt. It has class, professionalism and style etched in to every single micro-groove. — *Record Mirror***

Matt, Mickie and the children moved down to the seaside resort for several months. Mitchell and Iris came too, and the kids had a grand time together.

Opening for Delfont in *Showtime* was one of Matt's more testing bookings, for he had to handle nearly all the serious vocals in a laughter-filled bill. He shouldered his task with musical mastery in a brilliantly staged spot that was introduced by dancing girls, and enhanced by a series of striking lighting effects. With Russ Shepherd at the piano, he opened with 'Once in a Lifetime' before switching to a dramatic version of the *Exodus* theme. He ended his sextet of songs with an impressive stage adaptation of 'Somewhere'.

Matt and Mike and Bernie Winters were back together again, with the added bonus of Jimmy Tarbuck. Jimmy was a twenty-five year-old Liverpudlian who'd made an impressive showing in the Royal Variety Performance the previous year. Building on that success, he was offered his own television show, *It's Tarbuck 65*. When the summer

Jimmy Tarbuck, Bernie Winters, Matt & Mike Winters in Showtime

season first started, Jimmy was very quiet and deferential, and kept calling everyone 'sir', but once they got to know him his personality exploded, leaving in its wake one of the nuttiest, zaniest and most likeable and generous characters they'd ever met. He played practical jokes on the boys all the time and his maniacal donkey laugh brayed across the theatre. Mike Winters recalls: "Working with Tarbuck and Monro was a ball, the happiest and most successful show we've ever been in, and we set a record, which I doubt will ever be broken. We filled the house every single night, for sixteen weeks – except one. And then only two [seats] weren't taken."

Mike and Bernie's comedy was highly polished and expertly timed, but still appeared spontaneous. Jimmy joined the Winter brothers in their foolery, yet still made his own individual contribution. Bernie, Jimmy and Matt mucked around during rehearsals for a new sketch and fell about laughing so much that Mike became really cross and stropped around with his pipe jutting out of his mouth. This spectacle earned him the nickname 'Squire Trelawney', graciously bestowed by Jimmy. Mike took the act extremely seriously and when Matt and Bernie, the rubber-faced half of the act, over-stepped the mark he reprimanded them, but it didn't stop them messing about.

Matt first introduced Jimmy to golf in Yarmouth. They played their initial games at Gorleston Golf Club, as did Con, Jon and Dec of The Bachelors. They were the most determined to get a handicap before the end of the season. The Rockin' Berries were also at the ABC with The Bachelors and were equally keen golfers, while Joe Brown at the Britannia had a handicap of twenty-four. Matt and the others took part in a weekly competition at the Gorleston Links.

Matt & Jimmy Tarbuck

Matt certainly looked the part, nattily dressed in blue and wearing a matching polo cap with a long peak, but he never won any trophies. Eventually the guys felt sorry for him and presented him with an 'Early Bird' award. All the boys competed in the TV Times Showbiz Golf Challenge Cup, and while Matt might not have played well, there wasn't a fitter looking star when he came off the course.

Social time was something all the boys revelled in, and these seasons afforded them the luxury of staying in one place for more than a few days and keeping the same company, making friendships for life. There was just one problem for Mike and Bernie: they were starring in *Blackpool Night Out*, the follow up to their *Big Night Out* television series and that meant flying From Yarmouth to Blackpool every Saturday as soon as the curtain came down at 10.30pm.

Matt was also performing in Blackpool for a series of Sunday concerts throughout the season and would often hitch a lift on the plane with Mike and Bernie. He had travelled in many small light aircraft but said after one particularly bumpy flight, "It flew in a strong wind and I discovered I didn't like landing sideways."

At nearby Bungay there was a tarmac airstrip, belonging to a local flying club, which was kept especially open for us, and a Cessna waited there, ticking over. There were two rows of tin cans on the runway, twenty-five a side, filled with kerosene-soaked rags, and an old farmer fired them with a taper, to light our take off. When we were gone, he'd snuff them all out and take the cans away. There was a big concrete slab – probably a relic from the war – halfway up the runway, and every week Bernie, sitting in the back, with fingers, arms, toes and eyes crossed, could be heard muttering a prayer. Ninety minutes later we'd spot the lights of Blackpool Tower, then we'd roar down the promenade, and the pilot would boost the engines as we passed the Imperial Hotel. This was a signal to Philip Jones and Pat Johns, the producers, that we were on the way in. Blackpool Airport was usually closed overnight but was kept open for us by special arrangement. We'd get to the hotel about 1.00am, but before turning in the four of us would chat about the show. It was a long tiring day and we'd be up again for rehearsals at ten. After the show, Bernie and I would get all tensed up, worrying about the return flight. Finding a strip of tarmac with a concrete slab on it was not easy. There was no control tower to talk to, so when we got near Yarmouth, we'd all start looking out of the window. It got a bit twitchy, but our pilots were great. — Mike Winters

The television show was as madcap as the boys. It aired live and on one edition Bernie took an elephant, with its minder, into the audience. The production team pacified the boys by explaining it was perfectly safe, but Mike and Bernie were on tenterhooks the whole time, imagining all manner of unpleasantries if something startled the rather large beast But it wasn't a large animal that gave them their most entertaining moment. During one particular show, millions of viewers watched Bernie lead a donkey through a side door into the stalls, and the brothers stood, one each side of it, gagging away over its head. The audience were absolutely hooting with laughter, and Bernie and Mike exchanged puzzled looks, because they knew their material wasn't that funny. Then, glancing down, Mike saw a great, steaming pile on one of his shoes!

Showtime regularly put on a Carnival Day when all the artists got together and went around town promoting the show. Matt made an unusual appearance at the Beaconsfield Recreation Ground as one of the jockeys in Yarmouth Round Table's annual charity Donkey Derby. He got in a little pre-match practice on the beach with the help of Jimmy Tarbuck, who was also competing at the event along with Lonnie Donegan and Peter Goodwright.

> **I remember Matt was at the Wellington with Mike, Bernie and Jimmy while I was at the ABC with The Bachelors. We often met after the shows at the Greek restaurant in Yarmouth. We all used to go to a midnight horror film show at the cinema owned by Jack Jay on the promenade. Tarbuck and I were almost banned for shouting out funnies, which actually were better than the film.**
> **— Freddie Davies**

By the end of June 1965, Matt's album was still receiving solid reviews and had been voted 'Pop LP of the Month' by *Melody Maker,* but sadly the acclaim didn't help the disc climb the charts. Don Black pointed out on the new LP's sleeve that Ella Fitzgerald, Connie Francis, Steve Lawrence, Andy Williams, Perry Como, Vic Damone, Sammy Davis Jr and Sinatra were among those who had paid Matt the ultimate compliment of recording songs that Matt had originally introduced. The *Birmingham Evening Mail* even added a footnote: "and…none of them has yet been able to better the original version".

TV Times was equally complimentary: "Matt ranks way up with Sinatra, Sammy Davis Jr, Andy Williams, Como and all the world's leading ballad singers. Yet he is grossly under-rated in Britain. Listen to his *I Have Dreamed.* Fourteen titles including a tremendous performance of the moving *Exodus* theme, interpreted with warmth, sincerity and distinctive class. This one must rate as one of the major ballad albums of the year."

Even with the new album out George wanted to record tracks for a follow up, so Matt flew from Yarmouth to London to spend three Sundays at Abbey Road. One of the tracks, 'And Roses and Roses', was so good they decided to place it on the B-side of Matt's new single 'Before You Go', which was issued in August 1965. It was an earnestly sincere romantic ballad for which the singer was so well known, but it also missed the charts.

Two-hundred-and thrity-thousand theatre-goers watched *Showtime* over the course of the 1965 season; four thousand more than the previous year. It played to a record ninety-eight point seven per cent capacity, trumping the ninety-senve point eight per cent in 1964. The show was described as "the best we have had" and the Chairman of the Entertainment and Publicity Committee, Mr Stone, presented the artists with lighters as a token of his appreciation.

Alongside his work as Matt's manager, in 1965 Don Black began to find success in his own right as a lyricist. John Barry had taken note of Don's song-writing talent on 'Walk Away'. Like most of the music industry, Barry spent a fair amount of time in and around Denmark Street, and on one of those occasions bumped into the budding songwriter. Everyone in Tin Pan Alley would swap trade news and these two men were no exception. It was over lunch that Barry offered Don a commission, the chance to work on the next Bond film. This was an enormous opportunity to both write lyrics for a successful movie franchise and to work with John Barry, who was making quite a name for himself. *Thunderball* was a huge success when released in 1965 and the soundtrack earned the creative duo a gold disc. However, even more important for Don was that in Barry he had found a great writing partner. They reunited for Barry's next film, which would make Don his fortune. In fact, Don would soon find himself straddling two careers – as Matt's manager and as a burgeoning lyricist. For the moment, the partnership between Matt and Don benefited them both.

Don wasn't the only one who was busy. It seemed George had been making big plans for his future, and his long-term aims didn't include EMI. He had decided the time was ripe to set up his own company. However independently minded, he wasn't one to abandon old friends, and continued producing Matt's recordings throughout the late 1960s.

There was a pool of about eight people who were responsible for the creative work at EMI. Apart from George there was Norman Newell, Wally Ridley and Norrie Paramor together with their assistants. When the time came for George to leave EMI, he offered some of the younger key creative people the opportunity to go with him. John Burgess, Peter Sullivan and Ron Richards accepted the proposition and set off to start a new company in August 1965.

The artists they were jointly producing made up a fearsome roster: John Burgess had Adam Faith, Manfred Mann and Peter and Gordon; Peter Sullivan produced Tom Jones and Engelbert Humperdinck; Ron Richards was producing PJ Proby and The Hollies; and Martin himself had The Beatles, Cilla Black, Gerry and The Pacemakers, Billy J Kramer with The Dakotas, The Fourmost and, of course, Matt. That was how AIR Associated Independent Recording was established and when most of the artists chose to go with AIR to produce their records, EMI suffered a crippling loss.

In the early years of AIR, we had no studios of our own. We had to

rent whatever studio was available and suitable for that particular recording. The most difficult job was to find a suitable site... The choice was greatly affected by the fact that I wanted a multi-purpose studio, one that could be used for dubbing films as well as making records. We settled on the top of the Peter Robinson building at Oxford Circus. — George Martin, *All You Need is Ears*

Not one person could fault George for his decision to leave EMI. Simon Kavanaugh of *The Express* summed it up succinctly. The Beatles' first album *Please Please Me* took a day to make and cost four-hundred pounds; *Sergeant Pepper* took nearly six-hundred working hours and the bill neared a hefty six figures. Though Martin was guiding the group to the top, he wasn't sharing in any of the financial rewards. As an arranger, he was paid a flat fee on a ridiculously outdated scale. For orchestrating 'Eleanor Rigby' he was reported to have received fifteen pounds. It was now a different story altogether. He had struck out on his own, with his own company and contracts. An analysis of the sale of a million Beatles LPs in 1965 shows why: The Beatles as singers got seventy-two-thousand pounds, The Beatles as composers got sixty-thousand pounds, retailers four-hundred-fifty-thousand pounds, EMI seven-hundred-fifty-thousand pounds, Government purchase tax two-hundred-fifty-thousand pounds. Now Martin could finance his own sessions, and lease the tapes to record companies for royalties of between ten and twelve point five per cent.

Before George left EMI permanently, he had several commitments to honour. One was Matt's next recording session. The singer first heard the number 'Yesterday' whilst on summer season in Great Yarmouth. He was sitting at home one Sunday evening watching The Beatles on *Blackpool Night Out*, and halfway through their act Paul McCartney sang 'Yesterday'. Matt thought the number tremendous and phoned George the following day to say he'd like to record it for his next album.

Two weeks later, Matt was again on the phone to his producer discussing the coupling of songs for his next single. 'Just Yesterday' was selected for the A-side and George talked Matt in to putting 'Yesterday' on the flip side, not knowing that McCartney would soon take it to the top of the American charts. When they got into the studio and recorded 'Just Yesterday', it didn't turn out as well as they'd hoped. What's more, Jack Jones had also recorded it and Matt was not at all sure about the recording. So George came up with a different solution.

It was on 'Yesterday' that George first started to score The Beatles' music. He had played the piano when necessary on the 1964 album *A Hard Day's Night*, but this track was the first time he'd used instruments or musicians other than The Beatles or himself. Trying for something more experimental, McCartney's solo version featured a string quartet. George suggested that Matt release the track as the A-side because there was a clause in The Beatles' record contract in England prohibiting the issue of a 45rpm, either instrumentally or vocally, unless all four members of the group had taken part in the recording session. Since Paul McCartney recorded the song with a studio orchestra without all his partners, no single could be issued.

'Yesterday' isn't an easy piece to put across, and George approached Matt's version with the fixed opinion that nothing could match the composer's splendidly nostalgic, beautifully wistful rendition. Surprisingly, Matt's version was totally new and he made the number his own by giving it a thoroughly distinctive styling. Changing a few notes here and there, the singer used a full-strength orchestra positioned discreetly in the background, rather than Paul's gentle string quartet. The vast string section swells out the accompanying sound, but never threatens the clear, highly polished sound of Matt's voice.

Matt's version burst into the Top 50 on release, steadily climbing to the number eight spot and remaining in the charts for an impressive twelve weeks. Although a classic Lennon/McCartney song, Matt's version was the first to chart and even The Beatles original could only match Matt's peak when it was eventually released as a single in 1976. To capitalise on its success, Parlophone issued the *Hits of Yesterday* compilation featuring eight of Matt's most famous songs, but once again the album failed to chart.

The British singer's version was launched in America following plugs on American radio from pirated British copies. Originally the disc was not intended for the American market, but Matt was pressured into allowing Liberty to rush release the record into the shops for November.

Matt's rise to fame coincided with The Beatles era and although their styles were very different, through his association with George he successfully recorded several Lennon/McCartney tracks with his own arrangements. They included 'The Long and Winding Road', 'All My Loving', 'Michelle', 'Here, There and Everywhere', as well as 'Yesterday'.

After the recording of 'Just Yesterday', Matt had a farewell drink with George and headed to Club Fiesta in Stockton-on-Tees. The twelve-thousand members of the leading northern nightspot had just voted him 'Top Cabaret Artist'. Bill Hall was chaplain to the club, a new position created out of the Church's concern for the welfare of all members of the theatrical profession, especially when they were away from home and at their most vulnerable. Matt was topping the bill and the place was packed out. There were long bars at either side of the cabaret room, which remained open throughout the performance. But as Matt was announced, everyone left the bars and crowded forward to watch the show, and the club didn't sell a single drink while Matt was on stage.

Russ Shepherd introduced me to Matt and the conversation lasted some time, and I later remembered that I had included a comparison of his recording of 'I Have Dreamed' with Sinatra's. To a less secure star, it might have been threatening or insulting but it didn't faze Matt who put me straight on the significant differences. Matt was to return to the Fiesta the following February and then again in the first week of August 1966. This was an unprecedented three times in less than nine months at the same venue. Each time he played to a capacity room with an enthralled audience. — Canon Bill Hall

Those frequent appearances at the Fiesta helped to cement the friendship between Matt and Bill Hall. When the singer returned in August, Bill invited him for lunch. As a bachelor, he had to rely on his own culinary skills and the sympathy of the local butcher. Having explained that he was intending to cook steak for a friend, he was assured that theirs was the best but that he should cook it as slowly as possible. When Matt arrived, Bill's first concern was what the neighbours would make of the Rolls Royce parked outside the curate's terraced abode.

The men made their way through to the dining room at the back of the house while the neighbour's youngsters gathered on the wall behind the property, providing them with a grandstand view of the two men eating. Bill proudly presented his dish and was utterly dismayed when the knife made no impression in the meat. It was as tough as old tanned leather and, embarrassed, he admitted as much to Matt. The singer had already made a valiant attempt at eating the meal, but with Bill's acceptance of defeat, was relieved he didn't have to struggle with it anymore. Bill had indeed followed the butcher's advice and cooked it slowly... under the grill rather than in the oven! Fortunately, Matt had brought a bottle of cognac to help the vegetables digest!

From that moment on they dined out whenever Matt was in the northeast. Bill relates that on one occasion, while the two men were eating and deep in conversation, a piece of paper was thrust in Matt's face with a command for his autograph. He replaced the food back on the plate, smiled, obliged with the autograph and chatted with the 'intruder'. As she left, Bill made some comment about the unmannerly approach but his friend's only response was supportive of the autograph-hunter and, by implication, of all his fans that enjoyed what he was doing.

When Matt returned to the Fiesta in 1966, he asked about the invitation Bill had sent for his ordination to the priesthood in York two months earlier. He wanted to know how it was that Bill was a 'reverend' before this. Bill explained that in 1965 when they had first met, he had been ordained deacon. The usual practice for the Church of England was that, after a year in the parish, the deacon was then ordained a priest. Out of this conversation came the suggestion that ordination was like getting a second wing. Matt commented that, later in cabaret, he would dedicate one of his songs to the young chaplain, as it was relevant to their discussion. Bill was quite shy and admitted that he would be embarrassed if his name was mentioned on stage, so Matt agreed not to reveal his identity.

> **During the cabaret I was at one of the cocktail bars some distance from the stage. He came to the song and, without announcing the title, simply said he dedicated it to one of his friends in the audience. He started to sing 'You're Gonna Hear From Me' followed shortly by the words 'wings' and 'learning to fly'. The connection hit me like a ton of bricks and, almost forgetting where I was, I let out a gasp of recognition that he claimed he heard from the stage.**
> **— Canon Bill Hall**

During the weeks Matt was appearing in the northeast, the two men frequently met up. It was the tradition of the parish where Bill Hall was curate to be called Father followed by the Christian name, so he was addressed as Father Bill. Matt had his own contemporary version of this, greeting his good friend with 'Hi Daddio' whenever he answered the phone. Often it was just to chat or tell the chaplain he was about to leave for a tour abroad, but it was an important way of keeping alive a friendship that was separated by geography.

Before the start of his arduous American tour in autumn 1965, Matt and Mickie took a week's holiday in the Riviera Hotel in Palm Springs, and then on to Milwaukee for a three-week cabaret season. The singer didn't need to adapt the act for an American audience, although he did make it a little more English, using an umbrella and a bowler hat in a Cockney routine.

The sprawling industrial city of Milwaukee – situated on the banks of one of the Great

Lakes, about ninety miles from Chicago, and close enough to the Canadian border to feel the intense cold of winter – welcomed Matt Monro with open arms. Matt and Mickie spent a good deal of time sightseeing in the area. They were staying in La Leilane, which also housed the club where Matt was working. Across the street was an excellent diner where they used to eat, but it was so bitterly cold, at forty degrees below, that they regularly hailed a taxi to take them across the road.

It was only after the success of 'My Kind of Girl' that the American audience really knew Matt Monro. Now he could fill a room on the strength of his name, although a hit record can mean nothing in such a vast country. Having the top chart placement in New York didn't guarantee you'd be known by people on the West Coast. However, television really helped boost Matt's exposure, as he was booked on a circuit of shows with Red Skelton, Jack Benny, Johnnie Carson and Pat Boone.

One of the most enjoyable aspects of show business was spotting a familiar face, especially when touring. You were more likely to see someone thousands of miles from home than in your own country, and Milwaukee was no exception. While performing one evening, Matt saw The Four Freshmen standing at the side of the stage. They had just finished work downtown and Matt dragged them up on stage, gave them the mic and left them to it. Later, they all ended up sitting on the floor in Matt's room. Bill was playing guitar and the others were all singing five-part harmonies. These memories were among the nicest and warmest of Matt's career.

Gordon MacRae, Bobby Greco & Matt (middle three l to r)

The owner of the club in Milwaukee had money difficulties, and as a result Matt didn't get paid for his cabaret season. He later found out that Brenda Lee, who had worked the club several weeks before, had also not received her money. They had no option but to sue and eventually managed to reclaim part of their fee through a court judgement, but it was not settled until late 1966.

After Milwaukee, Matt and Mickie decided to drive to Chicago to catch their flight to Vegas. The weather was as bitingly cold as the last town and because of the thick incoming snowstorms, the couple decided to stay a few nights in the Windy City to break the journey. They caught Buddy Greco's show, who invited them up to his hotel suite. Mickie went to the bathroom and saw Buddy's socks and underpants hanging over the bath rail to dry. It hit her that it didn't matter how big a star you were, they still did their own smalls, Matt included.

Matt was scheduled to play his most important American engagement to date: a month in Las Vegas in the main room of the Fremont Hotel and Casino. It was then the tallest resort hotel in the world at thirty-two stories high. Las Vegas's newest showbiz impresario, booker Eddie Torres, had put together a tidy and talented package in his Fiesta Room. Other than Matt, the stars featured included: Ethel Ennis, a stylish lady with silky, sensuous tones; and George Matson, who did more than merely pantomime a song to a backstage record player. His gestures, timing and ribald material were top quality, adult fare.

One of the side effects of a successful career in entertainment is that it becomes totally absorbing. You think about it twenty-four hours a day. It is not a thing that you can switch off whenever you want to. To some degree, it also dictates your hours and can limit your circle of friends. But the fraternity of show business personalities is friendly, if not a bit cutthroat. And that is more apparent in Las Vegas than anywhere else on earth. In Vegas there are no stars. It is just a job you all do. After working hours you meet up for social get-togethers, go to each other's shows and stop backstage for drinks. — Matt Monro

Vegas may be all glitter but it certainly is not all gold, and anyone that thinks an artist's life is an easy affair needs to think again. Matt's stint at the Fremont included two shows a night, increasing to three performances on a Saturday and Sunday.

Big plans were being made for Matt Monro. During the previous few years, he had established himself in Europe and the Far East as a leading nightclub and recording star. He had earned the reputation of being the 'Singer's Singer' as evidenced by his celebrity following. Names like Sammy Davis Jr, Doris Day, Hoagy Carmichael, Steve Lawrence, Andy Williams, Frank Sinatra and Bobby Darin had all lauded his efforts. Every night he performed in Vegas there would be a liberal sprinkling of American show business personalities in the audience, such as Quincy Jones, William 'Count' Basie and Billy Eckstine.

Thanks to the hard work of Matt and his record label, Liberty Records, America was made aware of and soon became addicted to the smooth Monro style. To capitalise on his growing popularity, Matt's manager Don Black had coordinated a tour of leading American nightclubs, including his current engagement at the new Vegas hotel. Once the opening night curtain had come down everyone waited anxiously for the reviews. They weren't disappointed and Nat Kahn's write up in the *Las Vegas Journal* was typical of the press response.

Matt Monro, a new British import with a reputation as a disc bestseller in his home country, made his American debut an auspicious one over the weekend when he opened a four-week

engagement in the Fiesta Room at the Fremont Hotel. The diminutive young singer makes up in poise, know-how and ability what he lacks in physical stature. Monro is a pop singer with a neat flair for projecting a lyric. He sells with an unadulterated showmanship that could be an object lesson for many of his young American contemporaries. He sings simply, in straightforward style, and he knows how to pace himself adroitly. Monro is equally adept at both ballads and rhythm tunes, with his simple, though assured manner winning his audience from the start. — Nat Kahn

The Vegas debut was more important than Matt could know. After years of holding his dreams in check, he had reached a turning point in his career. Mickie could even pinpoint the exact time that she realised her husband had 'made it'; "We were in our room at the Freemont when the phone rang and it was Don Black. We had heard something was cooking at Capitol when Nat King Cole died. His death led them to look for someone of roughly the same singing style to replace him. We knew they had considered Matt and that Don had gone into a huddle with them. I could tell by Matt's reaction on the phone that something big had happened but I didn't realise how big. Matt put down the phone, came to where I was sitting, took my hands in his and looked down at me with a wonderful tender smile. 'I've just been offered a deal with Capitol for seven years with a million dollar guarantee,' he whispered."

You don't forget the date you are offered a million dollars, but the phone call was even more special because it came on Matt's birthday. This was the deserved pay-off for years of hard work, and Mickie was moved by her partner's triumph. It wasn't just Matt's efforts as a performer that were being richly rewarded, it was also her own dogged work behind the scenes that was finally paying off. Capitol immediately sent a letter of intent and a contract was shortly forthcoming with an offer for three years with two options of two years.

The Capitol signing of Matt Monro was something that was done over my head, but I didn't object to it because I thought Matt could be very successful in the United States if he was properly promoted. The best thing that came out of it was the popularity of Matt's recordings in Latin America. — George Martin

Matt and Mickie's world was changing once again and now the promoters offered a life of first-class air travel, hotel suites and black stretch limousines. A night off was in order to celebrate with friends, and the couple headed a short way up the Vegas strip to see Bobby Darin's show.

Instead of a conventional dressing room, Bobby had a deluxe trailer equipped with a changing area, bedrooms and a kitchen. The very front of the trailer, which accommodated the lounge, afforded floor to ceiling glass. Bobby sat in a chair with his back to the glass wall, and Matt and Mickie sat opposite him. They were playing records and jamming along with Bobby rocking back and forth in his seat. Before they knew what happened, Bobby had rocked himself straight back through the glass!

Mickie left Las Vegas on 14 December to travel back to England. She didn't like to leave the children for any length of time, and not only had she been away for nearly two months, but Christmas was approaching and Michele was due to break up from school. The separation was harder than ever. Matt still had eight days until the end of his contract in the States and then had to fly to Manila.

Unfortunately, during that period, Matt had to cancel a couple of shows in Vegas as he completely lost his voice. Not only did the rapid climate change play havoc with his vocal chords, but the hotel's air-conditioning was always set on full blast.

> **Christmas is going to be miserable without you. I developed a stinking cold and lost my voice completely. I had Wednesday and Thursday off and it looks as if I'll have today off as well, although it's a lot better. I've spoken to Ed Torres a few times and he is delighted that I've taken the trouble to go on and introduce the show and explain to the audience why I can't perform. I suppose it does do a bit of good really. Business here is just about the same, if not a little worse but then it is the same everywhere so nobody is too upset. I had a call from Bobby Grinola in the Philippines and he tells me that Bayside have opened a new nightclub and want me for one night at one-thousand dollars. I said I thought it would be OK. — Matt Monro, letter from Fremont Hotel.**

Matt's voice crackled over the inter-continental telephone line, "Call me the man who missed Christmas." While families all over the world were celebrating together, Matt's Christmas was the day that never was. On Christmas Eve, he boarded an aircraft in Vegas bound for Hong Kong. When he arrived in Hong Kong a day later en-route to Manila in the Philippines, the calendar had skipped an additional day because the plane had crossed the International Date Line. Matt was welcomed in Manila on Boxing Day with a local brass band, the glamour of a radio and press conference and a motorcade through town followed by an invitation to dine with President Marcos. But he had missed Christmas Day entirely!

Matt's appearance at the Araneta in Manila back in April was said to have been the most successful since the late Nat King Cole had performed there. But the question that had played on everyone's minds since then was: what had *really* packed every performance at the Big Dome? Was it the combo contest that ran simultaneously with the show which drew the crowds, or was it the singer himself as Matt's diehard fans claimed?

They were about to get their answer with Matt's Yuletide return from 29 December to 2 January with a scheduled nine shows. Local personalities were also cast with Matt, including Pilita Corrales, a veteran of many television, radio and stage shows; Ric Arrelano Jr, whose latest recording 'You' reportedly made the Top 10, and Orly Ilacad and The Ramrods.

The Cosmos Bottling Company was sponsoring the three-hour show, which was split into two parts: the first section was titled *Philippines A-Go-Go*, where the local talents provided lively entertainment. The second half saw Matt sing seventeen songs, including local and festive numbers.

One other unique event was arranged to coincide with the singer's arrival in their country. That year, a local promotional company in the Philippines launched a nationwide 'Miss Sweetheart of Matt Monro' contest and the search for the 'Mr Matt Monro of the Philippines'.

Beginning in November and lasting five weeks, the Miss Sweetheart contest was conducted during the top-rated noontime radio variety show *Talents Unlimited*, which was aired on DZXL, an ABS-CBN station located at their broadcast centre on Aduana Street. The show was aired from 1.00pm for half an hour on Monday through Saturday with a bevy of young and beautiful girls competing daily. The five daily winners then vied for the weekly title on the Saturday live broadcast, answering Matt-related questions and singing one of his songs. The search for Mr Matt Monro was conducted simultaneously, with male contestants singing Matt's songs and competing daily and weekly. There were a plethora of prizes on offer for the two winners, but the most sought after was the offer to be the British singer's special guest on stage during his opening night. Matt crowned Norma Fonollera as the reigning Miss Sweetheart of Matt Monro and Walter Bowman won the title of Mr Matt Monro of the Philippines.

Matt crowning Norma Robinson

The winners were both introduced on stage at the Araneta. For Norma, it was a night to remember: "Matt serenaded me on stage with his rendition of 'Portrait of My Love' and I was the envy of the whole female population; I might add the men folk too."

Winning the title paved the way for Norma to launch her own show business career. She had been working as an executive secretary at a local bank, but after winning the contest she was offered the female emcee job on the same radio programme that had sponsored the event. Her career took off and she received requests to host other shows, record voice-overs for product endorsements and star in a radio soap opera. She told the press, "I owe it to Matt for the realisation of my dream to be in show business."

During his stint at the Araneta, Matt answered all of his critic's doubts as to whether or not he could fill the Coliseum on his own merit. He appeared before the biggest audience of his career on his opening night in Manila, playing to a capacity crowd in the biggest music extravaganza of the year. He thrilled his fans with new songs, both ballad and lively, delivered in his very own captivating style. The audience found him to be charming and when he stepped off the stage and mixed with the crowd, shaking hands and serenading them, the place erupted.

The shows at the Araneta finished up great and I broke my last record there easily. We had three of the shows to absolute capacity, about twenty-four-thousand. They were going mad as on the last night they ran right out of tickets and that's never happened before, so you can't talk to me now; I've such a big head. As you can see from the notepaper I finally got to Davao. I only arrived here by plane from Manila at 9.30am, and by the time I got to the hotel the local radio stations were broadcasting the fact that I was here and phoning me for interviews. On Sunday I went (at my suggestion) to the prison about ? hour from Manila and did a show for them. It is such a dreadful place, I couldn't try to describe it. They had set up a stage in the exercise yard but of course they didn't have a piano, so I used the trio from our show and Russ did the opening song on a tiny accordion – it was hysterical! Then to follow that, he accompanied me on a tiny organ from the chapel, which he had to pump with his feet. It was one of the best comedy acts I've seen. The outcome, believe it or not, was one of the best audiences we've ever played to. — Matt Monro, letter from Davao Insular Hotel, Philippines

While Matt was in Manila he made a side trip to Clark Field US Military Airbase on Luzon Island to entertain the troops. Hearing about the singer's arrival, both the NCO and Officer Clubs were packed. Although there were countless bars off-base in Angeles City, the servicemen's clubs at camp provided a welcome alternative. All three were large scale operations: the Officer's Club (CABOOM) near the parade ground, the Top Hat Club for NCOs near Lily Hill, and the Coconut Grove Airmen's Club with indoor palm trees. The NCO Club was especially active, and regularly brought major bands and artists from the United States to perform.

I was a sergeant in the USAF and my home base was at Clark Field Air Force. I was in the 1st Mobile Communications Group and assigned to different locations in SE Asia for temporary duty. It was on one of those assignments that I heard Matt sing on the jukebox. This was in Cebu sometime in August of 1965 and it was shortly after that when I returned to Clark, that he was performing live.

> **Matt sang at the Officer's and NCO Clubs. No uniforms were required at these functions and audiences were not segregated. The military were the first to integrate in our society. Matt packed the clubs and it was standing room only. — Ed Harrod**

Matt should have arrived back in London on 12 January 1966. Instead he was attending court in Manila charged with breach of contract by Hong Kong theatrical agent Gerry Scott, manager of the Orbit Recording Company.

Matt had been in his hotel room preparing to pack when a sheriff arrived and delivered a writ preventing him from leaving the country. A civil case for breach of contract was not usually a matter for the police, but by adding perjury charges Orbit cunningly ensured the singer was arrested, denied an exit visa and prevented from travelling home.

Scott contended that she had booked the singer in the Philippines nine months previously and that the contract was applicable to his recent appearances at the Araneta. The writ alleged that Matt had violated a contract under which he agreed not to perform in the Philippines for one year after his last singing engagement there the previous May. Orbit Records was now seeking five-thousand pounds in damages.

Matt took legal advice immediately, and with a solicitor's help counter-sued for fifteen-thousand pounds damages, plus legal fees. Having employed a local law firm he spent several days shuttling between his hotel, the solicitor's office, the immigration authorities and the consulate. He was made to deposit several thousand dollars to the court as an act of faith and was anxiously waiting to leave. A judge set a hearing to determine whether legal cause existed to keep the British singer in the Philippines.

Back in England, a Foreign Office spokesman issued a statement saying, "Mr Monro has contacted the British consul in Manila and is getting all the help he wants. I gather he made a deposition in court, and that seems to be the reason for the perjury charge. He does not seem to be getting all the messages we sent him and is now being held in a hotel room, but has been allowed to ring his wife."

Matt was absolutely livid. As well as being under house arrest, he was also now responsible for the additional hotel bill. It also meant he missed the release of his newest single, the first of 1966, and, as it would later turn out, his last for Parlophone. He had to cancel several appearances that were to have promoted the new number, withdrawing from *Parade of the Pops*, Pete Murray's *Late Night Saturday* and *Easy Beat*.

As far as Matt was concerned, it was a simple business dispute over his right to accept engagements in Manila without consulting the recording company. He'd made the normal legal answer to their claim and thought he could leave the rest to his lawyer. Once the writ was issued, a fifty-eight page deposition was drawn up in which he admitted that he had been under contract to Orbit for any work that he took in Manila, but they'd waived their rights in a talk with his manager Don Black. Orbit was forced to reduce the perjury charge to that of 'false testimony' after they found that Matt hadn't actually signed the deposition. Finally on the 15 January 1966, City Fiscal Senor Ricardo Catindig – who under Filipino law determined whether there was evidence to warrant formal charges in court – dismissed the charges of breach of contract and false testimony through lack of evidence. Five days later than planned the Immigration Commissioner, Martianiano Vivo, allowed Matt clear passage out of the country.

Matt had never been quite so pleased to stand on British soil and arrived home to find Mickie waiting with outstretched arms for her little 'criminal'. She arranged a surprise Christmas for him in the middle of January, complete with tree, turkey, presents and friends, and Matt regaled them with stories of how he had almost ended up rotting in a Filipino jail.

A RAW EDGE

The first thing Matt attended to on his arrival back in the UK, following his adventure in the Philippines, was an appointment with Musgrove, his throat specialist. The Harley Street doctor reassured the singer that all was well.

In January 1966, Beatles' manager Brian Epstein's firm North End Road Music Stores Enterprises (NEMS) announced the merger with the Vic Lewis Organisation, together as NEMS they formed the biggest European company to handle popular music arts. Former bandleader Vic Lewis and composer Don Black joined the board of directors at NEMS on 1 February. As well as Matt Monro, the new company now represented Donovan, Nelson Riddle, Henry Mancini, David Rose and more than a dozen top American artists whom the Lewis Organisation represented in Europe. The sixteen acts handled by NEMS, combined with the seventeen represented by Lewis, as well as the American contingent, made for an enviable list.

For Vic, joining forces with Epstein technically meant that he was now part of the company that managed The Beatles. Epstein had equally gained access to Lewis's impressive list of artists, but the real coup was the reciprocal deal that Lewis had sealed with the GAC agency in America, by which Lewis would take care of their artists when they were in England.

The agency tried to convince Matt and Mickie that the new set-up would be beneficial, but they didn't see it as working to their advantage. Don's time was being divided: while persuading Matt to record another one of his lyrics on the new single 'Beyond the Hill', which George had coupled with 'How Do You Do', he was also working to make a name for himself within the new agency – Vic Lewis had a lot of artists to juggle and Don was only too happy to help out.

Matt was scheduled to spend three months in the States in the summer of 1966. In the meantime there were commitments in England. *Sunday Night at The Palladium* was

Lionel Bart, Matt & Russ Conway

filmed live and the February transmission saw the show swinging from the outset.
Sharing the honours with Matt was Libby Morris, who teamed up with Larry Adler
in their Ad-Lib Show. The *Daily Mirror* was critical of the duo and as staunch
supporters of former host Bruce Forsyth, they felt that new host Jimmy Tarbuck fell
short of the show's high standards. However, they boasted to their readership that
they had enjoyed every minute of Matt's performance. Matt hadn't wanted to do the
show but with his upcoming trip to the States keeping him away for several months,
he knew visibility was the key.

Before Matt left, he made time to meet up with his great friend Russ Conway
who'd recently suffered a stroke affecting one of his hands, the worst thing to happen
to a professional musician. At first Russ didn't think he would ever play again, but
after months of intense physiotherapy, he gradually regained the use of his hand.

Matt had switched from Parlophone to Capitol in a long-term deal, recording both
at Capitol Tower when in Hollywood and under the supervision of George Martin
when in England.

Matt's first single for Capitol was one of the songs he will forever be associated with.
The year before, producer Carl Foreman had forged with Columbia to film *Born Free*. It
was based on the true-life international bestselling book written by Joy Adamson about
her game warden husband George and Elsa, the orphaned lioness they raised while

living in Kenya. The simple tale about lions in captivity had already been translated into twenty-one languages and seemed an obvious choice for conversion to celluloid.

Carl Foreman and producer Sam Jaffe struggled to decide who was to write the music for the film. The fact that *Born Free* was set in Africa was actually what provided the solution, for although composer John Barry was known for his Bond contribution, he had also scored the music for another feature filmed in that same country: *Zulu*.

Barry had a few ideas of where to take the music but was nagged by the suspicion that this was nothing more than a sentimental family romp. He decided to treat the piece as a pastiche on a Disney-type adventure, and, although he had never scored for a Disney movie before, he admitted it could be a fun and challenging project.

The next stumbling block was the title song. With the success of Bond, film companies generally accepted soundtracks as an essential marketing tool for selling a film, and producers were paying close attention to the theme of any project. Columbia wanted to hire an American folk group to both write and perform the title song, but John gave them an ultimatum: either he would do it all or he would walk away from the project altogether. His threat carried weight and Foreman backed down, leaving the composer in peace.

Barry's first choice of lyricist was Leslie Bricusse, but he was spending most of his time in America at that time, so John was forced to look a little closer to home. He had collaborated successfully on *Thunderball* with Don Black, so he was an obvious second choice.

Barry decided that the lyrics should focus on the freedom theme and had already jotted down a few ideas. He shared his thoughts with Don and the lyricist went to work. Barry liked Black's finished piece and was happy to go straight into the recording studio, but Foreman felt differently. He disliked the song immensely, feeling the lyrics should centre around and encompass the lions themselves. However, Barry somehow persuaded the producer to stick with his vision, so now the only question that remained was: who should sing it?

Barry's choice was the Danish singing duo Nina & Frederick, not only were they friends of the composer, but they also had their own successes in the music field. Foreman's choice, on the other hand, was Matt Monro. Both Don and Barry agreed that the sincerity and tenderness of Matt's voice would be the ideal instrument for the piece, so he joined the team. However, the experience proved to be fraught with difficulty for all three men.

Working on 'Born Free' – Matt was effortless, he picked up the song so quickly, he never asked any deep questions, he just sang it. He

The Three Musketeers, Matt, Don Black & John Barry

was not over stylised, I hate people who come in with ideas and almost reinterpret the song. I liked Matt's directness and I liked the fact that he sung the song the way it was written and just added a wonderful sound and kept the simplicity there. — John Barry

It wasn't just the musical side of the film that experienced problems. The lead actors were having difficulty with the animals: they were, after all, not of the domestic variety and didn't take direction well. Progress on filming was laborious and agonisingly slow.

The problems with the film's music continued, James Hill the director and Sam Jaffe, the film's day-to-day producer, had their own thoughts about how the rest of John's score should fit into the film. They were adamant that the music should burst through when the animals were first introduced on screen. When he heard this, John got straight on the phone and begged Foreman to help prevent a crisis. The producer placated Barry by confirming that his score would be put in the film the way it was intended.

James Hill then wrote a letter to John not just outlining how unsuitable his music was, but that he hated it and that Barry hadn't even been his first choice as a composer. He further added he had serious doubts about how the Americans would receive it once it was released in the States. It was clear that Hill wanted Barry off the picture, but if Barry left the project then Don and Matt would follow suit. They had formed a strong bond and didn't want a division in the team.

Born Free *Premiere*

Carl Foreman surprised everybody with his solution – he replaced the director. It should have gone smoothly from then on, but Foreman was no pussycat and weighed down the project with yet more problems. He kept changing his mind on whether the film should even have a title song and thought Don's lyrics were too much of a social comment. Foreman couldn't see beyond what was obvious to him, that the lyrics should speak of lions, cages and bars. Don Black fought back declaring the song had to have a universal appeal *and* still fit with the theme of the film. Barry stated that the song was essential to the whole essence of the project and the narrative would lose impact if the score was cut. Barry and Black fought their corner vigorously and thought they had won the battle with Foreman, but they were in for an unpleasant surprise.

Matt and Mickie attended the Royal premiere of *Born Free* at London's Odeon Leicester Square on 14 March 1966 eagerly anticipating the reception the song would receive. Matt happily posed for the waiting press, answered the usual questions and then sat down to watch the film.

It wasn't long before Don received an anguished call from the singer telling him they'd cut the song from the final cut of the movie. Matt explained to the lyricist that

Carl Foreman had approached him in the lobby after the film's closing credits and apologised for the omission. He explained that they'd dropped the first reel of the movie and fractured the film so the soundtrack couldn't be used. But the truth was that he thought it was in the film's best interest to drop the song and he'd gone back into the cutting room and re-edited the film, removing the song and replacing it with an orchestral version for the opening.

Barry and Black had both been unable to attend the premiere, so if not for Matt, they would have remained blissfully unaware of what the producer had done and the music history books would have told a different story. The trio were apoplectic and called the producer to read him the riot act, but Foreman was adamant that his decision wouldn't be reversed.

However, as it transpired, Sam Jaffe had been wrong about Barry's music, the Americans had loved it. 'Born Free' had rocketed up the American charts soon after release, and the Roger Williams orchestral version, complete with backing choir, was now sitting in the number one position. Carl Foreman couldn't justify his decision any longer – he had to reverse it.

Columbia could see dollar signs but there was a slight problem: for a song to be eligible for an Academy Award, it had to feature in every print of the film. The heads of Columbia, the publishers, Screen Gems and the producers all clamoured to reclaim every piece of celluloid that had been distributed, so as to put the song back in, spending vast sums of money on an Oscar campaign to promote the new version.

In 1966, both the song 'Born Free' and John Barry's score were nominated for Academy Awards, but attending the ceremony was the last thing on Barry's mind, not only was he incredibly busy, but the experience had left a bad taste in his mouth and he had wiped his hands of the project. Don, however, had no such compunction; he was beside himself with excitement and flew over to America with his wife for a ringside seat at the most important annual event in Hollywood.

A motorcade of polished stretch limousines deposited their famous passengers at the entrance of the Santa Monica Auditorium. As each celebrity took their place on the red carpet, the adulating fans duly screamed their approval. Among them, Don was desperately trying to remain dignified but his composure crumbled as the importance of the occasion, and the company he was keeping, sunk in. Here were the high rollers of Hollywood, the makers of dreams, and as the celluloid stars made their way to their seats Don and Shirley found themselves sitting next to renowned lyricists Hal David and Jim Dale. The competition was fierce with Jim Dale and Tom Springfield for 'Georgy Girl', Burt Bacharach and Hal David for 'Alfie', Johnny Mandel and Paul Francis Webster for 'A Time for Love' and Elmer Bernstein and

The photograph Don sent Matt from the night at the Oscars, pictured with Dean Martin.

Mack David for 'My Wishing Doll' all in the running for the coveted prize.

At last it was time for the audience to hear all the songs nominated. Representing 'Born Free', Roger Williams and His Orchestra complete with a huge choir, with singers of all different races and backgrounds brought home the song's powerful message – that everyone could live in harmony, whatever their colour, race or religion. It was a typical over-indulgent Hollywood production and the audience lapped it up.

After what seemed like an eternity, the decision was read out – and 'Born Free' had won the Oscar! It was finally Don's turn to take to the stage and he proudly accepted his gold statuette from actor Dean Martin. In less than three minutes he was back in his seat but those 180 seconds changed his life for good.

Don sent Matt a photo of the occasion and signed it: "For Matt, if it wasn't for you, I wouldn't be in this picture, Donsie." Matt received another gold disc for his efforts.

In the early hours of the morning, a phone rang in London. With no thought to the vast time difference, Michael Crawford excitedly informed a bemused John Barry that he had just won two Oscars: for Best Song and Best Score. Barry had achieved what most people spent a lifetime pursuing. With the song-writing team of Barry and Black scooping the Academy Award for the Best Film Song of 1966, they gained the honour of becoming the first British partnership to ever earn this distinction.

> **Born Free was the ultimate, Matt made the movie even more special than it was; and put Don Black, Matt's manager, on an incredible writing career. Don had the words and Matt had a voice like melted chocolate: what a combination. — Jackie Trent**

'Born Free' became one of the most successful songs of the twentieth century but despite popular belief, the classic has never charted in the United Kingdom and even Matt's version in the States only reached No 126! The success came from further afield with the track soaring to the number one position in the Australian hit parade, knocking Sinatra's 'Strangers in the Night' off the top spot, No 1 in Singapore, No 1 in Matt's adopted country – the Philippines – and No 1 in the Jamaican hit parade.

The lyrics were interpreted as a message of freedom and were adopted by political and religious leaders the world over. Presidential candidates, preachers, cult leaders, gurus and devout sects heralded the lyrics and their subliminal meaning and in 1992, during a state of emergency in Thailand, the song was broadcast over the airwaves.

> **When Matt goes up and hits the high notes and sustains them there is a tremolo that comes into it which he doesn't have in the lower register, and there is a fascinating quiver. It never goes out of key but it introduces both vulnerability and suspense into the song and he comes to use it often and effectively, he only uses it a couple of times in each song but it becomes a trademark of his. — Paul Gambaccini, music critic and broadcaster**

> **'Born Free' was one of the most important theme tunes and of course John Barry wrote the score and Don wrote the lyrics. Don was a fledgling writer in those days and this was a very big chance. He naturally suggested it as a title for Matt Monro because he was starting to manage Matt at that time. All together it was a very successful collaboration. — George Martin**

'Born Free' will forever be associated with Matt Monro. Like The Beatles, his voice was to become the international sound of 1960s Britain. In the wake of the Bond craze, he became known as Hollywood's 'King of the movie soundtrack', reaching a

Matt & Mickie in Jamaica

massive worldwide audience who might otherwise never have heard his music.

**Matt's voice was cultivated and cultured. His diction, it's so classy
so he'd sing an ordinary song but with that approach and that
accent it really elevated it to some exalted arena. — Don Black**

Needing a break from an increasingly heavy schedule, Matt and Mickie nipped off to
Montego Bay in Jamaica on the 28 February for a twelve-day break. They stayed at
Breezy Point Hotel and, at the invitation of Errol Flynn's wife Patrice, hired a small
plane to visit the Flynn's one thousand-six-hundred-acre estate in Port Antonio. The
three of them spent the afternoon on a thirty-foot bamboo raft on the Rio Grande. It
was a truly spectacular trip, epitomising the tranquillity and beauty of the island. The
small vessel meandered through rainforests and farmland, spying singing
washerwomen and waving small children, who would run along the sides of the river
banks trying to keep up with the raft. There were no paparazzi hassling them, or
phone calls to answer, it was the perfect getaway.

Drinking in the hotel bar one afternoon, Matt and Mickie met American singer Ginny
Simms who had recently gone into real estate. Because of their initial introduction to

Jamaica, Matt and Mickie were tempted to invest in property and by the end of the afternoon they had put down a large deposit on a condominium.

Ginny first achieved fame as a big-band vocalist with the Kay Kyser Band. After her two previous marriages ended in divorce, she settled with her third husband, Washington's former Attorney General Don Eastvold. Together they bought Breezy Point Lodge in 1963, one of Minnesota's most famous resorts, and planned to develop the area into a country club community. Eastvold formed a company with his wife and other partners called Eastco, primarily for developing properties in Jamaica and Palm Springs.

After a huge building and renovation programme, Breezy Point reopened on 22 May 1964, and crowds flocked to the resort to hear musical greats such as Tommy Dorsey, Count Basie and Glenn Miller. To the locals, the revival of the resort was beyond belief, but had they taken a closer look, the distant rumbling of storm clouds may have raised some doubts.

The high-flying days of Don Eastvold and Ginny Simms came crashing down in September 1965. Their explosive growth of Breezy Point had pushed money out the door faster than it was coming in. At the end of 1965, three creditors sought to force Breezy Point Estates into involuntary bankruptcy. Though, as is often the case in the legal process, the wheels moved slowly.

When they met in Jamaica, Matt and Mickie had no idea that Ginny and Don were in financial trouble. The couple had shown professional presentations of the properties in their portfolio and everything looked above board. But unknown to the Monros, between the time the creditors sought bankruptcy, and until the declaration, Simms and Eastvold had set up another company in Jamaica, selling condominiums, including the property that Matt and Mickie had put three-thousand pounds against.

Once they returned to England, more than one person advised the couple that what they had signed for didn't exist. Matt and Mickie had befriended several people over on the island that had also been tempted into buying, and together they instigated a group action to get their money back. However, by the time solicitor's costs were paid, they got back very little, and it wasn't until May 1966 that Breezy Point Estate was finally declared bankrupt. More than two hundred creditors presented claims, estimated at nearly three million dollars. With that, the ownership by Simms and Eastvold was placed in receivership.

Matt was delighted to be asked to star in Rediffusion's television tribute to American composer Jule Styne, which was being produced by Styne's nephew, Buddy Bregman, and broadcast on 13 April 1966. *A Funny Thing Happened to Me on the Way to the Piano* was a musical profile of the composer, who flew over to take part and conduct the fifty-piece orchestra. The television programme also included performances by Bob Monkhouse and Millicent Martin. Perhaps better known for his songs than his name, Styne had been nominated for an Oscar nine times, and won the award with 'Three Coins in the Fountain'.

> I tried to pick the best English artists I could get. Millicent is tremendous, her songs have something to say dramatically. Matt sings a quartet of Oscar nominations, besides the award-winner, 'I'll Walk Alone' and 'I've Heard that Song Before'. — Buddy Bregman

The *Weekend Mail Ball* was another wonderful evening. It could have been mistaken for a Royal Variety night as outside the door of the Lyceum Ballroom star after star drove up. *Weekend Magazine* held the party with more than two thousand of their readers attending, not to mention some of the biggest names in show business, including Britt Ekland, Lionel Blair, Henry Cooper, Mitch Murray, Judy Geeson, Dorothy Squires and Graham Stark. Peter Sellers, who broke into a bit of 'Goodness Gracious Me', received the Show Business Personality of the Year Award from editor David Hill, while Matt went onstage to receive *Weekend's* Silver Star as the Top Male Singer of the Year, presented by compère Jimmy Savile. Savile had compèred the last three *Weekend Ball Nights* and fittingly won a star for Disc Jockey of the Year that evening.

After a flurry of private functions, BBC's *Parade of the Pops*, and a week's cabaret in Newcastle, Matt flew to Los Angeles on 20 April, three weeks earlier than expected, to spend the next eighteen days recording an album and two singles for his new record company.

A COUPLE OF FELLAS

Located on the corner of Sunset and Vine in Hollywood, The Capitol Records Company was founded by songwriter Johnny Mercer in 1942, meaning that New York based companies such as RCA-Victor, Columbia and Decca now had direct competition from the West Coast label. In addition to the Los Angeles-based recording studio, Capitol had an extra facility at West 46th Street in New York City.

By 1946, Capitol had more than forty-two million sales under its belt, helped in earlier years by artists Paul Whiteman, Martha Tilton and Ella Mae Morse and later by Bing Crosby, Peggy Lee, Stan Kenton, Les Baxter and Nat King Cole. The company soon established itself as one of the Big Six record labels. But the expansion didn't stop there and three years later they purchased the KHJ Studios on Melrose Avenue in Hollywood and added artists Frank Sinatra, Judy Garland, The Andrews Sisters, Jackie Gleason, Dean Martin, Nancy Wilson and The Four Freshmen to their ever-growing roster. In 1956 Capitol sold ninety-six percent of their record stock to the English company EMI and soon after built a new studio at Hollywood and Vine to match its state-of-the-art Abbey Road Studio in London.

The full glare of American media was soon to fall on Monro as the US record industry underwent dramatic changes. With Sinatra's defection to his own Reprise label in 1961 and the death of Nat King Cole in 1965, Capitol lost their two biggest selling male artists. Matt had consequently left England's shores at the request of the giant American label, having been coaxed over by an unheard-of million-dollar contract. The lad from Shoreditch was now expected to fill his boyhood idol's shoes so that Capitol could maintain an A&R balance and revive their great vocal tradition.

The parallels between Matt's life and passing and those of Nat King Cole bear mentioning. Both died of cancer in the same month, twenty years apart. Both had children who celebrated a birthday the month they died, and at least one of those children entered the same profession. Each man had a son who died relatively young (though years after they themselves had passed) and their performing children later recorded poignant tributes on compact disc, which through the procedural advances in technology allowed them to merge new arrangements of their own voices with those of their respective fathers', giving life to a series of duets. One other striking similarity was that both artists released albums in a foreign language. In 1958, Nat King Cole went to Havana, Cuba to record *Cole Español*, an album sung entirely in Spanish. The album was so popular in both the States and Latin America that two others followed in the same format. Matt recorded his first Spanish album in 1968, ten years after Cole, like his peer learning the lyrics purely by rote, and after the success of *Alguien Cantó* followed it up with several others in the same vein.

In 1966 Capitol gave Matt the golden opportunity of allowing him to work with such greats as Nelson Riddle and Henry Mancini and he was to turn out some of the finest recordings of his career during this period. Matt was primarily partnered with one of two arrangers, depending on the demands of the recording. If swinging through up-tempo, brass-driven charts were required, Monro was usually placed in the capable hands of Sinatra's old friend Billy May. If a more sombre or sentimental approach was desired, Sid Feller was called in for some of his inspired string-laden orchestrations.

Sid Feller was a conductor and arranger best known for his work with Ray Charles, who he had helped woo over to the ABC label. As well as acting as the star's conductor on tour, the two had turned out a series of albums, starting with *Genius Hits the Road*. Ray once said of him, "If they call me a genius, then Sid Feller must be Einstein," and he had a right to comment as they worked together for thirty years. Feller stayed with ABC until 1965 and had only recently moved to California to become a successful freelancer when he worked with Monro.

Matt was given Sinatra's former A&R man Dave Cavanaugh, who with his wife Mildred threw a cocktail party at their home to welcome Matt and Mickie and introduce the new singer from England. One of the introductions made on that evening was to Sid and Gert Feller and it wasn't long before the men were huddled in the corner talking shop. Gert left the men to it and sought out conversation with Matt's wife, who was sitting alone on the settee. She instantly felt as if she had known Mickie for years and the two women spent the whole afternoon talking. Gert was the only person Mickie had felt truly comfortable with since arriving in America, desperately needing a friend and confidante. She explained that Capitol expected them to move to America and, with Matt shortly going on the road for seven weeks, it was all a bit overwhelming. Gert contacted a real estate colleague and within a week

Matt & Mickie having dinner with Sid & Gert Feller

the Monros had found the perfect home less than a mile away from the Fellers, with a pool and a school right across the road on Roseda Street.

> Sid thought that Matt Monro and Ella Fitzgerald were two of the best singers in the world. He died saying that same thing. Everyone in this family thinks that Matt Monro is the best male singer ever. Sid was in love with Matt as a person, a friend and a singer. He has said in interviews as late as a couple of years ago that he enjoyed every minute working with Matt. Being that us two wives got on so well made it easy for them to work together. Even the kids got along wonderfully. — Gert Feller

The American market was a very difficult thing to break into for British artists in the 1960s, but Matt was readily accepted among his peers. Tony Bennett, Jack Jones and Frank Sinatra all loved his voice, and Sid was fussy about who he worked with, so his admiration for Matt was no small compliment. Matt was a refreshing commodity, a fantastic singer and a genuinely nice man with no Hollywood airs and graces.

Working in the Hollywood recording studios was a dream come true for Matt and he had lots of help and encouragement from the likes of Billy May, Hugo

Matt & Dave Cavanaugh

Winterhalter and Nelson Riddle. Under the direction of American recording manager Dave Cavanaugh, Matt's first Capitol sessions produced his label debut in 1966. *This is the Life* was laid down in barely four days, spending a single week in the chart at number twenty-five. Interestingly, it included his version of Udo Jürgens 1966 Eurovision winner 'Merci Cherie', which Capitol chose not to release as a single, leaving the honours to Vince Hill, who had chart success with it back in England.

> Respect – that's the only word that can really be used to describe the feeling surrounding Matt Monro. Matt's just finished cutting his first album in America and the sessions for that album really show the kind of entertainer he is. He was working with an entire new set of musicians, new arranger and a new producer. You'd think things would be a little strained just because they had never worked together before and didn't know each other. But Matt really showed his stuff during the four-day session. Unlike many artists, Matt cuts a record together with the entire orchestra at the same time – most artists like to cut each set of instruments individually and then add the voices. Not Matt, he walks into the recording booth, surrounded by a full orchestra, and cuts each

Matt & Sid Feller

record all at once. And he cuts a first-rate album in just four days –
no artistic temperament, no late night sessions, no hair pulling,
name calling or strained emotions... The greatest compliment a
performer can receive is from his fellow entertainers and the
people in the business. Overnight successes or gimmicks do not
impress these people. They respect consistency and talent. And
that's the way it is with Matt. After a session you hear an engineer
say, "I cut that same song with Nancy Wilson but I never heard the
song until this afternoon". You hear the arranger tell Matt, "You
phrase a lyric beautifully". You hear the musicians talk about how
easy-going he is and how he's the kind of guy you just naturally
want to do great things for. And that's the secret of Matt Monro.
He's a modest kind of guy who doesn't make demands, so you just
naturally want to give him the world. — Carol Deck, *KYA Beat*

Matt's talent blossomed and flourished under Capitol's guidance. His confidence
grew as he relaxed into the niche they had carved out for him. They needed a singer
of Matt's calibre to fill the void left in their table of artists and although he failed to
meet his commercial potential whilst with Capitol, there is no doubt that he recorded

some of his finest songs between 1966 and 1970. It seemed someone had finally unlocked the true essence of Matt Monro.

With his debut album in the can, Matt was eager to meet up with Mickie to tell her all about the sessions and they agreed it was best to meet in Los Angeles. She flew into LAX Airport and together they drove to Reno for Matt's 10 to 30 May engagement at Harold's Club. Billed as 'The Mad Greeks', the comedy team of Lewis and Christy shared the three-week run at the seventh floor nightspot. They dashed through a well-paced and perfectly timed routine that sparkled with fresh and extremely witty material.

Harold's second-floor Silver Dollar Room offered entertainment with the swinging song styles of Johnny Prophet, piano offerings of Freddie Henshaw, guitar and tunes of Ronnie Draper and banjo plucking of Curley Elder, so in between shows Matt and Johnnie Spence would often catch another act there. In fact, there was a lot of talent in the town, with Roger Miller and Shirley Bassey at the Sahara Hotel, Shecky Green at the Riviera, Buddy Rich and Jackie Mason at Aladdin's Hotel and Sammy Davis Jr at the Sands Hotel. Sadly, with two shows every night of the week and three on Saturday, there was little time for Matt to do anything other than perform.

Several nightclub operators around the country had put feelers out for months to land the English singer, but Matt chose to follow the Reno date with an engagement at Paul Catalana's San Jose Safari Room. The dates all proved highly successful, with promoters and club owners begging for repeat bookings before Matt had even left the building. The singer had no time for paperwork however, that was for Don to sort out. Matt was due back in the studios.

Matt spent three consecutive days at the beginning of June laying down tracks for his next album, even before the first one had been released. Everything seemed to be done so quickly and, this time, Matt didn't enjoy the process. Dave Cavanaugh was an experienced producer – he'd worked with The Four Seasons, Nancy Wilson and The Beach Boys – but as much as he liked the man, Matt didn't feel the same rapport he shared with George. Tracks were thrust at Matt and, as always, he was happy to go with the flow on most things – but he was adamant on others. There were certain songs he wouldn't sing.

I don't think songs should be philosophical. A song is basically a poem set to music. It shouldn't be a protest of the world in which we live, a protest against the government. I don't want to hear about the hellholes of Vietnam, about people dying. I don't want to be preached to. Good songs are those that last and become

> **standards, songs that are intentionally acclaimed by everyone, have masses of appeal, stand the test of time and even twenty years later, given a new treatment, could sound good.**
> **— Matt Monro**

Matt felt that music evoked memories and fond ones could be therapeutic; they gave calm to the pressured mind and could bring a brief moment of release from pain. None of that could be achieved with an organ in the musical line-up. Matt absolutely abhorred the instrument, thinking it the most unromantic sound in the world. The one other unmentionable was the use of fade-out, and about that Matt was adamant: "I hate fade-outs; all it means is that they couldn't think of how to end the song. It means they haven't put enough thought into it. That's ridiculous because they all know how they're going to start the song, why can't they work out how to end it?"

The single 'Honey on the Vine' came out on 10 June, but like all his Capitol singles, it failed to chart. The accompaniment was a knockout, with deep bass throbs forming the main rhythm patterns. For the first time in years, Matt had brought about a change in the typecasting of the Monro voice. This song was quietly but meaningfully delivered with added personality, if slightly less power. A rhythmical, almost semi-jazz drum backing complemented Matt's voice, creating a very warm atmosphere. It was subdued and bluesy with excellent orchestration.

> **Capitol had a selection of 'easy listening' artists on their roster and my father was trying to find ways of selling their records to a younger audience. Being thirteen, he brought home 'Honey on the Vine' to ask my opinion as to whether it would appeal to the teenage market. He used to tell me that hits were a 'luxury', and consistent artists like Lou Rawls, Peggy Lee and Matt kept the label afloat by steadily selling product. — John Gilmore**

Capitol had three main departments, A&R, Sales and Legal, and the head of each division was a vice president of the company. In 1963, Voyle Gilmore was named Vice President of the A&R department and subsequently spent less time in the studio than in the office. Without warning, the sales department began calling the shots, determining what products were 'cool' and should be marketed to the younger record buyers. Traditionally, the A&R department made the artistic decisions and the sales department did the selling, but the weekly singles meeting that Voyle had previously chaired was taken over by someone from sales, and his weekly album meeting soon

American Press Shot

went the same way. Young, inexperienced salesmen were making important calls and only trying to market what they felt made the grade, ignoring the other products in their stable. The tide was slowly turning and changes were being made at Capitol, but Matt didn't have time to hang around and find out what the changes were – he had a date with Hancock.

STOMPING AT THE SAVOY

Preparations for *The Blackpool Show* were well under way. It was a Sunday night variety series hosted by Tony Hancock and filmed in the Lancashire resort. The executives at ABC Television decided they wanted a pilot episode at their theatre in early June. They needn't have worried, as the show was wonderfully successful. A large venue with a lot of seats to fill didn't faze the comic, and he brought the house down. After the success of Mike and Bernie's humour of the previous year, Hancock continued the legacy, delivering high levels of entertainment to an appreciative crowd.

With the success of the pilot to build on, the producer decided to use the same script for the first show, but with a different cast to freshen up the delivery. Mark Stuart, the director of the eight-week series, was delighted with Matt's agreement to headline the 19 June opening instalment, with support from American jazz singer Marion Montgomery. The series, which replaced the *Palladium Show*, was an immediate top-ten hit in the ratings. ABC's confidence in Hancock's ability as a compère was confirmed. The Hancock genius was never in question, with sharply timed off-the-cuff remarks and ad-libs cleverly executed with impeccable split-second timing.

Matt would have loved to stay over and catch up with his mate, but he had a flight to catch the following day to Australia, where he was to be based for the next four weeks. The opening show on 23 June was terrific and Matt dedicated 'You Don't Have to Say You Love Me' to Dusty Springfield, who was sitting in the audience. She was so moved by the dedication and the beauty of the performance that she had tears running down her face. With 'Born Free' sitting in the number two position in the Australian charts, it was understandable that Sydney's Chequers Club was packed out every night.

Matt's contract for the Australian club specified that whoever appeared there also had an obligation to appear on a television special, either filmed at the club, or in this case in a studio. Called *Matt Monro Sings* the programme included his old friend Lorrae Desmond and singing group, the Flanagans. While Matt sat in Australia, Mickie attended George and Judy Martin's wedding reception. It was a wonderful day and the couple looked so blissfully happy. It had taken a while but now at least everything was legal.

> I started my spectacular TV yesterday. Would you believe a 9.00am call at the studios? It looks very good. Great producer. We're doing the thing in two halves, yesterday and next Saturday. We had a trio on the show called the Flanagans who do a medley and at the end of their spot I join them complete with bowlers and rolled umbrellas for a little dance. Would you believe 'DANCE'? It turned out great. Next week I do the medley with Lorrae Desmond, all London songs. Last night in Chequers, which seats 500 people, we had 600 – can't be bad. – Letter from Matt, Sydney Town House Hotel

Producer Ron Way went to Chequers to watch Matt work and listen to his arrangements. He liked to get a sense of the man, know his 'victim' and get a feel for Matt's character and personality. At a meeting the following day, Ron presented a concept of what he wanted to achieve. He didn't want the camera and the director competing against each other; everything had to be focussed on the person on the screen. He just wanted to let the cameras sit and watch the performance as a static audience, rather than try to be artistically clever. With each new camera angle taking twenty minutes to set up, it was important to Ron that he didn't lose the atmosphere. A cut would make the whole thing go flat in seconds.

> We spent about two weeks preparing for the television special, and there were quite a few rehearsals to finalise the programme. Matt brought a few orchestrations that were designed for the club dates in Sydney but I had a much larger orchestra so it was my job to enlarge the existing orchestrations and write new ones that were decided to be included in the programme... I have been fortunate and privileged to have conducted countless shows for international stars during my 63 years as a musician/arranger/conductor but I fondly remember my association with Matt because he was a nice human being, a perfect gentleman and a regular guy with no airs and graces, with a huge

Australian Television Special

**talent and a beautiful, instantly recognisable singing voice that has
catapulted him into super stardom. – Tommy Tycho**

Ron's vision was to do Matt's big numbers in an empty studio. It was difficult to be
creative when the production only had a limited budget of thirty thousand Australian
dollars, but it worked well. They did the shoot over two separate Saturdays, with the
first morning given to music rehearsals and the afternoon spent on the production
numbers with the Flanagans and Lorrae Desmond. Although the musicians
complained because they had worked late the night before, Matt arrived full of
enthusiasm, though slightly bleary eyed, and as soon as the band struck up the first
note he came alive. When there was a natural break he would slope off to the dressing
room and have a quick nap. The sails of the Sydney Opera House provided the motif
for one of Matt's sets in the pop singer's hour-long television special. Set designer Ken
Goodman said, "We haven't got the final cost yet but hope it's close to the original!"
On the second day's shoot they introduced a live audience, mainly made up of a party
from the show's sponsors, Dulux. Shot between five and six in the afternoon, the
audience witnessed Matt's production numbers, one with him in a dark business suit,
armed with a bowler hat and umbrella singing 'I'm a Pommie'. After the break they
filmed the British singer and Matt White bantering on stage, as well as Lorrae's duet

Matt & The Flanagans

with the star. The sponsors loved it. Although not shot until early evening, the day had started considerably earlier for Matt and the musicians. He was tired and still had his evening show at Chequers to do, but it had been worth the effort.

I thought Matt was a wonderful singer – one of the best in the world. In the 50s there was a little coffee shop in Denmark Street called 'Julie's' and that is where I met Matt, two young hopefuls looking for work. He had a terrific sense of humour and we would often belly laugh. When he was in Sydney I saw him perform at a club – an excellent act, great singer with a warm, natural personality – a real audience connector. The Dulux show was the only time we worked together. It was shot in two days with no party after, I think we were all too worn out and Matt still had his evening show to do. Matt was an exceptional talent, humble with a great sense of fun. It was a joy working with him and an honour to know him. – Lorrae Desmond

We were privileged to work with a great many international stars during that wonderful period, but Matt was a standout. I cherish the tape of the special that we did with him and will never forget

**his professionalism, his kindness and most of all his friendship. We
wined and dined with him on a few occasions and when we left
Australia I really felt proud to say that we were his 'mates'.
– Paul Flanagan**

The television special was highly successful and scheduled to broadcast on over
thirty Australian stations in November. With 'Born Free' still at No 1 in Singapore,
Jamaica and the Philippines, Matt flew back to England at the end of July satisfied,
more so because after sitting in the Australian charts at number two for a few
weeks the record had just knocked Sinatra's 'Strangers in the Night' off the top spot
as well. It had been a long four weeks, which he wouldn't have minded so much
if Mickie could have been there with him. Matt was torn between his love for the
business and his love for his wife. The simple fact was that the accolades didn't
mean as much without her to share them with.

It didn't take Matt too long to chalk up another record in England, this time as
being the only Top of the Bill star to play the famous Greasbrough Club for two
consecutive weeks. Also sharing Matt's unique distinction was his pianist Russ
Shepherd, who was elated that Matt had filled the place to capacity at every
performance.

**Playing Greasbrough was a great leveller after Australian living,
people in our business have an inflated ego at times and it's great
to be brought down to earth. – Matt Monro**

Greasbrough was a mining community and the club looked like an enormous
shed. Run on a non-profit basis, it housed a restaurant and concert hall complete
with club secretary and committee. Matt and Mickie travelled down to Rotherham
in the afternoon for rehearsals, after which they went back to the hotel, a few miles
outside the village. Even though he had done the club before, driving there on a
Sunday night was not quite as easy. Matt's Rolls Royce was laden with extra
passengers, friends coming along for the opening. They were rather wealthy
people garbed in mink coats and smoking Havana cigars. As they drove towards
the village, the area was completely pitch black, none of the lampposts seemed to
be working and Matt could hardly see a thing. After driving in circles he admitted
defeat, he was lost. At Meadow Bank Road he stopped the car.

Although there were no streetlights, he made out a lone figure walking down the
street and drove towards the shadowed outline to ask for directions to Greasbrough

Social Club. The car glided to a halt and the electric windows slipped down creating a link to the outside world. The guy pleasantly went through a very detailed route of how to get there. He spoke in a very strong Northern accent. "Ay you're goin' wrong way, turn round here, go down road couple hundred yards, you'll find a turn on the right, go right there, then go to top of rise and when you get to top look down the hill and you'll see a lot of lights in valley, that's Greasbrough Social." Matt thanked him profusely and just as he was about to drive off the local man added, "but you'll not get in, because Matt Monro's appearing there tonight."

In one show, the social secretary sat at the back of the room operating the lights and suddenly in the middle of 'Portrait', the lights were abruptly raised and the tannoy voice boomed, "Pies 'ave cum." Every chair was scraped back across the floor and the audience stood up en masse and raced to get in line for the food. Those clubs were the heart of what happened in the North, they were the centres of the community. Every week the same people would turn up, sit in the same seats and wait to be entertained for a few hours. They usually had a good time, although they didn't always show it. It didn't matter; Matt loved the surroundings of a stage, the audience, the lights and music. Never mind that it was an unsophisticated social cub with peeling paint and nicotine stains, serving warm beer to a sometimes frosty audience. He was on a high every night.

Two Sunday concerts at the Scarborough Futurist Theatre, two nights in the Isle of Man, a meeting with George Martin and then it was time to sneak quietly away for a two-week break in Benidorm. Evelyn was invited to come over with them and the children, and Marion and Johnnie joined the party with their new addition. The bond that had built between the two couples over the years was indestructible. Matt and Johnnie did their thing while the girls invariably looked on in bemusement. They acted like teenagers at times, belly flopping in the pool, inflating their chests, prancing and pranking about with each other, drinking a bottle of beer (or six) and then sleeping it off around the pool. They had set up camp on the beach and paid the local Spanish pool guy some pesos for umbrellas and loungers so the girls and children could sit in the shade. On one such afternoon, Matt and Johnnie were chest-deep in the sea breaking the waves with their bodies and calling over to their wives to watch them. The surf was strong and as the next wave hit them squarely head on, the boys disappeared from view. For a split second Marion and Mickie looked worried and jumped up to get a better view, when they suddenly saw both men emerge from the watery expanse and start hobbling towards them. It came as no surprise to the girls that after three hours in the local hospital, both men were declared fit but suffering

Matt, Johnnie and Marion enjoying a night at El Alcazar, Benidorm

from three broken ribs – each!

At least the timing wasn't bad, they had exactly seven weeks for the injuries to heal before the opening at the Savoy on 19 September for a three-week engagement. The Savoy Hotel was a prestigious event in professional circles and opening night saw much excitement. Len Matcham flew over especially from Jersey, to host a private dinner party for Matt and Mickie. Sue Groves flew over with him and invites included Marion, Bill Hall and George and Judy Martin. Marion was dressed up to the nines, it wasn't often she went to such an event or saw her husband work, so she was really looking forward to the evening. Matt and Johnnie joined the table for dinner in the show room; champagne was flowing, the guests were laughing and swapping stories when out of the blue Johnnie announced he wasn't feeling very well.

I was excited about the evening. It wasn't often that Johnnie and I got such an invite and I had dressed up for the occasion and was drinking champagne, which Len kept flowing. Everything was so expensive there so I wanted to enjoy every moment. When Johnnie said he wasn't feeling well, I was slightly irritated as I didn't want him to put a dampener on the evening and snapped that he should go and see the hotel doctor if he felt 'so' ill! Poor Johnnie, not wanting to cause

a fuss, kept his mouth shut and did the show. – Marion Spence

In 1966, Matt invited me to stay with him, Mickie and family at the time he was appearing at the Savoy. Mickie seemed unfazed by the fact that her husband had brought a clergyman to stay at such an important time. For me it was the beginning of a friendship that now included both of them. This was important because Matt often talked about his beloved Mickie and her role in his success. The first night at the Savoy was a great occasion – as, of course, was every Matt Monro performance. At this one, one of his friends hosted a dinner party, at which I was included among the guests. Matt's sense of occasion was then, as always, immaculate.

– Bill Hall

It was the most fantastic evening. Len played the perfect host, regaling everyone with stories about Brecqhou, the new island he had just purchased in the Channel Islands near Sark. Matt brought the house down and after changing into his lounge suit he came out to join the table. Meanwhile, Johnnie snuck off to see the hotel doctor. He didn't come back. He was rushed into the nearest hospital with a ruptured appendix, which was promptly removed!

With three weeks' work in his hometown it was obvious there would be a constant flow of old friends and visiting celebrities who would pop in to see the show. Johnnie received an unwelcome barrage of Matt's humour each day when he visited the hospital on his way to the hotel. Russ Shepherd stepped into the breach with a few hours' notice and everything continued as normal.

One point that I must mention is Matt was one hell of a performer. I saw him in cabaret at the Savoy. The world knows what a great singer he was; unfortunately, not enough people saw him perform 'live'. I miss him. I try to console myself by believing that like my brother Bernie, Matt didn't just take a sip out of life, he lived it, and drunk it down with enthusiasm and good humour. His heart was big enough for him to give love and affection to family and friends, and at the end, big enough to give him the courage that fortified him and inspired us all. – Mike Winters

Humour was a big part of Matt's life and an important element of all his friendships. He swapped stories with Bill all week, and he had the clergyman in stitches describing the comedic performances he had watched. Don Rickles himself could not have bettered Matt's re-creation of the comic's act in Vegas. Johnny Mathis was appearing at the Prince of Wales theatre, while Bill was staying with the family. With Matt working at night he took Bill to the matinee. After an excellent performance, they went backstage. Matt greeted Mathis with "John, what can I say? That was fantastic" – Johnny's face beamed only to change quickly as Matt completed the sentence "fantastically mediocre". The smile quickly returned: he was familiar with the Monro humour.

It wasn't just celebrities that popped into the Savoy. Sue Maull had driven up from Birmingham with Christine Inkles in tow. Even though the weekend was costly, it was worth every penny to the two die-hard fans. With the menus all in French, neither had a clue what they had ordered but it didn't matter, they couldn't wait for Matt to come on. Christine had never been very talkative and sitting in such a grand setting didn't help. She didn't say a word until they got to their hotel room and then Sue couldn't shut her up – she revelled in her idol's performance, dissecting every song with a glowing account and was still going strong at five in the morning!

Matt was a humble soul, never quite understanding what all the fuss was about. He was chuffed when he was told that in the Jamaican hit parade his records were sitting in the number one and two positions with 'Born Free' and 'Walk Away' respectively. He was always secretly pleased when he received a compliment from an artist he admired. While at the Savoy he received such a tribute from Hoagy Carmichael by way of a letter.

Dear Matt, Sitting here and listening to your rendition of 'One Morning in May' I had a strange feeling that not once had I thanked you for all the fine renditions you did for me – that's not right – so here I am thanking you, even though it might be a repeater. Believe me you balladed all those songs so believably good, 'One Morning in May' is a real achievement, most difficult, my little mother's favourite song of mine. Keep up the great work, sincerely, Hoagy

His biggest buzz came with the arrival of a letter from the Variety Artists Benevolent Fund confirming his appearance at the Royal Command, and asking that the matter be kept confidential until the official press release was made from Buckingham Palace. The East End boy had made good.

While in London, Matt was thrown into his usual working pattern with producer George Martin. 'Where in the World' was one of the songs that Matt had featured in his recent Palladium television appearance. Not the oldie of the same title but a beautiful ballad – tender, sentimental and unashamedly sugary with a slow lilting rhythm and a big-build crescendo. The disc was due for release early the following year and would be coupled with the soon-to-be-recorded 'The Lady Smiles' as its B-side.

John Barry and Matt's next outing was for Rank's *The Quiller Memorandum*, starring George Segal, Alec Guinness and Senta Berger, with a script by Harold Pinter which told the story of a lone British spy's quest to discover a neo-Nazi insurrection group's headquarters. The song's title was 'Wednesday's Child'. This haunting John Barry/Mack David ballad was poignant, appealing and somehow strangely mystic. Barry's scoring was first-rate with cellos, violins, clavioline and mandolin effect, and a gentle slow lilt, with background whistling in the lush orchestra reprise. On the flip side was 'When You Become a Man', another Vic Lewis/Don Black ballad that raised a lump in the throat of many a parent.

No sooner had Matt settled back into family life, than his suitcase was packed again and with passport in hand he flew to Los Angeles en route to Harvey's Resort in Lake Tahoe. The resort had fantastic gaming facilities, boasted six dining areas and ten bars, three adjacent to the entertainment areas. Having arrived a few days before his opening on 14 October, Matt and Mickie explored the area, bumping into Andy Williams in town. He extended an invitation to the couple to see his show and join him at his hotel for an after-show party.

> **A handsome, quiet, personable English gentleman has invaded Lake Tahoe. The gentleman by the name of Matt Monro, one of the most popular male vocalists on both sides of the Atlantic, is at Harvey's Resort Hotel Pavilion of Stars with his powerful voice and swinging styles. This is the third time Matt Monro has invaded the shore of the 'colonies' but the first time he's reached as far inland as Lake Tahoe. Matt Monro favours ballads, but his entire selection is well sprinkled with up-tempo numbers and some finger-snapping pop jazz. His musical arrangements, conducted by Johnnie Spence and played by the Al Tronti Orchestra are first class. His fine voice, good looks and easy-going manner combine to explain his international popularity. – *Nevada State Journal***

Although set in beautiful surroundings, the work was hard with Matt performing three shows a night, six days of the week. He was also expected to give press interviews and be available for local radio. The Americans certainly got their contract's worth.

Two weeks later, Matt flew to New York for rehearsals prior to his opening in the Persian Room at the Plaza Hotel. He was booked for three weeks as a replacement for Jack Jones, who had bowed out for a telespecial, but Matt's acceptance was based on the condition he be allowed to keep 14 November in his diary for his pre-booked Royal Variety Performance. Minor problems were overcome and the Plaza finally agreed to let him out of his contract for three days, allowing a day for travel, one to do the show and another to get back. It was an extremely tight schedule. Matt was also responsible for placing his own deputy. He finally found someone suitable, but they were on more money than him, so it proved a costly exercise. Matt didn't care. He felt so strongly about his British roots that had it been a choice, New York would have been left for someone else. Matt wasn't about to give up the opportunity of performing in front of the Queen Mother. It was a great honour for him so early into his career, and he would have the thrill of sharing a dressing room at the London Palladium with some of the biggest names in the business.

Matt was forced into the obligatory press rounds, appearing on both the *Johnny Carson* and *Mike Douglas* shows to promote his visit. Dusty Springfield's season was running almost simultaneously with Matt's New York cabaret and he attended her opening night along with Jackie Trent, with Dusty repaying the compliment a few nights later. Tony Bennett was another familiar face at Matt's first New York show and the two men talked shop well into the small hours.

Taking advantage of the fact the singer was in America, Dave Cavanaugh booked Matt into Capitol Records' recording studio in New York, laying down sixteen tracks over two days. Matt was extremely unhappy about one of the sessions, feeling the tracks had been butchered. Three songs particularly offended his ear: 'Sweetest Sound', 'Lover's Caravan' and – the worst offender – 'The Lady Smiles'. It seems that although recorded in New York, a large number of tracks were overdubbed at Capitol's Hollywood Tower.

> In one case I was in New York and Capitol came out there and we did an album with a trio, just head arrangements and then they took it back to LA and scored them. They did the arrangements round the trio and added strings and brass in California; you don't even know who the arrangers are. I won't mention his name but I

> went in to routine a song and it took this arranger three hours to
> transpose from the written key into my key, I was mad and asked
> what was going on. The guy said, "Well man I don't play piano", it
> was laughable; one of the arrangements was never finished
> because he didn't know how to do it. – Matt Monro

Matt remained in a tetchy mood for the rest of the day after that recording session. He was angry with the label for prostituting his music and didn't understand why everything was being rushed. That night, after the show, Matt was taking some private time in his dressing room. With the applause still ringing in his ears and sweat trickling down his face, he lit a cigarette and sat down. Suddenly a stranger barged in without knocking, and demanded that Matt go back on stage and sing some more songs. Matt was in no mood and politely told the man that he was finished for the evening. The uninvited guest kept insisting, needling and bugging the singer and when at last it was clearly evident that Matt had no intention of stepping back onto the stage, the guy pulled out a gun and stuck it into the singer's face yelling, "You will sing another song!" Matt was flaming and told him in no uncertain terms that whatever he chose to do he would not be singing again – at which point the man walked out, slamming the door behind him. When Matt flew back to London for the Royal Variety Performance the next morning, he wasn't sure whether he would return to finish the gig. The events of the previous night had unnerved him, and although outwardly belligerent at the time, it was certainly not what he had been feeling inside.

The annual Royal Variety show is as synonymous with November as a British pea-souper, and the always highly anticipated, hugely theatrical event is available to everyone through the medium of television, and now the Internet.

The first and the only *Royal Command Performance* in aid of the Variety Artists Benevolent Fund (VABF) at the Palace Theatre, London took place on 1 July 1912. Held in the presence of King George V, it was agreed that he would attend annually provided the profits went to the VABF. After that first show the official title became *The Royal Variety Performance*. It is televised to the public and the responsibility of producing and broadcasting the show is shared alternatively between the BBC and ITV networks, with the proceeds from that evening going to help members of the profession in need. It was not uncommon for hardship to fall upon an artist, and with this in mind a committee was formed to discuss how best to tackle this eventuality. The VABF was established and went from strength to strength, adding the purchase of Brinsworth House – an old people's home – to their portfolio. As well as helping

hundreds of pensioners, assisting with nursing fees and funding regular convalescence outings, the charity also helps in the matter of funerals.

Throughout the profession, it was considered an honour to perform before the Royal Family, and over the weekend the invited artists were frantically rehearsing for what would often be the highlight of their careers. Working for forty-eight hours straight, they stopped only for meals and a few hours sleep. Their main concern was the running order, timings and lighting around their moment on the stage. The production team meanwhile were busy looking for artists and hauling stand-ins on stage for lighting any absent stars.

Monday 14 November 1966 saw the Queen Mother, the Duke and Duchess of Kent and Prince Richard of Gloucester attend the performance, which was filmed by the BBC and broadcast six days later. After the arrival of the Royal Party and the National Anthem sounding throughout the theatre, the audience settled down for what they hoped would be a great night of entertainment. The London Palladium orchestra rose out of the ground arriving at stage level, like a submarine rising to the surface of the ocean. The overture played, the curtain rose and the opening number revealed The Palladium Boys and Girls with the Bel-Canto Singers presenting a colourful spectacle of music and dance. Des O'Connor compèred the evening and effortlessly warmed up this most hypercritical of audiences. His winning personality sparkled and with impeccable timing he introduced the Bachelors to the stage. With a change from their usual routine, they carried off a pastiche as white-faced minstrels, but the audience seemed to prefer it when they transposed back into what they were more commonly associated with, the slow ballad style number, 'Beautiful Dreamer'.

Jack Douglas, Des O'Connor, Gene Pitney and the Piero Brothers all took to the stage in the first half, although Gilbert Bécaud lost his voice completely at rehearsals and was unable to perform. The Anta Theatre in New York lay dark for the evening at an estimated cost of three thousand pounds to enable the French singer/composer to appear. He sat in the auditorium, tears rolling down his face, to be compensated in some measure later by being presented to the Queen Mother. The spectacular magic act of Marvo and Dolores (alias Morecambe and Wise) entertained one and all. Eric wandered around in his outsized magician's tailcoat in the guise of a bedraggled conjurer with Ernie kitted out in full drag as his enchanting blonde assistant. The pinnacle of the performance saw Ernie imprisoned in a Chinese box while lethal weapons were thrust in one side and out the other. It was one of the best skits ever seen at the Palladium, and recognised and applauded as such. It would have been mad to try and follow that with any other comic offering, so instead Juliette Greco rendered a French version of 'Autumn Leaves' with an elegant simplicity.

One of the surprise offerings came in a four-minute widescreen colour film showing highlights of the greatest British sporting event in recent history, the World Cup. At its conclusion, the curtain was raised to reveal the victorious English team holding the trophy triumphantly aloft. The crowd were ecstatic. The variety bill continued with a vocal presentation by Wayne Newton, who was virtually unknown in Britain, but the audience had no such problem identifying Tommy Steele. Celebrating ten years in show business, the singer invited audience participation with 'Little White Bull'. On a receding wave of enthusiasm the curtain came down on the first half, and a short interval allowed the multitudes to rush to an insufficient number of bathrooms.

Henry Mancini opened the second half conducting at the piano three of his own compositions, 'Days of Wine and Roses', 'Charade' and 'Moon River', backed by an enormous onstage orchestra. He was followed by the Bel-Caron Trio, The Seekers and the sombre talents of Frankie Howerd. In a growing paroxysm of mock rage, he ranted about his reprehensible treatment at the hands of the ever-tolerant Bernard Delfont. Howerd was a fine antique of flawless descent and the last authentic voice of Music Hall: hoarse, brassy, boozy and ever so often sharply demonstrative, reproving

the audience for their wilful misreading of double entendres.

Matt earned an ecstatic reception with his smooth, immaculately phrased singing, entertaining the masses with 'As Long as I'm Singing', 'Born Free' and the *West Side Story* number 'Somewhere'. He shared dressing room No 1 with Sammy Davis Jr, Jerry Lewis and Tommy Steele, with Morecambe and Wise in the adjoining room. Nerves played an important part of all the artists' performances on that night and although struggling himself, Matt later admitted his weren't nearly as bad as Bernie Winters', who when meeting Her Highness at the Royal Variety in 1962, called her

'Your Honour' and promised her tickets for their pantomime if she wanted them.

The Queen Mother saw Jerry Lewis making his third appearance at the London Palladium; his first was back in 1953, while he was in partnership with Dean Martin. He centred much of his comedy act on musical gags. The last act of the night was Sammy Davis Jr., making his third appearance in a Royal Variety show with his incomparable versatility. Coming on more than three hours after the start of proceedings, he began with 'You're Gonna Hear From Me', moving on to a memorable version of 'Birth of the Blues' and a medley of songs from the Newley/Bricusse stable, ending dramatically with 'What Kind of Fool Am I'. The crowd roared their appreciation.

Despite over-running by more than thirty minutes, the Royal party stayed in the foyer with the artists until nearly midnight, congratulating them and producer Bernard Delfont on a wonderful show.

Matt loved the evening, and performing for his country was something that he had dreamt of doing for quite a while. His appearance that night was hailed as a great success, but he was never given the opportunity to perform at another Royal Variety show. Matt wasn't the only one who was acutely aware of his absence from the more notable programmes, and the tabloids continuously printed comments asking for an explanation for his exclusion.

> **He was quite philosophical about his success; he used to say "what does it all mean son?" Same when he wasn't chosen for a Royal Variety Show. – Don Black**

There was no time to bask in the aftermath of that magical evening, as Matt was soon back on the same flight that had winged him over less than seventy-two hours before, to complete his stint at the Persian Room. Unfortunately, the journey wasn't without incident. Matt was carrying an empty suitcase after depositing some belongings in England, and when he arrived at Kennedy Airport, the customs official had a great deal of difficulty in coping with this fact, especially as the singer was in the throes of passport difficulty. The request for Matt's appearance at the Persian Room was last minute and it had been difficult obtaining an American visa quickly, but the real problem stemmed from the fact that Matt needed immediate re-entry to New York after the royal show. Everything was finally settled and Monro completed his six thousand mile round trip – only missing one performance at the Plaza.

BLACK OR WHITE

The late 1960s saw gambling and entertainment venues spring up all over England, the architects' briefs from their clients born of a burning proclivity to outclass the competition. But they made the mistake of over-extending themselves and, with the growing number of clubs clamouring for a finite number of acts, booking agents took advantage of the situation by quoting over-inflated fees for their artists to appear. The clubs had no other option but to give in to the excessive demands, but their acquiescence proved more costly than they first thought. It soon became apparent that they had no way of sustaining the ballooning fees and they started buckling under the strain, closing as quickly as they had opened.

While the North may have been considered less sophisticated than the South, the clubland scene there was extremely influential, with the major operators guaranteeing seating for over a thousand people. The Cabaret Club, Blighty's, Copperfields, The Golden Garter and the Talk of the North were just a few notable venues around the Manchester area. The rest of the north of England had the Night Out in Birmingham, Batley Variety Club, the Wakefield Theatre Club, Sheffield's Fiesta and Jollies at Stoke-on-Trent, to name a few. Arguably the biggest club company in England was the Bailey Group. Controlled by John Smith, there were very few major towns or cities in the North and North East that didn't have a Bailey's Club.

The South answered the Northern club scene with an equally strong stable of venues such as Caesars Palace in Luton, the Club Double Diamond at Caerphilly, Circus Tavern, Purfleet, and Lakeside at Camberley – all one-thousand-seater venues. Weston opened the Webbington and Wales had the White Wheat at Maesteg.

George Savva had just taken over the running of Caesars Palace, a venue with a magnificent auditorium with two tiers for diners and an overwhelmingly opulent ambience. Michael Black was the club's entertainment booker and worked from his office in London. The larger-than-life agent visited the club almost every night, occasionally taking it upon himself to compere the evening's entertainment. Savva remembers Michael as a force to be reckoned with: "He was a total extrovert, but wonderfully charismatic. He always gave me the impression that the whole of show business revolved around him."

> **Every table and every seat was taken in the 550-capacity audience. There was a feeling of intimacy, even in such a large room, further enhanced by the lighting, now dimmed so that the bright stage lighting could have maximum effect and be the focal point of the room for cabaret. — George Savva, *For Whom the Stars Came Out at Night***

George 'produced' an evening to perfection and hosted an event as if it was his own private party. He knew every regular's name and made each person feel as if they were the most important person to walk through the door that night. He was equally attentive with the artists, fulfilling any request with good cheer and establishing many a celebrity friendship in the process, Matt included.

Matt's opening week on 10 December was a sell-out and during afternoon rehearsals he tested out a new song he wanted to put into the act. The charts had been written for the musicians and he wanted to hear the new tune in action. "I'm going to do a thing that I've never done before since coming into the business", he told the audience later that night, and with that he produced the sheet music for 'The Impossible Dream' and began to sing. The audience was overwhelmed and, when Matt had sung the last note, they leapt to their feet in a standing ovation.

Savva went backstage after the show to make sure that Matt had everything he needed and to find out if he was available for autographs later in the evening. The singer was happy to oblige and asked if he could have a table and chair in the auditorium near the backstage door. George was pleasantly surprised by Matt's easy demeanor, as some artists would only accept a limited number of autograph books for signatures, others had signed photos to be handed out and a minority didn't want to be troubled with autograph hunters at all.

> **After the show almost the entire audience formed a queue right round the club like a snake. It wound its way round the entire circumference of each level. Matt met everybody, signed**

autographs and had his photo taken with those that had cameras. For well over three hours he worked his magic with all. How they loved it. Word got round that the great Matt Monro was meeting and greeting at Caesars. By the end of the week the public were fighting to get into an already-overcrowded club. — George Savva, *For Whom the Stars Came Out at Night*

The Castaways in Birmingham was another new club that opened in 1967 and Matt was booked there the week after his Luton appearance. It advertised a superb three-course meal sitting beneath the tropical palms of a South Sea island, and boasted a glittering floorshow of glamorous girls and star artists emerging from native huts or the deck of a wrecked schooner. The bars were inside the wreck itself, creating a unique character and atmosphere for the club. You could be served by one of the forty Castaway girls or laze around the beach hut bar and gaming tables. The novelty of the club brought people in droves, helped by the fact that they were booking all the top names in the business. In fact, the club charged the highest entrance fee they'd ever charged for Matt's debut week and every ticket was still snapped up.

Dave Allen was appearing ten minutes away at Dolce Vita with Kenny Baker as support and all the artists in town stayed at the same hotel. Kenny Baker remembers one particular evening well. "Matt and Dave were always messing about when they were in the same town. I was appearing with Dave and after our show we popped across to the Castaways. We had snuck in and were sitting in a balcony to avoid being noticed. Suddenly Dave sprang up and flung himself at one of the nearby palm trees. The audience fell about, as did Matt, and the two did a full ten-minute skit on the stage together before Matt kicked him off."

Matt and Dave spent most of the week trying to outdo each other and after performing they would sit in one of their hotel rooms playing cards, drinking Guinness and whiskey and cracking up over the night's antics. Their rooms were interconnecting and each day saw a barrage of rude notes exchanged under the door. It was a cardinal rule never to disturb one another in the morning, sleep being their most important commodity, but they would know when the other was up by the slip of paper that slid under the door. Dave would find room service delivering an order he hadn't put in, while Matt noticed extras on his bill for blue movies. Dave placed Clingfilm on Matt's toilet seat, while the singer snuck out and removed one of the shoes that Dave had placed outside his room for polishing the night before. Only when Matt heard Dave on the phone berating the management did he sheepishly produce the missing article.

Matt loved a good curry and one of the restaurants near the Bullring would stay open late if he rang ahead to say he would be coming in to eat. The singer was eager to take Dave for a meal there and made a reservation for after the show. As Matt was a seasoned regular, the owner would always rustle up something special for him personally and Dave, not wanting to appear a coward, said he would have whatever his mate was having. Unfortunately for the comic, on that particular night the chef had created a dish called phaal. It is widely regarded as one of the hottest forms of curry available and at that time was hardly ever seen on a Western menu. Dave spent the remainder of the evening downing pint after pint of water trying to extinguish the fire in his mouth. After that incident, Dave ordered for himself.

After the Castaways, with a gruelling couple of months on the horizon, Matt decided to spend a week at Henlow Grange Health Farm to lose a few pounds and get in shape. Meanwhile, Mickie was frantically trying to pack up the entire house for the family's move to Hollywood. There were a million things to do, not only with the house itself, but with pulling the children out of school and finding new ones overseas. It was a daunting prospect, which is why the couple had only chosen to rent a property in California for the near future, giving them the chance to get their bearings before making a final commitment to buy. Unfortunately for Mickie, her husband wasn't able to help much, as he was expected in South Africa for a run of shows.

Not only had Mickie packed the kitchen sink but she also travelled with two children, their nanny Renate, a whack of luggage and, of course, her mink coat. Leaving England on 15 January 1967 and after flying for more than twenty hours, she exited LAX airport to find a chauffeur waiting for her holding a sign saying 'Munro Party'. She wondered if the incorrect spelling was a sign of things to come.

> The journey here was quite a nightmare and I was certainly glad when it was over and we were 'home'. I rented a Ford Falcon and have been driving every day. It really is a different world and a different life. I like it very much. Bill Comstock and Dot Squires have called, everyone is being wonderful especially Sid & Gert.
> — Letter from Mickie to Langham Hotel, Johannesburg

Matt left England four days after his family had flown to the States so he was able to catch Dave Allen's opening at Talk of the Town as well as make a quick trip to the studio to sing the theme tune for a new Hayley Mills film, *Pretty Polly*, with the

French composer Michel Legrand.

With suitcases packed, Matt and Bob flew into South Africa's Jan Smut's Airport. Opening in Johannesburg, the tour would see Matt perform in Durban, Maritzburg, Port Elizabeth, East London, Cape Town and Pretoria. The Cape Town season ran from 10 to 14 January, with two performances nightly backed by the George Hayden Orchestra. The variety bill offered up Frankie Holmes, a new English comedy star, D'Angoly's Junior, a juggler with a curiously punctured name, and Pat and Olivier, who Matt had worked with a few weeks before at the Castaways. But the most applauded of the supporting cast was a lively puppet interlude by Les Regens, a couple who made eighteen-inch rag dolls dance and beat out music to rhythms that put George Hayden's orchestra to shame.

Matt insisted on meeting up with the former owner of Ciro's nightclub, Joe Kentridge, whilst in Johannesburg. Joe had recently made a remarkable recovery after being in a coma for three months and Matt was eager to visit his friend and see how he was doing. Having recorded 'It's a Breeze' back in 1964, Matt was also excited about the possibility of recording some of the newer material that Joe had written and left with a plethora of new compositions to take home and consider. Joe loved the way Matt had sung his original arrangement; he thought him one of the greatest jazz singers he'd ever met.

> **The show had great reviews and we have packed houses for both. Tell Michele her daddy's very proud of her for taking piano lessons, and how about you charging round in your Falcon. I remember when you couldn't drive a Mini Minor. Bob has been really great and well worth bringing, especially with all the schlepping around we've done. I'll be seeing Bob Monkhouse on Sunday so I'll give him your regards. Give my love to my babies. — Letter from Matt, Clifton Hotel, Cape Town**

Matt and Bob landed in rain-swept Durban en-route to the Playhouse Theatre. The singer and his road manager stepped off the jetliner at Louis Botha Airport and were whisked off to his suite at the Beverly Hills Hotel at Umhlanga Rocks. It was here that Matt met the 'elder statesman' of French entertainment Maurice Chevalier, who was in Durban for a short season and opening at City Hall the same night as Matt opened at the Playhouse. They shared a press conference and so it made perfect sense to also share a drink.

Opening night was rather challenging. First there was the faulty loudspeaker,

Matt & Maurice Chevalier

which crackled and thundered to the groans of the audience, then there was the band, who'd arrived for the performance completely unrehearsed, and then the microphones, which refused to co-operate. Matt earned Bob's undying admiration for his utter composure amid all of this chaos. He battled on against an unsure drummer and some very strange lighting effects.

> Our second night in Durban is over. I know you'll be very interested to know that last night I didn't get a standing ovation but, better still, they wouldn't move out of their seats. They just wouldn't go home until I sang another song. They just sat there and kept on applauding until I went back on stage. Baby it was fabulous. I was in my dressing room with my coat off, just about to take my tie off, when I realised that they were still cheering and had to go back on. Mind you, I didn't mind. The hotel here is fantastic. All it needs is you to make it complete. They have taken up the option for three days in Rhodesia. One day in Bulawayo and two in Salisbury.
> — Letter from Matt, Beverly Hills Hotel, Umhlanga Rocks

Radio interview, Bulawayo , South Africa

The Beverly Hills Hotel was owned by Sol Kerzner, a Jewish immigrant from the Ukraine who had started out with a small kosher guesthouse in Durban. Having built the Astra, his first hotel, when he was only twenty-seven, Sol opened the Beverly Hills, South Africa's first five-star hotel only two years later. But his ambitions did not stop there and within five years he had added the Southern Sun to his empire, which completely changed the face of the hotel industry and established South Africa as a tourist destination. It wasn't long before he was giving Matt the star treatment, beginning with an invitation to a small cocktail party at which Matt was introduced to Christiaan Barnard, the world's first heart transplant surgeon.

The tour was doing exceedingly well and Matt was given a very warm welcome when he arrived at DF Malan Airport for his four-day season at the Alhambra Theatre in Cape Town. One of the first things he did when he got there was to change into slacks and a leisure shirt and take a long walk along Clifton Sands. Bruce Forsyth and Max Bygraves had both extolled the virtues of the country, almost making it sound too good to be true, but Matt wasn't a bit disappointed.

"No non-white performance will be given." Mr John Clarke, regional manager of

African Consolidated Theatres, said, "It is a great pity that a permit could not be obtained because Mr Monro is especially popular among the coloured people, but we tried very hard."

Matt was livid. Given that his big break had come from a black woman, Winifred Atwell, and that Sammy Davis Jr was one of his close friends, he was particularly adamant that there should be no restrictions placed on who could attend his performances. Indeed, he had it stipulated in his contract for the tour that his concerts should not be segregated. Matt told the Cape Town authorities he would be very disappointed if a show was not arranged, even threatening not to appear at all if that were not a possibility.

> **When we reached Cape Town Hotel, the maitre d' approached Matt and urgently told him that the blacks were being warned away, but he pleaded, "We must hear you sing 'Born Free', it is an anthem to us." Matt was outraged and went to see the mayor of Cape Town. He was told the only way he would be allowed to sing to the black population was to give another concert after his contractual evening show, in private. Matt willingly agreed. — Bob West**

Two days later, a permit was grudgingly granted so Matt could appear before a non-white audience on the Monday evening, but not at the Alhambra itself. Matt arranged to give one show at the Gem Theatre, Woodstock, performing for free. What struck Bob West most about the situation was Matt's incredible generosity of spirit.

> **After one evening performance he went with his drummer, pianist and bass player to a small cinema on a street corner in the middle of one of Cape Town's black neighbourhoods. We had secretly rehearsed there in the afternoon and, when we got there that evening, Matt walked in through the auditorium. The entire black audience cheered and surrounded him so he couldn't get to the stage. He sang 'Born Free' right there on the floor and the audience went crazy. Finally making his way to the stage, he sang the number another three times in a row before they would let him continue to another song. And they had hooked up speakers in the streets, where immense crowds gathered. When he sang 'Born Free', we could hear the roar from outside. It was never reported. — Bob West**

Bob West & Matt arriving in Rhodesia

Nearly one thousand non-whites packed the Gem Theatre at midnight for that special performance by the visiting British singer. For some, 'Born Free' had become a powerful message of freedom, and the singer's arrival saw the whole auditorium out of their seats cheering and stamping their feet in appreciation.

While Matt was in South Africa, a few dates in Rhodesia were also added to the itinerary, but there was a small problem: officially, British people were not allowed into the country as Ian Smith, the Prime Minister of Rhodesia, was at loggerheads with the British Government. To get round the issue, Matt and his crew flew over on a plane that, landing in an isolated area, did not have a passport control. He appeared at the Palace Theatre for two shows and in a press interview later said that Equity, the British musician's union, had not tried to stand in his way, either on the question of his performing before segregated audiences in South Africa or singing in Rhodesia. They left the whole matter entirely to his conscience.

Neither good taste nor tact on the part of an interviewer were evident on that Tuesday night when the Information Department produced an interview with Matt in background to the 7.00pm news. The presenter seemed intent on forcing Matt into a corner, trying to make him say he would get into trouble overseas for performing in Rhodesia. It seemed not so much an interview as an interrogation. Time and again Matt was asked if Equity would penalise him for singing to segregated audiences in South Africa and for performing in Rhodesia. As it happened, the singer was fully equal to these clumsy tactics. If he had slipped once in the aggressive 'interview' he could have landed himself in a verbal trap, but he kept his temper and displayed remarkable diplomacy.

On the whole, Matt enjoyed the tour, but he especially loved South Africa and agreed to return if an opportunity presented itself. But for the time being, the singer set his sights on joining his family in California.

THE JUDGEMENT

Mickie and the children had settled in fairly quickly, adapting to the new lifestyle more easily than expected. Their rented bungalow on Merridy Street was only twenty-five miles from Los Angeles and had the obligatory swimming pool and orange trees scattered about the garden. Dave Cavanaugh gave Matt and Mickie a record player and a television set as a house-warming present, the perfect gift for Matt. The idea was that Matt would commute between LA and London for television, cabaret and business deals, but be based in Northridge so that he was available to the American club circuit.

> To make a serious impact in the American market – and it's a big one for a singer like myself because the competition is so much greater – you have to be there physically for a long time to consolidate yourself. There are so many singers of my style in the USA that the challenge is all that much greater than it is in Britain, where the competition is limited and so are the circuits. There are fresh fields to conquer, more rewards to gain, a new world to be won.
> — Matt Monro

The owner of Southern Music, Monique Peers, threw the couple a 'small' welcome-to-LA dinner party at her house. Monique, a large woman married to a stick of a husband, loved to entertain. The gathering was held in a room set up to accommodate seventy covers, leaving Mickie wondering if this was a small event, what constituted a large one? Matt, Mickie and Johnnie arrived to find Sid and Gert Feller and Johnny Mercer on the same table and they spent a wonderful evening in the company of some lovely people.

Capitol were very keen to have a theme for the next LP, so instead of deciding the

Matt, Johnny Mercer & Johnnie Spence

mood and then picking a title, this project saw the title picked first then used as a guide for the tracklist. A shortlist was made of forty songs from which the team selected the eleven they would go with. The pacing of the album was the most important element, and Matt wasted no time in sitting down with Johnnie to find the right key for the music so that the orchestrations could come together.

Here's to My Lady, the follow up album to *This is the Life*, was peppered with popular odes to famous women of song, but perhaps the album's stand-out track is a sensitive rendition of the David Raksin-Johnny Mercer classic 'Laura', lovingly arranged by Johnnie Spence. The second album missed the charts, as did the singles 'Where in the World' and 'These Years'.

In August, *Invitation to the Movies* sold a hundred thousand copies, eventually earning Matt another gold disc. Despite the disc's solid commercial performance, it only made it into the lower echelons of the charts, coming in at number eighty-six. It was to be Matt's final entry in the album charts for nearly thirteen years. After *Here's to My Lady*, theming had gone out of the window; there was never enough time.

These Years offered another collection from Matt. These eleven tracks benefited from excellent accompaniments by Billy May and Sid Feller. Billy was brassy and bouncy in 'Release Me' and 'The Happening'. Sid deployed a large body of strings in such songs as 'Don't Sleep in the Subway' and 'Here, There and Everywhere'. Matt came across as warm-voiced, expansive and immensely confident, with the *Halifax*

Guardian stating, "We haven't a ballad singer to touch him." Matt was certainly in superb musical company with directors Sid and Billy, whose inspired arranging and conducting truly suited his repertoire.

> I enjoyed Billy May and Sid Feller. Billy's such a character and it was such a thrill to work with the guy, he's a lovely guy. I enjoyed the thing he did on 'Spanish Eyes' and 'Georgy Girl' — they were fun to do. Can't fault the musicians, we had some great guys on the sessions, some real knock-out players and so competent, just sit down, start reading and bang you got one in the can. — Stan Britt

Billy May started out playing trumpet in big bands like Charlie Barnet's, but it was his talent as an arranger that was championed by Glenn Miller and Les Brown. He was hired as a staff arranger, first for the National Broadcasting Company, then for Capitol. It wasn't long before Billy's characteristic brisk tempos and intricate brass parts were being applied to mainline artists such as Frank Sinatra, Nat King Cole, Peggy Lee, Bobby Darin, Nancy Wilson, Bing Crosby and Rosemary Clooney. One distinctive feature of his style was his repeated use of trumpet mute devices, another a saxophone glissando widely known as his 'slurping saxes'.

Billy May and Matt Monro had a mutual-admiration society going. Each admired the other's professionalism, musical approach and artistic flair, but the icing on the cake of their relationship was the great fun they shared on the sessions.

> Matt had a very distinctive quality, it was similar to Sinatra and it was similar to Nat Cole, in the sense that the way they sang you knew all three of them were good musicians, in other words they had a good musical approach to things. Matt Monro was one of the finest guys I ever worked with; I mean I enjoyed him as a person and I enjoyed working with him. It was just one big laugh, the whole session, whether we were doing a sweet ballad or something like that. I just had a wonderful time with him. So you had a session like that and it would make up for all the garbage. — Billy May

All but one of the tracks on *These Years* was recorded in a single day. The albums were thrown together without the care that was taken in Matt's English recordings and Dave Cavanaugh was frustrated because he couldn't get anything done on the promotional side. The process was rushed and Matt was forced into singing over backing tracks for a lot of the songs. The diminished quality of the recordings didn't escape the singer's fans, indeed 'Spanish Eyes' caused much debate as to whether Matt was singing off-key. In fact, the arrangement and clash of sounds give the impression that the vocals are slightly out of tune. The arrangement is at counterpoint to his vocals at all times, the accompaniment never playing the tune or even a harmony line throughout. Matt is on his own all the way through with no melodic support and although he does bend notes it is totally in keeping with the performance. The arrangement is superb and shows just how brilliant Billy May was.

> **'Spanish Eyes' is a Matt Monro vocal masterpiece. His range on the song extends from a low A-flat to a high E – over one-and-a-half octaves. But even more impressive are the vocal techniques used throughout the recording: appoggiaturas, modents and turns, to name a few. On the first verse he teases us by going in and out of pitch – to great effect. The second time through the song, Matt's intriguing improvisation soars over the complex rhythms and blaring trumpets. For the song's final phrase, he holds the high note for an eternity and, again, plays with the pitch by creating dissonances with the orchestra – just brilliant! The listener is transported to a flamenco club in Andalusia. — Jeffrey Paul Hayes, Pianist**

Recording five albums over a six-month period is exhausting by anyone's standards. Capitol insisted that albums were a big market in the States, but it just seemed to Matt that the record company were rushing headlong into projects without much thought. The exception was *Here's to My Lady*, one of Matt's favourite Capitol albums. Living next door to Sid allowed the pair to sit down and work out what they wanted to do with the songs, much like he did in England with George Martin. They might take a couple of days to routine a few songs but at least by the time they got to the studio, those songs would be to the best of everyone's ability. As far as Matt was concerned, the English way might have been slower but it was more professional and the end product proved the worth of spending the extra time on an album. The mindset was completely different in America – they felt that if an album took two days rather than one, they were losing money. To Matt it appeared that American records used more brass and voices but England was better for strings, so the ideal combination would be a bit of both.

With tens of tracks in the Capitol bank, Matt left them to it. He had a date with

Kenny Clayton in Vancouver.

Although Matt had only seen Kenny play on one occasion in Singapore during April 1965 when he'd worked with Bassey, it was enough for him to know the man was a great talent. Interestingly, it was Johnnie Spence who had given Kenny his first break. In 1963, Kenny was looking for work when he was told about a Richard Rodgers show called *No Strings* being conducted by a man called Johnnie Spence. The show was opening in December and Spence needed a rehearsal pianist to start in November. That was ideal, as the rehearsals took place in the daytime, leaving Kenny free to work in Harry's Bar in the evenings.

During the show, Johnnie suggested that Kenny should conduct and the young pianist had to admit he didn't know how. Johnnie sat him down in the dressing room one afternoon and gave him a master class in the art of getting the musicians to perform as he wanted. By the end of the show's run Mr Clayton was performing and conducting all the matinees of the show himself. After the production ended its six-month run, Johnnie arranged for Kenny to audition for Bassey. "Be in Vic Lewis's office on 3 June. Shirley will come up and you will play for her." Nervously Kenny did as he was told and, by the end of the month, he was opening at the Talk of the Town with Ms Bassey herself.

Kenny Clayton had been working with Shirley Bassey for three years. They hadn't been particularly easy years, but Kenny didn't expect anything less. However, one incident tipped him over the edge, forcing him to reconsider his professional commitments. Bassey was booked to play a club in the Philippines called The Nile. En route from Australia, Vic Lewis, the agent at the time, called Kenny and said that Matt had just worked the room on his recent trip there and he'd had a great band who knew what they were doing. Based on Vic's information, Kenny allowed for a three-hour rehearsal, reckoning he would need the first hour himself to talk to the musicians and take a look at the music, before Bassey arrived to do a full run. Accordingly, he arrived at rehearsals at 2.00pm and introduced himself to the twenty-eight musicians, readying them for 'On a Wonderful Day Like Today'.

> **"Here's the opening number. I'll give you two bars in: 1, 2, 3, 4" –**
> **and you could hear chu chu chu chu chu, ten times slower than we**
> **needed. So I said to the drummer, "Let's try that again," and the**
> **same happened. It took me minutes to know that this wasn't the**
> **Cardin Cruz Band that Matt had used. We had rice growers,**
> **dustmen, anyone who thought they could play. Anyway: disaster.**
> **Shirley arrived at 3.30pm and after listening to the drummer,**

when Matt went on stage later that night, he found only a handful of people in the three-hundred-seater room. Unfazed, he started his performance and before long a couple strolled in, then another and another, until the place started to fill up. It was quite disconcerting, but Matt carried on regardless of the distraction. Several songs into the performance, three people snuck in and, instead of taking a table further back, they walked right to the front of the room and seated themselves beside the piano. Matt started the intro to 'Yesterday' but all Kenny could hear were the three newcomers talking and it was starting to affect his concentration. Matt continued blissfully unaware of any problem. Finally, Kenny's frustration got the better of him and he stood up, leaving the bass player and drummer to carry on, walked slowly over to the offending table and loudly said, "I can't hear what I'm doing, there's a guy singing 'Yesterday', can you wait until he's finished?" They kept quiet.

> **Working with Matt was like working with a brother and we became such good friends. We were both from the East End and apart from the respect I had for his talent we liked the same things and shared the same sense of humour. He appreciated his musicians, wonderful sound, great company, couldn't be better. Matt behaved like a normal person. There was absolutely no starry thing about him; he said, "Let's do the job," and that's what we did. Matt had the best instincts, his pitching was wonderful, his phrasing phenomenal and he could certainly hold his notes.**
> **— Kenny Clayton**

Ever since the boys had arrived in Montreal the hotel staff had insisted on speaking French instead of English, even though they were capable of it. Leaving for a radio interview early the next morning, the trio headed to the reception desk to hand their room keys in. Deciding to have a bit of fun at the Francophones' expense, Kenny said in broken English, "We are from England to visit Expo '67 and I would like you to expose yourself," leaving Bob and Matt collapsing in laughter behind him.

In Montreal, Kenny succeeded where others before him had failed – he managed to get Matt out during the day! Kenny was a classically trained musician and there was an orchestra giving a concert he was keen on seeing, so he planned the whole outing. The idea was to get Matt up in the morning, they'd go for a nice lunch together, then he'd take him to the afternoon concert. Matt was game. Everything went to plan and they got to the concert hall and sat in the front row of the circle. The orchestra started the overture. By the eighth bar, Matt was fast asleep. Even with the companionship of Bob and Kenny, who Matt loved, he was feeling very low – business was slow, it was bitterly cold and even though in Kenny, he had found the perfect drinking partner, it couldn't compensate for his deep longing for Mickie.

After yesterday's depression I'm feeling OK again and just hoping that tonight will be better, though I doubt it. I just had a call from Henry Miller asking if I wanted to play five weeks in Australia. I said if he got me more money and three fares so that I could take my wife, then I'd go, otherwise forget it. I'm choked about the Academy Awards programme but we've got the Red Skelton so I suppose that's something. It is so cold here it's unbelievable. Twenty-seven degrees [Fahrenheit] and they say, "You should have been here in the winter!" I get a day off on Friday so I might fly to New York and come back on Saturday, Bobby Darin is on at the Copa and I'd like to see how he works. — Letter from Matt, The Queen Elizabeth Hotel, Montreal, Canada

Don had taken time off and was still in Hollywood after attending the Academy Awards. Matt was choked that he'd not been invited to attend the ceremony or sing the song, which actually featured in the *Born Free* film. This was the moment when a small stab of resentment started to creep in over Don's managerial commitment. Matt felt Don was so wrapped up with the possibility of receiving an Oscar himself that he had overlooked pushing for Matt's appearance in the show. They'd used the Roger Miller instrumental version instead.

With Don miles away from his desk and his responsibilities to his artist, Matt had no option but to carry on, but he was desperately unhappy about things. He featured on a CBS Showcase special on radio singing six songs with a good thirteen-piece orchestra. He was hoping it might drum up more business. He found the French speaking province hard work and the people that did attend the show tended to be rather pompous and difficult to please.

By the end of the tour he was happy to leave Canada behind him and get back to his family and new home. Kenny was living in Vegas, so they parted company for a few days and Bob and Matt headed to Merridy Street.

General Artists Corporation, working under the auspices of NEMS, booked Matt the usual array of television appearances, *Gypsy Rose Lee*, *Pat Boone*, *Joey Bishop*, *Art Linkletter* and the *Red Skelton Show*. They all seemed to follow the same format, several sketches and a song. Matt had inveigled himself into the Hollywood lifestyle, but instead of nights on the town, he tended to spend his time off at Sid and Gert's house with Mickie. The wives spent nearly every day together with or without their husbands, and if Mickie wasn't at home she could be found at Gerts. When Evelyn flew over for the summer to spend time with her daughter and son-in-law she, like the nanny and children, spent most of her time at Gerts because Merridy Street didn't have air-conditioning and the hot afternoons could be unbearable.

Matt was booked into the Century Plaza Hotel in Los Angeles. It was considered a prestige booking and Don Black kept insisting on its importance. Don was sure that this opening night performance would mark the point when Matt would formally take over from Nat King Cole and went about inviting a celebrity audience, record company bigwigs and some important agents to Matt's debut in the Westside Room. Matt, a laid-back person by nature, felt highly-pressured by what his manager expected of him. Don was hovering around all day, at the one o'clock rehearsal, in the hotel room and backstage. Matt had taken to pouring himself several large drinks to try and steady his nerves – he never normally indulged until after a show, but the pressure was getting to him and he couldn't control it.

Matt's intro began and he walked steadily to the front of the stage and opened with 'Around the World'. The audience were excited about the presence of a new star and they lapped it up, applauding vigorously. Matt knew the importance of good patter, it was what made the difference between a singer and an entertainer and he peppered his performance with banter to engage the audience. But he was new to the American culture and the humour that might have done so well in other countries was falling slightly flat as the audience didn't quite understand the taglines. Matt was getting nervous, and when he got nervous, he tended to ramble. He could feel Don's presence in the audience, eyes begging him to stop, but he was trying to redeem himself.

Don was sitting next to Jack Benny when Matt launched into a Benny impression, which horrified the lyricist. In James Inverne's book *Wrestling with Elephants*, Don Black gives his perspective on the performance making it crystal clear that as far as he was concerned Matt's chance of superstardom had gone and he would never rank alongside Frank Sinatra or Nat King Cole. Dramatically, he states that he was dying while desperately praying for the singer to stop rambling and telling jokes. While he felt the audiences feeling of disappointment was palpable, it was more Don's own disappointment that was so obvious to everyone. One of the most telling remarks Don makes is that a star must have a mystique and air of mystery to elevate them above the masses. But Matt's lack of airs and graces was precisely what made him so popular, not just with the masses, but with his friends and colleagues in the business.

He was one of the people and that very quality endeared him to millions.

Interestingly, and in contrast to his previous statements about a singer needing to elevate himself above his audience, Don made another comment that seems to indicate that he knew the source of Matt's charm lay in his accessibility.

Matt and Sammy, their generation had one thing in common which you don't get nowadays, you had contact with them, the audience would think they knew them, they touched them, it was like spending an hour with a friend, they seemed to come across the footlights. — James Inverne, *Wrestling with Elephants – The Authorised Biography of Don Black*

Bob West said, "Don was more ambitious for Matt than Matt was – he wasn't driven". Matt wasn't of the character to elevate himself above anyone else, he was a normal guy who could sing well and part of his charm was that each member of the audience felt that he was only singing to them. His easy character transcended the footlights, he didn't want to be aloof and become 'affected' by the Hollywood players. That was one of the main reasons Matt grew to dislike living in America, he felt that the people in the business were mostly superficial and disingenuous.

It was the intense pressure and expectation that had been responsible for Matt's uneasy performance, not the couple of drinks Matt had downed before the show. He had tried too hard to please and suffered from a bad attack of nerves. It was probably Matt's most indulgent performance and he was the first to admit that the opening night was his worst concert. What Don saw and what the audience saw were two different things. Don was comparing it to Matt's usual presentation; the audience were looking with fresh eyes. They loved it, the reviewers loved it, the Plaza Hotel booked him back for another three-week appearance and Jack Benny specifically asked Matt to work with him in Las Vegas during the following year.

Matt Monro Makes Mark on Coast
What lured me over to Century City and the Westside Room of the Century Plaza was the first West Coast appearance of singer Matt Monro. Matt is, in my opinion, the finest male vocalist around today. Although the Britisher is not widely known in this country he has continued to gain fans and stature with every new engagement. You may recall that I reviewed Matt's New York appearance last fall at the Plaza's posh Persian Room. Gimmick-free Matt comes on at

this elegant new supper club and just sings. His 'Walk Away' is a big crowd pleaser, as are such numbers as 'Born Free', 'Once in a Lifetime', 'Yesterday' and 'As Long as I'm Singing'. If you don't know Matt Monro, when you hear one of his albums, you will soon become an avid fan as I. He is in the true sense of the word, a 'class' singer. — William E Sarmento, *The Sun of Lowell*

The audience that night was littered with celebrities. Bobby Darin, Petula Clark, Henry Mancini, George Montgomery, Mary Helen Stoddard, Nelson Riddle, Andy Williams, Woody Woodbury and Claude Akins all came to see the show and had nothing but praise for the singer's performance. Matt and Mickie had also invited a few friends themselves, including Sid and Gert Feller.

Matt and Mickie invited my friends and their husbands to the opening night dinner and the show. That was a beautiful thing to do and everyone loved the show. Matt was phenomenal. — Gert Feller

I think it would be fair to say that at this point Don lost faith in Matt and his ability to reach superstardom. Song writing was increasingly taking precedence over his managerial duties. Most of Don's time in 1967 wasn't focused on Matt's needs; indeed, by his own admission, that year alone he wrote scores for eight movies. His next success came from the movie *To Sir with Love,* recorded by Lulu, which hit the No 1 spot in the American charts and remained there for five weeks. Don should probably have walked away from Matt at this juncture his career, but he wasn't yet prepared to give up the connection. The singer wasn't blind to the effect of these competing demands on his manager's commitment, but it would take another ten years before he took a stand and parted ways with Don. Because of a sense of loyalty to his friend, Matt let matters drift on. But Matt's wry sense of humour usually carried him through the tough times and he found it easier to make light of difficult situations than to address them with open hostility. One newspaper he spoke to printed his remarks on the matter. "Don Black became my manager. He used to get £30.00 or 10%, whichever was the greater. He doesn't need me now for he's always writing hits – 'Born Free', 'Walk Away', 'Thunderball', 'To Sir, With Love' – In fact I wouldn't mind managing him."

While at the Westside Room, Gert and Sid brought along Claude Akins and his wife to see the show. Matt was not aware that they were coming along that night, otherwise

Therese 'Pie' Fairfield, Claude Akins & Matt

he would have introduced them from the stage. Instead, he rang them the next day, apologised and invited them to dinner. Matt then rang Gert and told her they were all doing dinner at her house. Unfortunately, Sid was recording with the singer John Gary that day, and it did not go well. By the end of the session Sid was beside himself with rage. He came home during the meal, didn't go in to say hello, went straight to his bedroom, got undressed in the dark and went to bed. Matt went in, sat on the edge of the bed and talked to Sid for thirty minutes in the dark, finally persuading him to come out and join everyone on the back patio for drinks. Soon after the two men had rejoined the group, Therese Akins took a fancy to a piece of furniture that was out on the deck, saying, "Oh, I have been looking for something like that for years. Where did you find it?" Before Gert knew what hit her, Sid told Therese she could have it. Gert was gobsmacked and could have killed her husband on the spot. To add insult to injury, Claude immediately went home in his car, returning a short time later in a station wagon. The Akins took the item home with them that evening and Sid and Gert never saw it or them again. Gert always said that Matt's ability to get Sid out of his bad mood had cost her a perfectly good piece of furniture.

During opening night at Century Plaza, Matt had also met Henry Mancini and, while Matt was away on the road sometime later, Mickie received a call from Mancini's wife, Ginny, saying, "Let us know when Matt comes back to town so we can get together?" Mickie graciously replied, "I do not need you when Matt comes

Henry Mancini, Matt & Andy Williams

back to town, it would be nice if you called me when I was alone." That was the fickle side of the business, if people couldn't rub shoulders with Matt, why would they waste time entertaining Mickie?

Another visitor to Century Plaza was the comedian Woody Woodbury. The comic was king of what was known as the 'Adults Only' genre and was an extraordinary phenomenon in the world of vinyl. He sold records well into the millions but he didn't have his sales boosted by the privilege most of the popular comics enjoyed: television exposure. When Jack Paar abandoned the *Tonight Show*, the hosting gig was up for grabs, and there were two candidates in the front running. Woody Woodbury was one, the other was Johnny Carson, who was hosting a popular game show on ABC titled *Who Do You Trust?* Woody was arguably the more qualified for the *Tonight Show* seat as he had already guest hosted the show during the Steve Allen era. Nevertheless, it was Carson who was finally given the job, but in a strange twist of fate, Woody was named the new host of the game show *Who Do You Trust?* He later went on to host *The Woody Woodbury Show.*

My wife, Sue and I went to see Matt perform several nights running... and I don't have to tell you he was enormously well received. 'Born Free' and 'Portrait' had catapulted him to real big-time stardom here in the States. My people there (the talent

coordinators) contacted Matt's representative to come and be my guest on *The Woody Woodbury Show* but Matt's contract with the hotel forbade him appearing in any other venue during or immediately following his show date there... that's actually the way some of these silly contracts were drawn up back then... Television would have tripled their hotel cabaret and room-suite business but they just couldn't see it that way. — Woody Woodbury

On 19 May 1967, Matt recorded with the USAF Band, the Airmen of Note. The recording was made at the Annex Studio in Hollywood under the direction of CWO Bob Bunton and broadcast on Armed Forces Radio in 1968 in their public radio series *Serenade in Blue*. The five tracks recorded that day, 'Georgy Girl', 'Born Free', 'Alfie', 'My Kind of Girl' and 'In the Arms of Love', were included on a private press box set released as a recruiting tool for the USAF.

Public relations had become a very important part of the Airmen of Note's objective. To improve the quality of the *Serenade in Blue* radio series, guest artists were invited to record with the band, including Joe Williams, Jon Hendricks, George Shearing, June Christy, Sandler and Young, Shirley Bassey and Matt Monro. When the guest artist recordings first started, few of the performers had ever heard of the Note, as they were called, and they weren't expecting much from a service band. But once the sessions got under way, it quickly became apparent that this was a great group of musicians. Lou Rawls was booked for a session, but his own rhythm section (which he'd insisted on using) were delayed en route to the studio. To save time, Rawls agreed to rehearse the charts using the Note's rhythm section. When his men finally arrived, they found themselves part of the audience instead of part of the band.

CWO Bob Bunton was a product of the field. He came to the Note after leading Air Force bands all over the world. In 1966, he produced the Note's first promotional LP *The Surprising Sounds of the Airmen of Note*, which was initially used to stimulate interest in potential sponsors and later to publicise the concerts. A subsequent album featured musical excerpts from the public radio series *Serenade in Blue* called *Airmen of Note and Friends*. Matt is featured on this album with 'Georgy Girl'.

REVIEWING THE SITUATION

The British had invaded the Roosevelt Hotel in New Orleans and established a beachhead for the first three weeks in June on the bandstand in the Blue Room. Known as the birthplace of jazz, Kenny and Matt were keen to roam the streets and soak up the atmosphere. There were hundreds of bars and restaurants dotted across the city, but the men made a beeline to a small steak house in the French Quarter, which had an old radiogram. They went in there nearly every night. Kenny remembers New Orleans very well and not so much because of the shows or the food or indeed the city itself.

We were working in the Hotel Roosevelt and we followed a lovely gentleman called Frankie Laine who did the first half, and after we had finished about 11.00pm Matt and I went for a bite to eat. New Orleans stays up as long as you want it to. Matt asked if I fancied a game of pool. We went into the pool room and it was like a film set with low lighting and a bar tucked in the corner, a pool table and the only people in there were a couple of guys sitting at the bar and the barman. We went and got the cues, which were hanging on the wall, began chalking the heads and started our game. It wasn't long before two Sonny Liston-type guys came in the door and asked what we were doing. "Playing pool" Matt answered. The guy replied, "That's our table." We sort of shrugged it off but the man blocked our path to the table and said, "I don't think you understand, this is our table." Again we laughingly shrugged it off but the guy didn't let it go - he said, whilst pulling a gun out of his jacket, "I don't think you understand this is definitely our table". We laid the cues carefully on the table and crept out. It was a weird moment but Matt wasn't fazed. — Kenny Clayton

Matt and Mickie flew to New York for Matt to make a commercial for Newport cigarettes and appear on *The Johnnie Carson Show*, before flying on to London.

While in the UK, Matt was recording two television shows for the American market and his own forty-five minute programme entitled *Matt Monro Meets Nelson Riddle* for the BBC. His new British single 'What to Do' was released on 30 June in conjunction with the singer's visit to Britain. The disc maintained Matt's unfailing high standard, a gorgeous ballad and a deliciously swaying rhythm. The flip side 'These Years' was a reflective nostalgic ballad with a gentle, sophisticated swing.

Also on this visit, an unexpected change of plan meant the star was back at Caesar's Palace in Luton for a booking with George Savva. Matt was originally set to play London's Talk of the Town for a three-week season, but at the special request of impresario Bernard Delfont had agreed to his date being switched with Shirley Bassey, enabling her to make her 'farewell' nightclub appearance. Bassey's manager Kenneth Hume expected an absence of three years because of lengthy commitments to *Josephine*, a new stage musical. So instead of three weeks at the Talk, Matt swapped to a week at Caesar's and a fortnight at Batley Variety Club and would play the London nightspot in March of the following year.

Matt's week at Caesar's was solidly booked as was always the case when he worked there, the locals loved him. George Savva couldn't have hoped for more, he liked nothing better than overseeing a full house and spending time with one of his favourite artists. What George couldn't know at this time was that within a few years his club would undergo a dramatic change when the Ladbroke Group suddenly bought it out. With Ladbroke's main focus lying with its very large bingo and gaming interests, George was left managing a very different set up.

Matt was booked for one of the new programmes that had been commissioned as a television vehicle called *Piccadilly Palace*, produced in England by ATV. It was part of a package of colour shows that Lew Grade sold to the ABC Network in America for two million dollars. The show starred Morecambe & Wise and was originally contracted for twelve episodes, but for some reason the comedic duo only recorded eight shows. Matt appeared after the duo had left with Millicent Martin as host and regular cast member Bruce Forsyth.

Matt's trip to the UK also afforded him the time to fit in a *Saturday Club*, a Cadbury television commercial and a return outing with Simon Dee and Bob Monkhouse. *Dee Time* was made for the BBC at the Dickenson Road Studios, a terrible old converted church in Manchester.

> **Simon Dee made a big thing about the show being extemporaneous, no cues of any kind, that it was all ad-lib. Matt gets introduced – "Here is my next guest Matt Monro." Matt says to Simon: "You didn't say my name right," and Simon says, "I said Matt Monro" Matt says, "It isn't Matt Monro, it's Matt Monro," Simon replies, "I said Matt Monro." Matt replies, "You didn't, my name is spelt MATT MONRO, you said MUNROE," Simon says, "How do you know?" and Matt says, "It's written on your cue card." Everyone fell about.**
> **— Bob Monkhouse**

Matt was very excited about working with Nelson Riddle, who he had met in May at the Century Plaza in Los Angeles. It was a landmark moment for both men, and although considered two of the finest performers of popular music by their peers, it was unfortunately the only time the two had a chance to work together. Both artists had a great passion and love for their art, especially concert touring and personal appearances, which gave them the chance to engage with their audience and cross the footlight barriers. Their worldwide recognition afforded them the opportunity to travel the world, each gaining a new fan base and greater audience appreciation. As well as a love for their music, they also had a great respect and admiration for each other and were able to understand some of the immense challenges that their work could throw at them.

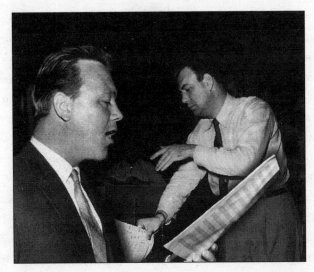

Matt & Nelson Riddle

The date was 14 July 1967 and the venue was Wood Lane Television Centre in London. The BBC had brought them together for a televised concert, which would allow both artists to show off their talents to a selected audience. The event was the brainchild of Vic Lewis – an exceptional bandleader in his own right – who had been Riddle's European manager since 1960. Within that capacity, he had already organised several successful television and radio shows for the American maestro, as well as a highly lucrative and well publicised concert tour with Shirley Bassey. Therefore it seemed natural that Nelson Riddle, regarded at the time as one of the finest arrangers in the world, should meet up with Matt Monro, regarded at the time as one of Britain's most outstanding singers.

12 July saw Riddle's three boxes of music parts and another box containing the scores arrive from Hollywood, courtesy of TWA. The production crew were in charge of ensuring everything was in place for the following day's rehearsal and with a programme budget set at a generous £7,538.00, they were able to easily meet everyone's needs.

A day later, Matt and Nelson were at the television centre rehearsing for the following night's concert. With an eight-hour time constraint it was a gruelling day, but both artists enjoyed the challenge of nurturing the handpicked orchestra to perform the music to the best of their ability. With a line up of twelve violins, four trumpets, two percussionists, four violas, four trombones, four cellos, five saxophones, one guitar, one bass, two horns, one harp, a xylophone, vibraphone, a C3 Hammond organ, a pair of pedal tymps and a Steinway six-foot eleven-inch piano this was music presented at its best with a theatrically produced ensemble and high end opulent lighting creating the most perfect of atmospheres.

The evening kicked off with Nelson performing 'Brother John' and concluded with Matt singing a version of 'Strike Up the Band' that Riddle had arranged especially for him. With a blistering saxophone solo by the great British jazzman Tubby Hayes, the high swing number culminated in a double encore that saw the 500-strong audience on their feet demanding more. Unfortunately, as with most of the early BBC footage, the televised concert was taped over, to maintain the company's stringent budget restraints.

Thirty years after the show was recorded, Bryan Officer, a former committee member of the Sinatra Music Society, stumbled across the reel-to-reel tape of the show in his attic, originally given to him by Dick Turpin. The recording was re-mastered and re-engineered by Alan Bunting and made available as a compact disc to the Nelson Riddle Appreciation Society.

In 2006 the Matt Monro Estate had the opportunity of buying the rights to the masters, and with the backing of EMI decided to release this exceptional concert to a wider audience. Restoration engineer Richard Moore had the arduous task of re-mastering the show from scratch. The source was a 3-3/4 inches per second, quarter track, reel to reel tape which had been recorded directly from a TV-line source. The recording had a number of technical problems that had to be addressed. The original restoration had dealt with some of the larger issues, but more work was needed to remove the hum caused by the mains electricity supply that ran throughout the tape and the high frequency distortion. The microphone that Matt used during this broadcast also had a minor flaw, which caused some strange 'clunking' noises to appear on the soundtrack but these and a considerable number of dropouts were digitally removed. The only thing that couldn't be restored were the bass frequencies, because there was nothing there to boost. Whilst it still has its imperfections, it now sounds much closer to how it was originally broadcast. It was finally released in the autumn of 2007 with the title: *Matt Sings, Nelson Swings*.

With the success of the show still ringing in his ears and 'Wednesday's Child' in the Top 10 in the Philippines, Matt left for two weeks at the Batley Variety Club. With the singer's imminent departure to the States a last-minute session at CTS Studios was arranged to lay down several tracks with George Martin. This was the first UK EMI Group recording outside of Abbey Road Studios. Matt's Capitol contract and Martin's independence now freed them to work elsewhere and with three tracks in the can Matt flew back to America on 31 July for his opening in Lake Tahoe four days later.

Lake Tahoe

Lake Tahoe is like Vegas in many ways, but rather than blazing neon from the edge of the desert, it sits on the bank of a shimmering lake and is altogether less showy than its sister town.

After Matt's appearance at Harvey's the previous year, the office had been contacted immediately to reschedule a second visit. Matt was headlining with support from American prestidigitator Channing Pollock, the man who had redefined the image of the stage magician. Flawlessly and elegantly dressed in white tie and tails with chiselled good looks, the conjurer stood with an almost patrician detachment, centre stage, and manufactured doves out of the air with technical perfection. Channing exuded sex appeal, which gave him the edge over the hundreds of other illusion acts on the circuits. He was a familiar face on the Reno/Tahoe circuit, stunning audiences nightly as he produced a surplus of doves from handkerchiefs or made a cage full of birds disappear from view under the drape of a black velvet cloth.

The Del Webb Corporation contracted the American comedian Don Rickles exclusively for both the Sahara Hotel in Vegas and in Lake Tahoe and he was now fulfilling the Tahoe portion of his agreement. Rickles was Matt and Kenny's favourite 'insult comic' and they took every opportunity to watch the master at work. When the boys went to see his act they'd try and sneak into the back quietly because the comic had a nasty habit of picking on people in the audience. One evening there was a woman dressed in a green outfit in the front row and he pounced – "What have you come dressed as? A well dressed asparagus tip?" – and

Matt, Mickie & Richard Harris

without pausing for breath he went on to his next victim. He had the most vicious sense of humour but it was hard to be cross with him when you were rolling about with laughter.

It was a fantastic time for everyone and with the memories of many laughter-filled nights, Matt and Mickie flew on to Bermuda on 21 August for a two-week engagement at the Forty Thieves Club in Hamilton and it was here that the singer met Richard Harris.

> **Richard met up with us several times and came to see the show most nights. We all went out to eat after one of the shows to a restaurant he'd suggested. The Robin Hood was a little shack and the service was appalling. Richard started a big singsong and then got impatient when the food didn't come out very quickly. Like a schoolboy he mounted the table striding up and down chanting at the top of his voice "We want food, we want food" while stomping his feet on the table. We nearly got arrested for disorderly conduct! — Mickie Monro**

Matt was a man's man, he loved nothing more than to hang out with a mate, but that usually meant reverting to juvenile behaviour, with schoolboy pranks, jokes and card games in the hotel suite. With someone like Richard Harris in your company, it was never going to be a low profile affair, he was a full-blooded Irishman and bursting with life. Richard was as renowned for his hell-raising lifestyle as for his ability as a performer and was everything a bad-boy Hollywood star should be. A handsome, boozing, brawling, womanising jet-setter, whose moody magnificence brought glamour to the weakest of movies. But beyond his headline-grabbing lifestyle he was an actor of real emotional depth. On that trip Richard spoke to Matt of his heartfelt aspirations to sing himself, and how he didn't think he had the confidence to take it further. Matt spent hours talking to him about his own singing career and what it brought him as a person.

Camelot was Harris' first musical triumph. It revealed the actor to be a singer of great feeling and with a greater confidence he stepped into the world of music. Richard's friend songwriter Jimmy Webb composed a twenty-two minute cantata that ended with a seven-minute coda called 'MacArthur Park', which he offered to Harris. He also crossed the Atlantic several times in order to produce the disc himself. The seminal recording topped the music charts in Europe and peaked at number two in the American listings. Harris released a string of singles from these two LPs, plus tracks from *Camelot*, and enjoyed radio coverage that rivalled The Beatles throughout 1968. Ever generous, Harris presented Webb with a Rolls Royce in gratitude for the song and sent a rather special bottle of vintage scotch, a Dunhill lighter and a thank you note to his mate Matt.

From the high jinks antics of Bermuda, Matt, Mickie, Kenny and Bob flew to the rather more serene island of Honolulu on 4 September. Matt had developed a nasty throat infection just before the contract ended in Bermuda necessitating him to cancel the last show, and although booked to perform at Honolulu's Ilikai Hotel from the thirteenth of the month, the Monros felt it would be prudent to fly there early and grab a few days rest before Matt's opening.

The rest did them all good. In front of the hotel was a beautiful lagoon, which afforded privacy to anyone swimming. This alone prompted Kenny to teach himself to swim, and by the time they left the island he was fairly proud of his accomplishments.

Mickie flew back to Los Angeles to be with the children, while Matt, Kenny and Bob flew to Sydney for two months. Two shows a night, six days a week with Sundays off was the deal.

First nights are always a big event for any entertainer but opening night in Sydney for Monro had something that smacked of an endurance test about it. He had just finished his first show, and with another coming up at 11.30pm, Matt was pondering the star billing outside Chequers, as he waited for a car to rush him to Don Lane's Tonight Show at TCN Studios. Any thoughts he might have had about Sydney treadmills was eclipsed by the absence of his name over the entrance to the venue in which he had done his opening performance. Not a mention of the English singer was to be found anywhere. Instead of listing Matt Monro as the headlining act, the sign unblushingly announced Gigi Galon and Mike Preston. There was a reason of course. The man who normally changed the sign had become ill and was sent to hospital, taking the key to the sign with him.

> Even so there are many entertainers who would have been furious at opening in a city with someone else billed as the star. Not Monro, who is claimed by those who work with him as the easiest performer in the world to get along with, a short guy with a giant's tolerance. On the way to the studio Monro, who sat in the front seat because he gets car sick in the back, grinned when I asked what he thought about sandwiching a television appearance between two floorshows on his opening night. "It doesn't bother me," he said and then asked for information he could use to send up Don Lane when he was being interviewed. It never occurred to him to ask for a script to know what he had to do when he went on camera. Joy Butler, Chequer's publicity girl, was shocked when she saw a wall of visitors blocking the entrance to the studio and urged that they seek another way in as a precaution against Monro being mobbed. He insisted on marching right through the crowd humming a couple of bars of 'Born Free'. I asked Monro after the second show how he managed to remain so tolerant on an opening night, where others were a bundle of nerves. "That's easy to answer," he replied. "This is my third visit here and I love the place and the people. I get a thrill when I hear people call out 'Welcome home Matt,' and you can't help feeling relaxed when you're home".
> — Matt White

It was now October 1967. Matt had officially left England in January of that year and since then he had hardly had time to put his feet up in any home, old or new.

He was getting the first pangs of homesickness for Britain. Mickie, on the other hand, loved the Californian lifestyle and had made several very good friends over there. But however settled Mickie was becoming, Matt was having second thoughts.

> **It's been so hectic here; for instance today I was up at 10.00am and had to travel twelve miles to do a panel television show, which everyone said was very important. At 4.00pm there was a press party at which I was the host and went on until 6.45pm. First show 7.00pm and second show 11.30pm, finished 1.00am. Would you believe it is 1.35am and I am at the hotel writing to you – that's a record. — Letter from Matt, The Town House, Sydney**

Matt's spirits were raised when his friend Tony Hancock arrived in the country. Hancock was being taken care of by Neil Harrold who worked for the film and TV production company NLT Productions in Sydney. NLT had an arrangement with the Chevron Hotel in Melbourne whereby it provided the entertainment for its Celebrity Room at no charge to the hotel, in return for a percentage of the gross revenue, and Neil Harrold's role was to book and promote the shows.

Hancock's latest television show hadn't fared very well and he'd returned to Australia to re-establish himself. The Willard King Organisation, a television production and entertainment group partly owned by NLT, had arranged for Hancock to appear in a number of stage engagements at the Dendy Theatre and Cinema in Melbourne, opening on 4 October 1967 for a three-week run. The plan was for Tony to do his forty-five-minute act in the first half, and after the interval the venue would screen the movie *Wages of Fear*.

Hancock bumped into Matt, Bob and Kenny, when he found himself staying at the same hotel, and when things went wrong on Hancock's opening night, Matt was able to help out his old friend.

> **Tony was working out of a place called Brighton, just on the edge of Melbourne in a theatre there. There was a call to our place while we were on stage, and as soon as we came off Matt said: "We've got to go, Tony's been taken sick, let's get a cab and get over there." They kept the audience waiting until we got there.**
> **— Kenny Clayton**

Several stories circulated about this incident. Roger Wilmut wrote in his book

Artiste that a party had been thrown for the star while he was 'on the wagon' and one of the guests, aware of Hancock's condition, had laced his drink with vodka. But most of the press reported the incident saying that Hancock was suffering the after-effects of cholera injections prior to his departure for Singapore. They also said that the comic was very obviously in a bad state of health when he insisted on going on with the show, despite several attempts by the management of the Dendy Theatre to take him off the stage. But what really happened? Had Tony had an allergic reaction to a travel injection or had his drink been spiked?

Before Hancock's arrival in Australia, NLT advised Neil Harrold that the comic had not had a drink for sometime and that he was to make sure that he stayed away from alcohol. Hancock was taking a great deal of medication to counteract withdrawal and Neil made sure that he took the correct dosage before he went to sleep each night. On the day before his opening, Neil and Tony arrived back from rehearsals at the Southern Cross Hotel and bumped into Matt in the foyer. Matt invited his mate to a get together with a few friends in his suite later that night, but Hancock declined saying he was a little tired and, as well as a television appearance the next morning, he also had his opening at the Dendy. He was very nervous about the live performance as he hadn't worked for sometime and wanted to spend the evening with his own thoughts. Neil left Tony getting ready for bed with his medication on the side table.

The next morning when Neil arrived to take Hancock to the television studio he couldn't get an answer from his hotel room so went to look for him in the coffee shop. He bumped into Bob West who explained that Tony had changed his mind about coming up for a nightcap the previous evening and that the last time he'd seen the comic, he was asleep in Matt's suite. Bob had a key and entering the suite the two men found Matt asleep in bed and Tony out cold on the couch in the next room. Neil only had ninety minutes to get Tony to the studios, so Bob offered to help. They managed to part undress the comic and put him in a cold bath to wake him up.

> That was the start of a horrific and very sad day, his TV performance was terrible and the head of production for the network, Norm Spencer, agreed not to put the whole performance to air. For the rest of the day, I did not let Tony out of my sight, except when I went home to change, which took less than an hour. We had arranged with the hotel management discreetly that there was to be no alcohol delivered on room service. Somehow the

understood the situation. I said, "We'll do the best we can. We'll do all the ballads with piano, bass and drums, but as far as jazz is concerned or anything that swings, it is going to be very hard." We get through about fifteen minutes of the show and it's agonising, so Shirley storms off... I thought, "Thank God that's over," picked up the music and walked past her dressing room. As I got level with the door Shirley says, "How dare you make me work with this fucking ridiculous band," as if it was my fault. I went to my room and thought things through, looked at my diary and the last gig we had was in Miami in March '67. Over the next few weeks I made my excuses, saying I wanted to work in America. — Kenny Clayton

Kenny wasn't the only one in the business who thought the lady was difficult. Anyone actually booking her would be subject to a contract and an accompanying list of demands. Michael Black recalls that Bassey's rider clause was four pages short of *Gone With the Wind*.

In March 1967, Kenny was doing his last week with Bassey when he received a call in his hotel from Don Black. Explaining that he had heard the musical director was leaving Bassey, Don mentioned that Matt was looking for someone new. Kenny replied that he loved Matt's music, but that the singer was based in Britain, whereas Kenny was trying to establish himself in America. Don told him that things had changed, that Matt had just rented a house over in LA for a year and most of his dates were overseas, with his first date in Vancouver, then Montreal, New Orleans and Bermuda. Don told him to think about it, but Kenny didn't need to think very hard and the young musical director soon joined Matt in Canada.

They were booked to play at the Cave Theatre on 8 March with the ingeniously named Tita and Rikko and the Dancing Nymphs as the support. Ten days later, after a hugely successful run in Vancouver, Air Canada winged its passengers to Montreal, making one stop in Winnipeg for a refuel and to pick up extra passengers. As the plane waited to board new travellers, a luggage truck went by the aircraft's window, crossing the tarmac and heading for the terminal. Matt suddenly jumped out of his seat and hightailed it off the airliner running after the truck shouting, "That's my case!" Catching up with the vehicle, Matt politely and somewhat breathlessly asked, in his best British accent, if the staff would mind kindly putting it back on the plane.

Luggage safely in hand, Matt, Bob and Kenny checked in to the Royal Elizabeth Hotel. It was Expo '67 year in Montreal as well as Holy Week and the place was empty. On top of that, the weather was lousy, making commuting impossible. So system didn't work and by the time I arrived to pick him up to take him to the theatre he was not in great shape. The theatre was booked out and as it got closer to show time Tony was looking the worse for wear. When he was introduced the audience rose to its feet and he rushed on stage and nearly fell over, it was terrible seeing this great comic perform so badly. The audience was in shock and there were calls from the audience "We love you, give us a show." In the end he fell over and couldn't get up. As there were no tabs, we had to go out on stage and carry him off.

Once off stage I called The Twenties and spoke to John Collins, the General Manager of the Willard King Organisation, who said he would call me back after speaking with Matt. The call came back in minutes that Matt and orchestra would come free of charge after their show at around 11.00pm to help out, which meant we would need to put the movie on first. When this was announced the audience stood and applauded, we also announced an apology from Tony stating that his condition was due to an adverse reaction from a cholera injection he'd had that day and there would be a complete refund or exchange for tickets for another performance.

The music stands had to come from the Twenties as well as transport for thirteen musicians and the sound and lighting crew. It was now 11.30pm, no one seemed to have left the theatre, in fact more people arrived after they had heard what had happened on the radio news. When Matt walked on stage the whole audience stood and applauded well into his opening song. I had seen him work many times but I never have seen him do a show as well as he did that night, it was just marvellous. The show finished with a standing ovation after which he came out and sat at the end of the stage signed autographs and chatted to the audience. — Neil Harrold

Matt and Tony spent a lot of time together on that trip, often attending social gatherings laid on by the promoter or hotel. There were always countless invitations, particularly on their days off, and they spent one particular Sunday at a beach barbecue. Bob West recalls the period with a hint of sadness: "Hancock was a very lonely man and clung to Matt and my being there. He was not a disciplined man and totally insecure."

Tony decided to have an evening. He said he was off the booze. That night we got in after the show, and Barry Humphries, as well as others that were there at the time, popped their heads in. It was after midnight when everyone started drifting out. Kenny and I were watching Tony going around picking up the near empty glasses and pouring them into one big glass. I thought, 'Well if that's giving it up!' — Bob West

It wasn't just Tony who was up to his old tricks, Matt hadn't been an angel himself. Without Mickie around, he had resorted to having a drink late morning to pep himself up for the day. Kenny had picked Matt up one morning in his hotel room and noticed a freshly delivered breakfast tray from room service on the table. "On it was laid the local paper, a Carlsberg Special and a shot of whiskey." Being away in a strange country, without the stability of your family was tough. Matt didn't tend to get up until midday and with television, radio and personal appearances there was little time for anything but work. Once a show was over, he could hang out with the boys, the musicians and friends working in the same town, and let loose. This was the way he needed to unwind when Mickie wasn't with him; he hated going back to an empty hotel room when the adrenalin was still pumping.

Tony had resumed his shows at the Dendy and was a knockout. Everything had returned to normal and the promoters were able to breathe a sigh of relief – well almost! One day Matt, Bob and Kenny had gone to one of their favourite haunts for lunch, the Shark Fin Restaurant on Little Collins Street. Matt, when able, always tried to have a nap before a show. But that day, after waking he felt slightly odd, but shook it off. Two hours before the show he was vomiting in his hotel suite and felt extremely shaky, but insisted on doing the show.

He was supposed to appear at 9.00pm but it was well after 10.00pm before he took to the stage. He managed two songs but halfway through 'Yesterday' he just stopped and then left the stage. The audience sat there stunned. John Collins was sitting in his office and could see that Matt was in difficulties. Oddly enough he was on the phone to Hancock and explained the situation.

Tony Hancock stood in for Matt last night when the singer became ill during his act at a Melbourne restaurant. Hancock was dining at another restaurant when he heard of Matt's illness. He called a cab and rushed to help out with a thirty-minute performance. The audience at the Dendy Theatre, Brighton, in sharp contrast to a

previous night's booing and jeering, gave Hancock a wild and warm welcome. Mr John Collins, one of the proprietors of the restaurant, said today that the doctor had diagnosed Monro's illness as a 24-hour virus... Hancock said, "In a way I'm glad it happened as I have cleaned the slate." — *Reuters News Agency*

Matt was very ill for the next two days but the doctor gave him an injection and something to manage the vomiting, so he would be able to perform the following night, but he remained weak and shaky. The press took umbrage to what they felt was a huge publicity stunt, with first the Hancock incident and then Matt's episode. The press had looked into the story and were suspicious when it was discovered that the same management company owned both the New Twenties and the Dendy Theatre.

Mickie was unaware of the dramas unfolding on the other side of the world and continued to keep Matt abreast of domestic and business developments. Because of their forthcoming commitments in London, the couple felt it prudent to give up the rental property on Merridy Street, rather than renew the lease on the house, and look to buy something permanent when they returned to the States. What Capitol Records and Mickie couldn't know then was that Matt wasn't going to return to the States at all.

Don was in touch with Voyle Gilmore this morning and said it is NOT necessary to record in the next few weeks. There are a lot of tracks in the can, but if you want you can always record in London. Let me know if you want to do a *Joey Bishop Show*, that's if the strike is off and also whether you want to go via New York to do *The Tonight Show*. You will have a single out by then 'Only the Night Wind Knows/Fourth Blue Monday'. Don will move Greasbrough back a week so that we will have at least a full month to pack up. If you are in agreement we can give up this house and store everything in the car, which Sid will garage. — Letter from Mickie to the Southern Cross Hotel, Melbourne

Matt had no idea when he left Australia that he would never see his friend again. Hancock's last performance at the Dendy was on 22 October 1967, but although relatively successful, his condition was worsening. He had just signed a contract with ATN7, a Sydney-based television station and he began writing the scripts in preparation.

He made the pilot in the early part of 1968, and it was a disaster. His drinking had spiralled out of control and he was in no fit state to be filming. The television company had no choice but to kill the show. They arranged for the star to undergo psychiatric care and with a real conscious effort over the next two months Tony sobered up. Filming resumed in May with slightly more success, but the pressures of work conspired against him and on the morning of 25 June 1968, he was found dead from a large cocktail of pills and alcohol. His parting words on a suicide note read: "Things seemed to go wrong too many times."

> **I had been on tour in Australia. I said goodbye to Tony on the steps of the hotel on this Friday and I was on the way to the airport and Tony said, "Where are you going?" and I said, "I'm going back to London." "You got any room in that case for me?" he said and that was that. When I got back to London, which was quite a while later because the flights in those days required a stop of twelve hours – the placards were saying that Tony had committed suicide, and you feel kinda maybe I should have put him in the case. — Dave Allen**

Matt was absolutely devastated by Tony's death. He couldn't take in that on their last night together he'd had no indication that Tony was at such a low ebb or that his life was spiralling out of control. He felt that if he'd known he might have been able to do something, or help in some way. The world had lost a great talent, and Matt had lost a wonderful friend.

October 1967 saw the release of the title song from the new Hayley Mills film *Pretty Polly* as Matt's new single. A delicate and illustrative ballad beautifully sung with lush strings and a gentle beat. 'Release Me' was chosen as the B-side, but unlike the Humperdinck number, it was treated as a sophisticated swinger with a punchy backing.

Although Matt was happy with his vocal, he had no illusions about the song charting and went off on a much-needed holiday to the Bahamas. Matt and Mickie had a lovely hotel cabana right on the beach and over the course of the first few days they befriended several other holidaymakers as well as the hotel musicians.

Even though the question of jealously had not come up often in the Monro's marriage, Matt was prone to attacks from the green-eyed monster. He was very protective of his wife and on this trip he got it into his head that Mickie had a crush on one of the musicians, when, in fact, it was the other way round.

One afternoon after a drink-laden lunch, Matt fell asleep next to the pool and awoke to find the musician having a drink with his wife and a few other people in their cabana. After politely throwing the men out, he started to rant and rave, acting as if it was Mickie's fault that the man had shown interest in her. Drink certainly fuelled both their tempers but after enough verbal abuse, Mickie smacked Matt hard across the face – something she had never done before. She then turned on her heel and went to bed.

Mickie woke early and donning her bikini placed herself gingerly on one of the loungers outside the cabana with a large cup of coffee to soothe her throbbing head. Matt came out some time later, his hand holding his face, and announced he was "Off." "Off, off where?" Mickie demanded. "The dentist," Matt replied, revealing a face that was swollen beyond recognition. He was given an emergency appointment at the local dentist who explained that the knock to his face had caused a massive abscess to erupt, and the tooth would have to be removed. Matt had to wear a bridge for the rest of his life. He didn't forgive his wife that quickly and she never hit him again.

Returning from the Bahamas on the last stop of the world tour on 30 November, the Monros headed to London for the star's television appearance on The Petula Clark Show. On their arrival in London, their entire luggage, all eight suitcases, were searched by customs, after which Matt and Mickie were led to a private customs office to answer a barrage of questions.

The cause of the trouble was an empty jewellery box and the suspicious item was a pair of cufflinks, which Mickie had bought her husband in Lake Tahoe, that he was actually wearing. The thirty-five year old singer was tired and tetchy after his fifteen-hour flight from the Bahamas and his mood wasn't helped by the fact that airport officials had held him from 8.30am until 11.30am. He was almost apoplectic when he was told that he wouldn't be released until he had paid a £21 duty for the cufflinks.

Having taken nearly three hours to clear customs at Heathrow, Matt strode forcibly out of the arrivals building leaving Mickie to try and keep up with him. It is best not to describe the singer's mood when he then found the airport police had towed away his Silver Cloud Rolls Royce from the parking bay!

Matt did the British television rounds to let everyone know he was back in the country. Apart from *This Is Petula Clark*, he was also booked on *Simon Dee*, *Val Doonican* and a new vehicle from ATV. The station's Sunday night viewing pattern underwent a radical change in December 1967 with the introduction of a new twelve-week series, *Showtime*. These were to be one-hour spectaculars screened in Britain, but primarily filmed for the American market. It was quite normal at the time for certain shows to be made for both markets, but it required the use of two sets of cameras because the technology didn't allow for the conversion of tape in the studio. England's was made in black and white in Pal at twenty-five frames per second and America's in colour for NTSC at thirty frames per second. Although England had broadcast programmes like Wimbledon in colour during 1967, it was still at an experimental stage and it wasn't until late 1969 that the country caught up and started to develop all their programmes in colour.

Showtime was offering a cross-section of some of the world's biggest and best variety acts over a run of three months. Bob Tamlin, the executive producer, laid on a format of straight variety with a true international flavour. Each show had a different performing host, most of them American stars. American comedian Shelley Berman took the reins for the opening broadcast with other headliners set to follow. The stunning troupe of London Line Dancers, Jack Parnell & His Orchestra and the Mike Samms Singers were regulars on the series. Though there was an impressive roster of guest stars in the running, name value was not the sole criteria for booking the series, they were also looking for acts that would be relevant to a nightclub atmosphere. One of the big reasons for taping the show in England was that it was possible to offer several acts that were difficult to get in America, and rather than bring the artists across the pond, it seemed simpler to take the emcees to London.

The show was taped at ATV Studios in Elstree, about twenty-five miles from London. Shelley Burman was a popular choice as host for the inaugural show. His satirical observations on modern-day living had made him one of the best-known and favourite comedians in the world. Matt Monro and Shirley Bassey headed the guest list and treated the audience to five musical numbers between them. A New Orleans jazz treatment by Acker Bilk and his Paramount Jazz Band and a vocal-instrumental number performed by the Paraguayan music group Los Paraguayos rounded out the evening.

1967 closed with an endless round of cabaret appearances across England and by the time the New Year rang in, Matt had made the decision to remain in his home country indefinitely. Although his contract was with Capitol, some of the recordings were made in England so Matt reasoned he could maintain his contractual obligations from his British base. Mickie knew he'd made his mind up when she overheard Matt gifting his white Chevrolet Caprice to Sid Feller in a telephone conversation.

Matt & Kenny Clayton in the studio

Although constantly in demand in the States, Matt had become increasingly homesick and he was always very proud of his roots. "I'm English first and British second and very proud of my country," he would say. But he came to regret his decision to return to British shores for good, saying later: "Career wise it was probably one of the worst moves I ever made."

Matt had once again returned to a changing Britain. The early 1960s had brought The Beatles and the real revolution in music had hit the British shores. The BBC hadn't really known how to handle this new sound and carried on regardless, seemingly ignoring its massive popularity. It wasn't long before the coast of Britain was awash with illegal pirate stations playing non-stop pop in between adverts.

In 1967, the BBC gave in and changed their line-up and thus Radio 1 was born. The Light Programme became Radio 2, the Third Programme turned into Radio 3 and the Home Service became Radio 4. By the late 1960s, the old-style popular vocalists had been eclipsed in terms of chart performance by the new beat and pop groups dominating the airwaves.

None of Matt's Capitol singles released in Britain between 1966 and 1970 made the charts, but he continued to record for Columbia and EMI under the guidance of George Martin.

Matt was underrated in this country, but I think, unlike America, which has well defined areas of music, all very successful: country, jazz, swing, rock and roll, blue grass and so on, in this country we seem to be dominated by whatever the young people want at any time, and I think that is why today's music isn't a patch on what we did in those early days. — George Martin

The arrival of the Mersey Beat Boom effectively spelled the beginning of the end for the old hierarchical record-business system. Throughout the 1960s, A&R men continued to wield power over artists, but gradually they began to assert their own creative identity and the fact that The Beatles wrote their own songs inspired others to do the same. Suddenly, having lost control of many artists' material, the influence of the A&R men drastically diminished.

Even though Matt had returned to England, his overseas popularity forced him to travel nine months out of every year, and he was as familiar to audiences in New Zealand, Singapore, Australia, Hong Kong, New York and the Philippines as he was to London, Blackpool, Glasgow, Manchester, Sheffield and Cardiff.

THE POWER GAME

Matt was back at Olympic studios at the beginning of February 1968, recording a themed album called *The Late Late Show* due for release the following month. The album was the brainchild of Cadbury, who ran a series of commercials for their 'late late drink'. A competition was run, which allowed the public to pick the songs they would most like Matt to sing out of a pre-determined selection. Matt was also in rehearsals for a special television programme that he was headlining called *International Cabaret at London's Talk of the Town*. The live transmission would be shot on 12 February, hosted by Kenneth Williams and also starring Roy Budd, Topo Gigio and Viola Talvi and Jackie Farn.

Matt had spent most of the previous year touring and, without the stability of Mickie's presence, he had been drinking on a regular basis, but since returning to England he had cut down drastically. With Matt refraining from Scotch and spending ten days at Henlow Grange Health Farm, he had lost over a stone in weight and looked tremendously fit.

Feeling refreshed, he returned to the studios to record one of the tracks from *West Side Story*. Kenny enthusiastically took up the challenge of creating an arrangement for 'Maria'. "I felt a bit nervous as I was living in the shadow of Johnnie Spence, but I did it, we recorded it and it worked. I always thought of that as securing my position with Matt because what you do on stage is one thing, but working with George Martin and all the best musicians in the world and getting away with it, that's something else."

Following on from his success the year before, Matt was back at the Castaway Club next, for two shows a night. Extraordinarily, Dave Allen was up the road at La Dolce Vita again and the two staunch friends couldn't resist getting together and returning to old habits.

Dave finished earlier than we did and came to see the show. Matt

called him up on stage and they did this gag – both on board ship, a *Mutiny on the Bounty*-type thing, it's the Napoleonic Wars and Dave says, "Ah, Captain, there are forty French Froggy Frigates at port side." So Matt says, "Aye." Then Dave says, "There's another fifty French Froggy Frigates to the starboard side. What should I do?" and Matt says, "Hand me my brown trousers please." The audience creased. — Kenny Clayton

Matt's diary was already crammed full for the next two years and, as with most venues he appeared in, as soon as he had packed his gear and left the dressing room, the booker was on the phone to the office to grab another date.

Popping in to catch Matt's act when he opened at the Castaway Club on Sunday, Dave Allen, in town for the week at rival club La Dolce Vita, must have left feeling he has a comic as well as a singer as opposition. For the simple fact is that Matt has now developed his between-numbers patter to such an extent that he raises far more laughs than many so-called comics.... He gives full value for money with a performance that is a lesson in the art of getting the most out of a popular song. It all adds up to a forty-minute act spelling professionalism. — Dennis Detheridge

Returning from Birmingham, Matt didn't have much time before his opening at Bernard Delfont's top London venue, but he still managed to squeeze in appearances on Cilla Black's show *Cilla* and *Doddy's Music Box*. There was also the small matter of a rushed recording session for George Martin, who wanted to release 'One Day Soon' as a new single within the next three weeks. Rushed or not, the critics were kind, saying it was a classy ballad and that Matt was untouchable when it came to stylish lyric-reading.

Matt wasn't the only one who was busy. Don was concentrating on his own writing career, and undertook ten separate projects during 1968, so it was understandable that the aides at NEMS were undertaking some of the workload.

Having dispensed with a photo session and dress rehearsal, Matt was ready for his month-long stint at London's Talk of the Town, the booking that had been deferred from the year before because of Shirley Bassey. Bernard Delfont's dazzling sequence of successful productions in the London nightspot had set new standards in the world of showmanship and the presentation of headline talent.

Robert Nesbitt had devised and produced spectacular shows throughout the world, but the Talk of the Town afforded him the opportunity of staging the most colourful and elaborate displays of his long and successful career. His newest floorshow, *Fine Feathers,* was an eye-dazzling production based on *Follies.* The costumes also happened to be the briefest yet, but that was not a cause for complaint.

Mickie hosted a table of specially invited guests for Matt's opening night, including Len and Sue Matcham, Johnnie and Marion Spence, George and Judy Martin, Don and Shirley Black, Vic and Jill Lewis and John and Joan Shakespeare as well as Mickie's mother Evelyn and her brother Ernie. It had been a long time since Matt and Mickie had seen some of these close friends and it was especially nice entertaining them in London. Ably backed by the Burt Rhodes Showband and Kenny Clayton at the piano, Matt swung gently through a fifty-minute act with the minimum of patter. Matt's programme was predictable, with standards such as 'My Kind of Girl', 'Love is a Many Splendoured Thing', 'Spanish Eyes', 'Portrait of My Love', 'The Shadow of Your Smile', 'It Was a Very Good Year', 'One Day Soon' and 'Born Free', before closing on 'Maria'. It was predictable because it was becoming increasingly difficult for the singer to include new material. When he'd tried to put an entirely new repertoire together, he received complaints from people who expected to hear the records he'd made famous.

While on stage, Matt caught sight of himself in one of the establishment's ornate mirrors. He was reminded of his resemblance to Patrick Wymark in *The Power Game* and spontaneously went into an impression of the actor to the delight of the crowd. George Martin enjoyed the night immensely. "Matt was essentially a very good cabaret artist and he had a really smart line of patter. He used to do impressions of people from time to time as part of his act. I think it's a kind of forgotten art now amongst singers of today, but it used to go down very well with the audiences of the time. He was enormously versatile."

Today the Monro-Wymark link is part of showbiz folklore. One well-known story has Wymark going with his eldest daughter to see Ken Dodd at the London Palladium. Just before the interval lights went up, the actor insisted on rushing to the bar to avoid being bothered by autograph hunters. There was one fan, however, who managed to catch him at the bar entrance – and asked if Mr Monro would mind signing his book! In a separate incident, Wymark went into the dimly-lit bar one lunchtime at Elstree Studios and spotted Matt. He launched into the story about the London Palladium, but Matt didn't seem to be taking much notice.

Dave Allen & Matt in the a television scene from The Power Game

Then, just as he was coming out with the punch line, the truth dawned on him – he was talking to Dickie Valentine!

Matt and Patrick only actually met the once. The occasion saw them sat at adjacent tables over lunch at a television studio, eyeing each other at intervals. Wymark certainly didn't want to repeat his prior mistake and stayed put. It wasn't until later in the day that the two men had a brief drink together in the hospitality suite, exchanging stories about the past mix-ups. Matt would later share his impression of the actor with the TV-viewing public when he appeared on *The Dave Allen Show* in a sketch based on *The Power Game*, with Matt cast in Wymark's role.

One man who caught Matt's show in Leicester Square was John Burgess. He was very impressed with the star's stage presence and vocal ability, little knowing that less than two years later he would take over the producer's role from George Martin.

The Late Late Show was released while Matt was working at London's top cabaret spot, and as a press opportunity Cadbury had asked Matt to present the prize to the winner of the contest during the show. The entrants had originally been asked to choose the ten most suitable songs from a list of twenty hits for Matt to sing, taking into consideration that the album was intended for late listening. The decider was the completion of a slogan for Cadbury's Drinking Chocolate.

Although Matt was able to go home every night after his show at the Talk of the Town, he wasn't able to put his feet up. He was needed at the studios for appearances on *Pete's People*, *Parade of the Pops*, *Saturday Club*, *The Billy Cotton Show*, *The Londoners*, *Dee Time*, *The Des O'Connor Show*, *The Val Doonican Show* and *The Morecambe & Wise Show*.

Matt & Leonardo Schultz

His superb singing technique, coupled with those classy arrangements, made him the best we ever had in our part of the world. — Val Doonican

In the 1960s, when I was a BBC TV producer, I used Matt in a Val Doonican 'special' and, soon afterwards, in one of the first series of BBC Morecambe & Wise Shows. A long time ago, yes, but it says a lot for Matt's distinctive talent that I still remember him, not only as a great singer, but also as a professional artist to work with – a view shared not only by stars such as Val and Eric and Ernie but by everybody else in the business, certainly including me. We all appreciated the high quality of that golden voice but also remember him as a very nice person. A gentleman, a joy and pleasure to work with, great voice and we always had a laugh. — John Ammonds

Unexpectedly, Don received a telephone call from Buenos Aires; it appeared that a South American agent wanted to bring Matt Monro over to his home country. The problem was that Mr Schultz spoke hardly any English, only Spanish and Yiddish. Don thought that Matt might be interested and asked the agent to write to him with more details. Some weeks later, Leonardo Schultz was knocking on the lyricist's door. Don's instructions had got lost in translation and the small Jewish South American had thought Don wanted him to travel to his address, rather than write to it. Such was Leonardo's excitement for the project that he had willingly got on a plane and flown over without hesitation for a face-to-face meeting.

It transpired that Leonardo wanted Matt to sing in Spanish, as he felt there was a large unexploited market that would fall for the charms of Mr Monro in a big way. Matt reluctantly agreed. It wasn't that he didn't want to record in Spanish, it was more a case of he didn't know how to sing in Spanish. Schultz did the adaptations from some of Matt's existing repertoire, adding a few new ones to the album they were working on. With *Alguien Canto* (The Music Played) recorded, the title track was released as a single and shot straight to the top of the charts in South America. The disc sold in excess of seven million units worldwide, earning Matt his first Platinum record.

> **I can't speak Spanish; I learn to sing the lyrics phonetically. A song I recorded in Spanish, 'The Music Played', is currently top of the charts in South America. — Matt Monro**

Interestingly, the very first Spanish track Matt had laid down was the controversial 'When I Look into Your Eyes', which, like its English predecessor, was shelved. In 1967, Matt and Billy May had worked on an English version of the song as a single. Both Matt and Capitol loved the track, and it was mastered for release, but at the last minute there was a problem with the publishers and the project came to a halt.

> **I did 'Spanish Eyes' for him (30 May 1967). It wasn't a big record but Matt loved it because it was a completely different version. We did it up-tempo with a Mexican rhythm and he loved it and so did the band. I played with him at Fairfield Halls in Croydon; we had a great time catching up. He also did 'When I Look into Your Eyes'. We were all fond of it, Capitol Records were very happy with it, but something happened with the publisher and they refused to let Capitol put the record out. It was a great disappointment to Matt. — Billy May**

Capitol was forced into shelving the song after it was discovered to have different lyrics to the official published version that appeared in the film *Doctor Dolittle*. In Matt's version he sings, "those eyes so pure, so warm, so wise, how I love the look in your eyes", but in the film the lyrics sung by Rex Harrison are, "those eyes so wise, so warm, so real, isn't it a pity you are a seal?" It would appear that after the film was released, all versions, including those recorded by Anthony Newley, Bobby Darin, Frank Sinatra and Tony Bennett, were changed to, "those eyes so wise, so warm so real, how I love the world, your eyes reveal". Matt's version was recorded before the official pop version was released and therefore disallowed by the publishers.

With a successful album in the can, Schultz flew back to his homeland having exacted Matt's promise to appear in South America during the following month. In the meantime, the singer had a date with Dave Allen. The comic was in the middle of filming for his highly successful television show with the BBC. Luckily for the comic, Matt wasn't too touchy about his height and Dave got away with a couple of jibes during filming: "They promised me a big singer," complained Dave. "You've got a big singer," Matt replied. "Yes, when you're sitting down I've got a big singer, but standing up…"

> We were sitting in a bar in Birmingham one night and Matt had the most extraordinary long body and very short legs – I'm just reasonably normal and I'm sitting on this stool and I know I'm about five inches bigger than Matt but he's looking down on me whilst he's sitting on the stool. And I straightened up, thinking I must be slouching, but he was still towering over me. I asked Matt to do me a favour and stand up. So we both stood up and now I'm looking down on him! — Dave Allen

Despite Matt's international star status, he would cheerfully play the stooge in Dave's routines. On one memorable occasion, after months of phone calls, Dave finally persuaded Matt to take part in a sketch cast as Sir John Wilder of *The Power Game*.

> Dave had a tremendous sense of fun and could be quite a prankster. We were rehearsing just off Baker Street one day, with Matt Monro, Dave and Edward Woodward. There were lots of dancers as well. It was going to be a really large show. I got an unexpected call telling me that I had won the Charles Chaplin Award in Geneva for the *Charlie Drake 812 Overture Show* that I had directed. Dave was

delighted for me and said that this was such a great honour that we needed to go out at lunchtime and celebrate. Matt, Dave, Edward and I went to the pub over the road for lunch. I am a teetotaller and never drank, but that day Dave said that it was such an occasion that I really should. He ordered four pints of Guinness to celebrate my success. I sipped a little, and we talked about the award. After about twenty minutes I noticed that my pint of Guinness hadn't gone down at all. Dave had been topping it up with champagne. I couldn't walk back to the rehearsal rooms. It was chaos, none of us could do anything for laughing, and I had to cancel the rehearsals for that day. — Ernest Maxin

Although Matt was not a fan of the time constraints and the sterility of most television shows, he loved taking part in skits in a Morecambe and Wise special or a Dave Allen comedy routine. Ernest Maxin had an outstanding resume in television, directing and producing some of the nations best-loved shows, including *Jack Benny*, *Dick Emery* and *Les Dawson*. He was also responsible for some of the most memorable choreographical sequences, such as the unforgettable 'Singin' in the Rain' sketch. So when Maxin invited Matt to do another show with Dave, he was delighted. A custard pie skit was casually mentioned, and the singer was told that it might be better if he wore an old suit to the shoot, but even though Matt took the hint and put on clothes he'd bought in Hong Kong years back, he hadn't anticipated on just how messy things would get.

The sketch's participants were organised into two teams and the flan cases, which were filled with flour and water rather than the foam Matt had expected, were hurled everywhere, with everyone slipping and slithering all over the studio. The show finished with Dave scooping up a bucketful of the stuff and dumping it over Matt's head. "I looked like a melting snowman, but what a lot of trouble I had to clean myself of the 'custard'. I found my shower wouldn't work – you need cold water to get the flour out of the hair, if you use hot then your head becomes a mass of dough. If you can visualise me kneeling in the bath, with my head under the cold-water tap, you can see there are funnier things happening off the screen than on."

The bucket plonked on Matt's head was Dave's revenge for being pushed into the biggest custard pie the world had ever seen. No one had been more surprised than Dave when it was wheeled out into the studio. Made in secret by the backroom boys of the programme, and a foot-deep with a diameter of six feet, the monstrosity was filled with gallons of flour, water, artificial plastic snow and any old junk the studio hands could find. As the twelve-dozen normal-sized custard pies were used up in the battle, technicians struggled on to the floor with their pièce de résistance. Dave Allen watched, puzzled, until suddenly he was nudged headfirst into the jelly-like substance. The technicians had taken Dave at his word – lots of surprises and no rehearsals. But it was good for the show, and that was all that mattered.

> I adored Matt; I think he was the greatest singer – even better than Sinatra. He had a magnificent voice. A pop song has a thirty-two-bar chorus, Matt made it sound like an MGM movie, with a beginning, a middle and an end and a 'this way out please'. When I first heard him sing on TV he came to the end of the song and my wife Leigh and I were holding hands. He had that effect.
>
> On one of the Dave Allen shows, I wrote a silent film sketch for Dave and Matt with a flicker wheel on it to add authenticity. Towards the end of the show Matt sang 'This is My Song For a New World'. It was followed by my favourite song, 'The Shadow of Your Smile', and was its first airing on television. I can still hear him singing it. I remember being in the control room. Usually it was a hive of activity, with cameras cutting from one to another, but I was totally mesmerized and at the end of the number my secretary was amazed to see that I was crying. I respected him so much; he was the greatest singer ever to come out of England. — Ernest Maxin

Dave thought Matt to be a natural actor and had him work on three of his television shows that year, in May, October and December. Dave, Matt, Johnnie Spence and Kenny Baker met up in the Green Room after one such appearance, and, once the bar had been drunk dry, they decided to continue the party back at Matt's house. Several hours later, Dave and Johnnie took their leave, but Kenny was too drunk to drive so Matt rolled the cinematic screen down, stuck a Western on and they sat, drank, smoked and laughed through most of the night. Eventually, Mickie moved Matthew out of his room and let Kenny use the boy's bed, leaving strict instructions with the children not to close any of the doors as, having been born with a form of dwarfism, their guest was too short to reach the doorknobs. But, of course, Kenny got locked in by mistake and there was nothing in the child's room for him to stand on. Initially unconcerned, and not wanting to wake anyone up, Kenny's plight soon became urgent when the call of Mother Nature got too painful to ignore. He started banging on the door and Matt, still in the same position on the settee where Kenny had left him hours before, burst out laughing – although in fairness he had tried to keep a straight face!

Matt kept his word to Leonardo Schultz and on 15 May, as soon as filming was completed on the BBC show he packed his bags and flew from London to Buenos Aires, Argentina, with Don Black, Kenny Clayton and Bob West in tow.

> **Don explained that Leonardo Schultz was laying on a big spread at his apartment. Leonardo picked us up at the airport, after an eighteen-hour flight, in a beautiful gleaming Mercedes. We neared the apartment at about 7.00pm local time and as we walked in we could see the table was beautifully laid out. We sat in the lounge for a pre-dinner drink and Leonardo looked round at Matt, who had chosen an overly large armchair for himself — he was fast asleep and stayed that way for the night. — Kenny Clayton**

Matt was scheduled to do a radio concert in a town south of Buenos Aires and, with a two hour drive ahead of them, Matt and his entourage headed out in separate cars. Matt and Leonardo were in the lead vehicle, being driven by George Gutmann, Leonardo's right-hand man. Kenny and Bob followed in the car behind. It was a long journey along dangerous coastal roads, but they eventually neared their destination. About a mile out from the venue, they could hear loudspeakers announcing the star's imminent arrival, and as they rounded a corner near the building they could see thousands of people swarming the area, and all the while the loudspeakers were hyping the crowds up.

The first car pulled in as near to the venue's door as possible and, with Gutmann and several police officers' help, they managed to cordon off a route through the crowd and get Matt and Leonardo safely into the building. However, as the multitudes surged after the star, Bob and Kenny got swept up in the melee. They had no help and were desperately trying to claw their way to the doors. The police, not realising the two men were with Matt, were unrelenting in their task of pushing people away from the entrance and they were thrust back into the masses. This changed once the constabulary heard the men's accents as they were calling for help and realised their mistake. They quickly organised a makeshift thoroughfare and Kenny and Bob, who were carrying the cases of music, were hustled along. Unfortunately, although the police were making way at the front of the party, no one was protecting the men from behind and, having finally muscled

Matt & Pelé

a route to the entranceway, the doors slammed on Bob, breaking three of his ribs in the process. Nevertheless, twelve thousand people were insistent on hearing the Englishman sing and, in order to stop any riots breaking out, Matt performed on the balcony of the building to a surging audience in the streets below.

In between giving concerts, Matt was invited to a football match with the Brazilian team Santos, where he was introduced to Pelé. Matt greatly admired the athlete; indeed he was the greatest player on the football field at the time. Wearing the number-ten shirt, he weaved across the field effortlessly and seemed to be able to make the ball do as he pleased. As with many such meetings, Matt was always pleasantly surprised to find that the people he admired wanted to meet him as well.

From Brazil, the party flew to Uruguay and moved quickly through Carrasco International Airport. Montevideo was the largest city, and the capital and chief port of Uruguay. It had the most beautiful beaches, scores of monuments and museums, and historic buildings and squares. Bob West accompanied Matt to some of the most exotic destinations around the world, but never got the chance to see any of them with his friend, as Matt would have been mobbed as soon as he stepped out of the hotel door. Though at least in South America, Leonardo drove him to the capital, a place Bob wanted to see.

The trip to South America had been squeezed into the diary after switching around other dates, but the most they could muster was ten days. With the tour nearly finished, Leonardo was desperate for a repeat booking and the Monro entourage left, promising to return the following year.

On 29 May Matt opened his two-week run at Harvey's in Lake Tahoe, his third trip there in as many years. With the success of 'Alguien Canto' still ringing in his ears, the decision was made to record the song in English as well, and it was officially due on the streets in the next few days. Matt invariably presented a song with an authority, smoothness and polish that was second-to-none and his latest disc was no exception. A lilting ballad with a poignant lyric encased in a glossy Johnnie Spence scoring of sweeping strings and concerto-type piano.

From Tahoe, Matt flew to Los Angeles for his repeat booking at Century Plaza's Westside Room, but before he had a chance to open, he had to step in for an ailing Connie Francis at Vegas's Congo Room at the Sahara Hotel for two nights. It was coincidental that Matt was due to open there himself a few weeks later with Jack Benny. Benny was in the audience when the singer opened in Los Angeles, as were Elmer Bernstein, Jack Jones and Jane Wyman. After a swinging opener, 'As Long as I'm Singing', he followed with a strong repertoire of 'Spanish Eyes', 'Yesterday', 'In the Still of the Night', 'Maria', 'It Was a Very Good Year', 'Born Free' and 'Walk Away', finishing with his new release, 'The Music Played'.

Something was evidently bothering Matt on the Tuesday night at his opening because he was extraordinarily quiet after his appearance in the Westside Room. It could have been the long delay by the management in getting him on stage. He had been ready to go on at 9.00pm, but when the show didn't get underway until 10.20pm, the needless waiting, delayed service, poor seating arrangements and abysmal microphone system, on top of the usual opening-night pressures, had become too much to bear. He joked with the audience about the delayed service and moved around the front tables, engaging the guests in conversation, but was openly relieved when the curtain finally came down. Matt's mood was not helped by the fact that Don wasn't there to sort the whole mess out, and his irritation came to a head when he was later seen having words with the management.

During Matt's Los Angeles shows, Kenny Clayton was staying at the Sunset Marquee, a little motel built round a pool. While lying out in full swimming costume splendour, with a large rum and coke in hand, he suddenly heard the dulcet tones of Ronnie Fraser. The actor explained that he was filming with Robert Altman, and Kenny replied that he was there working with Matt. Kenny subsequently arranged for Ronnie to come to one of the shows, though Ronnie asked that Kenny not mention seeing him, as he wanted to surprise his mate during his performance.

On the night, Ronnie made his entrance to the venue in full Scottish regalia –

l to r Irwin Molasky, Mickie, Matt, Pepi Molasky & Kenny Clayton

kilt, sporran, the whole works – and all eyes were on him as he sauntered to the front-row table. Scottish attire was not the normal dress code in America and it earned him more than one suspicious look from the crowd. Matt and Kenny were by the two kitchen doors behind the stage, waiting for their cue, when an Italian waiter came through the doors, tray in hand, and said, "Jesus Christ, some fucking guy in the front is wearing a dress!" Matt immediately turned to Kenny and said, "It's got to be Ronnie Fraser." Kenny was stunned; he didn't know how Matt could have possibly guessed. Matt went on stage and played to every part of the room – except the one chair whose tenant was desperate for Matt to notice him. Then, with ten minutes to go until the end of Matt's routine, he strode straight up to his expectant visitor and casually said, "Hi Ronnie." Ronnie was gutted. But they all had a good laugh about it in the hotel room later.

Mickie flew over to join Matt and while in Los Angeles, Kenny introduced the couple to Pepi and Irwin Molasky, who invited them down to a 'little club' they owned. The three thousand five hundred acre La Costa Resort and Spa opened in 1965 and was twenty-five years ahead of its time. Only eighty-five miles from LA, it was ideally placed and surrounded by scenic rolling hills, lush canyons and expansive views that stretched to the Pacific Ocean. Ever since those humble beginnings, the rich and famous had been coming to La Costa, which offered luxury custom-built homes. Frank Sinatra, Dean Martin, Humphrey Bogart and Lauren Bacall all had second homes on the estate. Matt, Mickie and Kenny were given a house to stay in for the weekend with an invitation to have drinks in the clubhouse at 7.00pm. They arrived to find Hoagy Carmichael sitting at the piano playing with the likes of Deborah Kerr dancing along. On the second night, which was advertised as a charity event, Matt did a few songs with Kenny at the piano.

Matt was arranging to host a surprise birthday party for his wife at the Century Plaza, with guests Phyllis Diller and her husband Warde Donovan, Shani Wallis, Davy Jones, Vince and Linda Edwards, Channing Pollack, the Paul Kenners and Sid and Gert Feller. After attending a meeting with the hotel management to ensure all the arrangements would be in place for the party, which was to be held in his suite after the show on his wife's special day, he returned to his twelfth floor hotel suite. Minutes later, an earthquake hit Los Angeles. Matt and Mickie had never experienced an earthquake tremor before. Suddenly the room started swaying and a heavily-laden room service trolley crashed into the wall.

> **I suppose it was the swaying that made me think of it, but I had the underlying thought that I should sing a song while the quake was in progress – you know, like they did in the movie about the sinking of the *Titanic*. But I was so dry-mouthed I couldn't sing a note. When the rumble had subsided I dashed to the balcony, and could see the telephone wires moving to and fro.**
>
> **I got the funniest feeling, because after all it happened on 4 July, and I'm from England and I'm in the Colonies. You're not still mad at us are you? — Matt Monro**

Matt had switched his contract with the Fairmont Hotel, Las Vegas, to August when he got the date with Jack Benny at the Congo Showroom. The singer was asked if he would go to Mr Benny's suite for rehearsals, as they were going to do a little comedy spot together. Matt walked in to find Benny in his pyjamas in bed, and that is where he stayed throughout their run-through together!

What made Benny one of the supreme artists in the tricky showbiz maelstrom was that he not only lived up to expectations, but routinely exceeded them. Recognised by both press and public for many years as a master of timing and the delayed pun, the Waukegan gent was a master in the art of spoofery. Whether he

Matt & Jack Benny

was chiding his wife, Mary Livingston, playing fiddle or engaging in delightful banter with the audience, you couldn't help but walk away from a Benny show completely entertained.

A brief overture by the Louis Basil Orchestra was all the introduction Benny needed. He walked nonchalantly on to the stage, without so much as a drum roll, fanfare or over-bleated announcement, delivering topical jests with impeccable timing and pacing, before strolling off with that familiar Benny stride to a rousing standing ovation. Matt charmed the room in equal measure. His aura of sincerity was immediately established with 'Maria' and 'Walk Away', captivating his audience, only to outdo himself with 'It Was a Very Good Year' and 'Younger Than Springtime'. In a brief but telling dialogue with Benny, the British singer displayed neat straight man proficiency as he laid on a 'critique' of the comedian's mannerisms. Monro encored with his renowned hit 'Born Free' to a standing ovation. Matt loved working with Benny, saying, "I had to take part in Benny's routine, which was a knock out. He's a thrill a second that man, and a gentleman."

Normally a British artist would go over and give them half an hour in a show where there was an American headliner. Even Bassey's

first time at the Sahara was only twenty-five minutes; the Osmond Brothers were top of the bill. So when we heard that Matt had been invited to go over and do the first half an hour for Jack Benny, Matt said, "You can't get much better than that", and was delighted. So we go over there and attend rehearsal. Jack's agent, Irving Vine, and Benny are talking about the show. Benny turns to Matt and says, "What we'll do is I will go on for half an hour and then I'll introduce you by saying, 'While I was in England I met this wonderful young man and I want you to listen to him, Matt Monro.'" So he reversed that whole warm up thing. Instead of Matt going on cold, Benny goes on first and the audience are comfortable. They've seen what they've paid for so when Matt comes on they're interested, he's not just somebody who passes through. For me it was one of the great stories of generosity in our profession. — Kenny Clayton

During Matt's tenure at the Sahara Hotel's Congo Room, Mickie hosted a table for dinner, inviting Dinah Shore, Connie Stevens and Gert and Sid Feller, who had driven down from LA for the night. That was one of the few nights she missed her liaison with Jack Benny, as they usually met at a designated one-armed bandit in the break between the two nightly performances and played the slots for half an hour. The comedian had become very friendly with the Monro couple and they often had drinks together or grabbed a snack after the show.

Matt very nearly stayed on at the Congo Room after his contract with Benny finished as he had received a phone call asking if he was available to act as standby for Judy Garland. She was apparently suffering the repercussions of long-term drug and alcohol abuse and the management were unsure if she could perform. However, Garland did end up taking the stage, and Matt and Mickie were guests at the show. It was the only time they saw her perform live, but it might have been better if she hadn't appeared that night. It was a very sad performance and the audience were left disappointed.

Matt thoroughly loved his time at The Sahara. Don Rickles was working in the Casbar Theatre in the same hotel and Frankie Laine, Eddie Fisher and Buddy Greco were in Vegas at other venues and there were plenty of opportunities for everyone to meet up, it was that kind of place. Len Matcham even flew over just to have dinner with Mickie and Matt and to see the singer perform. "Len only ever

went anywhere if he had a reason to go and seeing Matt perform was obviously a good enough one," said his companion Sue Groves.

The first order of business when arriving back in England was an appearance on *The Morecambe & Wise Show*. Matt shared the screen with Eric and Ernie as well as Kenny Ball and his Jazzmen and helped out with a sketch based on the Bing Crosby and Bob Hope road pictures. One part of the scene had the singer trying to serenade a rather rough-looking 'Dorothy Lamour'. Matt could barely get a note out for laughing, and no wonder; Dorothy was played by Ernie Wise.

September also saw the release of *Star Spectacular*. Here was a golden opportunity to help the United Nations Children's Fund carry on their work for the underprivileged children of the world. As well as the stars that took part in the recording, the music publishers and record companies all donated their royalties from the sales of the record to UNICEF. And what a line up it was: Paul Jones, Cliff Richard, Cilla Black, The Shadows, Acker Bilk, Shirley Bassey, The Hollies, Mrs Mills, Rolf Harris, Ken Dodd, The Seekers, Peter and Gordon, Vince Hill, Frank Ifield, Russ Conway and Matt all contributed to the success of the project.

The singer liked to help a range of charities wherever and whenever he could. On one occasion, sportswriter and broadcaster Michael Parkinson was booked as one of the speakers at a celebrity luncheon for the Variety Club of Great Britain, held at the Grand Hotel in Sheffield. When he couldn't attend owing to television commitments in London, Matt stepped in as a replacement speaker. The Variety Club's Sunshine Coach Scheme was important, and if his appearance could help raise funding to provide motor coaches for children's outings at three Sheffield special schools, it was worthwhile.

Leaving the Crystal Room in Lancashire after a run of successful shows, Matt went on to the Cavendish in Birmingham. The booker had handpicked Matt for this specific week because Norman Wisdom was the main attraction at the Cresta Theatre Club in Solihull, only a couple of miles away from the Cavendish. They felt that Matt was one of the few artists that could fill the club on a week where normally they would lose out to the competition – and they were right.

It wasn't long before Matt was in EMI's Studio 1 to lay down the title song for the forthcoming Columbia Pictures production *Southern Star*. George Martin, who was also scoring all the incidental music for the movie, produced the session. The film was due for release in the New Year, and Capitol wanted to issue a single of the title song to coincide with the premiere of the picture. The track used on *The Ultimate Matt Monro* is from the actual opening credits of the film rather than the Capitol single recorded at the beginning of December. Three days later, Matt went in to record the French version and on 9 July the following year, the Spanish adaptation.

Leonardo Schultz had kept in constant contact with the singer since his appearances in South America and, based on Matt's previous chart success in the Latin speaking countries, Schultz organised another session in the studio to record a new album of Spanish songs.

After finishing a show at the Wakefield Theatre Club, Matt, Kenny and Bob headed for the Ace of Spades, an after-show bolthole. The cab dropped them off and they commandeered a booth in the corner. Matt and Kenny sat next to each other and Bob West sat facing them. They ordered drinks and one of the girls who worked at the club, who was quite beautiful, came and sat down in the spare seat next to Bob. She was a fan of Matt and was hoping to get better acquainted with the star, but Bob was very protective of his charge and after about ten minutes Matt's road manager and the girl disappeared and never came back. Matt and Kenny were not sure what Bob had promised her, but whatever her expectations, she must have been disappointed to find out that Bob was gay.

Perpetually being hailed as England's answer to Frank Sinatra and advertised as such at every venue, including Wakefield, Matt couldn't escape the constant comparisons. The Sinatra tag was a little unfair, particularly so when it was only Britain that thought of him that way. In America, they treated him as a star in his own right.

> I felt like I had the perfect objective scenario through which to analyse the great singers of the 1960s. In the late seventies I heard all of this music for the first time on an 'MOR' radio station and all of the voices existed in a vacuum without the whirlwind of media attention that surrounded the original release of these songs. I could judge them without being prejudiced by commonly-held views about who was the best. After deciding for myself who was the best I became aware of 'conventional-wisdom' and had to conclude that Sinatra's pre-eminence was based less on quality and more on cult-of-personality, legendary romantic escapes, latter-day mob glorification, successes in other media, and so on. That Matt Monro was likened to Sinatra was always puzzling to me. Historically, I know that all singers who followed Sinatra owe him the fact that their name is on the label rather than that of the orchestra and that they shamelessly aped his style, but it's still just plain lazy to come up with 'Britain's Sinatra' as the common shorthand for 'Matt Monro'. He was so much more than a 'British Sinatra', and in many ways anything but. — David Durrett

Matt was back to working flat out. He recorded another commercial for the McDougall's flour company, who were using national television, an extremely large budget, and a redesigned pack to launch their new flour, Extrafine. A series of thirty-second commercials were made that featured a jingle and the theme, "You can feel it's finer flour". With the advertising campaign ready to go, Matt left for Leeds to rehearse and record Yorkshire Television's first colour special, *Mr & Mrs Music*. Hosted by Jackie Trent and Tony Hatch, the guests were Scott Walker and Matt. It was not the happiest experience for any of the cast.

> The programme that Jackie Trent and I did as the light entertainment launch for Yorkshire Television was a very traumatic experience. The studio in Leeds wasn't ready for such a huge show. Matt showed his usual patience although the pressure was enormous. The problems experienced at Yorkshire Television were

due to several factors. The studio wasn't large enough, but it was all new and recently installed equipment which had obviously been tested but had never been used before to make a programme as complex as a music show. Many difficulties were experienced, especially with regard to sound balance. Rehearsals were delayed as various other technical hitches surfaced. I'm sure our individual performances were compromised in the final rush to get the programme on tape. It was a one-off show so there was never a chance to get it right in subsequent programmes. — Tony Hatch

Jackie Trent was just sixteen years old when she met a twenty-six year old Matt in Tin Pan Alley. She had arrived in London, fresh from Stoke-on-Trent, to make her own claim to fame and everyone seemed to cross paths, searching for that route to stardom. She admits she got lucky when, ten years later, she co-wrote and recorded 'Where Are You Now', her own number one in the charts. Her co-writer, Tony Hatch, had also penned 'I Love the Little Things', Matt's Eurovision entry. "In those days the contest was about quality," Jackie said, "and Matt Monro was the 'crème de la crème. In the fifties, the music industry was rather like family: the music publishers all had pianists to ply the artist with new songs and even provided arrangers to score the music for them if they were lucky enough to land a broadcast, and of course Matt's 'radio voice' fitted in there with the velvet tones of pure magic."

The television audience, no doubt avidly watching their first Yorkshire TV colour transmission, would never realise that the set design was hopelessly wrong: a glorious cream pageant of colour, but with no space for the mussos to play. The set designer obviously hadn't realised that trombone players need extra space for their slides, so the poor old Sax players sat in front kept being hit behind the ear with brass sliders. The cello players also had difficulties playing in limited space, I mean where are you going to put a large cello between your legs and play the thing with no space to move. Oh Joy!! I'm proud to say I knew Matt Monro; not just proud, honoured. He was a gentleman, with a wonderful sense of humour and a generous heart, as with Mr Sinatra, who treated me with sensitivity and respect as a writer. And my good friend Sammy Davis Jr, who I will miss forever... All three, Sinatra, Davis and Monro, were diminutive in stature but giants as men: the finest voices in the

world, bestowing a rich legacy on mankind. — Jackie Trent

Matt Monro will never be forgotten because he was the best singer of that musical genre the UK ever had, with a unique easy style and sound. His technique was amazing. Notes were always perfectly pitched and he thought carefully about the lyrics. I think the opportunities for him to shine were always going to be less in the UK than in America. — Tony Hatch

While working at Yorkshire television Matt had some upsetting news. Eric Morecambe had been working a week of midnight performances at the Variety Club in Batley. Whilst driving home after the show he suffered a heart attack and had to spend two weeks in hospital. When Matt heard about Eric's attack he insisted that he and Kenny go to the hospital and check on him on their way back to London.

What was claimed to be Britain's largest theatre club, due to open in Middlesbrough on 7 November, was treated to a last-minute change of name. It was originally to be the Astoria, which was the name of the building before its conversion, but it had finally been decided to title it the Showboat Variety Club and the local papers were spearheading the story. The opening was to be a major event in a town that had been short on entertainment venues and the club had already pre-sold most of its tickets for Joe Brown and the Bruvvers, who were topping the bill for the opening three nights. Matt had originally been asked to front the cabaret that week himself, but was already committed elsewhere, so instead he appeared in the last week of November, with former Geraldo singer Jill Day booked to open the show.

By this time Matt was quite literally going through the motions – he was incredibly tired and desperately in need of some time off, but that was something still three months down the line. In the meantime, he had committed his time to once again appear alongside Val Doonican, another *Dee Time* performance, a date with Dave Allen and the New Year's Eve *Cilla Black Show*.

Although Matt was generous with his time when it came to charity work in general, he was leaning more towards supporting the Stars Organisation for Spastics and tried to help whenever he could. So the day after his thirty-eighth birthday, Matt, Mickie, Marion and Johnnie all bought tickets for the SOS Christmas Ball at The Dorchester Hotel in London. On the evening, they all had a considerable amount to drink and were having a thoroughly good time. One part of the entertainment was given over to a dog act. The dogs were all poodles, in an array of different colours, shapes and sizes, and the girls fell instantly in love with them. After the show, Matt and Johnnie approached the dog-handler to ask if he had any puppies for sale. He didn't, but gave them the address of a breeder in Wallington, and leaving the function in the wee small hours, the boozed up foursome were still discussing the merits of dog ownership on their way back to Dallas Road. Unfortunately for the boys, even in the cold light of the next day the girls still had their hearts set on having a poodle each, so with hangovers in check they all set off to the dog breeder in Warrington. Marion recalls, "I'm not sure how Mickie and I persuaded the boys, but somehow we did and the result was that we came home with two dinky black poodles, which were called Moet and Chandon. Matt named them such because he said we had all drunk too much of the stuff the night before." Matt kept Moet because the dog's name started with the lucky letter 'M' and Marion and Johnnie took Chandon home with them.

When Matt began to sing 'Walk Away' at the Aztec Club, Hornchurch, on a Saturday night in December, it was for him a forlorn hope. The capacity audience just wouldn't let him go. They couldn't get enough of the singer and Matt enjoyed himself so much that he sang for almost an hour and a half. That night he proved conclusively that there was no one who could sing with better timing and control. He hit top notes without effort in running through all his hit numbers.

As in past years, the Monro and Spence families' routine of spending Christmas together continued. Matt also received a letter from Don that year.

> At Christmas I was stony broke and borrowed £7.00 from Don, who was in the music publishing business. It took me a while to pay it back but I wound up with Don as my manager. That was seven years ago and this Christmas Don sent me seven one-pound notes with an accompanying letter saying, 'To insure the next seven years'. — Matt Monro

On Christmas Day, Matt's newest single, 'The Impossible Dream', was named Record of the Week by *Reveille Magazine*. The year had been good but Matt was hoping 1969 would be even better, even though it meant him only spending a handful of weeks in London. The offers were still pouring in and it wouldn't be too long before Mr Monro could add the role of thespian to his curriculum vitae.

Devil's Harvest

1969 saw the release of three more singles. Although there were no official album releases, there were, however, two compilations – *Here and Now*, and, in a rather odd pairing, *Tony Blackburn Meets Matt Monro*. The latter album featured all the songs that Matt recorded for Fontana in the late 1950s.

Don Black was commissioned to write a couple of songs for a British comedy crime caper. Charlie Croker, played by Michael Caine, masterminds a daring robbery and an escape plan that brings Turin's computerised traffic system to a standstill by creating a traffic jam so massive that it would prevent the gangsters and police pursuing the suspects after the heist. The film featured two songs, 'On Days Like These' sung over the opening credits and 'Getta Bloomin' Move On', better known as 'The Self Preservation Society', during the film's climactic car chase.

The huge success of the film created a wealth of work for Mr Black. The year would see him complete twelve new movie projects, though none of them equalled the success of *The Italian Job*.

But whether the songs were successful or not, they certainly kept Don unbelievably busy and he seldom moved away from his writing platform. Matt had no option but to leave him to it; he had a four-week season in Australia to contend with and it wasn't going to be easy. Indeed, when he'd returned from there a few years before he commented: "It wasn't all peaches and cream by any means, it was very hard work. They'd never heard of me out there, it was like doing an audition every night of the week."

Leaving for Australia on 2 January, Matt was mainly booked into workingman's clubs with names like The Eastern Suburbs Leagues and The Manly Club. Although it was incredibly hard work every night, it was obviously successful as the office had immediate offers for his return.

While Matt was in Australia, he received a call from George Montgomery, a giant of a man with a generosity of spirit to match. Matt was in total admiration of Montgomery's creative talent and was completely stunned when he asked if Matt would like to appear in his next movie, as well as sing the title track. Matt explained that he couldn't act, but George reassured the singer, saying that he was the director and Matt had his confidence. A package promptly arrived by special courier and after reading the script Matt agreed to take the role.

Following his Australia trip, Matt headed back to the UK. Leonardo Schultz took this opportunity to fly over to England in the hope that he could convince the British star to work in South America again. He spent two days with Matt and Mickie and took the time to interview them for a twenty-page magazine special. He was also the bearer of some very good news indeed: Matt was in the Argentinean charts with three separate placements. 'Todo Pasara' was in at No 3, 'Que Tiempo Tan Feliz' at No 11 and 'Alguien Canto' at No 17. By the time Schultz left that afternoon he had secured another tour for April of that year.

On 12 February, Matt had two recording sessions booked at Abbey Road. He recorded six tracks, four of which remain unreleased. 'Love Song' would only see release in America and would have to wait until 2006 for its appearance in the UK on *The Rare Monro*. The track 'Just a Heartbreak Ago', recorded at an earlier session, was brought out as the new single.

Matt was the first star attraction when the Penguin Club in Birmingham opened its doors on 16 February 1969. Owner Jon Kirkbright had spent fifty-thousand pounds on converting what was a bowling alley into a lush thousand-seater theatre club – and this was only the first of five clubs that he planned to open in the Midlands. A specially invited guest list and a packed celebrity audience thoroughly enjoyed the opening and even those that had travelled furthest in the most inclement weather found the warmth of the hospitality lavished on them well worth braving the sub-zero storms.

The resident compère expertly knitted the show together, announcing the opening number as a troupe of attractive dancers made their way to the floor. Samantha Steele performed a full repertoire of classic songs and was followed by American comedian Lenny Allen. The second half saw Matt entertain the masses with an hour-long repertoire, which had the audience barring his exit; in fact, had he agreed to every request, the show would have gone on all night.

Although the opening night was one to remember, it might not have been that successful had it not been for the staunch loyalty of Matt's number one fan: Sue Maull.

The Penguin Club at Aston Birmingham was due to open with Matt and there were posters, flyers, banners and newspaper advertisements all around the city. ALL had his name spelt wrong, MUNRO. When I went in to buy my tickets I told the girl in the booking office that Monro was spelt with an O not U. She didn't believe me, but had second thoughts when I purchased tickets for every night of the week, and called the manager. He was gob smacked and asked if I was sure... "One hundred per cent plus," I said. He was so grateful that he gave me the money back for the table of twelve I'd booked for the opening night. All the adverts were corrected before Matt's arrival. — Sue Parker nee Maul

It was a late night, with Matt spending time after the show with the specially invited guests including Tommy Docherty, who had come to the club to celebrate his wedding anniversary. The six-night booking was a resounding success and leaving Birmingham Matt hoped that his booking in Stockport would go equally well.

Vince Miller was the compere at the Poco Poco Club in Stockport, and he remembers Matt with fondness. The show was sold out every night and Matt, Bob, Kenny and Vince shared several curries together after the curtain came down.

Although business wasn't suffering, Matt was. He had felt unwell for days experiencing bouts of diarrhoea and vomiting and arrangements were made for him to see Dr Hadley at Harley Street.

Writing to the singer's GP, the specialist confirmed that he couldn't feel the patient's spleen because the liver was enlarged. At a conservative estimate he noted Matt's alcohol consumption to be half a bottle of scotch a day, a practice he felt had been going on for some years. His diagnosis was that it was likely to be some sort of infective gastroenteritis, but he arranged for liver function tests and a Barium Meal anyway.

If the results surprised Matt, he covered it very well. But Mickie didn't; she was shocked and stunned, not by the diagnosis of an enlarged liver, but by the fact that Matt's drinking had crept up to that level of consumption. You would never have suspected that he had been drinking if you didn't see the medical evidence. There were never any visible, telltale signs: he didn't stumble, he didn't slur, his eyes didn't glaze; he would just eventually fall into a fitful sleep.

I never thought of Matt as having a drink problem, only as having

Liberace, Mary Hopkin, Matt & Eve Arden

**a drinking buddy. I never saw him vomiting because of drink. I just
wish people would concentrate on his talent rather than discuss
whether or not he had a drinking problem. — Kenny Clayton**

Although the specialist had diagnosed gastroenteritis, Matt and Mickie were still
anxious to see the results of the further tests. It took several weeks before they heard
back from Dr Hadley. The Barium Meal and blood count were completely normal
but there was evidence of liver damage, which the specialist explained was most
certainly due to excessive alcohol consumption in the past.

Mickie was relieved by the results and Matt agreed to abstain for a month and then
cut down his intake to two whiskies a day. There had been lots of episodes of jaundice
over the years and Matt had just accepted that it was part of his disposition. However,
he didn't know that he had suffered from infective hepatitis as a child, and that he had
required a year of convalescence. Had his mother told him this, Matt might have gone
about things differently.

The gastroenteritis hadn't necessitated Matt taking any time off work, and he
managed an appearance on the *Morecambe & Wise Show* and a further outing with
Liberace. The flamboyant pianist's guests included American actress Eve Arden, Lord
Charles's personification of aristocratic inebriation, songbird Mary Hopkin and Matt.
The show received a very unsavoury review from the *Evening News*, which didn't
surprise Matt in the least. It was everything about America he hated, wrapped up in
one tight package.

Sid & Val James with Mickie

On a clear day you can see Matt Monro without propping him on a
platform that gives him an extra couple of feet. You can hear him
sing too, without surrounding him with a bunch of dancers who
moon around pointlessly, serving only as a distraction while Matt
gets on with it. It was nauseating, the grand piano dressed up like
a Union Jack and as it was wheeled into camera range, the
orchestra blew up a swift few bars of 'There'll always be an
England', (...) Liberace introduced 'Tea for Two' "I know a nice
American tune with a real English flavour." If there had been room
in the studio they would have fitted in cardboard replicas of the
fifty destroyers the Americans sent across to us in the bad old days.
No show on earth works as hard on the good pals act.
— *Evening News*/Associated Newspapers Ltd

Matt and Mickie flew out to South Africa on 7 March for a well-earned rest, staying
at Sol Kerzner's Beverly Hills Hotel in Umhlanga Rocks again. While they were
there, they bumped into Sid and Valerie James. Although a South African himself, Sid
had renounced his citizenship in the 1960s to become a British National.

The foursome arranged to meet up for dinner and Mickie chose that moment to
use cream hair remover under her arms for the first time, as she wanted to wear her
new strapless dress. Matt called her from the other room in the suite and she got

embroiled in a conversation, completely forgetting she had applied the corrosive cream. By the time she realised her mistake and rinsed the depilatory off, she had burnt her skin very badly and spent the next three days walking around with her arms outstretched as if ready for take-off!

The holiday did the job of recharging Matt's batteries, and with a golden tan he returned to England for just long enough to record his own television show for BBC2. Produced by Michael Hurl, it was filmed in colour at the Talk of the Town and aired on 8 May. He also managed an appearance on Des O'Connor's Show and attended the Royal Charity Premiere of *Mackenna's Gold* at the Odeon Leicester Square. At that event he and Mickie were presented to Princess Margaret and Lord Snowdon. Matt, ever the English boy, got a kick out of meeting the royals.

With Matt packing for a two-week tour of South America, Don Black penned his latest single 'All of a Sudden' with a little help from Leonardo Schultz. The flipside 'That's the Way it Goes' was written by Dennis King and actor John Junkin.

The trip to Buenos Aires started off badly. The press had written that Panamericana TV were upset by the singer's non-appearance on one of their shows and printed that Matt had simply failed to turn up – even though the singer wasn't in the country at the time. They added that they thought it had all been a publicity stunt to promote the singer's records and in their opinion Matt's music was not much better than Nat King Cole's! Although a promoter had told the television station the singer was coming to the studio, they admitted later that they didn't actually have a contract to that end anyway. Leonardo contacted Panamericana and explained that he in fact was the official promoter of the tour and gave them a date when Matt could come to the studio.

Matt flew to Ezeiza Airport in Buenos Aires. One important factor that had drawn Matt to travel to one of Latin America's largest cities was that Odeon Records, the record company that produced and distributed his discs in Argentina, were part of the promotion. Company representatives were at the airport to greet the star with flowers and quickly whisked Matt away to a private room in the terminal for a press conference.

On arrival at his city centre hotel, Matt attended another press conference. This time the hotel laid on food, wine and entertainment, and the record company invited local stars of film, stage and song. Ricardo Bavlero and his wife actress Gilda Lousek had a conversation with actress Julia Sandoval about the price of the imported whisky. Singers Yaco Monti and Leo Dan were asking the waiters to serve the local wine and complained they didn't like the caviar. Dancer Nelida Lobato was wearing a psychedelic dress with multi-coloured beads and was desperately trying to catch the photographer's attention so they'd take a picture of her with her husband. In the meantime songstress Ramona Galarza was talking to the English dancers The Bluebells about the models and their dresses. How they were all talking to each other was a mystery as they all spoke different languages.

At 8.00pm Matt had still not arrived at the conference but the crowd was too busy enjoying the lavish spread to get impatient. While they were waiting some of the guests burst into spontaneous renditions of the 'Todo Pasara' to pass the time. Fifteen minutes later, the singer, and his interpreter and manager Leonardo Schultz, finally arrived, making the appropriate grand entrance. All the photographers were desperate to be the first to take a picture of the star and a bevy of young models descended on Matt, trying to get close to him so their picture would appear in the paper. The record company executives anxiously tried to get Matt to safety, and finally managed to escort him to the waiting rostrum.

News of the star's arrival in the city was covered in every newspaper and radio station, and Channel 13 made a small documentary *The Voice and Art of Matt Monro* and screened the programme repeatedly, throughout the star's stay. The concert tickets sold out within a few hours, leaving hundreds of young girls sobbing with disappointment. One thing that didn't disappoint was Matt's performance.

> **Surely that artistic figure of Matt Monro is not one that the young public can understand. He's a bit short and a bit chubby and he's not that young, but the English artist covers all that with simple art and the purity of his songs. He interprets what he does with a natural honesty. His voice arrives with softness and his personality becomes naked in its song. When the Buenos Aires public met Matt through his songs 'Alguien Canto' and 'Todo Pasara' he immediately became an idol of us – millions of them can't be wrong. — *Magazine Trasande***

The Grand Rex theatre was elegantly impressive, with seating for nearly 4,000 people, and an underground car park. On Matt's first night, obsessed by a need to corner their idol after the show, fans purposely blocked the car park exit to street level, preventing the singer from leaving. Mobbed by thousands of frenzied teenagers, Matt was effectively trapped with nowhere to hide. The situation necessitated the police being called to calm the surging crowds and escort Matt to safety. A tow truck was needed to remove the car obstructing the exit and it was more than an hour before order was resumed. After the chaos of that first night, Matt used a back-street entrance for the remaining three shows.

For the next leg of his tour Matt flew to Santiago de Chile. He was late for the press conference on arrival because he was desperately trying to get a phone call through to England. It was his tenth wedding anniversary and he wanted to tell Mickie he loved her and missed the children. He sent a telegram reading: "The first ten years were delicious, the next ten will be sensational, I Love You, Matt."

Despite the fact that Matt wasn't stereotypical of a singer that would appeal to a teenage market, dressing conservatively rather than follow the latest fashions and with short hair, he was still one of the most in-demand singers in the country. The shows were a testament to Matt's popularity, as there wasn't an empty seat in the house. The crowd stood at every opportunity, roaring their approval at an introduction to a song, after a song and even when the singer's microphone started making funny noises and he kept singing. Leonardo told him he only needed his magnificent voice to enchant the public and make everything meaningful.

> **He has a great sense of communication and with 'Hava Nagila' he had everyone singing along and clapping, and the audience made him sing the chorus over and over again. He has a great sense of communication and is a very generous person; more sensitive than many professionals and puts his caring before his career. He was very emotional and thankful over the reaction from the audience and all the time they were screaming "Bravo" and singing along.**
> **— Leonardo Schultz**

Newspapers and magazine journalists followed Matt everywhere, right up until he boarded his Air Aerolineas Pervanas flight out of Santiago de Chile to Lima, waving goodbye from the aircraft door.

Matt had three shows booked in the Sky Room at the Crillon Hotel in Lima. Leonardo picked him up from the airport and apologised for parking some distance away, explaining that a car had exploded at the other terminal and the road was blocked! You don't see the best of a city driving from the airport to the downtown area but Lima was particularly unimpressive. There were very few tall buildings because of the risk of earthquake and almost all the structures were old, with peeling paint and crumbling foundations. The performances were televised for Panamericana and several of Matt's shows appeared on different channels throughout Peru.

From Lima, Matt flew to Rio for one show, where Mickie was waiting for him. They were scheduled to fly straight to South Africa after Matt's final performance the following day in San Paulo.

Although firmly labelled a ballad singer, Matt would have liked to broaden his horizons to the silver screen, but he never got around to seriously developing that side of his talents. He really wanted to act, and was wonderful in the small cameos he had done on various television shows, but the nearest he ever came to it was starring in the long forgotten *Devil's Harvest*, released in 1970. Matt said it was one of the best experiences of his life.

The singer flew to Johannesburg in South Africa for the film role. He'd been offered many movies in his life, but it was the offer to make a film with George Montgomery, as both director and star, that he'd accepted. In a statement to the press he commented: "It was nice not to be asked to appear in a film as a singing bus driver, yet again."

Montgomery had been raised on a large ranch in Montana, where as part of daily life he learned to ride horses and work cattle. This was good groundwork for living the cowboy life he portrayed in his films. Matt had previously been given the choice of roles but picked the character with the least lines: Bates, a tough bush pilot, with a story centred on drug smuggling in South Africa. What Matt didn't know, at this point, was that Montgomery had rewritten the script to give his character a much meatier role.

> I'll never forget our first meeting in Sydney, Australia, where Matt was doing his show. I was so taken by his personality and talent that I offered him a part in a film that I was doing in South Africa which he accepted, and for which I'm thankful. From that meeting and these many years, I've not only had a beautiful friendship with the wonderful Monro family, but memories that I'll cherish forever.
> — George Montgomery

The film started shooting on 8 May in a disused gold mine on the outskirts of Johannesburg. Matt had never been on a film set before, and his initial delight in finding he had been accorded his own personal trailer, turned to amusement when he discovered there was neither air-conditioning or running water. But Matt loved the sprawling plains of South Africa and was looking forward to living it rough, cooking on makeshift campfires and enjoying the camaraderie of the crew.

On Location with George Montgomery

George arranged for Matt and Mickie to tour the goldmine. The shaft entrance towered above them, and after donning safety equipment the couple made their descent in metal cages, which were then dropped 250 meters to the bottom of the mine. With every inch of descent the darkness enveloped them and the air turned cooler. At the base of the deep shaft, they were led into a tunnel lit only by their helmet lights and a couple of lanterns. The tunnel was only six feet high and so narrow they had to walk in single file. It was bitterly cold and wet and Mickie was the first to notice the swarms of rats, whose eyes turned red when the light hit them. She was absolutely petrified, and the fact that her hard hat kept slipping over her eyes didn't help the situation. They declined the offer from the guide to take them deeper into the mine and were rather pleased to see daylight again!

After a few days, they moved locations and spent several weeks near Beitbridge in Rhodesia, the country now known as Zimbabwe. Beitbridge is a border town lying just north of the Limpopo River and about one kilometre from the Alfred Beit Bridge, which spans the crocodile-infested Limpopo between South Africa and Zimbabwe. They travelled several hours into the bush and Matt was captivated by the purity of the land, its sheer vastness hiding secrets of long ago. Not a single telephone line,

On Location with George Montgomery & Tippi Hedren

house, shop or indeed any evidence of twentieth century technology broke the landscape.

Gofers were used to locate water sources, set up camp each day, light and manage the fires and maintain the petrol lanterns, zigzagging about on last-minute errands. One of the locals was responsible for maintaining the first aid boxes, ensuring that there were needles for draining blisters, gaffer tape to wrap splints, venom extractors and anti-venom.

Matt was given flat-soled leather boots, which were excellent for walking on the rough terrain and a wide brimmed hat that was mandatory in the harsh midday heat. They were told to wear long sleeved shirts and long trousers to cover up from the sun and protect against biting insects, which carried diseases like malaria.

Dehydration was a major concern, and everyone was on the lookout for possible symptoms. Another warning issued to the cast was not to wander out of camp without a guide. The sheer scale of the environment could be overwhelming, everything looked the same and with no visible landmarks on the horizon, it would be easy to get disorientated. And being lost and alone in the harsh terrain was nothing short of a death sentence.

Glamour aside, the accommodation left a lot to be desired. Housed in an outbuilding, Tippi Hedren, the American actress who also starred in the movie, and her husband got off lightly. Matt and Mickie found themselves staying at a white hunter's farm in the bush, having to share a room with several other members of the cast, all male. The only thing that separated them from everyone else was a single sheet hanging from the rafter.

Filming involved getting up at 4.30am and eating breakfast in the dark while waiting for the sun to come up, which arrived like clockwork at 6.27am. Matt loved every day, immersing himself in the Bates character and revelling in the interaction between the actors. After a hard days shoot, George would arrange for the local guides to take them on an impala hunt, cheetah safari or some such exotic adventure.

After the cast and crew left in the early morning light, George would arrange for the wives to go on a walking safari in the bush. After driving into the heart of the landscape, the team set off on foot through grassland that was interlaced with acacia trees, termite mounds and aardvark burrows. Their walk included sightings of spectacular birdlife, giraffe with their young, some nasty looking warthogs and a herd of buffalo. The guide had a keen eye for spotting local wildlife, but tracking game on foot slightly unnerved the ladies and they rather hoped they wouldn't bump into any of the larger beasts indigenous to the region.

The production company erected large steel cages around their camp, which housed the animals that were used in the film, including a dozen or so cheetahs, monkeys and several lions. Mickie didn't like to walk too close to the cages as it frightened her when the big cats pushed their bodies against the confines of their prison. She was convinced that the smell of caged animals must attract other wild animals, especially in the still of the night when the sudden snapping of twigs in the bush sparked a faint tingle down the back of her neck.

The nights and early mornings were bitterly cold but as soon as the sun came up it became unbearably hot very quickly. Layers of clothes were worn for breakfast, but it didn't take long for items to be discarded as the sun warmed their bodies. Dinner was taken as soon as the crew came back from the shoot and food was served at long trestle tables set up outside. The staff presented local delicacies and cold beers. Most of the time Mickie and Matt were not sure what it was they were eating, but on the whole it was good. One particular evening there was much talk about an impala that was being cooked for dinner but here Mickie drew the line; she couldn't face eating such a beautiful animal.

It was a sad time for all the crew and cast when the four-week shoot came to a close, as they had formed a close bond. George's work on the film was far from over, as he now had to go through each rush and edit the film together. It was during the editing period that the decision was made to change the film's title to *Satan's Harvest*.

Matt and Mickie returned to the Beverley Hills hotel at Umhlanga Rocks. Hotelier Sol Kerzner persuaded the star to appear at the club during their brief stay before returning to London. A contract hastily drawn up at 1.00am confirmed the deal.

Kenny Clayton flew out to join Matt and was impressed when Kerzner sent a chauffeur to pick him and Matt's music and suits up from the airport. The musical director also brought with him the news that in Matt's absence the soundtrack *Southern Star*, that had been recorded a few months before, had been released. *Record Mirror* were very generous in their praise: "Movie-theme ballad dressed up with the usual George Martin skill, plus the magnificent voice itself. My 'Record of the Week'. I'll trade in my record player the day Matt makes a bad record."

The four impromptu shows that Matt did at the Beverly Hills's Copacabana were so well received that Sol Kerzner begged Matt to return at Christmas. Matt explained that he didn't like to work abroad over the holidays, as he didn't see his children much as it was. The hotelier promptly offered Matt and his whole family complimentary flights and accommodation for an extended period so that they could be together over the festive season and combine the trip with a holiday. Matt and Mickie hastily agreed.

Matt's return to England saw him open in June for his third season at London's Talk of the Town. It was a wonderful venue for Matt; each time he returned he felt like he was coming home. Robert Nesbitt and Rosalyn Wilder were waiting to greet him at rehearsals. With the venue's capacity for a large orchestra, Matt was able to include 'Time After Time' in his repertoire; the song needed a good string section and conductor Burt Rhodes knew exactly the treatment the singer wanted.

His previous appearances at the Talk of the Town had drawn audiences from all over the continent and this five-week season was no different, with Matt playing to packed houses every night. There were always lots of laughs and copious amounts of celebrities popping in to pay their respects.

> **I would invariably be in London at the weekend recording some TV show or other and I would meet up with Matt and Mickie. We would always go to the Lotus House and do a Chinese meal after Matt's last show on a Saturday night. Matt was the consummate artist, always immaculately turned out. He had such an appealing manner on stage, which made him someone you could see time**

after time after time and never tire. — Freddie Davies

The London venue was host to the elite in the world of show business with artists from across the globe jostling to take residence. Each one felt that being asked to perform on the renowned stage was an honour, as Billy Marsh was always selective as to who he would have there. Over the years Shirley Bassey, Liza Minnelli, Tom Jones, Pearl Bailey, Buddy Greco, Johnnie Mathis, Cliff Richard, Sammy Davis Jr and Neil Sedaka all appeared on that celebrated rostrum. Matt was in excellent company.

The success of their collaboration on *Satan's Harvest* prompted George Montgomery to ask Matt to do another film. He gladly accepted and was scheduled to fly to the Philippines to shoot a Western on location in September. No title had yet been chosen and Matt hadn't been told whether he was going to be cast as the hero or a villain.

In readiness for the movie, Matt took riding lessons everyday at Richmond Park. Hollywood had invited him to play a gun-totting cowboy and 20th Century Fox set up a publicity shoot with Matt dressed in full cowboy attire, complete with holsters, six-shooters and spurs. Pictured as a typical gunslinger, Matt was dressed in faded jeans, cowboy boots and a Stetson pulled down low on the forehead, hands arched at his sides ready for a lightning quick draw from the gun-holster. The producer asked that Matt sit on the horse for an authentic shot but the animal that was brought out was so large that the singer had to use a stool to mount it. Unfortunately for its rider the horse was spooked by the flash photography, bolted and Matt was thrown from the saddle, fracturing his spine in five places! He later said that he would look for a modern Western in which they got about in jeeps. In the end the film was never made. George was besieged with problems from the beginning with civil unrest in the Philippines and trouble from the Union so he later decided to shelve the project.

The show business motto, 'the show must go on', was never more in evidence at this time in Matt's life. Despite the intense back pain and resulting depression Matt suffered because of his injury, he continued to work. Although he had the luxury of getting home every night after the Talk of the Town, he didn't have the luxury of being idle in the daytime, with bookings to appear on *Dee Time, Pete's People* and *It's Sunday Night with David Jacobs*. Add that to a photographic shoot with Dezo Hoffman and recording studio sessions for his next Spanish album *En Espana*, and it was clear that Matt wasn't going to have much time to recover.

On the night Matt appeared in Bradford a plane was on standby at Yeadon Airport ready to fly the star back down to London for his show at the Talk of the Town. A host of top stars were to appear in the Royal Gala Variety Performance being staged at the Alhambra Theatre. Produced by the BBC and attended by HRH The Duke of Edinburgh, the show featured several of Matt's friends, including Ron Moody, Malcolm Roberts, David Berglas, Freddie Davies, as well as Dave Allen, who was compering the show. Unfortunately Matt couldn't stay to 'play' with his mates, as he had to leave before the interval in order to make the 11.00pm start of his show.

Bob West drove Matt down to see Mitchell on his birthday on 16 July. The boy was now fourteen years old but did not have the closest of relationships with Matt. A television screen was often as close as he could get to his father. As he lurched into adolescence, the lonely boy was becoming more and more insular and Matt was perplexed as to why his eldest child was so introverted. Mitchell was acutely shy and often withdrawn, and it didn't help that he suffered from chronic acne. Having discussed the situation with Mickie, Matt asked his son to move in with them. Unfortunately Mitch didn't feel this would be the right move because he had taken up a fervent interest in flying and wanted to continue living near Biggin Airfield.

Matt's season at London's Talk of the Town had finished and Bob West had come to a painful decision. Having driven home extremely late from the venue one night, he fell into bed. He woke in the morning and realised he couldn't recall the drive home at all. It was then that he decided he couldn't do the job anymore. On his last working day, he drove Matt and Mickie to Heathrow Airport and took their luggage in to the porter. When he returned to the car there was an envelope on the seat addressed to him. Inside was a five hundred pound thank you present.

Matt flew into Palma for a television special and an engagement at the Tagomago nightclub. Whilst there he discovered he was one of the most popular non-Spanish singers in the Spanish-speaking world. His records were played all day long on the radio and were being snapped up at the record shops. He was riding high in the Spanish charts and 'Todo Pasara' was No 1 in South America. Matt was understandably shocked to find he was the biggest-selling recording star in Spain; he'd had five hits there in the last eighteen months and topped both the singles and album charts.

Matt's bookings towards the end of August were all over the place at this time. No sooner had he rushed back to England to tape *Mike and Bernie's Show*, he was travelling to Manchester to appear at the Golden Garter and meeting up with his old friend Bob Monkhouse on the game show *The Golden Shot*. Although his schedule was packed tight, it didn't stop him going to see Sammy Davis Jr on the opening night of his appearance at Talk of the Town. In fact the two friends took the opportunity to meet up several times either at the show or after it.

On 27 August, Matt flew from RAF Northolt to Germany for a day to repay a long-standing debt. He'd been in the REME for five years and spent four of those in Hong Kong with guys like Frankie Howard and Brian Rix flying out to entertain the troops out there. Matt wanted to show his gratitude by giving the troops in Germany the same enjoyment and encouragement those artists had given him during his army days. Matt was the star of a combined forces show in the thousand-seater Schutzenhof Hall in Gutersloh in aid of the Army and RAF Benevolent Funds.

Matt and his entourage arrived at RAF Gutersloh and myself and a few colleagues in four staff cars were ready to ferry everybody back to the hotel where Matt and everybody were staying in Bad Oyenhausen, a village near Herford. Matt was rather amused about being wined and dined in the officer's mess, something he never did whilst he served in the forces. Visits by famous people always help support troops morale. The show that Matt starred in has left a lasting memory for nearly fifty years; such was the impact of meeting such a star as Matt. A really nice bloke. — Brian Hayes

Returning to England, Matt spent two days at the studios, one dedicated to Spanish recordings and the other to a new concept album *Matt Sings Don Black*.

Don was riding high. He had got back together with Elmer Bernstein, working on the John Wayne film *True Grit*. Although nominated for an Oscar it was Burt Bacharach and Hal David who took the trophy for 'Raindrops Keep Falling on My Head' from *Butch Cassidy and the Sundance Kid*, evening the score for losing out to 'Born Free' a few years back.

With all the work Don had on his plate, he didn't need Matt's commission, but he liked the idea of a whole album dedicated to his music. There was no doubting that there were some very pleasant songs on the release; however, they did not bring Matt chart success. The trouble was that the music business was changing, and not just in Britain.

Dad's [Voyle Gilmore] last day at Capitol was the last day of the 1960s, 31 December 1969. Frankly, the A&R department had been so reduced in importance that he knew it was time to go. Matt and my father were part of a wonderful era when artistic integrity and musical quality were paramount. I think it's fantastic that Matt's records are so widely enjoyed to this day. It's really a testament to

how audiences still hunger for the best. — John Gilmore

Most of Matt's recordings were produced or overseen by George Martin, ensuring timelessness to both the artistic and technical qualities of the singer's discography. But finding winning songs was no longer easy. Ten years previously Matt was bombarded with demos from songwriters and publishers hungry for success. But this was no longer the case. Groups were all writing their own music and they were dominating the charts, leaving very little room for solo artists. Matt was still looking for that elusive No 1 in his own country, but it was becoming much harder to make that dream a reality. There were very few good writers around that didn't sing themselves and for the performer that relied on others to write their songs it meant the big hits were few and far between. But Matt didn't have the luxury of lamenting that fact for very long – he had a date in Manila.

For Matt the trip to the Philippines was the perfect opportunity to stop off in Hong Kong for two nights to see his mates. Matt got together with John Wallace, Bing Rodriguez, Ray Cordeiro and Carl Barriteau. It could have been described as a bachelor's night out save for the fact that Mickie went along as well. They commandeered one of the island's restaurants until four in the morning, before catching the ferry back to the hotel. Matt couldn't remember what time he crawled into bed, but his head hurt far too much to care. He was always sad to leave Hong Kong, having been there at such an impressionable age, those early memories stayed with him throughout his life.

After a delayed flight, Matt and Mickie finally disembarked at Manila only to find that the airline had left Matt's music behind in Hong Kong. The ground staff told them they would do what they could to get the case back as soon as possible, but Matt had a concert that evening. There would be no time to rehearse the thirty-piece orchestra and furthermore, the First Lady Imelda Marcos was due to attend the performance.

They checked in to the Philippines Village Hotel and waited for news. The music arrived an hour before Matt was due on stage, so the only thing they could do at band call was a talk through. It was a stroke of luck that several of the musicians had played for Matt at the Araneta Coliseum the last time he was in the country and were familiar with the music. Filipino singer Pilita Corrales had also been booked with Matt at the Coliseum and the shows were a complete sell-out.

The trip to the Philippines was a perfect example of what Kenny loved about touring, with different locations, different food and different sensations.

> The whole thing with my career has been made palatable by the travel aspect of it and learning something new, so you remain a student all your life. The last five years has made the aspect of travel lose its excitement. Who wants to endure an anal search every time you want to fly? I know a few people would but not me.
> — Kenny Clayton

First Lady Imelda Marcos attended several more shows. She never informed Matt in advance, but he always knew when she was there as she would sit in the first row flanked by several strapping bodyguards. On each visit she would insist on coming up on stage to sing 'Feelings' with Matt. Whatever the singer thought privately about her musical abilities, you couldn't escape the fact that Mrs Marcos's attendance was always guaranteed to be front-page news.

Next to President Marcos, Matt was the biggest thing in the country, if for no other reason than the fact that people credited Matt with getting Marcos elected four years previously. Now, 1969 was a new election year and Ferdinand Marcos had just been re-elected for an unprecedented second term. As far as the people were concerned, Matt was their lucky charm.

> I loved the Philippines, especially when we were shot at. It was an election year and a greeting dinner had been arranged for us. The event was in a large private club, which held about 200 people. We had a table of about twenty people, all to do with the show. We had some beautiful food and after about an hour a waiter was going around saying, "Down, down, down down." We all disappeared under a table to take cover. It was like a party game and once we got under, the next thing we hear is "clunk clunk". Then the waiter comes around and says, "Okay no problem, you get up now." Someone had come in and dispensed with one of the opposition who was sitting in the club. Apparently the mafia owned the club and there were bullet holes in the walls, the result of a previous shoot-out with the police.
>
> One of my most exciting moments was when I entered the Araneta Coliseum and saw 50,000 people or so, that was something. The pinnacle for me was standing next to the guy I loved the best in the world being accorded that fantastic thing.
> — Kenny Clayton

The Filipino concerts went better than Matt could have expected, and feeling rather self-satisfied he headed off to Melbourne. He picked up a bug when passing through the tropics and he was suffering from nausea and a throat infection, but the 350-strong audience at the Chevron Celebrity Room wouldn't have known Matt was anything less than fighting fit. Another week in Adelaide followed, and then Matt headed home for a few days.

With the huge success of Matt's Spanish recordings, EMI UK and Matt's management put together a Spanish tour in October 1969. Peter Jamieson was put in charge of handling the arrangements. Peter first started with EMI UK at the beginning of 1967. He'd worked in every department as a trainee, from royalties to marketing to sales. Now suddenly his official job was to go to Spain for the company as assistant to the MD, Phil Brody. He was a young executive apprentice and wet behind the ears. Everyone in the company spoke Spanish, except Phil Brody, and with Peter's bilingual abilities they based him in Barcelona.

With Matt arriving in the country, he nervously waited in the airport's arrival lounge anxious to meet the star. Peter had been assigned to the artist as interpreter and general factotum. Everywhere that Matt went, crowds besieged him. It was an exciting time for the duo as they took the journey together, seeing the impact of Matt's Spanish recordings first hand.

Matt was terrified of singing in the local language but he wanted to pay his respect to the people. His sentiment was: "I'm not great at this, but this is my best shot." But it didn't matter, the Spanish audiences were so impressed that he would bother to record in their mother tongue that it elevated him to phenomenal success. Matt and Peter travelled across all of Spain and the enterprise became so lucrative and important for EMI that Jamieson was taken off of his normal duties and permanently allocated to Matt for his Spanish recordings.

Matt was a man defined by his sense of humour and no experience was ever complete without a few laughs here and there. His tour with Peter was no exception. They lodged in quaint hotels, staying up at night sipping brandy, trying to rehearse the lyrics. Matt would practice in front of mirrors trying to get the accent right, but in some ways the fact that the accent was wrong helped make the song.

I remember the press conference in Barcelona and I'm sitting up on stage with him, just the two of us, the room is packed and I'm interpreting and that was a huge gig for me as I realised that I was

indispensable to the process. I had to be with Matt at all times, otherwise no one could speak to him; he didn't speak a word of the language. I remember being overwhelmed with the popularity and the way the press responded to him. I remember tour buses, helping behind the scenes at concerts. I remember the recording studios and Kenny Clayton. I remember mixed audiences, some would be packed out and some wouldn't be, and we'd get through it. It wasn't hugely provincial, it was major towns but we had no idea what the next place would be like, what the accommodation would be like, who was there, whether anyone would turn up. It was always hard work for Matt. He enjoyed it but he didn't enjoy it. He was a bit out of his comfort zone. It was a bit of a shoestring operation at times, a bit of hand to mouth. It was terrifying but every so often we would be overawed by the sympathy and warmth and understanding of the public, it was really quite special. We knew each other for a small focused period but in some ways I was closest to Matt than any other artist I have ever been in forty years in the recording industry. — Peter Jamieson

It was a combination of Matt's personality, his warmth and brilliant singing voice that made Hispanics fall in love with the boy from Shoreditch; his songs also struck a chord with the listener. But although Matt sang them beautifully on stage, he was terrified of singing them live, and tried to avoid it as much as possible. Matt and Peter went touring up and down Spain, performing concerts at big clubs, small clubs, smoky clubs and sleazy clubs. Matt, always the consummate professional, would look to Peter in the wings where he would be holding up the Spanish lyrics on big boards.

He'd sing his English songs he was famous for and then he knew he'd have to sing this Spanish song and watching him I could see him visibly weaken and then he's burst into it with this wonderful extraordinary style of his that endeared him to millions of Spanish-speaking people. As a record company employee it was not the norm to be able to get close to an artist so this period in my life was very special. The artist normally kept their distance from company people. I was like a manager, interpreter, record company rep and friend and the combination of all four made it by

Kenny Clayton, Peter Jamieson, Norma & Matt arriving in Barcelona

far my most over-riding memory. That situation has never repeated itself in all my years at EMI. Matt helped me understand the business and helped me grow and develop in stature; it was a great learning curve for me. — Peter Jamieson

Peter suddenly found himself in the studio with Matt recording the follow up to his first Spanish album. They started work on *En Espana*, and although Leonardo Schultz was very involved with the first album (recorded in England), he was absent from the studio for the second. Matt had brought out to Spain with him over forty tracks as possibilities, and they'd pour over the songs, working out which they could get lyrics to and what would work best. Peter was in and out of the studio because Matt needed help with the pronunciation. Peter was the first to admit: "Matt's accent was always awful, but it had this wonderful endearing quality that enabled him to sell millions of records across the world in Spanish."

The second album was not as popular as the first but it breathed new life into 'Alguien Canto'. Interestingly the Spanish songs that became the biggest hits were some of the least popular songs in England and visa versa. Peter knew Matt's relationship with the record company was rather special and he could understand why. Certainly a special bond formed between the two men and the result of this experimental tour was that the singer was more in demand than ever before. Prior to leaving the country, EMI exacted a promise that he would return to tour again in March of the following year.

Matt and Kenny flew to New York en-route to Indianapolis to appear at Bill Ball's North Meridian Street bistro, the Embers Club, for a week. Booked for two shows a night and three on weekends, the management requested that Matt's second show consist of different material than that of his first and third. So Matt and Kenny put their heads together to see what would work.

> "Reconstructing our whole library," that's what I call it. Sometimes I feel guilty when I hear one of my records because it sounds rather old-fashioned, you know you can't live on nostalgia forever.
> — Matt Monro

The trouble was that the audiences had come to see the nostalgic numbers and when 'My Kind of Girl' and 'Walk Away' were missing from Matt's show, there was uproar. The crowd refused to leave and started stamping their feet and banging the tables with their fists. So to avoid any unpleasantness, Matt did an encore that included the missing numbers. The management reluctantly admitted defeat, and for the rest of the contract Matt went back to the firm favourites.

After a week in Boston, he flew to Seattle for a booking at the Washington Plaza Hotel. Kenny arranged a birthday treat for Matt in the superb eatery at Space Needle Tower. The building is over 600-feet tall and boasted some of the world's fastest elevators, which ferried its passengers at fourteen feet per second. The boys' reservation was in The Sky City Restaurant, a 360-degree revolving dining room with the city's skyline and Mount Rainier as its backdrop.

> I went to Victor Borge's concert tonight with the Seattle Symphony Orchestra, fantastic. A three-hour show the man did, he's brilliant. We got out of the Opera House at 11.20pm and had a walk back to the hotel for a drink and then a meal. Would you believe, bars close here on Sunday at 10.00pm. Not even room service and I've given up keeping any in the room. I have a TV interview in the morning so I've got to look lovely as always. The shows have picked up enormously since we opened I'm glad to say, but I was told when we opened that Seattle is a weekend town anyway. It's a lovely

town right by the coast so next Sunday, our day off, we're taking the ferry to Victoria. It's about a three-hour trip each way so it could be a good day out. — Letter from Matt, Washington Plaza Hotel, Seattle, Washington

Michael Sullivan had the looks of a typical show business agent: lean and hungry. He'd clawed his way up the management ladder and become a director at Bernard Delfont's agency, looking after several names in the business, including Sid James, Charles Hawtry, Kenneth Williams and Bruce Forsyth. He had persistently tried to get Matt to sign with him, but the singer had refused. Mickie went to Michael's fifth wedding to French film star Dany Robin, held at the Fairmile Hotel in Esher.

Mike, who was Irish, was a loveable rogue who was my agent for a while. But he also had a crazy Jekyll and Hyde side to him, which wasn't so loveable. — Bruce Forsyth, *Bruce – The Autobiography*

Matt stopped off in London en route to South Africa to pick up Mickie for the Christmas booking with Sol Kerzner. They arranged to stay in Durban for a five-week visit combining work and pleasure. Because the festive season's flights were rather full, they'd arranged for Mickie's mother Evelyn and the children to fly there ahead of them.

We said goodbye to the children and my mother on Thursday evening. A few hours later they were back home, the doctor said Matthew had an ear infection. However that got sorted out. They left the following day but had missed their connections right along the way. Matt and I left London on Sunday evening and arrived in Durban within hours of the rest of the family. — Mickie Monro

This was the first time the whole family had been abroad for Christmas and it was a memorable experience for everyone. It was also the first time Michele had seen her father work to a live audience and, although she was very excited, she did wonder what all of the fuss was about. The shows were tremendous and the papers were full of positive headlines such as: "Mr Kerzner must be congratulated on giving Durban audiences the best Xmas present they have had in years."

Sol Kerzner was the perfect host and afforded the family every luxury imaginable, even arranging a two-day safari for Evelyn and the children to the Kruger National

Setting up for a Sunday evening barbecue

Park. Because Matt was staying at the same hotel that he was performing at, it was hard to maintain any real sense of privacy. Hotel guests were forever approaching the star around the pool for autographs or to congratulate him on his shows. Despite his best efforts, Sol couldn't do much about the situation, apart from making it very clear to staff that Matt was not to be disturbed for any reason whatsoever. That directive led to a disruption to the hotel's Sunday evening barbeque.

Matt was working at the Copacabana that night and was used to sneaking in a mid-afternoon nap. He had fallen asleep in a sun-lounger while Mickie and the family had gone out shopping for the day. At 4.00pm the hotel staff were ordered to collect in all the deck chairs and loungers and set up for the evening's buffet, but not one member of staff was prepared to go against the owner's strict instructions and wake the sleeping singer. An hour later the barbeque was set for the evening, save for a six-foot space where a sole sun-lounger lay undisturbed on the green, cradling one sleeping international star, blissfully unaware of the events going on around him!

THE END OF CAPITOL

A dark cloud had settled over Britain at the beginning of the 1970s. With a state of emergency declared over the Dockers' strike, the postal workers routinely out on strike and, most disruptive of all, the Miners' Strike in 1972, England was plunged into darkness except for emergency lighting and hurricane lamps. It was reminiscent of Victorian times, with the working week reduced to three days as a result. Even television programming suffered at the hands of the strikers, who held Britain to ransom.

It wasn't just television that was targeted. The 1970 Gaming Act inflicted numerous casualties across the entertainment industry. Club owners whose premises straddled entertainment and gambling were forced to separate the two purposes out. If it wasn't possible to create dedicated areas for each, they were forced to choose the one facility they wanted to remain open. A list of areas legislated to hold gaming licenses was issued and if an existing business fell outside that catchment area, they were also forced to close their doors. Clubs up and down the country crumbled like a domino run, most facing financial ruin. There had been more than a hundred venues with a thousand-person capacity or higher prior to the Act, but when the legislation took hold, only thirty percent remained.

While Britain's youth turned to the new sounds of the 1970s, Matt's popularity amongst the older mainstream audience never waned. With an insatiable worldwide audience, Matt's records continued to thrill crowds overseas, particularly in countries with a strong romantic ballad tradition. His popularity had reached cult proportions in Latin America, with record sales to match. What was even more remarkable was the fact that he didn't speak a word of the language and recorded all the songs phonetically. He currently had three hits in the Top 10 in South America and his Spanish version of 'My Way' was number one in Spain. His chart success wasn't restricted to the Latin countries either; in Australia 'On Days Like These' was also sitting in the number one position.

Good work in England was hard to come by and Matt had no option but to accept the countless overseas bookings that came into the office. He travelled approximately 150,000 miles each year, with a passport that looked like a compressed version of an airline's departure board.

Kenny Clayton resigned from his post as Matt's musical director at the beginning of 1970 after three years of happy employment. He was travel weary and wanted to try his hand at writing movie scores. John Barry advised him that it would be difficult to get any movie work if he didn't stay in one spot. Putting his affair with America on hold, the composer in Kenny surfaced and he went on to score *Ragman's Daughter*, *The Pied Piper*, *The 144*, *Brother Sun Sister Moon*, *The Savage Hunt* and the final Morecambe and Wise project *Night Train to Murder*. He also successfully scored for stage with *Bertie*, *Oedipus*, *Ring Your Mother*, *Box* and *The Mistress*. Matt was gutted, not only to lose a gifted musical director but also a close friend and confidante. Matt presented Kenny with an inscribed watch as a parting gift and the two remained close friends throughout Matt's life.

> **Had it lived up to my expectations of working with Matt and working in America? Yes, in fact it was enhanced by the fact it was with Matt because he delivered the goods, he was as good as anybody else on stage vocally. He was an easygoing artist who found it difficult to understand the excitement he created – a humble, loveable gentleman. — Kenny Clayton**

Choosing a musical director wasn't just about choosing someone with the right qualifications. With all the travelling Matt had to do, he would spend weeks or months at a time with his pianist, so personal chemistry was of the utmost importance. They would travel with each other, eat, drink and lose sleep together. It was by no means a normal employer–employee relationship, but rather more like a marriage of musical talents that allowed the finished performance to be its best. Matt was having difficulty relating to the deputies that Kenny provided, and was beginning to lose hope. That is, until a certain Mr Colin Keyes came along.

As Colin's wife Pam recalls it, Matt knew the couple casually from past show business events and they would catch up every so often. As she says, "In this business it's the phone call that starts it all. Would Colin be interested in meeting Matt with the possibility of being his MD? Wow, what a thought. They met up and both agreed the answer was yes. There was barely any time for the two of them to rehearse before flying off to Spain so I knew Colin was very nervous."

Mickie, Matt & Colin Keyes

I'd been working with Bruce Forsyth for four years when I got a phone call from Kenny Clayton's agent Aude Powell. Matt was offering me a job at three times my existing salary. Bruce was in America at the time so I asked his agent Mike Sullivan if he would contact him and ask if he would consider giving me a small increase in salary, not to match what Matt was offering, but just improve on what I was getting. The answer was a flat no! As Matt was due to begin a Spanish tour in ten days, I had to make a quick decision. Matt was easy to work with and we got on well, he was also easy to follow as an accompanist because of his natural ability to interpret a lyric. He was quite laid back about the show as long as everything was done properly. — Colin Keyes

As if changing musical directors wasn't enough, George Martin had spoken to Matt about how busy his workload had become and suggested that John Burgess might take over the reins. It didn't please Matt one bit, but there was little he could do in the circumstances. So for the first time since joining EMI, apart from one session with Ron Richards, Matt wouldn't have Martin's genius beside him in the studio. It was the end of an era and emotions ran high.

It was a real privilege to work with him, to know him as a person,
marvellous man. He was almost unique in that his career was
sustained through the 60s. I can't think of another, there's the odd
singer like Vince Hill that had a lot of work but wasn't making hits.
Matt's career lasted a long time, the people he started with fell by
the wayside, the Lita Rosas, Denis Lotis and those kind of people
who were band singers and if Matt were alive today he would be
every bit as big as, say, Shirley Bassey for example, he was of that
ilk, so distinguished and so individual. — George Martin

Before leaving England, Matt did a series of one-weekers including Talk of the
North, Tito's, the Cresta Club, Ace of Clubs, Wooky Hollow and the Poca Poca.
In addition to the club circuit there was the usual sprinkling of radio and television
engagements to fulfil. With Matt's new single 'Just a Heartbreak Ago' in the shops
it proved the ideal way of plugging the disc.

I had become a producer in my own right, and I remember a little
tentatively asking if Matt would consider coming in to do a session
for me. By this time radio had taken a bit of a back seat with
television and commercial radio both covering popular music.
Some artists didn't think it worthwhile to accept a date on 'steam'
radio. Matt always came in for me and we had some marvellous,
very special sessions whenever he was available. — Pam Cox

Kenny had agreed to work with Matt up until he left for Spain in March, and
joined him in the studio for an EMI session. Most of the tracks went towards the
forthcoming album *Close to You*, including 'Hava Nagila'. Although Matt had been
performing the Hasidic traditional song in his act for some time, he had never
recorded it, despite numerous fan requests.

In addition to the excellent diction, Matt brought an added
dimension to 'Hava Nagila'. I love the tempo break in the middle.
I believe it's the only recording where he sings Acapella. What a joy
to hear him singing without any backing. You can really hear his
pure voice. This recording illustrates his incredible range. He sings
a low C# (two octaves below middle C, which most basses can't
even sing) and then goes as high as an F above middle C. And he

Peter Jamieson going through the Spanish itinerary

sings it in full voice with no falsetto. Outstanding. — Jeffrey Paul Hayes, Pianist

Matt was off to keep his promise to Peter Jamieson and complete another tour of Spain. The trip didn't fill him with as much trepidation as the first tour as he knew what to expect and had the added confidence of having Peter by his side. Matt was so important to EMI Spain that Jamieson was taken off all other duties in the interest of Matt's tour. He became Matt's alter ego – Matt would do the singing, Peter would do the press and PR.

I was a young kid but I was hosting press conferences, there were people besieging Matt wherever he went, all the young girls in Spain were absolutely crazy about him because of his English charm and the fact he had bothered to spend time recording his songs in Spanish for them. It was just the most wonderful experience. We knew every town in Spain; it was a surreal, unusual time that was helpful and instrumental in his career and took him to a much broader public than almost any other English language singer. I didn't tour Southeast Asia with Matt but I've seen the

heritage of his popularity there. The reason is that although the Philippines isn't a Spanish speaking country as such, their native language has Hispanic roots and so the Spanish songs were particularly popular there. No one has been able to do it before or since. Matt was a pivotal part of EMI's stable. — Peter Jamieson

Because of prior commitments, Matt's time in Spain was short, only managing a few shows in Madrid, Valencia and Barcelona, with the promise of an August return. Colin Keyes joined Matt on his first official trip as musical director. He didn't speak a word of Spanish either, and both he and Matt struggled to communicate with the musicians. They managed to muddle through the language barrier, helped by a great deal of patience and a hearty dose of laughter. Although Colin had come with an impressive work pedigree, it was his sense of humour and warmth of character that ultimately endeared him to Matt.

When Pam Keyes wasn't performing herself, she would travel around with Colin and Matt. The boys would always grab something to eat after a show, generally heading out for a quick curry at a local dive. On one such occasion, Pam saw a large rat run up the stairs as they were tucking into their meals. Shocked, she told the guys, expecting to collect their things and leave. Instead, they both shrugged their shoulders and said they would put their feet up! A small rodent infestation wasn't enough for them to give up their curry. Matt just crushed the poppodums with his fist, dug in with relish while laughingly ordering another beer!

Colin and Matt shared many common interests. They didn't party after a show, preferring to go for a late meal or, if Don was around, play a game of cards. Don always beat Colin, so he was keener on a game of golf. The game was a passion that the two men shared and travelling afforded them the luxury of playing on some of the best courses in the world.

Colin's debut with Matt started well and with a successful tour behind them, he relaxed into the role. Returning to England Matt did another week at the Wakefield Theatre Club, missing another of his daughter's birthdays, though he made sure to send a telegram and telephone her before she went to bed. That was one of the toughest parts of the job. He just didn't get much time to spend with his children. This was particularly true of his first-born. As Matt found a bigger audience, Mitch had to compete with millions of others for his father's attention. Mitch wasn't alone in his frustration; Michele and Matthew were in much the same position.

Now that he was back at home, Matt spent two days in the studios recording Spanish tracks for the album *En Espana*, but managed to pop along to the Talk of the Town to catch Shirley Bassey's opening night. He was always interested in examining the repertoire other artists were performing and enjoyed catching up with old friends. But he wasn't prepared to witness his friend and colleague, Simon Dee's fall from grace. To make matters worse, Matt felt that it was somehow his fault. Simon Dee had hosted a variety of shows over the years, one being the popular BBC series *Dee Time*, which commanded ten million viewers and ran for three years. Just a few months before, at the beginning of the year, Dee had signed a brand new £100,000 two-year contract with London Weekend but was unceremoniously dismissed after only twenty-five shows due to a conflict with company officials.

It started as a difference of opinion over who Simon would interview on the show, and who got to make that ultimate decision. The host had recently invited the Archbishop of Canterbury to appear, but London Weekend vetoed the idea and Dee was left fuming. Sometime later, Dee invited Matt to appear but again company officials refused to honour the invitation. Dee threatened that illness might prevent him from appearing on air if his demands were not met, but producer Bimbi Harris wasn't a bit fazed and arranged to guest Cleo Lane against the host's wishes. Dee quickly changed his mind about not appearing after the company placed disc jockey Pete Murray on standby as a last minute replacement. Dee's opening comment on air was "Pete Murray couldn't make it."

Dee was a pillar of the business. He'd started his career at Radio Caroline, working as Britain's first pirate disc jockey before switching to the BBC in 1965. In a short space of time he rose from the ranks of spinning discs to the television chat world, becoming one of the highest paid performers on the company's payroll. His fall from grace was just as rapid as his ascent to fame. He was fired soon after the incident involving Matt's appearance and within months of his dismissal, he was signing onto the dole. That wasn't the end of his misfortune. Soon after, the former television personality was jailed for twenty-eight days for rate arrears. The months that followed saw him sell his beloved red Aston Martin, his wife's Mini, and move out of his West End flat. Eventually the strain caused his marriage to collapse and Simon was left poor, alone and without any hope of work. Matt could not quite believe how quickly someone could lose favour and it confirmed just how fickle the business could be. It was a huge wake-up call for many temperamental artists.

Although Kenny had officially left Matt's employment, he did conduct and arrange a session with the singer in April of 1970. Songs were filtering through the office and from a pile of six or seven, one number took the singer's fancy. Curious as to whether it would work or not, Matt asked if Kenny wouldn't mind running through the number with the spare studio time they had after the session. The track was so quirky that it was just asking to be heard and Matt and Kenny recorded it having no idea as to its value.

> **Normally when you release a new record you will hype it to the extent that you stop everything else. You record say on a Friday, then you mix it and the following Friday it will come out and you'll be doing this gig and that promotion with huge posters everywhere to endorse it. We recorded it without concentrating on any promotion. Kenny Everett insisted on playing the track, which was a B-side and made it a turntable hit. We had no idea it would be seized upon as a protest song. — Kenny Clayton**

It was because of Kenny Everett that 'We're Gonna Change the World' became a turntable hit. He absolutely loved the song and took every opportunity to play it on air. On one of the last BBC shows he did in May 1970, Everett unearthed and played a skit of Matt singing the song. It starts off with a type of 1950s American News Bulletin signal, then the announcer comes in with: "From the world, the nation and the Texas News Triangle, this is hourly news", followed by Everett's voice, "It's just been announced there's going to be a musician's strike, until we hear more here's some music." The intro starts and 'We're Gonna Change the World' begins. Partway through the song, we hear Kenny say "Everybody out, come on" followed by the sound of footsteps as everyone seemingly vacates the room, leaving Matt singing a cappella. When he reaches the chorus, he collapses into an uncontrollable coughing fit. Kenny's voice interjects, "Knew he couldn't keep it up."

The song was written by a couple of lads at Air London, the company with which Matt's former record producer, George Martin was involved. It was made as a demo and given to Matt for a listen. He liked it so much that he went into the studios there and then and recorded the song. It was one of those natural tunes that hits you like a ton of bricks, and Matt fell in love with it instantly. "You've just got to sing it, that's the way it was for me." It was so far removed from the artist's usual style that many people were shocked at his choice. Cultural historian Robert Hewison was such a person: "If you listen to the lyrics instead of just listening to the voice, they really are extraordinary because they are all about the revolution of the late 1960s. When he talks about putting life into people's wretched lives, going on marches and being done over by the police, it seems to be a complete contradiction to the bouncy cheerfulness of the song itself." Another weekly music magazine joined the conversation: "Here's a salute across that dark abyss, the generation gap, to Matt Monro whose 'We're Gonna Change The World' must rate as one of the best records of 1970. This fact alone will ensure its absence from our Top 30, but with what class and style he sings the song, and what a song. Well done Matt, your record is a prime example to other younger so-called singers of how it should be done." When the record came out in August, Matt also had another record on the go, 'If There Ever is a Next Time', a musical tale from the movie *Hoffman*, written – of course – by Don Black. Matt sings it three times during the film.

> **Matt is brilliant at lyrics. He's one of the few singers who actually read the words of a song so he knows what he is singing about. He was the fastest person I know to lay a song down. The art in recording is to rehearse at home first and then when the red light comes on in the studio you know what you're doing. You know they're paying a fortune for the orchestra, you rehearse once and you record twice, that should be enough for a 3 ? minute track. Left hand mike, right hand mike, 25 musicians who know what they're doing, vocal in a booth, press the button, George Martin, thank you, very nice. You can do a whole 12-track album in three days.**
> **— Kenny Clayton**

On 7 May Matt and Johnnie had a box reserved at the Royal Festival Hall for a Frank Sinatra concert, but unfortunately they'd been booked to do a recording session at St John's Wood, a commitment they couldn't get out of. Rather than waste the tickets, they persuaded Mickie and Marion to go in their place and arranged to meet up with them later at the White Elephant on the River. The girls went on their evening out and sat in the box feeling like a million bucks. They were equally excited about dinner, as the Elephant was a swanky place. They all met up later as planned. The boys ended up on stage, Johnnie on piano and Matt on vocals and closed the place down at 4.00am. The prestigious restaurant never stayed open that late and it wouldn't be the last time the boys shook the place up.

In fact, it was on another night at the White Elephant that Matt's jealousy reared its ugly head again. After one of his shows at the Talk of the Town, Matt took a large party down to the restaurant for dinner. Dave Allen was one of those invited. The drinks flowed, spirits were high and several couples took to the dance floor. Mickie wanted to dance but Matt didn't. She'd always said he'd married her under false pretences as when they were dating, he would often dance with her, and in fact he said he loved it. The truth was he hated dancing and rarely took his wife in his arms on the floor anymore – well, not in public! Not wanting to disappoint, Dave danced with Mickie several times and it appeared everyone was having fun – all except Matt, who sat quietly, fuming at the table. When the dancing couple returned to the table, Mickie was glowing and appeared quite flushed after her twirl around the floor and when Matt made a sarcastic comment, Mickie looked at him and shouted, "Bore, bore, bore." It was soon after that they realised that Matt had caught a cab and gone home!

There wasn't much time to sulk as Matt was about to join Frankie Vaughan, Dusty Springfield, Malcolm Roberts, Peter Sarstedt, David Bowie and Sandie Shaw to perform at the Ivor Novello Awards show at London's Talk of the Town. The 10 May event was transmitted live via satellite to over sixty closed-circuit outlets in America, including New York's Carnegie Hall. The Novello Awards recognise the top British compositions each year, awarding them with a Bronze Statuette of Euterpe, the Greek Muse of music.

Matt and Mickie planned a well-deserved holiday to Majorca on 16 May and arranged to spend the evening prior to their flight with friends Sid and Val James. Sid had promised Matt that he would repay a loan from some months back of a few hundred pounds, but it was never forthcoming. Sid was a gambler and this made him terribly unreliable when it came to money. Val had known about her husband's addiction from the very beginning of their relationship and had combated the problem by forming a limited company with herself and her accountants as sole directors. That ensured that Sid's contracts and payments were filtered through the company and he was given a weekly allowance to make sure he behaved. But Sid was clever enough to get around his wife's well-thought-out plan by getting his agent Michael Sullivan to arrange cash backhanders on some of his contracts. He also made a habit of going to his friends for top-ups when creditors came knocking at his door. It put Matt in a difficult position, because he wouldn't bring the debt up in front of Val out of a sense of loyalty, and all he could do was wait patiently.

Mickie wasn't about to be nearly so polite about the matter – she put her foot down and confronted Sid with the threat of revealing all to his wife. Matt got his money back with surprising speed.

It was with Michael and Dany Sullivan that Matt and Mickie flew for a five-day break to Majorca the following day. Mickie didn't like to leave the two boys on their own unsupervised, as Michael was constantly trying to get Matt to sign him as his agent. Business aside, she couldn't understand why the two men always reverted to infantile behaviour when they got together. It certainly didn't amuse her when, coming back from the hairdresser, she stopped off poolside to tell the boys she was back and Michael threw her, new hairstyle and all, in to the pool. Matt couldn't stop laughing, but Mickie was beside herself with irritation. On another occasion, she was dozing on a lilo in the pool and Michael swam underneath her and punctured the plastic without her noticing. Moments later the lilo deflated, with Mickie gripping on for dear life. She wasn't the strongest of swimmers and the incident frightened her to no end. The boys were quietly giggling and although she knew they must have somehow been involved she couldn't prove anything, which angered her even more.

The holiday flew by and Matt and Mickie were back in England before they knew it. Matt had to honour one diary commitment on 7 June for *The Des O'Connor Show* before packing up ten days later ready for several weeks in America. Matt had been looking forward to this gig for months; a two-week headliner stint at the Hotel Tropicana's Blue Room in Las Vegas, backed by the Woody Herman Orchestra. The first half of the show featured Woody and his band, with Matt charming the crowds with his usual repertoire in the second. The finale saw Herman and Matt in a wild duet, singing 'Sonny Boy' and bringing down the house. Matt felt that he'd been very lucky in his career, having the opportunity to work with some of the people he admired. Woody Herman was one of them – it was a tremendous thrill for Matt and it seemed that Woody felt the same way: "I had the good fortune of working with Matt on a couple of occasions in Las Vegas and he is a very fine singer, very consistent and a very astute gentleman. I really enjoyed working with him."

Matt loved the buzz of Vegas, the town was full of headline artists and each show was bigger and better than the previous year. Andy Williams was working at Caesar's Palace, Perry Como (who was making his first nightclub appearance in twenty-six years) was at the International, Dean Martin was at the Riviera and Pat Boone at the Fremont. Not bad company to be in at all.

With all the excitement going on around them, Matt and Mickie had their own surprise up their sleeves. They announced they were getting married again – the next day! After eleven years of wedded bliss, Matt remarried Mickie at the Little Chapel of the West in Vegas on 10 July 1970. This time Matt bought the ring and licence. The only people in the know were Colin Keyes, who was invited, Sid and Gert Feller, who they considered two of their closest friends, and Matt's American press relations manager Norm Winter and his wife Joy. Matt rang Evelyn and told her he was renewing his wedding vows to her daughter and when she asked why, he replied, "Because I love her very much." It was a very simple affair, but something Matt felt strongly about. He felt he owed his wife the wedding she'd never had, but more importantly he wanted to prove to everybody how much she meant to him.

We went to their wedding in Las Vegas. Mickie looked lovely. The piano player looked lovely. Matt looked lovely. Sid and I did not look lovely. We were not dressed properly which we didn't know until we

Wedding Vows Little Chapel of the West

got there. They were formal and we were casual. We were one of the few people with them; it was an honour to say the least. — Gert Feller

The festivities continued with an evening wedding breakfast. The party ate, drank, played the tables, drank, told jokes, played the roulette wheel, drank and finished on the slot machines. Matt was ready to call it a day and asked his wife to take him upstairs to bed. The only trouble was, they weren't in their own hotel!

Although Matt had just finished working one of the most prestigious gigs in Vegas and appeared on the *Johnny Carson, David Frost* and *Dick Cavett Shows,* he never forgot his early performances. His first appearance back in England was on 19 July at the Whitcombe Lodge in Cheltenham. During the week's booking, Matt took the opportunity to pay an informal visit to RAF Innsworth to record an interview with Ed Martin for the Innsworth Forces Network. He also managed to fit in an appearance on *It's Lulu,* a new television show featuring the singer and her guests Peter Cook, Jerry Reed and The Hollies.

Matt flew back to Malaga on 1 August ready to complete the Spanish tour with Peter Jamieson. The travelling itself would be arduous with the tour zigzagging back and forth across the country. Jamieson took his responsibility to Matt very seriously, going above and beyond what the label were prepared to pay him for, but Peter was committed to the cause and gave up his two-week holiday in order to tour with Matt around Spain at his own expense. "I looked after Matt, it was more important and more exciting doing that than anything else. The thought of him being in Marbella and doing stuff on his own was a no deal for me."

After picking Matt up from the airport, Peter took him to the Don Pepe Melia Hotel in Marbella. They needed to sort out the schedule and work out routes, timings and tour accommodation but Peter wanted to give Matt some breathing time and agreed to meet up at 3.30pm that afternoon in the lobby. Peter checked the prices at reception and realised that the trip was far too expensive for him and his wife Carol – but Peter had a plan!

> Matt was singing at one of the biggest clubs in Marbella and had the Penthouse Suite in the Don Pepe Melia courtesy of the concert promoter. On the first day, Matt checked in and we met up mid-afternoon for a drink on the terrace of his suite – Matt asked what room number we were in and we explained we were not staying at the hotel. He asked where we were staying and we pointed to a lone tent set up in the large field next door. From then on he insisted we came in for everything, bath, meals and showers, which we did – Matt couldn't stop laughing. Matt, God bless him would get up at the crack of dawn every morning and we'd come up and have breakfast with him in the suite and we'd be able to wash and clean up – it seems so bizarre now but we'd spend the day with Matt and then work together for the concert that night and at the end of the show Matt would go back to the Penthouse and we'd go back to the tent. What was bizarre is that I'd emerge from this tent dressed in a suit to go and see Matt in this 5 star hotel. It was such a contrast. We had so much fun.
>
> — Peter Jamieson

This would be Peter's last tour with Matt, as shortly after, EMI unceremoniously posted him to Greece, ending his working relationship with the singer he had grown so fond of.

Matt & Bruce in Sheffield

The week of 24 – 29 August saw Sheffield treated to two top entertainers competing for the crowds for the first time in years: Matt at the Club Fiesta and Bruce Forsyth at Baileys. Sheffield had seen two large nightclubs open within the previous three years, bringing with it more variety entertainment than the city had seen since the days of The Empire and the Lyceum. Matt and Bruce were both staying at the Grand Hotel and while the papers speculated on whether Sheffield could provide enough people to fill the 1,900 plush seats in the cabaret rooms of these two clubs, the boys lapped up their supposed rivalry. The truth was that both men commanded a strong pulling power and both venues did very well indeed.

Having just received the new album *We're Gonna Change the World*, Matt was beside himself with anger. It took a lot to rile him to a state of unbridled fury but this episode did just that. He wrote immediately to Art Mogull at Capitol but the response did nothing to calm his mood.

> Having just heard the 'sweetened' version of 'We're Gonna Change the World', I felt that I must write to you although I am lost for words. An artiste likes to be proud of their work but I feel anything but that, regarding this track. The editing of one verse has been so

badly done that it has unmistakably left nothing to the imagination. The so-called 'sweetening' has added nothing except that the clean crisp sound has been eliminated and I am left with a disc which is not as good as the original rough acetate in my possession. I am also extremely unhappy with 'Why Can't I Touch You' for obvious reasons, plus the fact that 'He Ain't Heavy' was used as a B-side when I had other intentions for this track. I feel that I should have been consulted, particularly as I was in California at the time. Surely, this is no way to treat an artist or his work. Please let me have your views. — Matt Monro

I am in receipt of your letter of August 28. I only I wish I could disagree with you. However, I think you are totally correct, and on behalf of everyone at Capitol I apologise. Please also accept my personal apology, but unfortunately, right after you were here, I went on vacation and never heard the single prior to its release. — Art Mogull, Executive Producer, Capitol Records USA

The singer's frustrations were wholly evident when he gave this telling interview to Stan Britt about the events leading up to the album.

The title song was recorded in England and they cocked that up as well. I took it to the States, walked into a board meeting, they all had their feet on the desks, all smoking, drinking coffee and doughnuts, "yeah baby that's great", and they took it away and added a bit more rhythm and the extra brass were playing the wrong figures. If you listen to the English original and the American version it's a different record. They cut out a whole chorus and the song doesn't make sense anymore, it's out of tune, terrible. I don't know whether they ever released it. It was very frustrating, and dissatisfactory, sometimes with my travelling it is difficult for me to get into the studio but you'd think that with Capitol, this multimillion-pound concern... and you can never get anybody who knew what was going on. Over here someone's always on the look out for material for you but over there, there's a lot of back scratching going on, you scratch my back, I'll scratch yours and I find myself recording some terrible songs from a

nothing show because someone's a pal of someone. A lot of the stuff I'm sent is show or production material which can't really be used as single material or even album material because taken out of context it doesn't really mean anything, also with what you get from amateur writers, you might find one in a hundred, they are all so trite and corny. — Matt Monro

The American single was indeed released with a whole verse and chorus missing. Whilst it doesn't necessarily destroy the enjoyment of the song, it cuts out some key narrative and poor Annie Harris never gets out of bed, making her a fairly pointless character! To add insult to injury, the record company actually dubbed the 'sweetening' to it on 22 June at Capitol Tower – the same day Matt was across town recording 'Why Can't I Touch You' and 'Close to You' at United Recorders. Capitol did at least act on Matt's complaint by using the English version on the American album release *Close to You,* but it was too late – the relationship was at an end. There was nothing to salvage. Matt felt the company had prostituted his art by hacking away at its very heart; they weren't interested in producing great albums, as long as they were brought in on time and under budget. Apologies were a bit too late in coming and after fifteen singles and seven albums, Capitol and Matt parted company.

HAVE SUITCASE WILL TRAVEL

Matt was back doing the circuit of clubs in England in September of 1970, thrilling crowds at the Talk of the North, the Double Diamond in Caerphilly and the Wooky Hollow Club in Liverpool. Although he was set to go to Australia, he didn't like to sit idle at home, not that he could ever have been accused of that. His need to keep working stemmed from the fact that he never knew if he would have work after his last contract. He hadn't had a big hit in a while and although it didn't affect his work in America, England was a different story. The fact that a lot of clubs had disappeared overnight with the introduction of the Gambling Act meant he couldn't afford to take any booking for granted, although there had been some better news on the work front.

Butlins had just announced a revolutionary change in their entertainment policy. During the 1970 season they piloted a brand new late night entertainment program at two of their sites. Minehead set the ball rolling with dancing and cabaret starting at midnight in the Beachcomber Club with Matt topping the bill to a packed house. The Queen's Club at Skegness followed suit with Hughie Green. With both experiments a resounding success, Bobby Butlin decided on making late-night entertainment a regular affair, featuring top-drawer names at all the camps the following season. This was a radical change to the Butlins format, as for the last twenty-five years all entertainment had closed at 11.15pm. It proved a wise move, with over a million people enjoying the additional shows the following year all more than happy to pay the premium.

On 8 October, just before leaving for Australia and Hong Kong, Matt took delivery of a brand new Rolls Royce Silver Shadow Convertible – an early birthday present from his wife. Unfortunately, not long after, a magazine commissioned a story on Matt and wanted to take pictures of the star inside the car, with the roof down, as it was a glorious day. Matt didn't notice that the photographer had placed his heavy camera equipment on the roof's mechanism, damaging it to such an extent that it never really closed properly after that.

Colin Keyes was looking forward to visiting a new country, especially as his wife was travelling with him. Sadly, as soon as they arrived in Adelaide, he came down with an attack of vertigo so severe that he couldn't get out of bed without losing the room. A deputy had to be found for the week, and fast. If that wasn't enough, someone had taken the trombone book as souvenir, apparently not realising that without it the musician couldn't play. There was much scurrying around as a result, with the trombonist trying to write a rough outline of the show.

Once Colin was back on his feet, he took to his surroundings like a fish to water. He loved Australia from the start, not just the landscape but also the culture and way of life. The gigs were good, as were the musicians, so it was a lot of fun. The only thing that fazed him slightly was some of the domestic flights they had to take. He had only taken three small aircraft flights in his life, and two of them were with Matt. One trip they took together was in a twin engine Beechcraft from Madrid to Gijon, a holiday resort on the Northern coast. Colin was quite happy until the pilot had to negotiate a tricky landing through thick woodland. It was like a Kamikaze pilot executing a near perfect dive for approach, leaving Colin's stomach somewhere in the atmosphere. When they finally landed, the pianist's hands had to be pried off the seat-rest, finger by finger. It put Colin off the small ones for life.

Having suitably soothed his friend for the ensuing flight, Matt and his entourage moved onto Sydney. As luck would have it, Val and Lynn Doonican were also staying at the Sebel Town House and extended an invitation to Matt and Mickie to join them in their suite for drinks. The men talked shop while overlooking the views of Sydney Harbour. These quiet moments with friends grabbed between engagements were some of the nicest moments of the business. Sadly, it was the last time the four friends would ever see each other.

Matt opened his Hong Kong season at the Hilton's Eagle's Nest. After the frenzied touring of Australia, being stationed in one place for a whole month was a luxury. It was also a good opportunity to show Mickie, Pam and Colin the country that he loved so much. The shows were a complete dream, the superb Lito Naba Orchestra, guided by Colin Keyes at the piano, were equal to the task of supporting Matt, making an evening at the Eagle's Nest a worthwhile experience.

Playing Matt Monro in front of a Hong Kong audience is a little like

> playing Strauss Waltzes in Vienna – you simply can't lose. Not only
> because he started his singing career here, in a long-defunct
> serviceman's club 25 storeys directly below the Hilton's Eagle Nest,
> but also because he's a top notch entertainer, the kind who would
> please almost any crowd in almost any town. — *South China*
> *Morning Post*

With Matt so well known in the Colony, it was hard for him to go out without
being mobbed by hundreds of fans. Three days after opening, the singer was
craving a quiet night in and ordered room service for the four of them in his suite.
Conversation drifted pleasantly from music to new songs and arrangements, until
suddenly Colin was spluttering and turning bright red.

> The four of us were having a meal and I bit into a very hot chilli.
> While the other three were falling about laughing, I went purple
> from the neck up and tried to drink every glass of water on the
> table. I would never have imagined that your body could actually
> react like that. You could see a physical line slowing moving up
> from my neck to my face. — Colin Keyes

> He'd swallowed a whole chilli and I'd never seen Matt laugh so
> much, he was holding on to the table in convulsions. Colin was
> begging for water to drink and Mickie and I rushed to get some but
> in the meantime Matt threw the whole jug of water over him. Colin
> did recover but we never laughed like us three did that night.
> — Pam Keyes

As the news swept the country that Matt was playing at the Hilton, phones were
ringing off the hook with people begging for seats in already capacity-filled venues.
The shows went from strength to strength and the press returned rave reviews
about the Englishman's performance. The only thing to spoil Matt's mood was the
request from the management that he take the Hebrew number 'Hava Nagila' out
of the show, as they had a group of Arabs booked in for the evening. Matt calmly
said, "And I have a Jewish wife and she will be watching the show tonight, the song
stays in", and it did. Regardless of the singer's refusal to comply with their wishes
the management pleaded with the star to extend his contract and as much as Matt
would have liked to oblige he had commitments elsewhere.

> Matt is a gentle purveyor of words of love, good cheer and confidence. And along the way is humour. Half bouncing and half sauntering on to the stage, Matt swung in to a combination of 'My Kind of Girl' and 'Lady is a Tramp'. And he brought the house down when he said, "If you have any favourite songs you'd like to hear – forget it, we don't do requests". The most remarkable thing about Mr M is his relaxed style – he not only entertains but reaches out to his audience as well. When he extends his warmth with some handshaking to the crowd – you know he means it. It seems every cabaret crooner does the tune 'My Way' – and Matt was no exception. Only his rendition WAS exceptional. Matt Monro may be diminutive in size – but he can sure belt them out. Even to the point of moving musical mountains. — Tony Bugay, *The China Mail*

Anyone who had missed out on tickets to Matt's show could tune into RTV and watch him perform live. The star guested on a television variety special hosted by Rebecca Pan, a top Chinese female singer. Renowned for her fashion sense as much as her singing, some of her costumes cost in excess of sixteen hundred dollars each.

> There was a thirty-piece orchestra and we'd decided that I would play piano and conduct. The string section sounded like authentic Chinese music! When we broke for dinner at six o' clock, two of the string players said they were going as they had another job! I didn't argue, deciding that two less out of tune violins was probably a good thing. Essentially the piano was out of tune but when you couple that with a violin section that's not greatly in tune with each other, it leads to disaster. Their intonation was awful and where they were placing their fingers on the violin's neck wasn't quite on the right pitch. The musicians would have thought it sounded fine as Chinese music can sometimes sound like that but it would have been painful and horrific with piano, so I ended up conducting rather than playing. — Colin Keyes

Matt was not paid for enduring such a fiasco. Instead Mickie and Pam were each given an authentic Chinese dress, made to order. The reception was always so warm in the Far East, and the hospitality so lavish that Matt couldn't stay cross at the lack of adequate facilities. Everyone meant well and they were genuinely

Matt's 40th birthday Hong Kong

appreciative of the singer's talents. Although the television appearances were a tool to promote the singer's shows, it was a moot exercise as all tickets had sold out long before the variety special aired.

Matt's fortieth birthday was celebrated in the same country as his twenty-first. Aside from the Rolls Royce convertible that Mickie had organised before leaving England, she had a second present waiting for her husband – a pair of custom-made diamond cufflinks she'd had commissioned in Hong Kong. She also hosted a surprise birthday party following his show with several Hong Kong buddies including Bing Rodriquez and Ted Thomas. There was a fantastic cake, presented in two halves, one featuring a message to Terry Parsons with the figure of a soldier, and the other commemorating his fourteen years in show business as Matt Monro. Ray Cordeiro, Radio Hong Kong's popular DJ, knew of the 'surprise' and arranged for the Beatles number 'Birthday' to be played on his *All The Way with Ray* programme at midnight. As if that wasn't enough of a birthday treat, another shock came with the arrival of 'surprise' guests Leonardo Schultz, Len Matcham and his lady Sue Groves, Sid and Gert Feller and Johnnie and Marion Spence, who had all flown in especially for the party. There was, however, no sign of Don Black.

Matt returned to a very cold Britain. After months away it would have been nice to put his feet up, but no such luxury was afforded. Within two days, he was on another plane heading to Munich to record the *Rolf Harris Show* and from there to Paris to record with the renowned composer Michel Legrand for *A Place in Paris*. This wasn't the first time Matt had recorded a Michel Legrand composition. The first was three years back in 1967, when he had gone into the studio with *Pretty Polly*. It was originally Hal Shaper who had recommended the singer to the composer after writing the song for the film *A Matter of Innocence*. Shaper had an inkling that Matt would be interested in recording the song and he was right. This second outing was no different. Matt loved the song and Michel Legrand was equally impressed: "I loved the way Matt sang. He was an extraordinary crooner and I was very proud that he accepted to record my songs. I loved him very much."

Arriving home on Christmas Eve, Marion and Johnnie were waiting at Dallas Road to kick off the festivities, and there, at least for a few days, Matt finally relaxed and chilled out with family and friends. Five days off wasn't nearly long enough, but it did recharge Matt's batteries and he finished the year by working on Jimmy's show, *It's Tarbuck*.

Don saw only four pieces of his work come to fruition in 1970. He had also been busy pursuing his passion for musical theatre but his first attempt *Maybe That's Your Problem* was a resounding failure.

> **Don felt dejection almost beyond anything he had known before. It was as though he had simply wasted a chunk of his life. It was a terrible feeling. — James Inverne, *Wrestling With Elephants – The Authorised Biography of Don Black***

Mickie felt that Don had also wasted a large chunk of Matt's life by concentrating all his time away from the singer. Matt didn't see much of Don that year, with the songwriter composing for five more film projects including the huge Hollywood triumph *Diamonds are Forever*.

In 1971, Matt moved to Columbia, another subsidiary of EMI, and his debut single was the George Harrison song 'Isn't It a Pity'. When the single failed to chart, it was flipped with 'Mama Packed a Picnic Tea', which was then credited as the A-side. Apart from a Decca compilation, there were no other official releases that year. A Dutch washing powder company, Bio-Tex, did, however, issue two compilation albums. The first one included the track 'People' and the second 'Close to You'. Customers had to collect three box lids and send five Dutch guilders into Bio-Tex and they would get one of the albums in return. But Matt wasn't all that interested in monitoring his releases; he was more concerned with ensuring the run-through at the Talk of the Town was to his satisfaction.

Adverse weather conditions reduced Matt's opening night audience, at the Talk of the Town on 4 January 1971, to only half of what it should have been, but he couldn't have received louder applause had the place been packed to the rafters. It would be fair to say that Colin Keyes added to the worth of what was a truly excellent performance. Pam Keyes was working with the Tiller Girls in the West End, and dashed across town after her show to catch Matt's act.

> The atmosphere front of house and backstage was throbbing with tension and excitement. Matt was putting in new material for the show so Colin, as usual, had stayed up all night putting finishing touches to the music. Both of the men were pacing the dressing room floor waiting to go on. Matt always had people visiting in the dressing room after shows so Mickie was busy setting up a bar and nibbles before we all went out front to watch the show. Matt won people over just by walking onto the stage. They had come to see a great singer and performer and as always Matt delivered. It always seemed as if all the West End's artists came round to the dressing room to congratulate him. Praise and laughter rang out until we were forced to leave so they could lock up for the night. Each time Matt performed at the Talk of the Town it was the same.
> — Pam Keyes

Matt rang and asked if I could help for two or three days by running the hospitality backstage. I had no idea what he meant but once explained said that I would be glad to help but it would mean taking time away from work and that I would need to cover the loss of earnings. Matt agreed to the amount. I spent my time with him as Don was away in America – I never got paid! He rang a week later and said that a number of people including Vic Lewis at NEMS had asked him what office/agency I worked for not realising I wasn't even in the business. Matt said if I wanted a change in career, he would open the door but I would have to find my own way in. This was a new start for me, and a couple of months later I

Reg Parsons, Matt, Mickie, Len Carron, Reg & Alice Parsons

was sitting at a desk in NEMS trying to book a UK tour, despite not having a clue what I was doing. — Reg Parsons

So in a bizarre twist of fate, Matt opened the door to a whole new world for his nephew. Although Reg was nervous about taking such a huge step, with Matt's guidance he started off by booking hotel shows, eventually adding producer and compère to his list of achievements. His network grew, as did his confidence, and he even booked Matt on a number of occasions, but the most memorable of those was at The Grosvenor House Hotel. Having introduced Matt on stage, the singer held his intro and called Reg back on to proudly introduce his nephew to the crowd.

Whenever Matt performed in London, you could bet that Ms Maull would turn up as well. She declared herself to be Matt's greatest fan and no one else made claim to her title. She chatted up the doormen at Talk of the Town and begged them to send her the full-sized cut-outs of Matt on display in the foyer after he'd finished his run – she succeeded twice.

Matt was always mindful of his fans, especially the ones who had followed him around the country. He had become very fond of Sue Maull and her family and always made a point of inviting her backstage where possible. He even sent her Christmas cards over the holidays. Sue always stayed in London overnight when visiting the Talk of the Town, as it was too far for her to travel home afterwards.

She nearly passed out when on one occasion Matt casually asked if she would like to come to Dallas Road the next morning before setting off home. She arrived thirty minutes early and sat outside the house trying to steady her nerves. She was so shaky that she barely remembers any details of that first visit to the Monro family home, but she certainly wouldn't forget it any time soon.

Matt was always heavily booked up whenever he was in London for a few weeks and this time was no exception. He did a whirlwind of radio appearances including *The Roger Whittaker Show*, and what was to be his last appearance on *The Morecambe & Wise Show*. Matt was desperate for a break. It didn't seem to matter what country they went to anymore, he was always swamped with fans. For Matt and Mickie, there was only one place to go if they were fed up with travelling thousands of miles a year, seeing millions of faces, journeying to countless destinations – Brecqhou. This seventy-four acre island was owned by their multi-millionaire friend Len Matcham and boasted a menagerie of free-roaming animals, few residents and even fewer visitors – it was paradise. The loudest things on the island were the seagulls.

Len bought Brecqhou for £44,000 in 1966 as a weekend retreat but he soon decided that he wanted to live in his new kingdom permanently. Relocating his business empire was no easy undertaking, and to help with operations and the renovations of the island's facilities he took his personal assistant Sue Groves along with him, who quickly assumed the role of island manager. She was delighted in her new role, she loved the outdoors and here she had a whole island to enjoy, housing a wealth of animals including Shetland ponies, Guernsey cows, chickens, ducks, donkeys, pigs, Ollie the parrot and Len's own dog Match, a German Shepherd.

The island was completely isolated so Len commissioned the construction of a helicopter pad, affording routes to the island by air and sea. The Monros would sail over to the island on board Len's personal forty-foot boat, *Brecqhou Chief*, and stay in a cottage at Jacob's Head overlooking the Gouliot Passage and Sark. They loved it so much that after their first trip Len had given them the cottage as a gift, renaming the area Monro's Point.

On one of their trips, Don arranged to come over to the island for the day, as he urgently wanted Matt to sign some papers. Matt and Mickie went down to Le Port to meet him. The weather conditions made for rather rough seas and Pat, the skipper, was having trouble aligning the vessel with the quay, so all hands were

Len Matcham & Matt in Brecqhou

used to fend the boat off. There were no problems until the skipper felt he ought to go round again to get a better approach. Everyone let go of the boat except Matt, who, as the gap between the quay and the boat widened, ended up in the drink. Only his Jackie Stewart 'flat cap' (which as it turned out was still attached to his head) was showing above the waves – a bit of a worry at the time but very funny after he emerged in one piece.

Matt had been on the island a few weeks when the children came to join them once school let out for the holidays. It was Matthew's seventh birthday and Matt wanted to make sure they were all together on his son's special day. This was a huge concession for Len, as he wasn't overly fond of children on the island. He didn't like any disruption to his peace and quiet but made a special exception for Matt and Mickie.

Matt's accident-prone days were certainly not behind him and his trips to the island was fraught with small misfortunes. The singer borrowed one of the bicycles on offer, and the first time he mounted it he lost control and came off in a spectacular display. Most of the time Matt 'styled it out', pretending the mishaps were inconsequential, much too proud to admit to others that he had actually hurt himself and his pride. On another occasion Matt was showing off his prowess on a horse. He was approaching La Grande Maison, which had a freestanding brick archway. The saddle slipped, resulting in the horse going through the archway and Matt being delivered sideways at the front door.

The most wonderful thing about visiting the island was the tranquillity its beauty offered and the lack of pressure exerted on the singer to do anything but relax. He took the opportunity of adopting a healthier lifestyle, with home-cooked meals and abstinence from all alcohol. Despite his sensible living, four days into his trip Matt suffered a fit in the middle of the night. A doctor was urgently summoned and Len immediately dispatched the helicopter to bring the physician over from the mainland.

> This patient had a fit about 4.00 am on Friday 29th January. It was well described by his wife with all its stages – tonic, clonic, flaccid, followed by a prolonged period of confusion, the whole attack lasting an hour. He has never had a fit before and the likelihood in this case is a result of alcohol withdrawal. He has been working solid for nearly two years without a break and drinking steadily all day to keep himself going. I gather you found an enlarged liver a year ago. He tells me that last October he stopped drinking for a fortnight and had a slight attack of the shakes. However on this occasion the alcohol withdrawal was precipitated by an attack of diarrhoea and vomiting and the shakes were much more pronounced. In addition he found himself almost totally unable to sleep and the fit occurred at four in the morning whilst he was still awake. When I saw him his only complaint was a pain in the centre of his back but this was a pulled muscle as a result of the fit. My other positive findings were a marked pharyngitis, slightly inflamed right eardrum, signs of bronchitis in the chest and the enlarged liver (two fingers), which you had already noted. In addition I had a suspicion that his eyes were more yellow than normal and this suspicion was strengthened as he had orange urine. I subsequently found that he had no bilirubin in the urine so I think the idea of hepatitis can reasonably be excluded. I suggested that he return home to your care but am told today he has gone against my advice and has decided to stay over here a while longer. Meanwhile I will be working on him with a view to talking him out of his alcoholism. — Doctor's Report

The epileptiform seizure was a huge shock to the family and everybody was understandably upset. However, despite the seriousness of the situation, Matt made the decision to continue with his holiday; there would be plenty of time for doctors later. Although the doctor did talk to his patient about alcoholism, Matt argued that he could stop whenever it was necessary, as he had proved on many occasions. The trouble was that Matt actually liked to drink and the pressures of the business had made it easy to reach for a bottle. He had come to the island with the sole purpose of abstaining from booze, not realising that instant withdrawal could produce such severe symptoms. Matt returned to the mainland feeling refreshed, but complained of intense backache. He went to see a specialist in Harley Street about the ongoing problem but the doctor could find no tangible explanation for the pain. However, he did note that Matt's lower dorsal region was mildly kyphotic and distinctly tender to pressure. This area was the site of the backache, which spread round the chest on either side. Dr Critchley felt it strongly suggested a local lesion on the vertebral column with damage to the roots.

The specialist carried out a number of tests. The EEG was normal, as was a straight x-ray of the chest but the images of Matt's back demonstrated some vertebral collapse. The problems seemed to have been of a long-standing nature, suggesting that Matt may have damaged his back in the past and the recent nocturnal fit had aggravated the problem. The doctor gave Matt permission to keep his engagements in the North but on his return two weeks later, still suffering from intense pain, he was referred to specialist Mr Braddock. Examination revealed marked tenderness in the area and an x-ray showed crush fractures of the thoracic spine. He advised Matt that his symptoms would persist, but should gradually improve over the next three months. Matt had no option but to carry on, although the pain was debilitating. He had an evening recording session at Air London booked on 5 April and they would not take too kindly to a last-minute cancellation, so with lyrics in hand Matt laid down seven tracks, one of which was 'Love Story'.

Engineer Richard Moore only uncovered the English version of 'Love Story' in the summer of 2007 after intensive research, but only three quarters of the track existed in the vaults of EMI. Engineer Peter Mew at Abbey Road Studios explained that some of the tape was accidentally wiped when the Spanish vocal was overdubbed in 1971. In order to release an English version of the song, the studio needed to recreate the missing section but they only had a Spanish take to complete it. However, at the original session it appears they dropped in too early, and clipped the last two thirds of the line before the end section. Because of that error the last three words are missing on the released track that was issued on *Matt at the Movies* in 2007.

On 12 April, Matt left for a week's booking at the Shakespeare Cabaret Club in Liverpool. He was there on the evening of his and Mickie's thirteenth wedding anniversary, and he was sad not to be spending the evening with her. No one was more stunned than he when, having made an impulsive dash from London to Liverpool Airport, Mickie walked into the club while Matt was performing. Club DJ Pete Price said, "Matt was absolutely shocked when he saw his wife blow in when he was on stage. Everyone was standing up and applauding, it was very moving." The club's management laid on a champagne reception for the couple after the show.

Even though Matt's records had seen no movement in the charts of late he was still in demand on the standard variety vehicles. In the last week of April he appeared on both *Moira Anderson Sings* and *Whittaker's World of Music*. Matt knew Roger Whittaker quite well and it appeared that the host was as busy on his travels as Matt. He had just finished a month of cabaret dates in Canada and moved straight into this, his first television series. The two performers swapped travel-weary stories, but however tired Whittaker was, it didn't show; he had a boundless energy on stage.

> **Matt Monro was a great character and one I liked a lot. We appeared on many TV shows together. One I recall for the BBC was down at the Riverside Studios. Matt, Lulu and I were on the show together and he was telling me how forgetting the words was no horror story to him because he could scat his way through, that is he could make up the words as he went along and no one would know the difference. I think they did that day, as the producer wasn't too happy with us! — Roger Whittaker**

The atmosphere was certainly informal in Studio Four at London Weekend Television's Wembley headquarters on 27 April, with Roger himself doing his bit by chatting and telling jokes to all his guests, who included The Fantastics, McGuiness Flint, Sandie Shaw, Alan Haven and American country singer/guitarist Jerry Reed. The finale was reminiscent of the defunct *Ready Steady Go,* with the audience invited to appear around and behind the stage in the huge studio. It saw audience members scrambling and pushing for the best positions in front of the camera. Matt liked this laidback approach to a television show, which didn't come around too often.

Four days after filming, Matt and Mickie took a two-week break at the Hotel Los Monteros in Marbella. Matt chose Marbella because he had sung at the Hotel Don Pepe the previous summer, and he had warm memories of the place. Although he had hoped to play some golf, his injuries were still painful and he thought it wiser just to rest his back. He was sensible to grab a few days of rest before his upcoming tour, as the itinerary was tight with ten shows over nine days in Madrid, Gerona, Reus and Barcelona, all at different venues and with flights squeezed in between, and a television appearance thrown in for good measure.

Although Matt and Mickie had enjoyed their Marbella break, the subsequent Spanish tour had left the singer exhausted, but almost as soon as the couple had touched down at London's Heathrow Airport, Matt had repacked and driven to Derby for a week's engagement at Talk of the Midlands.

Ever since journalists damaged Matt's new Rolls Royce, he had been unhappy with its performance. Where the electric roof had been damaged it leaked water in wet weather, but more irritating was the weird noise it made when driving at speed. On reflection Matt felt something more practical for the road, not just in size but also in petrol consumption, would be better. The excuses were just self-justification to buy another car and this time he ordered a metallic maroon Mercedes Benz, but there was a slight wait on delivery. In the meantime he decided to buy Mickie a surprise birthday present.

> **We were up North and Matt decided to buy Mickie a new Mercedes for her birthday. Colin also decided he would trade up our car and now I'm worried as I know I'm going to have to drive our car home. There's me driving the new Audi, Colin driving the Mercedes and Matt in his Rolls on the motorway in convoy with a warning from both men not to hit either of their cars. This was after a show so we didn't start off until midnight and after a very long journey I was glad to get back to Dallas Road. Mickie was delighted with her car but still told Matt off for spending so much money but beamed as she said it. — Pam Keyes**

In August, Matt was seen by Mr Braddock, and although the singer hadn't suffered any more blackouts he was referred back to the original specialist Dr Critchley for further tests, but no neurological abnormalities were noted in the resulting x-rays. Matt had stayed off alcohol for four months, but had recently started taking a little

Matt & Lisa Rosa on Tour

whisky again, although far less than was his normal practice. Dr Critchley wrote to Matt's GP, informing her that he had told the singer in no uncertain terms that he would do well to avoid alcohol altogether, but doubted very much whether the singer would take his advice.

Matt was certainly suffering from depression when he left for South Africa at the end of August, made worse by the fact that Mickie wasn't due to join him for a few weeks. Matt was headlining at the President Hotel in Johannesburg with Lita Roza as support, but she was struck down with illness on opening night, leading to some very cruel headlines. Rumours circulated that she had been too drunk to take to the stage, but the truth was that she was suffering the effects of low blood sugar. Lita had been diagnosed as a diabetic in 1950, and until then had managed to control her condition and hide it from the public, especially promoters, as she didn't want them to think she might be an insurance risk.

I was insulin dependent and didn't realise the levels would be different because of altitude so didn't alter my drugs accordingly. On opening night I walked out on stage and just stood there looking at the audience. I knew I was there for something but didn't know

what. It later transpired that I suffered a hypoglycaemic attack. Someone led me off stage and took me to my room where I went into a coma. A doctor was called immediately and while examining my arms for needle marks, Matt came in and explained that he thought I was a diabetic so I was duly administered Glocovan. The following morning the papers were soul-destroying with headlines "Was she drunk?" or implying I might have been on drugs. I went back on stage the second night and everything went well after that. Although I had always met up with Matt we had never worked together until South Africa. I used to watch him perform every night. He was just so brilliant. He had a voice to die for. He never said anything you could take offence at. There are certain people in life you liked immediately and Matt was in that category; he had instant contact with you and what a sense of humour. — Lita Roza

The trouble with overseas promoters was that when they put together a tour they never took into consideration the time it would take to travel to each town or city, squeezing the maximum amount of time from their acts. Matt and Colin hit the road after Johannesburg and travelled to Bloemfontein, Welkom, Kimberley, Pretoria, Klerksdorp, Durban, East London, Port Elizabeth, George, Parrow and Cape Town. The travelling was the worst part and Matt arrived in each town exhausted before he even stepped on stage.

Matt decided to hire a single-engine plane to make the journey from Welkom to Kimberly. It was a one-hour flight and the pilot was ex-RAF, and insisted on whistling the whole way. The assault on the small aircraft from hot-air turbulence was so severe that it threw the plane across the sky and the ordeal lasted the entire flight. When the battered machine finally landed, Matt was left with the task of trying to prise Colin's white fingers off the seat in front. He was so traumatised that he had to go to bed for two hours to recover. A few days later the duo flew to a place called George, a town so small that it only had one hotel and a circular hut with a straw roof that served as its bank, but nobody mentioned that it had a grass landing strip. As they were coming in to land Colin couldn't see any runway and freaked out. Although the flights didn't faze Matt in the slightest, it all got a bit much for Colin, who genuinely feared for his life. With his two feet gratefully planted on terra firma, he refused to fly any further.

The promoters, a married couple, were waiting at Kimberley Airport to take the travellers to the hotel, but things didn't improve for Colin. The woman took the wheel but was constantly turning around to talk to Matt and Colin in the back seat. She kept asking questions about their trip, taking her eyes off the road. Colin was looking nervously past her into the oncoming traffic. At the end of a stretch of road, he spotted a group of people crossing the road, but the driver was too busy chatting to notice them. Colin was forced to scream out and with that she stamped on the brakes, causing the car to nearly stand on its end!

It wasn't just the car journey that was fraught; Matt and Colin found the whole tour a nightmare from start to finish. With no credible management taking the reins, the weeks were plagued with problems and impossible schedules. Both men were exhausted and Matt sank deeper into a growing depression. He was extremely grateful when the tour ended six weeks later.

> Matt went through a period on the South Africa tour we did where it got a bit on top of him. It was done through Hugo Colletti, who was Eve Boswell's father and his management/agency/promotion, whatever you want to call it. There were a few situations that they introduced to the way we were doing the tour that were not right and Matt shouldn't have been subjected to those things. Matt was fraught so I ended up taking on the role of manager for a brief period, talking to Hugo about the numerous problems we had but the main thing was the schedules where we had a ridiculously short time to get from one place to another. There was no one else to do it and I ended up having shout ups with Hugo on Matt's behalf. — Colin Keyes

The song-writing talents of John Barry and Don Black came together again when they collaborated on the film *Mary, Queen of Scots*. Don called on Matt to record the two songs on 26 November. It was Colin's first recording session with Matt and was very special to the pianist. They recorded 'Wish Now Was Then' and 'This Way Mary', both of which Colin scored. Several days later they went back to Abbey Road to record Matt's new album, *The Other Side of the Stars*.

> The biggest high was being asked to arrange and conduct a whole album for Matt, *The Other Side of the Stars*. Unfortunately EMI managed to screw up the whole experience by not releasing it for two years and then unbelievably issuing the album unmixed including a glaring trumpet mistake. It happened on 'I'm Glad I'm Not Young Anymore'. The trumpets play a wrong note in the instrumental section

and it's the top note played by Stan Roderick, who was playing lead trumpet, and he just screwed it. We did an edit but they never actually used that version. It could have been so much better had they taken the trouble to mix it. If they did mix it, it was a very poor job and they missed a glaring mistake. I was very disappointed. — Colin Keyes

A week after his stint at the Talk of the North, Matt went on a series of engagements for Harold Landey, who had handled The New Seekers' British tour. Unlike the club circuit, these were all concert dates at top theatres in the country, all wanting two shows a night in the lead up to Christmas.

I remember working with Matt at Talk of the North and Blighty's as well as several television shows I worked on at Teddington. I was only in my early twenties and just starting out so I was slightly in awe of him. Matt had a great rapport with the musicians. Although he was a big star he was never aloof or had any airs or graces, he was just one of the guys. He was a great musician, so professional and his singing was impeccable. It was a great honour to work with him. — John Barclay, Musician/Lead Trumpet

Matt finished off the year with a week at the Cresta Club in Birmingham. The party season was in full swing and Matt and Mickie were naturally inundated with invitations. Sid James threw a lavish party at his home in Ivor for his wife's fortieth birthday. It was a wonderful evening and a relative who's who of the celebrity world. Matt talked to director Gerald Thomas, whom he'd met some months back, about his forthcoming film. Thomas had been involved in all of the *Carry On* movies, and taking a liking to the singer had offered him a role in the forthcoming *Carry on Henry*. Matt declined the offer, not only because his diary was packed as it was, but also because he just couldn't picture himself in a comedic role.

SUICIDE WATCH

Although Don Black was no doubt upset when *Maybe That's Your Problem* flopped the year before, it didn't stop him collaborating with John Barry for a second time. For this outing, a better subject matter was selected; in fact *Billy Liar* was one of Barry's favourite plays and he set about the task of writing a musical. Don was also to reconnect with Walter Scharf, working on an unusual project about a boy who befriended a rat. Michael Jackson was chosen to sing the song and 'Ben' went straight to the top of the American charts. His success didn't end there, and he followed it up with a lavish production of *Alice's Adventures in Wonderland*. The songs didn't have enough impact, though Matt happily recorded 'The Me I Never Knew' and 'Curiouser and Curiouser' for his friend.

Matt obviously knew Don was being kept busy and at this point, most of his contracted bookings were coming through NEMS. It seemed that while the agency were happy to pick up the phone and take enquiries, no one was actively chasing anything or drumming up any new business. Indeed, it appeared that phone calls or letters regarding Matt's work could go unanswered. On one occasion, this even led to an offer of work being withdrawn.

Letter to Don Black at NEMS
As you know I have telephoned your office on several occasions during this week. I learned from your secretary that Matt Monro had not come back to England as soon as expected and was finally due in Wednesday morning. I left a message for you on Wednesday and yesterday explained that the matter was now most urgent for our producer who still has a lot to do to organise everything. I stated that I would have to hear by mid-day today or I must assume that Matt Monro was no longer interested in the idea.

This, then is to confirm to you that, as I have received no word at all, our offer is withdrawn and we are offering the engagement elsewhere. Mary Ramonde, assistant to Light Entertainment Booking Manager: NDO Anniversary Concert (Northern Dance Orchestra)

Matt knew nothing about these sorts of incidents. Mickie had spoken strongly against Don to her husband, voicing her fears for his future. Her complaints and cautions mirrored everything Matt secretly feared, but he wasn't prepared to admit that his friend had turned his back on him. Matt eventually spoke to Don about his concerns, and his manager promised that he would find renewed vigour and that everything would be fine, explaining that his people at NEMS were on the case and Matt would be well taken care of.

Suitably reassured, Matt and Colin flew to Canada on 5 February 1972 for a gig at the Beverley Hills Hotel in Toronto. The hotel was impressive, but it was the first time Matt had come across armed security guards who patrolled up and down the hotel's corridors, which was slightly unsettling. The city was so bitterly cold that just crossing the road was an ordeal. Colin was convinced that his ears would snap off.

I will always remember Canada. We were due to open on the Sunday but arrived on Saturday and were invited to watch the show of the previous performers. I sat with Matt on one side and Oscar Peterson on the other and watched the Basie Band play their last show. We then went up to his suite and met Count Basie. — Colin Keyes

The papers announced that Tony Bennett was to star in his first British television series. The thirteen half-hour shows were to be recorded before an audience at London's famed Talk of the Town. Several television stations battled for the rights, but it was Thames Television that landed the show. Unlike similar variety formats that introduced comedy, Bennett's concept was a production of pure music with the minimum amount of stage banter. With a lavish budget at his disposal the singer opted for a 38-piece orchestra headed up by Robert Farnon, using the cream of British musicians including Stan Roderick, Kenny Baker, Don Lusher, Tony Fisher and Kenny Clare. As well as performing several songs himself, Bennett also acted as host to international guest stars Sarah Vaughan, Tommy Leonetti, Billy Eckstine, Cleo Laine and Matt Monro. But the Cockney lad from Shoreditch was the only artist asked to fill three guest spots for Mr B.

Incidentally, Tony also had a lady mentor who had helped launch his career. It was back in 1950 when a young commercial artist turned singer called Anthony Benedetto landed a one-week engagement at the Greenwich Village Inn in New York. The star of the show was Pearl Bailey and she admired the boy's singing so much that she helped him land full time work at the club. Bob Hope dropped in to hear Pearl sing, saw Benedetto and talked him into joining his tour. One change: Hope rechristened him Tony Bennett, and like his friend Matt, he suffered many misspellings of his name.

To make it a worthwhile experience for the audience, Thames recorded two episodes on each of the filming dates. *Colours Green* provided warm up music before filming started and also in between the two shows. The small interval saw Tony's pianist John Bunch, bassist Arthur Watts and drummer Kenny Clare treat the crowd to an informal jam session, keeping them engaged while they set up the next shots for filming. Matt recorded three programmes, two on 27 February and one on 5 March, with all three transmitted in the Spring. Even a twelve-hour workday didn't dampen anyone's spirits; it was a thrill to be there and not just for Matt, every musician felt the same way. It was an equally exciting prospect for Mr Keyes as he was a great admirer of Bennett's work, and felt honoured to have been selected – especially as Matt could have used Tony's own musical director John Bunch.

> **We went over to Bennett's apartment in Grosvenor Square for rehearsals and he had his rhythm section there. He was into his painting then and we'd be doing something and he suddenly disappeared on to the balcony of this little penthouse. He had an easel out there and was painting away and suddenly he'd pop back in again and do a bit more rehearsing. — Colin Keyes**

The wonderful thing for Matt was that not only was he working with a great friend but the twosome had also agreed to duet in each episode. Matt phrased his way flawlessly through the first show with 'The Second Time Around' and 'Time After Time', while Tony's numbers included 'Autumn Leaves', 'Baby Dream That Dream' and 'Here's That Rainy Day', later joining talents for the old standard 'I Want to be Happy'. Tony rated Matt as one of the world's top five singers, while Matt said he'd queue for hours in the rain to hear the American sing. They spent a lot of time with each other over those weeks, talking through the best routines and kicking back.

> **Matt was really a great friend of mine. I'm more than a fan of his,**

Tony Bennett & Matt

he's like a brother to me and treated me so well when I came to Britain the first time, he really worked hard at trying to help me out. To my mind Matt Monro is the best singer England has ever produced. — Tony Bennett

Colin was very excited; not only was he working with two of the greatest performers in the world, but he was also about to become a father. Whenever there was a break in filming he would slip away to ring home and check on his wife. The pace of the shows was brisk, but it was nothing compared to Colin's movements. As with most births, the process was a lengthy one and Colin spent all day between rehearsals and the live recording running backwards and forwards to the hospital. It certainly caused a buzz in the studio, but as it transpired Victoria Keyes didn't arrive until after midnight.

Those three shows represented the meeting of two artists separated by the Atlantic coming together to exemplify each other's unique talent. Instead of working against each other or trying to grab the limelight, you could see genuine camaraderie between the two men and a delight to be working together. The shows saw both artists at their most superlative, demonstrating to the world why they were considered the best at what they did.

After the adrenalin rush had ebbed, Matt was back making the rounds with visits to some of the biggest clubs in the country, completing two months on the road with an appearance at the Club Double Diamond in Caerphilly. The management were delighted with Matt's return to Wales, and so were the public, clamouring to snap up five thousand show tickets before they sold out.

Rehearsals for the *David Nixon Show* took place at Teddington over two days. Matt's good friend Freddie Davies was a regular on the series, as was Rod Hull and Emu. The bird caused its usual catalogue of problems for its owner, but Matt cleverly avoided a confrontation with the uncontrollable beast. Matt's spotlight included 'Sarah's Coming Home' and 'Witchcraft', which was sung during a magic skit he performed with the cast. The sketch was fairly long; Freddie, with his lisping dialogue, was hilarious as Nixon's assistant, but look to the top of the screen and you can spot the microphones hovering over the artists as they try to catch the audio. David's assistant Penny Meredith was stripping behind a screen and each item of clothing was passed to Nixon who then handed it to Matt to place in a suitcase. The end of the routine would see Nixon showing the audience an empty case, but before the end of the trick, bad camera angles meant you could see the false shelf in the case as Matt was packing it. Matt fell about laughing when watching the playback. It was brilliantly bad. Freddie was equally impressed: "The sketch we did together was one of the highlights of the entire series. I looked at an old video of the show recently and the magic came back immediately."

After Matt finished up the show, Len Matcham invited the Monros to spend a few days on his boat, which was docked at Port Gallice, Juan Les Pins in Nice. *Solaria Too* had a crew of three and afforded every luxury known to man. Len loved to sail and made regular trips back and forth to Menorca. The plan was for Matt and Mickie to travel on the boat as far as Marseilles and then fly home from there. Over the week they established a routine of sailing throughout the days, docking at a different port each night and enjoying dinner in one of the local restaurants. Matt was sunning himself aboard the holiday yacht off St Tropez when Len casually mentioned that the very plush vessel passing alongside them belonged to the famed film producer Sam Spiegel. Matt grabbed his cine camera and started filming, whereupon Mr Spiegel – outsized cigar in mouth – walked out on deck and waved a friendly hello in Matt's direction and said "Hi there." Matt had just got over the surprise when Yul Brynner followed the producer out on deck. There was lots of friendly hand waving all round.

The trip was fabulous apart from a passing mistral they encountered out at sea. Unable to beat the storm they had no choice but to see it through, so it didn't surprise anyone that Mickie wasn't hungry at dinnertime! Matt and Mickie would have loved a few more days relaxing with their friends, but there were commitments in England including a week's contract at The Kings in Ilford and a date at Air London. The session booked for 29 June included five tracks for Matt's new album *Close to You*, but the one that meant the most to him was 'Michelle', for that was his daughter's name. He took her to the studio with him, held her hand throughout the recording and sang from the heart.

> **It was the first time I had been to the studio with my father. I had no idea he was recording the track. Air London was full of people running back and forth but suddenly everything went quiet and dad held my hand and started singing 'Michelle' to me. It was such a special moment, the memory of which has stayed with me throughout my life. — Michele Monro**

Matt topped the bill on Anglia's *Saturday Variety*. Larry Grayson was booked in humorous support but after trouble from a stomach ulcer, he bowed out in readiness for his own series, which was due to start shortly. But very soon the roles were reversed when Matt had to cancel his appearance at Copford's Windmill in Essex when he was laid low with laryngitis.

One more session at Air London, a cholera shot, new suits delivered from his tailor and a trip to Qantas check-in at Heathrow on 25 August saw Matt heading back to Australia for a five-week tour. Tony and Jackie Trent were now living in Sydney and Matt made a point of seeing them whenever he was in town. The couple had kept in some form of contact ever since the Eurovision Song Contest and Matt had even recorded one of their songs, although it had been written for Frank Sinatra.

> **At the time Sinatra was dodging in and out of America to Acapulco to avoid the Establishment pursuing his alleged involvement with the Mafia. Frank cancelled the pre-booked recording session at the last minute, literally the day before, as other people would cancel a lunch appointment: studio, musicians – the lot. That was Frank! So we used up the recording time and orchestra with top session singers to make top class demos. They were sent out and Matt**

picked up on 'The Auction'. — Jackie Trent

Another familiar face was Shirley Bassey, who was now being managed by her husband Sergio Novak. There always seemed to be more time to relax with friends when he bumped into them abroad, without the distractions of the business at home. Matt also met up with Johnny Dankworth and Cleo Laine, who had come to see him in cabaret. After the show they went to a great steak restaurant that had been recommended. The T-bones were so big they hung off the plate. Cleo was amazed: "They put the biggest steak in front of us, which I couldn't get through, but Matt just kept going and going. He was one of my favourite singers. I loved him and he was great fun to be with. We saw more of each other on the road than we saw each other in Britain."

Matt had started drinking again. He had suffered from agonising pain since his trip to Brecqhou and later confessed to a doctor that he'd been plagued by bouts of depression. The suicide of two of his friends had affected the singer deeply, and he felt dreadful that he hadn't managed to do anything to prevent their deaths.

> **One could have been Mike Holiday. I remember when I was working with Matt and we were doing the Northern clubs. We were on a train either going or coming back from Manchester and Mike Holiday was on the train alone. I thought it so sad that he actually got that troubled by what he was doing because he was so popular.**
> **— Colin Keyes**

Though Mike's death saddened the singer deeply, he was more affected by Tony Hancock's suicide. Living with the knowledge that someone near and dear to you has not only died, but has given in to suicide is traumatic. You can only try and imagine the torment that must have coursed through their veins, tortured souls who, for those few minutes, lose their mind and make the ultimate sacrifice. Mickie herself was to lose her own brother Ernie to the disease nine years later. Thankfully Matt's depression was never severe enough for him to fall victim to moments of insanity. He loved life, loved his family and loved his friends. Unfortunately, it was that same intense emotional connection he had to his loved ones that led to Matt drinking when he was on tour. He felt bereft and sometimes singing wasn't enough. He was quoted as saying, "When I'm away I miss the family something terrible. If I'm away too long I start to do bad performances", but it is unlikely that anyone else was witness to a bad performance; it is something Matt felt, not what an audience observed. Hotel suites have no personality and they certainly don't exude a feeling of homeliness. With Matt spending so much time on the road, it is not surprising that he suffered from homesickness. He always said that he lived out of suitcases so much that he forgot what it was like to open a drawer. One thing that did help was his unique ability to sit down for hours and do absolutely nothing, not even think. It was an extraordinary gift of total relaxation.

Matt often lamented about his own siblings. He didn't see much of his brothers and sisters, although he always rang them after returning from long stretches abroad. His siblings never bothered to ring unless there was a particular reason, though they always accepted any free tickets that were offered to see their brother perform, and Caesar's Palace was near enough to all of them to be geographically viable. It hurt Matt terribly in earlier years that a gulf had grown between them, especially after the row he had with his sister Alice over their mother's wedding ring. Len didn't help the situation, fuelling his wife's emotions with opinions of Matt's selfishness and that he should have done more for the family. They felt they were owed something – in fact a letter after Matt's death from Len Carron stated just that. When Matt was a young lad his sister had lent him the odd pound here and there, as did all his brothers; after all he was the youngest and the only one living with and looking after their mother. Len felt that the debt still stood! Although full of bitterness after Matt's death, he never brought any of these feelings to the table while Matt was alive.

We all went to see him sing over the years. I last saw him at Caesar's Palace in Luton in the early 1970s where he spoke to me in the audience in the middle of his act. We spoke again after the show but unfortunately I had drunk too much and passed out in the loo – humiliating. — Christine Parsons

Spending time with Colin Keyes did, however, alleviate Matt's loneliness somewhat. They would spend hours talking about music and the friendship that grew would last them a lifetime and extend outside the parameters of work. Shortly after the tour concluded, Matt and Mickie solemnly undertook the task of acting as Godparents to Colin and Pam's daughter Victoria.

In between taping the *Nana Mouskouri Show*, *Saturday Variety* and the *Reg Varney Revue*, Matt attended rehearsals for that night's Grand Order of Water Rats Ball at London's Grosvenor House Hotel, which is always held on the last Sunday in

Brothers & Sisters

November. He was one of the surprise star guests taking part in the cabaret. Colin was leaving Matt's employment and arranged for new hopeful Tony Stenson to meet the singer during the band call.

> **The reason I left Matt was it reached a point where I desperately wanted to get into television on a regular basis. I'd met Des sometime earlier; of all places Newcastle station platform. He very fairly said, "I would never ask you to leave Matt, but if you ever feel that you want a change, give me a call." It just seemed the right move at the time. — Colin Keyes**

At the end of 1972, Equity Australia announced that certain British entertainers were to be barred from performing on their lucrative club circuit. They'd put together a blacklist, which included Matt, Max Bygraves, Ronnie Ronaldo and several others. The ban was designed to give Australian performers a greater share of the bookings at local clubs, which paid huge fees for top talent. Equity felt the venues were paying inflated fees to foreign artists and Hal Lashwood, president of the union, threatened that if bookers tried to import international performers the artists would be blackballed. The move was firmly resisted by the booking agencies and club managements. Nobody actually knew whether Equity had the power to impose the ban, but a spokesman for the clubs declared they would fight them all the way. Matt had been touring Australia successfully for years and a ban like that could have had a huge detrimental effect on business. Fortunately Equity's plans didn't hamper the singer's return as he wasn't due to play there until early 1975, and the arguments had all blown over by then.

1973 saw the release of Matt's first album of new material for three years, but neither *For the Present* nor the single 'I Am' made it to the charts. Hours after Big Ben rang in the New Year, Matt was already in the studios recording another album, *The Other Side of the Stars*, but nothing excited him musically; he didn't feel any of the material he had been given was worthy of a hit.

Matt took to the usual club circuit, appearing at the Wakefield Theatre Club, Alison's Theatre in Liverpool and the Broadway Club in Oldham before flying to Holland at the beginning of February. Although there was a lot of travelling involved in any one year, Matt's gigs were always in week blocks at the clubs, which gave him a chance to settle in to his surroundings. The Oldham gig was no different from any other except that he had a new musical director on board. Tony Stenson never actually auditioned for the job. Colin invited him to play keyboards on one of Matt's shows whilst he conducted, so a report could be written on the pianist's ability.

> Matt seldom came along to a band call, but always wanted to know how it went and what the band was like and if there were likely to be any problems. He was fairly laid back about the shows as a rule. Apart from changing the running order from time to time, very little new material was added. Matt told me he'd spent a considerable amount of time and money on a complete new set of songs only to realise that what people wanted to hear most were the old familiar ones that he was associated with. I loved conducting the gigs when we had a fuller orchestral backing with strings, brass and percussion and we could dig out those gorgeous Johnny Spence arrangements – what joy! — Tony Stenson

Matt and Mickie were nearly set for their trip to Caracas as guests of the Venezuelan government. There was just one slight problem. Mickie had recently slipped two discs in her lower back and the doctor's advice had been to wear a plaster cast but she had turned the suggestion down. Instead she had been laid up with agonising back pain and with the flight to South America looming it looked like she would have to stay behind. Living with constant pain is a miserable distortion of life. Living on heavy drugs is not much better and Matt's wife had suffered with disc problems for years. The night before flying to South America, her back gave out completely and she found herself on all fours unable to straighten up. Matt believed in spirit healing, despite doctors usually explaining away certain miraculous cure stories as spontaneous remission. He rang noted healer Ted Fricker, who agreed to see Mickie at a moment's notice. The pain was excruciating and even getting into the taxi was difficult. Looking more like a corporate executive than a spiritual healer, Fricker's cheerful personality and complete confidence soon put an apprehensive Mickie at ease. He began rubbing his hand over her back, and Mickie felt instantly relaxed. She didn't feel any change during the session but he did manage to straighten her back. The result was dramatic. She fell asleep on the plane and woke up in Guadeloupe, and while disembarking the aircraft realised that the pain was entirely gone.

The couple flew via Paris and Martinique before landing at Guadeloupe; this was Mickie's first flight on a jumbo jet and she marvelled at the technology, but like so many other passengers, she did quietly wonder how the metal monster was staying in the air. They travelled with John Barry, Vic and Jill Lewis and Don and Shirley Black to attend the National Concert and after an early night the party caught a flight to Caracas.

Katerina Valente and Matt were performing in Caracas for the Onda Nueva Festival, which opened at the Teatro Municipal. The arena erupted into chaos when bombs were suddenly detonated in the crowds, and several unknown gunmen opened fire. A blanket of armed guards rushed in to secure the scene while a traumatised crowd looked on in horror. The old adage 'the show must go on' was paramount to all the performers and after order had finally been restored Matt mounted the stage to perform his segment of the show. Although the singer presented a calm exterior, he felt rather vulnerable standing on the raised open platform and was secretly worried for his own safety and that of his wife and friends.

Although the trip was only a week, Matt enjoyed spending the time with John Barry. They hadn't seen each other for some time and the composer told Matt he was already formulating plans to leave England because of tax problems. In fact John was forced to leave the country in 1975, spending a year in Majorca. He was later commissioned to score an American special in Los Angeles, which required six weeks of his time. He stayed twenty years!

At Barry's insistence, the Monros tried out a new holiday destination. John was adamant Barbados was *the* place to go. In the early 70s package tours to these

Matt & Mickie, Settler's Beach Hotel, Barbados

remote Caribbean islands were a thing of the future; in fact, very few people in England had ever heard of the place. Flights had to be booked independently, as did the hotel, and the couple picked a small resort of only twenty-four bungalows right by the water, called Settler's Beach. It was the most wonderful place: total peace, quiet and relaxation. The bungalow even came equipped with a television set. Broadcasts were extremely limited but it didn't bother Matt, who used to sit watching black and white re-runs of *The Outer Limits* and *Peyton Place*. Another foible of the star was that whenever he was based abroad for a few weeks he had *The Daily Express* delivered from England. He used to sit on a lounger doing the daily crossword, while Mickie tanned herself.

Because of the seclusion of the island, it was a rarity for anyone to approach the singer looking for an autograph, although the hotel management weren't shy about coming forward. The island became the retreat for many artists over the next five years and Mickie and Matt often met up with Doreen and Ernie Wise, who stayed at The Coral Reef Resort next door. The holiday had only been booked for two weeks in case they hadn't liked it, but future trips were extended and included their children. By the time he got back to England, Matt looked tanned and refreshed and was

Matt & Ernie Wise in Barbados

raring to go back to work. Dropping Mickie off at home, he grabbed his working case and headed to Toronto with Tony Stenson. They were booked into the Beverley Hills Hotel and as well as twelve days playing in the Seaway Room, Matt also managed to squeeze in time to do *Open House Live* for BBC Radio and a CBS Television Special *Band Wagon*.

> **The first time we travelled abroad was to Toronto. The venue was a large hotel with an integral stage. I remember the Everly Brothers were just finishing their week's engagement and we caught their last show. Matt liked to socialize and have people to chat to after the shows. It was a sort of unwritten part of the contract that I stayed around and joined in whenever possible. Sometimes we went for a meal, sometimes we stayed on at the venue and sometimes he invited me back to his room at the hotel for a nightcap. It depended on the circumstances. I recall being in a recording studio once with Matt in Toronto and him saying that he'd like me to meet a friend of his who had just popped in to listen, and turning round to find Oscar Peterson sitting there! Wow! — Tony Stenson**

It was slightly surreal that one moment you were in Toronto enjoying the hospitality of the country and in one blink of an eye you were back in Blighty performing at Talk of the North in Eccles and then the Talk of the Midlands in Derby. The clubs were used to providing a trio but Matt wanted a better show and the only way to achieve that was to add extra musicians. Three trumpets, two trombones, one alto sax doubling as flute, one tenor sax doubling as clarinet and one baritone sax doubling bass clarinet gave Matt the sound he wanted, but he was left to pay the extra costs. The clubs were happy to have a better show but reluctant to pay for it. At an extra six pounds per man per night, Matt felt the audience deserved the expense.

His Dutch appearance a few months back had been received so well that the singer was offered his own television programme for TV Holland. It was simply called the *Matt Monro Special* and recorded on 11 May at Hilversum. Matt and Mickie checked into the hotel but were given a room with twin beds. They asked that the beds be pushed together after being told there were no double bedrooms available. The consequence was that sometime during the night, both Matt and Mickie fell through the gap between the beds as the castor legs gently rolled away from each other and landed on the floor. They stayed there for quite a while!

An unprecedented demand for tickets meant that Matt had to give three shows at Hereford's Crystal Room on the Thursday, Friday and Saturday following his return. The couple stayed at the Green Dragon Hotel. During the early hours of Friday morning the hotel's fire alarms were set off and several sleepy people congregated outside at the central safety point. Matt and Mickie slept through the whole evacuation. The hotel management were quickly able to determine there wasn't in fact a fire and left the singer and his wife asleep to catch up with events at breakfast the next morning.

> **Polish and poise. It's the essence of any performance by Matt Monro. And the minute he walked on stage last night it was apparent his audience knew how to appreciate such qualities. Seeing him perform live for the first time was to realise he is not just a superb singer, his between-numbers patter showed him also as an accomplished comedian. The audience was, no doubt, composed of Monro fans, but the way they cried for more and still more at the end of the night was quite a sight. The three times he returned to the stage seemed hardly to satisfy his admirers. I am glad to say I was one of them. — *Evening Echo***

Most stars are acutely aware of their celebrity and create a divide between themselves and members of the public. Matt was the complete opposite of the archetypal star. He didn't believe in official fan clubs, preferring to respond to each letter personally and in his own handwriting. He used to spend every day between shows catching up on mail. Every evening was a test; every audience you played, a new challenge.

Matt's popularity was the measure of the man; he had the durable talent as well as out-and-out class to survive any passing fad in the notoriously fickle world of pop music and he connected with his fans. It didn't just relate to one age bracket.

> The air in the Manchester nightclub was blue with smoke. Most of the evening had seeped away, and the tables were littered with full ashtrays and empty glasses. Noisy non-stop chatter echoed from table to table, and a group of long-haired lads beside me drummed the back of their chairs impatiently as they waited for the cabaret to begin. Who's Matt Monro anyway? the youngest asked sarcastically. Oh you know that oldie that sings like Frank Sinatra, his mate answered. It's going to be a bore, but we can always tell jokes. Ten minutes later the whole six of them were silent, cigarettes burning away unnoticed, eyes riveted on the stage. Then they were up on their feet applauding and cheering loudly. Oldie or not, forty-plus and singing the frankly sentimental 'Theme from the Godfather', Matt Monro had his audience from teenagers upwards, conquered by the sheer power of his personality and the superb mature strength of his singing. By the end of the act the top of the pops contingent at the next table were eating out of his hand.(...) It was the kind of performance that had STAR written all over it in big letters, and explained why Matt Monro is one of the biggest international draws in Las Vegas, Australia, America, Canada, Hong Kong, South America, the Philippines, Japan, and all points exotic. — *Scottish Daily Express*

But not every audience was as accommodating. One night a man was continuously blowing raspberries, another was giving Matt two fingers throughout the act, and yet another was being sick all over his table.

> The previous day can depress you as a singer, just as a bad previous result can put a football team back on their heels and cause them to lose confidence. When I go on tonight I'll have self-doubts and

Talk of the Town

really have to start from square one. That is why the people around me like my musical director Tony Stenson are so important. You've just got to have a good team with you.
— Matt Monro

The lead up to Matt's sixth appearance at London's Talk of the Town saw rehearsals take place in the Dubarry Suite in the Café Royal. The four-week run in Robert Nesbitt's *Dream Machine Revue* was as well received as any other. This outing saw Matt add a string section plus an extra trombone and saxophone player.

One of the joys of working London's premier venue was that as well as getting home to his own bed every night, many friends would pop their heads in and the room afforded the most wonderful atmosphere. It wasn't just Matt that was affected by extensive touring and long stints on the road. The downside of touring for Tony was being away from home. He was married with two young children and you had to be totally committed to your art to give up seeing your children grow up. Matt missed nearly every birthday and holiday with his family, and over the years a multitude of telegrams piled up for all the missed occasions. Matt was, however, in England when Michele was rushed into University College Hospital to have her tonsils removed. Having been unwell for weeks with suspected tonsillitis, it was only on seeing a specialist after Michele's symptoms had worsened that quinsy was diagnosed. The infection is more serious than tonsillitis, with potentially devastating or fatal consequences, and because the large pus sac attached to her tonsil was in danger of bursting at any moment it necessitated emergency surgery. Though Matt missed the main event, he turned up at his daughter's hospital bedside after a function at the Palladium with an autograph from Elton John in hand. The extraverted pop showman was one of Michele's favourite singers at the time, so Matt was forgiven.

It wouldn't be long before Matt would see himself resident in the private wing of the University College Hospital, facing a sinus operation. Matt was surprisingly relaxed for a man who could have a totally different voice in a few weeks. Surely he had a few nagging fears as to what this relatively common surgery with Mr Musgrove would hold for him? At worst it could affect the resonance of his voice so that the days of hits like 'Born Free' and 'Walk Away' would be gone for good, or only repeated if he could retrain his voice to an equally relaxed and pleasing style. Matt was philosophical about the surgery, and in fact was quick to point out that, far from reducing the quality of his singing, it might even give him more power by aiding his breathing and giving him a new range and control.

> **I've had this problem some time and it's not helped by my smoking, as much as I do. Once I've had the operation I'll convalesce and then fit in a holiday with my family. And I'll test my new voice out in the bathroom and then I'll know just how much life there is left in this old guy. — Matt Monro**

There was plenty of life left in the singer at Bailey's nightclub, even though the odds were against him in that the audience was not totally 'his by nature'. He was topping the bill on a night that had opened with the semi-final of a nationwide talent contest. The competition was won, amid thunderous applause, by Showaddywaddy, a Leicester rock and roll group whose electrifying act did a good deal to pack the two thousand capacity club in Leicester. While there was no out-and-out disregard for the calmer Monro style, the high spot of the evening had obviously come and gone for a good many of the patrons. Youngsters agitatedly waited for the restart of the disco, and the supporters of the losing semi-finalists filed out to catch buses back home.

It was amazing how totally unsuitable some of these bookings were; his management consistently failed to check the clubs out or determine what age groups the venues attracted. Matt could only put his foot down after such an appearance. He didn't feel it was his job to vet the venues – that should have been done for him.

Coming home was always a comfort and even though Matt had just been told that Dallas Road was now valued at considerably more than he'd paid for it, he would certainly not consider moving anytime soon, not after having the builders in for nearly two years at the outset. Four years later Matt and Mickie had braved the process again and added an extension to the side of the house, creating two more rooms, a downstairs den for the children and their friends and a separate en-suite dressing room area for Matt. The builders had been there constantly since the previous August, and Matt and Mickie were glad to see the back of them. Having finally created the perfect family home, the couple were very proud of the results, so much so that, eight years after moving in, they at long last threw a house-warming party. With over a hundred guests, Mickie did the sensible thing and hired a caterer. Gold chairs to match the décor were brought in and a bar set up in the hallway. Maurice Woodruff, Mike and Bernie Winters, Russ Conway, Sid and Val James, Warren and Connie Mitchell, Tom Jones, Petula Clark, Val Doonican and Glenda Kentridge were just a few of the guests that came to raise a glass.

ONCE A RAT, ALWAYS A RAT

The Grand Order of Water Rats is the oldest and most famous show business charity organisation in the world. They were formed by a group of Music Hall artists in 1889 that owned a trotting horse called 'The Magpie', the winner of several races in London. They used the winnings to help other performers who were in need and to fund soup kitchens in London's East End. The name came from a bus driver who passed comment during a downpour – "Trotting pony? It looks more like a drowned rat!" That gave inspiration to the group, who excitedly realised that 'rats' spelled backwards was STAR. It couldn't have been more perfect, and so the fraternity was born.

These are the Freemasons of show business. It was, and is still not easy to join the society, as a prospective candidate requires a vote from ninety percent of the members. To belong to such an exclusive fraternity is therefore a much-prized honour for performers. Members include some of the biggest star names in Britain and Hollywood; others are as widely dispersed as Australia, Africa and Spain.

The little golden Water Rat emblem is worn with pride and signifies membership of a special brotherhood, in which race, colour or creed has no relevance. The emblem must be worn at all times and being caught without it could lead to an instant fine from another member. The GOWR base was the Eccentric Club in Ryder Street, although the organisation has since moved to Gray's Inn Road in London, with Lodge taking place every Sunday. If you had an ear to the door you could hear the members chanting the signature song that opens every meeting.

'This is the emblem of our society
Each member acts with the greatest propriety
Jolly Old Sports! To us they raise their hats

Mickie, Freddie & Vanessa Davies & Matt

A jolly lot of fellows are the Water Rats
Rats, Rats, Rats'

Matt was initiated into the Order on 7 October 1973 and paid £40.95 for his entrance fee and annual subscription. It was probably one of the more exciting cheques he had written in his life. Proposed by David Nixon and seconded by Past King Rat George Martin, Matt was now a member of one of the most elite show business groups in the world. At each meeting, every member wore their own collar designating their rank in the society. The ultimate accolade for a member was to be voted King Rat. Their task was to preside for one year over the Lodges and oversee the charitable works of the Order.

> My friend Matt was also a brother Water Rat and I had great pleasure in picking him up from his house in Ealing and taking him for his initiation ceremony at the Eccentric Club in St James. I remember how nervous he was and how thrilled and proud to be admitted as a member of this wonderful theatrical charitable organisation. — Freddie Davies

Although Matt's commitment to the Water Rats was no less than one hundred percent, he still felt very strongly for a charity he had supported for years. Pupils at Crosshill School, Blackburn got an extraordinary surprise when their new coach pulled up outside the main gates, driven by one international singing star! The Manchester branch of the Variety Club of Great Britain provided the vehicle so that the children with learning difficulties would be able to get out and about with ease.

After the last of his dates in Manchester, Matt drove through the night so he could keep to his schedule. He was booked into Air London to record a new single, which was to be issued twelve days later. Earlier that year, Simon Park had taken 'Eye Level' to number one in the British charts. The instrumental was the theme to a popular television series about a Dutch detective called *Van Der Valk* and it spent nearly six months in the chart. Matt had just moved back to EMI and his first single was a vocal version of the successful theme. Once again the *Van Der Valk* magic spawned a hit single and Matt took 'And You Smiled' into the Top 30.

You may have felt you'd had a sufficiency of the Eye Level theme from *Van Der Valk*, but now they've added words to it, and there's none better to sing that kind of melodious mixture than Matt. He really is a remarkable professional at-ease sort of singer – and I'm herewith guaranteeing the tune will be a big hit all over again. — *Record Mirror*

Matt wasn't particularly happy about his recording sessions. He had nothing against John Burgess, who was a competent producer, but unlike his times with George Martin, he was now paired with a medley of A&R men including Peter Sullivan, another partner at Air London, and later Terry Brown. It was all rather disconcerting. Matt liked stability in the studio and he resented the presence of these minders who watched over him. It made him feel that he had lost the company's confidence – not vocally but in his ability to produce another chart hit. It was Catch 22 – he wasn't getting the right material to record, so hit records were very hard to come by. A rush of compilations appeared on the market to cash in on Matt's chart return, but surprisingly EMI didn't release a follow-up single until eight months later with 'Darling Come Home Soon'. That was to be the only 'new' release in 1974.

The *Van Der Valk* theme had to be incorporated into Matt's act. The New Cresta, Birmingham, Wooky Hollow, Liverpool and Helmaen Country Club in Usk were all treated to the chart topper. The Helmaen was way out in the sticks but within easy reach from a variety of directions. It would have been a relatively short journey from London if Matt hadn't got lost on the final leg of the journey.

Matt and I worked together in cabaret and on one occasion we appeared at a theatre club in Usk, South Wales. We were following Tommy Cooper who had just finished his week at the club on the Saturday. We arrived at the hotel on Sunday afternoon and found Tommy sat at the bar, taxi waiting outside – it had been there since the previous evening! Saying our hellos and goodbyes we went off to rehearsal at the club leaving Tommy at the bar and he was still there after we'd finished that night at midnight – the taxi was still waiting. — Freddie Davies

Leaving Tommy Cooper propping up the bar at the hotel, Matt, Freddie and Johnnie Spence headed off for rehearsals. Johnnie had been conducting with Matt as 'special guest' whenever time permitted. Although he had plenty of work in the book, he was loath to give up gigs with the singer as they always had the best of times. Unfortunately for Johnnie, that was not the case at Usk. The stage lights were so powerful that they blinded every artist they were trained on, making it impossible to see anything. Johnnie was attempting to lay white tape strips along the stage floor to act as a buffer, so Matt didn't fall off the raised stage during the performance. Matt didn't – but Johnnie did, straight into the orchestra pit, breaking his leg in the process. Vic Lewis was requisitioned to push the tetchy musician's wheelchair. He accompanied Johnnie everywhere including the studios, where the maestro led the orchestra from a seated position. He even took him to have the plaster checked. Unfortunately Vic banged his chair-bound hostage into one of the hospital's double barrel doors, which did not assume the swing position. It was a good job that Johnnie was already in the hospital, as he had to have the plaster removed and a new one put on.

Matt's depression had escalated over the past few months. He wasn't happy with EMI or about the work Don and his team were providing. While the diary was not empty, it certainly wasn't brimming with the prestige dates Matt might have expected, and he was being passed over for engagements such as the London Palladium and the Royal Variety Show. It had been eight years since Matt had been invited to appear on the show, and he didn't seem to be any closer to a second booking or indeed an offer of his own series. Matt's drinking had increased over the weeks. There were no outward indications, but he was pouring a scotch in the mornings to get himself through the day.

Matt was suddenly taken ill and was in bed with a stomach ailment. He had to cancel a New York cabaret spot, a trip to Holland and an appearance on ITV's *The*

Golden Shot. The doctor diagnosed gastro-enteritis and that's what the newspapers reported.

> **Mr Monro stated the problem was simply that he enjoys having a drink. There have been times during the last three or four years when he has felt that it was getting too much, mainly because of morning sickness and a few amnesic blackouts. He has never until the past week missed an engagement because of alcohol and has never had the DT's. About two years ago he suffered an epileptic fit, this was carefully investigated and no organic cause was found. He knows that liver tests in 1969 and 1971 were abnormal. In the last few weeks he has been drinking more and the weekend before I saw him had been unable to perform because he was so ill on a Sunday morning. He has cut down his drinking and had experienced two further fits. His appetite has been much less and he has lost about a stone of weight. He occasionally has depressed feelings but these never amount to much. I did not think he was significantly depressed and I think that his alcoholism is largely environmental. I outlined the various pieces of evidence pointing to the damage that alcohol was doing to him and he agreed to stop. I have arranged to see him again on the 18 January. — Doctor's Report**

> **I saw Mr Monro again today and was pleased with his progress. He told me that he was drinking one whisky at night but nothing else and was feeling much better. He was free of tremor and looked much fitter. He told me he was sleeping well and had regained about 5lbs of his weight loss. His only problem was that he had not yet acquired his full vitality and was planning to start playing golf again, after a lapse of two years. Consequently I was dismayed to hear your report on the telephone today. I will see him on 25 January unless I hear contrary from you. — Doctor's Report**

Matt and Mickie flew to Barbados for a couple of weeks. It was thought the best way to get him away from his habitual environment where the need to socialise was of paramount importance. It would also be easier for Mickie to monitor her husband's drinking if they were in close quarters. The rest did him good and with the aid of sun-

bronzed skin he looked healthier each day. Returning to England, Matt saw Mr Baker, a specialist in Harley Street on a regular basis and admitted his consumption had been increasing and had been clearly excessive on one or two occasions. He agreed to stop completely. Now he was over the stomach illness he was back at work, and after a successful week at the Wakefield Theatre Club he flew to Holland to sing at a big charity gala for UNICEF.

Don had been absorbed in writing a second musical and now finally *Billy Liar* was to open at the Theatre Royal in Drury Lane. Michael Crawford took the title role and turned *Billy* into a hit, establishing himself as a major star in the process. Don invited every big name he could think of to the opening, including the British Prime Minister Edward Heath. The reviews were excellent and the show would go on to play for almost three years. The lyricist also developed six more musical movie scores, including another outing with Bond and an Oscar nomination for 'Wherever Love Takes Me' for the film *Gold*.

Matt's booking at Drake's Country & Leisure Hotel was in the aftermath of a terrible UVF (Ulster Volunteer Force) bombing in Dublin on 17 May, which had killed thirty-eight people and injured one hundred. Entire families were wiped out and the area was awash with misery. There was heightened security everywhere and Matt entered the auditorium flanked by several burly minders. Frederick Boylan was sitting in the audience with his parents. He had been a fan since his youth but this was his first opportunity of seeing the singer perform live.

I have fond memories of the one and only time I saw the great Matt Monro perform live. It was in my native Dublin in 1974. Bombs had gone off in the city and the atmosphere was one of shock and disbelief. Performers were edgy and I recall Cliff Richard cancelled his dates, as did the group Paper Lace. One man however was not going to be deterred... Matt Monro appeared on RTE (Irish National Broadcaster) and said, "I'm here to make people happy... I'll appear no matter what" and that's just what he did. — Frederick Boylan

Safely back from Dublin, Matt's next outing was three days with the legendary comedic magician Tommy Cooper. Matt absolutely loved Cooper and his ability to make things look outside of his control. He worked extremely hard at ensuring that everything he touched had disastrous consequences – his props would either fall apart, crumble, collapse, disintegrate, topple over or refuse to work. His genius lay in his expert timing and his ham-fisted portrayal of a gawky magician whose every failure captivated his audience. The biggest laughs came from his quick-fire magic tricks and his cheerfulness following each disastrous outcome. He would show his audience a white handkerchief with black spots, promising the spots would vanish, which they did – when he shook them to the floor. While the crowd were still laughing from his clownish behaviour he was already into his next gag. "I went out for a meal and ordered the whole menu in French – my friends were impressed – it was a Chinese restaurant." "I went to the doctor and said doctor it hurts when I touch my neck – he says don't touch your neck." The audience didn't care how silly the joke was, it was nonsense at its best. Matt enjoyed doing the shows, and his drinking buddies over the week included Tommy, Bob Todd, Tommy Godfrey and Kerry Jewel. Despite promises to his doctor to the contrary, Matt joined in helping his friends drink the bar dry.

Kerry Jewel had been booked to do the warm up and was delighted to find he was working with Matt again. He had compèred a couple of Sunday concerts with him in the past and they'd got on like a house on fire. Kerry's father was the legendary Jimmy Jewel who had worked a double act with partner Ben Warris. Kerry's disadvantage as a comic was he was never a very funny man, but he was an excellent raconteur who knew his stagecraft and had impeccable timing. He presented himself

Michael Black, Sid James, Matt & Jack Slipper

well, wearing handmade suits by Cyril Castle in Saville Row and Robbie Stanford, tailor to the stars. He was never aggressive with an audience and never swore on stage but at home he had a steel worker's mouth. Kerry very nearly left the business after a booking arranged for him by Michael Black.

His agent Tito Burns had placed Kerry on a long tour with Sacha Distel, ending with a season at the Palladium. Lindsay De Paul and Mike Reid were also on the bill and the show was very successful, so it remained a mystery to Kerry as to why he wasn't getting much work. Tito arranged a meeting with Michael Black. Kerry was suitably impressed on entering the office to find the walls full of framed photographs of Michael with a catalogue of prominent people, including Sammy Davis Jr, Frank Sinatra and even the Pope. It took him a while to realise that Michael's head had been superimposed on other people's bodies! The agent was an outlandish character, with a wonderful sense of humour. Sometimes, when ringing the office, you would hear Sinatra singing in the background with Michael shouting, "Take five Frank. I can't hear a bloody thing." Or on another occasion his secretary would answer and say Michael was in the pool and would ring you back later. Michael didn't have a pool!

Michael convinced Kerry that not only did he have the perfect job for him, but it would also make him the most sought after comic on the circuit. The venue was the American Sporting Club in the Grand Ballroom of the Grosvenor House Hotel, where Kerry was meant to entertain the crowds at a boxing match. Kerry had never done a stag night in his life and was intimidated by an audience full of contrast: thugs and villains bearing the scars of broken noses and cauliflower ears dressed in the best that Savile Row had to offer. He sat at the top table with Jack Solomon, Henry Cooper, Michael Black and Reg Gutteridge, a sports commentator and writer for the *Evening Standard*. In the middle of the smoky room sat the boxing ring. Kerry's job was that of the 'last bell ringer', which was the fifteen-minute spot before the last big fight of the night. Reg Gutteridge was the first speaker of the evening and used the opening line, "What the fuck am I doing talking to you fucking cunts," which raised spontaneous laughter around the room. Fear surged through Kerry's body and he knew he was about to be battered worse than any boxer that night. And he was (albeit verbally). As soon as he could, he fled the scene and sought solace with his friend Roy Castle, who was doing a cabaret spot at the Royal Lancaster a few minutes away. Several large drinks later he was still shaking and visibly upset. That was the last of his dealings with Michael Black.

Not many new record companies could claim to start with such a spectacular introduction as Sunday's show at the London Palladium to launch the Charlie Stable record label. On 27 June, The Henry Hadaway Organisation presented Matt with support from Tommy Trinder, Bill McGuffie, Dailey and Wayne, Max Wall, Alton Douglas, Garfield Demango, Austin Kent, Sid Gately and Anne Beverley with backing from Bert Rhodes and his Talk of the Town Orchestra.

Compère of the proceedings and the first comedian on stage was Tommy Trinder. He was marvellous, as was Max Wall, who was regarded in and out of show business as a comic genius. Matt, the star of the show, had the audience eating out of the palm of his hand. His medley of songs showcased the very limits of his excellent voice and proved beyond doubt that he was still right up there in the superstar class. The show was a roaring success.

Matt talked at length to British Music Hall veteran Tommy Trinder. He was a fellow Cockney, and although Matt recognised his undoubtable talent he was at a loss to know how Trinder had played twelve Royal Variety Performances, as well as appearances before royalty at Windsor Castle, Balmoral and Buckingham Palace, while he was ignored when it came to booking these same shows.

Matt was still not feeling well, and had been referred to Professor Sheila Sherlock at the Royal Free Hospital in London. On examination the patient's liver was found to be enlarged and a needle biopsy showed acute alcoholic hepatitis. There was considerable fibrosis but no clear-cut evidence of cirrhosis. The biopsy results were surprisingly good for the size of the liver and taking into consideration the number of years that the patient had been drinking. The Professor felt that if Matt could be persuaded to abstain, he should do very well indeed.

The subsequent follow-up appointment saw Professor Sherlock extremely pleased with Matt's efforts. His biochemical tests continued to improve, enzyme levels had fallen and proteins had risen. A further appointment was booked for six months later. Life carried on for the singer, and the month brought the fruition of a new album – this time a compilation of what were considered his best presentations.

On 29 July 1974 Matt had a date with BBC Radio 2 at Golders Green, where he recorded four programmes in the one day: *The Early Show*, *The Joe Henderson Show*, *The Tony Brandon Show* and *Night Ride*. It was a pleasure working with such great musicians, unlike his Wakefield Festival opening. Matt opened his show with 'Around the World', which went down well, but as the evening passed, he and the orchestra lost co-ordination. One realised that apart from Monro having had no time for a full rehearsal, the orchestra, including instrumentalists from the Halle, Willie Hirst's Orchestra and the Northern Lights Orchestra had all suffered the same problem. However, after the interval everything seemed to fall into place and the musicians became more polished. The encore number 'Born Free' attracted so much applause that Matt returned with 'Portrait', which earned a standing ovation.

The whole family headed off to Barbados for three weeks. Matt loved spending time with his children and was a caring and excellent father. Incredibly, thanks to Mickie's sacrifice in staying home with them in their formative years, they had both grown up protected from unwanted media attention. This of course was largely due to Matt having to absent himself from school sports days, ballet recitals, football games and Girl Guide badge presentations. If he did attend, the focus was aimed towards him, and the event would turn into an autograph-grabbing debacle rather than a private family moment.

Although well grounded, Matthew did go through phases of craving attention from his absentee parents: the doorbell rang and the vicar politely asked for his pool table back; he cooked marshmallows in the back garden using petrol to light the fire (nearly burning the house down in the process); he sent blackmail letters to neighbours (but was found out because he'd put his address on them) and he even took an accidental overdose while Matt and Mickie were in South Africa.

Michele, on the other hand, got away with murder. One day, the house was rather too quiet and Mickie went to see where the children were. Michele and her cousin Gary had spent the afternoon drawing pretty pictures on the garage walls with crayons. She successfully blamed her brother! She also wrapped Matthew up in her

Michele & Matt

dolls' pram and took him for a walk round the block, letting go of the carriage at the peak of the hill to see what would happen. Nothing did happen to her sibling, but a Vauxhall did incur a few bumps when it swerved to avoid the oncoming contraption and hit a lamppost instead. She also thought it fun to wrap him up in cling film, although she did gouge out slots for his nose and mouth, leaving him to fend for himself when she got bored. Hugely excited at the prospect of being left alone in the house when her parents went away on one of their trips, Michele decided to throw a large party in the back garden without her parents' knowledge. Though she had secretly harboured the fantasy of an unsupervised shindig and the anticipation of something so taboo had been shamelessly exhilarating, the reality of the evening was not what she expected. She was so fed up by the end of the night with gatecrashers and thrower-uppers that she rang the police anonymously and complained about the noise. It didn't take them long to turn up and throw everyone out!

These were all merely cries for attention, but the extended trips on holidays with their parents made up for a lot. They both knew their father loved them unequivocally and when they did spend time together, he always listened to the mundane stories of their world, feigning huge interest in the little details of their lives.

News of the popularity of the Caribbean island had spread and Matt himself had extolled the virtues of the exotic location to countless friends and colleagues. He even encouraged John Burgess to take his holiday there – but John very nearly didn't come back!

> **One year he persuaded my family to take a villa in Barbados close to his. We all decided to take the local cruise on the Jolly Roger pirate ship, which was lashing out ridiculous amounts of the local rum punch. I well over indulged and back at our beach decided to walk out to sea, aiming to reach the far horizon. I would have drowned quite happily if Matt had not followed me, well out of his depth, and dragged me to safety. — John Burgess**

Matt always felt so much better after a break with his family, but although he needed the stability of firm roots he also felt an enormous draw to take to the road. When he didn't work he missed the applause and the adrenalin rush – he needed his audience. In fact he was in such a hurry to get to a gig in Caerphilly that he was fined eighteen pounds for driving at over ninety miles per hour on the M1.

He returned to Professor Sherlock and further blood tests were deemed excellent. The specialist reassured Matt about his liver but urged him to keep off alcohol. He was also complaining about various aches and pains, so he was referred on to Dr A T Richardson, their Consultant in Rheumatology.

Matt finally secured a solo concert spot with his own show *Matt Sings Monro*. Backed by a big band in Manchester, he sang some of his hit numbers as well as a few less familiar songs. Kerry Jewel was asked by the BBC to do the warm up for the television programme and the two men enjoyed catching up. After his debacle at the boxing evening he thought he'd never work again, but BBC producer Peter Ridsdale Scott had used Kerry for a programme called *Playschool* and booked him for Matt's television special on the strength of that performance. Between rehearsals Matt and Kerry went for a drink and indulged again after the show. Kerry was due to catch the last train back to London but woke up at Euston Station the next morning with an empty bottle of brandy beside him. He had no recollection of getting on the train. A week later he was doing his warm up for Thames Television and Matt filled him in on the details. They had gone to a club that was run by Johnnie Burns for drinks after the show. Kerry was slightly the worse for wear at the end of the night and Matt had driven the comic to Stockport and personally put him on a train home.

In the early days there was no late night television or video, so socialising was the only form of entertainment after a show. Every time I met up with Matt it was dangerous, because we would get pissed. We did a lot of shows together including a tour of Northern Ireland for four or five days for the Services. Matt was seventeen years older than me, the elder statesman of the drinkers. — Kerry Jewel

Matt's charity work was not neglected: as well as the numerous calls on his time by the Water Rats he also attended a Variety Club of Great Britain dinner in Leeds. It was a grand affair and the Queens Hotel was packed with visiting celebrities, the cream of the crop. Roger Moore, Cary Grant, David Niven, Dickie Henderson, Douglas Fairbanks Jr and Matt Monro were presented to Princess Alexander. In fact Mickie's legs had gone quite weak when Cary Grant sat next to her at breakfast the next morning. It would be a long time before she would forget that meal!

Matt's Christmas season was committed to London's Talk of the Town and he attended rehearsals with Tony Stenson and Burt Rhodes on 14 December. Burt was more than a little familiar with the singer's act after so many appearances at the prime venue that short work was made of band-call. Any artist who is invited back to Delfont's eatery with regularity must be an entertainer of distinction, and Matt, who was enjoying his sixth season there in ten years, justified the recognition. Robert Nesbitt's floorshow curtain raiser *A Touch of Venus* was a stalwart success, his ability to deliver consistent high-class revues was the reason the venue was recognised as one of the best nightclubs in the world. Performers often find cabaret tough going because of its constant chattering audience. Matt proved that even the most talkative could be silenced if there was something worth listening to.

The season finished on 4 January 1975, and within the week Matt, Mickie and Tony Stenson were heading off to Melbourne. Matt hadn't been back in nearly three years and his return was hailed as a great success. Malcolm Cooke, in association with HSV Channel Seven, laid on a twenty-three-piece orchestra for the star of *Summer in the City Music Festival*, which was held at the Sidney Myer Music Bowl. Even though it was supposed to be summer, the weather was cold and wintry. Matt's entrance was from the top of a huge flight of stairs that travelled down through the centre of the orchestra and onto the stage. His overture began and Matt stood at the top, paused for a few seconds and then made a slow descent, wrapped in a thick wool blanket. At the bottom of the stairs, while walking centre stage he threw it off, discarding it for the remainder of the show. The crowd went nuts, cheering and stamping their feet for several minutes. It was one of the best entrances Matt ever made.

Mickie had hoped the trip to Australia would have afforded them both some free time in between commitments, especially as her nephew Andy was living there. When her brother's divorce had come through, Diane took Andy and went to live in Australia while Ernie and their son Gary stayed in England. It was a shame that so many miles separated the young brothers, but it seemed to be the fairest solution for all parties at the time. Diane had remarried a young man called Graham Satterley, and it was Mickie's hope to visit everyone while they were there.

> **In Auckland everything was even more hectic as it was our first visit, more radio, television, newspaper interviews, press reception etc. The audiences have been simply terrific but of course so were the shows. Tonight is our last performance here and tomorrow night we leave for LA. In fact we leave at 12.40am Monday morning and arrive in California at 6.00pm on Sunday – work that out. That's because we cross the International Date Line. We have many people to see, many things to do so it will not be very restful but we are really looking forward to seeing Sid and Gert. We have not told them we are coming so it will be a big surprise. We will be home on the 12 February and then daddy will leave on Valentine's Day for three days in Dublin. — Letter from Mickie, White Heron Lodge, Auckland**

Crossing the International Date Line is one thing when you are on an aircraft, it had happened to Matt numerous time throughout his travels, but whilst appearing on the Gold Coast in Australia, he nearly missed a show when he didn't realise that the time in the club across the road where he was performing that night was actually one hour later than in his hotel. The time zone went right through the road between the two locations. He came off stage and was back in his hotel room before he had even technically gone on stage, which made for hilarious confusion.

Arriving in New Zealand, the seasoned traveller took to the stage at both Morris's Peter Pan and the Ranch House on the North Shore in Auckland. It was his first trip to the area, but Matt couldn't have hoped for a warmer reception. Sadly, even though the business was good, Matt was left with a bitter taste in his mouth. Ranch Enterprises filed a writ against the singer claiming $9,760 damages for breach of contract. Morris Enterprises and Takapuna theatrical promoter Christopher Cambridge were also named as second and third defendants. The writ alleged that Ranch Enterprises had entered into a $3,000 deal with Matt for him to appear at their venue. According to the small print in his contract he wasn't allowed to appear anywhere else in the surrounding area during his engagement. An unfortunate oversight! The case dragged on for months, and was eventually settled out of court.

The song that launched a pirate radio ship and an English bus driver to international stardom took centre stage in Auckland that week. 'Born Free' was the theme song of Radio Hauraki when it broadcast from the *Tiri* in the Hauraki Gulf. Ian Fergusson, one of the original announcers, presented Matt with a tape-recording of the last hour the station was on air before coming ashore as a licensed station. 'Born Free' was the last song played at sea.

Matt caught a plane as often as most would catch a bus. His brief stopover in LA gave him a chance to meet up with Sid and Gert and regale them with stories of his Australian experiences. John Barry was renting a house in the Golden State and invited them over for a liquid lunch. He also persuaded them to listen to a new star in the business, playing a promo of Barry Manilow's new album *Tryin' to Get the Feeling*. John suggested that some of the material might suit Matt. The singer took his friend's advice and he went on to perform 'I Write the Songs' and 'One Voice'.

Those few days in California gave Matt a chance to catch his breath. It had been an arduous five weeks and although he was looking forward to getting home, he wasn't looking forward to seeing his specialist – he knew he was due a lecture.

Matt had had several talks with Don about the dissatisfaction he felt and his manager's seeming neglect of his duties, but Don still refused to give up the mantle. Matt clung to the hope that Don's reassurances would be justified, but inside he felt his world was coming apart and the sense of betrayal was too much to handle. It wasn't easy to speak to his wife about the subject as she had begged him to dispense with Don's services on countless occasions and Matt didn't want to admit he'd been wrong. His stubbornness to confront the problem led to intense inner turmoil, and a rapidly shrinking diary. He wasn't short of radio broadcasts, they were lining up for his services, but the prestige bookings were waning with alarming speed. Michael Sullivan again approached Matt, begging him to sign with his agency, but loyalty prevailed and the singer declined the offer. He still had bookings in the diary, but some of them had been placed over a year before and Matt didn't realise that the advance bookings for the following year were non-existent. It seemed that no one at NEMS had really taken over the reins in Don's absence. Matt's dependence on alcohol grew as a way to escape the way he felt – that he had been comprehensively let down by someone he considered a friend.

Matt's drinking, although spiralling enough to affect his health, wasn't outwardly visible and his performances were not affected. He appeared on BBC television's screening of *Miss England* and on Radio 4's *Desert Island Discs*, enjoying several lunches with producer Ronald Cook and host Roy Plomley, who had also devised the programme. Matt picked the records he would take to a desert island and discussed his choices. The unscripted discussion was very interesting, revealing Matt's deep love for popular opera. He owned several recordings by Beniamino Gigli and Ezio Pinza.

> **I have always felt very humble about the dedication of opera singers – they have to keep learning all the time. They may go on for years without earning a great deal of money. The amount of work and study they have to cope with would drive me mad. When I think of the vast technical skill they achieve, it would make me embarrassed just to be in the same room. — Matt Monro**

Matt's love of music was varied and one of his biggest thrills and fondest memories were of a jam session he had shared with the Four Freshmen. Les Gilbert, who used to play lead alto with the Heath band, had a pub quite near to Dallas Road. After Matt's tour with the Freshmen, most of the cast including Dennis Lotis, Ted Heath, Kenny Baker and a few other marvellous musicians headed over to Les' bar. An impromptu end of tour party followed, which didn't finish until the small wee hours. The whole team launched into a rendition of 'Tom Dooley', which absolutely paralysed Matt. It was moments like that which made the whole business worthwhile.

Matt was forced to see yet another specialist after a rather nasty incident following a show. Coming out of Jollies to sign autographs, several overzealous fans surged forward when the star appeared, knocking him off of his feet. Matt didn't know the severity of his injuries until he saw George Braddock, but he had in fact suffered a shoulder fracture. The singer was advised that he could expect recovery to take at least three months, but arranged to see the doctor again in three or four weeks. Matt was not in a position to cancel work; the one thing he loathed to do was let an audience down. He couldn't take the painkillers the specialist had given him as they made him woozy. Instead he ended up self-medicating with scotch at the end of each night. A series of one-nighters and week blocks at Birkenhead, Cork, Swansea, Dublin and Eccles all followed with Matt in the most excruciating pain he had felt in years.

Taking a rare social night, Matt and Mickie were among the guests at the opening night of the Queen Mary Suite at the Cunard International Hotel, starring Dionne Warwick and Frank Gorshin. Also in attendance were Tony Blackburn, his actress wife Tessa Wyatt, Fred Pontin and Matt's old adversary Jeffrey Kruger. Another festive event was the birth of Ernie's son Darren. Ernie had re-married a short time back and Mickie was really hoping that with the birth her brother would settle down happily. His divorce had been extremely hard on him, and losing one son to Australia had broken his heart, so it was especially important that the newborn give him a brighter outlook.

Michael Black's fiftieth birthday held at Quaglino's gave Matt one last chance to speak to his manager before he left for America. Don was moving lock, stock and barrel to Los Angeles. He'd spent months packing up and putting the house in order and was soon heading across the Atlantic, to take up residency in a house in Bel Air, with Fred Astaire, Cannonball Adderley and Tony Curtis as neighbours. The Blacks met the elite of society and mixed with Elvis Presley, Muhammad Ali, Michael Jackson and Olivia Newton John. Don Black had finally arrived.

On the 10 October 1975, impresario Alan Blackburn announced that he had joined NEMS as deputy managing director and that his theatrical agency, together with his clients and own personal staff had all merged with the bigger agency. NEMS already represented some of the most important clients in show business, whom Blackburn would now be handling together with managing director Vic Lewis. They included Cilla Black, Elton John and Matt Monro.

John Ashby remembers that he had been working for the Alan Blackburn Agency when it was taken over by NEMS. "I remember being told I was the responsible agent for Matt Monro, which for me was a big thrill because he was the first international star that I ever had the honour of working with. I'd first met Matt in Australia and it struck me what a very nice guy he was for the status he had in the business." Don had moved to America and in his absence Bernie Lee had been looking after the bookings for Matt. John was horrified by the state of the diary he inherited. As far as he was concerned, Matt Monro was a big star and he couldn't understand why there were only two bookings in the diary; two nights at Hendon Hall and two nights in the Midlands.

Shortly after merging with NEMS, John was due in Plymouth as part of the tour he was doing with Cilla Black. He travelled to the venue by train, as did Matt and Tony Stenson who were working the week at Talk of the West, St Agnus in Cornwall. John recalls, "We took the train on Friday morning and those three or four hours gave me a chance to get to know Matt quite well as a man, a real regular guy. He was a man's man and we became great friends right from the word go." John felt totally embarrassed by Matt's work situation. It wasn't that nobody wanted to book the singer; it was that staff were in sufficiently proactive, not always chasing enquiries and converting them into contracts. John immediately set out to remedy the matter.

Matt's diary might not have been marked with paying jobs, but he was busy offering his support where it was needed. A galaxy of stars converged on Lakeside Country Club when the Water Rats held a charity ball at the Frimley Green nightspot. Among those supporting the evening were Dick Emery, Tommy Trinder, Roy Hudd, Harry Worth, Billy Dainty, John Inman and Matt. The singer also attended the Society's Grand Ball, which was always staged on the last Sunday in November. Although strictly a male society, the Ball was an opportunity for all the Rats to come together socially and bring wives and friends. Each year a cabaret was staged to entertain the crowd and fellow Rats would help out where they could; some hosted tables, others sold raffle tickets, those qualified staged and produced the show and yet others helped with the after-dinner speeches. Matt hosted his own table and it felt good to just sit back for an evening and watch his fellow performers entertain a jam-packed room.

Mickie slipped a disc in her back the week before Christmas and she encouraged her husband to use his 'gift'. Matt laid his hands on his wife's spine and to his surprise felt a burning sensation in his palms – almost immediately Mickie felt fine. Famous healer Ted Fricker was responsible for Matt's new role. He'd recognised the singer's latent gift when Mickie had previously been to him with serious disc trouble and encouraged Matt to use it for others' benefit. It was a particularly dramatic intercession. Ted suggested Matt give up show business and go in to healing permanently, but entertaining was far more lucrative a career.

Matt felt he should experiment whenever an opportunity presented itself to see whether he could repeat the result. It happened unexpectedly with his multi-millionaire friend Len Matcham, who owned the Isle of Brecqhou. He had suffered from back trouble for some time and tried a multitude of treatments.

> I always get embarrassed when someone says, "Try to do something for me." Len was at my house when he exclaimed, "If you are so clever do something for my back." I went through the Fricker-like motions. I felt depressed as nothing much happened. But next day Len phoned me from Paris where he had gone on business. He said he had enjoyed the best night's sleep for years. And his pain had completely vanished. This incident really convinced me I possessed the healing gift. To help someone out of pain and distress is a marvellous uplifting experience. — Matt Monro, Peter Green/Psychic News

When, as a guest on *Desert Island Discs*, Matt was asked if he had a religious faith, he had replied without hesitation, "I am a Spiritualist." He also spoke of his firm conviction of an after-life. He was interviewed by Peter Green of the *Psychic News* who wanted to place on record the manner of Matt's early introduction to the Spiritualist movement. Matt explained that while in the army, he became good friends with another soldier in his R.E.M.E unit, Stephen Hiscott. He was a Spiritualist and the two discussed the subject for many hours, convincing Matt of its truth. Matt witnessed a remarkable scene generated by psychic phenomena while he was there. Four people were playing Mah-jong. They were thrown into a state of hysteria when they discovered five pairs of hands in play. The players ran out screaming. Even the police were called. Matt had also had an impressive precognitive dream. He described in minute detail a room, the people and how they were dressed. Hiscott showed him a photo of the same room. His description tallied in every respect. It was an incredible experience.

Matt's brother Harry also became interested in Spiritualism, but was largely a sceptic. He took Matt and Mickie to a medium living near his home in Watford, Hertfordshire. Everything she told the trio was accurate and everyone was impressed, although Harry seemed shocked and frightened by the experience. Matt knew many people were scared of Spiritualism; they tended to conjure up theatrical images of holding hands around a table, contacting the dead, with someone going into a trance and speaking in strange detached voices. Although those preconceptions were quite far-fetched, Matt didn't begin to presume it was his place to explain or force his religious beliefs on others. For the most part he kept that part of his life private.

In 1976, EMI re-issued 'Yesterday' coupled with 'Michelle', which had been recorded in 1973 as a tribute to his daughter, but this time the single didn't chart. The timing of the release was strange, as EMI had just re-issued the entire Beatles' singles back catalogue, which included the British debut of 'Yesterday' on seven inch by the Fab Four. 'The Little Things' was rushed out instead, but this also missed the charts. The fact that Matt failed to chart wasn't at all surprising given the appearance of another passing musical fad, punk music. The charts were awash with such delicacies as 'Anarchy in the UK' by the Sex Pistols.

The clubs were in trouble and during the first few months of 1976 the Showboat Club in Cardiff, the Fiesta in Sheffield and Talk of the Midlands in Derby shut their doors, as one by one they were declared bankrupt. Others would be affected as the year progressed. The smaller venues started juggling their finances and became slow at paying debts, resulting in agents and managements around the country demanding fees to be paid up front. The clubs had no one else to blame but themselves, having paid out exorbitant fees to guarantee the services of international headliners in the past. In some cases, these bore no relation to their drawing power, resulting in huge loses. Having run the Talk of the Town for years and knowing the business inside out, Rosalyn Wilder was astonished at what was happening: "I didn't understand why artists were hiking up their fees from one engagement to the next when the economic situation in our business was so uncertain. It was ludicrous, as they were cutting off the hand that fed them. Even when certain artists knew the economic situation they refused to lower their fees."

The first booking John Ashby secured for Matt at the New Cresta Club in Solihull wasn't the greatest success, although it was an evening they would both never forget. On 5 January, Matt complained of being unwell before his show. Ian Reid, general manager of the club, said the singer, who was starting a one-week engagement, went on out of theatrical tradition. He made his entrance at 10.30pm to a capacity audience of more than seven hundred people and struggled though the first three numbers. During 'Yesterday' Matt became unsteady and collapsed from his stool without warning, striking the side of his head and breaking his right collarbone. Several members of the audience rushed onto the stage to offer help, including a doctor who pushed through the crowd and took Matt to the dressing room. Suffering from severe shock, the singer was rushed by ambulance to a local hospital while the club waited for further notice of the singer's condition before arranging a programme change.

Sue Maull and her family had been in the audience, her father dashing round to the dressing room to check the status of the star. Seeing that he was now conscious he relayed the news back to his anxious party. Tony Stenson was walking around like a lost sheep and when questioned, admitted he hadn't contacted the singer's wife as he didn't know the number. Mike Parker took matters into his own hands, ringing Mickie and offering to pick her up from London and drive her to Solihull.

As he lay in hospital with his arm in a sling, the forty-five year old singer was still puzzling over what had happened. He knew he'd been in the middle of singing 'Yesterday', but that was the last thing he remembered until he came round in the dressing room. Matt had suffered a brief spell of generalised shaking and frothing at the mouth, and told the doctor that he'd had a pain in the lower left chest for about ten days, which he attributed to an old injury. He also explained that he'd had a previous blackout two years before and that although he had been drinking rather heavily the day before the incident, he hadn't drunk anything on this particular evening. The next morning he told the press that although the doctors had advised him against going back on stage that night, he was hoping to give a show the following day.

> **Apart from his fractured clavicle and a bruised eye, he looked ill with mild jaundice, coarse liver flap and had agitation and confusion verging on delirium tremors. The liver was enlarged five fingers breadth, and there was slight spider naevi. Although he was clearly unwell, he was unwilling to stay in hospital owing to his commitments. It was not clear whether his blackout was due to a minor cerebral 'spasm' or whether it was true epilepsy. I warned him about the state of his liver of which he is well aware, and he knows what must be done about it. — Doctor's Report**

Matt wasn't able to return to work at all, he was far too ill. John Ashby got straight on the phone to Singapore to postpone Matt's imminent appearance at The Neptune in February. Once Matt was stable, Mickie drove him back home and together they sat and had a heart to heart. Matt's drinking had escalated to the point where he was extremely ill. Matt had to confront the reality that his liver was not strong enough to sustain the daily punishment from the whisky bottle. Not only was he killing himself, he was also killing Mickie. She was petrified that she would lose him and was determined to make him face the fact that he needed help and he needed it now.

HUNG OUT TO DRY

Matt agreed to treatment at the Priory and was admitted on the 21 January 1976. He spoke to the chief psychiatrist Austin Tate at length. The root of the problem seemed to be that Matt simply enjoyed drinking. They established that his drinking did not interfere with his normal life: he was quite competent and able to go about his normal day without it having a detrimental effect on his routine.

Unfortunately, it did have a detrimental effect on his liver. It was damaged and with regular jaundice attacks it was evident that alcohol and Matt did not get on with each other. If Matt or the doctors had known that he had suffered infective hepatitis as a child and had been extremely ill for a year, it might have ensured a better understanding of these sudden attacks. Matt's medical history concerning his skeletal system did actually lead to a deeper understanding of the immense pain the singer had suffered for several years, and he admitted that because of prolonged discomfort and depression he had been drinking more than usual.

Matt's introduction to rehabilitation was several lengthy meetings with the doctors and an introduction to the other patients in his group. He wasn't allowed visitors or phone calls, although Mickie had contact with the clinic. He was cut off from the outside world, including newspapers, television and radio with the purpose of removing any external stimulus that would distract him from recovery and so focus on the underlying cause of his drinking.

The community was made up of sixty people with a variety of conditions. The clinic wasn't just set up for alcohol withdrawal, but detoxification of every kind of addiction, including drug addicts, sex addicts, obsessive compulsive disorders, eating disorders, manic-depressives, gamblers and self-harmers. The clinic housed people from every walk of life: pub landlords, racehorse owners, chefs and entertainers. Matt also met a stockbroker, a member of the bar, several doctors and a surgeon. Their first name and the initial of their surname introduced everyone in the group and a councillor was in attendance to encourage them to speak openly and freely.

The clinic observed a very strict regime reminiscent of army drills with breakfast and rounds starting at 7.30am. Patients were monitored around the clock and medication was administered to combat serious withdrawal symptoms. Lectures were given and videos were shown, all instilling the same message. AA meetings were an integral part of the treatment and these were held at outside venues, with the patient being escorted both ways with no chance to sneak their addictive preference. The only requirement of AA was the desire to stop your addictive behaviour. The staff's sole purpose was to instil into your mind that you had a disease and that their help was needed to combat the problem.

Matt went through rehabilitation for two weeks, his body detoxed, his liver started regenerating and he told the doctors everything they wanted to hear. He was the ideal patient. On his departure, he was given relevant literature and encouraged to attend AA meetings. He was allocated a sponsor, whose purpose was to offer comfort and support if he needed help and was in danger of relapse.

Matt took it easy after coming home, taking a week to get together with old friends. Siggi and Bernie Winters came over for dinner, as did Marion and Johnnie. Matt hadn't seen Johnnie for quite a while. Since he had started working with Gilbert O'Sullivan, the arranger/pianist/conductor had endured a non-stop travel regime. It was nice to kick back and talk about the early years.

Matt's illness had caused a delay in his Singapore booking, but with a clean bill of health, the 9 March saw him fly off to the Far East with John Ashby to enjoy the facilities of the Mandarin Hotel. Opening at the Neptune Theatre the following night, after two months away from the stage, Matt obviously had concerns, but as soon as he walked out on the stage they disappeared into the night.

The tour would certainly be challenging, for straight after Singapore he was expected in Kuala Lumpur, Bangkok, Jakarta, Australia, Hong Kong and Manila before returning to London in two months' time.

I travelled the world with Matt and we had wonderful times together. The Neptune Theatre is probably to this day the greatest night I've ever had in show business with an artist. I think we had 2,000 people there in the theatre. When Matt sang a song he made it his own. The audience were there from all over the world and every song he sang they literally stood up and cheered. It was such a wonderful, wonderful experience and when Matt came off stage, I said to him,

Matt, John Ashby & Mickie

**"I've never seen anything like that." I still remember it to this day as
one of the greatest concerts I've ever seen. — John Ashby**

Matt certainly had a special affinity with the Far East, he loved the people and they
certainly loved him. The shows in Singapore, entitled *An Evening with Matt Monro*, were
a knockout. The theatre was bursting at the seams. You couldn't help but compare the
receptions he received abroad to the recognition he received in his own country. For
some reason he never received the same status in England as he did abroad. Matt's
record producer John Burgess made the same observation as George Martin before
him, but could find no real reason for the disparity.

**Although Matt had been in show business nearly thirty years, he
never quite got the acclaim in his own country that he got abroad.
He was an enormous star in the Philippines, South Africa, Australia,
South America and Spain. He was one of the best ambassadors of
British music but was never really acknowledged as that here. I think
in his heart, Matt was very sad about that. — Mickie Monro**

In a volatile and ostentatious industry, Matt's down-to-earth qualities remained
constant. Every performance was equally important, whether a workingman's club or

a date at the Araneta – to him every audience deserved his best.

Matt rang home to see how Michele was. She had just had her appendix out at Hammersmith Hospital and Matt arranged to send his daughter a telegram from Singapore to add to her growing pile of absentee good wishes. It wasn't his fault he was never around for big moments in his children's lives; it was simply the sacrifice he had made when he entered the business. He was often forced to work abroad, mainly because there was more work on offer, as well as more money. Which is harder to take, being homesick, or having 83% of your income sliced off in taxes? Australia gave Matt the best return for his endeavours: 40% of his income went in taxes there compared with 53% in America.

The singer told his wife how well the tour was going and what a difference John Ashby's presence made. He was impressed by the agent's enthusiasm to get things right. John had come on this, the first overseas tour under his jurisdiction, to make sure everything ran smoothly. In short, all Matt had to worry about was his performance. For the first time in years, he felt that he was afforded the attention fitting for a star of his calibre. He didn't want to worry about the mundane details or any behind-the-scenes chaos, and he could relax in the knowledge that John Ashby was filling his diary. A huge weight was lifted off his shoulders.

His shows at the Merlin Hotel in Kuala Lumpur were equally good and Matt was on a natural high. He really hadn't felt this good in years and it showed in his performance – he nailed every single one. The story was the same at the Dusit Thani Hotel in Bangkok, the Danau Toba Hotel in Medan, likewise the Borobudur and Hilton Hotels in Jakarta. Matt couldn't have asked for a better reception.

On the 22 March, Matt, John Ashby and Tony Stenson flew to Australia for his three-week commitment with the promoter John Harrigan. The itinerary was ridiculous from a geographical point of view, with each gig doubling back on the other, making for hundreds of miles of unnecessary travel. Matt was only scheduled for two days off, but both had to be spent deadheading to other areas. And all that hard work ended up being for nothing as Harrigan knocked Matt for the majority of the money anyway.

The hospitality abroad was always first rate, except the time Tony Stenson finished a gig in Australia, went back to his motel room, turned down the sheets only to find the whole bed covered in red ants! A shiver goes up his spine every time he recalls the experience. It wasn't only the hotel room that made him slightly uncomfortable on that trip, but also the internal flights on small aircrafts. Like Colin Keyes before him, he preferred to drive, however long the road journey. John Ashby also wasn't a lover of the tiny tin bucket trips and to this day hates flying, especially after his trip to

Aubrey with Matt.

Matt was working in Canberra in a venue that was quite literally in the middle of nowhere. The place was jam-packed and by the time the curtain came down it was well after midnight. The owner offered Matt and his entourage the large snooker room attached to the venue to relax in after the show. At 3.00am John Ashby was getting slightly concerned, as they had to be in Aubrey the next day and it was a five-hour drive on the tour bus. Fortunately, or so he thought, one of the club owner's friends offered to fly them to the next town.

> The next morning the reality was there, a single engine Cessna plane sitting on the runway with a mountain in front of it that we had to fly across. The plane started taxiing and at the end of the runway I had to ask them to stop the plane. I then ran straight to the nearest toilet and was literally shitting myself. We took off, John and me in the back. Harrigan's veins in his neck were bulging out. Matt was at the front with no expression. I looked ahead and saw these dark clouds and I asked if we could go around them rather than through them. The pilot said it would be another $45 and add about an hour to the journey. John readily agreed but Matt said, "No let's go straight through." I never forgave him for that. We were thrown all over the sky. The flight should have only taken an hour but took two because of the head winds. When we finally landed I actually kissed the grass. — John Ashby

On the 21 April, Matt flew to Manila with a stopover in Hong Kong for the night. He never let an opportunity of a visit go by, and this trip was no different from other jaunts: a night on the town with Ray Cordeiro and Bing Rodriquez was in order. Matt introduced John to a whole new world.

> I remember sitting around a table in Hong Kong having dinner with Billy Eckstine, Al Martino and Matt - they were all respected people. The American public respected and loved artists for what they did, but the British don't show it in the same way. It's a British trait. The recognition was big but not what it should have been. — John Ashby

Matt's contracts had changed from those humble beginnings; now each promoter had to guarantee first class travel, a suite for Matt and accommodation for two others,

'Uncle Ray' Cordeiro & Matt

luxury chauffeur-driven cars, first class venues and musicians to match – and most importantly no food or drink service during his performance. Matt was lucky in so far as he could dictate his aircraft routes and stop offs. He would pop into somewhere like Hong Kong or Manila as casually as a New Yorker would change trains.

In a striking contrast to the luxury he had been afforded on his travels, Matt accepted a charity request to sing to the underprivileged on one of the smaller Philippine islands. It involved a flight on a small prop plane, so John was visibly relieved when Matt told him he could stay put. Unfortunately, Tony Stenson wasn't offered the same 'get-out' clause because Matt needed his pianist. Rehearsals were in a local boxing hall, with the ring, minus the ropes, acting as the stage. The area was open house for everyone and anyone during the afternoon's four-hour rehearsal, including pet dogs and chickens roaming around at will. The concert went very well and the local musicians played their hearts out.

Back in Manila, the hotel management were hugely excited about such a big star staying at their establishment and Matt's suite was adorned with large floral arrangements, handmade chocolates and silver trays laden with local fruits. And all this for doing something he loved. He was never happier than when entertaining a hushed, captive audience, his lavish tones smouldering like a smoking gun to their heads.

First Lady Imelda Marcos welcomes Matt

The Marcos' hospitality was as overwhelming as ever and Imelda was in her usual front row seat in the Araneta Coliseum. As always, she extended an invitation to Matt and his musical director to come to their residence after the performance. It was a matter of protocol, it didn't matter how tired the singer might have been, it was impossible to turn the invitation down.

> **I remember a concert we gave at the Araneta in Manila. There were so many musicians on stage I could hardly get on to start the show! During our stay we were invited to dine with the Marcos' at their town residence. It was quite a splendid affair with lots of people using gold cutlery. — Tony Stenson**

The only thing that soured Matt's trip was the news that came on 26 April, the day before he was leaving for England. Mickie rang to tell him that Sid James had collapsed on stage at the Sunderland Empire Theatre, aged only sixty-two. He'd suffered a heart attack during the opening night of *The Mating Season*, and despite all attempts to resuscitate him, he died on the way to the hospital. The tragedy hit Matt hard, losing a friend was never easy and he felt desperately sorry that he couldn't be there to comfort Val.

There is nothing nicer in the business than to receive an accolade from one of your peers and Matt felt blessed as not only had he received so many over the years, but he was now officially known as 'The Singer's Singer'. Bing Crosby had referred to Matt several times when giving interviews.

> **I was thinking the other day: There's three fellows who, for me, sing pure songs. They sing the songs with no tricks, no gimmicks, no attempts at anything but good singing, listenable quality. The first is Buddy Clark, the second is Matt Monro and the third is Barry Manilow. I'm talking about a straight song. If you want to listen to a song and hear it sung beautifully, that's it. Those guys could do it. Matt Monro's got a song, 'I Get Along Without You Very Well' – that record is one of the most beautiful records I've ever heard.**
> **— Bing Crosby**

After the lavish facilities of the Far East, it rather tickled Matt that back in the UK, working the week at the Circus Tavern in Purfleet for Bob Wheatley, his dressing room was in fact a caravan. The venue had established itself as Essex's leading cabaret club, attracting the finest international stars to its stage, and Matt was happy to add it to his curriculum vitae.

Matt also recorded a tribute to Hoagy Carmichael with a fifty-six-piece orchestra for BBC Radio 2 before jetting off with Mickie for a much needed holiday in Barbados. Settler's Beach had become a second home for the couple and Matt relished the peace and tranquillity of the island.

The couple were away a month and although they wrote a couple of letters to the children, they only highlighted what Matthew and Michele were missing. Joy Huggins was the manager of the hotel, and she was a wonderful, warm and caring soul who ensured that everything was waiting for the Monros whenever they arrived back on the island. Michele and her brother had enjoyed several trips to the Caribbean with their parents and it was such a fantastic experience that it was really hard to be left at home on this occasion, but Matthew was still at school and they were very strict about unauthorised absences during term time.

It wasn't long after Matt returned to England than he was back at work, this time working the Butlins circuit. Starting off at the Pig & Whistle Showbar at Bognor on 19 July, Matt was contracted for eighteen nights over six weeks. With Butlins' revolutionary change to their entertainment policy, all the shows were midnight performances giving the venue license to charge the public. It made a big difference to the artists as the audiences were there because they wanted to be and not just because it was freely on offer.

During his season at Butlins in Barry Island, John Ashby and Hugh Sadler travelled down to see the singer. Sadler was an Australian promoter and he wanted to talk to Matt about doing a deal over there. Having just been knocked by John Harrigan, Matt was honest in his concerns. As the hours passed and more drinks were poured Sadler was able to convince the star that he worked more honourably than his predecessor. By the time negotiations had ended Sadler was pissed out of his head, but it was a small price to pay as he had exacted a promise that Matt would travel to Australia in seven weeks' time.

Before leaving British shores, Matt opened Edward House – the Dorset Spastic's Society residential home at Wallisdown. The singer was an old friend of nineteen-year-old Karen Groves, who had been unable to speak for the first seven years of her life, until her parents happened to buy the Matt Monro LP *Hits of Yesterday*. When the record was played, Karen began to mouth the words of the song and gradually her speech became near normal. When Matt appeared in Bournemouth, Karen's parents took her to the show and she met the singer backstage. She instantly became a firm friend of Matt and Mickie's, and they corresponded with her, sending cards at Christmas, Easter and birthdays. When the new centre in Poole was completed, Matt was the obvious choice to perform the opening ceremony and unveil a commemorative plaque. Karen was there and presented the singer with a dolphin in Poole pottery.

> **Matt 'adopted' a little handicapped girl called Karen Groves and kept in constant touch with her. Her parents Pam and Brian Groves felt that Matt brought a joy to Karen's life that she didn't have before, and Matt in turn worked hard at seeing her as often as possible. It meant a lot to him that he was able to play such an important role in her development and rehabilitation.**
> **— Mickie Monro**

At the same time as Matt was packing for his second trip to Australia that year, Johnnie and Marion Spence were also packing, but for a more permanent move. Over the year they had discussed the merits of moving to Los Angeles so that Johnnie could take over as Tom Jones's musical director. He had been flying back and forth across the Atlantic for several years now, working for Gilbert O'Sullivan, Tom Jones and

Engelbert Humperdinck, but now was the time to settle down somewhat and spend more time with his family.

Matt was far happier with the work ethic of Hugh Sadler, whose company Vidette Productions went out of their way to make sure the star was happy. Matt had already completed ten trips to Australia, but Sadler had his eye on convincing the singer to do several more for his company. The bottom line was Matt Monro had the drawing power to sell seats – all of them.

> **Opening night was followed by a dinner thrown in Daddy's honour. The shows have been just terrific – in fact Saturday night the show went with a great bang – everything fused just as Daddy was going to sing 'Born Free'. That's show business. The shows, this week and next, are all over the place. On Tuesday we drive to a place called Newcastle – about three hours from here. We could have gone by plane – one of those small ones – but I didn't fancy that. We've done quite enough flying during the last three weeks. Saw Ronnie Corbett in Melbourne and here in Sydney we've seen Winifred Atwell and Jimmy Edwards, to name just two. We are in good company here at the hotel. Mrs Thatcher's been and David Frost and Stirling Moss are here at the moment. The sign in the foyer welcomes all these famous people and Daddy's name is on top – of course. Probably because he spends more than anyone else!! — Letter from Mickie, the Boulevard Hotel, NSW**

Matt's first appearance was on 16 September at the South Sydney Juniors Clubs, where he was booked for four straight nights. It was so successful that the owners begged for more, so four more shows were added to the following week. With the singer based in one place for a number of days, the tour was far less strenuous than in previous years and gave Matt and Mickie the chance to see family and friends.

Although it was an easy trip as far as Matt was concerned, Tony Stenson found it a real challenge. There was already talk about a return trip to Australia and he realised that he didn't want to venture that far away from home again. He desperately missed his family and decided he needed a job that didn't involve travelling. After two and a half years he decided it was time to move on

Tom Jones & Matt

We left Sydney eight hours ago having stopped at Pago Pago and are now on our way to Honolulu. Travelling the way we have, from London over the Far East to Sydney and back home this way, means we'll have travelled right around the world. We crossed the International Date Line and will arrive in LA on the same date we left but ninety minutes later, work that out! We are excited about going to LA, although a little sad to leave Australia. It was really a marvellous trip, both in business and pleasure. The shows were very successful and our friends, old and new, made the whole thing something to remember. — Letter from Mickie on flight Sydney to Los Angeles

As well as seeing Sid and Gert Feller the trip to Los Angeles gave them the chance to see how Johnnie and Marion were getting on. They had rented a house in the foothills of the city and were looking for somewhere more permanent to live. They spent a marvellous week together and Matt even got the chance to see Johnnie work with Tom Jones. It felt strange seeing his friend on stage with someone else.

I first met Tom Jones after he made his first record. He's a funny fellow with a deep Welsh accent. He's quiet and he loves his cups of coffee. But when he's on stage he's dynamic, he's the greatest. He completely changes. He sings soul; it's what he feels. — Matt Monro

The time went far too quickly and soon Matt and Mickie had to say goodbye to their friends. They had spent a totally relaxed week shopping, eating and sunning themselves. Johnnie had the ability to make Matt roar with laughter at the slightest provocation. One evening he was out working and Matt, Mickie and Marion were at the house waiting on his return so they could grab dinner. But Johnnie came home a little worse for wear. On his way back from the studios he had taken one of his extremely expensive cowboy boots off and was happily swinging it around in big circles outside the vehicle's window. He was seemingly unaware that at some point the boot had gone missing, totally oblivious to the fact that it had taken flight, or that it had flown effortlessly across the freeway and landed on top of a camper van going in the opposite direction, for he was still swinging his arm around in circles outside the car! Johnnie hobbled up the walk with one boot on and came through the door to the utter bewilderment of everyone in the house. His driver, bringing the music cases to the door, explained to the stunned party what had happened. Matt had tears rolling down his face, made worse by the sight of Johnnie crashed out on the settee with the one boot still on!

It was a difficult and emotional farewell for the four staunch friends who had spent the better part of the last twenty years together. They had worked, sweated, partied, drunk, laughed and cried together. Matt would have cried a lot more had he known it would be the last time he would see his best friend.

A Different Perspective

Having returned from Los Angeles, Matt had two weeks of gigs before flying out to Athens for the first time. John Ashby had lined up some good venues for his artist and Matt's diary was much healthier than in the months before Don left. After a week at Jollee's in Stoke-on-Trent and several nights at the Beaverwood Country Club, Matt's appearance at Baths Hall received cracking reviews from local paper the *Scunthorpe Star*: "Matt Monro as suave and polished as ever, with a voice as satisfying as a big bite of rich milk chocolate, received a rapturous reception from a large band of Monro buffs." Matt loved working with a big accompaniment, and ten extra musicians from the BBC augmented the Bobby Quinn Set (the club's resident band) for his appearance.

Athens was a short flight and Matt was able to enjoy the evening relaxing at the Hilton. After an encouraging Greek reception, Matt headed back to more familiar surroundings with an engagement in Ireland. Working a week in Dublin at the Chariot Inn was rather different from his previous trips, where the threat of bombing had tempered the audiences' mood. Matt didn't need to worry about safeguarding himself from outside threats; there were more immediate risks to his health, right on his doorstep. Four days into the Irish contract, Matt slipped in the bath at the Burlington Hotel. Lying down eased the pain in his left shoulder, but over subsequent days the pain got increasingly worse and he developed a bronchial cough that produced a distinct heaviness in his chest. At Mickie's insistence he was forced into seeing Dr Dawson on his return and learnt he had hurt his shoulder and developed a chest infection, although Dawson was far more concerned with his enlarged liver. After performing a biopsy, the doctor gave his patient the hard truth. If Matt wasn't prepared to stop drinking, the next stage of a diseased liver would be cirrhosis – and that was untreatable. The copious injuries and excruciating pain Matt had suffered over the years, coupled with the need to continue working without adequate rest, had driven the singer to self-medicate in order to cope. He was very good at giving up alcohol, but also very good at taking it up again. Matt was forced to face facts and promised Mickie that he would stop again, this time for good.

At a follow-up appointment several weeks later, the specialist was delighted with the singer's progress. He had virtually cut out alcohol and was sleeping well on the prescribed Surmontil and Mogadon. Although Dawson told Matt that he had to give up drinking altogether, the doctor felt it would be difficult for his patient to be abstemious in his line of work, especially over the Christmas period. Nevertheless, he expressed the wish to see Matt in a month, after the liver function tests had been repeated.

Even with Matt and Mickie away so often, it was rare for the house to be left unattended. It therefore came as quite a shock when thieves raided Dallas Road and made off with nine thousand pounds of jewellery, including Mickie's second wedding ring. It was several days later before the missing items were noticed, and Mickie was devastated. She had to tell Matt about the incident over the phone, as he had left to entertain the troops in Germany. By the time Matt returned, the police had established that it had been an inside job, suspecting some of the builders that had recently worked on the house. Even with a generous reward, the items were never recovered.

Tony Stenson's departure saw Matt take on Paul Jury, a talented young man who worked very well. He was a nice enough person, but Matt wasn't able to replicate the close relationships he had previously enjoyed with Spence, Clayton or Keyes. His musicianship certainly couldn't be questioned and that was good enough for the moment.

On the eve of the Queen's Jubilee Year, many of the artists who had contributed to popular music over the past twenty-five years were invited to take part in *A Jubilee of Music*. Vera Lynn, Acker Bilk, Max Bygraves, Petula Clark, Ken Dodd, Val Doonican, Rolf Harris, Kathy Kirby, Lulu, Cliff Richard, Helen Shapiro, Norman Wisdom and Matt were all invited to appear. It was like a reunion of old souls in the Green Room after the taping. Matt hadn't seen some of his colleagues for years and it was wonderful to play catch up. His year finished in the Stardust Room on Hayling Island and as the clock struck midnight, Matt rang in the New Year with a soda water.

Sue and Mike Parker were sitting front row when Matt opened at the Talk of the North on 9 January 1977. Matt's biggest fan had finally married, but it didn't stop her pursuing Matt across the country. Mickie asked her: "What does Mike think about the other man in your life?" To which Sue replied, "Mike is the other man in my life! Matt's been there longer."

Being the partner of a dedicated super-fan brought its own challenges, especially when Matt's show hit town. If Sue got wind that Matt was playing a week in Birmingham, Mike's life changed dramatically, as prior arrangements were cancelled and his chauffeur's hat had to be dusted down. There was a whole network of people to be contacted and tickets booked for the large party that would grace the venue's front table for each of the six nights. The men were given strict instructions not to talk during the performance and, at the end of the show, they waited patiently while their significant others went backstage to get an autograph or three! Venues more distant than Birmingham, and there were many, created different problems... there were itineraries to plan and hotels to book. One-nighters were equally hectic, particularly weekdays, as days off work had to be begged for and suitable arrangements made. Last nights were never too late because Matt usually wanted to rush home afterwards, but they were good times, a focal point for get-togethers, a great show, a meal out and a little liquid indulgence.

> **Passing the Barbican on our drive down to London for a meeting, we saw a big picture of Matt outside the venue - he was appearing that night! Sue jumped out of the car and into the box-office and managed to get two returned tickets. We arrived home in the early hours, and still had to go to work the next day! There were other incidents like that where we just happened to be passing a poster and all of a sudden our world turned inside out and upside down. Once we were on holiday in Torquay, pleasant stroll along the promenade.... then bang!! This is a flavour of life on the edge of sanity – we're not all locked up you know! — Mike Parker**

Matt saw Dr Dawson again on his return from the North and, although he'd had a small relapse over Christmas, all in all there had been a steady improvement. His nausea had dissipated and he generally felt better in himself. He still took the occasional Chlorpromazine tablet and was taking the Surmontil regularly at night. Dr Dawson wrote to Matt's GP confiding: "I'm afraid we are going to get these relapses from time to time but I am sure it is worth persevering."

Although Matt occasionally took small holidays, he always returned to punishing schedules, working weeks on end without a day's break. Following Talk

of the North, he travelled to Heart of the Midlands in Nottingham, The Nite Spot
in Bedford, Caesar's Palace, Luton and the Fiesta Club in Sheffield. The Fiesta had
announced the first of many big name artists in its bid to attract waning crowds.
The new format started with Matt topping the bill. It was a sell-out. Even after this
gruelling run of engagements, another appointment with Dr Dawson produced
favourable results.

> **Things seem to be more under control here. For the last two weeks
> he has been completely teetotal, he is feeling much fitter and
> certainly the liver has shrunk. The liver tests however remain
> slightly abnormal and I doubt if they will ever become completely
> normal. — Doctor's Report**

Matt was buoyed by the news and booked himself into Henlow Grange Health
Farm for a week in a bid to get trimmer and fitter before his appearance at Talk of
the Town in a few weeks time. Four days before the opening, Matt was at Wembley
recording his new single 'If I Never Sing Another Song'. It was co-written by Don
Black and Udo Jurgens and features one of Matt's finest vocal performances. Matt
felt it was the perfect marriage between singer, composer, lyricist and musical
arrangement, a true classic. Although he really loved the track, he did wonder if it
wasn't prophetic. The British charts were full of punk and new wave music, and
there was little room for established artists of Matt's calibre. The song failed to
chart. Someone at EMI obviously had faith in the singer because it was re-issued
in 1979 and was also used as the title of what was to be Matt's final album of new
material.

Matt was about to open his five-week run at the Talk of the Town for his seventh
season at the London venue. After weeks of rehearsal, Robert Nesbitt's revue
Razzle Dazzle was now ready, with a cast of forty taking the audience on a
sensational musical fantasy. Early afternoon saw final rehearsals taking place centre
stage. Matt was celebrating his 21st year in show business and a photographic
shoot, complete with showgirls, was booked to capture the moment when Eamonn
Andrews, dressed as a chef, surprised him with his famous Red Book.

In a small open plan office at Teddington Studios, a highly covert operation was
being planned. Room 226 is no ordinary workplace; it is the nerve centre of *This
is Your Life*, one of television's most successful shows. The focus is a large
conference table in the centre of the room where production staff converge for

script meetings and in-depth discussions on their targets.

Candidate selection was down to the associate producer, John Grantham. His decision was then passed to the research teams who analysed mountains of data on their subject, filtering out anything relevant. The phone lines were constantly jammed, used as a tracking machine to hunt down friends, relatives and old acquaintances with the photocopier and fax machines constantly bleeding information. The team's ultimate objective was to distil thousands of pieces of information and shape the pages of the famous Big Red Book. Such was the level of security, each subject was given a codename and referred to by it throughout the process, which was only revealed on the closing credits of the programme.

Meetings were arranged and permission sought to make the 'hit'. Usually it was a wife, husband or close family member that was contacted and sworn to secrecy. That confidante's collaboration was crucial to the show's success as they were ultimately responsible for supplying the list of people they felt should be included in the programme and granting access to private photographs, press cuttings and cine footage. Not every guest was available for the live feed and in that instance a film crew would be dispatched to gather that all-important message for the small screen.

The day of transmission started with a script conference. Camera operators tested equipment, spare bodies were used for dummy shots, cues timed, filmed inserts examined and the floor manager ensuring everyone was happy. Finally the studio control room were ready and a break for lunch was called. A second crew and its director were readied for dispatch to film the pick-up and, while Eamonn Andrews was en-route to spring his big surprise, two additional rehearsals took place. The first involved a run through, with the scriptwriter standing in for Eamonn Andrews, and the second took place with the guests who had gradually been arriving over the last hour. They rehearsed their entrances and exits before visiting the make-up room. A real sense of excitement grew as they dressed for their big moment and everyone waited anxiously for the official call confirming that the special guest was en-route

Having led their 'mark' to a luxury trailer, champagne was served to steady the nerves. The studio control room was given the pre-arranged signal and a button pushed to start the VT rolling, so the guests and studio audience could see the moment Eamonn Andrews sprung his surprise with the Big Red Book. As the signature theme tune filled the studio, the famous presenter walked onto the set with his subject. 1505 seconds later, the show was a thing of the past and all the months of meticulous planning, tattered first-run scripts and discarded paper piles could be archived in the vaults of Thames Television.

Once Mickie had given permission for her husband to be the target of the programme, the production team sprung into action. With Matt away so often, she liked to spend all her time with him when he was home, but suddenly she was disappearing for meetings with the crew. There were hushed phone calls and on several occasions when Matt answered the phone, it went dead in his hand. His suspicions were raised. Mickie, without divulging why, roped her dressmaker into the plot to act as an alibi. Mickie didn't want anything to jeopardise the surprise, as the production staff were adamant that should Matt stumble upon the truth, the programme would be cancelled.

> **Matt's codename was 'carpet'. I was so excited that he had been picked for the programme but it was very difficult hiding the truth. Even though there was a valid reason I felt awful lying to him and deep down I worried that he might be cross with me for agreeing to the programme. I didn't tell a soul, even though I was dying to, but my main concern was that the surprise didn't get out.**
> **— Mickie Monro**

Thames Television had previously made contact with Rosalyn Wilder, explaining they wanted to film the opening sequence of the show at the London venue. The photo shoot was a ploy to lure the singer into the venue early. Rosalyn was left to organise the finer details and ensure Matt was in the auditorium at the exact time, but that proved to be rather difficult. Mickie arranged for one of Matt's friends to ask him to lunch at the Curzon Club so he'd be safely out of the way whilst she and the children went to the studios. At 1.15pm, while en route to the restaurant, Matt decided to pick up some new music from his dressing room to run through at lunch. With Thames rehearsing in the auditorium, Rosalyn was standing by the box office explaining the filming schedule to the staff when the face of one of the girls turned a rather strange colour. Matt had just walked through the door and was looking for someone to explain to him why he'd been refused entry at the stage door. Rosalyn, thinking on her feet, said that a television company was shooting a commercial and had paid a lot of money on the understanding that no one had access except the film crew. She offered to try and get the item for him, but he said he'd rather do it himself and asked when he could come back. She stumbled through the conversation, mumbling a pre-arranged time of 4.00pm and was relieved when Matt took his leave, albeit not in the greatest of moods.

It was a very close call. What Matt didn't know was that by 1.00pm Thames Television had already commandeered the cabaret room. Eamonn Andrews, with a specially crafted twenty-first anniversary cake, was to make his entrance dressed as a chef on the scenic bridge, which would be lowered to the floor during the photo shoot. The crew were testing all the electronic equipment, and if Matt had walked in on proceedings the game would have been up.

Mickie and the children arrived at the studios and were anxiously waiting in the Green Room for news that the 'surprise' had been successful. The hospitality suite was full of family and friends, which was a nerve-racking time for everyone. One guest was given special permission to turn up later than the others and that was because he had flown several thousand miles to attend. A black stretch limousine pulled up at Euston Road and out of it emerged a small wiry black man flanked by two burly six-foot white bodyguards. The scene would have been nearly absurd, if the diminutive entertainer hadn't commanded so much respect. After all, it wasn't often you were in the presence of Sammy Davis Jr. Entering the revolving doors a runner stood to attention and at exactly the right minute he handed the superstar a long tall glass of Dubonet and soda. It was the ultimate accolade that Sammy thought this event important enough to fly in for.

Matt's photo shoot was well under way. He was surrounded by a bevy of beautiful showgirls and his music was being played through the in-house entertainment system. The singer was oblivious to the activity above him and on signal the floating platform was lowered. Eamonn Andrews made his entrance, carrying the Big Red Book, and uttered those momentous words: "Tonight Matt Monro – This is Your Life." Leaving Euston Road, several cars raced across London to the studios where everyone was waiting. Matt made his entrance to rousing applause, and was completely bowled over by the event. It was the first time all his relatives had been together in years, and as well as Michele and Matthew, his eldest son Mitchell was there to complete the family picture.

Throughout the show, many stars gave their testimony about how Matt had touched their lives. Val Doonican explained that he'd been a fan since he'd been a lad and said Matt brought real class to the English pop scene. He remembered they'd been working in a TV studio in Manchester with PJ Proby. As soon as they'd finished they wanted to jump in a taxi, head for the airport and hotfoot it back to London, but that seemed unlikely due to the huge crowds outside the stage door. When the commissioner opened the door the kids all started screaming and surging forward, waving autograph books in the air. When the fans saw who was coming, one shouted "Don't worry; it's nobody good, just Val Doonican and Matt Monro."

Ken Brown welcomed his old army mate and Harry Leader told how he had taken the young Terry Parsons on as a singer with his band many years ago. Filmed tributes from Winifred Atwell, Bing Rodriguez and Frankie Vaughan were emotional for Matt, even more so when Bing Rodriguez walked through the double doors to give his old mate a big hug. Bing had never travelled outside Hong Kong before, and it was the thrill of a lifetime to share a stage with his friend again. It meant so much to the bandleader that he was near tears.

> I was due to do a Boys Club Tour in Cornwall eighteen months
> previously but was taken rather ill. Matt rang my wife Stella and
> told her "Tell the silly sod to stay in bed, I'll do the rest of the tour"
> and he did. It was a wonderful gesture and one I didn't forget.
> — Frankie Vaughan

Matt White flew twelve thousand miles from Australia to explain how Matt had borrowed half his name and Don Black reminded everybody of the hard times in the early days. The man who produced Matt's first hit, George Martin, flew in

Matt & Sammy Davis Jr, This is Your Life

from America to pay his tribute to his old recording star. Of course the programme wouldn't have been complete without a splattering of hugs and embarrassing stories from Mike and Bernie Winters and The Bachelors who told of Matt's golfing prowess. But there was still one person left to come. Sammy Davis Jr, who'd recorded an LP of tributes to his favourite singers and dedicated the song *My Kind of Girl* to the man who'd made it famous, came striding through those famous doors.

> **I wanted to pay my respects to Matt from one performer to another, even though we live on different sides of the water. We became friends and the real reason I forgave him for singing so good was because I'm taller than him. — Sammy Davis Jr**

After the credits rolled, the guests made their way to the green room, but unfortunately Matt couldn't stay for his own party since he was due on stage at the Talk of the Town. Instead, he invited several people to the venue to watch his show. Rosalyn arranged a table for Matt's unexpected guests and while Mickie played host, her husband went backstage to get ready for his performance. There was an excited buzz in the air as the audience patiently waited for the singer to

make his entrance. On Mickie's table, family and friends were happily talking about the day's events when suddenly Matt's brother Arthur collapsed and slumped across the table. An ambulance was called while those around tried their best not to panic. Arthur was taken to Westminster Hospital, where it was confirmed that he had suffered a heart attack and was in a critical, though stable condition. Matt, totally unaware of the events that had taken place, walked on to rapturous applause and gave a stupendous performance. Mickie had thought it better not to tell Matt about Arthur until after the show. Over the week Arthur was in hospital, Matt made sure to visit him several times.

Every week, scores of invitations arrived through Matt's door. He agreed to perform at a special event on Sunday 27 March for his old friend George Savva, who was being presented the 'Club of the Year Award' at Caesar's Palace in Luton. Recorded by Anglia Television and networked throughout ITV, the scene was set for an unforgettable evening involving a host of top show business personalities. The club was closed to the public, but eight hundred guests were invited to eat, drink and be entertained on the house. Compered by Ron Moody, it featured what felt like a cast of hundreds. Matt was in good company backstage, chatting to Madeleine Bell, Bernie Clifton, Mike Reed and Les Dawson, although he kept a wide berth of Rod Hull. There was nothing actually wrong with Rod, but he had a rather unpleasant emu as his sidekick, who sometimes took on a life of his own!

Matt was also delighted to talk boxing with Joe Bugner, who had lost on a split-points decision to Ron Lyle in Las Vegas the week before.

His season at the Talk of the Town finally came to a close, and as before, it had been hugely successful. Feeling buoyant and fit, Matt visited the specialist for some further blood work. He had slipped back into his old ways in the last month, enjoying the odd drink, but the results weren't as bad as he expected.

> **I am afraid once again he has relapsed a bit. However the tests are good and he is reasonably fit. I thought we ought to repeat the blood tests before he goes to Hong Kong and try and get him teetotal during that time. When he comes back if things do not settle down it would probably be wise to repeat the biopsy to see if overt cirrhosis is present. — Doctor's Report**

Though Matt had failed to chart with 'If I Never Sing Another Song', he was convinced that with the right material he could still make an impact. As good as Don was, he was writing showstoppers and movie themes rather than songs aimed at the charts. Describing Matt as one of Britain's inveterate singers, *The North Cheshire Herald* was of the same opinion: "Although chart success has eluded him in recent years, he still continues to produce splendid works, which his many followers, recruited during his expansive career, continue to buy. His voice sounds as good today as it did in the early 60s when he enjoyed considerable chart success. I feel quite confident that should the right composition emerge, we would see him in the charts again. Regrettably this is not that special single but his fans will find it quite gratifying."

Leaving the hope of chart success behind him for the time being, Matt flew into Hong Kong on 12 May at the invitation of RTV, dropped off his bags at the Hilton hotel and went straight on a shopping prowl through the back streets of Kowloon. He wasn't required until the following day, when he was to make a guest appearance in the finals of the Second Asian Amateur Singing Contest. The Rediffusion programme was recorded live and the judging was determined between Matt, his musical director and the producers.

Five days after leaving London Matt was back at home, but this time the trip had left him feeling tired. Not one to normally suffer from jet lag, it caught him unawares, although he didn't have time to stop as he was participating in the GOWR Silver Jubilee Float. Show business stars and dance bands visited twenty-four London boroughs in that first week of June to give free open-air performances as part of the Queen's Silver Jubilee celebrations. Leaving from two central points, Tufnell Park and the Elephant and Castle, the stars paraded to the centres in twelve decorated floats, each equipped with its own sophisticated amplification system enabling the artists to perform. Lord Delfont arranged the appearances, and among those who volunteered their services were Max Bygraves, Russ Conway, Rolf Harris, the Beverley Sisters, Ray Ellington and his Quartet, Marion Montgomery and, of course, Matt himself.

The singer was becoming slightly disillusioned with England. It seemed to have crept up on him slowly, but now he felt it at the pit of his stomach, like an annoying ulcer that keeps playing up. Although he was one of the luckier ones in the business, and didn't need to look for extra work, he was having to work harder for it. In previous years, Matt would have performed in week blocks at each venue, but with so many clubs facing financial hardship, many had stripped back their entertainment programme to weekends only. It hadn't taken him long to realise that coming back from the States had been a huge mistake, but it took him longer to openly admit it. Not only was there a wealth of work overseas, the money was infinitely better. In an interview to the *Sunday Express* he candidly admitted his mistake.

> I make no secret of the fact that one of the main reasons for going to America, apart from the work opportunities, was to avoid paying British tax. But while my early morning swims in my pool and the weekly barbecues and the glorious suntans were very enticing indeed, not to mention the lovely lolly of course, I woke up one morning and felt homesick for England. I missed my friends, the pubs, the grey skies. I don't know, just homesick. So we packed up and came home. Got rid of the house in California, bade the sunshine adieu and here we are. In retrospect I think it was a mistake. I should have just flown back for a month or six weeks, got England out of my system and flown back to Los Angeles. The trouble is he said, getting England out of one's system is easier said than done. I don't miss California nearly as much as I missed England. There has to be a message in that somewhere. — Matt Monro, *Sunday Express*

Even though Matt felt rueful about past decisions, he pushed such thoughts to the back of his mind and set his sights firmly on the future, making an appointment to see top Harley Street plastic surgeon Percy Jayes. Although Matt was not prone to attacks of vanity, seeing himself on the *This is Your Life* playback he couldn't dismiss

the huge puffy sacks below his eyes and decided to do something about it. Dr Gallen had recommended Jayes, and Matt had consulted him on the feasibility of the operation. The surgeon considered him a suitable candidate and a date was diarised for the end of July. It was considered to be a simple procedure.

> Much is written about the vanity of celebrities; especially it might appear those who have nothing to celebrate other than their celebrity status. There was much about Matt that could have led him to be vain. His was a towering international musical talent. In addition, his was clearly a powerful attractive personality with a great sense of humour and he was always immaculately dressed. He was also totally devoid of vanity. — Bill Hall

Although not openly concerned about his looks, the consequent ugly bruising over his eyes was something he didn't think the newspapers should print. After spending a week in hospital, he flew out of Heathrow, wearing dark glasses, and headed for Barbados with his family. On the 27 August 1977, less than a week into the trip, Matt received some of the most devastating news of his life. His beloved friend Johnnie Spence had died of a heart attack in Los Angeles aged forty-two.

The funeral took place five days later. Tom Jones cancelled a concert in New York to act as pallbearer, and Gilbert O'Sullivan also flew out to enact the same role. Matt was stuck on what was still considered by the travel industry as a remote holiday destination. There was only one flight a week and, however hard he tried, it was impossible to get a connection to Los Angeles in time. Matt was devastated and beside himself with grief. Although he flew over to comfort Marion a week later, it didn't compensate for missing his best friend's funeral.

Johnnie was highly regarded on both sides of the Atlantic for his talent as a composer, musical director and arranger. Just before his untimely death, he'd also managed to realise his long-time ambition of working in television. He had just signed a contract with the *Joey Bishop Show* for the ABC network, which would have given him more stability. The tragedy for his widow was made worse because the insurance papers on their brand new house had not yet been signed. Johnnie and Marion had moved into Lake Encino Drive just a few days before the tragedy and the insurance people were bringing over the papers on the morning of 27 August. Not only had Marion lost her husband and the father of her two small children, they had also moved lock, stock and barrel across the world and she now had a house that wasn't paid for. Matt and Mickie were terribly upset and angry at the situation, but Kenny Clayton was actually fuming. He categorically blamed Gordon Mills for Johnnie's death. Mills ran MAM, one of the most successful show business agencies in America. The sole reason Johnnie had moved to the States was the promise of working as Tom Jones' musical director. But once Tom's tour finished Mills instructed Johnnie to work with Gilbert O'Sullivan and from then on he was continually passed to whichever one of Mill's artists needed him.

> **Gordon Mills killed him. Johnnie wasn't Tom Jones MD, he was Gordon Mills MAM do-what-I-tell-you-to-do man and he did it for nearly five years non-stop with either Engelbert or Tom or Gilbert. Gordon worked him into the ground. Marion and the children never saw him because he was always on the road.**
> **— Kenny Clayton**

THAT INCH MAKES ALL THE DIFFERENCE

After spending time with Marion in Los Angeles, Matt and Mickie flew straight back to England. Matt was beside himself with grief; he felt as if his heart had been ripped out, all he felt was raw pain, and being in Johnnie's house – with all the reminders of his good friend – was too much to bear. Matt threw himself into his work, but it didn't ease the pain of losing someone so close. He started drinking again to dull the heartache and soldiered on as usual.

'Berlin greets London' was the theme of *Big Band Night*. The show was being recorded from the Fairfield Hall, Croydon, and Katerina Valente, with Paul Kuhn and the SFB Big Band, represented the German offering while Matt and the Alan Ainsworth Orchestra with the BBC Radio Big Band made up the British side.

The issue of fees paid to artists for BBC-promoted public concerts was a tricky one, and the company had done well to put a cap on the fees they offered artists for such engagements. They inevitably paid more for a concert at which they were taking money at the door than for a studio engagement, normally offering a fee ten to twenty pounds higher than the studio fee plus the addition of a relay fee. This worked well with the more serious artists appearing in the *Proms* and for those appearing in a *Friday Night is Music Night*-type of concert. The problem occurred with the 'pop' type of artist, like Matt, who could command very high fees in the commercial world as their managements saw no reason why the BBC couldn't match those amounts.

The BBC thought it was clearly wrong for them to pay commercial rates for Matt's performance yet carry on paying what was tantamount to studio fees for other types of artist. They had tried with each public concert to maintain some sort of fee scale, making the point to artists and agents that whereas thousands might hear an engagement in a concert hall, millions would hear a radio broadcast. However, because of the unusual circumstances surrounding the Matt Monro booking, the BBC agreed to an especially high fee. Matt received more than three times his studio fee – the highest amount the Drama and Light Entertainment Department had ever paid any British artist for a public concert. The concession was made because, having been turned down by the singer when they first approached him, the BBC had subsequently managed to convince Matt to change his travel arrangements and fly back on a red-eye flight a day earlier than planned. Despite the special circumstances, there were still concerns that the arrangement would set an uncomfortable precedent and that an offer of a public concert to Matt in the future would be harder to secure at a lower fee.

Matt wasn't interested in the back office's rumblings. In fact, he wasn't interested in much at the time and, having initially agreed to the concert, he subsequently pulled out of the show. The initial shock of Johnnie's death had worn off, but the reality was only just sinking in and it took stern words from Mickie to pull him out of his deepening depression. Understandably, Mickie was worried about her husband as he'd been so low in these last weeks and his drinking had escalated to a worrying degree. There wasn't much she could do to ease her husband's growing melancholy apart from offer comfort and solace.

> I am afraid this chap relapsed pretty severely while on holiday and was drinking half a bottle of scotch a day. On examination the liver is once again enlarged and the transaminase back to square one. However, he is not retching and his general health is quite good. I think it would be wise to repeat the biopsy and it may well be sensible to get a psychiatrist to see him. — Doctor's Report

> I performed a biopsy, which showed that the alcoholic hepatitis has progressed to hepatic cirrhosis. I therefore got him to see Dr Maurice Lipsedge who is a psychiatrist with an interest in alcoholism in an attempt to try and help Mr Monro more. They have met but to be quite candid we are not terribly optimistic for, as Dr Lipsedge pointed out, he drinks for fun and because he enjoys it. However he is going to see him again in two months and will keep me informed of his progress. — Doctor's Report

Matt ran into a little trouble with his old adversary Jeff Kruger in October. While at Henlow Grange, Matt had got talking to a lady called Sandra Leslie about the business, especially his run in with Jeff Kruger years back. He forgot himself for a moment and, venting, went on to say that Kruger was a thief and had released material that he had no right to publish, resulting in Matt taking him to court. Unfortunately, Sandra Leslie happened to be the record company director's sister and he went after Matt, citing slander and demanding a written apology and damages. Kruger wrote that the original case had not been pursued as he had acquired a good legal title from the owner of the master tapes, Merrick Farren. The case was dropped on 20 December 1977 after Kruger received the apology and £25.00.

1978 saw a new collaboration. Matt had been introduced to Roy Budd at the recording studios and his pedigree was outstanding. Budd had developed his great keyboard facility and broad musical command by playing the piano entirely by ear. His early influences were jazz pianist Oscar Peterson and he went on to gain modest international fame as an author of more than fifty film scores. Matt and Roy met to discuss a new project, and at the end of the meeting the singer had agreed to record the composer's latest film soundtrack 'Alone Am I' for the film *Tomorrow Never Comes*. Matt liked the song, but it had a strange feel to it that a lot of people didn't really understand. Budd also chose a controversial twist in 1980 when he teamed up with Matt again for a film called *The Sea Wolves*, this time changing the 'Warsaw Concerto' into 'The Precious Moments'.

> **'Alone Am I' shows the pure technical wizardry of Matt Monro. The song appears to change key throughout, with many unusual intervals... not to mention the complex rhythms. Matt accomplishes all with perfect pitch and timing. Rare is the vocalist who can combine technical prowess with so much emotion. Listen to his tonal painting with the lyrics; one feels the pain in his voice of missing someone special. — Jeffrey Paul Hayes, Pianist**

Matt played a variety of diverse engagements over a seven-week period, flying to Amsterdam then on to Dublin. He covered thousands of miles as his contracts took him to some of the more notable clubs around the country as well as appearances on *Stars on Sunday* and the popular programme *Pebble Mill at One*.

The singer seemed to believe that the most graceful way of growing old was to relax and have fun with it, indeed a lot of his humour was gently self-mocking. He feigned genuine offence at the press's continual reference to his height as being five foot five inches, when he was actually five foot six – "and that inch makes all the difference!"

Matt Monro was one of the best we produced in this country. He was a singing contemporary of mine. He was a man of whom Frank Sinatra said in a notable line, "If that guy was a foot taller he'd be a superstar", and Sinatra was obviously right. — Jimmy Young

Comic Johnny More was playing at the Heart of the Midlands in Nottingham and Matt was working up the road. The singer quietly slipped into Johnny's show after his own had finished while the comedian was in the middle of a spate of impressions. One of the audience members yelled out, "Can you do Matt Monro?" Without missing a beat, Johnny replied, "No – my legs are too long!"

On 15 March, Matt took his short stature abroad, where it didn't seem to bother anyone, and for the next eight weeks played Bangkok, Malaysia, Kuala Lumpur, Jakarta, Singapore, Hong Kong and Bahrain. While he was in the Far East, an offer was put on the table for Matt to play the summer season at the Windmill Theatre in Great Yarmouth. Matt was making a concentrated effort to spend more time with his family, so he agreed to the proposal, as it would give him three months at one UK venue, something he hadn't done since the 1960s. Jack and Peter Jay presented the summer show on a bill that also included impressionist Aiden J Harvey, comedy duo Lambert & Ross and Irish-born singer Clodagh Rodgers. The excellent Paul Jury Orchestra provided the backing and The Shades of Love linked the two halves of the show.

Peter Lambert and Willie Ross were sharp, smart and easy on the ear. They used no blue material and mixed quick-fire stand-up patter with expert slapstick clowning. Willie was rather outspoken, but shared Matt's legendary sense of humour and the two got on wonderfully.

The Monros rented a cottage in the grounds of a manor house, which was being rented by Larry Grayson who was also in season in Great Yarmouth at the Wellington Theatre. Freddie Starr had been the previous occupier of the cottage and had reportedly left it in such utter chaos that the owners had no option but to redecorate the premises. The children had a wonderful time in the seaside town and often visited other shows in the area.

The mayor held a special midnight screening of the Peter Sellers film *Revenge of the Pink Panther* at the local cinema for all the artists in the area and their families. When Mickie went to take her seat, the seat kept going down until she ended up on the floor. Matt and Michele couldn't stop laughing, and the more they tried to help her off the floor the more they fell about. The lights eventually went down for the opening credits of Blake Edwards' newest offering, the fifth Pink Panther

Donkey Derby Winner

movie and the last to star Peter Sellers. At one point Chief Inspector Jacques Clouseau, on the trail of some drug smugglers, disguises himself as a large Godfather-like gangster character. When he gets in a lift, just as the elevator doors close the typical gag of breaking wind takes place. Matt couldn't stop laughing at the scene and had tears running down his face. It was hard to know which was funnier, the scene on screen or the sight of Matt in fits of contagious laughter.

The movie screening was a great opportunity to bring together all the artists in the area, guaranteeing good press coverage, so other suitable activities were duly organised. Unfortunately, rain lowered attendance at the Yarmouth and District Round Table's Annual Donkey Derby at the racecourse, but the organisers reported an otherwise successful and entertaining day. Nearly seven thousand people attended to see the stars from the theatres all turn out in full force. Larry Grayson opened the event and star charioteers included Little and Large and Norman Collier (ABC), Matt and Clodagh Rodgers (Windmill), Keith Harris, Lenny Henry and Bobby Knutt (Britannia) and Neil Martin and Leah Bell (Wellington). Despite the tough competition, it was Matt who carried off the star's trophy, much to the delight of Michele and Matthew.

Matt Jnr's singing debut

Syd Little recalls a wonderful moment at the Windmill. A lone spotlight lit the stage to evoke an intense mood. Matt started singing the opening bars to 'Maria', "The most beautiful sound you ever heard" – when several police cars with sirens blaring raced past the theatre, breaking the whole atmosphere of the song. The audience fell about and Matt wasn't far behind them. The incident was related backstage in all the theatres that week and Matt's fellow artists on the circuit ensured that wherever the singer went, rude siren noises were sure to follow.

One of the most special moments in Matt's son's life took place during that season in Great Yarmouth and is a memory Matthew will forever cherish. He was sitting in the audience watching his father's show. Matt was just about to start the finale when he called his young son up on stage so they could sing a duet of 'Yesterday' together. The youngster was terrified, but exhilarated, and that one experience would go on to carve out the young boy's future in show business.

I had no idea dad was going to call me up on stage. I was fourteen years old and the idea of climbing the platform in front of a packed audience was frightening, and when Dad suggested we sing

together I couldn't stop shaking. It was one of the greatest moments in my life but also the scariest. — Matt Monro Jnr

The highs of the night before quickly dissipated when Matt suddenly realised that his bracelet was missing. Mickie had given it to her husband in 1962, saving up for ages and having it inscribed with a personal message. Matt was gutted, and more than a little apprehensive about revealing the loss to his wife. Amazingly, it was returned to him within a few days when a couple holidaying in Yarmouth found it during an early morning walk and reported the find to the police. Matt was overjoyed to get the bracelet back as it held great sentimental value, and extended an invitation to the couple to see his show. Later he tried to offer the couple a reward. Anne Turner recalls that "Matt pushed some money into my husband's pocket, but I didn't need that kind of reward, his smile was enough."

One thing that wiped the smile off Matt's face during the summer season was an altercation he had with Larry Grayson. There were very few things that made Matt's blood boil, but any danger to his family was definitely one of them. Matthew had spent several afternoons playing snooker in the grand manor house with Grayson and his entourage. Matthew was too young to know that each time the comic offered to help him with his shot and got behind him to show him how to hold the cue, it was not an innocent offer of help. But Matthew did realise things weren't quite right when Grayson asked the boy to sit on his lap and he felt embarrassingly uncomfortable. As soon as he could make his exit, he ran from the house and told his father. If it hadn't been for Mickie, Matt would have done the comic some serious physical damage. After calming down somewhat, Matt talked to Grayson and told him in no uncertain terms that if he as much as went within a hundred yards of his son again, the only appearance he would be making would be at the local hospital.

During the Yarmouth season, Matt finally saw sense. Don had returned from Los Angeles and, after many talks with John Ashby, Matt realised that Mickie had been right all along and he should have walked away from Don years ago. With a heavy heart, he said goodbye to his friend of twenty years and wished him well. There was nothing Don could do but accept Matt's decision. They remained friends, but deep down Matt was disappointed with Don and resented all the years of what he felt were neglect and missed opportunities.

Tony Lewis had been on Matt's case for months to sign with him. Matt finally promised that as soon as he had extracted himself from the contract with Don he would join Tony's company. Vic Lewis was the first to leave NEMS, complaining he wasn't getting paid. Then Matt announced his departure. This was a blow to John Ashby who had been secretly planning his departure from the company. He had been plotting with Cilla Black and her husband Bobbie to set up their own business and they had hoped Matt would come with them. Despite the setback, they took Cilla, Los Riales and Julie Rogers and set up Hindworth Management. On the 21 August 1978, Tony Lewis Enterprises became the sole representative of Matt Monro. The relationship was set to be short-lived however, and within three years John Ashby would get his wish, with Matt joining Hindworth.

In October, Matt undertook a series of fifteen one-nighters for Bernard Parr before starting rehearsals for his eighth outing at London's Talk of the Town. The booking for a month in their Razzle Dazzle Revue meant that year, for the first time, he had managed to spend time with his children.

Dave Allen was a regular visitor to the show over the weeks. He was opening at the Vaudeville at the end of November in *An Evening with Dave Allen* and was in rehearsals every day. With the singer's season finishing three days before Dave's show started, Matt and Mickie were able to attend the comic's opening night, which meant a lot to him.

Soon after, Paul Jury and Matt flew to Thailand ready for the singer's Christmas Eve opening at the Dusit Thani Hotel in Bangkok. Though it wasn't a long trip and the duo were back on 2 January, it didn't appease their families. The Monros were acutely aware of Marion and Johnnie's absence over the Christmas period and it was at these moments that the loss really hit home.

The first part of 1979 saw Matt at the Kings in Birmingham, Silver Skillet, Maidenhead, King's Lodge in Kent, Crystal Rooms, Hereford, Beaverwood Country Club in Chislehurst and Talk of the North, Eccles. This already exhausting schedule was made even more tiring with a series of one-nighters in Byfleet, Welwyn Garden City, Harlow, Aylesbury, Swansea, Clwyd and St Helens. Matt's children weren't seeing much of him, but they forgave him as they had been promised a four-week trip to Barbados as soon as this run of dates ended.

Matt was true to his word and the Monros flew out to the Caribbean island. Life couldn't have been more perfect; balmy days on the beach and evenings spent at barbecues and cocktail parties around the island. Michele and Matthew had become proficient in all water sports, having spent so much time in Barbados over the years. Michele worked on the speedboats with the owner, Dalton, and she was rewarded for her help with free waterskiing time. The family had also befriended Nick Hudson, the owner of Bagatelle, a local restaurant, which played host to all the top stars, including Mick Jagger and Michael Winner. Although born in England, Nick considered himself a white Bajan, having successfully integrated himself into island life. The area was rife with gossip about the colourful character. Rumours circulated that he had won Bagatelle in a poker game. It was also said that his small island hopper plane had come down in the Caribbean seas some years before, while he was on vacation, and he had lain in a yellow inflatable boat for days before a rescue craft found him, unconscious and severely dehydrated. He was taken to the nearest hospital, in Barbados, and after recuperating he vowed to stay there forever. He never did return to England.

Alexander's was the main nightspot on the island, and Michele often frequented the disco with her beach friends. The Merry Boys were the top group on Barbados and Michele was often invited up to their mansion on the crest of the island. After finishing a gig the boys would often go crayfishing in the freshwater rivers behind the house, using homemade spears. Whatever was caught was cooked over a campfire and eaten with fingers to the sounds of several of the boys strumming guitars well into the small hours.

Matt and Mickie were quite content to leave the partying to their children. There was nothing nicer after a good meal than to sit back in their loungers on the bungalow's private veranda and listen to the frogs and crickets singing their night song in the sugarcane-scented air.

Each week the Coral Reef had a grand buffet and barbeque, which included typical Bajan entertainment from steel bands, fire-eaters and limbo dancers. Matt had seen the show a hundred times, enough to last a lifetime. But Michele begged him to take her for her birthday and he duly obliged, inwardly cringing when the limbo dancers made their entrance. After the dinner plates were cleared, the staff approached the family table with a Baked Alaska cake adorned with lit sparklers to acknowledge the special occasion. It had the requisite twenty candles and, with the restaurant patrons singing their birthday wishes, Michele basked in the moment.

The family had made a great number of friends on the island over the years and it wasn't unusual to see the same faces on those trips. Gordon and Rita Walker lived in Antigua and always tried to time their trips to coincide with Matt and Mickie's. They had four children, and in the earlier years they had played together with Michele and Matthew – there was no time to get bored.

Unfortunately, this trip ended slightly differently from any of the others. Michele had gone waterskiing. Legally each boat should have had a driver and a look-out, but Dalton took her out for an hour's fun on her own. She was a largely competent skier, but while attempting a 360-degree turn, the rope encircled her arm without her knowledge and when it grew taut it threw her into the sea. Dalton didn't witness the accident so didn't realise what had happened until he noticed the boat was dragging. He turned round and saw no sign of the skier. He rationalised that Michele must have fallen and circled the boat looking for her. He had no idea she was caught underneath the vessel and the rope drag was pulling her under. The last thing Michele remembered was looking at the surface above her – then total blackness.

By the time Dalton grasped what was actually happening, Michele was unconscious. He jumped into the water to rescue her, cutting the offending rope and attempting to get her lifeless body back in the boat. Responding to the mayday call, dozens of locals raced through the waters on a myriad of vessels to attend to the emergency. They sped the girl to shore and someone administered the kiss of life. Coming to, Michele had no recollection of the accident. She felt no pain, but was acutely aware that her bikini top was missing, but decency prevailed and a towel was quickly draped over her bare torso.

An ambulance raced Michele to the hospital while someone was given the task of informing her parents of the accident. Unfortunately, the towel wasn't just protecting the girl's modesty; it was also concealing the fact that the rope that had dragged her into the ocean depths was deeply embedded in her arm. Doctors were afraid that they might be forced to amputate. After sedation, they set about the task of cutting the sisal away from her skin, it had severed through all of the tendons, muscle and sinews and, although the operation was a success, Michele had no feeling or movement in her arm when she regained consciousness. Matt and Mickie were beside themselves with fear, firstly the fear of the unknown when they'd been told their daughter was lying in the hospital but didn't know why. Once they found out she was alive and in no immediate danger they felt floods of relief, but the fear soon returned when they learned that she might lose her arm. Matt was all for flying to a hospital in Miami, but he soon realised there was nothing they could do there that hadn't been done already. Then the anger set in – he wanted to know who was responsible and exact vengeance. He, however, knew his daughter all too well; she was a bright, confident young woman who had a wilful mind and was quite frankly a bit of a show off. She was always experimenting on skis and had actually been one of the first white people to barefoot ski on the island, suffering the most horrendous falls in the process. Once she came round from the anaesthetic she told her father it had been a freak accident and he knew it to be true.

The island was small and news travelled like a bush fire to each parish. The locals had known the Monros since their first trip in 1973 and had seen the children grow up over the years. Matt and Mickie didn't harbour any bitter feelings toward Dalton, they knew it had simply been an unfortunate accident and if they had pressed charges of negligence, he would have lost his business and livelihood. The singer put Dalton's mind at rest. The ski instructor had spent the better part of the night at the hospital and was deeply concerned about his friend. The next morning the Monros were sitting on the beach. Michele was lying on a lounger under an umbrella with her arm bandaged and in a sling. Over the course of the morning hundreds of locals, most of them perfect strangers, walked past to pay their respects and wish the girl well, offering up flowers, beads, coral and gifts. The gesture was enormous and it made the family realise that what affected one person in fact affected the whole island. Michele made a full recovery, although the injury took the best part of a year to heal and it was months before she got back the full use of her arm, but the scars remain as a reminder.

With his family safely at home, Matt boarded the 11.50am flight to Colombo. The BOAC VC10 landed the following morning at 5.25am, and because of the early hour Matt had thought he could quietly enter the country unnoticed. He was sorely mistaken. Hundreds upon hundreds of fans lined the streets waiting for the singer to exit the arrivals building, and after fifteen minutes of photographs and autograph signing he was whisked away in the patiently-waiting limousine. Located on the west coast of Sri Lanka, the capital city was busy, vibrant and multi-ethnic, with a mixture of modern life and colonial buildings and ruins. It always amazed Matt that driving on rural roads the natural beauty of the country suddenly made way for modern high-rise super structures, shopping malls and condominiums.

Staying at the Intercontinental Hotel, Matt was booked to work four nights at Bandaranaika Memorial Conference Hall (BMIC) on Buller's Road. The building was an outright gift of the Government of the People's Republic of China and one of Asia's leading and most up-to-date conference venues, located in a tropical paradise.

The island knew of Matt's arrival, with loudspeakers around the city announcing where he was working and when. Banners adorned the streets, walls, buses and taxicabs. Matt could have played there a month and still sold more tickets, the demand was amazing. Bodyguards flanked the singer at every turn, and two were stationed outside his suite throughout the night. It was impossible for the singer to be inconspicuous; the security put paid to a walk in the city or a midday swim. Matt had been to the pool once, but the armed guards cleared such a wide space around him and the chairs that he felt isolated from the other guests. He didn't speak the language so when he tried to tell the guards to let people approach him, they merely smiled at him and kept ushering the intruders away. In short it was an intense experience, not exactly unpleasant but strange, and although the shows were exhilarating and the welcome warm he was secretly pleased when Swiss Air took him back to London on 1 May. Six days later he was working the Phoenix Rooms in Rotherham. The stark contrast of Matt's two worlds was never more in evidence.

After the success of his season in Great Yarmouth the previous year, Matt had been persuaded to commit to three months in Jersey at the Inn for the Night in *Seaside Special '79*, where the singer worked the majority of the season with the outrageous comedic support of Bobby Knoxall. It was not the wisest of decisions and the season was fraught with problems – mainly financial. Opening night started well and the press reviewed the show favourably, but tempers were fraying on the holiday island. The accommodation the Monro family were promised never materialised, and they were moved from pillar to post with empty assurances from the promoters that they would sort the problems out.

> **We had a contract with a company called Elite International, who were supposed to pay us at the end of each week. But there were delays and when it got to the stage that they were three weeks behind in paying Matt, Equity, the actor's union, suggested he should pack up. Matt was also working in very difficult and frustrating conditions. Under the contract we were supposed to be provided with first-class accommodation. We moved four times, and were due to make a fifth move. It is all very annoying, as the shows were successful with very responsive audiences – despite the fact that there had been little advertising. — Mickie Monro**

On Equity's recommendation, Matt flew back to London three weeks before his contract was due to finish and was ready to take action to retrieve the ten thousand pounds still owed to him. His annoyance was compounded by the fact that he had turned down a lot of other work to take the booking. Elite Promotions, who were responsible for putting on the tour, refused to comment on the matter, although the owner of Inn for the Night, Harry Swanson, told the newspapers, "I did not employ Mr Monro or organise his show. My only comment is that I was glad to see him go. He was rude to the audience on many occasions." Matt was outraged. Insulting an audience was the last thing the singer would ever consider doing. Matt wrote a letter of rebuttal to Mr Swanson.

> **Further to your comments in the *Jersey Evening Post*, I would like to point out that at no time did I, my wife or my management ask for drink service to be stopped. I have never made a practice of this anywhere. With regard to the food service however, there are many artists like myself, who do make this a condition or request. It is quite impossible to create any magic while people are looking down at what they are eating and not at the artist on stage. I would further like to point out that it was British Actor's Equity who pulled me out of the show, something they do not do lightly. I would therefore suggest that you look to Elite International and Bill Thompson for any professional concern you may wish to register.**
>
> **I have been working under great pressure and very difficult and frustrating conditions, unlike any I have ever experienced. I would hardly say that I have been difficult or demanding, although under the circumstances it would have been easy to be so. However, I think it is quite in order for me to ask why last year's show was being advertised outside the showroom for the last 2 weeks and not a mention of my name. When bandleader, Keith Allen walked out of the show, I immediately gave permission for my MD, Paul Jury, to take over knowing what difficulties would be experienced otherwise. What is more, on leaving I agreed to Paul Jury staying on, knowing that otherwise there would probably be no show at all. I would hardly say that this action makes me the man you seem to think I am and I therefore feel your comments were quite uncalled for.**

Matt and Mickie sued Elite International for the lost funds. The company was comprised of David Dunn, P Squire, Ian Symonds, William Thompson and Ronald Prenelle. Matt's solicitor named William Thompson and Ronald Prenelle as the prime movers but the legal papers named all five in the action. The case took years to come to fruition and during that time David Dunn was made an undisclosed bankrupt following a serious illness in 1982. Squires and Symonds paid an out of court settlement of eleven thousand pounds on 10 February 1984.

Matt's appearance at Blazers, Windsor, during the week of 23 October, was a first, but the feeling of familiarity came from its manager George Savva. 1977 saw Savva's move from Caesars Palace to The Helmaen Club at Usk. His arrival heralded big changes, not the least of which was the name of the venue, which Savva christened Stardust. While George was able to add to the success of the club, his relationship with the club's owners wasn't nearly so successful, and the manager left within a year. Savva moved instead to Pat Cowan's new project at William Street in Windsor.

Blazers was accessed by an elevator which took its passenger to the top floor and deposited the new manager in a large open reception area. This led to the auditorium, which straddled the entire top of the multi-purpose building, enabling it to seat a thousand comfortably. George was anxious to make Blazers as much of a success as the other clubs under his management, and the first thing on his list was to ensure all the big names in the business were booked. Matt loved the hospitality afforded by George and his wife Pam, he really did make it his business to make sure all his stars were happy, and the upshot was that Matt, like others, were happy to play the club whenever George asked.

Instead of week blocks, a lot of the clubs were now reduced to booking their entertainment on only one or two nights of the week, so Matt was swamped with requests to do a series of one-nighters. Johnny Laycock's three-week tour was put in the diary, but the reality meant that Matt had to travel to a different venue for each of the eighteen nights arranged. Although the singer had agreed to the booking, he realised he was getting tired. He was doing more travelling than ever before and he was getting bored of seeing the inside of one soulless hotel room after another. The only other option was to turn his back on England and work abroad. It deserved serious consideration.

Matt's thirteenth trip to Australia saw him touch down in Sydney during November of that year. He was booked in at the Sebel Town House Hotel and Hugh Sadler sent a chauffeur-driven limousine to meet his charge outside the customs hall. With only a few hours sleep, Matt was whisked to the studios for an appearance on the *Mike Walsh Show*, Australia's highest rating television variety programme. It was watched by five million viewers weekly on one hundred and thirty stations nationally for both the Nine and Ten networks. It was easy work; to Matt it was like talking to an old friend. The men had indeed forged a friendship over the many visits Matt made to the country, and the singer was always sure to grant Mike an appearance. The same applied to the show's main competitor, Don Lane, who was purportedly the highest paid performer on Australian television. Don loved to make fun of Matt's height; it became a familiar running gag every year and the host regularly included comments in his monologue about the British star's stature. After a solo spot and the prerequisite plug for that year's show, the programme saw the two men perform a duet. A memorable routine started with a close-up shot of the two men singing, but when the camera panned out, it revealed Matt to be standing on a box, to match Don's towering six-foot stature.

The five weeks flew by and Matt was as successful as ever. Regardless of the fact that he had not had a hit record in years, the crowds couldn't get enough of the singer. After much thanks and handshakes all around, Matt flew straight home. With all the wonderful countries he had visited in his career he hardly saw any of them save the inside of hotels, studios and performance venues.

Back in England, he managed a quick appearance on the BBC's *Larry Grayson's Generation Game*, although he steered clear of the host – he hadn't forgotten Yarmouth and he wasn't the forgiving type.

In 1980, a new ten-year contract was signed with Supreme Records in Los Angeles in conjunction with EMI to record in Spanish. In the years running up to the signing, EMI had discovered that television advertising could breathe new sales into the company's back catalogue. Having returned The Beach Boys, The Hollies, Cliff Richard, Nat King Cole and Frank Sinatra to the upper reaches of the charts, EMI decided to try something similar with Matt Monro. The decision was prudent and the release of *Heartbreakers* took Matt into the Top 5, giving him his best album placing ever and earning the singer another gold disc.

To help promote the album, the record company enlisted the services of Britain's favourite star-crossed lovers, pandas Chi Chi and An An, for the television campaign. The heart-rending commercial hit the airwaves on 3 March with the backing of £120,000 spent promoting it on ATV, Granada and Trident. EMI also featured the pandas on the artwork of a special release of 'Born Free'/'We're Gonna Change the World' as a double A-side. It was quickly followed up by another classic track, 'The Precious Moments', taken from the film *Sea Wolves*. Although Matt had been a stranger to the charts in recent years, the *Heartbreakers* compilation proved that the Monro magic could still woo the public.

By the end of the first week sales topped one hundred and fifty thousand units and the album stayed in the charts for nearly three months.

Matt had been asked to work on the La Puerla cruise ship, along with a few other Water Rats. However, with less than a week to go, the Greek ship was arrested and deemed unfit to take passengers. With two week's work lost, Matt and Mickie decided to make the most of a bad lot and excitedly flew to Los Angeles.

> **Not a great start as it is now 3.10pm and we should have taken off half an hour ago. We've got to have our 'black box' (whatever that is) changed. However they have just told us that the flight will only take 10 hours, which is 40 minutes faster than usual. Everyone was fabulous to us at the airport and Daddy never stopped signing autographs. Can't believe that I am really on my way to one of my favourite places to see my special friend and my godchildren not to mention Sid and Gert after such a long time. Should have travelled tourist though as there is hardly anyone on board and only eight in first class. Ah well the taxman's loss is our gain.**
> **— Letter from Mickie en route to LA**

Marion was still living in Lake Encino and although Johnnie had been gone nearly three years, she was still single and proud of it. With two children to raise on her own, it hadn't been easy, but with the support of family and friends she had managed to cope, deciding to stay in America rather than uproot and return to England. The girls had a wonderful time shopping, while Matt put his feet up and had an affair with the twenty-four-hour non-stop television. Sid and Gert Feller didn't live far away and the days were crammed with social calls, dinners, drinks and gossip – in between the television of course!

There were tears all round when it came time to leave. Matt was furious, however, to find that he could have stayed longer. Bernard Parr had booked him for ten one-nighters, which by his own admission were "shit" venues. They were actually so bad that Matt was forced to cancel the shows, something he had never done before. Instead, he worked two performances at The Alfred Beck Centre in Hayes, and even though the booking was put in at the last minute the two shows sold out in hours.

Michele's twenty-first birthday was celebrated at the White Elephant on the River. Her parents had invited her closest friends and the champagne flowed. Matt actually danced with his daughter, but she was so nervous that she stepped on his

foot within the opening bars of the song, at which point her father announced, "That's enough", and left her standing on the dance floor. Regardless, it was a wonderful evening, with Matt taking to the microphone to sing a special rendition of 'Michelle', followed by several numbers with Ray Ellington, which had the patrons on their feet. The night ended with Michele receiving a letter announcing that she was now the sole owner of a black Mini Clubman, which was sitting in the drive when they got home. She was gobsmacked, as there had been no inkling that her parents were planning that big a surprise. The evening was wonderful and exceeded all her expectations.

Matt was back doing one-nighters with a commitment on his time of nearly three months. Of course, in between bookings he managed another week at Blazers for Savva, a photographic session with Dezo Hoffman and an appearance on *Pebble Mill at One,* where he was presented with a gold disc for his new album, which had now sold in excess of 200,000 copies.

Certainly the ten odd weeks that Matt had just spent on the road were a huge contrast to the ten weeks he was booked to do in South Africa, starting on 28 June, with one night at the Mmabatho Sun Hotel, then four weeks in Sun City, three in Durban and three in Port Elizabeth. David Allen was taken on as Matt's new musical director at short notice. With three quarters of the singer's year now spent working overseas, Paul Jury had decided to throw in the towel. On paper the job of working on stage with Matt Monro looked a glamorous one, but the reality of travelling thousands of miles on gruelling schedules each year saw most of Matt's MDs hang up their hats in defeat.

"I'm not only a singer, I'm a mind reader and I can tell exactly what you're all thinking... Isn't he short." The characteristic self-effacing opening gambit by Matt was amusing in its accuracy and significant in its summing up of an artist who could afford to be totally unpretentious. The shows were a testament to his ability to entertain any nationality, regardless of the languages they spoke. Sol Kerzner was delighted. His Sun City complex was only 187 kilometres from Johannesburg, situated in the Bushveld of South Africa's North West Province and surrounded by the imposing mountains of the Pilanesberg. Sol still owned the Beverly Hotels in Durban and Matt made himself at home for the three-week booking playing the Copacabana.

I had the privilege of playing guitar for Matt during his stint at the Copacabana Club. David Allen was on piano and acting Musical Director. I had a great time doing that gig although there was one little faux pas... just one.... I'd arrived on my first night a little early and set up, putting my amplifier where I was told. Earlier that day I'd bought myself a brand new Korg Guitar Tuner. You just plugged the guitar chord in and turned a little dial to match the string you wanted to tune and off you went. David Allen was sat at the piano and asked, "Would you like to tune up?" In my infinite wisdom and lack of experience I said, "No that's OK thanks, I have this brand new tuner, I will just tune to that." He asked if I was quite sure and I said I was fine. And so I tuned up my Fender Stratocaster using my brand new gadget and set my guitar on the stand and read through the charts as I waited for the gig to start.

So the moment arrives and we are all set up and ready, the big drum roll starts and then the announcement, "Ladies and Gentlemen, Mr Matt Monro..." and off we go into the first song and I am somewhere near a semitone OUT OF TUNE!!!! The MD is looking daggers over at me but it didn't occur to me that I was the culprit. I thought I must be playing the wrong chart and the only thing I could think to do was to turn off my volume. The problem

Cooking up a storm

was that the piano was not tuned to concert A440; it was a bit off
and using the tuner was my undoing. Everyone else in the band
had just tuned to the piano. I should have checked the tuner
against the piano but did not have the experience to think about
doing that. I was so embarrassed. I was able to tune by ear while
Matt was greeting the audience after the first song and all was well
for the rest of the three-week engagement.

Matt never looked back. Even though it was just a couple of
seconds, I knew he heard it, he was just too professional to
mention it but it was the last mistake I made behind him, I made
very sure about that. — Lister Coleman

The press reviews were very generous and broadcast Matt's arrival at the Hotel
Elizabeth's Room at the Top for a three week season. An artist was as good as his
backing and in musical director David Allen, assisted by local guitarist Jerome
Dempsey and the resident Gerry Fitzgerald Trio, Matt had nothing to worry
about. Famous for his many film recordings, the singer aptly chose 'Born Free' as

his finale, and left the stage still a lion among entertainers.

> **Velvet-voiced singer Matt Monro, who has just completed a four-week July stint at the Copacabana nightclub in Umhlanga Rocks, will return there for another four-week season on August 19. Mr Monro, who is appearing in cabaret in Port Elizabeth at the moment, would have left for his native land before 19 August but was persuaded to stay on in SA following his successful season at the Copacabana. Almost every night was booked up and on Saturday 26 July at least 50 bookings had to be refused.**
> **— The Daily News**

Port Elizabeth was not quite what Matt and Mickie had expected after their other experiences of South Africa. There was very little to do, the weather was awful and, worst of all, English television didn't start until 4.00pm and reverted back to Afrikaans at 8.00pm. Within that time there was a religious programme called *Tick Tock Time, Cross Questions*, with a panel of ministers discussing interesting subjects, *Thy Kingdom Come*, a studio service conducted by the Rev Alex Thompson, and the highlight of the evening at 6.00pm, *Little House on the Prairie*. Matt could hardly contain himself!

> **Only three days more, three shows and then on to Durban and some normality. Really don't like this place, the people – what people? Don't see many till show time. Those we do see don't even know they're here! It's dead, dull and a bore. Even the suite isn't comfortable because it's so cold, Daddy is reading his book dressed in his pyjamas, a sweater and his red cardigan, he may be warmer but he really looks a scream. Had lunch on board a cargo ship with the captain and crew, which was really enjoyable except they all came to the show drunk and almost spoilt the evening. Went to a barbeque last Sunday, all musicians appearing in a Jazz Festival here at the hotel. Spent the evening at their show and Daddy was asked to join them on stage. He sang three swingers and brought the house down. Think it was the highlight of our stay here.**
> **— Letter from Mickie, Port Elizabeth Hotel, South Africa**

Port Elizabeth was a bland town with lots of racial undertones, and Matt and Mickie had to have an escort whenever they ventured out. It was not a comfortable feeling and the couple felt they had to stay confined to the hotel. Mickie had never wanted to leave a place as badly before, it just felt as if it would never end. They were thrilled to land back in Durban, and as they approached the hotel they saw a huge banner proudly displaying the words 'Beverly Hills Welcomes Back Matt Monro'. It was a knock-out, as was the suite with its bar, peanuts, olives, fresh fruit and strawberries. The couple couldn't have been more pleased.

Matt willingly gave a free show at the Copacabana to help the KwaZulu Drought Relief, with all the proceeds going to the victims of the drought. Matt felt good that his contribution could make such a difference and that one show helped distribute five hundred tons of food.

The singer and his wife had been having the most wonderful time in South Africa, enjoying everything the country had to offer, until disaster struck. Back in England, Matthew had taken an accidental overdose of drugs while experimenting with friends. Michele had managed to carry his unconscious body to the car and drive him to the hospital and, after having his stomach pumped, the young boy's condition was deemed stable. Michele had hidden many things from her parents throughout their travels over the years, but she didn't feel it was the wisest of choices to execute a cover up operation under the circumstances. She decided to tell her parents and let them take control of the situation. Mickie immediately packed and flew home on the next flight. She was terribly torn, as her husband had not been feeling one hundred percent the last few days. With a weakness in his collarbone from a previous fall, he had managed to aggravate the injury. The pain wasn't intolerable and he concealed the fact that he had suffered several bouts of vomiting in the previous days. Matt promised that he would be fine and saw his wife off, after all he was due back in a few days himself. Matt was admitted to Parklands Hospital the day after Mickie left South Africa.

I saw Mr Monro whilst he was in Umhlanga Rocks. He presented with an acute alcoholic gastritis with persistent vomiting. As you know he has compromised liver function, associated with liver cirrhosis. His vomiting persisted in spite of conventional treatment and he was admitted to Parklands Hospital in early liver failure. He settled on intravenous fluids, electrolyte replacement and antiemetics. As you can see he has rather gross liver disturbance and possibly secondary Hyperaldosteronism. He may also have a degree of Hypersplenism. Unfortunately, I never checked his serum amylase and since discharged him. He has complained of

**mid-abdominal pain. Anyway I have advised him never to indulge
in any alcoholic drinks of any sort and have given him daily
Parentrovite and a low protein diet to minimise his nitrogenous
load and lactulose. He obviously has a cirrhotic liver, but I am
rather concerned about the large nodule in his left lobe. No doubt
you will decide on any further investigations. — Doctor's Report**

Matt was able to leave South Africa on 15 September. It was incredible to think
that however ill he must have been, it did not prevent him from performing every
night nor did it stop him from travelling to Scotland for a series of one night stands
for Johnny Kildare the week after he got home. Once again the venues welcomed
the prodigal singer with outstretched arms, and he received a standing ovation
from over two hundred guests at a charity evening in Barrow's Victoria Park
Hotel.

The week was like most others except that Matt had now tendered his
resignation to Tony Lewis, giving six months notice. It was a huge weight off the
singer's shoulders, as the relationship really hadn't worked out the way Matt had
hoped. Whenever possible, Matt would travel home, preferring to drive four or
five hours than sleep in yet another hotel without his wife. Although he loved a
drink, he never drank after a show if he was driving. On this night, 13 November
1980, his son Matthew travelled to the venue with him. Matt was proud to have
his namesake in the audience, especially as it was a full house and the fans had
roared their approval and cried out for more. After signing the requisite number of
autographs and packing up his stuff in the dressing room, Matt loaded his car and
thanked the manger of the Thurrock Civic Hall in Essex for his hospitality.

The accident happened on New Road, Dagenham, at 1.00am. Pedestrian James
Galvin was hit by the star's car and died of multiple injuries shortly after being
taken to Oldchurch Hospital in Romford. Matt and his son were both in a state of
shock following the road accident, but didn't suffer any injuries themselves.

Matt told the police that the man seemed to run straight out in front of the car
and he didn't quite understand what had happened. After the crash, the police
gave him permission to have a drink in a nearby public house because he was so
shaken. PC Michael Palmer gave evidence that the star was perfectly sober and
had admitted to having one scotch and soda before the show. He told the singer
there was nothing more he could do and to go home. Matt didn't even remember
the journey after that. A local garage towed his car and the police organised a taxi
company to come out to the scene and drive Matt and his son back to Ealing. He

was far too distraught to go on stage the following night and cancelled his concert at the Forum in Hatfield.

The inquest took place two months later. Matt was still acutely distressed, he couldn't get the incident out of his mind. The court heard that Matt was speeding when his Mercedes collided with twenty-year-old James Galvin and killed him. Monro had pulled away from traffic lights and was travelling at forty-seven miles an hour when the accident happened. Hornsey Coroners' Court was told that Mr Monro was not to blame. Accident investigation expert PC Barry Sharkey said Mr Monro was driving in a road limited to forty miles per hour. He added such speeds could hardly be regarded as dangerous. Coroner Dr Harold Price was told that Galvin of South Street, Rainham, Essex, had consumed a massive amount of alcohol and his blood level was three and a half times the legal limit for drivers when he walked from a pub forecourt into the path of the singer's car on a stretch of the A13 at Dagenham. Friends told the hearing that the boy had drunk about seven pints of lager and a number of shorts before the crash. It seemed that the local pub had stayed open way past what the licensing laws dictated.

> **I was not in a great hurry to get home and it was an easy drive. As always I was driving with dipped headlights. I stopped at a set of red lights and when they turned to green I pulled away. The next thing I knew there was a figure right in front of my headlights. I braked, but hit it. It happened so quickly there was nothing I could do about it. It seemed almost as if he ran into me. The first thing I saw was his face in my headlights. — Matt Monro**

Matt was completely exonerated by the inquest and a verdict of accident was recorded in the court records. The national media were awash with the news and pictures showed the singer to be pale and gaunt. Although the incident was worthy of several columns, none of the newspapers insinuated it was anything more than a terrible accident. Matt was far too upset to talk about the incident and told his wife that "the face in his car headlights would haunt him forever."

DAMAGE CONTROL

On 18 November 1980, the family left for a five-week break to Barbados. It was the perfect opportunity for Matt to unwind, away from the prying eyes of the press. Rita and Gordon Walker flew over from Trinidad along with several other familiar faces. The lovely thing about Settler's Beach was the intimacy afforded by the mere twenty-four bungalows. Although you could be sure of all the privacy you wanted, all of the home-owners or rentals operated an open-door policy and cocktail invitations were extended on a regular basis.

One week into the trip Matt received a phone call from Michael Black. He was raving about the deal of the century. It seemed he had bought into a condominium project in Florida and was ringing all his friends to give them the heads up. Matt and Mickie flew over to Florida for a couple of days, leaving the kids on the Caribbean island. Just two days later, Matt rang his daughter and explained they had bought a holiday property and were not coming back to Barbados, rather organising flights for her and her brother to join them in America.

> **Dad rang us in Barbados and explained he had bought a property in America. He was so excited and told me that there was no point in him coming back to the island as he wanted to use the time off he had left to furnish the property and spend time getting to know the area. It was so unlike him to do anything that rash but it turned out to be a sound decision and although he didn't know it at the time, it was to be a whole new beginning. I had to pack all the cases and hightail it over to Florida. It was hugely exciting. — Michele Monro**

The Monros rushed around the American state in an effort to furnish the property, and after just a few nights in a hotel they moved in to their Deerfield Beach two-bedroom property. Matt bought a white Chrysler Cordoba to run around in, and run around he did. The purchase gave him a new lease on life and having a project seemed to lift the singer's spirits tremendously. Dickie Davies and his wife Liz had also bought one of the condominiums in the complex and the two men spent lazy afternoons playing golf in between naps beside the communal pool.

Woody Woodbury had left his own television show several years before and had headed over to Florida for a change of scenery, first working the Beach Club Hotel and then the Bahama, a famous Fort Lauderdale watering hole. Matt and the kids spent several nights at the club watching his special brand of humour. On one of those occasions Woody pulled Matt and actor Fred MacMurray out of the audience and convinced them to perform. Fred tried to play the saxophone, something he hadn't done in years, but it was quite a duet – a new 'high' in sheer merriment with Matt trying to sing over Fred's strange sounds.

Woody's humour was contagious and word spread like wildfire that this was someone worth seeing. He sat at a thirty-six-inch high, 'spinet type' piano with a full eighty-eight-note keyboard and performed a routine based almost entirely on booze and boozers. He was such a devotee of drink that he founded a club based on alcohol consumption called BITOA (Booze Is The Only Answer) and to everyone's amazement it soon had more than a million members. Crowds flocked to the venue and stood grouped around his piano while he played, joked and made merry with general fun and nonsense. Woody was also the most marvellous golf partner. With a regular playing companion, Matt bought his own set of golf clubs and took to playing every morning. Unfortunately he spent the last few weeks of 1980 in Florida on crutches after wrenching his ankle while playing out of a sand trap. Accidents notwithstanding, Matt promised Woody he would join him on the golf course when he returned from England in April.

This was not the start Matt had hoped for in the New Year. He had suffered so many injuries over the previous months it was like something out of a bad sitcom – very unfunny and in his case extremely painful. The trouble started when he'd slipped and broken his collarbone about six months back and he was just getting over the fall when he slammed his thumb in the car door, breaking it in the process. Now on crutches, he'd awkwardly reached out to pick up a cup and strained his back. The continual assault on his body had become so bad that Matt was almost afraid to get out of bed.

With a conscious effort to become somewhat trimmer and fitter he had made the New Year's resolution to stop drinking, but this well-intentioned move came with its own problems. Two days later, he was admitted to Central Middlesex

Hospital as an emergency admission after suffering a grand mal convulsion. Matt had suffered a similar incident several years before, and on both occasions the convulsions were precipitated by a sudden abstention from alcohol. Investigations failed to reveal any other cause for the fits than alcohol withdrawal. For the first few days following admission, he was treated with a decreasing dose of Chlormethiazole and intravenous vitamins in the form of Parentrovite. He was finally discharged on 8 January.

He went to see his private specialist who advised him there was little doubt that alcoholism was at the root of the singer's problems. This had been well documented in the past by Dr Dawson and Professor Sherlock. The recent investigations at the Central Middlesex Hospital confirmed the diagnosis, showing abnormal liver function and alcoholic bone marrow disease. Dr Gallen, Matt's general practitioner, received a letter from the specialist outlining his findings.

Matt was well enough to work Fairfield Halls in Croydon. His platelets had now come up to within normal range. His haemogram showed him to have a macrocytosis and his enzyme levels were elevated, but the other liver function tests were normal. Dr Misiewicz told him this was in line with alcoholic damage and persuaded him to see Dr Paul Gwinner, who specialised in cases of alcoholism, when he returned from the Far East.

Matt flew Thai Airlines to Bangkok at the end of January with a new musical director in tow – Mike Hatchard. During his audition with Matt the pianist had only played the first four bars of 'On a Clear Day' when the singer stopped him. Mike felt it unfair that having travelled all the way from Bournemouth for the try-out he hadn't been allowed to play the whole number. He didn't realise he'd got the job. The gig required him to work the next two weeks at the Dusit Thani Hotel followed by three weeks at the Hilton Hotel in Kuala Lumpur. When he was first offered the gig, he didn't think it was that big a deal. "Certainly I had no idea of just how good he was. I thought he was a good singer but when I listen to him now, I suddenly realise with quite a jolt that I accompanied one of the best singers the world has ever produced."

Mike didn't quite know what to expect from his new job but sharing a suite with the singer, he soon got the measure of the man. "We really got on well although Matt never went out of his room, except once when I persuaded him to sit by the pool. He had various visitors including some wealthy golf-playing football manager. The night after he left, two hookers the manager had organised as a gift for Matt turned up, but the singer didn't want to know and sent them packing." Mike was knocked out by the success of the shows, but was slightly nervous when the singer received a message from the management of the hotel informing him that the King of Malaya was coming in the next night. The show was fantastic and the atmosphere Matt created on stage was nothing short of electric. Consequently he was invited over to the sovereign's table for refreshments after the show and again for lunch the following day.

> **Matt told me about the invitation to lunch the next day and insisted I went with him, which I thought was really nice. The Master of Ceremonies announced each person's arrival and the audience dutifully applauded. It went something like, "Please welcome Major General Montmorency of Lower Moldavia (applause) and please welcome Princess Gertha of Hertzog-Slatvinia (lots of applause). Please welcome the King of Malaya (huge applause) and please welcome international singing star Matt Monro (even more applause) and...er...Mike Hatchard (faint ripple) and please welcome Duke Esterhazy of Peregrinavia (standard applause resumed). — Mike Hatchard**

It seemed that there was all manner of royalty popping into the showroom at the top of the Kula Lumpur Hilton. One such gentleman broke into a private conversation Matt was having with some old friends he had invited down for the evening. The 'royal arse' kept butting in and insisted that Matt go back on stage and entertain him and his important guests. Matt had finished for the evening and had no intention of going back on as the band members had disassembled their instruments and were sitting at another table with Mike Hatchard enjoying a quiet drink. The man became belligerent, spoiling for a fight, insulted Matt's friends and threw his glass of red wine into Matt's face. Matt's right fist swiftly connected with the man's facial tissue.

The guy was out for the count and Matt was ushered out of the room by the management. They apologised to the star for any inconvenience caused and offered to have his suit cleaned, sending complimentary champagne up to the suite for Matt and his friends. Although Matt had felt quite pleased with himself for standing up to defend his corner, he later became a little nervous about possible retribution. He wasn't sure how high up this guy was in royal circles, but over the years he himself had made friends in high places and they promised to get him out of the country safely if the need arose. Matt never did find out who the dignitary was or get the chance to revisit Kuala Lumpur.

Ernie Schuller & Matt

Things were changing. After several long discussions, Matt and Mickie had decided to live in Florida whilst retaining their London home. The decision was taken in order to cut down on the vast amount of commuting Matt was doing because of overseas engagements. Britain had become boring, with Matt forever working the same clubs, and he was left wanting a new challenge, one that he didn't think England could offer him. He blamed Britain's predictable, if shrinking, club scene for many of the ills of the business and decided to apply some damage control. With the children grown up now, Mickie and Matt didn't have to worry so much for their stability. Michele was already settled in Florida and, with his visa approved, Matthew was due to fly to Australia in November. The couple decided to wait until June as Matt still had several commitments in England, and it would give Mickie a chance to put things in order. Luckily she was still in England when she received the news that her brother had died after overdosing on barbiturates. His wife Eliane had found him when she came downstairs in the morning. He lay in the lounge with a suicide note next to his body. It was one of the saddest moments in Mickie's life and she couldn't get over the fact that Ernie had given no indication that he was so unhappy. It was a hard thing to come to terms with.

Moving to Florida allowed Matt to indulge in one of his favourite pastimes – golf. He was not, by his own admission, a particularly talented player and would often joke that "his clubs were not used to him yet!" Matthew on *This Is Your Life* summed it up most eloquently by remarking that "he had two ambitions; one was to be a singer just like his dad and the other was to play golf – but not like his dad!" One of the oddest moments was when he was playing Crystal Lake in Florida. There is a par three hole over water with a carry of 185 yards to clear the lake before hitting the green. Matt was playing a four ball and the others had all taken their shots. Matt placed his tee, lined himself up and just when he got to the top of his swing a crocodile came lumbering out of the water. Matt nearly had a heart attack; his club flew out of his hands in the reverse direction and the ball stayed just where it was.

Matt and Matt Jnr were playing golf in Jakarta. Undeniably Matt's son was a much better player than his father and wanted to show off his ability. Teeing off at the first hole he was in such a hurry to get to his next shot, he tore off in the buggy, zigzagging along the small lanes and took the turning too sharply. The buggy overturned and trapped Matt underneath, his brand new five-wood lying beside him in two pieces. Matthew made the wise decision to let his father win that game!

Guest of Honour at the Governor's House , Jakarta

Florida was a golf player's dream with hundreds of lush fairways and greens to choose from. Matt bought all the kit possible; after all he had to look the part. Dressed in a coordinated outfit including a new pair of Footjoy 'Aqualites', he set off for his round with Woody. At the eleventh hole his ball didn't quite make the distance, falling short of the green at the side of the lake. Woody played an almost identical shot. The two men went to the side of the lake to retrieve their balls. Matt's was just out of arms reach so he used his seven-iron to try and steer the ball back to the edge. It just needed a bit more effort, and leaning over too far, he lost his balance and fell head first into the water. After the incident with the crocodile, Matt didn't wait around; you have never seen anyone clamber out of the water so quickly. His new outfit clung to his body and his shoes were anything but Footjoy!

The month flew by and before long the couple were making plans to retrace their steps over the Atlantic. Three days before flying back to England, Matt had the opportunity to see Frank Sinatra. Finally, he was to meet the artist he had been compared to for years. But sadly it was not meant to be.

When we were all in Fort Lauderdale, I got Matt, Dickie Davies and Gareth Hunt a condo and I also had one in Meadowridge. Matt's over there and I said you'll never guess who's playing here Sunday

Dickie Davies & Matt

week – Frank Sinatra. We got the tickets for the Sunrise Theatre,
Matt, Mickie and me, the three of us, we had seats upstairs – gold
dust - with concrete steps all the way up. Mickie felt sick and Matt
said she should go outside for some air and while helping her up
the stairs he slipped. I saw the bone come right up through his
hand. The paramedics came, that was in the first half of the show,
we never got to the end and there's me, I don't know what to do.
Matt was out like a light when the paramedics took both him and
Mickie to hospital. — Michael Black

On the same day that Matt had his plaster cast removed he signed with Hindworth
Management and was now represented by John Ashby. In May he recorded a new
single called 'Diana', a tribute to the Princess of Wales, co-written by Don Black
and Vic Lewis. The song was to be released in June, prior to the worldwide
broadcast of Diana's marriage to Prince Charles on 29 July. Matt wasn't thrilled
with the record, as he didn't want to be seen to be cashing in on the royal wedding.
He was also mystified as to why EMI had asked him to release a single at a time
he wouldn't be in the country to promote the song.

Monro left Britain just as the new single hit the shops. Asked what he would do if the record hit the charts and he was required in England for promotional work, he said, "Too bad, I'll be in Miami." The advent of cheap charter flights had drawn thousands of British holidaymakers to the Miami area, and some entertainers had moved their summer seasons there too. Matt was offered a four night a week season over four months at the Newport Beach Hotel in the capitol but turned the contract down. He was tired and felt that he had earned the right to relax his pace.

Matt and Mickie met Ron and Mo Miller in Meadowridge. Dickie Davies had lent the couple his condominium for a few weeks while the Millers furnished their own recent purchase within the complex. The Millers threw a housewarming party and Mickie had got a little drunk. When it was time to leave Ron came to the rescue: "I carried her down the stairs, got her in the car, drove round to their place and got absolutely drenched in the rain. Matt lent me one of his silk shirts, which felt very expensive, so I told Mo to take extra care when washing it. When we returned it, Mo went to great lengths to explain how careful she had been with it. Matt roared and said he had bought it in the Philippines for a couple of quid."

Ron was Sales and Marketing Director for London Weekend Television and was full of stories about the industry. The two men hit it off immediately, shared the same sense of humour and fun and were perfectly at ease in each other's company. Their friendship continued well after the Millers' departure from America.

Despite the success of *Heartbreakers,* Matt had shifted his focus to his Hispanic recordings. He released *Recital* that year and made plans to go back in the studio with Leonardo Schultz. Since his first Spanish album *Alguien Canto* had reached the number one spot in South America, subsequent releases were equally successful. It was in fact Matt's Spanish recordings that earned the singer his first platinum disc. Between 1967 and 1983 he brought more than twenty Spanish language singles and at least sixteen albums to the market. Matt's fans were always more important to him than chart position. Never was that more obvious than when he arrived in the Philippines and played to more than 100,000 overexcited fans over four nights, having only been booked to play one. They could not get enough of him and Monro mania was everywhere. Schultz wrote a letter to USA Immigration in March 1984 on Matt's behalf regarding his application for a green card and verified that *Alguien Canto* had sold in excess of seven million units worldwide and that *En Español* had done equally well.

Matt's Hispanic fans found his accent irresistible and had an insatiable appetite for adding even more of the star's releases to their growing collection. But

Photo shoot with Gary Mason

Leonardo complained that Matt's Spanish intonation was getting too good, and didn't want to ruin the winning formula. He asked the singer to read his phonetic pronunciations rather than the original text so that he would occasionally get the phrasing wrong, claiming, "that is your charm".

In July, Matt went into Quadradial Studios in Miami with Leonardo and his new partner Gary Mason. The two men had met and become partners in the early 1970s and had collaborated with Jose Feliciano, Demis Roussos and Shirley Bassey.

As Leonardo had previously worked on a Spanish album with Matt and secured a massive hit with *Alguien Canto*, Gary didn't object to his partner's proposal of doing another Spanish album with the star. Gary knew of the singer's pedigree, because *Born Free* and *From Russia with Love* had both been big hits in the American market, so he was more than happy to put up the finance for the new project and negotiate a tour with the singer to promote future products. At a meeting at Matt's condominium, Leonardo and Gary presented the singer with contracts with Supreme Enterprises for signature. The paperwork specified that Matt would commit to three tours over a two and a half year period and perform three working weeks out of four, with a maximum of nine shows a week. Although Matt signed the contracts, he never got the opportunity to go on another South American tour.

Un Toque de Distinción was laid down in stages. Mason and Schultz recorded the music at George Martin's AIR London Studio between 12 and 24 June and then hooked up with Matt in Miami in July. Matt's vocals were recorded in two days and they shot the album cover at the Doral Hotel in Miami Beach. Gary and Leonardo then flew to New York to have the album mixed at Phil Ramone's A&R Studios with engineer Tom Greto. The final stage saw Gary take the mixed album back to LA, where it was mastered at Hitsville Recording Studios with John Matousek.

> The sessions originally started at Criterian Studios but we were unhappy with the facilities and moved over to Quadradial in Miami. Matt was recording and we just couldn't get the right echo. I suggested he try singing in the studio's bathroom, it worked, and Matt ended up recording all his vocals in there. He had a drink in one hand and a cigarette in the other and I asked him "how the hell he could smoke, drink and sing". He pointed up to the sky and said God. Matt was easy to work with. In the studio he knew if his intonation was off and would ask to re-record. Once he was warmed up Matt's vocals were excellent and he was able to record all his songs in two days. Because he couldn't speak Spanish it was done line by line phonetically. ... The biggest problem we had was my constant fighting with Leonardo not to let Matt drink Johnny Walker Red Label and smoke while he was recording. I was more concerned with his health; Leonardo was more concerned with the recordings. — Gary Mason

Unfortunately the album did not fare as well as the others. Leonardo was an artist, not a businessman, and bad production decisions, with massive overspending made the album extremely expensive to produce. There was absolutely no reason for Supreme Enterprises to record in London, one of the world's most expensive cities, especially as Matt wasn't doing his vocals there. Leonardo spent as much on hotels and airfares as he did in studio time, when the whole thing could have been done for half the cost in Los Angeles. Leonardo also thought that using four different locations would make the album more prestigious and sound better. Gary felt that his partner was still living in the 1960s, when it was nearly unheard of for an Anglo artist to record in Spanish. In the 1980s that fact alone would not guarantee record sales. Spanish ballad singers were already emerging as major players in the business and standards were much higher than they were in years past.

With all that said Gary Mason did enjoy the sessions and his time with Matt. Artists like Paul McCartney and Lulu popped into the studios to say hello and there were plenty of jovial moments. Leonardo introduced Gary to Don Black when they recorded in London and the two spent some time together. In fact, he remembers one occasion very well. Having taken his Swedish girlfriend along for dinner, he was fairly miffed that Don spent most of the evening talking to her and came away perplexed as to why Matt had trusted Don with his career for so many years.

> Just because Don wrote a hit song for Matt, 'Born Free', it didn't mean he should have been his manager. Writer - yes. Manager - no. There were so many missed opportunities. He is a very talented writer, and a nice fellow. He knew a lot of people, but I do not think he had the knowledge and contacts necessary to move Matt to the next level. Don was known as a great writer in the business, not a great manager. To this day, I doubt if anyone even knew that Don Black at one time managed Matt. If Matt had had an Irving Azoff, or Ken Kramer, he would have been a much bigger star, especially in the U.S. — Gary Mason

Gary Mason was not alone in this assumption, it seemed that friendship had clouded a sound business judgement in the early days. Don Black was working for a music publisher, he knew nothing about the inside workings of the business and while it was easy to pick up a phone call and process an enquiry, he didn't have the knowledge, expertise or business acumen to take it any further than that.

> We were with Evelyn Taylor; she fought for us. If Matt had been with the right management or agency he would have been a huge star. — Mike Winters

Matt's sense of humour was always in evidence and he managed to convince Gary Mason that he was seriously thinking about having surgery in Hong Kong to make himself a foot taller. He told the producer he felt his height was holding back his career, and Gary bought the story, hook, line and sinker. He told Matt that height was irrelevant and that there were plenty of tall people who were very small and a lot of short people who were very big. The next day while shooting a photographic session for the album cover at the Doral Beach Hotel, Gary took off his shoes, placed his knees on them and stood next to Matt. It was a great moment.

While Matt was in Miami, he was introduced to the Bee Gees. The brothers all lived on the same piece of real estate in Bay Road, Miami Beach. A gated entrance protected each of their individual homes and there was a purpose-built studio within the compound. Matt got very friendly with Maurice Gibb in particular; the men had a lot in common, especially the fact that both entertainers were alcoholics.

Maurice had been clean for some time and spent days talking to Matt about his apparent difficulty in giving up alcohol. There was no question that Matt's drinking was out of control again, but more importantly, it was starting to really affect his family and Mickie was worried sick. A few days previously he had woken up disorientated on the settee and fallen through a glass-topped table whilst struggling to get up. He could have been seriously injured – it was time to address the problem.

Maurice Gibb immediately drove over to Meadowridge to see Matt and spent six hours with him. He told the singer that he was a member of Alcoholics Anonymous and relied heavily on the program, sometimes going as often as twice a day and at his worst he was hiding bottles of alcohol around the house so his wife couldn't find them. He even hid bottles in the toilet cistern. At that time celebrity stories about drug addiction or alcohol abuse were not as readily accepted as they are today. There were many in the business that felt that if they came clean or the press caught wind of their problems, it could end their careers. By the end of the session, Maurice had convinced Matt to go back to England and enter a rehabilitation centre. As soon as Maurice had Matt's agreement, he immediately made all the arrangements, not giving the star the opportunity to change his mind or to come up with any excuses as to why he couldn't go. Matt's flight left the next day.

TWELVE STEPS

Thank you for asking us to look after this man. He was admitted on
3 September. Physical examination and his very high liver function
tests supported the notion that he was a chronic alcoholic. There
was also evidence of chronic bronchitis from smoking and he had
pain over his sternum and adjacent ribs. The latter was caused by
a fall. X-ray revealed no fractures in that area but old compression
fractures of the mid dorsal vertebrae and a healed left clavicle.
— Galsworthy House

Matt's room at Galsworthy House contained the bare minimum, but he was
comfortable enough. He had been through a similar routine at The Priory
five years before, so nothing came as too much of a shock. The nursing team took
vital signs twice a day. Detoxification is designed to purge the body of intoxicating
substances and is the first step taken in overcoming addiction. To avoid withdrawal
symptoms, benzodiazepines such as diazepam or chlordiazepoxide are prescribed.
Matt was quite shaky on arrival and was given Librium to calm his nerves.

It is perfectly normal in a clinic of this kind for a breathalyser to be taken on
arrival as well as a strip search to ensure no hidden substances are being carried
in. Suitcases are scrutinised and anything, however innocent looking, is confiscated
if it is deemed to contain alcohol. Patients are always amazed when products like
cologne, shampoo, aftershave, hairspray, mouthwash, toothpaste and certain
shaving products are taken off them.

Matt was amazed by some of the people and their stories. A few had been there
more than six times, some actually turned up intoxicated having had a wee dram
up the road to give them the strength to enter the grounds, and some turned up
stoned even though they had stopped drinking two days before.

The clinical remedial team offered the very best medical attention and health education during the patient's withdrawal from drugs or alcohol in a twelve-step rolling programme. The nursing brigade were there to control symptoms and maximise the client's physical wellbeing. The health scheme was as in-depth as the attention given to drug control, with a focus on good nutrition, sleep, hygiene and anxiety management.

Group counselling took place midmorning and the group comprised of men and women from all walks of life. As well as addressing alcoholism and addiction, the clinic offered psychological services and treatments for a range of conditions. Everyone wore a nametag, which was handy, as Matt couldn't remember the other patient's names. Group therapy is essential for the client to make a connection with their peers and begin to understand the consequences of their addiction. Four weeks is a long time and it is amazing how close everybody becomes. The rules are strict: group confidentiality is a given policy and there can be no disruptions when someone else is talking. Listening is as important as sharing as it's a hard enough task to bare your soul to complete strangers without dealing with interruptions. Having to start again was far harder.

Galsworthy's philosophy was based on the principals used by Alcoholics Anonymous. The programme is a key element in the treatment of drug and alcohol addiction, and enables each client to begin their journey to recovery by reflecting on their needs, their beliefs and their sense of meaning and purpose. Their in-house meetings saw the whole group come together to talk candidly about their addiction.

When it was Matt's turn the group all acknowledged him: "Hi Matt," and encouraged him to start. "My name is Matt and I am an alcoholic" – those nine words can change your life, and in Matt's case they did. His outing to the Priory had been different: he had only gone there to keep everybody happy and hadn't really applied himself as much as he could have done. His commitment was real this time around, and he attended all the lectures and classes on offer. He accepted his shortcomings and admitted that his wife had taken away the burden of responsibility throughout their lives together, so that all he had to do was perform. He had gone through life seeking approval, acceptance and applause.

After a live show, I would stand in the dressing room, with all these guests coming in and congratulating me on the show. The excitement of a standing ovation is the biggest high a performer can have. — Matt Monro

It was impossible to sustain those types of high on a twenty-four-hour basis. There was no doubt that all the anxiety of performing, the loneliness of travelling and forced sociability had in part caused Matt to abuse alcohol. The doctor made him face the lowest and most telling moments of his life: that he was born into a very poor family, that he had lost his father aged three, that he had watched his mother struggle to bring up his four eldest siblings, as well as himself, that he had endured the horrors of war, that he'd married his first wife because of the pregnancy, and that the forced estrangement of his eldest son and his mother's death played a vital role in his dependence on alcohol. Those past events were deep-rooted, but there were other significant moments that came into play, the agony and pain of relentless injury to his body, the loss of close friends, the disappointment in others and the self-reproach of taking someone's life. It didn't matter that it wasn't his fault; he was racked with remorse and guilt.

Matt was encouraged to make a list of all his guilty thoughts, resentments and fears and the standards he had set other people, usually the cause of so much bitterness. He had to learn to accept his past and stop willing things to be different. He was told that while he was experiencing these negative emotions, he couldn't be truly happy. He made a gratitude list and ignored what he wanted to change, instead looking at what he had achieved and the wonderful things he had in his life.

The psychiatrist felt that there was no doubt that Matt was a highly dependent man, especially on women. Undoubtedly this was the legacy of being his mother's pet, and part of the reason why he was so devoted and dependant on his second wife, who shouldered all of life's larger responsibilities. As a result of these strong female forces in his life, he had never truly matured, his state being perpetuated by being 'spoilt' by enthusiastic audiences. Matt came to realise that he was the problem and that his reactions to life's events had caused his meltdown. It made little sense to him that after coming to terms with the cause of his pain, and recognising the defects of his character, that he would then go out and do those things again; it could only lead to more heartache and self-harm. But the hardest thing to accept was that his life wouldn't change over night; it was a slow process that would involve a lot of patience and tolerance on the part of himself and his loved ones.

The sessions were incredibly emotional for all the patients, and it wasn't unusual for someone to break down and sob uncontrollably. In extremely low moments, there was always someone to offer a hug and several took God into their hearts. Matt was a Spiritualist and believed in its message, and his faith helped him through the process.

Individual therapy was also part of the regime, so the client was able to communicate some of the more difficult issues that might be too overwhelming to discuss in group therapy. It also provided a safe space for Matt to connect with his own process and consider what options there were for the future. He was encouraged to write down what had happened to him the last time he'd had a drink: the guilt, fear and regret that it created, the harm he was doing to himself and others, the psychological, mental, and relationship damage it had caused and how it affected his self esteem. The 'unmanageability' – guilt, resentment, hatred, anxiety, fear and self loathing all caused 'disease' and that disease caused him to crave. He accepted that he had tried to run away from the anguish of disappointment, pain and death, but it was now time to accept life on life's terms. Matt went down on his knees with his councillor and prayed. It was that small act of humility that finally released him. He felt he had a duty to help other people and ensure they didn't follow his path or replicate his mistakes.

Outside of the meetings, lectures, therapy sessions, meditation, workshops, assignments, films and slide shows, Matt's day was taken up with chores to keep him busy. He was allowed limited telephone time and family visits.

Addiction is an illness that affects not only the primary sufferer but also has knock-on effects for family and close friends. The pain of addiction is just as severe for those who have relationships with addicts. The family group gave Mickie the help and support she needed and allowed her to finally talk about how she felt about what had been happening to their lives. More importantly, it gave her the skills and tools necessary to begin her own healing process.

The underlying focus was on 'graduation day' and the exit interview. During Matt's stay several people left which was sad in one way, as there was always a sense of loss, but also of elation, cheers and hugs and the hope that the graduate would stay strong on the outside. Matt was very friendly with two residents, Connie and Harry. When Harry left, he lapsed after only four months and sadly died from liver failure as a result.

Maurice Gibb remained Matt's sponsor. He had shared his addictive experience with his fellow entertainer and was enjoying a long and successful sobriety. He was there to give support should Matt lapse or offer encouragement if he had a weak moment.

> **I'm feeling more rested and at peace now and quite thrilled about Daddy's progress. He's getting on so well in all respects – mentally most of all, which is what it's all about. Matthew came with me to the family evening last night and was very surprised to see Daddy not only looking so well, but to hear him talk so openly about his problem. I think Matthew is more at peace now. — Letter from Mickie in London**

Matt accepted that he didn't just have a disease of his liver but a disease of the mind that was causing him to self-destruct. Rehabilitation taught him it was possible to have a good life without a drink and to live one day at a time. He felt ready to face the world again. Before Matt's release one of the people who ran Alcoholics Anonymous encouraged him to come to one of their outside meetings, but there was no outward pressure and they left him a selection of reading material to take home. Matt was discharged on the 30 September 1981. He never had to attend an AA meeting, but he never drank again, either.

Matt felt and looked twenty years younger. It was the first time in years that he hadn't relied on alcohol as a crutch and the transformation was astounding. With a renewed vigour for life, he was raring to get back to work. His fourteenth tour to Australia was being negotiated under a new promoter, Tony Brady, who ran a company called ATA Allstar Artists.

> I travelled to London in 1981 to meet various entertainment managers and agents for the purpose of contracting some artists to tour Australia. I was always a great fan of Matt Monro and so when the opportunity came to meet his agent of the day, John Ashby, I caught a taxi to 235 Regent Street and headed upstairs to John's office. The news wasn't all that good. John explained that Matt wasn't quite ready to work; however, he suggested I should meet him personally as he felt it might at least give Matt some confidence in what I was proposing for a tour. — Tony Brady

On 31 October, six months after first meeting Tony Brady, Matt and Mickie arrived in Sydney to tour five weeks around Australia. While Matt's regular musical director was unavailable, good fortune had it that Arthur Greenslade was living in Australia at the time and Matt asked him to join the tour. They added guitar, bass, drums and string machine to the mix and rehearsed at Cashmore Sound Studios before starting off on their travels, which was to take in Sydney, Queensland, South Australia and Perth. Tony remembers the time fondly: "Needless to say the shows were great and the audiences loved Matt!"

Tony wanted a car to impress the singer. He bought a second-hand Jaguar at the eleventh hour, but wasn't quite sure what all the dials and instruments did. That was certainly in evidence when driving to the South Coast as he desperately tried to get the air-conditioning to work. He fiddled with all the knobs throughout the journey, the car fogged up, the radio came on, the windows opened, the windscreen wipers swatted away everything in their path and the trunk even sprung open – in fact everything was deployed except the air-con! They made it safely to Wollongong, did the show and drove back to Sydney with the windows wound down.

Matt always stayed at the Sebel Town House when in Sydney and from there the first batch of press and radio interviews took place. Matt was one of two Water Rats enjoying Sydney's summer: the other was female impersonator Danny La Rue. The Water Rats have strict rules, so when the two members met at the Town House one Saturday night, Matt fined Danny for failing to wear his Rat emblem, breaking one of the Order's cardinal rules.

One of the nice things about travelling to Australia on a regular basis was it gave the Monros the opportunity of visiting their relatives. Two of Ernie's children, Gary and Andrew, were living there, as well as Matthew who was over on a year's visa. It was strange for Matt to have his children so scattered: Michele was living in Florida, Matthew in Australia and Mitchell was in England sitting his instructor's rating. He was training to be a pilot and doing very well indeed.

> **This will be our fifth flight since arriving and having always said that I would never do one of these tours, I don't know why I had to start at my ripe old age. We arrived Saturday morning in Sydney, Monday was press and radio all day but managed lunch with Matt White, then band call on Tuesday before flying to Melbourne. Spent that evening and Wednesday with the family. Did the television on Thursday and flew back to Sydney on Friday. Opened that night – and then flew out again. On Saturday morning we were booked on this funny little plane – a Bandeirante – seats sixteen people. Daddy was told at the airport that there was no stewardess on board, that we couldn't smoke and there was no toilet, he asked if there was a First Class! — Letter from Mickie, Sebel Town House, Sydney**

Had a very good flight here, could have done without the Aussie Test Cricket team, but they didn't fly First Class! Apart from Daddy we all wore windcheaters in navy and white which have 'Matt Monro Australian Tour 1981' on the back. Our luggage has similar labels so you can see that Tony Brady has really gone to a great deal of trouble. Daddy did press and radio all day long plus band call. It was opening night and the show was fantastic.

Daddy wrote: As Mummy said it is hard work but very rewarding. I'm enjoying working again so much; I'd forgotten what a good life it can be. — Letter from Mickie, Sheraton Perth

We are now in our sixth hotel, with seven flights behind us, not to mention the car rides, band calls, press, radio, TV and the shows! Getting laundry done is not easy; we don't seem to be in any one place long enough. Last Monday we flew back to Sydney on our way to Brisbane and it was the worst flight I've ever been on, there was an earthquake tremor! Had a real ball in Perth and we enjoyed every minute. Daddy's shows were a joy; the last night was just sensational. Danny La Rue plus gang came and Daddy had two standing ovations while Mummy was in tears. Our two nights in Brisbane were great too and I'm now looking forward to tonight. Shows in Sydney tomorrow, Saturday and Sunday, all at different venues of course, and then we have a day off on Monday. We will be leaving Sydney for the USA on 14 December and will arrive in Miami on that date if we don't stop off in LA. It would be nice to see Marion and it seems a shame not to utilise the airfares.

— Letter from Mickie, Telford Toowoomba Hotel, Queensland

Tickets sold out everywhere and the show was a smash wherever it went. This was quite a comeback for Matt, considering he had taken almost six months out to recover from his health problems. He was understandably concerned that having cancelled an Australian tour earlier in the year, he might not have been welcomed back quite so enthusiastically but he couldn't have been more wrong. He was in fact singing better than ever, looked fitter and slimmer than he had in years and was enjoying every moment of the tour.

A minor earthquake, measuring 3.6 on the Richter scale, rumbled through Sydney's suburbs and most of eastern NSW. Thousands of people were woken by the tremor, timed at 3.58am, as their homes shook for several seconds. Mickie woke up to feel the room moving and she promptly woke her husband. While they were deciding what to do, the tremor stopped. Although the Town House wasn't affected, one could clearly see that most of the suburb was blacked out. There was not much to be done except go back to sleep!

Matt appeared on the *Mike Walsh Show* again; in fact it was on the same show that Winifred Atwell had recently announced her official retirement. Asked whether Matt might make a similar announcement in the near future, he replied that nothing could be further from his mind. He felt as if he had been given a new lease on life and still had mountains to conquer. He celebrated his fifty-first birthday on the Gold Coast. It was a slightly worrying time for Mickie as she wasn't sure if Matt would succumb to the temptation of drink, after all he had given up before only to start again. But this time was different; Matt was absolutely resolute and his willpower was astounding. He was clean and proud of his achievement.

> We are on the Gold Coast, Surfer's Paradise, now. Daddy opens here tonight for five days. The club is beautiful and the resort is really 'paradise'. I know where we are, I know what day it is but I don't know the time! We are on the boundary of a time zone area here so by crossing the road there is one hour's difference. Also you listen to one radio station, which gives you a time check, which is completely different to the one on another station. The same goes for television so it is certainly confusing. Daddy has really not stopped but he has been doing tremendous shows and business has been terrific. Tony Brady threw a birthday lunch for Daddy today. I think he's really enjoyed his birthday this year – as you know we had to make do with drinks with Sammy! In two days time – the 4th – we will celebrate 'Meadowridge' one year since we moved in.
>
> Daddy writes: I must rush as it is 8.50pm and I'm being picked up at 9.15pm although I'm not on till 10.15pm but I don't know what side of the road the club is on! — Letter from Mickie, Cook's Endeavour Motor Inn, Tweed Heads

Sammy Davis Jr was working in one of the elite hotels in Sydney and the couple popped in to catch his act. Sammy invited them for drinks the following night and

Matt found the most amazing birthday cake waiting for him, as well as a completely non-alcoholic bar. Sammy also gave his friend a specially signed copy of his new book *Hollywood in a Suitcase* and a beautiful black lacquer Dunhill lighter. Matt was touched at the lengths that his friend had gone to and had no idea how Sammy knew it was his birthday. It was a funny thing now that he had stopped drinking, some people were now embarrassed to drink in front of him, they certainly didn't want the blame for leading Matt into temptation. But the smell of alcohol and its presence didn't bother Matt and he continued to keep a fully stocked bar at both his homes for when friends visited. When he was in England, he still dropped into his local public house, as he would have missed the camaraderie much more than the drink.

Matt's old friend Kerry Jewel had moved to Australia in 1978 and under the management of Tony Brady was booked out as comic and compere. Nearly every act that Brady brought out to Australia, Kerry worked the support. This year he was offered the tour with Matt, but was afraid to accept it as he had himself been on the wagon for three months. Remembering the drinking sessions he and Matt had shared in the past, he was scared he might be tempted away from sobriety. After much deliberation he decided to accept the contract, not realising that Matt was also off the booze.

Before drying out, Kerry attended a couple of AA meetings but found them so depressing that he ended up going to the pub to get pissed! Although AA was a marvellous programme it wasn't right for Matt and Kerry. One thing the men didn't give up was cigarettes and both men were heavy smokers. Kerry used to stand in the wings with a radio mike and make the intros for Matt. The singer would take a last puff and hand the cigarette to Kerry as he took the stage. As Matt walked on singing the opening bars all you could see was a cloud of smoke coming out of his mouth!

Kerry had been a heavy drinker and staying dry was a big achievement. It was not unusual to see Arthur Greenslade, Kerry and Matt enjoying a pub lunch, all of them drinking mineral water. Matt was very supportive of his friend's sobriety and there followed long talks into the night about abstinence. He insisted that Kerry telephone him if he ever needed to talk, even if it was in the middle of the night. Matt made a point of calling his friend once a month to check up on him and offer words of encouragement.

Some of the tour dates were not well planned and it meant that they were continually criss-crossing across the country. One of the gigs necessitated travelling from Cairns to Mount Isa, a twenty-four-hour non-stop drive. The musicians were not happy and rumours were circulating that Matt was flying there. Kerry approached Brady and said: "I hear we're going to Mount Isa, I might not live that long! If you want me with the 'Little Star' tomorrow night, I'm on the plane with you." Kerry was put on the flight.

Mickie had definitely got touring down to a fine art with all the years of practice she'd had. Matt was very particular about the way he looked on stage, but keeping things immaculate was extremely hard when you were living out of a suitcase. Kerry was constantly amazed at the way Mickie looked after the singer's stage attire.

> **Matt and Mickie were joined at the hip; you didn't see one without the other. Mickie used to disappear to play the poker machines. She had a way of hanging trousers that no one else had ever seen.**
> **— Kerry Jewel**

Just because Matt wasn't drinking alcohol, it didn't stop him buying anyone else a drink, and he remained generous to the end. After a show he liked to treat the musicians to a beer and he would often be seen at the bar with Arthur Greenslade, Bruce Kerr, Bruce Morley, Jim Gannon and Mike Hope. The tour was a huge financial success for Tony Brady and a personal success for the singer. Having already discussed a return trip in fourteen months' time with the promoter, Matt and Mickie took their leave and headed for their home in Florida just in time for Christmas.

FIFTEEN AND COUNTING

Even though 1982 brought with it a new chart trend, rap music, Matt's style of music continued to be popular among the mainstream fans and he was in constant demand. Having returned to England after a Christmas break, he was swamped with requests for radio, not just Ed Stewart on the BBC, but Tony Myatt on Capitol and Bob Holness on LBC. Now that he had based himself out of the country, the media were desperate to know what the lad from Shoreditch was getting up to.

He had flown back especially for his ninth appearance at London's Talk of the Town, with Bernard Delfont presenting *Gala Galaxy Revue*. Due to Matt's world travels and his stay at Galsworthy, it had been over a year since he had sung in Britain. After his season at the London venue he would be touring Britain with the Syd Lawrence Orchestra and in the spring, star in a special concert with Billy May and his Orchestra. John Ashby had come up with the concept of Matt touring with the big bands and it proved an exciting collaboration. The shows were a reminder that there were few things more musically satisfying than a good singer with a big band.

> **The series of concerts with Syd Lawrence were very successful,**
> **because the pubic could hear the music with the arrangements,**
> **and how they'd been written for a big band. It was quite a feat.**
> **— John Ashby**

"I like a family-type audience but they didn't tell me it was going to be just one family," Matt quipped, with pointed reference to empty seats on opening night, courtesy of the rail strike. But that didn't stop his season at The Talk of the Town being as successful as ever and once the strike was over, the room was filled to capacity. Matt loved working there, it was after all the most prestigious venue in the capital and he had a raft of wonderful memories from performing on that stage. As he took his final bow of the season, he had no way of knowing that it would be his last appearance there. It was a shock when the news was suddenly announced that the venue would be closing its doors later that year.

> Matt was one of the - no, actually, I think he was THE best singer of his type that we have ever had. He was a great interpreter of songs and he understood that it took a mixture of great arrangements, great musicians and musical directors to make it all happen and the amount of hits he had proves that. Look at the scene now – they don't know anything about music, compositions, and orchestras. — Rosalyn Wilder

On 2 March 1982, Matt opened at the Guild Hall in Preston in the first of a string of concerts with Syd Lawrence. Jeff Hooper was the lead singer with the orchestra. He absolutely adored Matt and spent as much time with the star as possible. They became fast friends over the length of the tour. The first leg took in Bedworth, Preston, Sunderland, Derby, Scarborough, Hanley, Stockport and Poole. John Ashby's idea was a cracker: the shows were storming everywhere and ticket offices had to turn people away. It seemed people had been deprived of the big band sound for far too long and now they came out in their droves.

> I first become aware of Matt's music at the age of fifteen and I became interested not just in the stars of that particular time but how they performed, the way they sounded and why they sounded the way they did, breath control and all that. I was trying to learn as much as I possibly could, so I listened very closely to all the singers – and Matt was one of the very best. He had such a warm sound and it was such a relaxed style he had, his voice was second to none. — Jeff Hooper

Matt took time to see his old pal Sammy Davis Jr, who was playing a private gig at the Grosvenor House Hotel. It didn't matter how much time had passed without seeing each other, they carried on exactly where they had left off.

While he was in England, Matt also took on a Scottish tour for the agent Frank Taylor, visiting Edinburgh, Blantyre, Perth, Dundee, Fife and Airedale. Although he was back doing one-nighters it didn't bother him so much, as the big draw of

Matt & Jeff Hooper

coming back to British shores had been his appearance at the Talk of the Town coupled with the promised concert with Billy May and the BBC Radio Big Band.

Matt was delighted to meet up with his buddy from the Capitol days and was equally chuffed that this was in fact Billy's first trip to Europe – and he had chosen to work with Matt from what must have been a large choice of singers. The show, presented as *Big Band Parade*, was recorded at the Fairfield Hall, Croydon on 23 April 1982, although it was not broadcast on Radio 2 until 15 May. A 29-piece accompanied Billy May and there was no doubting that in the presence of a big orchestra, Matt came into his own.

As well as the Syd Lawrence contract and the series of one-nighters, Matt had a heavy work commitment for the next few years. He decided he needed a resident musical director. By the age of eighteen, Dave Mellor was working in clubs, accompanying all of the acts booked on the bill six nights of every week, often without rehearsal. Whenever he had a night off he used to visit a local cabaret venue called Cranberry Fold, which had been purchased and renovated by a local property magnate. The place hosted all the top national and international artists. This was when cabaret and live music was at its height, in the mid to late 1960s.

Dave Mellor, Mickie, Kim & Jack Jones & Matt

There were no drink and drive laws to hinder business and life was good. One week he went up to Cranberry Fold to see Matt Monro. The place was full as always, but as well as punters there was also several prominent local musicians who had travelled over from Manchester especially to see the singer perform.

That night was a watershed moment in Dave Mellor's career. He was obviously knocked out by the singer, his phrasing, his tonality – but his eyes were on his pianist. Watching the large orchestra swinging away under his direction led to his ambition to become a musical director himself. He'd fostered the idea of conducting from the age of eight, but suddenly before his very eyes was what he wanted to do, and more importantly it was the style of music that he wanted to do it in. The fact that some years later he'd be working for that very artist has never failed to amaze him. Colin Keyes had recommended the musician to Matt and an audition was arranged. Following the call Dave went to Dallas Road to meet the singer and the two men hit it off straight away. He ran through a couple of charts on Matt's Knight spinet and that was that.

> We travelled thousands of miles around the UK, most of the time
> in fits of laughter; it wouldn't be the first time Matt had to pull
> over because we were laughing so much. After one of the first
> shows, driving back I commented to him about his comedic timing

during the middle of the show chat section, and the ripostes he gave to any 'mouths' from the audience – which was rare. I said that the ad-libs seemed to be straight 'off the cuff' and he responded with a line I have never forgotten but which I apply to just about everything I have done since. He said "Dave, there is not one thing I do on stage that has not been thought about, thoroughly practiced and rehearsed and honed." He was meticulous over the shows; however I don't remember one time when he had anything derogatory to say other than observing individual musicians who may not have been up to it. Later on I took responsibility for booking the band and this problem for the most part evaporated. He was also meticulous in his appearance. This was a performance and that was what you got, black tie, white shirt, smart and well cut black dinner suit and a red, sometimes white handkerchief. — Dave Mellor

Local newspapers proclaimed that lovers of the Big Band sound and beautiful ballads were in for a double treat, when the Syd Lawrence Orchestra joined forces with Matt for a memorable evening of music at the Spectrum Arena. The Syd Lawrence Orchestra had adopted the much sought after Glenn Miller sound far more effectively than many of their rivals. They were discovered in an upstairs room of a pub by Granada television executives and had since appeared with such show business greats as Bob Hope, Shirley Bassey, Petula Clark, Johnny Mathis and Tony Bennett.

Matt had only been to Malta once before, back in 1950 when he was in the army. Leaving England for his overseas posting in Hong Kong, his unit had spent one night in transit there. Now he was flying to the country with his wife to give three performances at the Grand Hotel in Rabat. Dave Mellor had settled in to his new job over the past weeks and felt comfortable enough to take his wife Yvonne, giving the ladies time to get to know each other. The shows were marvellous and there was no doubt that the star was singing better than ever and enjoying himself in the process.

Returning from Malta, the singer finished off his stint in England with another four nights with Syd Lawrence. For Matt, there was no better feeling than commanding the stage with a big band behind him. He certainly came alive with the proper backing and support of the expert musicians with whom he shared the stage. It was also rather nice that the concerts started much earlier in the evening

Grand Hotel Verdala Rabat, Malta

than cabaret and most nights he was off stage before 11.00pm.

Matt and Mickie flew back home to Florida as scheduled but the tour had been so successful that it had seen John Ashby's office inundated with requests for the show. After an absence of six weeks, Matt flew back to England in August to honour the extra dates that John had persuaded him to take. As well as the Big Band outing, he also undertook a series of one-nighters for Scott McKenzie and another for Roy Hastings and although he had only intended to return to England for four weeks, he ended up working right through until the end of December.

During that time, Matt only left England's shores once, and that was to perform at his friend Tony Dali's club in Marbella. A famous crooner of the 1950s, Tony had retired and opened an impressively lavish restaurant in Spain. Marbella had been a lovely small fishing village before the tourists invaded and it had lost its soul amongst all the money and nouveau riche. If you drove a few miles inland you could still find the true Andalucia, which was desperately trying to hold onto its Spanish roots.

> **All the tables were around the large swimming pool and there were candles floating on the water. It was quite a spectacle but for me the highlight of the night was when Matt came on stage. It was a wonderful evening and he was certainly surprised to see one of his British fans there. — Joan Jowett**

The one nice thing about being back in England on a temporary basis was that it gave Matt a chance to meet up with friends, both old and new. He hadn't seen Ron Miller since their time together in Meadowridge but the television executive had since invited him to dinner at Langhams and they sat and played catch-up. The two men got on famously; anyone looking in on the conversation would have thought they'd known each other for years rather than a number of months. Ron had also gone to see Matt work at a few of his recent concert bookings and had enthused about his friend's masterful talent. Matt's confidence had returned full hilt with the success of the shows in England and any doubts as to his own ability after his recent illness were quashed permanently.

> **The golden-voiced songster tops a terrific variety bill tonight when he is supported by one of Britain's most exciting new vocalists Terri Christopher, xylophone ace Syd Wright and as comedian compere one of the funniest men you'll meet in a long while Johnny Mans. Matt Monro is currently doing great business on his one nighter tour, brought out the house full boards at the Gordon Craig Theatre, where Brian Shaw presented him. — *Reuters News Agency***

Bob and Linda Marr first met Matt in Nottingham. Bob was Syd Lawrence's road manager and travelled with the band on occasion. Bob was a huge Matt Monro fan and after meeting the singer couldn't believe that an artist who was such a big international star was so down to earth. He was amazed that he was quite literally a humble soul, who had no airs or graces and was unconvinced by his own celebrity. Matt went up in the manager's estimation tenfold. Bob had been in Margate since mid-afternoon and was sitting in the band room eating fish and chips. Arriving for band call, Matt couldn't resist the smell and went to the fish and chip shop round the corner, stood in line and got his own. Two ladies were whispering as to whether it could possibly be Matt Monro. On leaving the shop with his take-away he leaned into the ladies and confirmed their suspicions – they nearly fainted.

The New Concert Hall was a sell out performance and although it was already a couple of day's after Matt's birthday, a fan walked right from the back of the auditorium, down the aisle and straight up to the stage carrying the biggest birthday cake you had ever seen. It stopped the show right in its tracks and the entire audience burst into 'Happy Birthday'. It was a wonderful moment and after the show Matt shared the cake amongst the band members.

That year The Stars Organisation for Spastics Christmas Carol Concert was held at the Royal Festival Hall. Alongside Matt, artists included Vera Lynn, Jeffrey Archer, Gloria Hunniford and John Mills. Matt sang the Bobby Scott and Bob Russell song, *'He Ain't Heavy He's My Brother'* and Barry Manilow's *'One Voice'* to close the first half. Not known for singing Christmas carols, his choice of *'Once in Royal David's City'* in the second half brought the house down.

In the second week of December Matt took to the road on a string of Granada dates for Roy Hastings before rounding down the year with an appearance on *Pebble Mill* with Syd Lawrence to promote their collaboration on the New Year's Eve television programme *The Big Ben Show*. The big band sound from the Syd Lawrence Orchestra featured many of the swing hits made famous on both sides of the Atlantic by Glen Miller, Count Basie and Tommy Dorsey. Matt was featured as a special guest with impressionist Joe Longthorne, singer Tina Cross and the group Shakatak. The show would be repeated the following year under the name *Strike up the Band* although there was no explanation from the television company as to why they effected such a change. Having taped the special, Matt left England to spend Christmas in Florida and formulate a new work strategy for 1983.

The strategy involved taking on an American agent and publicist. Derek Boulton would deal with bookings in America and Gene Shefrin would handle press relations. Since Matt had officially made the move to America, he had ended up spending nearing six months of the year in England but he now wanted to concentrate more on the American side of the business. Not only was he serious about the move, he was equally focussed on driving his career forward. He wanted the right calibre of work that would propel him to a position in the show business chain he should have achieved years ago, if he'd only had the right direction. He started the process by applying for residency status in Florida. In the meantime entrepreneur Larry Esquerra had persuaded the star to come to Manila.

Opening night in a couple of hours. The flight was 23 hours from London; bumpy nearly all the way, we loved that! Once we landed in Manila Daddy was home. He just disappeared in a crowd of press, photographers and fans. Not to mention all the officials at the airport – no customs for us. Finally, all with lei's round us, we were driven to the Hilton. When we got out the car, it looked so crowded. What no one realised is that it was all for Daddy. The whole foyer, which is huge, was full of people as well as the balconies on two more floors. There was applause; Daddy's music

played by a live band, champagne everywhere and flowers. A beautiful spray of roses for me, and daddy got lei'd again, if you'll pardon the expression! I was almost in tears and Dave couldn't believe it. Wouldn't have missed this for anything. Our suite here is quite something, pounds of fresh fruit, cigars, a huge bar (all free), sweets, cheeses, chocolates, matches with our name, as well as personalised notepaper. The day after we arrived Daddy did a television in the morning. He walked through a guard of honour on the set. Daddy is loving it all but the poor man can't walk two steps before he disappears among people who want to take a photo or get his autograph. If we go for a drink or a meal, he is introduced and his music played. — Letter from Mickie, Manila Hilton

There was no doubting Matt's love for this country. He described the Filipinos as a beautiful, romantic and appreciative audience of music lovers. The beauty of the country had drawn him back for a limited five-day appearance at the Manila Hilton and the star received an emotionally warm welcome. First Lady Imelda Marcos attended the farewell Valentine Show at which Matt was honoured by the Philippine Institute of Awards.

Matt Monro is hereby conferred this "Top Award of Honour" in recognition of the awardee's dedicated efforts in his chosen field of human endeavour or profession, having reached a level of merit and excellence, he is hereby honoured with this citation and award. The most sincere, sweet and cool, appreciative and loveable balladeer who ever sang here in Manila. Among the three top balladeers of the Western World, you are the most beloved here by the Filipinos.

It didn't matter how long Matt stayed away from the Philippines, it in no way detracted from the level of affection they held for the singer, his popularity never waned. On the 9 December 2006, twenty-one years after Matt's passing, EMI Music Philippines and Dyna Records posthumously awarded a Plaque of Distinction to the Monro family.

To Matt Monro in recognition of being the biggest selling foreign male solo artist in our company and for giving us a legacy of timeless songs, which have touched the hearts of millions of Filipinos.

First Lady Imelda Marcos, Araneta Coliseum

Matt Monro Jnr first toured the Philippines in 2005 as an unknown singer. His passion to enter the business was born of that one night in 1978 when he joined his father on stage in Great Yarmouth and he had gone on to become a singer in his own right. It seems the Filipino people have long memories. By the end of the first week the country had also taken Matt's son into their hearts with the streets lined with thousands of people and Imelda Marcos sitting in the front row once again. Even today the shops are full of Matt's products and he remains the country's most pirated artist. Filipino promoter Danee Samonte says the reaction has been remarkable. If the country had lost their number one idol, they were quite happy to take his son under their wing to ensure that the legacy continued. First Lady Marcos has attended several shows each and every trip and has even honoured Matt Jnr with her presence on stage. She walked proudly down the auditorium aisle flanked by a team of bodyguards and shrugged them off at the stairway to the stage. Matt Jnr was terribly nervous when he realised that she wished to sing a duet with him. They sang 'Feelings', the same song she had shared on stage with Matt Monro all those years ago. Some things never change and it is apparent that the Filipinos' feelings for Matt won't either.

Before Matt left Manila, James Dy, the Chairman and President of Dyna Records, sent a couple of songs over to the singer in advance of his April return. Dyna had spent weeks convincing Matt to release a recording in their country, and having secured the singer's agreement the recording session was diarised. EMI gave special permission for the collaboration, but retained the rights to release the song in other territories. The final choice was 'Be My Lady' and 'Memory'.

> **It was one of the most wonderful and unforgettable weeks of my life. We were invited to the Palace the night before but we were both so shattered we declined and had to hope that the President and his wife wouldn't take offence but we knew it was OK when we were told that the First Lady was coming to see the show. Security was in force all day and when she arrived the only calm one was, of course, Daddy. As usual he changed into a barong, their traditional evening dress, during the piano solo in 'Softly'. It always brings the house down but tonight it took the roof off. Daddy sang one ballad after the other and it was still not enough. Daddy presented the First Lady with a bouquet of orchids after singing a special request from her of 'Feelings'. The whole room stood, including her and she was in tears. At the end of the show flowers were thrown onto the stage but Madame Marcos then gave Daddy her own bouquet, it was amazing. The President phoned the next day wanting to throw a special dinner for us but we couldn't accept due to our flight schedule. Leaving Manila was something too. Daddy was treated like royalty and we were shown straight through into the VIP room while Cliff Richard was still in line! — Letter from Mickie, Hilton International, Singapore**

Dave Mellor was enjoying the experience immensely and felt so strongly about his time with Matt that he dropped him a line in England to thank him "for the enjoyable work over the last few months. Rarely have I enjoyed my work so much in recent years, I thank you most sincerely." But like others before him, he found working abroad difficult because of the miles that separated him from his family.

Matt could empathise with how Dave felt; he himself had spent years on the road, having no choice but to leave his wife and children at home while he tried to eke out a living. As wonderful as the 'highs' were after a performance the loneliness of travelling and a string of empty hotel rooms was extremely hard to bear. But Matt had paid his dues and having clawed his way up the ladder was now in a position to enjoy the benefits of his art. Having Mickie with him on the road was a priority, she had always been his anchor and her presence on these tours was the icing on the cake. There seemed no point in blowing an audience away if he couldn't share the incredible thrill he took from every performance. When the curtain came down and the venue went dark, Matt was content to enjoy the stillness of the moment, the aftermath of a battle that had left several scars over the years – he had finally exorcised his demons.

Now when a contract was offered it was only up for consideration if airline tickets and provision were made for his wife to accompany him and most bookers were happy to honour the singer's wishes. This trip was no exception, and with the cases re-packed Matt and Mickie left for the next leg of the journey, a ten-day stint at The Top of the Hilton in Singapore.

> **We arrived safely in Singapore after an emotional farewell to the Philippines. Our suite is so big that everywhere in it is a really long walk. Opened last night and it was quite different to what we expected. It was really a fantastic show with a fantastic audience. Daddy is walking round with a very big smile. Tomorrow is off, then back to work with two shows on Wednesday, Thursday and Friday but only one a night here. Singapore is quite a place but nothing goes on in the evenings now. They have a big clean up campaign so everything exciting has disappeared, there is no kissing on the TV and they have even banned *Cosmopolitan* magazine, bore, bore, bore. — Letter from Mickie, Hilton Hotel, Singapore**

Kerry Jewel tacked another date onto the tour with an appearance at the Tanglin Club. It was considered fairly upmarket and the idea was to work the show with Matt topping the bill and the comic doubling as compère. Performing in Singapore necessitated each artist having a special work permit. The Tamlin Club would make the application on behalf of the artists but the entertainer had to pick up the permit in person. There were no exceptions. Kerry picked Matt up from the airport and together they went to the oversized governmental office. They stood in a queue with 140,000 Chinese people and a variety of livestock. There was absolutely nowhere to sit and the two men stood for hours while the staff were "putting the chopsticks on it" (the saying for authorising a contract). Matt told Kerry to remind him never to work an extra gig for him again!

With two legs of the journey behind them, Matt and Mickie set off for a second tour with Tony Brady and once again Kerry Jewel was the support of choice. Merton Ciddor, the tour co-ordinator, picked the Monros up from Melbourne airport. After flying through the night, Matt had little time before he was due at GTV9 television studios to record *The Don Lane Show*. He was tired and slightly stressed and the last thing he needed was anything to add to it – but unfortunately he was just about to receive some very sad news.

> I was in Singapore and supposed to go to Sydney and spend two days there and then go on to Melbourne to do a TV show, which I thought was stupid. It made more sense to bring the TV show forward and fly to Melbourne direct. I was in the make-up room of the television studios and five minutes before going on I was told that Winnie had died – it was very hard to perform. It's fate because on Thursday I was in Sydney, which I shouldn't have been if I'd stuck to the original plan. I was able to go to her service – she was Catholic, which I didn't know and I was asked if I would present the offertory to the priest. It was a great privilege to be asked to do it. Unfortunately I didn't go to the cemetery as she was buried quite a few miles away from Sydney with her husband. She was the first black person to be granted citizenship of Australia. After Lew died some years earlier she was never quite the same. She relied on him for everything and loved him to death. He was responsible for any fame that Winnie had and she was the first to admit it. Her house got burnt out just a few weeks ago and when looking at new flats she said, "I don't know why I'm looking for something new, I won't be here in a few weeks time." — Matt Monro

Matt was broken up by Winnie's death but was grateful that at least he was able to attend the service at Lismore. As soon as *The Don Lane Show* was in the can he flew on to Sydney on the noon Ansett flight so that he could take full advantage of his two days off.

EMI had made a deal with Brian Nichols and partner John Evans of J&B Records and given the company permission to release an exclusive album for the Australian market. The album contained twenty tracks including the hard-to-find 'When a Child is Born' and 'Mary's Boy Child'. The tracks were only released on two LPs over the years, the J&B *All My Loving* and Columbia's *If I Never Sing Another Song*. Matt's video shoot for the new album's television commercial took place on a motor launch in Sydney Harbour and new photographs were shot for the cover. It

Photo Shoot J&B Records

made a nice change from the more traditional indoor studio shots, especially as the weather was so nice. In fact it had been Sydney's warmest weather for that time of the year for more than a century.

It was forty degrees in the shade and Matt suggested Mickie spend the day at the hotel rather than make the long car journey to that evening's show. She was round the rooftop pool when the wind started, and that was hot too. She'd never experienced anything like it and as the speed increased to gale force proportions it became extremely unnerving. Tables, chairs, glasses and bottles – everything started flying everywhere and it was even a hardship to move towards the elevator. She would most certainly have panicked if not for the presence of other guests to help her to safety. Even in the shelter of the suite, the hotel seemed to be shaking. She was certainly not sorry to see Matt walk through the door hours later.

The shows were marvellous but the travelling was definitely a challenge. Tony Brady had everyone running across country only to come back to where they'd started. Matt and Kerry worked a RSL (Returned Soldiers League) club in Orange near where the local crematorium had burnt down. Kerry revolved his whole act around an Irishman putting too much coal on the furnace and got the giggles. They also worked a Cootamundra Club, which they nicknamed the Cootabloodymundra Palladium. It was "the town that God forgot, a sheep area on the edge of the desert".

However tough being on the road could be, the two men shared a barrel of laughs. Kerry had been brought up in the business. His father Jimmy Jewel had teamed up with first cousin Ben Warriss, and together they were one of the great acts of British comedy. His father-in-law was Alan Clare, a gifted pianist who was considered a 'musician's musician' among his peers and who coincidently had worked with Matt on one of his earlier compositions, 'Mirage'.

> We were collected for a lunch at the Philippines Embassy, at the request of the Consul General. Matt Monro records were playing full volume and I think that half the Filipinos in Sydney came for a 'look see'. Lunch was, eat what is put before you, and Daddy enjoyed most of it but I did NOT. I really don't like these 'guess what you're eating dishes'. After lunch we all went into the reception room where we were entertained by a Filipino singer, accompanied by piano only. I'm sure you've guessed that Daddy then had to get up and sing. This is not too easy when the pianist doesn't really know your music. I did everything I could think of not to start giggling, nearly impossible, in fact when the Consul General got up to play his violin, very badly I might add, I really nearly wee'd myself.
>
> The shows are fantastic and I can only say that Daddy is just superb – the standing ovations bear that out. The TV video starts today so I'll be able to watch Daddy several times a day, if I want. We've seen a private showing of it and it's excellent. We were Billy Connolly's guests on his opening night; outrageously blue, even purple I would say but extremely funny. He was on for two hours and forty minutes. A party afterwards and we met John Cleese; he had just flown in and was feeling no pain! Yesterday we had lunch with Jackie Trent and Tony Hatch: they were charming. One never meets all these people in London but Sydney is always full of names. — Letter from Mickie, Sebel Town House, Sydney

Matt and Mickie posed for a souvenir picture of their visit to the residence of the Philippine Consul General in Sydney. Ambassador Nicasio Valderrama and his wife Mila were lunch hosts of the Monro couple, and later in the day they met with David Baxter of EMI Australia to discuss the new album with J&B Records.

Romanos was a pleasant change from the usual raft of one-nighters, as it afforded everyone three nights in the one place. The nightclub had opened in 1964 and was owned by Alberto Ferrante. Following his retirement the club was taken over by his daughter Lieta and her husband Michael Acquarola, and they were considered two of Perth's most popular hosts. The couple invited the Monros to a farewell dinner they were throwing at the club for the comic Ken Goodwin, who was leaving the next day for London.

The tour was relentless, the hours of driving between venues made for very long days and where possible Matt would come off stage and drive three or four hours onto the next town just so that he could fall into bed and stay there until show time. Geelong was the only spanner in the works. Their suite was full of fruit of all kinds; pineapples, melon, three kinds of grapes, bananas, apples, pears and some unpronounceable specimens for good measure. It must have weighed at least sixteen pounds, but Mickie was sure its primary function was to distract the couple from looking around the accommodation! An hour later they were at the venue and everything was wrong. They had a new sound and lighting crew who they felt knew nothing. Matt found the sound so bad that he actually stopped the show in the middle of his second song so they could sort it out – that was a first. He thought the lighting appalling and the band, who'd had a few days off while in Perth, weren't too hot either. Matt wasn't in the best of moods and decided to leave straight after the show and drive to Melbourne.

John Ashby rang to confirm a trip to Dubai and Abu Dhabi with the Syd Lawrence Orchestra. The show was in high demand and John had the enviable job of turning dates down because Matt was so busy working overseas. Matt was particularly thrilled with the American office, who had secured prestigious dates in Los Angeles and Las Vegas for later in the year. This was what he had been waiting for, the opportunity to work in America at some good old-fashioned show rooms. It was a far cry from the clubs that were left in England and Matt and Mickie decided that accepting hotel venues in some of the busiest tourist places in the world for three or four weeks at a time was better than schlepping around England day after day in a different town each night. Although in reality he was doing exactly that in Australia, it was completely different. The venues might not have had the most salubrious names but the clubs were fabulous. The Unions spent a lot of money on their workingmen and social clubs and promoted gaming in all the venues with one-arm bandits bringing in a big slice of their income. The hospitality abroad was second to none and Matt didn't feel he had much to go back to in England, or that he was wanted!

> Your mother is busy at the moment cheating the taxman so it's my turn to write. Brisbane is a really beautiful city but we haven't seen very much as you can imagine. Just one more show here then a day off which we both need and then HK for a week, a chance to unpack at least. The Philippines have got permission for me to record while I'm there, there's a possibility I may record 'Truly' but I don't know yet. I'm doing a Philippines song in English called 'Be My Lady'. Not bad; I think we can make a good recording of it especially for the Filipinos.
>
> I'm doing three concerts in the Philippines and everyone seems quite excited about it, so keep your fingers crossed. Had a very quiet time on our anniversary, a couple of the boys came back to our suite for a drink. I was drunk as a skunk. Those tonics get to you in the end! Your mother was unspeakable as usual falling about all over the place, it was disgusting! I had to put her to bed, and then the party started! I can't say too much as she reads the letters. — Letter from Matt, Crest International Hotel, Brisbane, Queensland

The fifteenth tour of Australia was a knock-out for all concerned and Tony Brady was keen to get another return date put in the diary as soon as possible. It was agreed that Matt would fly back on 15 August the following year for another six-week engagement.

The Sands of Time

Henry Parwani had tempted the singer over to Hong Kong to perform at several prestigious venues including the Banker Club, the Nautilus Club, the Sheraton Silver Ballroom, the Hyatt Hotel Macau and the Hong Kong Club. Matt's romance with the island over the years had grown stronger with each visit, but he was now shocked at the dramatic changes he witnessed in the Colony.

> **Here we are in Hong Kong and quite honestly we can't wait to leave, it's changed so much. There is a lot of smog covering the island and the buildings are covering the fresh air! I'm sure you would enjoy seeing it for the first time, but for your mother and me the glamour has gone. We've done two shows here so far, both in private clubs. Fantastic. Tonight we start here in the hotel; I'll let you know. The one good thing here that they can't change is the food. I can't tell you, it makes the Chinese in London look like McDonalds. Evidently they're swamping the radio and television with ads and one station is devoting the whole day to MM records. I hope to Christ it's not while I'm here, what a bore. I ordered six shirts here and cancelled five of them. The guy said they would fit me after 10 washes! — Letter from Matt, Sheraton Hong Kong Hotel, Kowloon**

Hong Kong's rapid industrialisation was a bitter blow to Matt, and his letter home disappointed Michele to an equal degree. She had nagged her father to take her to the island on every trip he had been on, but there was always a reason why it wasn't possible, and now it seemed very unlikely that she would have the chance. After all of her father's stories over the years of the sights, sounds, smells, food, restaurants and hustle and bustle of the exotic city, it looked as if they would stay just that – stories.

Matt's disappointment didn't extend to his shows; he couldn't have asked for a better reception and the hospitality was, as always, beyond reproach. He did six shows in total and gave himself one free day to visit his friends. It was impossible to sneak into Hong Kong, everyone knew of Matt's arrival from the press and radio and within a few hours Ray Cordeiro, Bing Rodriguez and Ted Thomas had made contact and the old gang made plans to hit the town.

The week passed far too quickly and by the 26 April 1983, Matt and Mickie were back in the Philippines. Matt had worked the Manila Hotel in February, but the venue had proved far too small and it had been next to impossible to get tickets to see the singer. For Matt's return visit, Lawrence Esguerra commandeered the Araneta Coliseum. Matt did wonder if he could still fill the stadium, nearly twenty years after his debut there, but he needn't have worried. *Matt Monro: By Popular Acclaim* was a sell-out. The return engagement of the world-famous singer, reunited with Asia's Queen of Song Pilita Corrales, thrilled the fans. One of the highlights of the concert was a special duet by the two internationally renowned stars.

> I will never forget the wonderful concerts I did with Matt. He was the favourite of the Filipino nation because of his wonderful songs. He filled the Araneta in all his performances. For me, Mr Matt Monro's voice will never be equalled. He will always be the greatest voice ever heard. He was not only a great voice, but a wonderful human being, so easy to talk to, so nice to work with, never asking too much and always in a wonderful mood. I had a lot of laughing moments with him. I've had the chance to sing with many international artists, but he was the kindest and most giving. I will always be thankful for knowing him in the span of my career.
> — Pilita Corrales

Matt made the time to guest with piano wizard Joselito Pascual during the taping of the TV show *Uncle Bob and Friends*. It was filmed in the auditorium and followed by a press conference. Matt also paid a return visit to the NCO Open Mess Top Hat Club in Clark Airbase.

> The first lady has been in the hotel a couple of times - I have to be so discreet, people are talking!! It's the big one tonight at the Araneta. It's been a long time since I was there so I'm delighted with the business – 15,000 sold out. I played an American Air Force

Matt & Pilita Corrales, Araneta Coliseum

**base last night, 90% Filipino audience; the Yanks didn't know what
hit them. The photographer made a fortune. — Letter from Matt,
Philippine Plaza Hotel**

Sponsors, Dyna Products Inc and Philippine Airlines begged the singer to add another
show at the Philippine Plaza's Grand Ballroom. First Lady Imelda Marcos was the
guest of honour and greeted Matt as if it had been years since their last meeting, rather
than a few months. Regardless, Matt felt honoured by the reception and the extra
publicity didn't hurt. If Matt had any lingering concerns as to the success of his shows,
they were quickly dispelled with the arrival of a letter from Lawrence Esguerra a few
weeks later.

Dear Matt and Mickie
My special wish that my dearest friends are in the best of health.

**After your successful performances here in February and April
this year, my enthusiasm to bring you back for two performances
at the Manila Hotel and one at the Araneta Coliseum could no
longer be equalled by any agent in town. I have the same
enthusiasm to have the original Four Aces back, so in this context,
would you accept to do a back-to-back concert with the original**

Four Aces on February 14, 15 at the Manila Hotel and February 17, 18 at the Araneta Coliseum? Knowing that you would prefer actual strings from the string machine, I leave it to you to decide the musician's line up. A big hotel in Kuala Lumpur is also interested to book the same act before or after your Manila stint.

I shall truly be grateful to you if you could give me your response and terms should you decide to accept my invitation. Not knowing in which address you will be at this time of year, I have sent three letters to three addresses including that of John Ashby.

My warmest regards to Dave and your children.

Till I hear from you, I remain... Very truly yours

As much as Matt would have loved to accept Lawrence's proposal, he was already booked out for the foreseeable future. He told the promoter he would definitely return as soon as he could clear some dates, but he was never able to make good on that promise.

On 2 May, Matt recorded a new single at AD & AD Studios in Manila. Dyna Records had selected 'Be My Lady' as the A-side and 'Memory' as the flip, both of which were to be included on the new album, which took the same name as the main release. The studio work had to be completed in one day as Matt and Mickie were leaving the following morning for Dubai.

John Ashby's winning concept of combining the Syd Lawrence orchestra with Matt's vocals didn't just attract the attention of English audiences – the Middle East also vied for the chance to host the show. With seven dates in Dubai, the Gala Spring Ball was hailed as the social event of the year. As well as working at the Hyatt Regency Hotel, Matt and his twenty-three-strong entourage were also staying there, which made for quite a sight poolside. Sitting in ninety-five-degree heat, Matt and the band played cards by the pool. In between hands, the singer swam several lengths before immersing himself under the water for long periods of time.

Matt used to hold his breath underwater, by doing that his lung capacity would increase – he had fantastic power when he wanted to. The power in his voice was quite staggering on stage. He could really come down from double forte belting it out and then slide down to nothing at all. That sweet sound which I thought was gorgeous. — Jeff Hooper

Jeff plucked up the nerve to ask Matt how he tied his bow ties. Unlike many singers at the time, Matt didn't go the way of clip-on ties; he always wore the real thing. Matt walked back to his room and returned with two such articles, putting one around his own thigh and gave Jeff the other to replicate the process. It took a couple of hours but Matt didn't give up until Jeff could tie it with his eyes closed!

This particular gig was extremely special to Jeff, he had admired the star from the wings for some time and was excited to be joining him on stage. Jeff had joined the Syd Lawrence Orchestra two years before as a twenty-one year-old and was anxious to learn from the best. Matt took the young Welsh singer under his wing and would often watch Jeff perform, and give him valuable pointers. He was very encouraging. Jeff travelled with Bob and Linda Marr and on the flight going home he was bowled away when Matt asked him to listen to eight songs on his cassette player for his viewpoint. None of those tracks ended up a winner, but Jeff certainly felt like one, he was chuffed that the elder statesman would seek his opinion at all.

Back in London, Matt decided to accept a few dates from agents Scott Mackenzie and Johnny Kildare, figuring that he might as well earn some extra money if he was already in the country. After six one-nighters in England, he opened for a week at the Adam Smith Theatre in Kirkcaldy, one of Fife's largest towns in the East of Scotland.

> **A packed audience on Monday night found plenty to enjoy in *The Matt Monro Show*, which is this week's attraction at the Adam Smith Theatre. Matt Monro takes hold of the proceeding in the second half. Is it my imagination or is he singing better than ever? Probably he is, and watching his perfectly relaxed performance one cannot help wondering why he is not up on a pedestal alongside Sinatra – not that he can be very far behind. All the familiar hits are there and many more, but none of them have become tarnished over the years. Possibly the reason is that Matt is such a perfect singer that whatever he sings is bound to please. He is the ideal proof that you do not need to be appearing continually in the Top Ten to remain right at the top of the singing profession. What is needed is the personality and the talent, and there can be no doubt that Matt has this in abundance. — *Fife Free Press***

Based at the Park Way Hotel, Matt held court with the press. There was no doubting how good Matt looked or that he was singing better than ever. When questioned about the transformation, he was quite candid about his newfound sobriety, admitting that the booze would have killed him if he had carried on drinking as his liver was shot and he'd had chronic hepatitis. It was two years since he had looked death in the face and upon the advice of his specialist had come up with the only solution he could – he had to stop. Now in great shape, he'd discovered that his wallet was a lot healthier too, his bar bills at Talk of the Town had been hitting £400 a week!

Having been away the best part of four months, the Monros headed back to Florida to put their feet up for a few weeks. Matt was on the golf course every day with Woody and friends, and Mickie was trying to sort through sixteen weeks of unopened mail. Now that they had based themselves in America there were more requests than ever to work in England, or maybe it just seemed that way. Matt was a workaholic and although he had amassed enough money to live comfortably for the rest of his life, he felt the need to keep on performing. The lad from Shoreditch never truly forgot the poverty of his youth and ever since the day he turned professional, he couldn't shake the nagging fear that the work might dry up.

When the offer of a summer season on the Isle of Wight came in from Hindworth Management, Matt agreed to do a three-week stint. Matt opened in *Startime 83* at the Sandown Pavilion on the 11 July with special guest star Mr Crackerjack himself, Stu Francis. Los Reales Del Paraguay provided South American music in the classic style and Pavlov's Puppets enhanced the summer show with their amazing range of novelty and comic characters.

The Monro family, including all three children, travelled over by Ferry and settled themselves at the Cliff Tops Hotel in Shanklin. It was easy work for Matt with only eight thirty-minute spots a week, allowing him to leave the theatre at a civilised 10:30pm each night.

Mickie celebrated her fiftieth birthday at the holiday resort. Matt pretended he had forgotten the event and made no mention of her birthday all day. Mickie was secretly hurt and bust his chops about it but felt rather silly later, when in the restaurant a beautiful cake was delivered and a small box surreptitiously appeared bearing a diamond bracelet. The night was made even more special by the presence of the entire family, a rare occasion in itself.

Mitchell and Matt had become much closer over the past ten years and the singer was especially pleased that his first born had been able to join them on this trip. Matt's first wife had chosen to remarry – several times. As time passed she seemed to harbour a bitterness that she wasn't still Mrs Matt Monro and enjoying a lifestyle she thought should have been hers. When Iris married her third husband, she moved to

Matt, Mickie & Mitchell, Isle of Wight

America. She had since borne another son, Simon, and found that she didn't have the relevant papers to take the child in the country. She made the decision to go anyway leaving Simon with his father. Mitchell, who was in his early teens, hadn't been invited to go anyway, and lived with various relatives over the years, later turning down an offer to move in with Matt and Mickie, preferring to complete his pilot training rather than uproot. But the events of his early life scarred him and he came to hate his mother, turning to Mickie for the love and attention he hadn't received from his own.

Mitchell and his sister Michele had also grown very close and gradually the older boy came out of his shell. He had been over to Florida several times to see the family and had even taken Michele up in one of the light aircrafts he was licensed to fly. Once they were airborne, he thought he would show off his abilities and looped the plane. Michele was so not impressed and very nearly never spoke to her brother again – and even though that might have changed, her resolution never to take to the skies with him again didn't!

Mitchell's flying career had prospered and he was thrilled when he was offered the job of private pilot for the Brazilian racing car driver Nelson Piquet. It meant travelling the world, and like his father he lived out of suitcases for most of the year. But it combined his two great passions, flying and mingling on the Formula One circuit with his schoolboy idols Ayrton Senna, Jackie Stewart and Niki Lauda.

Several years into the job, Mitch was suddenly taken ill in Brazil and airlifted to

Uxbridge Hospital in England with a serious tropical infection. His condition remained critical for days, with liver, heart and lung failure. Michele was anxious for Mitch to mend the rift between him and his mother and rang Iris in America, but she chose not to fly over, sending a bunch of flowers instead. Mitch's health recovered and with it so did his anger. After he had thrown the flowers in the bin, he berated his sister for going behind his back and told her never to do anything like it again, whatever the circumstances.

Years after his father's death, Mitch mellowed somewhat. In an effort to bury the hatchet with his mother, he invited her over for a holiday. She accepted and stayed with him in Sevenoaks for a few weeks. Mitch had not long bought his house and the place was not ready for critical assessment. Iris wasn't satisfied with Mitch's way of life, she bought bookshelves, moved furniture and rearranged the house according to her tastes. She admonished him for his bohemian lifestyle and told him to settle down and conform. In previous years she had opened an unsuccessful business with her current husband, leading to bankruptcy. Heavily in debt and forced to work as a cleaner, she felt that it was her right to extract money from her son. She was adept at making Mitch feel responsible for her hardship, damaging her son's self-worth in the process.

Several weeks after she had returned home, she wrote Mitch a blistering letter, attacking his character, and telling him he lived like a slob and was not the son she had hoped for. Secretly Mitch felt that she was jealous of his relationship with his father's family, refusing to meet either Michele or Matthew on her previous stay, and it was eating away at her. He had taken the first step to repair their relationship, but the letter was the last straw. He realised that he loathed his mother for all of the years of lack of care. The damage was permanent. All talk of Mitchell's mother was thereafter taboo, and if she came up in conversation, his whole demeanour changed and he became heavily agitated.

On changeover day, the singer and family packed up and left the Isle of Wight. Matt was due in Worthing the next night to kick off the first of ten dates for agent Johnny Laycock before flying to LA.

He purposely flew to the States eight days early so that he and Mickie could spend some quality time in LA with Marion, away from the time constraints of work. Marion wouldn't hear of the couple staying in a hotel and the Monros moved into Lake Encino Drive and immediately felt at home. If they hadn't known differently, they would have thought that Johnnie was due home at any moment. His Steinway Grand Piano, with its incomparable sound, satin ebony finish and keys of Bavarian spruce still sat majestically awaiting its master.

Five months back, Matt had been deeply shocked by the changes he observed in Hong Kong, and he felt similarly affected about the developments in LA since his last visit.

> **California was very over-crowded with constant rush hours and the freeways bumper to bumper. It doesn't matter where you go; it's just a frantic group of city suburbs looking for a city centre. — Matt Monro**

The appearance at The Shrine Auditorium was an important one for Matt. This was the first of several prestige dates lined up for the star since making the decision to move to America. It was make or break – Matt had reinvented himself and was ready to storm the city and prove himself capable of playing with the big boys.

Almen Productions were presenting the show at its Jefferson Street address. Matt was headlining the bill, with support from Amado Del Paraguay, Alice Mendez, Tony Escario and Pilita Corrales. Tom Bradley, the mayor of the city, not only made arrangements to see the show but also wrote a glowing letter to the promoters.

> **As the Mayor of the City of Los Angeles, it is a pleasure for me to extend my greeting to Almen Promotions, Inc, in sponsoring the combined musical engagement of talented personalities, Mr Matt Monro from England and Miss Pilita Corrales from the Philippines to be held at the Shrine Civic Auditorium on September 16, 1983. This is certainly a very special event and I am honoured to congratulate the promoters in holding this event that enriches the cultural heritage of those two people, which represents the diverse multi-cultural society of the city of Los Angeles.**

The Shrine Auditorium was the single largest theatre in North America with some 6,700 seats. Its design is an engineering marvel. The cantilevered balcony, built without pillars, seats more patrons than the floor and does not obstruct viewing from any seat in the house.

On his opening night, Matt received his five-minute warning before curtain call and slowly took his position in the wings. He quietly inhaled his cigarette and took stock. He felt he had something to prove and he wouldn't get a second chance.

The show was a monster; Matt received a six-minute standing ovation and the crowd refused to let him leave. With the phone ringing off the hook from ABC, CBS and half a dozen other television stations, press agencies, agents and bookers were frustrated by the fact that Matt was nowhere to be found – he had left for Vegas.

Sammy Davis Jr had rung as soon as he heard Matt and Mickie had hit LA and invited them down to Vegas as his guest for three days. A private aircraft was waiting at LAX to take them to McCarran International Airport and a limousine whisked them over to the Aladdin Hotel. The Monros were taken to a somewhat shabby room on the tenth floor. Before Matt had time to ring reception to complain, there was a knock at the door and the manager stood there bowing, scrapping and apologising for the mistake. He had failed to realise they were Mr Davis's special guests and begged them to follow him to one of the grand suites several floors up. The doors were opened to reveal a lavish lounge, dining room, two bedrooms and two bathrooms. Matt's only thought was "Christ, what is this going to cost me?" Every luxury was afforded and although Sammy was aware that Matt didn't drink, he still made sure the fridge was well-stocked with champagne for Mickie.

They spent a fabulous time with the legendary entertainer. As big a star as Matt was, he was always a little in awe of the respect his friend commanded after such a hard start to the business. Sammy's bodyguards were a permanent fixture, and when their charge entered a room everyone snapped to attention. The transformation of this small, wiry, black, Jewish singer to this giant of an entertainer when he mounted the stage was miraculous and no one could fail to be impressed by his performance. While the couple were watching the maestro sing, Sammy grabbed his mate on stage and the two men delighted the audience with a duet of 'My Kind of Girl'.

> **This hotel is the only one that had a suite big enough for my ego!**
> **Mickie can explain that I'm sure. Sammy made us very welcome,**
> **great show. It's now 5.00am and we leave for Frisco tomorrow.**
> **— Postcard from Matt, Aladdin Hotel, Las Vegas**

It was an incredible three days and when it came time to check out, Matt found that Sammy had settled the bill! The concert at the Shrine Auditorium was part of a double venue deal and now the second, at the Louise M Davies Symphony Hall in San Francisco loomed large. With shot nerves creeping in from those around him, Matt remained calm. He had just had confirmation that Vegas wanted him to headline in a few weeks and he excitedly dispatched a postcard to his daughter telling her the news. An invitation to perform in the entertainment capitol of the world was the ultimate accolade for an artist.

This is the place [referring to front of postcard] 10th October 1983. Headline Matt Monro. Wish me a broken leg or something! — Postcard from Matt, Sands Hotel, Las Vegas

The San Francisco concert was everything Matt could have hoped for. People were still reeling from his concert at the Shrine and there wasn't a seat to be had in the house. It was amazing how quickly news spread of Matt's success. People he hardly knew rang and hundreds of messages came flooding in. He was flying high.

Can't tell you how excited I am. I've been videoing all afternoon for a special in Manila so we haven't seen any of San Francisco at all. Leaving on Monday for Las Vegas. — Postcard from Matt, San Francisco Hilton & Tower

Matt and Mickie flew straight back to Los Angeles for an appearance on the *Merv Griffin Show*. Applause was still ringing in Matt's ears and it was hard to come back down to earth. The only bit of bad news was John Ashby's resignation. The fact that it was over something so petty made it ridiculous, but John had made up his mind. The phone had rung fairly early in the morning after a late night gig and drowsily Mickie picked up the receiver. Not recognising the voice on the other end of the line, she asked who it was and after an answer of John, she further asked, "John who?" The agent took great umbrage, thinking the comment was a deliberate snub, and stewing with humiliation, he wrote a letter terminating his employment. It was unfortunate but that was that. Matt was certainly not going to grovel or apologise for what was a perfectly innocent question under the circumstances.

Matt had been anxiously waiting for news on the album he had recorded five months back in the Philippines for Dyna Records. He didn't write too many letters in his life, especially in haste or anger, but he was furious when the cover of the Filipino LP was delivered to his hotel and immediately penned his feeling to James Dy.

I have just seen the cover of the new album and must say that I'm deeply saddened! What picture your 'artist'?! used to copy from I don't know, but it certainly was not taken within the last ten years. Buddy Medina knew that Fae Corrales had many recent photographs, some even in my Barong, and I fail to see why this very bad artist's impression of me was used. When you see it,

because I assume you haven't, I feel sure you will have it changed at once for both our sakes.

Having said that, now to the record itself. I spent a lot of time and trouble going through local songs to choose one which I thought would suit the local market. I spent time re-writing the lyrics to make them more acceptable internationally, hoping to have a possible worldwide release. I waived advances and expenses to record, at your request, a Filipino composition in the Philippines. The result was 'Be My Lady'. Buddy Medina, following the recording session, put in writing that the two singles would be 'hits', the other being 'Memory'. I find since my departure from Manila that there is already a hit single by a local artist and that mine was never released as a single. I hope this is because Buddy is no longer in the Philippines and left no on-going instructions.

I was told it would be called 'Be My Lady' for obvious reasons, and now find it's yet another 'Best of', 'Greatest Hits', etc., etc. Once again James, I am very disappointed and feel very let down. In the hope that we have many more years together in the future, perhaps we could have more communication on these things. I am not hard to contact, should you feel it is necessary. — Letter from Matt, San Francisco Hilton & Tower

Matt was livid that the specially recorded tracks were not released as a single – that was, after all, the whole point of recording them. James Dy's reply stated that "regarding the sale of your album the local market indicates favourable demand. As for the local artist's version of the song 'Be My Lady', it is picking up more sales simply because the said artist has all the chances for promoting the song in almost all the radio and TV stations, not to mention that he has his own TV show." It seemed politics was at play, and Dy's closing line of "I am sorry but I did not mean it to happen this way" didn't amount to a satisfactory explanation. With regard to the album's artwork, which was truly atrocious and never did get changed, James laid the blame with Buddy Medina, saying he had given him free hand and total charge of the album.

Notwithstanding recent disappointments, Matt was delighted with the flurry of press around his opening night at the Sands Hotel in Las Vegas. The Copa Room would present two shows a night and go dark on Mondays, and Matt would headline Russ Gary's three-week production *A Time to Remember*, with guest support from Johnnie

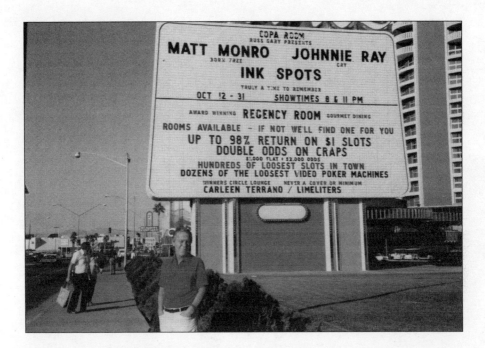

Ray and the Ink Spots. The town was buzzing with expectation. While regulars Debbie Reynolds and Jack Jones were opening on Thursday at the Riviera Hotel, Don Rickles at the Sahara and Siegfried and Roy at the Frontier, here was a new name on the block. Opening night was looming.

> **So now it is THE MORNING OF THE NIGHT – 12 October 1983. Daddy's name went up in lights yesterday morning and I can only say it looks great, a really wonderful achievement for Daddy and how he deserves it. We have taken one or two photos of the billing. The act and the running order is ready so now we can just look forward to a great evening, and it will be. — Letter from Mickie, Sands Hotel, Las Vegas**

There was one final rehearsal hours before opening and everything seemed primed and ready to go. There was a unique air about working Las Vegas; it was bigger, better, grander and showier than any of its contemporaries, you felt you were getting the best that entertainment could offer.

Matt's dressing room was filled with flowers and telegrams from all over the world, but the one from Sammy Davis Jr took pride of place. With five minutes to go Matt stood in the wings, drawing a puff on his cigarette, tapped his top pocket to make sure his red handkerchief was in place and had a word with Him upstairs. Dave Mellor

Matt & Johnnie Ray

struck up the intro and at 8.03pm precisely blinding spots followed Matt Monro's short journey across the boards to take his rightful place – centre stage Las Vegas – with a dutiful ripple of applause from the onlookers ringing through the showroom.

Monro had been absent from Vegas for thirteen years, but all of that time fell away with the opening notes of 'Around the World'. He was back – the room sat transfixed. On the opening bars of 'Born Free' the whole room rose like a tidal wave and rapturous applause and shouts of approval filled the room. By the end of the last note, Matt was drained; he had given everything. The crowd knew it and showed their appreciation, the press knew it and wrote accordingly and the management knew it and scurried away to phone in their reports.

Matt was close to tears and swept away by the emotion of the evening. Mickie's fears evaporated into the night and she was left exhausted and content, standing strong and proud next to her husband, the man she had always believed in and who now had proved his mettle once again. His courage, bravery, spirit, resolve and determination had seen him reach the very top for a second time, and she knew he would never relinquish the title again. During those three weeks at the Sands his future was discussed behind closed doors, but there were others that were opening up to him, giving him access to another world.

A friend told me that he'd seen Matt on the *Merv Griffin Show* and had mentioned an upcoming Las Vegas engagement at the Sands. We drove to Vegas to spend a couple of days and see the show. Like me, he was and is a lifetime fan of Matt's. The Ink Spots were OK – a bit of pure nostalgia. Johnnie Ray was frankly sad to see, appearing very feeble. Matt came on with a back up band of eight pieces. He sounded exactly as he had on all his records. I mean exactly! The wonderful aspects of his performance were there as always: his command of the material was complete and the performance as smooth and elegant as I remembered from seeing him at the Century Plaza in LA in 1968. Matt always sang in what my father called "the middle of the pitch", that is, exactly in tune.
— John Gilmore

Matt received a surprise on stage at the Sands. He had just started singing 'Born Free' when Otto Berosini, an exotic cat trainer, walked on stage left, followed by Simba, a 550lb lion. At first Matt didn't realise what was happening on stage behind him, but when he saw the animal, he stopped dead in his tracks. It seemed that the Board of Clark County Commissioners wanted to present the singer with a proclamation, in appreciation for his part in maintaining Las Vegas as the Entertainment Capitol of the World. Instead of making the Award privately, they wanted a showstopper and the lion did exactly that. Matt was in a state of shock after seeing a lion coming towards him on stage and after its presentation had to carry on singing 'Born Free' and finish the show with his heart racing wildly. He later said that it was one of the most frightening experiences of his life. Having finished the show, he came off stage to find the lion lying in the wings with the trainer nowhere to be seen. It wasn't tethered to anything and Matt's trousers nearly had to be sent to the cleaners!

The last time I saw Matt perform was in Las Vegas at the famous Sands Hotel. Matt was starring with Johnny Ray and the Ink Spots and closing the show. Mickie had told me there was a small surprise to come and we were not to say a word about it to Matt. My wife and I had gone to see one of the other shows in Vegas that night and we arranged to meet Mickie and Matt in the bar after the show. Matt was as white as a sheet and not too happy – apparently the 'surprise' turned out to be a disaster. As Matt was singing his big hit 'Born Free' a real lion wandered onto the stage from one of

the many animal acts in Vegas. It was tame of course but Matt just wet himself as he turned to see what the fuss was all about. Needless to say Matt and Mickie were not speaking to one another for quite a few hours! — Freddie Davies

Matt was signed to Derek Boulton, who was also Don Rickles' manager, and it didn't take long before the legendary comic asked for his old pal to join him on tour in Atlantic City the following February. Matt would have loved to start before, but he had just had word that the Sands wanted him back, and soon. It was a wonderful feeling to know that his hard work had paid off and that with the right contacts, you got the right work. He didn't have time to record and after lengthy calls from Capitol it was agreed that they would release a *Love Songs* collection on cassette in November and RCA Latino planned a US release of *Un Toque De Distincion* to LP the same month.

Matt had a small surprise arranged for his children but before that could be implemented he had to fulfil a few contracts that had been signed months back. Just because the prestige work was now pouring in fast and furiously, he was not about to pull the gigs that he had given his word on before he had taken America by storm.

Our last meeting was at a club by the riverside in Sunderland. The show was as wonderful as ever. I told him how only recently I had bought a copy of 'If I Never Sing Another Song' – one of his songs in that evening's performance and how much I enjoyed it. He gently told me that I should have asked him for a copy rather than buy one. Here among the last of my memories was a typical example of the generosity that was one of the most important marks of the man. — Bill Hall

BASF had asked Matt to consider working from the 24 to the 31 December in Jakarta and he turned it down flat. He had made a promise that where possible he would spend Christmas at home with the family. But BASF were persistent, asking if there was anything that could change his mind. He decided there was one thing that could sway him. They gratefully accepted his conditions.

On 16 December, Matt, Mickie, Michele and Matthew departed from Heathrow Airport on Singapore Airlines for Jakarta – or so the children thought. Sixteen hours later, the aircraft stopped in Hong Kong for a refuel. It was only then that Matt and Mickie sprang their surprise – they would have six days in Hong Kong together before flying on to Indonesia! The children couldn't believe it; Michele had begged her father to take her there for so many years that she was overwhelmed by the news.

Matt hailed a cab outside the terminal and gave directions to the Hong Kong Hilton, unaware that the Presidential Suite was waiting for him at the Mandarin Hotel, compliments of the management. Matt's unexpected arrival at the Hilton had the management in a frenzy. It was an honour that the superstar had chosen to stay with them and they afforded every luxury and privilege to the family. There was no time to sleep and within an hour of dumping their luggage they hit the town. Ted Thomas had come to meet them at the Ferry and for the next six hours Matt and Ted delighted the children with all that Hong Kong had to offer.

They went all over the island during the next few days. First stop was Hong Kong Island. It was the heart of the country, the centre of economy, politics, entertainment and shopping sectors. Matt took the kids on the Tramway to Victoria Peak. There they gazed down on the jungle of skyscrapers and Victoria Harbour where ferries and junks glided by. Aberdeen provided a glimpse of the essence of Hong Kong, with hundreds of trawlers housing fisherman and their families. They hired a sampan, which allowed a close-up view of waterborne life. Back at Aberdeen, they ate in the much talked about Jumbo Floating Restaurant. Matt introduced them to Yum Cha (tea drinking) and Dim Sum. Tea drinking is a very important part of Chinese life and

Matt taught the kids that when the waiter refreshed their cup with tea, you lightly tapped the table with three fingers, the traditional way to thank the server.

Bing Rodriguez and Ray Cordeiro joined them for dinner that evening at Maxim's Palace and Matt was in charge of ordering for the group. Before the meal came, a local from the kitchen emerged and entertained the crowd by making Chinese noodles from a lump of dough. He lifted the ball, flinging it over his head, and thinning it out until it became a virtual flying saucer hovering above their heads. He used a machine to cut the mix and suddenly before their very eyes he had created the thinnest, longest noodles you had ever seen in your life. The food began to arrive and when the traditional duck and pancakes were served, Michele thought she might faint – for this was no Western society restaurant, this was the real deal, and the duck appeared with its head still on.

Matthew had everyone in fits when he was caught coming out of the local McDonald's, which was ideally situated behind the hotel. He couldn't resist the temptation to see if it tasted the same as it did back home – he concluded that it did.

Stanley Market satisfied most epicureans with its multitude of stands, shops, original restaurants, outdoor cafes and authentic entertainment such as Chinese rhythmic dancers, jugglers and acrobats. Michele and Mickie couldn't choose between the colourful arrays of kimonos and ended up buying ten to share out between friends and family. Matt stopped by his 'tailor' and ordered a few shirts to take home but the highlight for him was looking through the newest electronic gadgets in Yau Ma Tei's Temple Street Night Market.

Matt took them to Nathan Street in Kowloon, a thoroughfare that ran in a south-north direction from Tsim Sha Tsui to Mong Kok. Lined with restaurants, shops and a multitude of tourists, the street was known as The Golden Mile in the post-war years, but the name is rarely used today. Memories from Matt's army days came flooding back as he tried to explain what it had been like back then.

Mickie was left at the hotel to get her breath back. They hadn't stopped since they had touched down and the kids didn't want to waste a moment of their precious time. Matt enjoyed playing the perfect guide to the city he knew and loved.

Pat Sephton, the former host of Hong Kong's radio show *The Hospital Request Hour*, was the appointed hostess at the most famous club on the scene and she invited Matt and his family over as her guests. Bottoms Up was a girlie bar in Tsim Sha Tsui (relocated to Wanchai in 2004), made famous for its appearance in the Bond movie *The Man with the Golden Gun* but the scene that was shot for the movie has a glaring mistake: James Bond comes out of *Bottoms Up* and goes to the waterfront. He jumps on a boat and tells the boatman to take him to "Kowloon side". In fact the club is on the Kowloon side of Hong Kong harbor. He should have asked for "Hong Kong side". The set up was an array of small round bars with about twenty seats around each and a beautiful topless girl in the middle of every one. They would play party games with the guests. One trick was to rub ice on the girl's nipples to make them erect and then see who could hang the most cocktail sticks on there. Matthew had a fabulous time and was gob-smacked that his father would take him to such a place, but he wasn't as impressed when on leaving the club, his father told him that they were all men!

There was nothing like Hong Kong. The people, sights, sounds, smells and startling array of colours in the bustling vibrant city with its seductive neon lights were unique and the memories of that trip would never be forgotten. With very little sleep but very big smiles, the family boarded a plane for Jakarta.

From the moment the aircraft touched down, until their chauffeured black stretch limousine took them back to the airport the Monro family were waited on hand and foot. The luxury car drew up to the Mandarin Hotel and the staff lined the entrance waiting to greet their special VIP guests. Ten people escorted them to the Presidential Suite; some carried silver platters of fruit, others chocolates, and still others with arrangements of flowers. The kids had never seen anything like it; they had never travelled to the Far East with their father, and it slowly sunk in that to these people their father was a superstar. The kids thought it a dream.

On Christmas Eve, Matt opened at the Grand Ballroom and Michele and Matthew were taken aback by the audience response. They were actually in awe of their own father. It was an incredible realisation that the man they saw in his dressing gown and slippers, with a day's growth of whiskers when not working, was loved and revered by others. It was a shock to the system.

They attended the show every night except one, when they went to see Bill Haley's Comets at the Hotel Indonesia. The last night's show was later than normal, with Matt leaving the stage just before the clock struck midnight. With the crowd still on their feet cheering and applauding, 1984 was counted in. Matt's family was called up on stage to share the moment with the man who had made all of this possible and as they hugged and kissed they hoped that the following year would be just as bountiful.

OYSTERS TO GO

Matt and family returned to London for a few days, just long enough to sort out a few business and legal matters. With work pouring in stateside, Matt made the decision to sign for personal management with Michael Gardener Associates in America, retaining the Shefrin Company for public relations. On 23 January 1984 the couple flew to Las Vegas for Matt's return engagement at the Sands Hotel.

We will never be able to forget 23 January 1984 – the beginning of our American adventure, we just can't take it all in. We will be staying at the Sands till about 19 February and will be doing Wayland Flowers and Madame (that very rude puppet) at a later date. Have been offered eight days on the Norway, well one has to try everything once, at least. We've been invited to Phyllis Diller's party at the MGM. I will have to get dressed soon – well it's only 1.10AM!! It's been a hectic time since we got here and yesterday was a really hard day. Rehearsals began at 1.00pm and Daddy just never stopped till well after the second show. We had a lovely opening; a great first show and a superb second show tonight – Daddy took the roof off. Shecky Greene is wonderful to work with, he adores dad and says on stage, "He is the greatest singer of them all", quite right. — Letters from Mickie, Sands Hotel, Las Vegas

Musical director Kenny Harkins had first met Matt in South Lake Tahoe in August 1967 when he was working with Louis Prima at Harrah's Casino. Matt was playing the main room across the street at Harvey's Resort and Kenny went to see the show with a couple of guys from Louis's band. "The first thing that struck me

when he walked out on stage was how diminutive he was in stature; but the second he started singing that was washed away with the absolute richness and resonance of his voice. I've played with a lot of famous singers and listened to a lot more and not one comes close to the sensual richness of his vocals. That and absolutely 'dead on' pitch."

On this return visit to the Copa Room, Matt was teamed with the comedy talents of Shecky Green. It was the first time they had worked together but it wouldn't be the last – they were already re-booked for a week in February. Matt's shows were at 8.00pm and midnight, and this time round, because Dave Mellor needed time with his family, he used Kenny Harkins. The stage can be a very lonely place, so having someone you trust up there with you is essential. Matt connected with Kenny straight away; apart from being a fabulous musician, they shared the same dry sense of humour. Kenny had to take a few days off in the middle of Matt's gig to cover some pre-contracted dates with Sinatra, but he hired a pianist named Billy T to fill in for him at the Sands. Before leaving Kenny attended rehearsals to ensure Matt was happy with everything. Matt walked up to the band, pointed to Billy and said, "So that's how it's supposed to sound." Kenny creased up with laughter. The musical director also introduced Matt to Ron Bavington, who ran a car rental agency in Vegas. Every time Matt was in town Ron would lend him his Rolls Royce to drive whilst performing there, and Matt couldn't resist using it to pick up a special passenger.

Phyllis Diller & Matt

In those days I used to commute to LA every six weeks and one of those trips coincided with when Matt was playing Vegas working with Shecky Green. Matt met me at McCarran Int. Airport driving a powder blue Roller with a chauffeur's hat on. — Roger Hancock

The Copa was followed by a booking to work with another old friend Don Rickles at the Resorts International Hotel in Atlantic City. Storming Los Angeles and San Francisco wasn't enough; it was just the stepping-stone for entry into Vegas – now the real work had to be done. Matt regarded it as one long audition, the powers that be wanted to see for themselves if Matt was good enough to headline the city. The shows had all gone well – actually much better than he could have hoped for, and now it was a matter of waiting for the verdict.

We flew American Airlines from Vegas to Atlantic City on the 2 February. We'd set a rehearsal time for Matt and the band in the afternoon and, as it turned out, my mum and dad had taken the bus from Allentown PA to come and see me but had to get home that

Matt & Shecky Green

night and weren't going to be able to see the show. So I brought them
along to rehearsals in this big showroom and sat them in one of the
VIP booths in the middle of the theatre. When I explained to Matt
what was happening he sat on a stool at stage centre and played the
whole rehearsal as if he were doing a private performance just for my
parents. He then invited them up to his suite and proceeded to make
coffee and serve it to them. Well, forget about it from that point on.
My mother told every one of her friends about how Matt Monro had
served them coffee in his suite in Atlantic City. Just another example
of what made Matt so special. I worked with everyone from Sinatra to
Mel Torme but some of my favourite moments were spent playing
piano and conducting for Matt. Of all the singers who abounded in
those days I have to admit it was Matt's voice that had the most rich
and musical quality to it. He was always a joy to be around and had a
great sense of ironic humour. — Kenny Harkins

With Mickie amusing herself in Vegas, Kenny took Matt to the Golden Nugget after
finishing their show to see a friend of his. Frankie Randall had been asking Kenny for
days to bring the singer down so he could meet him, as he was a big fan. He was
singing in the lounge when the two men walked in. During the performance Frankie
asked Matt if he'd mind getting up and singing a tune. Kenny said, "Of course Matt
did and it was one of the most beautiful renditions of 'My Funny Valentine' ever

592 The Singer's Singer

performed anywhere on any stage."

It was on this trip that Matt met Billy Eckstine, who was playing in one of the lounge bars, and being a huge admirer, Matt took in his show before his own. He also spent time with Rickles over the two-night booking, reflecting on the business and chatting about mutual friends. Just before the curtain went up on the second day, Matt received the news he had so hoped for, a headline contract in Vegas for the following year for at least twenty-six weeks. He'd hoped for good results from Atlantic City but this exceeded his wildest imagination. Matt was beside himself with excitement and spent the better part of the night on the phone sharing the good news. There were no direct flights back to Las Vegas from Atlantic City so the next morning saw him fly back from Philadelphia via Chicago landing into Nevada three hours later. He was booked back at the Sands with Shecky for the next four nights and he couldn't wait to see his wife and discuss what the news would mean for the family.

> **This is the place, just to think that they have the exclusive services of MM for a year, if they want it. — Postcard from Matt, Resorts International Hotel & Casino**

That wasn't the only shock that week. On 6 February the Monros were surprised to receive a letter in their suite from the hotel management:

> **Dear Hotel Guests:**
> **We are proud to advise that President Reagan is in Las Vegas and staying at the Sands Hotel tonight – on his birthday. In honour of this prestigious occasion, the Sands pastry shop has baked a giant cake to be presented to the President. At 4.00pm this afternoon, it will be made available to our guests and we would like to extend an invitation to you to stop by the casino for a piece of this special cake, while it lasts.**

But they were even more surprised when they received a phone call from the President's Press Secretary asking them if they would like to join the leader of the American people for cocktails early evening. It was a huge honour for Matt.

The Sands went dark on Thursdays, so Matt had a welcome day off on 9 February. The following day, he opened his show sharing top billing with Wayland Flowers and Madame for the next ten nights. The days flew by, Matt was on a natural high and invitations were pouring in from everyone in town. It was impossible to accept more than a handful but Matt promised the ones he turned down that he would catch them next trip. Having flown back to Florida and digested the news that the following year was booked solid with work in America, Matt and Mickie made a huge decision – to buy a house and live permanently in America. The green card application was progressing and there was no reason why Matt wouldn't be approved for residency. After spending days looking at real estate they found exactly what they were looking for in a complex called San Simeon in Boca Raton.

> I have been driving all day and every day to and from the house. Tiles, carpets, colours, you name it. The tiles and carpets have been changed so many times I can't tell you! Went to Palm Beach the other day for lunch with Richard Afton. Had a great curry. On the way back, darkness falling, we have to go via the HOUSE. There we are stumbling around in the dark when I hear a shriek (of delight) and a cry "My bath is here". There it was in the middle of the floor in the dark. Can you picture your mother crouching and crawling around with a cigarette lighter checking the colour? She's definitely on the way, where I don't know!! — Letter from Matt, Deerfield Beach, Florida

Matt had settled into his new life in America very well. He played a lot of golf with his friend Woody and they often made up a four-ball with friends. He had been to the Doral Country Club to watch the Doral Open and even met Nick Faldo. He stayed in touch with Ernie Wise and he was meeting up with Eric later in the day – they were always pleased to hear from Matt.

Mickie had done well with her driving, even venturing onto the freeway when she drove Matt to Palm Beach Airport when he had to fly to Vegas unexpectedly to see the lawyer about his residency papers. The attorney indicated it would probably take another eight months for the paperwork to go through, but the process should be straightforward.

Matt and Mickie celebrated their twenty-fifth wedding anniversary with presents for their new house. Michele flew out for the closing legalities on Sam Simeon and on 12 May the house became officially theirs. It was an exciting time for the whole family. Nothing could dampen their spirits, although Matt was deeply saddened to hear the news that Tommy Cooper had collapsed and died of a heart attack on stage in front of a live audience. It was particularly awkward as the comedic magician was in the middle of a routine, pulling all sorts of ridiculous items out of a handbag when he suddenly sank to his knees. Unfortunately, the audience thought it was part of the act and continued laughing. It was an extraordinary final curtain for one of Britain's most unrivalled talents but that was probably how he would have wanted to go – doing what he loved best. Matt would never forget their times together, especially Tommy using his sleight of hand skills to continually con him out of drinks.

Matt flew to London for two weeks to sign some paperwork and to spend some time in the recording studio. Columbia later issued 'You Bring Out the Best in Me' as a single coupled with 'I Don't Want to Run Your Life'. John Burgess wanted to talk about a new project but Matt had to put discussions on hold until he was back in England. Left without any new material, EMI continued to trawl their back catalogue for more compilations, culminating in *More Heartbreakers*.

The dates in Atlantic City had gone so well that Matt was asked to work with Rickles again and this time Michele flew out to Resorts International with him. It was always so exciting when she had a chance to watch her father work. Everybody was saying he looked good and was singing better than ever, and she had to admit that American living seemed to be agreeing with him. .

Meeting Don Rickles was also a great thrill for Michele. The man's comedic timing and well-pitched insults at the crowd were hilarious and she understood why he and her father got on so well. Mickie always enjoyed herself but it was made sweeter by the abundance of slot machines that littered the floor. Florida imposed a no-gambling law so Mickie made up for the country's discrepancy by indulging elsewhere whenever she got the chance. There was an air of expectancy in the Resorts complex; whether the accommodation, the food or the entertainment, you knew you were getting the best. America had a way of doing that and Michele was beside herself with excitement as she took her seat before curtain up. One would think by looking at her that this was the first time she had seen the show, but the truth of the matter was that it all felt so new, so fresh, so full of suspense, and when her father made his stage entrance bathed in spotlights to thunderous applause, she realised she was holding her breath. The audience's acceptance of him before he had even sung a note brought a lump to her throat. She felt so proud that this singing sensation was her father. By the time Matt took his final bow she had tears in her eyes and hugging her father backstage she was so overcome with emotion she could hardly talk, but she savoured that private moment. The spell was broken minutes later as the dressing room was overtaken by a deluge of well-wishers and show folk wanting to bask in Matt's glory and he was lost to her in the crowd. A sudden feeling of panic washed over her and

Don Rickles & Matt

she berated herself for feeling envious of the attention her father was lavishing on strangers. The trip was fabulous, but Michele had no way of knowing it would be the last one she made with her father.

The day after finishing at Atlantic City, Matt and Mickie flew to Australia for the sixteenth time. The journey had taken more than twenty-seven hours; they'd flown across the International Date Line again and lost 14 August along the way. By the time they'd landed Mickie felt upside down as well as down under! ATA Allstar had put together a six-week tour, confident that their star would have another sell-out season. They wouldn't be disappointed. Yorkshire comedian Dave Burke shared the first part of the tour with Matt and the singer invited him to his dressing room in the evenings to talk shop.

Kerry Jewel was another familiar face booked for the occasion. The comic had managed to stay dry since giving up the demon drink and Matt was extremely proud of him. Musical director Peter Warren completed the picture as Dave Mellor had decided to work only the British venues. It was just as well, as this set-up meant that Matt didn't have to keep paying for flights back and forth, and there were some great musicians to choose from in America.

The tour schedule were very much like the year before, however this time Matt and I started to seriously talk about scheduling concerts for the next tour at the end of 1985 using a larger orchestra. We had some great plans and it was in my mind to do some rather prestigious concert halls such as the Sydney Opera House and the Melbourne City Hall. We had just confirmed all the details and were set to go.
— Tony Brady

Whenever Matt made a visit to Australia he would invariably be booked on the most popular television talk shows. This time was no different except he appeared on *The Mike Walsh Show* twice two weeks apart and *Tonight with Bert Newton*. Don Lane had hosted his own variety show on GTV-9 since 1975 with co-host Bert Newton cast in the role of sidekick. The show had gone dark the year before and Newton was given his own vehicle, a significant move as he was the first host to present a variety show four nights of every week. The format felt no different to Matt except for the fact that Don Lane was missing from the set.

We always had a lot of laughs. The one-nighters meant a long time travelling in cars some for ten or twelve hours between shows. Tony Brady was a very good tour promoter but counted his pennies. The dates were always a mixture of capitol cities and regional theatres.
— Kerry Jewel

Matt was also asked to do a charity show with Jackie Trent and Tony Hatch, with Arthur Greenslade as musical director and Kerry Jewel the compère. Matt and Tony had flipped a coin to see who would close the show and having lost the call, Matt was able to join Mickie and Kerry at the back of the room after closing the first half to watch the Trent's act, which included a fifteen-minute medley of their biggest hits. After the show they all went for dinner, counting off all the hits the dynamic duo had written as they ate.

Several hotels around the area offered their guests automatic temporary membership of the Manly Warringah Leagues Club. With most gaming clubs, especially in England, you were required to be a member of the establishment before you could enter the premises and gamble, so this meant you could get around the rules. With Matt's appearance they were also advertising *Big Band Night of the 40s* prior to the star cabaret. This was a stroke of luck for Matt, as it gave him access to the magnificent fifteen-piece orchestra for a much bigger sound. The comedian Billy

Burton was booked as support and the evening was considered one of the club's best.

Nestled between the sandy white beaches of the Gold Coast and the sparkling blue waters of the Tweed, Twin Towns was the largest services club in Australia, and Matt was booked for five nights in the twelve-hundred-seater venue. It was considered an extremely prestigious location and Matt's first morning was taken up with an interview and photographic shoot for the *Gold Coast Bulletin* and an appearance on Dave Grey's television show.

Matt had his audience mesmerised – perfectly silent at times, singing, clapping, laughing and on their feet with excitement at others. The band was excellent; they were all seasoned musicians and complimented Matt's vocals perfectly. Opening with 'One Voice' he held the crowd in the palm of his hand as the speakers carried his voice to every corner of the concert hall. The audience lapped up standards like 'Second Time Around', 'Georgia on My Mind', 'Impossible Dream' and 'Birth of the Blues', but with the opening bars of 'From Russia with Love' and 'Born Free' they rose to their feet. He finished his set with 'Softly As I Leave You', and then did just that. It was the last time he would entertain at Twin Towns.

There was a 'meet and greet' after the show and the queue was at least a mile long. It was apparent that no one wanted to leave without a few personal words or a treasured signature from the star. Matt came home with a cassette tape of the performance and it laid for twenty-four years in a box of odds and ends until in 2004, when Michele had the good fortune of meeting up with Richard Moore, a sound engineer and staunch fan of the singer. He lovingly restored and remastered the performance, leaving it sounding every bit as good as a professional capture. Released in 2008, *Live in Australia* is one of only a few live concerts that sit in the archives and is considered a rare treasure. The difference between a live show and a studio session is enormous, not only for the authenticity of the performance, with no tweaking or tampering to the texture or timing, but also because the personality of the performer shines through.

I've stopped my world for a moment to pen a few words to you both. I can't add much to that which your mother has already written except to tell you that I've been quite superb again. The multitudes have been going berserk as usual at my performances and next year they're thinking of taking me out of tents and outing me in real venues. How about that?! The tour has been much easier than previous years. We're going up the coast a little way today for lunch on the beach with Tony Brady and then seeing Richard Harris for

dinner, also saw him last night, The beauty of these towns is that we rarely go inland so we're on the coast all the time and it really is beautiful. — Letter from Matt, Sebel Town House, Sydney, Australia

We really have had a tremendous tour, which we've enjoyed more than any other. We will be home on 26 September Air India Flight No AI125 arriving at 5.45pm. We leave Adelaide on Tuesday, change planes in Perth, then Singapore, Bombay, Delhi, Rome, Paris and some 40 hours later – from Adelaide that is – London. Change planes in Bombay too but if we had wanted a shorter flight we wouldn't have been home until Friday. We didn't want to wait a moment longer than necessary to see you even though we could have spent two days in Bombay!
— Letter from Mickie, Sebel Town House Hotel, Sydney, Australia

Whenever possible, Matt visited Doyles oyster bar in the Eastern Suburbs. It was one of his favourite places to eat. Towards the end of the tour, the couple went to the restaurant to eat rock oysters but shortly afterwards Matt became ill. Mickie persuaded him to see a doctor as soon as they reached Adelaide. The singer was diagnosed as having chronic indigestion and prescribed an antacid.

I've come across some strange names here in OZ but how about a place called Mypolonga!! Got some great pictures of Richard Harris – it's bloody cold, the hotel is good, the food isn't, a carsie last night, tonight not much better and they say it's the best venue in town! Only four to go. I can't complain though, when you mother's finished there's nothing left to complain about. — Letter from Matt, Hotel Oberoi, North Adelaide, Australia

Matt, Mickie and seven suitcases inched their way along the concourse of Heathrow Airport. The couple were completely exhausted from the long flight, which had brought them back from the other side of the world, but fortunately Matt had five days off to recover from both the flight and his recent illness. He still felt nauseous at times and had a dull ache over his liver, and the prescribed medicine he'd been taking was hard on his stomach. Looking slim, tanned but slightly tired he made an appearance on the BBC's *Russell Harty Show*, which was filmed at the Greenwood Theatre in South East London.

After being away from England for so long, Mickie had a busy week ahead of her.

There was a mountain of mail to address, Matt's suits to be cleaned and dozens of unanswered phone calls to deal with. She decided to stay at home and tackle the domestic administration while Matt went off to the Isle of Man. Billy Marsh and Kenneth Earle had put together a Royal Gala Variety Performance in the presence of HRH The Princess Anne at the Gaiety Theatre and Matt had been asked to take part.

The theatre opened at 8.00pm and the Royal Marines Band's music greeted Princess Anne on the half hour. As on most of these occasions a star line-up had been cemented in place including appearances from Bob Carolgees and Spit the Dog, the Barron Knights, Stella Starr, Bobby Crush, Leslie Crowther, Dickie Henderson and Matt, who had been allocated a fifteen-minute spot.

Matt was thrilled to see his fellow Water Rat and old golfing partner Dickie Henderson on the bill. His admiration for Dickie extended beyond his talent as an entertainer – he was also in awe of his discipline when it came to golf. Matt was only a fair-weather player, but Dickie was a fanatic and managed a game nearly every day no matter the weather. He'd been playing for thirty-odd years and had a handicap of eight. Matt's handicap was his clubs!

Matt's other mate on the bill was Mr *Crackerjack* himself, Leslie Crowther. Leslie was one of the busiest and most in-demand entertainers in the business. Not only did he have several top television series under his belt, along with numerous concert and cabaret engagements across Britain, he had just landed the plum job of host of a new show called *The Price is Right*. Matt always joked that with his wife Jean, four girls and a boy to feed, Leslie had to keep working! Bobby Crush also shared the stage having just emerged from six winning appearances on television's *Opportunity Knocks*, co-starring on three separate occasions at the London Palladium alongside Jack Jones, Vic Damone and Julie Andrews. After the finale, according to the usual custom, artists were presented to HRH on stage. It was a marvellous night for everyone but it was that much sweeter for bumping into old friends.

> 'My Kind of Girl' was one of the first records I owned as a kid and Matt's music has been a part of my life ever since. Listening to Matt's CDs is a reminder of what a truly magnificent singer he was. I had the privilege of working with him on a number of occasions, the final time being the Gaiety Theatre on the Isle of Man and found him to be an exceptionally nice man. I've come to the conclusion that he was undoubtedly the closest we ever had to having our own Sinatra. How proud Matt would be to know that a whole new generation is thrilling to that marvellous voice. — Bobby Crush

Once the doors had finally closed on London's Talk of the Town, Rosalyn Wilder had gone to work at the Barbican Centre as one of the main bookers for the venue. She'd thought of Matt straight away and booked him in to the theatre together with the New Squadronaires through the singer's new agent Mervyn Conn.

Sitting on Silk Street in the heart of the City of London, the Barbican was Europe's largest arts venue, and also home to the London Symphony Orchestra and the BBC Symphony Orchestra. Matt appeared on John Dunn's BBC show to plug the event, but he needn't have bothered as the eleven-hundred seater had long been sold out.

Band call was at 2:30pm and with a highly skilled orchestra under the leadership of Dave Mellor, Matt had the perfect support. With budget cuts worldwide most venues had cut down on the amount of musicians they hired but now with a line-up of eight brass, five saxophones and a rhythm section, Matt was able to include songs suited to a big band sound and he was delighted at the prospect.

One person who was not delighted by the events was the singer Julie Rogers. She was offered the support slot at Matt's Barbican appearance, but before accepting the booking, Derek Block rang and offered her a six-week tour with Bob Hope. She accepted the offer, weighing up the fees for one night's work against nearly forty, but the deal fell through. Rogers wouldn't have got the Barbican booking anyway. Matt, unaware that Mervyn Conn had made the offer, subsequently asked him to withdraw it, as he wanted to present the evening as a solo concert.

Matt was truly looking forward to the performance. After travelling abroad for so many years it felt like coming home. The trouble was that Matt didn't feel at all well when he woke up and had been sick several times throughout the day. If he was honest with himself he had felt off colour since his last trip to Australia and couldn't seem to shake whatever was wearing on him. Matt made it through band call and although he could have sloped off early, the show was important to him and he wanted to make sure the sound, lighting and microphone checks were as he wanted. There were several hours before the performance, but not a long enough period to pop home, so he went to have a rest in his dressing room. Mickie was worried about him. He had lost quite a bit of weight, his skin had gone a pasty grey and his eyes seemed to be slightly sunken in their sockets, but she reasoned that he was just feeling run down after his recent illness in Australia. Matt was adamant that the show would go on and there was no talking him out of it. Standing by the side of the stage waiting for his musical intro, small drops of perspiration were visible on his brow. His theatrical greasepaint used to ensure that under the punishing glare of spotlights he didn't look ghostly pale, belied the evidence of illness.

> He was so not well and it was the first time we can remember that he asked someone off stage to bring him a glass of water. He was in terrific pain. — Mickie Monro

Despite his failing health, the show was magnificent, a flawless performance with a fully deserved standing ovation of over nine minutes. Peter Hepple of *Stage and Television Today* was in the audience.

> If Matt Monro had been a six-foot Italian-American instead of a 64inch Londoner, even the British would have recognised him as the international singing star that he is. All the same I was delighted when a full house turned up at the Barbican and gave a standing ovation to an artist whom I have long considered to be more than the equal of the American masters of his branch of the singing trade. After more than 30 years in the business, it is no exaggeration to say that Matt Monro is singing better than ever, with a technique to challenge the best, marvellous sustained notes, phrasing which occasionally teeters on the edge of dangerous originality and a knack of emphasising

certain words in a way that Sinatra himself might envy. Reading through the list of numbers he sang, one is struck by the fact that he has had more hits in this country than any other singer of his type, most of them, as it happens, with lyrics by Don Black, who can have found no better interpreter of his words. — Reproduced with the permission of *The Stage Newspaper Ltd*

Matt had satisfied that harshest of critics – himself. He knew he had sung well and just for a short time he thought that Britain had finally shown their appreciation. It didn't matter how far he strayed or what country he hung his hat in – his roots were in London and it was the approval of his home city that he craved most of all.

Britain takes their artists for granted and they certainly took Matt for granted. He was such a big success in so many countries across the world, never without work, but happily that night he was shown by a British audience that they really loved him. — John Ashby

I was looking forward to the show at the Barbican enormously but when I saw Matt I was really shocked that he didn't look at all well. He did a fantastic show but I was deeply concerned at the effort I thought it cost him. I had a dreadful feeling that I might not see him again. — Rosalyn Wilder

After changing and washing his make up off he entered the hospitality suite to a tumultuous round of applause from the packed room and an ensuing stampede of people who wanted to be the first to congratulate him. Matt wasn't even sure who some of them were, but he made the rounds and thanked everyone for coming. The burst of adrenalin and endorphin release from his performance had made the star feel and look slightly better and this sense of well-being and buoyancy carried him through the next hour. No one knew that after his 'high' had dissipated, the singer who had been a giant on stage was near to collapse.

FALSE TABS

M att knew something was wrong. He had been feeling ill for too long and he urgently requested an appointment with Mr Roger Williams at Kings College Hospital. He was seen on 17 October 1984, two days after his appearance at the Barbican.

> **Thank you for referring this patient who was, as you know, doing very well having given up alcohol in September 1981. His present illness started with a gastrointestinal upset and it is likely that this did lead to temporary upset of liver function. This I am checking and am also having a liver scan carried out. I will see him again in a few days and let you know the results. — Doctor's Report**

The specialist gave his patient no cause for concern. Matt went through the symptoms he had been experiencing during the last month and relayed the diagnosis of chronic indigestion from eating rock oysters! He also categorically confirmed that he had not had so much as a drop of alcohol since going into Galsworthy House in September 1981. Williams carried out tests and an appointment was made in nine days; in the meantime Matt was told he could go back to work if he felt well enough to take to the stage.

Matt pressed on with an appearance on Thames TV's *Des O'Connor Tonight Show*. Des couldn't believe it had been fourteen years since Matt appeared on his ATV show, and as well as singing his new single 'You Bring Out the Best in Me', Des and Matt dueted with 'My Kind of Girl'. Not everyone enjoyed the performance – a by-line was added to the TV listing with the message, "You're great at the chat bit Des, but PLEASE give up singing with your guests."

The show had a great bunch of people with guests including Ted Rogers, Jill Gascoine, the Tremeloes and Stan Boardman. Stan very nearly took the show off the air when he memorably courted controversy on the live edition with a joke about reminiscences of the German 'Fokker' aeroplanes. Some have since claimed the outrage effectively ended Stan's television career. Whatever the response from the viewing public, it was one of the funniest routines Matt had ever heard, and both he and Des had tears running down their faces.

Matt's outing with the New Squadronaires was so successfully received, not only with the public but by Harry Bence himself, that they arranged a repeat offering at several venues, including Quaffers in Stockport. Although the standing ovation was shorter than at the Barbican, people were nonetheless on their feet. It was apparent that this combination of talent was equally as successful as the Syd Lawrence pairing.

Having seen Mr Williams again on 26 October, it appeared that the specialist could see no new evidence of any disease. The liver function tests were good, showing excellent compensation of the liver. Matt admitted to feeling slightly better, so they decided to monitor the situation and make a follow up appointment in three months.

Matt flew to the Isle of Wight to play at the Savoy Country Club for the Yarmouth Lifeboat Diamond Jubilee Gala Night, with support from the brilliant Royal Marines

Band of the Blues. His performance didn't go unrecognised.

> In his first-ever cabaret performance here, Matt proved beyond all doubt that he is way up there among the world's top singing stylists. In Britain he is in a class of his own. His quality outlives all music's changing fads. Following his Yarmouth show Matt was presented with a painting of the local lifeboat. — John Hannam, *Isle of Wight Weekly Post*

Ron Miller was equally impressed, not only by the performance but by the generosity of his friend in agreeing to appear: Ron was trying to raise thirty five thousand pounds to refurbish the lifeboat that covered the Yarmouth and Isle of Wight coasts. "The deal I did with Matt was that he would do the Yarmouth gig for nothing and I would book him as the cabaret for the TV conference in Monte Carlo. He did the Yarmouth show and as ever went down a storm."

Matt did an interview at the house with Richard Afton's son of the same name, as well as a telephone interview with Debbie Newton of the *South Wales Echo*. He worked St David's Hall in Cardiff with the New Squadronaires, followed the next night by a show at the Grosvenor House Hotel's Vision Ball, a charity for the blind. It was an extremely long day and Matt didn't get home until 3.00am. There wasn't much time to rest, as he had to leave at noon the next day for his appearance with the New Squadronaires at the Floral Hall in Southport. The show was another great success, but instead of staying at a hotel for the night and kicking back, he insisted on driving the four hours home after the show to be with Mickie.

On 7 November Matt had an afternoon meeting with John Burgess and Vic Lanza to talk plans for the future. Matt had been under contract with EMI/Capitol Records since 1959. 'Fred Flange' had marked a peculiar beginning to a twenty-five year relationship with EMI. Matt was one of the only artists of his genre that still held a contract, and if talks that day were anything to go by, the relationship would carry on indefinitely.

Later that evening the Monro couple went to see a show at London's Ritz Hotel. Don Black had set up a meeting for Matt, Mickie and Alan Jay Lerner, who had long wanted to write a song for the singer. Although Lerner submitted the song, Matt never got a chance to record it.

> I can't tell you what a joy it was to meet you last night. I am a fan of very few singers but I must tell you in all honesty that you are high among them. I am enclosing a copy of 'Dance a little Closer' – which, frankly, was a little slow last night. Anyhow, I hope you like it and it would be the answer to my fondest dreams if you should decide to record it. Whether you do or not, I hope we will meet again soon. Thank you for coming last night. You have all my good wishes and admiration always. — Letter from Alan Jay Lerner

Matt did one more show with the Squads that week, a repeat performance at Quaffers in Stockport, followed by a reunion with Syd Lawrence and his Orchestra at the Queen Elizabeth Hall in Oldham. There was a day's break between shows so Matt ensconced himself at The Four Seasons Hotel for two nights. Oldham had certainly had fair warning he was coming, courtesy of the *Evening Chronicle* who printed an article the week before the singer was due.

> Perhaps it is because he has never been very pushy: perhaps he is content to have a loyal band of true fans rather than members of the trendy, concert going set. Whatever it is, Matt Monro has never had the public acclaim he deserves. After all he has been a star for

almost 25 years, since his first big hit, 'Portrait', back in 1960: he has a number of gold discs and sold no fewer than 23 million records during his career. Bing Crosby rated him as one of his favourite singers. And not only Bing Crosby; Tony Bennett says of Matt, that he has done more for good music in Great Britain than any other artist. One article about him recently suggested that the only reason Matt isn't one of the world's international stars – like Bennett or even Sinatra – is because he is small and English rather than charismatic and American. You'll get the chance to hear just how good Matt's voice is a week today when the star plays the Queen Elizabeth Hall as part of a short tour to coincide with the release of a new record 'You Bring Out the Best in Me'.

— *Oldham Evening Chronicle*

Once he'd made up his mind, it was incredible how easily Matt had been able to dispense with alcohol, especially after all the years he was rather partial to a drop. But even though he didn't champion AA meetings or need support from his sponsor, there were many others that weren't so determined in their resolve. Matt had taken up the sponsorship of John Brown after completing his own treatment at Galsworthy House and he didn't take his responsibilities lightly. John had lapsed several times and now after a number of phone calls, Matt had persuaded his charge to sign into the clinic, with the promise he would drive him there personally to ease the transition and offer the support he needed to carry through with the treatment.

> **Matt wasn't just a great singer, he was a great human being. I'll never forget him. I owe him my life – no one will ever know what I owe that man. I couldn't go an hour without a drink. I was drinking over two bottles a day. I called Matt on the Monday and admitted I had a problem. He asked me if I was an alcoholic. He was the first person I ever admitted it to. "Do you want my help?" the singer asked and after accepting that fact we agreed that I would meet him at the house. Matt asked me what I was drinking and I told him half a bottle a day – he called out to Mickie, "We've got a bullshitter on the phone." I made sure I had a couple of slugs from a bottle of gin before Matt drove me down to Galsworthy. As soon as I came out of solitary Matt took time out from his schedule to visit and as usual his humour was in evidence. Tony, the one-on-one councillor talked to Matt about being my sponsor and his reply was, "What's it going to cost me?" It was hard going but the doctor was encouraging and it was important to have the support of the staff, family and friends. I have been sober twenty-four years and am now a sponsor myself. Yes, I owe Matt everything.**
> **— John Brown**

In the last week of November, Matt supported the Grand Order of Water Rats by agreeing to star as their main cabaret with the backing of the Ray McVay Orchestra. The singer received a standing ovation from his brother Rats and the performance was talked about for weeks afterward. The one thing everyone seemed to agree on was that Matt was singing better than ever, and that also appeared to be the consensus of opinion of the patrons at the Sports Centre in Bolton. Matt was certainly in the best of humour, and his mood carried over to the next day, when he appeared on his golfing buddy's LWT show *Tarby and Friends*. Matt and Jimmy were seen laughing and joking after the show, which wasn't a surprise if you consider the comedic ability of another guest, Michael Barrymore. The Green Room saw Shakin' Stevens, David Copperfield and Shirley Bassey in attendance, and by anyone's standards the show was packed with talent from all ends of the spectrum. It was to be Matt's last television appearance.

> **I was the Sales and Marketing Director of London Weekend Television. I used to talk to the Head of Light Entertainment at LWT, David Bell about Matt but he had by then a reputation for being a bit unreliable. I was trying to get Matt a spot on *Live From Her Majesty's Theatre* but David would not budge. Eventually I got him a spot on *Tarby and Friends*. — Ron Miller**

It's not clear why David Bell thought Matt unreliable, as the people interviewed for this book were unaware of any such 'reputation' and certainly Matt was always punctual. Admittedly, he had cancelled a tour to the Far East and a few one-nighters at the height of his illness in order to enter Galsworthy House, but as anyone could testify, Matt hadn't touched a drop of alcohol in over three years.

Matt and Mickie were never aware of a possible problem or that his reputation had been sullied. And considering how gossip travelled in the business, if it affected one television station's decision you can bet that it affected others. Matt had always been deeply hurt that he had never been offered any of the prime time shows or his own series, or the fact that in his twenty-five years in the business he had only been invited to do one Royal Command Show. He hadn't heard a whisper, hint or indication of anything wrong, no one told him on the quiet or gave him reason to suspect that he had been blacklisted. It seems stranger still considering that every single one of his television appearances – from the very first with Cyril Stapleton in 1957 – was nothing less than sterling. Whether cast in a comedic role, as an interviewee or as a provider of music, his voice had never let him, a host, a producer, director or an audience down. With more than three hundred television credits to his name, it might have been wiser to base booking decisions on his track record, rather than the whispers of the rumour mill. It wasn't only evident to Matt; his absence from the screen had been a constant feature in newspaper remarks and protests from fans. It was an insult to someone who was passionate about his roots, a true royalist and an ambassador of music for his country.

> **I never saw Matt throw up in his dressing room before or after a show and never saw him drunk before a performance. When Matt was drinking rather heavily you wouldn't really have known. That was the way he was. There would be times when he would have a**

drink in the morning and it was almost as if he was topping up from the day before. Matt always drank from the time that I joined him but his performance was never affected and I would certainly remember any times when the voice didn't happen. I really don't recall any point ever when I would have said it was noticeable. I also don't recall him ever being late through all the radio broadcasts, rehearsals and televisions we did. — Colin Keyes

Matt's health was getting visibly worse. He had lost a lot of weight and his appearance was rather drawn, but he was putting on a brave face. He was having difficulty eating, and it was obvious to all around him that his appetite wasn't what it should have been. There were hours of the day when Matt felt fine within himself and then great moments of pain, discomfort and nausea, and he calculated that the symptoms were more pronounced after eating.

Although Matt wasn't getting any better, the doctors were seemingly unimpressed with his symptoms. He could no longer ignore the fact that he had been experiencing discomfort for the past three months, so he decided to take matters into his own hands. He went to see Ted Fricker; in fact he saw the healer twice, and although he felt slightly better following the sessions it didn't dispel his overwhelming feeling of malaise.

Matt was in good spirits when he was interviewed by Radio 2's John Dunn. He was at the studios a number of hours and the programme came across well. No one could tell there was anything untoward, but Mitchell knew of his father's ill health and for that reason he made plans to travel with his dad to the show at the Grand in Wolverhampton on 15 December 1984. It was a good idea as Mitch could take over the driving if Matt got too tired and it was important that the two shared some time together on their own.

When the Grand re-opened its doors after its refurbishment it was one of the best-equipped theatres in the country and Matt felt privileged to play such a fine venue. The sound was crisp, echo and reverb came in at just the right levels, the fold back was perfect and he couldn't have been happier with the acoustics.

Matt stood in the wings, a solitary figure whose silhouette could just be made out in the shadows. Was he contemplating the performance, or focussing on Dave Mellor's cue to the musicians? Was he thinking about his son in the audience, or his wife at home? Was he running through that night's routine once again or talking to the man upstairs? Whatever he was thinking, it couldn't have been that this would be his last public performance.

Final Tabs

Matt continued to feel unwell but hid his discomfort from the rest of the family, especially his children. The family planned to travel to Florida on 16 December and spend Christmas together and he didn't want to disrupt anything. He persuaded Michele to fly off as scheduled and to get the house ready for his arrival, explaining that he wanted to see the specialist once more before he flew overseas.

Michele received phone calls with progress reports but Matt being Matt played the whole thing down. The Christmas period was incredibly busy for all professions including the medical trade and the first appointment they could get with Mr Williams wasn't until 27 December. It was very disappointing, as it would mean they would now spend the holidays apart. Both Matt and Mickie said it would be ridiculous to waste a fare for Michele to travel back to London and that it would only be a matter of days before they would be flying out themselves. They would be together for New Year and in the meantime Michele was to stay put.

How ill Matt thought he was at that point in time is never ascertained. He was a private, proud and selfless man who wouldn't have wanted to worry those around him and he kept any personal reservations to himself. Matt and Mickie each had their own secret fears but things were best left unsaid until he had seen a doctor.

It was a very lonely Christmas for all of them. Michele spent the holidays eating bagels with her friend Monette in Boca Raton's 85 degree heat. The small Christmas tree laden with presents in readiness for her parent's arrival was the only clue that the holiday season was upon them.

Michele really had no idea of the severity of the situation. She, like others, had disregarded the idea of chronic indigestion that the Australian physician had diagnosed and thought it much more likely that her father had suffered a severe strain of food poisoning from the rock oysters that, unless properly treated, would continually cause problems. Mr Williams was convinced by the tests that he had already conducted that there was nothing that should give cause for concern. Whatever each of them thought, there was nothing that could be done except wait.

At 10.15am on 27 December, Matt presented himself at King's College Hospital for another consultation with the specialist. He was suffering from lassitude, abdominal pain and weight loss. Hours later he was admitted to the Cromwell Hospital in London.

> I saw this patient, who as you know has not been well over the past few weeks with increasing abdominal pain and distension. On examination the liver has enlarged significantly and there is a tender lump, which is very suggestive of a hepatoma development. I have therefore arranged for his admission to Cromwell Hospital immediately. — Doctor's Report

Symptoms of malignant hepatoma are often similar to those of liver disease and include pain and swelling, especially in the abdominal area, loss of appetite and weight, jaundice, fatigue and fever. To make an accurate diagnosis the specialist called for a battery of tests including blood work, a chest x-ray, a hepatic arteriogram, an abdominal ultrasound, a computed tomography scan of the abdomen, a TC scan of the liver and spleen, an isotope bone scan and a liver biopsy. It was then that Matt and Mickie were told that the investigations had confirmed the presence of liver cancer.

> I went to see Matt twice in hospital. The first time he seemed sure that things would be OK. Les Dawson had just been in to see him. Matt had been given some drug or other and the effect was that he was peeing blue, Les found that hilarious. — Ron Miller

Matt had plenty of visitors, in fact so many that they had to be limited so as not to tire him. Outwardly he was in good spirits, he spoke to his daughter on the phone, telling her that once these tests were run he would be out there, surmising it would probably be another week, but he neglected to mention the doctor's findings.

Michael Black visited, as did Bernie Winters and Dec Clusky. When Don Black arrived Matt was in the middle of watching Steve Davis and Jimmy White playing snooker and he said, "Hang on son, he's on for the big break." Dave Allen's trip to the Cromwell was rather traumatic for the comic. A known claustrophobic, Dave cautiously entered the empty lift and while it made its slow upward climb, he nervously counted the seconds until it reached its destination on the fourth floor. The contraption stopped but nothing happened. Dave was sweating profusely and started randomly pressing buttons, still nothing – now he was openly petrified and pummelled his fists against the steel doors. A lone voice asked if he was all right and, turning, Dave found that the doors had opened behind him. He made a rather embarrassed and hasty exit and despite the fact that he now knew that the lift had duel doors at either end, he never used it again. Matt thought it the funniest story he'd heard and fell about laughing, offering up his bed to the pale and shaken comic in case he felt faint.

John Ashby had spoken to Matt after his return from Australia and told him that he was going to the USA for Christmas and the New Year and would be back in four weeks. As Matt was also planning a quiet time over the holidays, they agreed to talk about what they were going to do work-wise when they next met up.

> **I got back on 10 January and the fifth message on the answer machine went, "Hello son, I'd like a word, ring me on this number, room so and so." I thought it was strange. I rang the number and it was the Cromwell Hospital. That was the first inkling that I knew he was sick. At that moment I didn't know how ill he was, he'd never mentioned he wasn't well after getting back from Australia. — John Ashby**

John visited nearly every day and got upset by how many people were visiting at one time, but it was extremely hard for Mickie to distinguish who should have priority. Matt had so many good friends and if the visits perked him up, she didn't want to deny him that pleasure.

Extensive investigations were performed to define any extra-hepatic spread. Because the malignant cells were in an area of fat in the liver biopsy specimen, which only suggested local spread, it was felt that a liver transplant was worthy of consideration. Matt was referred to Professor R Y Calne, the Professor of Surgery at Addenbrooke's Hospital in Cambridge.

Michele had an extremely bad night. She woke up drenched in sweat and knew with absolute conviction that something was very wrong. All she had been told up to this point was that her father was waiting for the results of tests and that, all being equal, her parents would fly out the following week. It was 4.00am, and with a shaking hand she dialled the house number in England. Her mother answered the phone, explaining that she had just walked in and was about to call anyway. Mickie disclosed that the tests had shown primary cancer in the liver but that it hadn't travelled to any other organs. This was good news in the grand scheme of things because it meant that Matt was a good candidate for a transplant. They were going to transfer her father to Cambridge on 12 January.

Michele felt sick to the stomach; her father was seriously ill and she was thousands of miles away. She berated herself for not going home sooner, but her parents had been adamant that it wasn't necessary and that they would be joining her in America in a matter of days. She phoned British Airways to make immediate plans to fly home the next day. The flight was full. She explained that having been an air stewardess in her early twenties, she could be allowed (at the captain's discretion) to sit in the cockpit's jump seat for the journey. The airline rang back with the news that unfortunately the captain's wife was on the flight and she would be using the extra seat herself. Becoming hysterical, Michele was put through to the managerial office, where she explained exactly who she was and why it was imperative that she be on the flight the next day. Again she waited anxiously by the phone. This time she was told there was nothing they could do with regard to the flight as it was full and that although she could be added to the waiting list it was extremely unlikely that a space would materialise. They could, however, offer her a seat on Concorde, which left at about the same time as the Jumbo jet the next evening. She explained she didn't have that sort of money at her disposal but the airline told her the seat was complimentary. They knew and loved her father and it would be their pleasure to help her get home. They promised her confidentiality as Michele was worried that they would leak the story to the newspapers, but she needn't have worried as the papers in England were already awash with news of Matt's illness.

Michele's flight actually landed on 8 January, nine hours before the scheduled aircraft she should have been on, and she hotfooted it across to the Cromwell. It was 10.45pm and the security guard was loathe to give her access as it was way past visiting hours, but she wasn't about to let that stand in the way of seeing her father. She needed to see and touch him, she needed a hug from her knight in shining armour and no hospital policy was going to stop that from happening. Tiptoeing into his room, she found him sitting up in bed doing the crossword and, on seeing her, a big smile lit his face. Mickie had left about two hours before and Matt rang his wife to tell her Michele was safely in England and sitting right beside him. Father and daughter spent an hour together and, feeling reassured by her father's high spirits, she left him to sleep for the night.

On 12 January, a private ambulance transferred the star from the London hospital to Addenbrooke's in Cambridge. It became an ordeal, as one of the nursing staff had leaked the star's departure to the press and they were camped out at all the exits. As the electronic doors of the hospital peeled open and the stretcher was carried out, the paparazzi surged forward, jostling to get the best picture. It was a huge intrusion on what was an intensely painful and private time for the family. Flashlights went off in their faces and they had to push their way through to gain access to the vehicle. The press had tried all possible ways to gain entry to the star's hospital room, even resorting to donning doctor's whites and parading along the floors with stethoscopes dangling round their necks. Thankfully the ruse wasn't successful, as the hospital had the foresight to give Matt an alias. Had they looked at Mr Smith's admission chart, they would have found their prey.

An organ transplant is an extremely delicate and difficult procedure and not a decision to be taken lightly. However, Professor Calne thought his patient an ideal candidate for the operation and considered the prognosis promising. The growth was contained in one area and the patient was otherwise in good health and young enough to benefit from another twenty-plus years of life. Although Matt was a smoker, there was no indication that the habit had any bearing on the current disease and the patient's lungs were extremely healthy. The family were introduced to Celia Wight, the transplant co-ordinator, and she explained what they should expect in the coming days. The first steps had been taken; Matt's name had been entered on the National Transplant Database.

Awaiting a transplant is an agonising experience, for in essence you are wishing time away and fervently hoping that someone else's time on Earth comes to an abrupt end. It wasn't enough that a bereaved family, in their darkest hour, would give permission for you to have their loved one's organ, but it had to cross-match on so many different levels. Incredibly, only seven days later a match was found. A liver was rushed from North Wales in a desperate bid to save the singer's life. Surgeons flew by air ambulance and RAF helicopter to Glan Clwyd hospital near Rhyl where they removed the liver from the donor. A police car then took the team on part of the return journey to Cambridge after low cloud and ice forced the helicopter to land.

The family walked with the gurney to the doors that would take Matt through to the anaesthesia antechamber and there they said their goodbyes. Although it was important to put on a brave face for the patient's benefit, the risk of the operation was not lost on the Monro family. There was nothing more they could do now except wait and pray. They had been told the operation would likely take twelve hours and they prepared themselves for a long wait.

Matt had undergone at least twenty different tests prior to the procedure to establish that the cancer hadn't spread to other parts of his body, but the start of the operation revealed extensive abdominal spread of the tumour. The incision was closed without further intervention.

> **Don and I saw Matt at Addenbrooke's with his family; he had just had his pre-med and was so pleased to see us. He said he didn't want to go back to work for about six months, that he wanted to go to Florida and just relax. We stayed until lunchtime, which was when Matt went down to theatre, and we promised that we would drive back up the next day. Don and I went to the University Arms Hotel in Cambridge and had lunch. There was only one other table in the restaurant that was occupied. They had background music playing and about 1.30pm Don said, "Listen to that", and they were playing 'Softly As I Leave You'. Later that day at about 5.00pm Don rang me and told me that he had heard from the hospital that the operation had been aborted because of the spread of cancer. It was quite poignant that they should play that song at that time, at that moment. — John Ashby**

Matt had never suffered major surgery before but still made an excellent recovery from the operation. Although the procedure had not been completed he had still undergone anaesthesia and sustained a Mercedes Benz incision and the regulatory drips protruded from different parts of his body. After spending time in recovery, Matt was wheeled to his room and made comfortable. The family were called for a conference with Professor Calne and his team and there they explained the harsh facts of Matt's case, that the growth was not confined to the liver. They concluded that the best chance of recovery was to start a course of chemotherapy, but that the specialist Mr Williams would make the final decision on treatment.

Returning to Matt's room, the family were shocked to see it was completely empty. They approached the nursing staff but they were as perplexed as everyone else. It didn't take them long to find the singer in the patients' lounge. He was smoking a cigarette and regaling a captive audience with tales of his operation, looking relaxed and cheerful. He had woken up and inched his way to the lounge, wheeling the stand that held the drips and tubes attached to his body.

Matt was unaware of the discoveries made during the procedure and, when he first woke up in recovery to a cacophony of machines, tubes and monitors, there was no indication that the transplant had been aborted. It was the aftercare nurse who apparently told him that the operation hadn't been successful, but Matt had taken that to mean that the liver wasn't a match and settled himself to wait for another donor. It was a heartbreaking moment for the family, for the reality was very different.

Once Matt learned the truth he stayed philosophical; he reasoned that it wasn't meant to be and that there would be an alternative. But, of course, there wasn't and he knew it and his family knew he knew it. There was nothing much the hospital could do except make their charge as comfortable as possible, but Matt didn't want to loiter around and made arrangements for the hospital to transfer him back to the Cromwell.

He knew he was dying. When I visited Matt in Addenbrooke's after the failed surgery, I found him in the family room smoking. "What are you doing?" I asked. He replied, "It doesn't matter now!"
— John Brown

Matt's chemotherapy treatment began with Mitozanthrone in a dose of twelve milligrams per metre-squared. This amounted to twenty milligrams diluted in a hundred millilitres of normal saline, infused over thirty minutes. The drug was given at three or four week intervals. Prednisolone was also administered. This was used as an immunosuppressant and was a common drug for organ transplants, but it could cause unpleasant side effects, which included fluid retention in the face, muscle cramps, muscle weakness, nausea, pain in back, hips, ribs, arms, shoulders or legs, reddish purple lines on arms, face, legs, trunk or groin, thin and shiny skin, unusual bruising, weight gain, decreased or blurred vision, increased thirst, confusion and nervousness! You had to wonder if the end justified the means.

Four days after the treatment was started Matt had had enough. He didn't want to stay in hospital, he felt vulnerable and wanted to get to the comfort of his own bed, away from prying eyes. He didn't see any point in sitting there for countless weeks until the next course of chemotherapy was due.

He was incredibly weak and the humiliation he felt when the nursing staff dropped him on the way to the bathroom was too much for the family to bear. Mickie knew she could administer to his needs and if necessary would employ a nurse to monitor her husband at home. The doctors finally agreed that their patient could go home. Mickie was delighted to gather Matt's few possessions and get ready for their return. She asked the hospital for a box of refuse bags, as that was the easiest way of transporting the thousands of cards, letters and fan mail that had accumulated since the singer had been admitted into hospital.

I spoke to Mickie and told her that I would pick Matt up and drive him home to Ealing. I parked the car at the Cromwell and Matt came down in his pyjamas and dressing gown (there was no point dressing, it was too much effort). I'm a strict non-smoker and I'd just bought this brand-new car. As soon as we were in the car, I said to Matt, "If you need to smoke that's fine, but I would prefer if you don't." He said, "Well, you know me, I'm going to have a cigarette". He smoked one and stubbed it out in the new ashtray. — John Ashby

Although John removed the ash he kept the cigarette stub in the ashtray for the next three years. He couldn't bear to throw it out.

Matt was only home for four days. Although he had tried his best, he was unable to eat because of the nausea and the drugs had made him extremely weak and befuddled. He was loath to be readmitted to hospital as he had enjoyed the peace and security of the family home and having his wife and children around him. He lay on his settee in the lounge watching television and Michele would sit in the armchair watching over him. It didn't matter if her father didn't want to talk, she was perfectly happy with the silence as long as she could stay with him. Mickie hardly slept. She didn't want the intrusion of a nurse if it wasn't necessary, desperate to maintain some sense of normality for her husband. Their home doctor was available twenty-four-seven and was at the end of the phone whenever needed. They didn't attempt to move Matt for bedtimes, as he was too weak to climb the stairs and he was perfectly happy to sleep on his sofa, a place where he had fallen asleep in front of the television a thousand times in the past. It meant that Mickie also slept downstairs as she didn't want to leave her husband unattended at any moment in case he needed something. Despite the family's best efforts, Matt's inability to eat or drink caused him to become dehydrated and he needed to return to the hospital to stabilise his condition.

Mickie promised her husband it would just be for a few days, but she was more worried than ever. He was so thin and frail that he looked as if he would blow over in a strong wind. Michele got his Mercedes out of the garage and brought it round to the front door. Mickie had held up pretty well in the circumstances, but privately she shed tears that she might be losing her best friend, her confidante, her lover, and the father of her children. She didn't let Matt see the cracks that were starting to appear in her resolve, but as he was helped to the car, his wedding ring slipped off his finger and that moment defined everything for Mickie. She knew she was going to lose him.

Matt's condition stabilised within thirty-six hours. He was treated with glucose and insulin together with calcium resonium. Further tests showed leucopoenia, a condition in which the numbers of white blood cells circulating in the blood were abnormally low and the nursing staff administered something to combat the problem. Mickie limited visitors but there were a few people Matt wanted to see.

> The second time I went to visit Matt was when I had been to Monte Carlo to walk the course at the conference Matt was going to sing at. I flew into Heathrow in the early afternoon and was going to go straight home. I bought the *Evening Standard* and in the 'stop press' it said, "Matt Monro fighting for his life". I went straight up to the Cromwell. — Ron Miller

John Ashby went in almost every day, and on this particular day Matt was beaming as he showed his former manager a telegram that had just arrived from Frank Sinatra. He was absolutely thrilled. It arrived just in time.

> Dear Matt,
> Sorry to hear that you've taken ill and hope you'll soon be on the mend and up and about.
> I send you love and prayers.
> Your fellow boy singer,
> Frank Sinatra

As soon as Matt was readmitted to the Cromwell, Michele made it her personal crusade to contact an eminent doctor in Switzerland who had controversially treated Yul Brynner with a degree of success. Miraculously, she managed to track him down to a small village and phoned him immediately. He was charming and considerate of the emotional state of his caller. A fee of ten thousand pounds could have been charged to fly over and treat the star, but it would have been taken under false pretences, for after listening to a description of her father's condition and hearing the answer to a set of questions he posed, the doctor admitted that it was too late. He softly explained what was likely to happen next so as to prepare Michele for the inevitable. The euphoria of tracking the doctor down across Europe dissipated abruptly, and Michele was left feeling only despair and devastation.

Matt's condition continued to decline despite his white cell count rising and his

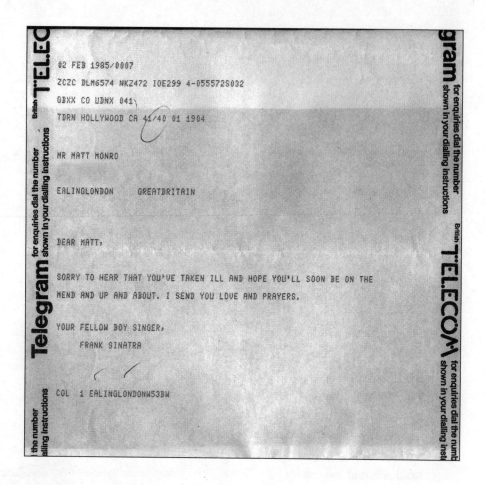

02 FEB 1985/0007

ZCZC DLN6574 NKZ472 IOE299 4-0555728032

GBXX CO UDNX 041

TDRN HOLLYWOOD CA 41/40 01 1904

MR MATT MONRO

EALINGLONDON   GREATBRITAIN

DEAR MATT,

SORRY TO HEAR THAT YOU'VE TAKEN ILL AND HOPE YOU'LL SOON BE ON THE
MEND AND UP AND ABOUT. I SEND YOU LOVE AND PRAYERS.

YOUR FELLOW BOY SINGER,
      FRANK SINATRA

COL 1 EALINGLONDONW53BW

electrolytes stabilising. The cause of his deterioration was now bronchopneumonia and, after fighting against the onslaught of the disease, Matt fell into a coma after being given Diamorphine to control his agitation. Despite all efforts, he died peacefully at 3.45pm. It was 7 February 1985 – cause of death hepatic failure secondary to hepatocellular carcinoma and bronchopneumonia.

CRY ME A RIVER

I remember exactly where I was when I read the news in the morning paper. The last time I'd seen Matt was on the Des O'Connor show a few weeks before when Des proclaimed he was "singing better than ever" and I had to agree. It felt like a member of my own family had gone. Did a woman ever love a man more than Mickie loved Matt? I doubt it. — James Creaton

Matt was quite a spiritual man and we often discussed this and other aspects of mortality during our long drives. In the final days I was working at the Dominion Theatre, and following a matinee walked out of the theatre to see the Evening Standard placard 'Matt Monro Dead', I was at the crowded junction of Oxford Street and Tottenham Court Road at 5.00pm on the 7 February 1985 and I felt empty, I had lost a good and close friend. He may have been a famous singer and myself just the accompanist, but our relationship was much deeper than that. — Dave Mellor

The next time Mickie rang was to invite me to officiate at Matt's funeral. During my address at the funeral, I told of how one of the great theologians of the twentieth century had emphasised the importance of music. He claimed that, on reaching heaven, there were a number of people he would want to meet. He named half a dozen famous theologians, but then added, perhaps surprisingly, that before all of them he would first enquire about Mozart. For many, rather than Mozart, it will be Matt Monro about whom they will enquire. — Canon Bill Hall

To me he was a star who never lived like a star. He didn't have a great ego. What made him so special was the fact that he never pretended to be anything or anyone other than what he was, and he never forgot his roots. To me he was a lovely, lovely man who in some respects was quite ordinary, except for the fact that he had a truly wonderful voice and really made the lyrics come alive. He didn't court celebrity and that's possibly why people might say he could have gone further, but I suspect those that represented him didn't do a great job there. I only knew Matt for four years but I cannot impress upon you how fond I was of him. I just regret that I didn't know him for much longer.
— Ron Miller

When Matt was taken to hospital, Mickie never left his side. We would visit and try and get her to rest but she never did. Then we had the terrible phone call. I'd never seen Colin cry before or since, but he just crumbled into tears. Mickie asked Colin to play 'Softly' onto tape to be played at the end of the funeral. It took Colin ages, he just couldn't do it without breaking down, and Colin had played that tune for years. — Pam Keyes

The funeral was hugely crowded and I was standing inside the church and they brought Matt's coffin in to the strains of 'Softly' and I've never been more moved in my life by anything, either before or since. It was to do with Matt, it was to do with the occasion and it was to do with the music and the linking of that song. That was the moment I completely and totally lost control and broke down and had to be carried out. I walked for two hours with that song in my head – that is what Matt's music and his songs can do to a person. — Peter Jamieson

My last personal memory is going to Golders Green Crematorium with an incredible crowd of musicians and stars, to celebrate his life and to see him on his way after he had died. He didn't want us to be sad and we tried hard, with many happy memories, but to hear 'Softly' as his coffin was taken away still brings tears and an ache to my heart. Every other memory,

Floral Tributes

though, is of fun and warmth and of a superb talent and a wonderful man. My personal opinion is that Matt Monro was the very best singer of popular music this country has ever produced. — Pam Cox

Matt's reputation among fellow pros was evident when I went along to pay my respects at his Memorial Service in Golders Green some time later. The place was packed and I had to stand at the back like so many more. I stood beside Dave Allen, Vince Hill and Spike Milligan and we all said farewell to the man I always described as 'the best'. — Val Doonican

When Matt was readmitted to the Cromwell he made Mickie promise that she would take him home as soon as possible. She kept her promise to her husband and arranged for the casket to be delivered to the house. Canon Bill Hall travelled down to spend the night with the family and held a special prayer service for his friend. Matt's coffin rested in the lounge until the given time when the hearse came to collect its special passenger.

Matt never acquired the 'superstar' tag, but quality was his code, and he earned the reputation for being a class act with a superlative gift. Gimmicks and effects that might leave writers breathless, carry little weight with a seasoned performer who recognises the rarity and worth of a sincere ballad delivered without affectation. That Matt Monro was indeed a Singer's Singer is neatly confirmed by the fact that Bing Crosby, Sammy Davis Jr and Frank Sinatra were all numbered among his admirers. Sinatra singled out Matt Monro as the only British singer he ever listened to, and later covered the singer's songs for his Reprise label. Matt's intense feelings for his profession were deep-rooted. He felt it was a calling, a vocation. He loved the business and saw only the good side of everything and everyone – but it was the accolades from his contemporaries that gave him the biggest thrill of all.

> In all my years in the vocalist business, I have listened to all my co-working boy singers constantly, not only enjoying their work, but hoping I might learn something from them. So we come to Matt Monro ...If I had to choose three of the finest male vocalists in the singing business, Matt would be one of them. His pitch was right on the nose; his word enunciations letter perfect; his understanding of a song thorough. He will be missed very much not only by myself, but by his fans all over the world. — Frank Sinatra

> In my line of singing, in this country, when you use the word 'class' you automatically think of one man. When it came to classy singers there was Matt Monro and the rest of us simply followed. — Vince Hill

> He was a great talent with the most beautiful voice.
> — Michael Jackson

> Matt Monro obviously possesses a poet's soul. You can hear it in the romance of his recordings. Matt's voice makes you listen not just with your ears, but with your heart. — Nancy Sinatra

Matt, Kenny Everett & Mitch

The inimitable vocal style of Matt Monro will never be forgotten. My memories of Matt will remain with me always. Not only a wonderful voice, but a wonderful man. — Maurice Gibb

When I look back on my twenty-five years in the entertainment business Matt stands out as one of the most honest, humorous, warm and talented people I have had the privilege of knowing. He is one of those people, the mention of whose name will always be engender a wisp of sad mist in the soul; until we ourselves are lost to this life. — Roger Whittaker

Working with Matt was a delight, he was always open to song suggestions, but in the studio he was the vocal maestro. I would sit back in the control room and marvel at his superb interpretation of the chosen songs. He rarely needed many takes and he loved recording with the full orchestra, and that feeling comes across in all his records. — John Burgess

Once Matt's funeral had taken place it seemed the world of show business turned its back on the legacy he had left behind. Two years past without a single tribute being organised and Michele grew increasingly cross, deciding to take matters into her own hands. On the 22 February 1987, hundreds of stars and fans turned up for a Gala evening staged in Matt's honour at London's Grosvenor House Hotel. *By Request* was a lavish affair and the room was littered with personalities from all areas of the business. Bob Monkhouse, Barry Cryer and Dave Allen were the main speakers of the evening, but all eyes were trained on Mickie as she spoke to the crowd.

My dear friends, ladies and gentlemen. Matt Monro, my husband, my very best friend, a great singer, a great artist and an even greater man. Above all, he had the most wonderful warm sense of humour that never ever left him at any time – and so I know exactly what he is saying watching us honour him this evening: 'About bloody time!'

Whenever Matt walked into a concert hall, theatre or club, one of the first questions he would ask was: "How's business?" Well wouldn't he be just knocked out by the 'House Full' signs tonight? This is just a wonderful party.

I am happy and lucky to have my family around me – Mitchell and Matt Jnr, a chip off the old block in more ways than one – and my daughter Michele. Michele had a dream which she was determined would come true, and it has tonight. Almost single-handedly, against all odds, she took on the enormous task of putting together this tribute. It took sheer guts, very, very hard work and a great deal of faith. She has done an absolutely fabulous job and your father would be very proud of you.

Of course none of this would have been possible without each and every one of you. You have been magnificent and I just don't have the words for what I feel. You have all given me enormous strength and from tonight I shall only go forward and keep Matt's name brightly lit. I thank you all for showing Matt so much love.

I promised to love and honour Matt, which was never hard – it was the obeying that was difficult! Of course we had our rows, especially after a few drinks – well quite a lot of drinks – and he would always end up saying: 'You just like being Mrs Matt Monro' and I'd say, 'You're damn right!' Well, if you are listening darling, and I'm sure you are, you're still right – I still like being Mrs Matt Monro and I shall always proudly be Mrs Matt Monro.

It would be another ten years before the BBC decided to put together a programme on Matt's life. The decision not to screen *The Man with The Golden Voice* on terrestrial television was a gross misconception of the singer's popularity, but after

Bob West & Bernie Winters

unprecedented viewing figures on satellite channels a decision was finally made to broadcast the biography on BBC 2. Despite competition from the World Cup, the programme still managed nearly 1.8 million in its viewing figures and featured in the channel's top 30 most popular programmes of the week.

Nearly twenty-five years on, his music remains as popular as ever, and with renewed interest in the crooners of the 1960s, Matt Monro has been discovered all over again by a new generation.

> **As people grow up beyond their early teenage years and have an appreciation of the music of the twentieth century, they pick up from people that were good, they should pick up on a few Matt Monro songs, even if it's only half a dozen. Those half a dozen are great and deserve to survive and he will survive. Matt Monro found me when I wasn't looking for him. He came to me over WMCA New York in 1961 with his American top twenty hit 'My Kind of Girl'. He jumped at me from the silver screen in 1963 with 'From Russia with Love'. In 1964 he broke my heart with Don Black's moving 'Walk Away'. Bowled over by his emotion and his musicianship, I discovered he was the originator of the instant standards 'Portrait of My Love' and 'Softly as I Leave You'. Now that I had him in my home, I couldn't let him go. He has been a part of my life ever since. — Paul Gambaccini**

Matt was not just a great singer; he was also a great entertainer. He was still singing in the same key as when he started in the business. He was one of the lucky ones who didn't have to have a hit to survive. It seems that this travelling salesman of songs had something unique that transcended chart success. Fred Flange had indeed come a long way.

Millions of admirers still hold Matt's recorded legacy in the highest esteem. In the decades that have passed since his untimely death there has been no dip in the singer's appeal and it is likely that his performances will endure, to be numbered among the most lasting contributions to popular music. In recent years, many singers riding the resurging wave of retro-pop have cited Matt Monro as a strong influence, including Monica Mancini, Rick Astley and Michael Buble. Many musician's biographers note his stylistic influence on their subjects, including those of Cass Elliott and Karen Carpenter.

> Any number of times, I have seen or heard Matt Monro described, in so many words, as one of the best pop baritones to hail from England in the early '60s. Talk about an understatement filled with qualifications! Matt Monro was one of the finest pop baritones who ever lived, possessing perfect intonation, remarkable enunciation and articulation, a natural feel for a song and a warmth of tone that gives the listener goosebumps. Karen and I did not hear of Matt Monro until the 1964 release of 'Walk Away'. I bought the single and proceeded to turn the groove grey. Soon after, I purchased the 'From Hollywood with Love' album - also packaged as 'From Russia with Love' - and was blown away by the work of all concerned: Matt, producer George Martin, arranger Johnnie Spence and engineer Stuart Eltham. From then on Karen and I were sold. I was greatly saddened by Matt's passing, and only two years after Karen's death. Two greats – gone too soon.
> — Richard Carpenter

Since Matt's premature death, his recordings have been regularly repackaged and the advent of compact discs saw a rush of compilations hit the market. The first to be issued on the new format was *Heartbreakers*, and in the subsequent years EMI have issued more than fifty collections of recordings in the UK alone. In 2001, Steve Woof of EMI Gold started working with Michele, with the decision that instead of a conveyor belt of 'the best of' and 'greatest hits' offerings, they would put their heads together and come up with unique ideas to give the listeners a chance to hear more interesting material. For the casual fan *The Ultimate Matt Monro*, issued in 2005 is probably the best overview of his career, but the lesser-known recordings of the singer has caused the most interest of late. When EMI and the Matt Monro Estate released *The Rare Monro,* it was hailed by both *In-Tune* magazine and *The Record Collector*, the latter citing it as one of the most important releases of 2006.

Matt Monro was admired by so many, not just his fans, but his friends, peers and fellow singers. Cliff Richard said that although he never wanted to change his voice, he wouldn't have minded some of Matt's quality. Dick Haynes rated him as perhaps the greatest of the lot, not just on the technical side of his singing but because of the mood and warmth behind his performance. There doesn't seem to be a bad word to be said about the singer who touched hearts with his music and touched the lives of those that were lucky enough to count Matt among their friends.

Matt was a credit to the music industry and praised by the highest names in showbiz around the world. He was Frank Sinatra and Tony Bennett's favourite singer, and it doesn't come any better than that. He will always be remembered as the man who left us with some of the greatest classic songs of the twentieth century. He touched me deeply; both as a man, and as one of the finest voices I have ever heard. His recording of 'If I Never Sing Another Song' was my greatest inspiration when it came to me coming to terms with my own inability to sing any more. Matt will always be remembered and revered by the generations that grew up with his music, but times have changed and the new generation have yet to discover good music. They say that things come in cycles and hopefully this will mean that his music will be rediscovered – it certainly deserves to be.
— Frank Ifield

Matt Monro was the finest singer of ballads that I have ever had the good fortune to produce. Like that other great one, Nat "King" Cole, he had the rare gift of getting to the heart of a lyric, and with his superb voice, delivering it in such a way that it became a personal message to his audience. And this quality showed in his personal life. Always outward looking, he had a terrific sense of humour and seemed to find only the best in other people. In an age when a more raucous sound became common, his popularity remained undiminished. Matt will sing on and I shall always hear him. — George Martin

Matt had an infectious laugh and a wild sense of humour, they don't make 'em like that any more, no, they don't — they never made another one. — Michael Black

He was the most balanced, generous, talented, well-behaved individual I ever met. — Kenny Clayton

He was my friend and he was one of the best singers I have ever heard. From my point of view in both categories he was very special. — Sammy Davis Jr

I have never heard a Matt Monro recording that wasn't of the highest taste and sensitivity. He was my friend and I thank him for leaving a legacy of fine recordings for all of us to enjoy forever. — Henry Mancini

Matt was one of the nicest, most talented and genuine people I have had the pleasure of knowing. A good man, a most treasured friend and a possessor of that rare gift — a sense of humour. I am honoured he considered me his friend. I hope he knew the affection, respect and admiration I held for him. Somehow, I believe he did. Matt was no fool and he instinctively sensed the real from the phoney. I feel grateful Matt graced my life. I will always miss him. — Mike Winters

Matt was charming and totally compelling, from the easy smile to the laughing eyes to the deep vibrant voice. The music industry used hit records as its measure of success, but for Matt the real joy came from singing to live audiences in all their unpredictable variety. "Every show is a challenge, you can never get complacent, you've got to go out and sound as though you mean it, you can't fool the audience."

Matt's biggest disappointment was that he never had a number one hit in his own country during his lifetime. Although a topper of the charts all over the world, Matt still craved that same recognition in his home country. He regretted not being sensible and admitted he should have stayed in America. He should have stood up to the people who disappointed him, rather than endure them. Bruce Forsyth sums up exactly what Matt had secretly thought.

Morriston Orpheus Choir

I should have been more upfront and involved in directing how my career should go, instead of waiting in the wings for everything to come to me. But it was not in my nature to push myself, to make myself be seen in all the right places at the right time. If I had been blessed with a different type of temperament, I could probably have done even more things I would have been very proud of.
— Bruce Forsyth

The same characteristics that stopped Bruce from confronting these problems also stopped Matt. It was not in his nature to be cold, calculating or aloof, and unfortunately he left his career in the hands of others.

It is a tragedy that the BBC's policy of the time to wipe the tapes of its television and radio broadcasts, with few exceptions, means that very little exists of Matt's timeless performances. Only copies held privately by collectors might mean some of the material will eventually come to light. The Monro family themselves were guilty of withholding footage. For nearly forty years an unknown film reel of Matt Monro performing live lay discarded in the family garage. Its discovery by Michele was momentous: the only known film of Britain's greatest singer had at last been found. This was an invitation and a once in a lifetime opportunity to spend – *An Evening with Matt Monro*. The concert release shot to the top of the DVD Music charts, knocking off the likes of Eminem and Usher, giving Matt his first No 1 hit in England.

In 1985, Matt Monro received a posthumous award from the British Academy of Songwriters, Composers and Authors. Val Doonican presented the family with a Gold Badge of Merit at a special lunch at London's Hilton on Park Lane. He was never awarded an honour from the palace for his contribution to the British music industry or acknowledged for being the ambassador of British music that he was.

> **There's something about the purity of his voice that must be commented on. It is like a camera lens on which there is no dust whatsoever. You listen to it and wait for the imperfection, you wait for the dust, a speck, it doesn't come. And yet somehow when it came to singing he was able to keep it crisp clear, it's a beautiful instrument.**
> **— Paul Gambaccini**

The one word used more than any other to describe Matt Monro's show business image is professionalism. He gave his audience his best, he gave his musicians respect, he possessed unmistakable tone, flawless diction, was subtly sparing in the use of grace notes and sang in the accent of his speaking voice. He made a huge impact on the business when talent and style still had a role to play. That he was surely one of Britain's greatest exports is not in question. His record career alone must be a significant milestone in the annals of the music business. But go beyond the tabloid image and you find a staunch and supportive friend, a man who cared deeply about other people, a humble man with no ego who didn't believe his own hype. But this is a man of so many different parts, a meditative soul who was overwhelmed by his own press and seemed genuinely surprised that people would want to listen to him. He was the most wonderful husband and father who cherished his family deeply. That he was sparing of the time he could give them was unfortunate, but he was not sparing of the love he gave. He was caught in the headlights of an industry that exuded magic, at times torn between the two, but he made the right choices – his family wouldn't have wanted it any other way.

To really understand Matt Monro all you have to do is one simple thing – listen – his voice is the clue to his humanity. Through his music Matt lives on.

He is irreplaceable.

THE LAST WORD

Matt was indeed a unique vocalist and very dedicated to his art. He was the kind of artist who could touch one with his richness of soul. A compassionate human being who always gave his all. I believe Matt's spirit and music will be a memorable experience for everyone.

Quincy Jones

Besides enjoying working with Matt, he was always a perfect gentleman, a fine singer and always a joy to be around. We all miss him.

Perry Como

I met him in England and I really loved the guy. He was one of the best singers I ever heard in my life.

Mel Torme

The most generous man I ever met.

Tony Bennett

Matt Monro's recording of "I Get Along Without You Very Well" is one of the most beautiful I've ever heard.

Bing Crosby

"Let There Be Love" – Great singers can take a classic and make it their own – Matt made this his own.

Cliff Richard

Matt was a great artiste. Whenever I met him he was always a pleasure to be with and I remember him fondly.

Paul McCartney

The inimitable vocal style of Matt Monro will never be forgotten. My memories of Matt will remain with me always. Not only a wonderful voice, but a wonderful man.

Maurice Gibb

Real friendship is a rare commodity in today's world and I remember Matt as a true friend. We worked together many times and shared a great working relationship. Apart from being a wonderful singer and marvellous entrepreneur of lyrics, he was also the ultimate professional – with his records he will always be with us

Shirley Bassey

I can't say that I knew Matt well – yet I always felt close to him – musically. His voice is very rare – warm but never going for the 'easy way out' even when he takes on the most poignant of songs "If I Never Sing Another Song" or "Look For Small Pleasures".

Petula Clark

He always gave me and a lot of singers a great deal to live up to, both as an artist and a human being, and still does. When we singers talk shop his name always comes up.

Jack Jones

Matt was a great buddy of mine, and someone other singers always looked up to. He had the creamiest voice, I must say, and the greatest musical instinct.

Henry Mancini

He was as warm as his voice and I miss him.

Harry Secombe

If I could have sung like Matt, I would never have given up singing.

Adam Faith

Matt was a great talent and lovely man, and while they keep playing his songs how can we possibly forget him. The Matt Monro magic goes on and on.

Roger Moore

When I look back on my twenty-five years in the entertainment business Matt stands out as one of the most honest, humorous, warm and talented people I have had the privilege of knowing. He is one of those people, the mention of whose name will always engender a wisp of sad mist in the soul; until we ourselves are lost to this life.

Roger Whittaker

Matt was not only a great singer, but a man whose smile made everyone in the room come alive. We all miss him.

Don Rickles

As a golfing partner, quite frankly he wasn't very good, as a singer he was supreme, as a companion, he was great company, and oh don't we all miss him.

Jimmy Tarbuck

We were always the very best of friends wherever we met in our tours around the world and I can say, with sincerity, that the one thing that stands out above all about Matt was the deep love he had for his family, his profession and his friends and he was always genuinely pleased for other people's success and happiness. That was my friend, Matt.

Frankie Vaughan

With a voice like his and the friendly persuasion of his personality he will never leave us.

Tommy Steele

Dear Matt, I still hear you singing.

John Barry

I backed Frank Sinatra, Nat King Cole, Ella Fitzgerald, Sarah Vaughan, Dick Haymes and Dean Martin. My favourite – Matt Monro!!

Johnnie Gray

When we lost Matt we lost a truly great artist. His wife Mickie and family can be in no doubt of the real affection that Matt was held in by his millions of fans, of which I am but one. An everlasting fan.
Cilla Black

Back in the late fifties while still working on one quarter of a popular singing group I became a Matt Monro fan, judging him to be the best singer of popular songs Britain has produced. As the years passed and success came my way I had the pleasure of sharing the stage, the microphone and the television camera with him on numerous occasions. Now that I can look back over forty years of songs my opinion has not altered. Matt was the best.
Val Doonican

Singing magnificently was only one of Matt's God given gifts. He was the most hypnotic storyteller. If he was conjuring up a sad scenario, goose pimples would be inevitable. If it was a big band swinging mood, the fingers and feet would start jumping. Matt could play with the listeners' emotions and take them on extraordinary journeys. I have had made many unforgettable trips listening to the best voice this country has ever produced.
Don Black

I am proud to have known and worked with Matt. He was the first artist I met as a young EMI apprentice in 1968. It was my business to help him, but in fact he made it his business to help me. I will never forget his friendship and inspiration across four countries and seventeen years.
Peter Jamieson

Matt – he had something 'unexplainable' in his voice – I try and analyze it whenever I can and the only thing I can think of is that without even trying every word uttered by him "comes from the heart"- with "heartfelt meaning" and I know if he had to lecture on it he himself wouldn't be able to explain it – which is "heartfelt magic unto itself"! Matt Monro was the best male singer – pure and simple – I ever worked with.
Buddy Bregman

ACKNOWLEDGEMENTS

This book has been over twenty years in the making. Several authors approached the family along the way but none seemed willing to give an in-depth overview of the artist and his contribution to the music industry, preferring instead to glorify and focus on just one aspect. It was in fact my friend and colleague at EMI, Steve Woof, who finally persuaded me that this book should be written and that it should come from me, as he felt it would ensure the book's historical accuracy.

The final deciding factor was the thought that when I die, my son would only know that his grandfather was a singer; he would know nothing of the stature of the artist or what Matt Monro brought to his profession. He would be ignorant of his true roots and unaware of the great esteem that everyone held for his grandfather. It is a great success story with a sad ending that nevertheless needed quantifying.

This book could not have been written without the vast amount of help I received from all corners of the globe. Some offered reams of material while others contributed one fact, a single date or one piece of the jigsaw, but they all were equally important.

My deepest love and admiration must go to my mother who was not only instrumental in helping Terry Parsons achieve his dreams but helped me achieve mine in writing this book. Reliving past events has been somewhat painful and brought strong emotions to the surface, but without drawing on her memories, notes, diaries, contracts and letters, this book could not even have been attempted.

My heartfelt thanks have to go to Richard Moore, who has been my right arm, my co-conspirator, my rock and my confidante. We have spurred each other on, leaving no stone unturned even when a piece of paperwork looked irretrievable. Everyone should be lucky enough to have such a friend in their lives.

It isn't just the people I am grateful to but the vast sources I have drawn from that helped in the creation of this book.

BOOKS:

Abbey Road – The Story of the World's Most Famous Recording Studio – Brian Southall, Peter Vince, Allan Rouse, Sir Paul McCartney, *Omnibus Press, UK (1997)*

All You Need is Ears – George Martin, *St Martin's Press, New York (1979)*

Brecqhou – A Very Private Island – Peter J Rivett, *Planetesinal Publishing Ltd, UK (2002)*

Bruce: The Autobiography – Bruce Forsyth, *Sidgwick & Jackson, UK (2001)*

The Complete Eurovision Song Contest Companion – Paul Gambaccini, Tim Rice, Jonathon Rice, Tony Brown, *Pavilion Books Ltd, UK (1998)*

Dave Allen: The Biography – Carolyn Soutar, *Orion, UK (2005)*

For Whom the Stars Came Out At Night – George Savva, *Boulevard Publishing UK, UK (2003)*

Jacob's Ladder – David Jacobs, *Peter Davies Ltd, UK (1963)*

John Barry: A Sixties Theme – Eddi Fiegel, *Constable & Co Ltd, UK (1998)*

Life in the Twenties and Thirties – James Cochrane, *The Readers Digest Association Ltd, UK (1995)*

Morecambe & Wise – Graham McCann, *Fourth Estate Ltd, UK (1998)*

My East End – Memories of Life in Cockney London – Gilda O'Neil, *Viking, UK (1999)*

Playback – George Martin, *Genesis Publications, UK (2003)*

Shake a Pagoda Tree – Mike & Bernie Winters, *WH Allen & Co Ltd, UK (1975)*

Sid James – Cliff Goodwin, *Century Ltd, UK (1995)*

The Rough Guide to Frank Sinatra – Chris Ingham, *Rough Guides Ltd, UK (2005)*

The Way We Lived – Richard Tames, *The Readers Digest Association Ltd, UK (1997)*

There's No People Like Show People – Confessions of a Showbiz Agent – Michael Sullivan, *Quadrant Books Ltd, UK (1984)*

This is Your Life: The Story of Television's Famous Big Red Book – Roy Bottomley, *Metheun London, UK (1999)*

Tommy Cooper: Always Leave Them Laughing: The Definitive Biography of a Comic Legend – John Fisher, *Harper Collins, UK (2007)*

Tony Hancock 'Artiste' – Roger Wilmut, *Eyre Metheun Ltd, UK (1978)*

When the Wind Changed: The Life and Death of Tony Hancock – Cliff Goodwin, *Century, UK (1999)*

Wrestling with Elephants – The Authorised Biography of Don Black – James Inverne, *Sanctuary Publishing Ltd, UK (2003)*

PERIODICALS AND NEWSPAPERS:

BASCA News

Best of British

The China Mail

Daily Express

Daily Mail/Associated Newspapers Ltd

Daily Sketch

Disc

The Evening Echo

The Evening News/Associated Newspapers Ltd

The Evening Telegraph

The Evening Times

Hong Kong Sunday Post-Herald

Isle of Wight Weekly Post

Islington Gazette

Jersey Evening Post

KYA Beat

Magazine Trasande

Melody Maker/ IPC Media Ltd/IPC + Syndication

Memory Lane – Ray Palette

Nelson Riddle Society

The Nevada State Journal (now The Reno Gazette-Journal

Newcastle News

New Musical Express/ IPC Media Ltd/ IPC + Syndication

News of the World

North Cheshire Herald

Oldham Evening Chronicle

Perfectly Frank – Pat and Frank Harvey

Picture Goer

Psychic News

Record Mirror

Reuters News Agency (Thomson Reuters)

Scottish Daily Express

Scunthorpe Star

Soldier

South China Morning Post

The Stage Newspaper Ltd

The Standard – Hong Kong

The Sun of Lowell

The Sunday Express

The Sunday Gleaner

The Sunday Times

Tit-Bits Magazine

TV Times/IPC Media Ltd/IPC + Syndication

Vision – Richard Crane and Thomas Latham

INSTITUTIONS:

Abbey Road

Airmen of Note – Joe Jackson, SMS, USAF

BBC Worldwide

BBC Written Archive, Caversham

British Library Newspapers – Colindale

British Library National Sound Archive

Capitol Records – Don Andes

Decca Music Group – Andrew Dalton

Dyna Music Entertainment Corporation

EMI Archives, Hayes – Gary Pietronave

EMI Records – Steve Woof

GOWR – John Adrian

Islington Local History Centre

J&B Records – Brian Nicholls/John Evans

London Metropolitan Archives

London Transport (Driver's Records)

R.E.M.E Museum of Technology/ Major Derek Gilliam

SEI Corporation – Gary Mason

St Leonard's Hospital

The United States Air Force Band – Joe Tersero

RADIO QUOTES:

Alan Whicker

Billy May

Bing Crosby

Buddy Greco

Cleo Laine

Dennis Lotis

Don Black

Frankie Vaughan

Henry Mancini

Jimmy Young

Scott Walker

Tony Bennett

PHOTOGRAPHS:

Alamy Images

Anthony Middleton

Associated Press Images

BBC Stills Library

Bill Francis/ Flair Photography

Caroline Foster

Crescendo Magazine

Dave Allen

Doug McKenzie

EMI Music UK

Fairfax Photos

Fremantle Media Ltd

Gary Mason/ Supreme Records

Gary Pietronave/ EMI Photo Archive

Getty Images

Harry Goodwin

Helen Shapiro

Jean Riley

Maria Butt

Neil Dalrymple

Norma Robinson

Pictorial Press

Ray Palette/ Memory Lane

Redferns Music Picture Library

Reg McCallum

Rex Features

Times Picture Library

TopFoto

PERSONAL INTERVIEWS & QUOTES:

I wish to thank the following people, whom I had the pleasure of interviewing or corresponding with during the research for this book.

Alan Fox

Alan Whicker

Alice Parsons

Anthony Clarke

Bert Weedon

Bill Betteley

Bill Comstock – Four Freshmen

Bill Pertwee, MBE

Bob DeMuth

Bobby Crush

Bob Monkhouse

Brian Hayes

Bruce Forsyth

Buddy Bregman

Canon Bill Hall

Caroline Foster

Chris Woodward

Christine Parsons

Colin Keyes

Dave Allen

Dave Burke

Dave Mellor

David Berglas

David Jacobs

Don Cole

Ed Harrod

Emrys Bryson

Ernest Maxim

Frank Sinatra

Frankie Vaughan

Frank Ifield

Freddie Davies

Frederick Boylan

George Jones

George Martin

George Skelly

Gerard Kenny

Gerry Sieling

Gert Feller

Gilbert O'Sullivan

Gordon Holland

Grace Watson

Harry Killey

Helen Shapiro

Jack Hutton

Jackie Trent

James Creaton

Jeff Hooper

Jeff Kruger, Dr. MBE

Jess Conrad

Jimmy Tarbuck

Joan Regan

John Ammonds

John Ashby

John Barclay

John Browell

John Burgess

John Casson

John Gilmore

Johnnie Gray

Johnny More

June Marlow

Kathy Kirby

Keith Cowper
Keith Good
Kenny Baker
Ken Brown
Ken Bruno
Kenny Cantor
Kenny Clayton
Kenny Harkins
Kerry Jewel
Lance Raymond.
Laraine Kentridge
Larry Jordan
Lister Coleman
Lita Roza
Lorrae Desmond
Maurice Gibb
Marion Spence
Matt Monro Jnr.
Max Bygraves, OBE
Michael Black
Michael Sigman
Michel Legrand
Mike and Sue Parker
Mike Hatchard
Mike Winters
Mickie Monro
Nancy Sinatra
Neil Harrold
Nick Chapman
Norma Robinson
Pam Cox
Pam Keyes
Paul and Margaret Flanagan - The Flanagans
Paul Gambaccini
Paul Griffin
Peter Jamieson
Petula Clark
Pilita Corrales
Ray and Joan Jowett
Ray Cordeiro
Reg Parsons
Richard Carpenter

Richard Crook
Roger Hancock
Roger Whittaker
Ron Miller
Ron Way
Rosalyn Wilder
Rosemary Squires, MBE
Roy Hudd
Sammy Davis Jr
Sue Groves
Ted Thomas
Tommy Tycho
Tony Brady
Tony Hatch
Tony Stenson
Val Doonican
Vic Fraser
Woody Woodbury

For background and insight material on Matt Monro's life I am also indebted to:

Alan Bailey
Anthony Middleton
Audrey Purr
Barry Simcoe
Bert Bossink
Bob Day
Chris Woodward
Colin Kilgour
Craig Douglas
Danee Samonte
Darren Harte
Dave Carey – The Stargazers
David Durrett
Derek Mannering
Don Henderson – Capitol Engineer
George Jones
George Patterson
Ian Billingham
Jack Jackson
Jeffrey Paul Hayes
Jim Sterling
John Casson

John Hannam.
John Highton
Joyce McGowan
Major Derek Gilliam – REME
Marion and Peter Down
Mark Farenden
Mark Willerton –Kathy Kirby Organisation
Marta Alvarez
Michael Ellis
Mike James
Mike Martin
Mike Redway
Paul Howes – Dusty Springfield Fan Club
Paul Roy Goodhead – Anthony Newley Society
Pearl Bowman
Peter Fusea
Peter Lim
Peter 'Yorky' McEvoy
Robert Blythe (KCC GM)
Robert Earl
Sally Wiseman
Sandra Honeysett
Siggi Winters
Stan Britt
Simon Spillett
Stephen Garner
Stephen Pattinson
Steve and Lonnie Race
Steve Ellis
Stuart Eltham
Tony Fisher
Vince Miller
Wikepedia
Will Fyffe Jr

Every effort has been made to trace and seek permission from those holding the copyright to material used in this book. My deepest apologies to anyone I may have inadvertently omitted.

The author and publishers have made all reasonable efforts to contact copyright holders for permission, and any omission or errors in the form of credit will be corrected in future printings.

THE GREATEST

25 Classic Songs including the previously unreleased 'I'll Never Fall In Love Again'.

THE COMPLETE SINGLES COLLECTION

This 5 CD set, features all of Matt's A and B sides from his years with Fontana, Decca, EMI, Parlophone and Capitol Records, all completely remastered.

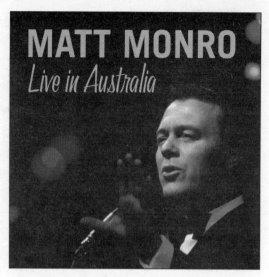

LIVE IN AUSTRALIA

Recorded in 1984, this concert is one of Matt's very few live performances that exist. His warm personality and wonderful sense of humour is evident throughout the performance.

MATT AT THE BBC

This CD features Matt's sessions with the Ted Heath Orchestra plus three tracks with Johnnie Spence from *Saturday Club*. The DVD is a wonderful array of Matt's TV appearances on the BBC.

THE RARE MONRO

This double album contains some wonderful gems that have been unearthed from the vaults of EMI. 51 tracks make up this set which include rare sessions, live performances and a mixture of jingles.

AVAILABLE FROM EMI